The Sublime
From Antiquity to the Present

This volume offers readers a unique and comprehensive overview of theoretical perspectives on "the sublime," the singular aesthetic response elicited by phenomena that move viewers by transcending and overwhelming them. The book consists of an editor's introduction and fifteen chapters written from a variety of disciplinary perspectives. Part One examines philosophical approaches advanced historically to account for the phenomenon, beginning with Longinus; moving through eighteenth- and nineteenth-century writers in Britain, France, and Germany; and concluding with developments in contemporary continental philosophy. Part Two explores the sublime with respect to particular disciplines and areas of study, viz., Dutch literature, early modern America, the environment, religion, British Romanticism, the fine arts, and architecture. Each chapter both is accessible for nonspecialists and offers an original contribution to its respective field of inquiry.

Timothy M. Costelloe is Associate Professor of Philosophy at the College of William & Mary. He is the author of *Aesthetics and Morals in the Philosophy of David Hume* (2008) and *The British Aesthetic Tradition: From Shaftesbury to Wittgenstein* (Cambridge, forthcoming).

The Sublime

From Antiquity to the Present

Edited by
TIMOTHY M. COSTELLOE
College of William & Mary

CAMBRIDGE UNIVERSITY PRESS
Cambridge, New York, Melbourne, Madrid, Cape Town,
Singapore, São Paulo, Delhi, Mexico City

Cambridge University Press
32 Avenue of the Americas, New York, NY 10013-2473, USA

www.cambridge.org
Information on this title: www.cambridge.org/9780521143677

© Cambridge University Press 2012

This publication is in copyright. Subject to statutory exception
and to the provisions of relevant collective licensing agreements,
no reproduction of any part may take place without the written
permission of Cambridge University Press.

First published 2012

Printed in the United States of America

A catalog record for this publication is available from the British Library.

Library of Congress Cataloging in Publication data
The sublime : from antiquity to the present / [edited by] Timothy M. Costelloe,
College of William & Mary.
p. cm.
Includes bibliographical references and index.
ISBN 978-0-521-19437-2 (hardback) – ISBN 978-0-521-14367-7 (paperback)
1. Sublime, The.   I. Costelloe, Timothy M.
BH301.S7S833   2012
111′.85–dc23   2011047623

ISBN 978-0-521-19437-2 Hardback
ISBN 978-0-521-14367-7 Paperback

Cambridge University Press has no responsibility for the persistence or accuracy of URLs
for external or third-party Internet Web sites referred to in this publication and does not
guarantee that any content on such Web sites is, or will remain, accurate or appropriate.

For Sarah and Andrew

Contents

List of Illustrations		page ix
Contributors		xi
Acknowledgments		xiii
	The Sublime: A Short Introduction to a Long History Timothy M. Costelloe	1

PART ONE. PHILOSOPHICAL HISTORY OF THE SUBLIME

1	Longinus and the Ancient Sublime Malcolm Heath	11
2	…And the Beautiful? Revisiting Edmund Burke's "Double Aesthetics" Rodolphe Gasché	24
3	The Moral Source of the Kantian Sublime Melissa McBay Merritt	37
4	Imagination and Internal Sense: The Sublime in Shaftesbury, Reid, Addison, and Reynolds Timothy M. Costelloe	50
5	The Associative Sublime: Gerard, Kames, Alison, and Stewart Rachel Zuckert	64
6	The "Prehistory" of the Sublime in Early Modern France: An Interdisciplinary Perspective Éva Madeleine Martin	77
7	The German Sublime After Kant Paul Guyer	102
8	The Postmodern Sublime: Presentation and Its Limits David B. Johnson	118

PART TWO. DISCIPLINARY AND OTHER PERSPECTIVES

9	The "Subtler" Sublime in Modern Dutch Aesthetics John R. J. Eyck	135
10	The First American Sublime Chandos Michael Brown	147

11	The Environmental Sublime *Emily Brady*	171
12	Religion and the Sublime *Andrew Chignell and Matthew C. Halteman*	183
13	The British Romantic Sublime *Adam Potkay*	203
14	The Sublime and the Fine Arts *Theodore Gracyk*	217
15	Architecture and the Sublime *Richard A. Etlin*	230

Bibliography 275
Index 295

List of Illustrations

3.1	Modes of the sublime	page 47
6.1	Nicolas Poussin, *L'hiver*, or *Le déluge* (*Winter*, or *The Flood*)	81
6.2	Louis Le Nain, *Famille de paysans dans un intérieur* (*Peasant Family in an Interior*)	86
6.3	Georges de La Tour, *La Madeleine à la veilleuse* (*The Magdalen with the Nightlight*)	87
6.4	Lubin Baugin, *Le dessert aux gaufrettes* (*Still Life with Wafers*)	88
6.5	Charles Le Brun, *Surprise et admiration* (*Admiration and Astonishment*)	90
6.6	Charles Poerson, *Louis XIV en Jupiter, vainqueur de la Fronde* (*Louis XIV as Jupiter, Conquerer of the Fronde*)	91
6.7	Charles Le Brun, *La Franche-Comté conquise pour la seconde fois* (*The Second Conquest of the Franche-Comté*)	92
6.8	Jeremias Wachsmuth (after Gottfried Eichler the Younger), *Magnificentia*	93
6.9	Charles Le Brun, *Entrée d'Alexandre dans Babylone* (*Entrance of Alexander into Babylon*), detail	95
6.10	Jean Audran, *Ravissement* (*Rapture*), after Charles Le Brun's drawing of the same title	96
6.11	Michel Natalis, *Le ravissement de saint Paul* (*The Ecstasy of Saint Paul*), after Nicolas Poussin's painting of the same title, detail	97
6.12	Nicolas Poussin, *L'inspiration du poète* (*Inspiration of the Poet*), detail	98
6.13	Philippe de Champaigne, *Saint Augustine*	99
6.14	Philippe de Champaigne, *Portrait de mère Agnès Arnauld et de soeur Catherine de Sainte-Suzanne* (*Portrait of Mother Agnès Arnauld and Sister Catherine de Sainte-Suzanne*), also known as *Ex-voto*	100
10.1	Frederick Edwin Church, *The Natural Bridge, Virginia*	155
10.2	*Great Falls of the Potomac*, drawn by G. Beck, Philadelphia; engraved by J. Cartwright	156
10.3	Thomas Cole, *View of the Round-Top in the Catskill Mountains (Sunny Morning on the Hudson)*	161
10.4	Thomas Cole, *View of the Mountain Pass Called the Notch of the White Mountains (Crawford Notch)*	162

10.5	*A Map of Lewis and Clark's Track, across the Western Portion of North America from the Mississippi to the Pacific Ocean: By Order of the Executive of the United States in 1804, 5 & 6 / Copied by Samuel Lewis from the Original Drawing of Wm. Clark; Saml. Harrison, fct.*	165
10.6	Thomas Cole, *The Course of Empire: Destruction*	167
10.7	Thomas Cole, *The Course of Empire: Desolation*	168
10.8	Plate XXVI, *Marietta Works*, in Squier and Davis, *Ancient Monuments of the Mississippi Valley*	169
12.1	Lucas Cranach the Elder, *The Crucifixion with the Converted Centurion*	190
12.2	Unknown, *Doukhobors Looking for Christ in Canada in Winter*	196
12.3	Sarah-Jane Lynagh, *Mute*	200
15.1	Étienne-Louis Boullée, Cenotaph to Sir Isaac Newton (project)	231
15.2	Étienne-Louis Boullée, Metropolitan Church (project)	235
15.3	Stuccoed dome (lost), Domus Aurea (Golden House), Rome	242
15.4	Pantheon, Rome	244
15.5	Pantheon, Rome, detail of attic zone with alteration of 1746–1748 and partial restoration of the original in 1929–1934	245
15.6	Mausoleum of Diocletian, split	248
15.7	Orthodox Baptistery, Ravenna	249
15.8	Mausoleum of Theodoric, Ravenna	250
15.9	Hagia Sophia, Constantinople (Istanbul)	252
15.10	Giulio Romano, Hall of Giants, Palazzo del Te, Mantua	255
15.11	Giulio Romano, Hall of Giants, Palazzo del Te, Mantua	256
15.12	Philibert Delorme, chapel, Château d'Anet, dome	259
15.13	Philibert Delorme, chapel, Château d'Anet, floor	260

Contributors

Emily Brady is a Reader in the Institute of Geography at the University of Edinburgh. Her research interests include aesthetics, environmental ethics, and eighteenth-century philosophy. She is the author of *Aesthetics of the Natural Environment* (Edinburgh University Press, 2003) and *The Sublime in Modern Philosophy: Aesthetics, Ethics, and Nature* (Cambridge University Press, forthcoming).

Chandos Michael Brown is Associate Professor in the Lyon Gardiner Tyler Department of History and Director of the American Studies Program at the College of William & Mary. He has published articles on early modern America and is author of *Benjamin Silliman: A Life in the Young Republic* (Princeton University Press, 1989).

Andrew Chignell is Associate Professor of Philosophy in the Sage School of Philosophy at Cornell University. He specializes in Kant and early modern philosophy, with interests in philosophy of religion, epistemology, and aesthetics. His work has appeared in *Noûs*, *Mind*, and *Philosophical Review*.

Timothy M. Costelloe is Associate Professor of Philosophy at the College of William & Mary. His research focuses on seventeenth- and eighteenth-century philosophy and aesthetics. He is the author of *Aesthetics and Morals in the Philosophy of David Hume* (Routledge, 2008) and *The British Aesthetic Tradition: From Shaftesbury to Wittgenstein* (Cambridge University Press, forthcoming).

Richard A. Etlin is Distinguished University Professor in the School of Architecture, Planning, and Preservation of the University of Maryland and a Fellow of the American Academy of Rome. He is the author of five books and editor of two, most recently, *In Defense of Humanism: Value in the Arts and Letters* (Cambridge University Press, 1996) and *Art, Culture, and Media under the Third Reich* (ed., Chicago University Press, 2002).

John R. J. Eyck has taught Germanic and Dutch studies at a number of universities, including the University of California, Berkeley, where he held the Queen Beatrix Chair. His work has appeared in *German Quarterly* and the *American Association of Netherlandic Studies*. He currently resides in New York City, where he works as a professional translator and is completing a book on sentimentalism and politics in the Enlightenment.

Rodolphe Gasché is SUNY Distinguished Professor and Eugenio Donato Professor of Comparative Literature at the State University of New York at Buffalo. He is the author of twelve books on themes in philosophy and literature, including, most recently, *The Stelliferous Fold: Toward a Virtual Law of Literature's Self-Formation* (Fordham University Press, 2011).

Theodore Gracyk is Professor of Philosophy at Minnesota State University, Moorhead. He is the author of many articles on aesthetics and its history and three books on music, including *Listening to Popular Music* (University of Michigan Press, 2007). He is also co-editor of *The Routledge Companion to Philosophy and Music* (Routledge, 2011).

Paul Guyer is Jonathan Nelson Professor of Humanities and Philosophy at Brown University. He is the author of nine books and editor of six anthologies on the work of Kant and has co-translated the *Critique of Pure Reason, Critique of the Power of Judgment*, and *Notes and Fragments* for the Cambridge edition of Kant, of which he is general co-editor. His three-volume *A History of Modern Aesthetics* is to be published by Cambridge University Press.

Matthew C. Halteman is Associate Professor of Philosophy at Calvin College and a Fellow in the Oxford Centre for Animal Ethics (UK). His research interests include hermeneutics, deconstruction, philosophy of religion, and human/animal studies. His work has appeared in *Continental Philosophy Review* and *Journal of Animal Ethics*.

Malcolm Heath is Professor of Greek Language and Literature at the University of Leeds. He has written six books, including, most recently, *Menander: A Rhetor in Context* (Oxford University Press, 2004). He has translated Aristotle's *Poetics* (Penguin, 1996) and is the author of a book on ancient philosophical poetics (Cambridge University Press, 2012).

David B. Johnson is a doctoral student in the Department of Philosophy at Northwestern University. His research focuses on aesthetics and twentieth-century continental philosophy, and he is currently completing a dissertation on the concept of intensity in the aesthetics of Gilles Deleuze.

Éva Madeleine Martin teaches French literature and culture at Princeton University, where she also received her doctoral degree. She specializes in the relations between the arts, philosophy, literature, and religion in early modern France. Her publications include *Esthétiques de Port-Royal* (Nolin, 2012).

Melissa McBay Merritt is Lecturer in Philosophy in the School of Humanities at the University of New South Wales. She focuses on Kant, and her work has appeared most recently in the *European Journal of Philosophy* and the *Southern Journal of Philosophy*. She is currently working on a book on enlightenment and cognitive virtue in Kant's critical philosophy.

Adam Potkay is William R. Kenan Professor of Humanities and Professor of English at the College of William & Mary. He is the author of four books, including *The Story of Joy from the Bible to Late Romanticism* (Cambridge University Press, 2007), which won the Harry Levin Prize of the American Comparative Literature Association for best book in literary history and criticism, 2006–8. His latest book, *Wordsworth's Ethics*, will be published by the Johns Hopkins University Press in 2012.

Rachel Zuckert is Associate Professor of Philosophy at Northwestern University. Her current research focuses primarily on eighteenth-century aesthetics. She has recently published articles on J. G. Herder, Lord Kames, and Immanuel Kant and is the author of *Kant on Beauty and Biology* (Cambridge University Press, 2007), an examination of Kant's *Critique of the Power of Judgment*.

Acknowledgments

This book began life in discussions with other participants of the NEH Summer Seminar, "Aesthetics of the Scottish Enlightenment and Beyond," organized by Paul Guyer and Rachel Zuckert, held at St. Andrews University, Scotland, in July and August 2007. Some contributors to the volume also participated in the seminar. I would like to express my thanks to the NEH and organizers of the seminar, without which the idea for this volume would not have been even a twinkle in my eye. I would also like to acknowledge the College of William & Mary for a summer research grant in 2010 that supported work on the book. I am grateful to Beatrice Rehl, Publishing Director, Humanities and Social Sciences, at Cambridge University Press, for her enthusiastic support and guidance at all stages of the project and to Laura Wilmot for her excellent job of copyediting the long and complicated manuscript. My thanks, finally, to the contributors, without whom the volume would be nothing. I am grateful for their hard work, for their graciousness in listening to and (for the most part) accepting my editorial suggestions, and for accomplishing their tasks in a timely fashion. Whether the chapters bear any marks of the great sublime they draw is for the reader to decide.

The Sublime

A Short Introduction to a Long History

Timothy M. Costelloe

It is almost as fashionable in the history of philosophy to declare certain concepts dead and buried as it is, periodically at least, to announce the discipline itself to be at an "end." "The sublime" seems to have undergone a similar fate in recent years, and one writer on the subject has even penned a "Farewell to the Sublime," placing himself proudly in the company of other savants to declare, in their collective terminology, the sublime anemic, bourgeois, elitist, feeble, ideological, ineffective, irrelevant, irresponsible, nostalgic, poor, and weak – in a word, dead. Drawing on the concept, moreover, does not "do much philosophic work or result in much understanding," readers are informed, and because the sublime is so clearly "damaged goods," they might be willing to accept a "moratorium on the word" and replace it with others that are "fresh and exact."[1] This is bad news indeed and, one has to admit, comes as something of a surprise.

To what, however, is one here saying farewell? What could it mean to declare the sublime dead or, at best, as the preceding litany of adjectives suggests, enervated and decadent? Fortunately, declarations of demise have a poor track record in philosophy, even when they come from the likes of Kant, Hegel, and Wittgenstein, and moratoriums imposed on the free spirit of philosophical thought tend to have the same traction as King Canute commanding the tide to stop. Hyperbole aside, such declarations can refer only to some inadequacy in the *philosophical concept* of the sublime, rather than signaling the disappearance of the *human experience* to which the concept refers or in some way delineates. These are two distinct spheres, but they are effectively elided when "sublime" is treated, as its naysayers apparently do, generically: "What could it mean to define the sublime, once and for all, when it has changed so much since the first appearance of the word – later taken to be the same as the eighteenth-century sublime – in a classical text by Longinus?"[2] Hegel is instructive in this context. Toward the end of the preface to the *Elements of the Philosophy of Right*, he reminds readers that philosophy comes late to subjects it treats, swooping, in his now famous image, like the Owl of Minerva in the gathering dusk of the day to paint its "grey in grey."[3] Hegel provides a powerful way of framing the relationship between experience and the attempt to grasp, explain, and express it in philosophical terms. In particular, the metaphor highlights a gulf between the two realms and, in Hegel's somewhat gloomy vision, the inability of mind to overcome the temporal and existential lag, the veritable rupture, between practice and its theoretical adumbration.

---

[1] James Elkins, "Against the Sublime," in *Beyond the Finite: The Sublime in Art and Science*, ed. Roald Hoffman and Iain Boyd White (Oxford: Oxford University Press, 2011), 75–90. I quote from 75 and 88. Elkins cites Richard Rorty, Philippe Lacoue-Labarthe, and Terry Eagleton in support of his contention.

[2] Elkins, "Against the Sublime," 79.

[3] See G. W. F. Hegel, *Elements of the Philosophy of Right* (1821), trans. H. B. Nisbet; ed. Allen W. Wood (Cambridge: Cambridge University Press, 1991), 23.

There is much here to aid reflection on the history of aesthetics, a discipline that, as common lore now teaches, was born at a particular time and place as an offspring of that complex of social, cultural, and political forces subsequently known as the Enlightenment.[4] The term "aesthetics" – from the Greek αισθητικός (*aisthetikos*, "sensitive" or "sentient") – was first minted as philosophical coin in 1735 as a Germanized Latinism (*Ästhetik*) by Alexander Gottlieb Baumgarten (1714–1762),[5] and although across the Channel the Anglicized version was not widespread until the middle of the following century,[6] British writers like Lord Shaftesbury and Joseph Addison gave the currency value under the auspices of its equivalent, "taste." Francis Hutcheson's *Inquiry into the Original of Our Ideas of Beauty and Virtue* (1726) is heralded, retrospectively, as a handy presentiment of what the fledgling discipline would accomplish when pursued, as it has been ever since, in a systematic and focused way.[7] To the realm of affective experience ("the aesthetic"), then – as Hegel's metaphor would have it – Minerva's Owl came late indeed, and at one fell swoop, in the shape of a new science ("aesthetics"), and the same is true, *pari passu*, of the various questions raised and issues gathered under the discipline's banner, inter alia the nature of beauty, art, and genius; the relationship between moral and aesthetic value; and – the focus of the present volume – the origin and defining features of the sublime.

To speak of the "birth" of the discipline and its desiderata, however, is to say little or nothing about the pleasure (or pain) people have long taken in the states they experience. This is certainly true of the sublime, which, at its etymological heart, carries the long history of the relationship between human beings and those aspects of their world that excite in them particular emotions, powerful enough to evoke transcendence, shock, awe, and terror. The term has its origins in the Greek noun ὕψος (*hupsos*) and its grammatical variations (ὕψοθεν, ὕψοι, *hupsothen, hupsoi*), meaning height, from high, from above, upwards, and, metaphorically, summit or crown.[8] The same range of meanings is found in the Latin equivalent, *sublīmis*: high up, aloft, elevated, tall, or towering; of heavenly bodies and meteorological phenomena; denoting the sky of the Northern Hemisphere, or birds in flight; imposingly tall (of men and animals); exalted in

---

[4] On this latter point, see the editors' introduction in Andrew Ashfield and Peter de Bolla, eds., *The Sublime: A Reader in British Eighteenth-Century Aesthetic Theory* (Cambridge: Cambridge University Press, 1996), 1–16. More detailed explorations along these lines are to be found in Peter de Bolla, *The Education of the Eye. Painting, Landscape, and Architecture in Eighteenth Century Britain* (Stanford, CA: Stanford University Press, 2003), esp. Introduction and chap. 1.

[5] Alexander Gottlieb Baumgarten, *Meditationes philosophicae de nonnullis ad poema pertinentibus/Philosophische Betrachtungen über einige Bedingungen des Gedichtes*, ed. Heinz Paetzold (Hamburg: Felix Meiner Verlag, 1983 [1735]); *Reflections on Poetry: Alexander Gottlieb Baumgarten's Meditationes philosophicae de nonnullis ad poema pertinentibus*, trans. Karl Aschenbrenner and William B. Holther (Berkeley: University of California Press, 1954); and *Ästhetik*, Latin text edited with facing German translation by Dagmar Mirbach, 2 vols. (Hamburg: Felix Meiner Verlag, 2007 [1750/1758]). For useful overviews, see Paul Guyer, "Eighteenth Century German Aesthetics," *Stanford Encyclopedia of Philosophy* (2007), http://plato.stanford.edu/entries/aesthetics-18th-german, and Kai Hammermeister, *The German Aesthetic Tradition* (Cambridge: Cambridge University Press, 2002).

[6] Samuel Johnson does not include it his *Dictionary* (1755), and only in the late 1830s does one find William Hamilton reporting (reluctantly) that the "term is now in general acceptation, not only in Germany, but throughout the other countries of Europe." See *Works of Sir William Hamilton*, 7 vols. (London, 1859), 1:124.

[7] Francis Hutcheson, *An Inquiry into the Original of Our Ideas of Beauty and Virtue in Two Treatises*, 2nd ed. (Indianapolis, IN: Liberty Fund, 2004 [1726]). For an informative account of the early history of the discipline, see Paul Guyer, "The Origins of Modern Aesthetics: 1711–35," in *The Blackwell Guide to Aesthetics*, ed. Peter Kivy (Oxford: Blackwell, 2004), 15–44.

[8] See *Greek-English Lexicon, New Edition*, compiled by H. G. Liddell and R. Scott; rev. Henry Stuart Jones (Oxford: Oxford University Press, 1995), 1910. For a useful overview of the term and its history in Greek literature, see the editor's introduction to *"Longinus" On the Sublime*, ed. Donald A. Russell (Oxford: Clarendon Press, 1964), xxx–xlii. My thanks to William Hutton for advice on Greek and Latin sources and help with translations.

rank or position and thus illustrious or eminent; and said of those with lofty ambition, noble or heroic character, and of elevated style or sentiments.[9]

This variety reflects the complicated history of the word and the competing etymologies available.[10] The most straightforward (and the one given by the OED) derives the term from *sub* (up to) and *līmin/līmen* (lintel or threshold of a building); the related word "subliminal" has similar roots, but with the sense of "below the threshold" rather than "up to the lintel." The other etymology, by contrast, suggested by A. Ernout and A. Meillet in their *Dictionnaire étymologique de la langue latine, histoire des mots* (1967), involves the connection made over time between *sub* (under or at the bottom) and *super* (to raise, to bring to a standing position from below), and the postclassical confusion among three different words and, consequently, three possible roots from which it might arise: *līmen* (threshold or lintel), *līmes* (a road bordering and delimiting a field), and *līmus* (sidelong/oblique). Ernout and Meillet argue for *līmus*, rendering *sublīmis* as "moving upward from a position below: hence rising diagonally, or more specifically from below to above, along a diagonal path."[11] "Sublime" and its relatives then entered the vernacular French and English, starting in the fourteenth century through the alchemical tradition meaning "to purify" (hence the verb "to sublimate"), and was associated with fire, violence, and pure essence.[12] From there it developed its now-familiar range of figurative meanings: honor, promotion, and high rank; to set on high and lift up; of flight and architecture; religious and secular indications of loftiness and purification; and, toward the end of the century, style – that is, the expression of lofty ideas in an elevated manner and, eventually, those ideas themselves.[13]

Distinct from the etymology of the term and the natural history of experience it reflects, the sublime also has a tale to tell as a *philosophical* concept, and it is with the last of these figurative meanings – style – that, for all intents and purposes, the story begins. It does so in the shape of περὶ ὕψους (*Peri hupsous*), a treatise that survives in a single manuscript routinely ascribed to the author called Longinus, a rhetorician, literary scholar, and philosopher of the first or third century AD.[14] The text was clearly known in the ancient world but was essentially lost until reintroduced in the early modern period through three sixteenth-century versions published in

---

[9] See *Oxford Latin Dictionary*, ed. P. G. W. Glare (Oxford: Oxford University Press, 1983), 1843.

[10] For the details of the etymology I am indebted to Jan Cohn and Thomas H. Miles, "The Sublime: In Alchemy, Aesthetics and Psychoanalysis," *Modern Philology* 74, 3 (1977), 289–304.

[11] See Cohn and Miles, "The Sublime," 290–2.

[12] German, Cohn and Miles point out, resisted the extension of the alchemical meaning of the term into figurative uses and employed native words instead to denote the same meaning: *erhöhen* (to increase), *veredeln* (to ennoble/enrich), and *erhaben* (to raise aloft/elevate); the latter yields the substantive, *das Erhabene*, which came to denote philosophically the equivalent to the English "sublime."

[13] See Cohn and Miles, "The Sublime," 294ff. In this shift from sublime style to sublime ideas, Cohn and Miles identify what they consider to be the corresponding philosophical shift from object to subject, and an increasing equation of sublimity with pain and (largely on the basis of Kant) moral imperatives: "The most important alteration of meaning, however, occurs when the *sublime* is used by English critics in the Longinian sense to describe not the external cause of a particular aesthetic state in the beholder, but that state itself; the sublime has moved from the object to the subject" (p. 296). As the chapters in Part One of the current volume show, this is a somewhat superficial gloss on a considerably more complicated and nuanced canvas.

[14] See Malcolm Heath, "Longinus and the Ancient Sublime," chap. 1 of the current volume; and "Longinus *On Sublimity*," *Proceedings of the Cambridge Philological Society* 45 (1999), 43–74; and Russell, "Longinus," xxii–xxx. For details of the early editions of the work, I draw on Bernard Weinberg, "Translations and Commentaries of Longinus, *On the Sublime*, to 1600: A Bibliography," *Modern Philology* 57, 3 (1950), 145–51, and Samuel Holt Monk, *The Sublime: A Study of Critical Theories in XVIII-Century England* (Ann Arbor: University of Michigan Press, 1935), chap. 1. Weinberg's research updates and corrects Monk, who relies on A. Rosenberg, *Longinus in England bis zur Ende des 18: Jahrhunderts* (Berlin: Meyer und Müller, 1917), 1–19, and app. D, 247–61, in W. Rhys Roberts's translation, *On the Sublime* (Cambridge: Cambridge University Press, 1899). A more recent treatment is to be found in the introduction to Karl Axelsson's dissertation, published as *The Sublime: Precursors and British Eighteenth Century Conceptions* (Oxford: Peter Lang, 2007). Axelsson uncovers nothing new and effectively summarizes the research of Rosenberg et al.

the original Greek by Francesco Robortello (Basel, 1554), Paulus Manutius (Venice, 1555), and Franciscus Portus (Geneva, 1569–1570). The first translation into Latin by Domenico Pizzimenti appeared in 1566 (Napoli), followed by those of Petrus Paganus in 1572 and Gabriel de Petra in 1612; the earliest extant vernacular translation is into Italian by Niccolò da Falgano (Florence, 1575). As the titles of these and other editions show, the term *sublīmis* was neither an obvious nor an automatic rendering of the Greek, with editors, translators, and commentators employing a variety of terminology: *de altitudine & granditate orationis* (undated, probably of the first half of the sixteenth century); *de grande, sive sublimi orationis* (Robortello); *de grandi orationis genere* (Pizzimenti), and *della altezza* (height/greatness) *del dire* (da Falgano). Other editions use "sublime" alone: *de sublimi genere* (Manutius); *de sublimi genere dicendi* (reprint of Pizzimenti edition 1644); *de sublimitate* ([Franciscus Portus] commentary 1581), and *de sublimi dicendi genere* (Paganus).

One thing these editions of *Peri hupsous* do have in common, however, is the emphasis that each puts on the sublime (great/elevated) *of* discourse rather than the sublime (great/elevated) *in* discourse. As Éva Madeleine Martin emphasizes in the current volume,[15] this distinction was central to and informed the most influential translation of the early modern period, Nicolas Boileau's *Traité du sublime ou du merveilleux dans le discours, traduit de grec de Longin* (1674), which was responsible for the wide dissemination of the treatise throughout the European republic of letters. As Martin argues persuasively, the "prehistory" of the sublime in early modern France shows how deeply indebted was Boileau to an older tradition of translation and commentary, including Guez de Balzac (who used the term *sublimité* as early as in 1636 and again in 1644), Tanneguy Le Fèvre (who published a critical Latin edition of Longinus in 1663), and, intriguingly, an anonymous translator at the court of Louis XVI who produced the first French translation in 1644, "De la sublimité du discours." There seems to have been an association of the term with rhetoric before Boileau (the *Dictionnaire étymologique de la langue française* cites an example of 1212 in which sublime means "placed very high"),[16] but, as Martin points out, no doubt drawing on this extant tradition Boileau transforms the Latin evaluative qualifier *sublīmis* into a substantive neologism – *sublime/sublimité* – to reflect the original Greek noun ὕψους, denoting it, in a conceptual sleight of hand, as an essence or independent existence expressed *in* and *through* language rather than *belonging to* or *of* language. Boileau insisted, in an oft-quoted passage from the preface to the *Traité*, that

par sublime, Longin n'entend pas ce que les orateurs appellent le style sublime, mais cet extraordinaire et ce merveilleux qui frappe dans le discours, et qui fait qu'un ouvrage enlève, ravit, transporte. Le style sublime veut toujours de grands mots; mais le sublime se peut trouver dans une seule pensée, dans une seule figure, dans un seul tour de paroles.[17]

by sublime, Longinus does not mean what the orators call sublime style, but this extraordinary and the marvelous that strikes in discourse, and what in a work elevates, ravishes, and transports. The sublime style always concerns elevated diction, but the Sublime can be found in a single thought, a single figure, a single turn of phrase. (translation mine)

Whether or not Boileau in fact drew on Balzac and colleagues, his choice of terminology effectively declared an allegiance to those who rejected the interpretation of Longinus's text as a method for teaching *le stile sublime* in favor of understanding it to be an exploration of *le Sublime* in writing and, by extension, other kinds of arts as well. Boileau's *Traité* thus marks a watershed in the philosophical concept of the sublime, although not due primarily to the *content*

---

[15] Éva Madeleine Martin, "The 'Prehistory' of the Sublime in Early Modern France: An Interdisciplinary Perspective," chap. 6.
[16] See Cohn and Miles, "The Sublime," 292.
[17] Nicolas Boileau Despréaux, *Traité du sublime ou du merveilleux dans le discours*, in *Oeuvres complètes* (Paris: Firmin Didot Frères, 1837; Elibron Classics Replica, 2007), 316–48, p. 318.

of the treatise it translates – rhetorical style was of ancient lineage and *Peri hupsous* itself long in circulation and known by French and English critics alike – but because, as Samuel Monk urges, its "*interpretation* of Longinus ... was heretical." Boileau recognized that the "greatest thought in simple language is the highest form of the sublime." Monk observes,

> since the thought operates directly and with no let or hindrance to the reader's mind, filling it with awe and awakening emotions of a very intense kind. Thus at one blow the sublime is severed from rhetoric and becomes art, a matter of the revelation of a quality of thought and the emotions which that quality, vividly presented, evokes.... Boileau's terms ... indubitably tell us that the sublime apart from sublime style, must be a great thought and that it must awaken strong emotions in the reader of the audience. This is the new, the eighteenth-century, sublime for which Boileau is responsible.[18]

Expressed *linguistically*, then, Boileau bequeaths to the tradition a term of Gallicized Latin (*sublime/sublimité*), a neologism consisting of a Latin adjective (*sublīmis*) to translate a Greek noun (ὕψους); expressed *philosophically*, however, he isolates a subject matter that not only occupies – as the tale is traditionally told – writers of the "age of taste" and first decades of the nineteenth century, but continues to fascinate up to and including those of the present day.

When the sublime became an object of interest for British writers during the early modern period, it was under the influence of this French tradition encapsulated in and purveyed by Boileau's *Traité*. This is not say that the term did not have at least a marginal presence in Britain already: in addition to the extant sixteenth-century editions, a Latin translation by Gerard Langbaine had appeared at Oxford in 1636 – the first such publication by an Englishman printed at an English press – as well as an English translation by John Hall in 1652 with the title *Peri Hupsous, or Dionysius Longinus of the Height of Eloquence*.[19] Geoffrey Chaucer, moreover, had earlier spoken of "high style" and Herbert Spenser of "lofty style" – neither with any decipherable reference to Longinus – and "sublime" had been used in connection to style more generally as early as 1586 and even with a hint of its modern usage in 1638.[20] John Milton had also referred to Longinus, although only on a single occasion, ironic given that subsequent generations were to see his work as an example par excellence of sublime style.[21] Such intimations notwithstanding, only *after* Boileau's *Traité* of 1674 does the influence of Longinus begin to be felt and the sublime take root as a feature of the British literary and philosophical landscape. Indeed, the second English translation of 1680 by J. Pulteney was not from the Greek but "out of the French" of Boileau,[22] and – even more telling – the first rendering of ὕψους with the

---

[18] Monk, *The Sublime*, 29 and 31–2. Cohn and Miles, "The Sublime," 292, gloss the same point, remarking that Boileau was "careful to distinguish between the [extant] rhetorical sense and the new emotional-aesthetic meaning he gives to *sublime* in his translation of Longinus." See also Meyer H. Abrams, *The Mirror and the Lamp: Romantic Theory and Critical Theory* (Oxford: Oxford University Press, 1953), 72ff.; Russell, "*Longinus*," xlii–xlviii, and A. F. B. Clark, *Boileau and the French Classical Critics in England* (New York: Russell & Russell, 1965 [1925]), esp. 369ff., all of whom draw a similar conclusion.

[19] *Peri Hupsous, or Dionysius Longinus of the Height of Eloquence Rendred out of the Originall by J[ohn] H[all]. Esq.* (London, 1652).

[20] On the former, see Monk, *The Sublime*, 18–19, and for latter the *Oxford English Dictionary*, which cites Sir Thomas Herbert (1606–1682), *Some Yeares Travels into Divers Parts of Asia and Afrique, Describing Especially the Two Famous Empires the Persian and Great Mogull Weaved with the History of These Later Time*, &c., 2nd ed. (London, 1638 [1634]), 33: "The element grew dreadfull, ... the sea sublime and wrathfull."

[21] In his essay "Of Education," Milton refers to Longinus as one of the teachers of "a graceful and ornate rhetoric." Quoted in Monk, *The Sublime*, 20. See in this context Addison's papers on the "Divine Genius" of Milton, in *The Spectator*, ed. Donald F. Bond, 5 vols. (Oxford: Clarendon Press, 1965), 2, nos. 267, 273, 279, and 3, nos. 285, 291, 297, 303, 309, 315, 321, 327, 333, 339, 345, 351, 357, 363, 369. On Milton's familiarity with Longinus, see Nigel Smith, *Is Milton Better than Shakespeare?* (Cambridge, MA: Harvard University Press, 2008).

[22] *A Treatise of the Loftiness or Elegance of Speech. Written Originally in Greek by Longinus; and Now Translated out of the French by Mr. J. P[ulteney]* (London, 1680). See Cohn and Miles, "The Sublime," who must be mistaken in citing Pulteney's as one of the two translations "before Boileau's work." It is thus not quite true, as they suggest, that "after Boileau, all English titles used the world sublime" (293n9).

English equivalent of Boileau's neologism comes with an anonymous translation of 1698 – from the Greek but "compared with the French" – to produce a title close to its modern and now-familiar form: *An Essay on Sublime*.[23] This was solidified and established with William Smith's translation of 1739, *On the Sublime*, the standard edition for the rest of the century and the period in which Longinus's text reached the height of its fame and influence.[24] Smith's translation went to its fifth and final edition in 1800, and the intervening years saw two new editions of the Greek by J. Hudson (Oxford, 1710) and Z. Pearce (London, 1724), which were collectively reprinted some fourteen times; other translations were to follow.[25]

When Samuel Johnson wrote the entry under "sublime" in the first edition of his *Dictionary* (1755), then, the term had already seen a good deal of action and arrived with a substantial weight of conceptual baggage belied by his charmingly simple definition: "SUBLIME, n.s. The grand or lofty stile," Johnson writes. "*The sublime* is a Gallicism, but now naturalized."[26] What he reveals, no doubt unwittingly, is – no pun intended – a veritable sublimation in which Boileau is at once absorbed into the soil of the English language and simultaneously transformed at the hands of the eighteenth-century British philosophers who tilled it. Johnson follows the French and distinguishes the *nominal* from the *adjectival* form of "sublime," tracing the latter, not the former, to *sublîmis*. To the English adjective Johnson thus attaches the same range of meanings encompassed by the Latin original and reserves the noun exclusively for Longinian style. His examples are Alexander Pope's now-famous lines from *An Essay on Criticism* (themselves a borrowing from Boileau):

> Longinus strengthens all his laws,
> And is himself the great *sublime* he draws[27]

and a remark by Addison: "The *sublime* rises from the nobleness of thoughts, the magnificence of the words, or the harmonious and livery turn of the phrase; the perfect *sublime* arises from all three together."[28]

---

[23] *An Essay on the Sublime: Translated from the Greek of Dionysius Longinus Cassius the Rhetorician. Compared with the French of Sieur Despréaux Boileau* (Oxford, 1698).

[24] Dionysius Longinus, *On the Sublime*, trans. from the Greek by William Smith (London: J. Watts, 1739).

[25] See Monk, *The Sublime*, 21.

[26] *A Dictionary of the English Language; in Which the Words Are Deduced from Their Originals and Illustrated in Their Different Significations by Examples from the Best Writers. To Which Are Prefixed, a History of the Language, and an English Grammar. By Samuel Johnson, A. M. In Two Volumes* (London, 1755). Dictionaries up to Johnson's did not include the term. See Theodore E. B. Wood, *The Word "Sublime" and Its Context, 1650–1760* (Den Haag: Mouton, 1972), app. 2, 214–16.

[27] Pope's lines in full read:

> Thee, bold Longinus! All the Nine inspire,
> And bless *their Critick* with a *Poet's Fire*.
> An ardent *Judge*, who Jealous in his Trust,
> With *Warmth* gives Sentence, yet is always *Just*;
> Whose *own Example* strengthens all his Laws,
> And *Is himself* that great *Sublime* he draws. (675–80)

Alexander Pope, *An Essay on Criticism*, in *The Twickenham Edition of the Poems of Alexander Pope*, 6 vols. (London: Methuen, 1961), vol. 1, *Pastoral Poetry and An Essay on Criticism*, ed. E. Audra and Aubrey Williams, 1:316. The last line echoes Boileau: "Souvent il fait la figure qu'il enseigne, et, en parlant du sublime, il est lui-même très sublime" (Often he imitates that which he teaches, and, in speaking of the sublime, he is himself very sublime) (*Traité*, 316), although Russell ("Longinus," xlii–xliiin2) traces the sentiment back further to a Latin letter of Stephanus de Castrobello dated 1612: "Quid enim praeter ipsam sublimitatem ipso Longino sublimis? ... ipsum typum exemplar sublimis et grandis orationis expressissimum" (For what is sublime for Longinus himself beyond sublimity itself? ... The very model [is] the most distinct example of sublime and grand oratory) (translations mine).

[28] The quotation comes from the *Guardian*, July 25, 1713. I am indebted to Robert DeMaria for identification of the source. Addison routinely reserves "sublime" for literary style and effect and uses "grand" for what strikes as

Johnson's entry and examples reflect the Anglicized French – English *sublime/sublimity* from French *sublime/sublimité* – and thus take over the emphasis on *sublime dans le discours*, the sublime as an essence not *of* but expressed *in* language, reserving the nominative "sublime" for sublime style. This reflects the convention followed early in the century by the likes of John Dennis, Shaftesbury, and Addison, who employ the term in reference to Longinus and rhetorical effect and use "great" or "grand" to indicate what later writers mean by the term "sublime": those features of objects (such as magnitude, height, and elevation) and the affective states (such as transcendence, awe, fear, and terror) they produce. Traces of this terminology are evident in David Hume and remain as late as Thomas Reid's "Of Beauty," the final essay in *Essays on the Intellectual Powers of Man* (1785); Lord Kames distinguishes "grand" (size) from "sublime" (elevation) in his *Elements of Criticism* (1763), but neither refer to the sublime of style.[29] As the century progressed the terms became interchangeable and, in the wake of Edmund Burke's *Philosophical Enquiry into the Sublime and Beautiful* (1757), and cemented by Immanuel Kant's *Critique of the Power of Judgment* (1792), the Longinian sublime all but disappeared. Under the influence of Romanticism at the turn of the century, *sublime style* and *sublimity* were uncoupled conceptually once and for all.

It is clear then, to return to the question raised at the outset, that any farewell to the sublime can be little more than a rhetorical flourish in reference to the purported inadequacy of the philosophical concept, and even there, to invoke Hegel and Minerva's Owl once again, we should not be surprised to find reflection lagging behind its subject matter, which, strive as it might, it can never capture entirely. Granted, like its mother discipline, aesthetics, the sublime has undergone considerable change from its inception in Longinus, and subsequent birth and growth in the late seventeenth and early eighteenth centuries. As this short introduction to a long history shows, however, in the sublime we inherit a concept with a pedigree that only the breeding of many generations can bestow. In addition, the sublime has insinuated itself into a range of disciplines and has taken on a rich variety of perspectives, and through its various liaisons has undergone a process of change and maturity.

This fact is nowhere more evident than in the chapters that compose the current volume. Part One covers the philosophical history of the sublime, the range of theoretical treatments the concept has occasioned from Longinus in antiquity; through British, French, and German writers of the eighteenth and nineteenth centuries; to its place in contemporary postmodern thought. Part Two shows how amenable the sublime is to take on a range of adjectival qualifications that denote, variously, national predilections (Dutch and American), aesthetic sensibilities (British Romanticism), worldviews (the religious and the environmental), and different creative practices (the fine arts and architecture). The fifteen chapters have no pretension to be exhaustive – that would be to close prematurely a concept very much open – but together they offer in a humbler spirit a fascinating narrative, in the warp and weave of which one discerns the deep, rich colors of a concept alive and well. Indeed, the sublime can no more disappear than the experiences to which it refers; for that we should be grateful and wish it in return a long and healthy life.

---

a whole and surpasses the capacity of the imagination to contain. See Addison's papers on Milton (n21 above) and the eleven essays on "The Pleasures of the Imagination" written between June 21st and July 3rd, 1712, in *The Spectator* 3:535–82, nos. 409–21. I consider Addison's view in more detail in the following, Timothy M. Costelloe, "Imagination and Internal Sense: The Sublime in Shaftesbury, Reid, Addison, and Reynolds," chap. 4 of the current volume.

[29] This goes hand in hand on the part of some – Hugh Blair, James Beattie, and James Mill, for example – who fault Longinus for being narrow and overly rhetorical. See Monk, *The Sublime*, 25.

PART ONE

PHILOSOPHICAL HISTORY OF THE SUBLIME

I

Longinus and the Ancient Sublime

Malcolm Heath

INTRODUCTION

Plato's *Timaeus* opens with an unexpected absence. The previous day, Socrates had led the discussion; his four companions were due to make their contributions today: "One, two, three … and yet our fourth, my dear Timaeus, is – where? (The fourth) of those who yesterday were guests at the feast, but are now the banquet's hosts?" (*Timaeus* 17a1–3). The first clause is a bare enumeration: it could not be simpler in construction, or plainer in diction. The shift from cardinal numbers to ordinal adjective signals a change at the start of the second clause: the diction is less plain, the syntax more elaborate; the displacement of the interrogative, as striking in Greek as in English,[1] enacts Socrates' surprise. The third clause, with its refined vocabulary and striking metaphor, rises to another level altogether. From a dull beginning, the sentence has blossomed by stages into a display that confers sublimity on the whole.

We owe that analysis to Cassius Longinus, a rhetorician, literary scholar, and philosopher of the third century AD, in a fragment preserved by the fifth-century neo-Platonist Proclus.[2] Proclus's source was probably a lost commentary by Porphyry, the most distinguished of Longinus's pupils. Porphyry described Longinus as the greatest critic of the age; he was still renowned in the following century for his scholarship and authoritative literary judgment.[3] It was once taken for granted that this Longinus was the author of the treatise *On Sublimity*. That attribution came under attack early in the nineteenth century and is now generally discounted. But before we consider this and other philological problems, it may be helpful to begin by undertaking a preliminary survey of what I shall, without prejudice, call Longinus's conception of the sublime.[4]

---

[1] English, not Greek, word order requires the clumsy repetition of "the fourth."
[2] Proclus, *In Tim.*, 1.14.7–20 equals Longinus, fr. 24. See English translation in Harold Tarrant, *Proclus: Commentary on Plato's Timaeus* (Cambridge: Cambridge University Press, 2007), 1:108–9. All references to the fragments (fr.) of Longinus (Greek with French translation) are to Michel Patillon and Luc Brisson, *Longin. Fragments. Art Rhétorique. Rufus. Art Rhétorique* (Paris: Les Belles Lettres, 2001).
[3] A. H. Armstrong, ed., *Porphyry: Life of Plotinus* 20, Greek and English, in *Plotinus* (Cambridge, MA: Harvard University Press, 1966), vol. 1; Eunapius, *Lives of the Sophists*, 4.1: Greek and English in Wilmer Cave Wright, ed., *Philostratus and Eunapius: Lives of the Sophists* (Cambridge, MA: Harvard University Press, 1921).
[4] All translations in the present chapter are my own. The best published translation of *On Sublimity* into English is that by Donald A. Russell, in *Classical Literary Criticism*, ed. Donald A. Russell and Michael Winterbottom (Oxford: Oxford University Press, 1989). Russell has also edited the Greek text, with an excellent commentary, in Donald A. Russell, ed., *"Longinus" On the Sublime* (Oxford: Clarendon Press, 1964), and produced a revised text alongside a revision of W. Hamilton Fyfe's translation in *Aristotle: Poetics. Longinus: On the Sublime. Demetrius: On Style*, ed. Stephen Halliwell, Donald A. Russell, and Doreen C. Innes (Cambridge, MA: Harvard University Press, 1995). Rewarding starting points for further study of Longinus on sublimity will be found in D. C. Innes, "Longinus: Structure and Unity," in *Greek Literary Theory after Aristotle: A Collection of Papers in Honour of*

LONGINUS'S CONCEPTION OF THE SUBLIME

Terminology offers only limited assistance. "Sublimity" renders *hupsos* (height); *megethos* (greatness) is used freely as an equivalent. These two roots provide a range of cognate adjectives, verbs, and compound derivatives; other terms denoting what is elevated or exceptional also occur. But these metaphors, although suggestive, are not precise enough to mark crucial qualitative distinctions. The pursuit of sublimity is at risk from false substitutes. We will not achieve genuine elevation by being "up in the air" (3.2) and must not confuse "greatness" with obesity (3.3). Moreover, Longinus's usage cuts across traditional categorizations. Neither Sappho, source of a famous illustration (10.1–3), nor Xenophon, one of Longinus's "heroes" (4.4), was an exemplar of the high or grand style in ancient literary criticism.

Yet Longinus never straightforwardly defines sublimity. In the opening chapter, under cover of acknowledging that his addressee does not need to be told what sublimity is, he offers only a series of oblique characterizations (1.3–4). First, it is "a certain pinnacle and excellence of discourse." Second, it is the one thing that secures the preeminence and enduring fame of all the greatest writers of poetry and prose. Third, it can be recognized by its effect: it produces ecstasy; it astounds and does not (merely) persuade; it controls or irresistibly compels the audience. Fourth and finally, it is a local rather than a global effect: it comes at a single stroke, like lightning, and is not achieved by content or structure on a larger scale.

The first of these characterizations is only a vague gesture. The second directs us to look for examples of sublimity in authors of acknowledged greatness, but one might doubt whether any *single* quality is the shared source of enduring fame for authors who seem extremely diverse. That diversity demands caution in the conclusions we draw from the third and fourth points. In a short piece like Sappho's lyric, the local context may be the whole composition; we will also be shown how sublimity can be achieved through techniques of accumulation in a relatively extended local context (11–13). In a more carefully qualified statement, Longinus says that "sublimity is *often* to be found in a single thought" (12.1): therefore, not *always*. There are many ways to overwhelm an audience. Demosthenes may be compared to a thunderbolt or lightning, but Cicero is like an inexorably expanding conflagration (12.3–4), and Plato's grandeur is the flow of a smooth, silent stream (13.1). There is, indeed, no thunder and lightning in the opening sentence of *Timaeus*: if it overwhelms us, it is with astonishment at the perfect control of variation in structure and diction, of trope and metaphor. We may infer that certain kinds of literary excellence lie beyond the remit of this treatise (for example, the skillful construction of a large-scale text, or sustained subtlety of characterization). But the full scope of its conception of sublimity remains to be seen.

Longinus's cautiously oblique approach is understandable. After a detour through some deviations from true sublimity (3–4), he notes that, as is often the case, faults have the very same origin as the real thing (5, cf. 32.7). So "a pure understanding and appreciation of true sublimity" is essential but hard to acquire: "Literary judgment is the final fruition of much experience" (6). If you do not have sufficient expertise and judgment to recognize sublimity when you meet it, a definition will not help you. Hence the notable display of hesitancy with which Longinus goes on to introduce some markers of the real thing: "It is, perhaps, not impossible to furnish discernment ... from some such source as this." These markers are, in part, the effects

---

D.M. Schenkeveld, ed. J. G. J. Abbenes, S. R. Slings, and I. Sluiter (Amsterdam: VU University Press, 1995), 111–24; D. C. Innes, "Longinus and Caecilius: Models of the Sublime," *Mnemosyne* 55 (2002), 259–84; E. Matelli, "Struttura e stile del περὶ ὕψους," *Aevum* 61 (1987), 137–247; Donald A. Russell, "Longinus Revisited," *Mnemosyne* 34 (1981), 72–86; C. P. Segal, "ὕψος and the Problem of Cultural Decline in the *De sublimitate*," *Harvard Studies in Classical Philosophy* 64 (1959), 121–46; and G. B. Walsh, "Sublime Method: Longinus on Language and Imitation," *Classical Antiquity* 7 (1988), 252–69.

on the individual – or, at least, on the right individual, "a man [sic] of good sense and literary expertise." His soul is uplifted, filled with "joy and exultation." This effect survives close examination and repeated readings; it is irresistible and unforgettable (7.2–3). But there is also a universal effect: genuine sublimity gives delight always and to all, and the consensus of people of many different backgrounds provides incontrovertible corroboration (7.4).

Universal consent was a recognized argument for truth in ancient thought – an argument, paradoxically, that need only be invoked in the face of dissent. For example, the popularizing philosopher Maximus of Tyre (second century AD) appeals to the universality of belief in gods, undeterred by a handful of materialists, atheists, and agnostics. These contrary voices can be dismissed, or pressed into service: "They know, though they do not want to; they speak against their will."[5] Longinus implicitly executes a similar maneuver in a later appeal to universal consensus: when he asserts its immunity to envy (36.2), he simultaneously concedes the existence of dissent and disqualifies it. Because envy is only felt by those who recognize excellence and resent it, the dissenters testify against their denigrations.

Longinus therefore restricts the scope of the relevant consensus on moral grounds, as well as on the grounds of a lack of literary expertise; the two deficiencies will prove to be related. This restriction is surprisingly severe. The reference to envy comes toward the end of a lengthy excursus arguing against those who denigrate Plato because of his errors of judgment (32.7–36). The target is Caecilius, a critic who taught in Rome at the end of the first century BC, and who wrote the only other attested ancient work on sublimity (now lost). Longinus tells us at the outset that his own treatise was evoked by the inadequacies of Caecilius's treatment, which was "lowlier" than the subject requires (1.1–2). This criticism goes deeper than at first appears. Throughout the treatise, "lowly" designates the antithesis of sublimity, and also the moral condition that makes sublimity unattainable (3.4; 8.2; 9.3; 9.10; 33.2; 35.2; 43.3; 43.6). Caecilius's denigration of Plato suggests that he is one with the "lowly and mediocre natures" who are risk averse (33.2); he shares the human tendency to remember the mistakes of great writers, and readily forget their good points (33.3). Perhaps he is one of the envious (36.2); certainly he is motivated by hatred of Plato and contentiousness (32.8). If one of the most distinguished of Greek critics can go so badly astray on the subject of sublimity, then the argument from universal consent will be based on a very limited sample indeed.

Whereas the "lowliness" of Caecilius's treatment of the subject hints at his personal inadequacies, more explicit criticisms of his treatise in the opening chapter reveal Longinus's conception of his own project. Caecilius's work is evaluated as technical discourse. This genre is subject to two requirements: first, to show what the subject matter is and, secondly, and more importantly, to show the methods by which it can be achieved (1.1). Caecilius fulfilled the first requirement (although only by collecting a superfluity of examples, as if writing for ignoramuses), but he totally failed in the second. Consequently, his work was of little benefit to its readers.[6] Longinus aims to rectify this deficiency by providing something that will be of practical use (1.2; cf. 36.1: "usefulness and benefit"; 2.3; 44.1: "useful instruction"). Specifically, it will be of practical use to "political men" (1.2). In ancient rhetorical theory, "political" includes forensic as well as deliberative oratory; so the target audience is anyone who uses skilled discourse to persuade in public contexts.

"Political" may be contrasted with what is "excessively sophistic" (23.4). The reference is not to the sophists of the classical period, but to the distinguished teachers of rhetoric of the

---

[5] *Oration*, 11.4–5. Greek text: Michael Trapp, ed., *Maximus Tyrius: Dissertationes* (Stuttgart: B.G. Teubner, 1994); English translation: Michael Trapp, *Maximus of Tyre: The Philosophical Orations* (Oxford: Oxford University Press, 1996).
[6] "However, perhaps that fellow deserves not to be criticised for his shortcomings so much as praised for his idea and his effort" (1.2). Longinus, always deft in polemic, takes care to show that *he* is no malicious denigrator.

Hellenistic and Roman imperial world. Because many of these were politically active in the relevant sense, the distinction is not primarily between politicians and sophists but between the contrasting styles appropriate to the oratory of forensic and deliberative debate and the oratory of sophistic display. One person may control both styles, but importing the extravagances of the sophistic style into political discourse was widely criticized. Longinus comments sardonically on "our eloquent modern orators" (15.8) whose excessively poetic imagination is inappropriate to oratory, and he is clear that he is concerned with what is appropriate to "genuine speeches" (3.1). Hence the treatise refers insistently to the orator (1.4), the true orator (9.3), the expert orator (17.1), and what the orator needs to know (11.2).[7]

Longinus thus situates his treatise within the tradition of didactic technical writing on rhetoric. Like other texts in that tradition, it recognizes that "political" orators can learn effective techniques from other forms of discourse and draws examples from a wide range of genres. Although it emphasizes the need to keep a firm grip on the difference between poetry and oratory (15.2–10), as those "eloquent" contemporary orators do not (15.8), its use of poetic illustrations is unusually lavish. The crucial point is that sublimity is a common but distinctive excellence of *discourse* (1.3). The treatise is therefore not a work of general aesthetics. The visual arts are judged by other criteria (36.3–4), music unaccompanied by discourse is downgraded (39.2–3), and although grandeur is admired in nature (35.2–36.3), it is in the discursive response to natural greatness that sublimity is found (36.1–2).

Yet the treatise is far from typical of a technographic tradition that often confronts us with the paradox of experts in fine speech who explain their art in arid and rebarbative prose. Some texts are more stylish than others, but nothing resembles *On Sublimity*. Its style is ambitious and idiosyncratic. Language is stretched in extraordinary ways: consider, for example, the oxymoronic expression "great-natured toadies" (44.3), which yokes greatness of nature, a defining characteristic of true sublimity (2.1; 9.1; 9.14; 13.2; 15.3; 33.3; 34.4; 36.1; 36.4), to its self-abasing antithesis. This gift for stretching language places considerable demands on the reader: pedantic literalism will often suspect Longinus of confusion or inconsistency. We have already noted that he does not define the sublime: he meets the first requirement of technography obliquely, by cumulative illustration. He goes out of his way to avoid a stable terminology, often sidestepping established technical terms of rhetoric and rarely defining them (except in 12.1, in which he wishes to show that the standard technographic definition obscures distinctions crucial to the subject of sublimity). He is apologetic when he is drawn into technical ("philological") treatment (29.2). His preferred expository device is the illustrative example. He mentions or quotes many examples but also *furnishes* examples of what he describes – often implicitly, and offset from the discussion of the technique being illustrated. That is one symptom of the treatise's studied avoidance of pedantically systematic order: its careful structure is masked by a no less carefully contrived façade of casualness in the organization of the material. This, too, is in accord with its own precepts: "In this way, his order is disorderly, and conversely his disorder encompasses a kind of order" (20.3, on Demosthenes; cf. 22.1). To an extent, these features can be rationalized: this is not a basic school text but is addressed to an advanced student (1.3), and Longinus does not wish to insult the reader's intelligence in the way that Caecilius did (1.1). However, the avoidance of technographic norms goes beyond that. These features contribute to making the text self-exemplifying: "Bold Longinus … is himself that great Sublime he draws."[8] In exemplifying what he describes, Longinus aspires to sublimity in his own right.

---

[7] For the rhetorical culture described here, see Malcolm Heath, *Menander: A Rhetor in Context* (Oxford: Oxford University Press, 2004), 217–331.

[8] Alexander Pope, *An Essay on Criticism*, in *The Twickenham Edition of the Poems of Alexander Pope*, 6 vols. (London: Methuen, 1961), vol. 1, *Pastoral Poetry and An Essay on Criticism*, ed. E. Audra and Aubrey Williams, 1:316. Cf. Boileau (preface to Traité du Sublime, 1674): "En traitant des beautez de l'Elocution, il a employé toutes les finesses de l'Elocution. Souvent il fait la figure qu'il enseigne, et, en parlant du sublime, il est lui-même

TRANSMISSION AND ATTRIBUTION

Before delving deeper into Longinus's exposition of his theme, we must take up some philological issues, including that of attribution. In the single manuscript to which we owe the text's survival, the treatise is headed "Dionysius Longinus *On Sublimity*," but the manuscript's table of contents has "Dionysius *or* Longinus."[9] These are alternative attributions to two of the most famous ancient critics: Dionysius of Halicarnassus (a contemporary of Caecilius) and Cassius Longinus. At least one of these attributions must be conjectural; at least one must be false; we have no guarantee that either is correct. Even if the manuscript attribution had been unequivocal, that guarantee would be lacking. Some ancient rhetorical treatises have been transmitted anonymously; others have acquired a demonstrably false attribution in the course of their transmission, and still others have acquired false attributions to more than one author.

Incompatibilities of style and content mean that the attribution to Dionysius has found almost no advocates. Until the early nineteenth century, it was taken for granted that the author was Cassius Longinus. The modern consensus against his authorship depends primarily on the contention that the last chapter presupposes a political situation inconsistent with a third-century date but appropriate to the early first century AD (the most widely accepted of a range of alternative datings). This objection does not, in my view, stand up to scrutiny. I have made that case at length elsewhere.[10] Here I will briefly outline some considerations, which suggest that, if the attribution to Longinus was conjectural, it was a good conjecture.

One misconception needs first to be set aside. Toward the end of his life, Cassius Longinus was associated with Zenobia of Palmyra in her revolt against Rome. A memorable passage of Gibbon records his amazement that "in the heart of Syria, and at the Court of an Eastern Monarch, Longinus could produce a work worthy of the best and freest days of Athens."[11] That bewitchingly romantic image is pure fantasy. Longinus taught for most of his career in Athens, one of the leading intellectual centers of the time. Many high-status Romans visited Athens for a period of advanced study. The treatise is addressed to Terentianus, a Roman (12.5), a young man (15.1), and an advanced student already educated to expert level (1.3), with whom the author had been reading Caecilius (1.1). The mundane reality is that, if Longinus is the author, *On Sublimity* is the work of a distinguished, middle-aged academic.

Caecilius's critical writings were read and cited in Longinus's intellectual circle: a fragment of Porphyry recounts a (perhaps fictional) discussion of plagiarism at a dinner party given by Longinus, in the course of which Caecilius is cited as an authority.[12] Caecilius is mentioned in accounts of the classical orators preserved by the ninth-century compiler Photius, and there is reason to believe that Longinus was the source.[13] Longinus would have had particular reason to study Caecilius's work on sublimity, because (as his analysis of the opening sentence of Plato's *Timaeus* shows) he was interested in the topic himself. Longinus, like the author of *On Sublimity*, was an admirer of Plato's literary style, but not an uncritical admirer: the fragments acknowledge faults in Plato.[14] The famous citation of Genesis (9.9) sits easily in Longinus's

---

très-sublime." Nicolas Boileau Despréaux, *Traité du sublime ou du merveilleux dans le discours*, in *Oeuvres complètes* (Paris: Firmin Didot Frères, 1837; Elibron Classics Replica, 2007), 316–48, p. 316.

[9] Donald A. Russell, ed., *"Longinus" On the Sublime* (Oxford: Clarendon Press, 1964), xxii–xxiii.

[10] Malcolm Heath, "Longinus *On Sublimity*," *Proceedings of the Cambridge Philological Society* 45 (1999), 43–74.

[11] Journal for September 11, 1762, in David M. Low, *Gibbon's Journal to January 28th, 1763* (London: Chatto & Windus, 1929), 139. Gibbon's amazement was compounded by his total failure to appreciate the strength of third-century intellectual culture.

[12] Porphyry, fr. 408, Smith (which equals Eusebius, *Praep. Evang.*, 10.3). See Andrew Smith, ed., *Porphyrii philosophi fragmenta* (Stuttgart: B.G. Teubner, 1993).

[13] See Malcolm Heath, "Caecilius, Longinus and Photius," *Greek, Roman and Byzantine Studies* 39 (1998), 271–92.

[14] Longinus, fr. 31 (which equals Proclus, *In Tim.*, 1.68.3–12); fr. 49.108–9.

intellectual milieu: the second-century philosopher Numenius, whose work Longinus knew, cited Genesis 1.2, and Longinus's pupil Porphyry cited Genesis 2.7 in an essay on embryology.[15] The author of *On Sublimity* was an expert on rhetoric and literature but also was alert to the philosophical implications of his theme; that breadth of interests matches Longinus's intellectual profile.[16]

When there is an attested author whose candidacy is intrinsically plausible, positing an otherwise unknown author is uneconomical. I shall therefore proceed on the assumption that *On Sublimity* was written by Longinus. But this is a working hypothesis: certainty is impossible. We therefore face formidable obstacles. This is a text of contested authorship and date. We cannot be sure of the intellectual context in which it should be read. Moreover, we have no independent access to the work by Caecilius to which it is a response (no other trace survives). Worse, Longinus's work itself came close to being lost and is only partially preserved. We owe its survival to a single tenth-century manuscript, from which a number of pages went missing before any copies had been made. The loss amounts to a little more than 35 percent of the original, leaving six lacunae of varying sizes scattered through the text (the last few lines are also missing).

In addition to the physical damage suffered by the manuscript, the treatise (like all classical texts) has suffered the copying errors inevitable in manuscript transmission. Some are easily healed or make no substantive difference to our understanding of Longinus's argument, but there are potentially significant uncertainties. For example, in all modern editions and translations Longinus says that Lysias falls short of Plato in the scale and number of his excellences but exceeds him in faults even more than he falls short in excellences (35.1). Lysias's appearance here depends on the suggestion, made by Paulus Manutius in 1555, that the manuscript reading *apousias* (of absence) is a corruption of *ho Lusias* (Lysias). The manuscript text certainly makes no sense, and the conjecture has superficial plausibility: Longinus is arguing against Caecilius, who prefers the faultless Lysias to the often-faulty Plato (32.8), and if Lysias were faultier than Plato, Caecilius's preference would be refuted. Despite its seductive neatness, however, Manutius's conjecture makes no coherent sense in context. A claim so much at odds with Lysias's literary reputation would have been credible to few, if any, ancient readers; denigrating Lysias for his abundant faults would therefore have exposed Longinus to the charge of contentiousness that he brings against Caecilius's attack on Plato (32.8). Moreover, Caecilius's verdict on Lysias and Plato provides a point of departure for a sustained argument to the effect that great achievement is of greater worth, despite its inevitable miscarriages, than flawless mediocrity (33–38): an abundance of faults would make Lysias an irrelevant distraction from that argument. A conjecture that attributes to Longinus a claim that would discredit him and that he does not need is reckless, and it is better to accept that we do not know what Longinus wrote here.[17]

THE SOURCES OF SUBLIMITY

We may now turn our attention to the substance of Longinus's argument. His advocacy of great, if risky, achievement in preference to flawless mediocrity helps to explain his circuitous

---

[15] Numenius, fr. 30, des Places (which equals Porphyry, *On the Cave of the Nymphs*, 10); Longinus, fr. 2 (which equals Porphyry, *Life of Plotinus*, 20); Porphyry, *Ad Gaurum*, 11.1 (48.18, Kalbfleisch). See Édouard des Places, ed., *Numénius. Fragments* (Paris: Les Belles Lettres, 1973), and *Porphyry: ad Gaurum*, Greek, in K. Kalbfleisch, "Die neuplatonische, fälschlich dem Galen zugeschriebene Schrift πρὸς Γαῦρον περὶ τοῦ πῶς ἐμψυχοῦται τὰ ἔμβρυα," *Abhandlungen der Preussischen Akadamie der Wissenschaft, philosophisch-historische Klasse* (1895), 33–62.

[16] For a discussion of the treatise in its philosophical context, see Malcolm Heath, *Ancient Philosophical Poetics* (Cambridge: Cambridge University Press, 2012); for Longinus's place in the third-century rhetorical context, see Heath, *Menander*, 52–89, and on Platonist rhetoric more generally, Malcolm Heath, "Platonists and the Teaching of Rhetoric in Late Antiquity," in *Late Antique Epistemology: Other Ways to Truth*, ed. Panayiota Vassilopoulou and Stephen R. L. Clark (London: Palgrave Macmillan, 2009), 143–59.

[17] See Malcolm Heath, "Longinus *On Sublimity* 35.1," *Classical Quarterly* 50 (2000), 320–3.

approach to his subject. After the introduction, and a section on the relationship between nature and art (to which we shall return), he addresses himself not to sublimity but to deviations from it, their cause, and how to avoid them (3–7). If he is setting out to teach us how to achieve something that is inherently risky, it is a sensible precaution to put in place this preparatory defense against miscarriage. But having steered us away from the risks that are destructive of genuine sublimity, he must also, at some point, steer us away from the timidity that will leave us incapable of achieving it. Some risks must be avoided, but some must be embraced. We must be willing to take the kind of risk that is necessary to (sometimes) achieving sublimity, undeterred by the possibility of failure. The ground is prepared early on: even Xenophon (4.4–5) and Plato (4.6) sometimes fail. An extended exhibition of Homer's genius (9.5–10) ends with the first of the treatise's excursuses, in which the *Odyssey* (a product, Longinus believes, of Homer's old age, when his powers were ebbing) is used to make the point that even exceptional talent can sometimes lapse into "drivel" (9.14).

Longinus's positive agenda is advanced in the treatise's technographic core, an analysis of sublimity's five sources (8.1): thought, emotion, figures of thought and speech, diction (vocabulary and tropes, including metaphor), and composition (word order, rhythm, and euphony). This analysis, together with its richly illustrated elaboration, is the basis of the text's claim to practical usefulness – its capacity to show us, as Caecilius did not, how to achieve sublimity. Longinus draws particular attention to emotion, which Caecilius omitted. Longinus suggests that he must have thought either that emotion is identical with sublimity (and did not need to be named separately) or that it contributes nothing to sublimity (and was therefore irrelevant). He was seriously mistaken either way: there is sublimity without emotion, and some emotions are "lowly," but the right kind of emotion can make an incomparable contribution to sublimity (8.2–4). Thus the initial assault on Caecilius is renewed to authorize Longinus's analysis. Later, criticisms of Caecilius's views on metaphor (31.1; 32.1) remind us of his shaky authority, as preparation for the crucial excursus on risk taking, which is staged as a critique of Caecilius (32.8). Longinus consistently exploits his predecessor as a device for launching the exposition of key points in his own program.

Emotion makes its presence felt throughout the treatise, but there is no systematic discussion: we progress directly from thought (15.12) to figures (16.1). The last surviving lines of text (44.12) mark a transition to emotion, mentioning a promise to discuss the topic in a separate treatise. That promise is not made anywhere in the extant text, and we can only guess whether the need for a separate treatise was revealed in one of the lacunae. There are also obscurities in the discussion of the first and most important source of sublimity (9–15). In Longinus's initial formulation, this first source is designated "powerful effect with regard to ideas" (8.1). The concluding summary speaks of "sublimities in respect of the ideas" (15.12) and lists three main divisions: sublimities achieved by greatness of thought, imitation, or imagination. Yet at 10.1 Longinus introduces a second factor capable of elevating discourse: the selection and combination of details, illustrated by Sappho's meticulous description of the symptoms of love. Then at 11.1 he introduces a further factor, "amplification," in which greatness is achieved by gradual accumulation or intensification. Why are these not mentioned in the summary? Almost half of this section has been swallowed by a long lacuna after 9.4, and a shorter interruption after 12.2. Again, we can only guess whether the missing portion of text, if recovered, would make the underlying logic of the exposition more explicit. The most probable explanation is that greatness of thought, the first main division in the summary triad, itself has three subdivisions. The discussions of selection and combination and of amplification cover the second and third subdivisions. The first will be what is described in 9.3 as "not having a low or ignoble mind" because "great discourses belong, in all probability, to those whose ideas are weighty and dignified." But further work is needed to unpack the logic of this layered structure.

The first of the five sources of sublimity is also described as "greatness of nature" (9.1). How are we to achieve this? Longinus quotes his own epigram: "Sublimity is an echo of a great mind."

The first example is a deliberate paradox: Ajax's silence in *Odyssey* 11.563–4, which is "more sublime than any discourse" because of the intrinsic greatness of the unspoken thought (9.2). It is this greatness of thought that is beyond the reach of a "low or ignoble mind." Longinus is embarking on another illustration, an anecdote about Alexander the Great, when the lacuna cuts him off. When the text resumes, he is discussing images of the divine, primarily in Homer's *Iliad*. Clearly, images of the divine convey "weighty and dignified" ideas if they succeed in portraying the divine appropriately. Longinus has worries in this regard. A superhuman image of a god may amaze us, creating the characteristic effect of sublimity (1.4; 9.2–3), but what is superhuman is still subdivine, and some images (such as poetic battles between gods, which had been subject to philosophical criticism for centuries) are so subdivine as to be "completely irreligious and improper" unless understood allegorically (9.7). Read allegorically, the superhuman dimension of such descriptions may be allowed to have its effect without raising theological objections. Nevertheless, images that present the divine as "something truly undefiled and great and pure" are superior – this is the context of the passing reference to "the lawgiver of the Jews" (9.9). From gods Longinus moves back to the heroic level, with a passage about Ajax from the *Iliad* (9.10).

Sappho's love poem, illustrating selection and combination, takes us into very different territory from "weighty and dignified" conceptions of heroic, superhuman, or divine greatness. The symptoms described are, as Longinus notes (10.3), typical of lovers. What amazes us is the compelling force of the perfect selection and combination of elements. The implication is that greatness of thought may consist also in the insight that enables this perfect integration even of the phenomena of ordinary human life – although they are not trivial, and (importantly) the effect is intensified by emotion. The following contrast between Homer's emotionally gripping treatment of a storm at sea with similar passages from other poets, in which the emotional effect is missed or spoiled, carries the same implication. The fact that even a single misjudged phrase can ruin the effect shows why success in such descriptive passages exhibits greatness of thought.

Amplification is achieved by applying techniques of cumulative intensification (11.1): "Comprehensive coverage of all the aspects and topics inherent in the facts, strengthening the point that has been demonstrated by dwelling on it" (12.2). Amplification *as such* is not sublime; something more is needed (11.2). The point is not a contrast between sublimity, achieved at a stroke, and the expansiveness of amplification – Longinus is careful to say that sublimity is *often* (but therefore not always) achieved in a single thought (12.1) – but to emphasize (against the standard technographic definition) that amplification and sublimity are not coextensive. Sublimity has elevation but not necessarily extension; amplification is always expansive but is not necessarily elevated. To make amplification sublime requires not something *other* than amplification, but a quality *of* the amplification that raises its level in the same way that sustained emotional intensity secures the sublime effect of selection and combination. Here, too, the greatness of thought will consist in the insight that enables this expansive accumulation to proceed without missing or spoiling the effect.

"Imitation," the second main division of the first source, refers not to narrative or dramatic representation (as, for example, in Aristotle's *Poetics*) but to the emulation of classical models (13.2; cf. 28.4; 34.2). Imitation in this sense was an important part of ancient rhetorical training. It does not mean copying, because the idea is not to say something that X said, but to say what X *would* have said in this situation (14.1).[18] Hence it requires not superficial mimicry but entering into the model's way of thinking. By daring to emulate the "heroes" of the past, we can amplify our native resources: the greatness of the ancients flows into our souls in a process compared to prophetic inspiration (13.2). This was true even for someone as undeniably great

---

[18] See Heath, *Menander*, 244.

as Plato, who drew inspiration from Homer, and without doing so could not have achieved what he did, either in philosophy or in literature (13.3–4). This claim may surprise those familiar with Plato's scathing critique of Homer in the *Republic*, but among Platonists in late antiquity it was a commonplace. A fragment of Longinus describes Plato as "the person who first, and best, transferred into prose the weightiness of Homer" (fr. 50.9). The great thoughts need not, therefore, be wholly our own: we can draw on external inspiration for reinforcement. So whereas greatness of thought is typically achieved by conceptions that are of heroic, superhuman, or divine greatness drawn from the speaker's own conceptual resources, imitation provides a means of extending one's conceptual reach.

The third main division, imagination, may be understood in the same way. Making an imaginary scene concrete in our minds through visualization takes us out of ourselves, as if we were possessed (15.1) and gives access to thoughts beyond our normal reach. These might be well beyond our reach if we are poets imagining the Furies or Phaethon's ride in the chariot of the sun (15.2–4); less so, but still with powerful emotional impact, if we are an orator concretizing the effects of a contested legislative proposal as virtually equivalent to an organized jailbreak (15.9, citing Demosthenes 24.204), or even (more adventurously) concretizing the necessity of a controversial emergency measure by imagining the defeat that occasioned it as the proposer of the legislation (15.10, citing a lost speech of Hyperides). It is a striking testimony to the power of imagination to extend one's reach that it enabled Euripides, who was "not in the least great-natured," to *force* his own nature to become tragic and achieve great things (15.3).

Imitation and imagination therefore provide ways to stretch our intrinsic capacity for great thought. That capacity is itself manifested in various ways: through the adequate representation of inherently weighty conceptions and through the insight needed to achieve full success in selection and combination or in amplification. Further evidence of the diversity of the literary sublime can be found within the treatment of amplification. The text resumes after a lacuna in the middle of an excursus that has apparently diverted Longinus from a discussion of Plato into a comparison of Cicero and Demosthenes (12.3–5). Demosthenes achieves his effects in abrupt strokes, like bolts of lightning, whereas Cicero's sublimity, compared to a spreading fire, is more diffuse, a characteristic that shows how amplification is consistent with sublimity. This must have been the point that Longinus was making about Plato before the lacuna: when he returns to Plato (13.1), the comparison is to the flow of a smooth, silent stream. This is something quieter than Ciceronian amplification, but also effective in its quietly persistent way. The three-cornered comparison reinforces the point that sublimity cannot be equated with any single style or technique.

What, then, are the limits of this diversity? It is not necessary for all five sources to be present – sublimity can be achieved without emotion, for example (8.2–3) – but is the first and most important source (great thought) indispensable? Obviously, low or trivial thoughts will spoil sublimity, as will triviality resulting from defects of expression such as poor rhythm, composition, or choice of vocabulary (41–43). The norm is the interdependence of thought and expression: "The thought in discourse and its expression are for the most part mutually implicated" (30.1). At a minimum, this means that sublimity is destroyed by triviality in any one of the sources, but not everything that falls short of sublimity is trivial or lowly. Greatness of thought is not dependent on sublime expression, because the limiting case of Ajax's bare unspoken thought (9.2) shows that all of the sources that depend on verbal expression are in principle dispensable. But can expression achieve sublimity in the absence of great thought? Longinus's discussion of Demosthenes' Marathon Oath takes us a step further (16.2–4, on Demosthenes 18.208). The "natural," unfigured, formulation has no sublimity, but the effect of Demosthenes' figuration is stunning. In this case, then, there is no thought capable of achieving sublimity independently of the way Demosthenes has expressed it.

NATURE AND ART

Longinus writes that "many authors of prose and poetry who are not sublime by nature, perhaps even wholly lacking in greatness, nevertheless, when using for the most part ordinary, everyday vocabulary that contributes no special effect, simply by arranging them and fitting them together ... have achieved weightiness and distinction and the appearance of not being lowly" (40.2). Here it is important to note that, although these authors give a misleading impression of their own powers, the compositional effect confers genuine sublimity on what they write. Euripides, we recall, could rise above his natural level by means of imagination (15.3). He could do so by means of composition, too: in *Heracles* 1245, "what is said is very commonplace," but it achieves a sublimity that is entirely dependent on the arrangement of the words (40.3). If Euripides, who was "not in the least great-natured" (15.3), could achieve sublimity through composition, it is not surprising that a genuinely great-natured author like Plato could do so, too, as in the opening sentence of *Timaeus*.

"Nature" in Longinus is a complex and potentially confusing term. This does not arise from conceptual confusion on his part, however, but reflects the complexity of natural phenomena. A brief survey may help to orient us. First, "nature" may designate the productive source of (nonartificial) phenomena; hence "nature the craftsman" (43.5) and "works of nature" (36.3). Second, each of nature's works has its own nature. This can be specified at different levels. A natural kind, such as an animal species, has a common nature. It is in this sense that Longinus speaks of "human nature" (39.3) and applies the expressions "natural to," "naturally," and "by nature" to humans in general, explicitly (36.3; 39.1) or implicitly ("we": 7.2; 15.11; 33.3; 35.4). But most animal species display some degree of behavioral diversity and plasticity. So we might say that a certain breed of dog is naturally aggressive, but that an individual dog has a placid nature. Hence Longinus can also speak of the nature of individual persons (1.1; 1.2; 9.11; 15.3; 33.2; 40.2; 44.1; 44.11). However, the normal course of nature is disrupted by abnormal circumstances: if you poke the placid dog with a stick it will, naturally enough, react aggressively. Hence violations of natural word order may, at another level of analysis, be natural (10.6; 16.2). People under emotional stress speak in abnormal ways, distorting the natural sequence of their words and thoughts, but authors who use hyperbaton to reproduce this effect are imitating the "effects of nature" (22.1). There is no inconsistency on Longinus's part therefore in saying both that there is a natural word order and that departures from this order can be natural: there are circumstances (such as emotional agitation) in which it is natural to depart from natural (default) word order (10.6; 16.2; 22.1; 22.3).

Nature, then, is complex. It is also normative: writing should be in accordance with nature, at some level of analysis. That poses a challenge to rhetorical technography, for if we aim to be natural, why do we need art? "Some think that those who reduce such matters to technical precepts are wholly deceived," Longinus writes. "Greatness, it is said, is innate; it does not come about by teaching, and the one 'art' that produces it is to be born. The works of nature, so they suppose, are rendered utterly feeble when technical discourse has made skeletons out of them" (2.1). Longinus must confront this challenge to vindicate his programmatic claim to practical usefulness. In doing so, he enters into a debate familiar from the rhetorical literature[19] and also starts off a thematic thread that will lead ultimately to the political and ethical debate staged in the final chapter.

THE ETHICS OF SUBLIMITY

Longinus infiltrates the theme of nature at the very start of the treatise, in a way that challenges a fundamental premise of the naturist position. The initial characterization of the treatise's

---

[19] See, for example, Quintilian, *Institutio Oratoria*, 2.11–13. Latin text with English translation in Donald A. Russell, *Quintilian: The Orator's Education* (Cambridge, MA: Harvard University Press, 2001).

more important task (by what methods can sublimity be achieved?) is almost immediately rephrased in terms that discount the idea of a *fixed* natural endowment: "In what manner we might be able to advance our own natures to a certain degree of greatness" (1.1). Our nature, then, is something that we can and ought to cultivate. When Longinus turns to the first and most important of the sources, "greatness of nature," he continues to think of nature as something that can be developed: "Since it has a greater part to play than the others ... here, too, even if the thing is more a gift than an acquisition, nevertheless we must train our souls towards great things" (9.1).

This theme returns in the final chapter, which purports to recount a discussion with "one of the philosophers," who posed the question why "sublime and exceptionally great natures no longer arise, or only rarely" (44.1). We have already seen Longinus's adverse comment on contemporary orators' inability to distinguish between the norms of poetry and oratory (15.8); he also condemns his contemporaries for their mania for the contrived novelty of thought that is the common cause of every variety of false sublimity (5.1). The philosopher brings a degree of balance to the assessment of contemporary oratory: the age produces natures that are "in the highest degree persuasive ..., penetrating and vigorous and above all rich in literary delight." But that only makes the scarcity of truly sublime, great natures more puzzling. The puzzle leaves the philosopher at a loss. He can only fall back on what he himself describes as a "cliché": that great oratory begins and ends with democracy. Freedom and political competition stimulate ambition and therefore achievement, and enslavement stunts our spiritual growth (44.2–5).

The philosopher shares Longinus's developmentalist view of nature, but the determinist slant of his political explanation is incompatible with Longinus's conviction that we can and should try to develop our own natures to achieve sublimity. Longinus accordingly shifts the terms of the debate from politics to ethics – a devastating maneuver because it exposes the philosopher's explanation as carping, and self-servingly evasive of personal responsibility. "It is easy, and characteristically human, to find fault with the current state of affairs. But perhaps it is not world peace that is destroying great natures..." (44.6). Whereas the philosopher's explanation characterized the autocratic imperial regime in negative terms, as a loss of freedom, Longinus redescribes it in positive terms as a guarantor of peace. The philosopher has thus fallen into the error of focusing on the bad rather than the good, which Longinus has already criticized in another context (33.3). But the positive redescription also provides the stepping-stone to a more fundamental objection: "... but much rather this unlimited war that has our desires in its grip" (44.6). The philosopher's explanation made the destruction of great natures an automatic product of political circumstance, placing it beyond the individual's responsibility; the shift in focus from world peace to inner strife brings it back within the realm of individual responsibility, restoring the possibility that we can influence the development of our own nature. We can aspire to greatness, even if the social environment is unfavorable.

Indeed, the political circumstances can be placed in a still more positive light. Far from withholding the stimulus to development that makes greatness possible, the autocratic regime supplies the constraints needed to curb the further moral decline that would make it utterly impossible. Political autonomy is not in the interests of those who lack moral self-control. Because we are enslaved to love of money and pleasure (44.6), and the vices that descend from wealth and lack of self-discipline are despots in our souls (44.7), it is better for us to be ruled than to be free (44.10). Compare the reference to wealth, status, reputation, and power in 7.1, which implies that a preoccupation with such things precludes the greatness needed to achieve sublimity. The early advice on avoiding false sublimity foreshadows the moral protreptic of the final chapter.

The argument of the final chapter therefore reassures us that, in principle, greatness is within our power to achieve (with the corollary that if we fail to achieve it, that is our fault). On reflection, it also offers another kind of reassurance. In the opening chapter Longinus distinguished persuasion, which generally depends on the listener, from sublimity, the effects of which, "exerting irresistible power and force, have the upper hand over every listener" (1.4). Do we, then, have no control over or responsibility for the effects that sublimity has on us? Or worse – if technography can tell us how to achieve sublimity, does that put the means of irresistible psychological control into the hands of those who might use it manipulatively and amorally? Sublimity, we now see, is beyond the reach of anyone who would wish to abuse it, because achieving sublimity requires not merely mastery of technique but also the ethical development of our nature.

It is true that debased natures may produce oratory with many positive, persuasive qualities and may persuade people of things of which they should not be persuaded. If so, the audience's own debased nature is at fault (even more so if the effect is achieved by means of false sublimities). Great natures are immune to such persuasion, and although great natures can achieve the irresistible power of sublimity, they cannot (by their very nature) abuse that power. Even the irresistible force of sublimity is qualified: it is not reliably recognized except by competent judges, and even Caecilius could resist Plato's sublimity. But that failure to be overwhelmed is also the fault of the audience. In corrupt times, it may be difficult to avoid these faults, but it is our responsibility to make the effort. If nature inspires an unconquerable love of the great in us (35.2), adverse environments cannot entirely suppress it. It is within our power to achieve greatness if we make the effort. Cultivating an appreciation of sublime authors, and imitating them, is itself a way for us to progress toward sublimity and may therefore help us out of the moral trap. But there is more – much more.

SUBLIMITY AND TRANSCENDENCE

Let us return to the relationship between nature and art. Longinus has to defend his technographic project against the naturists. Denying the role of natural talent had never been a plausible response: rhetoricians always acknowledged that nature and technique are both needed. A fragment of Longinus remarks that "often, because of a deficiency of nature, even experts fail in execution" (fr. 50.10). So the contrast is not between untutored natural genius and talentless technique (an obviously rigged comparison). The question is whether natural talent is eviscerated or enhanced by technique. Longinus's initial response is that, although nature is necessary, lack of technical expertise can annul it. Crucially, "the very fact that some things in discourse depend on nature alone is one that we must learn from no other source than art" (2.3). Technical expertise can assess the things it cannot achieve; if nature is fallible, we need technical judgment to determine which of the spontaneous products of our nature are genuine.

Of the five sources of sublimity, thought and emotion are *largely* endogenous; figures, diction, and composition come through art *in addition* (8.1). Longinus does not recognize a neat division between what is owed to nature and what to art: thought and emotion are not *entirely* independent of art, and figures, diction, and composition are not *without* nature. Nature and art are always implicated with each other, a reciprocity reasserted in 22.1, in which Longinus proposes that art is perfect when it appears to be natural, and nature successful when it contains latent art. The former point arises from the suspicion in which overt artifice is held – it can antagonize the audience (17.3). The latter point acknowledges once more the fallibility of art, and the need for art to assess nature's spontaneous products and (if necessary) correct them. The corrective function of art is especially important because the pursuit of sublimity is risky. This brings us back to the excursus that starts from Caecilius's perverse preference for Lysias over Plato (32.8). Ultimately, the conclusion is that because art produces correctness, and erratic excellence is the product of greatness of nature, art should assist nature: "Their reciprocity would perhaps be perfection" (36.4, with a cross-reference to the beginning of the treatise).

The argument of this excursus, as we have seen, is that faultlessness is not to be preferred to greatness, despite the faults that attend the latter. Precision in every detail becomes triviality; "lowly and mediocre natures" achieve faultlessness by running no risks, but at the cost of low achievement (33.2). Longinus compares (among others) Hyperides and Demosthenes to prove his point. Hyperides is a more challenging test of his position than Lysias, because he has all the excellences of Lysias, and more: he has almost all the excellences of Demosthenes, and many excellences in which Demosthenes is deficient (34.2–3). Even so, he is manifestly not as great an orator as Demosthenes (34.4). Plato is a more extreme case: Demosthenes lacks many excellences, but Plato is often positively faulty (35.1).

Plato's abundant faults[20] prompt the question that follows: "What, then, was the vision of those equals of the gods [*isotheoi*] who, aspiring to the greatest things in writing, despised precision in every detail?" (35.2). Longinus's answer breathtakingly expands the scope of his discussion. The role to which humans are assigned by nature is analogous to that of spectators (*theatai*) and ambitious athletes competing in a festival – but the festival venue is the whole universe. Hence nature has inspired our souls with an invincible passion for what is great and more divine than ourselves – so much so that even the limits of the universe do not constrain our intellectual vision (*theōria*). We are naturally drawn to amazed admiration of great rivers and the ocean rather than small streams, and of the heavenly bodies or volcanic eruptions rather than the fires we light ourselves (35.2–5). It is that instinct for greatness that drives writers of genius (36.2). The mistakes consequent on their risk-taking ambition are a small price to pay for the transcendent prize that they attain thereby: "Sublimity raises them near to the greatness of the mind of god" (36.1).[21]

---

[20] Not the abundant faults of Lysias! It is even clearer now that Manutius's conjecture, noted previously, which claims that the manuscript reading *apousias* (of absence) is a corruption of *ho Lusias* (Lysias), misses Longinus's train of thought completely.

[21] For the philosophical background to this conclusion see further Heath, *Ancient Philosophical Poetics*.

2

...And the Beautiful?

Revisiting Edmund Burke's "Double Aesthetics"

Rodolphe Gasché

Needless to say, Edmund Burke's *A Philosophical Enquiry into the Sublime and Beautiful* (1757, 2nd ed. 1759) – the sole contribution to aesthetics by this writer, whose work is primarily devoted to questions of political history, political theory, and the foundations of the commonwealth[1] – is profoundly indebted to all those British thinkers before him who in the first half of the eighteenth century undertook a critical review of the aesthetic norms of classicism, and of the classicist ideal of the education of a gentleman. Although Burke relied on many ideas found in Francis Hutcheson and Joseph Addison, to name only these, his *Enquiry*, by declaring, as has been noted, an "open revolt against neo-classical principles,"[2] also thoroughly distinguishes itself from his predecessors. It is true, of course, that all of eighteenth-century British aesthetics is inseparable from the thought of John Locke and David Hume. But Burke was the first to propose an uncompromising empiricist – that is, sensualistic – account of aesthetic experience, and to have radically uncoupled this experience from extrinsic considerations (particularly, moral and religious), which still dominate Hutcheson's *An Inquiry into the Original of Our Ideas of Beauty and Virtue* (1725).

In seeking to account for aesthetic experience on the basis of sober empirical observation alone, Burke stresses the sensualistic nature of aesthetic impressions by conceiving of the beautiful and the sublime primarily in terms of ideas and passions. By the same stroke, the sensual qualities of the particular objects that affect the senses and the imagination in such a way as to provoke these ideas, or passions, acquire major importance. It is on these premises that Burke, in the spirit of Isaac Newton, seeks to establish "an exact theory of our passions."[3] It is a theory

---

[1] The *Enquiry* is commonly read with complete disregard for Burke's political writings. However, as Neal Wood has shown, the two basic aesthetic categories of the sublime and the beautiful also inform and shape Burke's fundamental political ideas, which thus in turn shed light on the socioanthropological underpinnings of Burke's aesthetics. See Neal Wood, "The Aesthetic Dimension of Burke's Political Thought," *Journal of British Studies* 4, 1 (1964), 41–64. See also in this context the excellent work by Robert Zimmer, *Edmund Burke: Zur Einführung* (Hamburg: Junius Verlag, 1995), whose discussion of Burke's *A Vindication of Natural Society* further illuminates the socioanthropological tenets of Burke's thoughts on aesthetics (see pp. 29–39). Other recent works of note, although not addressed directly in this chapter, include Richard Shusterman, "Somaesthetics and Burke's Sublime," *British Journal of Aesthetics* 45, 4 (2005), 323–41; Vanessa L. Ryan, "The Physiological Sublime: Burke's Critique of Reason," *Journal of the History of Ideas* 62, 2 (2001), 265–79; Stephen K. White, *Edmund Burke: Modernity, Politics, and Aesthetics* (Newbury Park, CA: Sage, 1994); Linda M. G. Zerilli, *Signifying Women: Culture and Chaos in Rousseau, Burke, and Mill* (Ithaca, NY: Cornell University Press, 1994); and Frances Ferguson, *Solitude and the Sublime: Romanticism and the Aesthetics of Individuation* (New York: Routledge, 1992).
[2] James T. Boulton, "Editor's Introduction," in Edmund Burke, *A Philosophical Enquiry into the Origin of Our Ideas of the Sublime and Beautiful*, ed. James T. Boulton (London: Routledge and Kegan Paul, 1958 [1759, 1st ed. 1757]), lv. Unless otherwise noted, all references to Burke's text are to part, section, and page number as given in this edition. All roman numerals refer to Boulton's introduction.
[3] Burke, *Enquiry*, preface to the first edition, 1.

that inquires into their efficient – that is, physiological – causes, and that rigorously coordinates the feelings of the sublime and beautiful with the affections caused by the objects from which they spring. It is precisely the utmost consistency with which Burke applies Locke's empiricism to aesthetics, as well as his Newtonian methodology for discovering fixed laws regulating the domain of the passions, that allowed him to approach aesthetic experience as a realm of its own. The addition in 1759 of the chapter "Introduction to Taste" to the second edition of the *Enquiry*, which in all likelihood was written as a reply to Hume's essay "Of the Standard of Taste" (1757), is further proof of Burke's understanding of the realm of the aesthetic as a realm in its own right. Indeed, his assumption that "the conformation of their organs are nearly, or altogether the same in all men"[4] allows him to recognize the existence of a "ground-work of Taste [that] is common to all" (IT 24), and thus to provide his own contribution to the question of the general communicability of taste that occupied the eighteenth century. But in distinction from Hume's standard of taste, which is based on experience, cultivation, and expertise, Burke's standard, which "is the same in all, high or low, learned or unlearned" (IT 17), is rooted within the interplay in all human beings "of a perception of the primary pleasures of sense, of the secondary pleasures of the imagination, and of the conclusions of the reasoning faculty" (IT 24), so long as all these faculties "operate naturally" (IT 15), rather than being conditioned by custom or acquirement. This conception of a standard of taste, as well as Burke's reference to "a logic of Taste" (IT 13), which points to his attempt at rationally accounting for a domain that previously had been considered recalcitrant to rationality, is clear evidence of a significant breakthrough that would not be possible without the recognition of an independent nature of aesthetic experience.

Compared to his predecessors, Burke also devises a much sharper differential conceptual instrumentarium to analyze aesthetic experience and articulate the sensuous properties of the objects that cause the passions. For Joseph Addison, for instance, "the sight of what is great, uncommon, or beautiful" in outward objects is the source of the pleasures of the imagination, but according to him the "horror or loathsomeness" of any of these same objects may also overrule the pleasures in question, "in which case there will be such a mixture of delight in the very disgust [they give] us, as any of these three qualifications [greatness, uncommonness, and beauty] are most conspicuous and prevailing."[5] Not only are pleasure and delight not clearly distinguished from each other, but the sources of the pleasures of the imagination themselves lack clear borders. By contrast, Burke's approach to aesthetic experience is characterized by distinctions that allow for no overlapping. Precisely by hardening the distinctions and radically setting the sublime over against the beautiful, the *Enquiry* was able to develop a theory of the sublime whose extremism caught the immediate attention not only of his British but also of his French and German contemporaries. Indeed, by thoroughly distinguishing the sublime from the beautiful, Burke was able to give prominence to a form of aesthetic experience that, given its irrationalist underpinnings, had been neglected by classicist sensibility. Rooted in the most powerful of the passions of which the human being is capable, the feeling of terror associated with the sublime brought to light a dark side, as it were, of the Enlightenment and its rationalist conception of the world. For his contemporaries, this new conception of the sublime, whose power derives from an object so terrifying that it suspends the motions of the soul and fills the mind "entirely with its object," to a such a degree, indeed, "that it cannot entertain any other, nor by consequence reason on that object which employs it" (2.1.57), represented a novel insight.

Especially after Boileau's French translation of the *Peri hupsous* in 1674, Longinus's rhetorical and stylistic conception of the sublime, that is, as an effect of elevated language, had become

---

[4] "Introduction on Taste," in *Enquiry*, 11–27, p. 14 (hereafter IT followed by page number).
[5] Joseph Addison, essay no. 412, in Joseph Addison and Richard Steele, *The Spectator*, ed. Donald F. Bond, 5 vols. (Oxford: Clarendon Press, 1965), 3:540.

known in England. Whereas in France Boileau's classicist interpretation of Longinus turned the sublime into "a simple superlative of the beautiful,"[6] Shaftesbury, Addison, and John Baillie, in contrast, pursued Longinus's claim that nature "has implanted in our souls an unconquerable passion for all that is great and for all that is more divine than ourselves"[7] in order to expand the concept of the sublime beyond its rhetorical framework, and they suggested that it was the experience by which one is carried up by grand, natural spectacles "to where one is close to the majestic mind of God."[8] Addison, in a correlative move, staged the sublime as the experience of "the proper limits, as well as the defectiveness, of our imagination."[9] Yet Burke breaks with these conceptions indebted to Longinus when, in the preface to the first edition of the *Enquiry*, he writes that "even Longinus, in his incomparable discourse upon a part of this subject [the distinction of the beautiful and the sublime], has comprehended things extremely repugnant to each other, under one common name of the *Sublime*. The abuse of the word Beauty, has been still more general, and attended with still worse consequences."[10]

Although Burke's strict opposition of the sublime to the beautiful had the effect of giving this latter passion special significance in the eyes of his contemporaries, the beautiful is just as important and cannot simply be relegated to backstage. By drawing a sharp line between both passions, aesthetic experience is shown to consist of two equally important, although mutually incompatible, experiences. Indeed, by radically setting off the sublime from the beautiful, and arguing in a critical debate with the Enlightenment that aesthetic experience contains both passions, Burke owns the distinction of having been the first to have shown that aesthetics – or, in any case, modern aesthetics – is, in Carsten Zelle's words, a "double aesthetics."[11] It is thus in principle not permissible to privilege one of the passions in question over the other.

And yet, in spite of the explicit favor Burke demands from his reader, "that no part of this discourse may be judged of by itself and independently of the rest" (1.19.54), only his theory of the sublime has so far made history. From early on Burke's discussion of the beautiful has been judged unsatisfactory. August Wilhelm Schlegel, for one, calls Burke's empirical deduction of the beautiful a mechanistic effect, coarse, or heavy handed, and even James T. Boulton notes that "by reserving to sublimity all that is impressive and awe-inspiring, [Burke] robs beauty of any power to be intensively moving, and leaves it a weak and sentimentalized conception." He ventures "that the qualities Burke attributes to beauty are insipid," and that a "lack of energy and vitality characteri[zes] Burke's concept of beauty."[12]

In the following, I wish to argue that the theory of the sublime and the beautiful are intrinsically linked, and that one cannot have one without the other, except at the price of amputating one of the two constitutive drives that, according to the socioanthropological underpinnings of the *Enquiry*, make up the core of the human being. But I also wish to suggest that, although his theory of the sublime radically put classicist sensibility into question, Burke's account of beauty is not only as innovative as his treatment of the sublime; from today's perspective, beauty is perhaps the intrinsically more important and stimulating part of Burke's aesthetics.

---

[6] Baldine Saint Girons, "Avant-propos," in Edmund Burke, *Recherche philosophique sur l'origine de nos idées du sublime et du beau*, trans. Baldine Saint Girons (Paris: Vrin, 1990), 22.
[7] Longinus, "On the Sublime," in *Aristotle/Horace/Longinus, Classical Literary Criticism*, trans. T. S. Dorsch (London: Penguin Books, 1965), 146.
[8] Longinus, "On the Sublime," 147.
[9] Addison and Steele, *Spectator*, 3:576 (no. 420).
[10] Burke, *Enquiry*, preface to the first edition, 1.
[11] Carsten Zelle, *Die doppelte Aesthetik der Moderne: Revisionen des Schönen von Boileau bis Nietzsche* (Stuttgart: J. B. Metzler, 1995). Zelle is also the author of a study on Burke entitled *Angenehmes Grauen* (Hamburg: Meiner, 1987).
[12] See August Wilhelm Schlegel, *Kritische Schriften und Briefe* (Stuttgart: Kohlhammer, 1963), 2:57, *Die Kunstlehre*, and Boulton, "Editor's Introduction," lxxiv and cx.

As a preliminary to this contention, it is necessary to evoke the two most elementary ideas "to the ends ... of which all our passions are calculated to answer," namely, "*self-preservation and society*" (1.6.38). By combining two mutually distinct philosophical conceptions – one in which the human being is seen to be driven primarily by self-preservation (Hobbes) and another according to which the human being is above all oriented by a desire for community (Locke and Shaftesbury) – Burke defines the human being in terms of a double and antagonist vocation that models all of men's social behavior: "self-preservation" drives the subject to recoil upon himself, whereas "society" drives him toward the other.[13] Whatever causes on the mind a powerful impression of pain and pleasure, or a modification thereof, can be reduced to these two antagonistic heads. Whereas pain, as Hume had already suggested, "is an ultimate end, and is never referred to by any other object" and is therefore a state in which one senses nothing but oneself, pleasure, rather than enjoying itself, is directed on something besides itself, the object of the enjoyment.[14]

Now, the impressions of pleasure and pain that derive from the properties of objects are, first of all, sense impressions. But we recall that for Burke the groundwork of taste is made up of the senses, the imagination, and judgment. In contrast to the merely receptive nature of the senses, the imagination is "a creative power of its own" (IT 17), although only in the sense of reproducing and recombining sense impressions at its own pleasure, rather than creating something absolutely new. Burke writes, "Now imagination is the most extensive province of pleasure and pain, as it is the region of our fears and our hopes, and of all our passions that are connected with them" (IT 18). In other words, the imagination is the faculty by which that which the mind has received from the senses, the feelings of pleasure and pain, becomes connected to the commanding ideas of our fears and hopes, and the respective passions. The imagination, then, is the place where our fears and hopes – that is, our concern with ourselves and with others – bring about the polarization of our affects, or passions, in terms of the association of the sublime with pain, and the beautiful with pleasure. Imagination is, as it were, the root that founds Burke's "double aesthetics." If this role of the imagination with respect to taste were not yet sufficient to invalidate the accusation that Burke's empirical approach is limited to a mechanistic explanation of aesthetic experience, his acknowledgment of judgment as the third constitutive element of the groundwork of taste should at least further complicate such an assertion.

If Burke contends that "whatever is fitted in any sort to excite the idea of pain, and danger, that is to say, whatever is in any sort terrible, or is conversant about terrible objects, or operates in a manner analogous to terror, is a source of the *sublime*; that is, it is productive of the strongest emotion which the mind is capable of feeling" (1.7.39), this is because terrible objects are a threat to our well-being or, in his words, to "the preservation of the individual" (1.6.38). However, what is painful and terrible does not mechanistically cause this strongest of all feeling by itself. It is not the terrible object as such that produces the feeling of the sublime. Only after having become an idea, or a representation in the imagination, by which a certain distance from the terrible object is achieved, does the terrible incite a feeling of the sublime. Burke writes, "When danger or pain press too nearly they are incapable of giving any delight, and are simply terrible" (1.7.40). However powerful, the feeling of the sublime thus presupposes the removal of the direct threat to self-preservation and the fear of death that accompanies it. Rather than a pleasure, which is a feeling that is caused by a direct and immediate affection of the self by an external object, the feeling that makes up the sublime depends on the removal or cessation of another feeling. The sublime is, in spite of all its force, a derivative feeling, more precisely, only "a species of relative pleasure" (1.4.36), as opposed to the beautiful, which, although it is said to

---

[13] See Wood, "The Aesthetic Dimension of Burke's Political Thought," 64.
[14] David Hume, *An Inquiry Concerning the Principles of Morals*, ed. Tom Beauchamp (Oxford: Oxford University Press, 1998), appx. 1, 163.

be less intense, is a positive pleasure. Distinct from the positive feeling of pleasure, Burke calls the relative pleasure of the sublime "delight."

Terror, then, "is in all cases whatsoever, either more openly or latently the ruling principle of the sublime" (2.2.58). At its most fundamental, or "in its highest degree," the passion caused by the sublime, particularly "the great and sublime in *nature*," is astonishment, that is, "that state of the soul, in which all its motions are suspended, with some degree of horror" (2.1.57). Overwhelmed by its object, filled with it to such an extent "that it cannot entertain any other, nor by consequence reason on that object which employs it" (2.1.57), all reasoning is suspended by the exclusive attention to the one object that fills the mind, and that inhibits all comparison with other objects. Yet, as Burke holds, this very paralysis of the motions of the mind also "anticipates our reasonings, and hurries us on by an irresistible force" (2.1.57). From what we have said so far about delight as the affect that necessarily accompanies the sublime, it is clear that for astonishment to be the ground of a feeling of the sublime, the paralysis that it creates must be of such a kind as to animate reason and, at the same time, to reflect on it. Whatever causes the terror or fear that gives way to a feeling of the sublime, such astonishment is the fundamental state of the soul that subtends all of the various forms of sublime experience. It is, in fact, the operator, as it were, that turns terror into delight.

While attempting to explain "how pain can be a cause of delight," Burke makes the general observation that exercise and labor are required to keep our bodies and minds alert, in short, alive. Without them "all the parts of our bodies ... fall into a relaxation, that not only disables the members from performing their functions, but takes away the vigorous tone of fibre which is requisite for carrying on the natural and necessary secretions" (4.4.133). In addition, a languid inactive state of the body leads one to take a gloomy view of things. And so Burke holds that "the best remedy for all these evils is exercise or *labour*; and labour is a surmounting of *difficulties*, an exertion of the contracting power of the muscles; and as such resembles pain, which consists in tension or contraction, in every thing but degree" (4.4.133). Yet, precisely because exercise and labor resemble pain, these activities that make life more vigorous, that render it more awake and more alive, are therefore also tied to a certain delight.

Now, after having declared that "imagination, and perhaps the other mental powers ... make use of some fine corporeal instruments" (as opposed to the "coarser organs" that are the muscles) in their operations (4.6.135), Burke makes the point that exercise is also necessary for preventing the mental powers from becoming languid. In order to boost their vitality, nothing less than terror is required. He writes, "As common labor, which is a mode of pain, is the exercise of the grosser, a mode of terror is the exercise of the finer parts of the system" (4.7.136). These finer parts "must be shaken and worked to a proper degree" (4.6.135), not only occasionally but regularly. In fact, for the mind to remain animated, exercise through a mode of terror is required constantly. Such exposure to terror is instrumental in preventing the mind from slipping into a languid state. Burke adds,

If the pain and terror are so modified as not to be actually noxious; if the pain is not carried to violence, and the terror is not conversant about the present destruction of the person, as these emotions clear the parts, whether fine, or gross, of a dangerous and troublesome incumbrance, they are capable of producing delight; not pleasure, but a sort of delightful horror, a sort of tranquility tinged with terror; which as it belongs to self-preservation is one of the strongest of all the passions. Its object is the sublime. Its highest degree I call *astonishment*. (4.7.136)

In sum, terror not only has a cathartic effect on the body and the mind; it is above all the means to regularly, if not constantly, reanimate, that is, re-create, the bodily and mentally vital principles. Quickening the life forces, terror is at the service of self-preservation, of which the body and mind are in constant need not only when they are threatened with annihilation by outward objects but also because of the tendency from within to render the mental functions inert.

Terror and pain, if they do not press too close, accomplish this animation and thus produce a state of sublime delight whose strongest form Burke calls astonishment. Astonishment, the state of "delightful horror," is nothing but the sudden awareness of being alive. In astonishment life becomes preserved in that it is constantly renewed. Without astonishment, without this "delightful horror," there is no life to begin with. But if, ultimately, the function of the sublime consists in making such animating astonishment possible, thus preserving life from regressing into a state of languid stupor, the sublime accomplishes not only a highly elementary operation but one that is extraordinary only insofar as it is the condition for everything ordinary.

Indeed, while situating the experience of sublime delight within the encounter with terrible things, Burke makes an observation that to my knowledge has been overlooked so far by his critics and commentators. He writes that only "at certain distances, and with certain modifications, [danger or pain] may be, and they are delightful, *as we every day experience*" (1.7.40; my emphasis). As already pointed out, Burke's accomplishment is to have opened classicist aesthetic experience to the existence of irrationalist affects such as fear and terror, and to have secured them a firm place in the "logic of Taste." But because for the British theoreticians of aesthetics the objects of the sublime are generally extraordinary objects, the affects of fear and terror would seem to be intrinsically linked to things that are grand and overpowering. However, although Burke continues, of course, to highlight such properties of objects as the causes of the sublime, his remark that every day we have the experience of sublimity suggests not only that life-threatening experiences are not out of the ordinary, but also that the grandeur of the objects that cause them is relative. While inquiring into the efficient cause of the sublime, and of not only how the body affects the mind but also how the mind affects the body, Burke recalls that "whatever is qualified to cause terror, is a foundation capable of the sublime" in order to add "that not only these, but many things from which we cannot probably apprehend any danger have a similar effect, because they operate in a similar manner" (4.1.129). In short, if the sublime emerges apart from the everyday incidence of actual threats to our self-preservation and if the sublime is also encountered through association, then it is a rather frequent, and not uncommon, experience. Compared to his predecessors, and especially his romantic followers, there is, as it were, nothing particularly sublime about Burke's sublime.

Commentators unanimously agree that, for Burke, the sublime is the strongest emotional response of which the human being is capable. Indeed, does not Burke clearly assert "that the idea of pain, in its highest degree, is much stronger than the highest degree of pleasure" (2.5.64)? However, the passion of the sublime is also characterized as only "one of the strongest of all the passions" (4.5.134). We should not lose sight of this unresolved hesitation as we now turn to the beautiful, and the positive pleasure to which it gives rise and that Burke calls "the highest pleasure of sense" (1.8.40).

If the passion of the sublime is calculated to answer to the ends of self-preservation, the passion associated with the beautiful concerns society. Society, Burke contends, "may be divided into two sorts. 1. The society of the *sexes*, which answers the purposes of propagation; and next, that more *general society*, which we have with men and with other animals, and which we may in some sort be said to have even with the inanimate world" (1.8.40). As opposed to the source capable of producing pain and delight – namely, the sublime, a source that is solely centered on the relation to oneself – the source of positive pleasure, that is, of the beautiful, is, from the start, double and, as far as general society is concerned, multiple, inasmuch as it includes relations not only to other human beings but to animals and the animate world as well. In contrast to "the passions belonging to the preservation of the individual, [which] turn wholly on pain and danger," those that concern the society of the sexes, and that thus "belong to *generation*," originate from gratifications and pleasures that are "confessedly the highest pleasure[s] of sense" (1.8.40). However "lively ... rapturous and violent" (1.8.40), the pleasure that accompanies human procreation (as opposed to that of animals) is nonetheless not lust. Lust, "merely as such" is "the passion which belongs to generation." Moreover, even though the pleasures of love are the highest pleasures of sense, they are not simply sensuous pleasures: although their intensity is a function of the "great purpose" – "the generation of mankind" – reason, which guides human beings, makes here all the difference. Distinct from the animals, the passions that belong to generation in man are mixed passions (1.10.42). Furthermore, if such pleasure is a positive pleasure, then the highest pleasure of sense does not leave sadness in its wake, as Aquinas remarked, and though, unlike animals, the human being is at all times disposed to the pleasures of love, no great pain arises from the want of this satisfaction. Burke writes, "Had any great pain arisen from the want of this satisfaction, reason, I am afraid, would find great difficulties in the performance of its office" (1.9.42). Characterized as positive, the pleasures of the beautiful are not merely sensual or sensuous pleasures – they are heightened pleasures.

As is indicated by the title of the head – society – to whose ends pleasure answers, the passion of beauty is in both types a social passion. As "a creature adapted to a greater variety and intricacy of relation," the human being

connects with the general passion [of procreation], the idea of some social qualities, which direct and heighten the appetite which he has in common with all the other animals; and as he is not designed like them to live at large, it is fit that he should have something to create a preference, and fix his choice; and this in general should be some sensible quality; as no other can so quickly, so powerfully, or so surely produce its effect. The object therefore of this mixed passion which we call love, is the *beauty* of the *sex*. (1.10.42)

Beauty, itself "a social quality," is the object of the passion in question, which is therefore not merely an animal drive; it is a mixed passion, namely love, in that the respective partners "are attached to particulars by personal *beauty*" (1.10.42). Beauty, Burke writes, "is a name I shall apply to all such qualities in things as induce in us a sense of affection and tenderness, or some other passion the most nearly resembling these" (1.18.51). Love, which springs from the particulars of the other, from his or her beauty, and which is always necessarily a particular – rather than generic – relation, is for Burke a sentiment of affection and tenderness toward others, of men for women, as far as their persons are concerned. Although subtended by the purpose of procreation, love is a relation to another individual, rather than to a member of the same species, and beauty indexes that this relation is one to him or her as a distinct other.

"The second branch of the social passions, is that which administers to *society in general*" (1.11.43). Even though societal life in general, like life itself, is not explicitly the source of a positive pleasure, "the habitudes of *particular society*, are sensations of pleasure" (1.11.43). Just as certain sensible qualities make a desired other beautiful, so singularizing qualities that particularize general society endow it with social enjoyment. In both cases, positive pleasure is a function of particularity. Schematically, then: if the beautiful, which is linked to particular sensible qualities that individualize the other sex, is the source of love, the pleasure of a particular society must also crystallize in a social passion of some kind.

Burke distinguishes three such passions: sympathy, imitation, and ambition. All of these are predicated on a recognition of others as singular others. But, as Burke emphasizes, these passions are "of a complicated kind, and branch out into a variety of forms" (1.12.44). Indeed, these kinds of social passions form an intermediate zone between love and terror, between the beautiful strictly speaking and the sublime. If they are "of a complicated kind," it is because they can generate either pleasure or delight, depending on whether the particular concerns of others by which we are moved, we imitate, or we seek to excel foster or threaten our life in society.

For reasons of economy, I will only briefly take up the case of ambition. Even though imitation of others, and the pleasure we take in it, "is one of the great instruments used by providence in bringing our nature towards its perfection" (1.17.50), it alone would only lead to the homogenization of all men. In order for improvement to occur, a passion for differentiation is needed, and this is ambition. Burke writes, "It is this passion that drives men to all the ways we see in use of signalizing themselves, and that tends to make whatever excites in a man the idea of this distinction so very pleasant" (1.17.50). However, more often than not this passion for distinction takes on imaginary and self-delusory forms, or, as Burke argues, "raises a man in his own opinion, [and] produces a sort of swelling and triumph that is extremely grateful to the human mind" (1.17.50). And he adds that "this swelling is never more perceived, nor operates with more force, than when without danger we are conversant with terrible objects, the mind always claiming to itself some part of the dignity and importance of the things which it contemplates" (1.17.50). In other words, the social passion of ambition can be abused for individual self-infatuation when the delight of having escaped a threat to one's own self-preservation turns into a "glorying and sense of inward greatness" (1.17.50). In short, the experience of the sublime, which is a function of self-preservation and of the re-creation of life, is also an experience capable of being abused. Such is the case when this experience perverts the social passion of ambition by producing self-aggrandizement in order to create a however illusory distance between oneself and all others.

But let me return to the question of the beautiful, and the passion of love that the latter induces in us. In his attempt to show that, contrary to opinion, beauty is based on a "fixed principle," Burke offers a first definition of beauty: "By beauty I mean, that quality or those qualities in bodies by which they cause love, or some passion similar to it" (3.1.91). This definition immediately calls for three remarks: (1) If Burke confines these qualities to "the merely sensible qualities," it is not, as many critics hold, because of his sensualistic approach, but "for the sake of preserving the utmost simplicity." Indeed, the privilege of those sensible qualities derives from their visual evidence – that is, "from the direct force which they have merely on being viewed." But Burke explicitly acknowledges also "secondary considerations," caused by the sympathy that attaches us to other persons or things (3.1.91). (2) The "passion caused by beauty, which I call love, is different from desire," Burke writes, though "desire may sometimes operate along with it" (3.1.91). Following Hutcheson, who had already uncoupled the pleasures of beauty from the "Prospect of Advantage,"[15] Burke disconnects love from "the possession of certain objects" (3.1.91), because this is the specific characteristic of desire or lust. Love is a disinterested relation to its object, a relation that, as we will see, respects the other person or thing in its very independence from oneself. (3) By resting beauty on "merely sensible qualities," Burke takes on the whole tradition that culminated in Albrecht Dürer's *Four Books on Human Proportions*, according to which beauty "consists in certain proportions of parts" (3.2.92). Burke encountered this tradition, which has its origin in Pythagorism, in Hutcheson, among others, who states that "what we call Beautiful in Objects, to speak in the Mathematical Style, seem to be in a compound Ratio of Uniformity and Variety."[16] For Burke, by contrast, proportion is "a creature of the understanding, rather than a primary cause acting on the senses and the imagination" (1.2.92). Proportionality, as an intelligible quality whose perception presupposes reasoning, that is, "long attention and enquiry," is opposed to the beautiful, which, on account of its sensible qualities, pleases immediately. This has nothing "to do with calculation and geometry" (3.2.92–3).

While providing empirical evidence in often very humorous ways (as opposed to the definitely humorless developments on the sublime) to refute the traditional way of conceiving natural beauty, Burke extends the critique of proportionality – which, as he emphasizes, is an artificial idea projected onto nature and not borrowed from thence – to the idea that the shape of objects and living beings is responsible for their beauty. There is nothing beautiful about

---

[15] Francis Hutcheson, *An Inquiry into the Original of Our Ideas of Beauty and Virtue in Two Treatises*, 2nd ed. (Indianapolis, IN: Liberty Fund, 2004 [1725]), 1.1.15.
[16] Hutcheson, *Inquiry*, 1.2.3.

"squares, triangles, and other angular figures" (3.14.121), Burke holds. Nor are admittedly handsome bodies, even though they may display certain proportions, pleasing on account of "measure, but [only of] manner, that creates all the beauty which belongs to shape" (3.4.99). By rejecting proportionality as the source of beauty, whether natural or customary, and hence a consideration of shape defined by intelligible relations of parts and whole, Burke is, indeed, to my knowledge, the first to dissociate beauty from form as a harmonious and well-ordered whole.

As he notes, the opposite of beauty is not deformity or disproportion, as is generally and erroneously believed, but ugliness, "for *deformity* is opposed, not to beauty, but to *compleat, common form*" (3.5.102). If deformity is the opposite of common form (of the individuals of a species, for example), beauty has nothing to do with customary proportion, nor with the idea of form based on perfect proportionality and harmonious arrangements of parts. Even though certain proportions may be found in beautiful bodies, their existence does not necessarily make a body beautiful. They may even, as Burke emphasizes, "be least perfect in some of the most beautiful" (3.4.97). Furthermore, "very different, and even contrary forms and dispositions are consistent with beauty" (3.3.96). The beauty of a human being is not only based on an entirely different principle than perfect proportionality, which, whether natural or customary, is rather common in that it "is generally found in all mankind" (3.6.104) and thus is without any relation to beauty. Beauty is also a relatively rare thing, and the passion of love to which it gives rise is an unusual, extraordinary experience that is therefore contrary to the everydayness of the experience of the sublime.

In the context of his attempt to disconnect the beautiful from proportionality, Burke critically takes issue with another conception according to which "the idea of utility, or of a part's being well adapted to answer its end, is the cause of beauty, or indeed beauty itself" (3.6.104–5). But the opinion that fitness is the cause of the beautiful is not just another misconception of the nature of beauty. Indeed, as Burke remarks, "if it were not for this opinion, it had been impossible for the doctrine of proportion to have held its ground very long" (3.6.105). The conception that beauty consists in perfect proportionality rests on the common idea of a "suitableness of means to certain ends," or a "fitness to answer some end" (3.6.105), in short, on purposiveness and finality. Yet, "many things," Burke writes, "are very beautiful, in which it is impossible to discern any idea of use" (3.6.107). By thus freeing the beautiful from all formal proportionality, and refusing to consider it in terms of utility or fitness, Burke endows the beautiful thing, or human body, with an autonomy and integrity of its own. It follows from this that love, insofar as it is distinct from desire and lust, is not only a disinterested relation but also one of full respect for what is beautiful, letting it be what it is.

By excluding proportion and fitness from playing any role in the perception of the beautiful, Burke does not, of course, mean to suggest that both would have to be absent from anything beautiful. On the contrary, "works of art are the proper sphere of their power; and here it is that they have their full effect" (3.7.107). Yet, what this means is also that proportion and fitness have their strongest aesthetic effect precisely when they are not perceived through understanding and reason, and they thus lack any definite idea of convenience, order, or determined purpose, as is indeed the case in works of art in which proportion and fitness affect the senses and the imagination directly. Such is also the case with the idea of perfection, which, according to opinion, is another cause of beauty. By forcefully rejecting perfection not only in sensible objects but also in the shape of moral perfection, as a constituent of beauty, Burke, in my view, is again the first to break with a tradition that reaches back to neo-Platonism and that in the eighteenth century still found in Shaftesbury a strong defender. As Burke had already pointed out, contrary to the theories that highlight proportion and fitness as defining traits of beauty, empirical evidence shows that beauty is only to be found where a considerable deviation from expected proportions occurs, and where forms, rather than fitting some task, are characterized by uselessness. A certain imperfection of form is also needed for something to strike us as beautiful.

Burke's rather strange examples to make his point should draw our attention, especially because they prepare his own elaboration on the real causes of beauty. In sensible objects, he claims,

> so far is perfection, considered as such, from being the cause of beauty; that this quality, where it is highest in the female sex, almost always carries with it an idea of weakness and imperfection. Women are very sensible of this; for which reason, they learn to lisp, to totter in their walk, to counterfeit weakness, and even sickness. In all this they are guided by nature. Beauty in distress is much the most affecting beauty. (3.9.109)

Let us first take note that because the passion of beauty is a social quality, women are necessarily the paradigm of beauty. But, if the female sex is capable of the greatest beauty, this is an advantage they have over men that "will hardly be attributed to the superior exactness of proportion in the fair sex" (3.4.98). Nor is their superior beauty due to fitness or use. If the latter were criteria of beauty, the strength and agility of Hercules would make him more beautiful than Venus. It is precisely a positive freedom not only from ends and purposes such as self-preservation but also from possessive objectification by desire and lust that gives women an air of self-containment that sensibly shines forth as their beauty.

In the same way, imperfection compared to male strength, as well as modesty as regards qualities of the mind like the virtues – modesty, Burke remarks, "is a tacit allowance of imperfection" – is constitutive of female beauty. Indeed, if a beautiful other is not to be an object of possession or lust but to cause the disinterested affection of love for this other herself (free from all considerations of fitness, usefulness, possession, etc.), she is not to be perfect; she is not, in other words, to fit a preexisting concept of the understanding. These remarks on female beauty and its vulnerability, which for Burke's time, moreover, were something quite new, are not to be dismissed, therefore, simply as male fantasies. They are, indeed, paradigmatic of an openness to the other as other, to the other itself independent of preconceived expectations. But something else is at stake here, because the notion of perfection extends beyond sensible objects to the moral sphere. Thus, when Burke asks, "Who ever said that we *ought* to love a fine woman?" (3.9.110), it is clear that as with congruity, fitness, and finality, moral concerns must be excluded from aesthetic experience. Consequently, love is not of the order of a moral obligation that men have to others who would thus be loved because of their moral perfection and virtue; rather, it is a relation in which others demand to be loved for themselves. And women, therefore, to Burke, make themselves look both physically and morally imperfect, that is, beautiful.

With these negative determinations of the aesthetic experience of the beautiful, and the passion to which it gives rise, Burke has paved the way for an elucidation of their positive characteristics. Having freed the beautiful from all intelligible determinations that "produce approbation, the acquiescence of the understanding, but not love" (3.7.108), Burke concludes "that beauty is, for the greater part, some quality in bodies, acting mechanically upon the human mind by the intervention of the senses" (3.12.112). The qualities in question are, as we have already seen, "merely sensible qualities" (3.18.117), which Burke discusses in relation to categories that are forms of aesthetic experience rather than aesthetic judgment, or, as he writes with respect to "extent or quantity," to "the most obvious point[s] that present [themselves] to us in examining any object" (3.8.113).

These qualities are, needless to say, in all cases the counterpart of the aesthetic experience of the sublime. Because "there is something so over-ruling in whatever inspires awe, in all things which belong ever so remotely to terror, that nothing else can stand in their presence [with the result that] there lie the qualities of beauty either dead and unoperative; or at most exerted to mollify the rigour and sternness of terror" (4.22.157), Burke's commentators have mostly underrated the beautiful and, in light of the sublime, held it to be of inferior quality and judged its attributes to be insipid. We wish, however, to bear in mind that however prevalent the sublime seems to be, the beautiful admittedly also gives rise to one of the strongest affects of the senses. Furthermore, precisely because it cannot be a question of privileging the beautiful over the sublime – the sublime is, for ontological reasons, certainly the stronger passion – it is only fair to do justice to the beautiful by making its qualities appear as powerful as possible. To do this, we wish to look for implications of Burke's analysis of beauty and love that may not only deflate the importance attributed to the sublime but also provide incentives for a deeper exploration of the social passions. Indeed, as we have seen, the social passion of ambition is not only a limit case of the beautiful that borders on the sublime but one that shows the sublime to produce self-inflation. By contrast, it is hard to see what in the passion of love for beauty could provoke any such self-delusion.

"Extent or quantity" is the first category under which the sensible qualities of the beautiful may be considered in opposition to those of the sublime. "Attending to their quantity, beautiful objects are comparatively small" (3.13.114), Burke remarks. In terms of quality, the "property constantly observable" in beautiful objects is smoothness, as opposed to the ruggedness, sudden projection, and sharp angles that characterize sublime objects (3.14.114). The next property of beautiful objects concerns the spatial shape of the whole they form, or the delineation of their outline – that is, the "gradual variation" of their parts, "for whose beginning or end you will find it difficult to ascertain a point," and perpetual change of the line that delimits the whole it forms, as a result of which "the whole is continually changing" (3.15.115). As opposed to sublime objects, which have "an air of robustness and strength," "an appearance of *delicacy*, and even of fragility, is almost essential" to beautiful things. The fourth category thus concerns the temporal quality of beautiful objects: "Weakness and momentary duration ... gives us the liveliest idea of beauty" (3.16.116). Finally, speaking of the colors found in beautiful bodies, Burke notes that although "clean and fair" (as opposed to dusky or muddy, which are presumably sublime), they must not be of the strongest kind. In order to be beautiful, they must be "mixed in such a manner, and with such gradations, that it is impossible to fix the bounds" (3.17.117).

What then are the essential characteristics of beautiful objects or bodies, and by extension of the passion of love to which beauty gives rise? "Attending to their quantity, beautiful objects are comparatively small" (3.13.114), Burke contends. That is, they are not small as such but only small in *relation* to the grand objects of the sublime. This comparative smallness also suggests that, unlike the manifold objects that constantly threaten our self-preservation, beautiful ones are fewer, if not even rare. The overpowering nature of the sublime is such that the beautiful, and the passion of love, can only come into being once they are wrenched from that power, which also indicates that beauty and its passion are extremely fragile and are constantly in danger of being overrun by the power of the sublime. As Burke notes, "the sublime suffers less by being united to some of the qualities of beauty, than beauty does by being joined to greatness of quantity, or any other properties of the sublime" (4.24.157).

In distinction from the great and terrible objects of the sublime, love dwells "on small ones, and pleasing; we submit to what we admire, but we love what submits to us; in one case we are forced, in the other we are flattered into compliance" (3.13.113). Whereas the terrible objects of the sublime overwhelm us and leave no room for freedom but, on the contrary, force us to submit to them, the objects of love seem to submit to us in that they offer us the freedom to relate to them without being forced into such a relation, and in that they hence also make it possible for us to comply. As Burke points out, when we are afflicted by a power superior to us, "we never submit to pain willingly" (2.5.65). Power is adverse to the enjoyment of pleasure, which, by contrast, "must be stolen, and not forced upon us; pleasure follows the will; and therefore we are generally affected with it by many things of a force greatly inferior to our own" (2.5.65).

Burke's language about pleasure here is, of course, premised on its opposite, fear and terror, with the result that the things that cause it are often things inferior in force, and that consent into submission. But from the passage it is also clear that if pleasure must be stolen, rather than forced upon us, it requires freedom on our part. We must be free to relate to a beautiful thing or body in order to find it pleasurable. Vice versa, if force cannot make us enjoy pleasure, neither can pleasure be taken by force from things or others that are inferior in force than ourselves. Beauty and pleasure are attributes of things and bodies that provide the index of a relation based on a recognition and respect for the other in all his or her particularities.

In comparison to ruggedness, sudden projection, and sharp angles, smoothness – one of the most frequent words in the *Enquiry* – is "indeed the most considerable" (3.14.114) quality of anything beautiful. With this quality, which Burke claims to have been the first to associate with beauty, a difference opens within the sense of the visual that dominates the experience of the sublime. Undoubtedly, smoothness as a quality of surfaces is also of the order of the visual, but it is experienced primarily by the sense of touch. Smoothness names not only a sensible quality of the object that is perceived by the eye, but one that can, at the same time, "produce a similar effect through the touch" (3.24.120) called *feeling*. But smoothness is also a quality that demands a kind of vision that – rather than grasping, encompassing, and hence dominating the object – is, as Addison already noted, a sight that "may be considered as a more delicate and diffusive kind of touch."[17]

If, indeed, vision takes place through the picture of an object "painted in one piece" (4.9.137) on the retina, visual objects of great dimensions are a particular cause of terror, and hence the cause of the sublime. As Burke argues, when the object is large, the eye must painfully strain its fine organs in order to take it in. The sense of sight itself is subject to terror when it must grasp as one an object that is so great that vision does not readily arrive at its bounds. Visual beauty, by contrast, causes a relaxation of the organs, including that of vision. In the case of beauty, the eye is relieved of its need to take in uniformly and comprehensively an object that threatens well-being. Rather than taking in the object, the vision that corresponds to anything beautiful is one that gently touches it by sliding over its smooth and soft surface. Faced with a beautiful thing, vision becomes a caressing glance. In turn, the kind of pleasure that such a seeing instills is constitutive of the relation to the beautiful: it is "a smooth and voluptuous satisfaction" (1.5.38), or what Burke also refers to as relaxation.

But if such a tactile mode of sight does not arrest its object, fixing it in a manner such that it can be comprehended and dominated, but instead glides over and along the object, respectful of its integrity, it is also because the beautiful bodies "are not composed of angular paths ... their parts never continue long in the same right line. They carry their direction every moment, and they change under the eye by a deviation continually carrying on, but for whose beginning or end you will find it difficult to ascertain a point" (3.15.114–15). The eye that slides caressingly over a thing or body whose line, like Hogarth's line of beauty to which Burke refers, is "perpetually changing," so that it never becomes arrested as a whole, is a sight that has been relieved of the finality of having to grasp, determine, and possess the object of its gaze. Burke writes:

Observe that part of a beautiful woman where she is perhaps the most beautiful, about the neck and the breasts; the smoothness; the softness; the easy and insensible swell; the variety of the surface, which is never for the smallest space the same; the deceitful maze, through which the unsteady eye slides giddily, without knowing where to fix, or whither it is carried. (3.15.115)

In what has been incisively called an "aesthetics of tenderness," the eye is not threatened and thus does not need to master what it sees and touches by sliding over it.[18] Free of finality, it can

---

[17] Addison and Steele, *Spectator*, 3:536 (no. 411).
[18] Saint Girons, "Avant-propos," 39.

let itself be carried unsteadily along all the lines of a beautiful object or body whose whole is constantly changing, without ever having to dominate it.

The eye here is no longer the theoretical agent, as it was in the case of the sublime. As a consequence, in the fragile passion that is love – a passion that, as we have suggested, arises only in a resisting contrast to the daily terror of self-preservation and its attendant sublime experience – the beautiful object or body is set free in all its fledging individuality and wholeness. More generally, wrenched from everyday experience, Burke's aesthetics of the beautiful is the aesthetics of what, in each particular case, is an "event" – the encounter of the other. It is, therefore, also no accident that Burke qualifies "the passion excited by beauty [as] in fact nearer to a species of melancholy, than to jollity or mirth" (3.25.123). Considering the overwhelming might of the sublime, love of what is beautiful is a passion so fleeting that barely has it come into its own before it is threatened with extinction. Undoubtedly, the experience of the sublime as one of distance serves the self to overcome threats to his integrity and is the strongest of all passions, but love as a limit experience in which the self encounters the other, or rather in which the other approaches the self, is, for all its fragility, quite the opposite of an insipid experience.

3

The Moral Source of the Kantian Sublime

Melissa McBay Merritt

We see other worlds in the distance, but gravity forces us to remain on the earth; we can see other perfections in the spirits above us, but our nature forces us to remain human beings.[1]

INTRODUCTION

A distinctive feature of Kant's account of the sublime is that the term "sublime" does not properly apply to any object in nature: no craggy peak, turbulent sea, or thunderous sky is sublime *sensu stricto*. Rather, "true sublimity must be sought only in the mind of one who judges, not in the object in nature."[2] Indeed, no *sensible* object – be it St. Peter's or the Matterhorn – is truly sublime. Such a thing may be dubbed "sublime" only by courtesy, just inasmuch as it "awakens a feeling of a supersensible faculty in us" (CJ 5:250). Only a *state of mind* can truly be sublime (CJ 5:245–6, 257, and 264). Any account of the Kantian sublime must examine and account for this state of mind. Kant likens the sublime state of mind to a "vibration, i.e., to a rapidly alternating repulsion from, and attraction to, one and the same object" (CJ 5:258; see also CJ 5:245). But this clue about the phenomenology of the sublime does not adequately specify this state of mind, because other states of mind, such as weakness of will, might be described in similar terms.

In order to specify the sublime state of mind appropriately, we need to appreciate the significance of the sublime in the broader scope of Kant's critical project.[3] The received view – which Kant analyzes and corrects rather than dismisses outright – was that the sublime refers to something great or mighty in nature or art that arouses a distinctive pleasure in the subject. The pleasure is distinctive because it is mixed with a measure of pain or fear. In the *Critique of the Power of Judgment*, Kant explicitly acknowledges Edmund Burke's *A Philosophical Enquiry into the Origin of Our Ideas of the Sublime and Beautiful*.[4] Burke traces our enjoyment of the

---

[1] The epigraph is a remark from notes Kant inserted into his own copy of *Beobachtungen über das Gefühl des Schönen und Erhabenen* (*Observations on the Feeling of the Beautiful and Sublime*) sometime after its publication in 1764. See *Kant's gesammelte Schriften*, Königlichen Preussischen (later Deutschen) Akademie der Wissenschaften, 29 vols. (Berlin: Reimer [later de Gruyter], 1900–), vol. 20 (KGS); *Notes and Fragments*, ed. Paul Guyer; trans. Curtis Bowman, Paul Guyer, and Frederick Rauscher (Cambridge: Cambridge University Press, 2005), 20:153. References to all of Kant's works (with the exception of the *Critique of Pure Reason*) are to volume and page of the Akademie edition.
[2] *Kritik der Urteilskraft*, KGS 5; *Critique of the Power of Judgment*, ed. Paul Guyer; trans. Paul Guyer and Eric Matthews (Cambridge: Cambridge University Press, 2000), 5:256 (CJ).
[3] As we will see, Kant discusses the sublime in a variety of contexts. I focus here on Kant's "critical-period" (i.e., post-1781) view of the sublime. I have relatively little to say about the precritical *Observations*, a putatively descriptive catalog of the "beautiful" and "sublime" qualities of human beings according to sex, nationality, and race.
[4] Kant discusses the empirical approach of the British tradition and quotes twice from Burke's work, which he read in translation (see CJ 5:277 and the first introduction to *Critique of the Power of Judgment*, 20:238). The burgeoning

sublime in nature to the "passions" related to self-preservation. Whatever can "excite the ideas of pain, and danger," he maintains, "... whatever is in any sort terrible, ... or operates in a manner analogous to terror, is a source of the *sublime*."[5] We must respond viscerally to the idea of a physical threat on our existence, while at the same time recognizing our real safety from it. For if we really were in pain or danger, we would simply move to escape the threat. But then we would not be in any position to savor the passions of "pain and danger" – passions Burke takes to be the most powerful that we are capable of feeling. He thus implies that the sublime makes available to reflection a fundamental impulse of our animal nature.

Kant learns from this that the sublime might be pressed into service for a reflective, or self-examining, philosophy.[6] For Kant, however, our enjoyment of the sublime in nature makes available to reflection something about our essence as rational beings, not our instincts as animal beings. For Kant takes up the sublime under the rubric of his critical philosophy, that is, the collective work of the three *Critiques*, a project that (in broadest overview) is concerned with the nature of human reason. Admittedly, the theory of the sublime does not directly contribute to what is arguably the central task of the critical project, to establish fundamental principles of rational *cognition*.[7] The sublime instead contributes to the reflective work of critical philosophy by illuminating the moral psychology of the *rational animal*. Kant conceives of human nature according to this ancient formula and claims that our appreciation of the sublime in the sensible world has its "foundation in human nature," and, specifically, in our propensity to be affected by "practical" or "moral" ideas of reason (CJ 5:262; 5:265).

However, although Kant insists on the moral source of the sublime in the *Critique of the Power of Judgment*, he provides little in the way of an actual account. The reader is left to connect the dots between the sublime as it figures in Kant's aesthetics and the sublime as it figures in his moral philosophy. My aim in this chapter is to show how this connection is to be drawn and thereby to demonstrate that the sublime has greater, and more pervasive, significance for Kant's critical philosophy than is commonly supposed.[8]

I begin with the aesthetic theory, showing how Kant attributes the characteristic "vibration" to the conflicting directives of our capacity to represent sensible things (imagination) versus

---

industry of travelogues provided another source for the received view: Kant mentions Claude-Étienne Savary's *Lettres sur L'Égypte* (CJ 5:252) and Horace Bénédict de Saussure's *Voyage dans les Alps* (CJ 5:265 and 276).

[5] Edmund Burke, *A Philosophical Enquiry into the Origin of Our Ideas of the Sublime and Beautiful*, ed. James T. Boulton (London: Routledge and Kegan Paul, 1958 [1759, 1st ed. 1757]), 1.7.39.

[6] By that I simply mean a philosophical project in which the human mind examines itself. Although many of the canonical works of early modern philosophy are presented in such terms, for Kant a reflective philosophy is one in which human reason examines its own cognitive capacity: see *Kritik der reinen Vernunft*, KGS 3 and 4; *Critique of Pure Reason*, trans. Paul Guyer and Allen W. Wood (Cambridge: Cambridge University Press, 1999), Axi and Bxxxv, see also A877/B849. All references are to the pagination of the first (1781) and second (1787) Akademie editions, abbreviated CPR A/B.

[7] For this reason, the *Analytic of the Sublime* is offered as a mere "appendix" to the *Analytic of the Beautiful*; it does not directly contribute to the overall project of the *Critique of the Power of Judgment* (CJ 5:246). Kant finds in the judgment of taste – our appreciation of the *beautiful* rather than the sublime – the resources to ground the teleological view of nature that he in turn supposes must be invoked to bridge a "gulf" between nature and freedom, and hence to unify theoretical and practical reason (see CJ 5:175–6ff.).

[8] Most commentators on the Kantian sublime focus almost exclusively on the sublime in nature and overlook the moral sublime. For exceptions to this general rule, see Paul Guyer, "Symbols of Freedom in Kant's Aesthetics," in *Values of Beauty: Historical Essays in Aesthetics* (Cambridge: Cambridge University Press, 2005), 222–41, who addresses aspects of the connection; Paul Crowther, *The Kantian Sublime: From Morality to Art* (Oxford: Clarendon Press, 1989), who gives attention to the moral context of Kant's sublime, although he has little say about its bearing on the sublimity of nature; and Malcolm Budd, *The Aesthetic Appreciation of Nature* (Oxford: Oxford University Press, 2002), who notes Kant's suggestion that our enjoyment of the sublimity of nature might give rise to "a vivid consciousness of a respect in which we are sublime, a feeling of our own sublimity as rational agents." Budd does not explore the issue, however, and chalks up Kant's suggestion of a moral source for the sublime to his "inveterate tendency ... to moralize, in one way or another, any experience that he valued" (see pp. 68 and 84).

our capacity to represent the supersensible (reason). A sublime state of mind is one in which we take pleasure in the failure of sensible representation, because this failure enables us to appreciate the power of reason to conceive of what can never be met with in the senses, or rendered in sensible representation. I then show how the struggle between imagination and reason in Kant's aesthetic theory has its roots in his conception of a conflict fundamental to human nature – a conflict that cannot be overcome as long as we are both rational and animal. We are, in Kant's view, simultaneously repulsed by the demands of morality and yet attracted to the ideal of perfect rationality that can only be conceived through the moral law. According to Kant, sound moral disposition exercises a certain sublimity of mind, one that is analogous to the aesthetic response to the sublime in nature. Thus my aim is to show how we can understand the Kantian sublime by tracing it to its roots in the moral psychology of the rational animal.

THE SUBLIME IN NATURE

The *Analytic of the Sublime* in the *Critique of the Power of Judgment* deals primarily with the representation of the sublime in nature. Kant sets out with a general explication of the sublime as that which is "absolutely great" or "great beyond all comparison" (CJ 5:248). He then distinguishes the "mathematical" from the "dynamical" sublime: the former concerns what is great in spatial extension; the latter what is great in power.[9]

Kant's account of the mathematical sublime begins with a discussion of ordinary measurement, or the determination of magnitude according to a fixed and repeatable unit. There is always an appropriate standard of measurement for anything that we can encounter in space: not even the breadth of a galaxy is absolutely great (CJ 5:250). Thus ordinary measurement, which Kant refers to as the "logical estimation of magnitude," is inherently comparative (CJ 5:248). For this reason, it is not a candidate for the sublime, because the sublime is the representation of something as great beyond all comparison.

The mathematical sublime instead exercises an "aesthetic" estimation of magnitude, as when we take in the size of something merely by eye (CJ 5:251). An object can be represented as sublime when a subject attempts an aesthetic estimation of its magnitude and finds that it is beyond her capacity. Much of this rests, as Kant points out, on the subject's vantage point. The subject needs to stand in a sweet spot: she must not stand so close to the object that she takes in only a mass that spreads on all sides, extending into and filling her peripheral vision, but she must not stand so far that the boundaries of the entire object easily register in a single glance. In the sweet spot, the subject struggles to attain a comprehensive view of the thing but just fails – managing only to have parts in view as others fall out of view. Kant attributes this failure to the power of the *imagination*, or the capacity to represent sensible particulars. With the exercise of the imagination, the subject is able to "apprehend," or take in, the object bit by bit, but she cannot "comprehend" the object, or represent it as a whole (CJ 5:251–2). Thus it feels to the subject as if the apprehension would need to go on ad infinitum if the magnitude of the object were ever to be represented as a comprehensive whole. However, we are unable to represent an infinitely extensive, yet comprehensive, magnitude in sensible representation; anything that we can represent as a whole by means of the senses has boundaries in our sensory field. The representation of the "given infinite" (CJ 5:254), or "infinity comprehended" (CJ 5:255), can only be an *idea of reason*, that is, an intellectual representation to which no sensible representation can ever be adequate. Thus the mathematical sublime brings to light our capacity to represent the supersensible, which is reason.

[9] For insightful discussions of the distinction between the mathematical and dynamical sublime, see Crowther, *The Kantian Sublime*, 41–135, and Paul Guyer, *Kant and the Experience of Freedom: Essays on Aesthetics and Morality* (Cambridge: Cambridge University Press, 1996), 187–228.

In the dynamical sublime, the greatness is one of power: we find it in "threatening cliffs, thunder clouds towering up into the heavens, bringing with them flashes of lightning and crashes of thunder, volcanoes with their all-destroying violence, hurricanes with the devastation they leave behind, the boundless ocean set into a rage, a lofty waterfall on a mighty river" (CJ 5:261). We must represent the object as "fearful" – capable of arousing fear in us – without our actually being afraid of it. For if the subject were actually afraid, the impulse to avoid further engagement with the object would take hold. To represent the object as sublime, the subject must be able to dwell on the representation of a physical force incomparably greater than any she finds in herself. The subject who is able to contemplate a threat to her physical existence – without fleeing, as it were, from the representation of it – thereby finds within herself grounds for supposing that she is in some respect "independent of" this threat, or in some way superior to nature (CJ 5:261). The dynamical sublime brings to light "a self-preservation of quite another kind than that which can be threatened and endangered by nature outside us" (CJ 5:261–2).

Let us consider now what is common to the mathematical and the dynamical sublime. As I noted at the outset, Kant characterizes the sublime state of mind as "a rapidly alternating repulsion from and attraction to one and the same object" (CJ 5:258). Although this gloss appears in the discussion of the mathematical sublime, it would evidently hold for the dynamical sublime as well, in which, if anything, the aspect of repulsion is easier to identify. Because we naturally avoid physical threats, the representation of a physical threat would be repulsive even if we recognize our safety and engage in no real avoidance. In the case of the mathematical sublime, the difficulty of taking in the object figures as a kind of threat on our ability to make sense of the physical world around us: this is fearful and thus would introduce the element of repulsion. Both the mathematical and the dynamical sublime involve the representation of a threat on our physical capacities, broadly understood.

But Kant is vague about the attractive aspect of the sublime in the *Critique of the Power of Judgment*. He tells us that we are attracted to the large or mighty object in nature, but only because it stands in for an attraction to "the idea of humanity" in ourselves (CJ 5:257). Kant offers a further clue when he remarks that such large or powerful things are potentially *useful*, because the representation of them can "make palpable in ourselves a purposiveness that is entirely independent of nature" (CJ 5:246; see also 5:259). By "a purposiveness ... independent of nature," Kant indicates that we are determined toward some end other than animal self-preservation; the enjoyment of the sublime in nature apparently helps us to appreciate this end, or reinforces an existing appreciation of it. Kant reformulates this point when he claims that the enjoyment of the sublime arouses a certain "feeling" for our "supersensible vocation" (CJ 5:257). He later identifies this as "moral feeling": a feeling for the "vocation of the mind" that "entirely oversteps the domain of [nature]" (CJ 5:268). He even claims that this "vocation" is itself "sublime" (CJ 5:264; see also 5:262). We must ascertain what Kant is gesturing toward with these remarks in order to have an adequate account of his conception of the sublime. Hence the *Critique of the Power of Judgment* cannot be our sole text for interpreting the Kantian sublime, because it fails to explain the *attractive* aspect of the sublime.

To understand what Kant is saying here about moral feeling and our sublime "vocation," we need to consider his view of human nature – or, to be more specific, the moral psychology of the rational animal. However, we must first get a clearer view of the distinction between the sensible and the supersensible that is at work in Kant's theory of the sublime. We will then be in a better position to make sense of Kant's remarks about our "sublime" or "supersensible vocation" as rational beings. To understand Kant's distinction between the sensible and the supersensible, we must take a step back and consider it in light of the broader aims of Kant's critical philosophy.

THE SENSIBLE AND THE SUPERSENSIBLE

Although Kant's theory of the sublime does not contribute directly to the epistemological aims of critical philosophy, it cannot be understood in abstraction from those aims. So we must begin with Kant's famous lament about the "peculiar fate" of human reason: it is "burdened by questions" that it is neither able to ignore nor able to answer (CPR Avii). Kant has in mind the classic problems of metaphysics, such as the attempt to demonstrate the existence of God, the immortality of the soul, and the freedom of the will. Like most philosophers of the modern era, Kant addresses the challenges of metaphysics by providing first an assessment of the limits of our cognitive capacity. Unlike many of his predecessors, however, Kant does not set out to suppress reason's irksome tendency to raise questions that it cannot answer. Instead, Kant advocates finding a way of handling these questions that respects their rational origin and epistemological significance – while guarding against being led by them into speculative temptation, and thereupon into error.

For Kant, handling these questions properly requires maintaining a clear distinction between two modes of knowledge: the theoretical and the practical.[10] Theoretical knowledge concerns *what is the case* in the domain of nature: it is concerned with the sensible. The most basic epistemological lesson of the *Critique of Pure Reason* is that theoretical knowledge is limited to objects of possible experience: we cannot have theoretical knowledge about the supersensible. Hence we cannot determine that God exists, that the soul is immortal, or that the will really is free.

Practical knowledge, on the other hand, concerns the *good to be brought about through action*. It is in this context that Kant addresses the issue of freedom. We cannot invoke the notion of agency without invoking the notion of freedom. For if we take ourselves to be rightfully held responsible for what we do, then we must suppose that our agency is not brute force of nature; there must be some respect in which we are properly free from being determined by the causal order of material nature. We cannot make determinations about the good to be brought about through action if we do not conceive of ourselves as intentional agents, and this we can do only if we think of the supersensible. So as agents, we implicitly distinguish between the sensible and the supersensible. And yet, we cannot have theoretical knowledge of the supersensible. Hence we cannot introspect and determine of some particular action that it in fact results from the freedom that is proper to a rational being. The action may well have been the expression of some appropriately refined animal instinct – something that depends on sensuous inclination and answers to our desire to get on well in the sensible world.[11]

Practical knowledge concerns what *ought* to be done. If there is genuine *knowledge* to be had here, then the determination of what ought to be done must rest on objective grounds: it cannot be a matter of what a particular agent just happens to want. An objective determination of the good concerns what any rational being, in the unobstructed exercise of reason, would recognize as something that ought to be pursued. This is why Kant supposes that the fundamental principle of practical knowledge – the source of all knowledge about the good to be brought about through action – stems from reason alone, without regard to our existence as sensible

---

[10] For Kant's distinction between theoretical and practical knowledge, see CPR Bix–x, A547–8/B575–6, A802/B830, and *Kritik der praktischen Vernunft*, KGS 5, *Critique of Practical Reason*, in *Practical Philosophy*, trans. and ed. Mary J. Gregor (Cambridge University Press, 1996), 5:3–14 and 89–106 (CPrR).

[11] Kant makes this point often. See, for example, CPrR 5:28–30; CJ 5:275; CPR A802/B830; *Grundlegung zur Metaphysik der Sitten*, KGS 4, *Groundwork of the Metaphysics of Morals*, in Immanuel Kant, *Practical Philosophy*, 4:407 (G), and *Die Religion innerhalb der Grenzen der bloßen Vernunft*, KGS 6, *Religion within the Boundaries of Mere Reason*, in Immanuel Kant, *Religion and Rational Theology*, trans. and ed. Allen E. Wood and George Di Giovanni (Cambridge: Cambridge University Press, 1996), 6:21–22, 31, and 41 (R).

beings in material nature. This principle is the moral law, which is expressed as an imperative binding categorically on finite rational beings.[12]

For the purposes of this chapter, it is necessary to grant Kant's (not uncontroversial) epistemological claim that the moral law, or categorical imperative, is the source of all knowledge about the good to be brought about through action. In establishing the moral law as the fundamental principle of pure practical reason, Kant abstracts from facts about the *embodiment* of reason in us. Kant's conception of the moral sublime emerges only after the categorical imperative is established, and the fact of our embodiment is brought back into view. Thus it is with the moral psychology of the rational animal that our account of the sublime resumes.

THE SUBLIME VOCATION OF THE RATIONAL ANIMAL

Kant, as we saw earlier, repeatedly suggests that there is something sublime about human nature: he speaks of our "sublime vocation" (CJ 5:264 and 262), the "sublimity of our moral vocation" (R 6:50; see also 6:22n), and "the sublimity of our nature (in its vocation)" (CPrR 5:87; cf. CPrR 5:117). To understand these remarks, we must bear in mind what we have just learned about Kant's distinction between the sensible and the supersensible. To recognize that one can be held responsible for what one does is to suppose that there must be some respect in which one is free from being determined by the causal order of material nature. And so, although we find ourselves in the sensible world, we must also think of ourselves as belonging somehow to a supersensible, or merely intelligible, order of reason.

When Kant talks about the "vocation" of our kind, the term he uses is *Bestimmung*. In logical contexts, this is commonly translated as "determination," in the sense that the judgment "this is green" represents the determination of a singular representation under the concept *green*. Likewise the *Bestimmung* of our species is what determines our species to be the species it is. Following ancient tradition, Kant conceives of our species as *rational animal*, with rationality being the determining feature. However, Kant also gives special emphasis to the point that no individual is perfectly or infallibly rational. Rationality may be our essence, but it is something to be cultivated and developed – as best we can, with an eye to an ideal with respect to which we always fall short. Hence Kant takes our "natural vocation" to consist in "continual progress toward the better";[13] the progress can only be continual because perfect rationality is unattainable. Hence the term *Bestimmung* takes on a normative and teleological sense in this context.[14] Our *Bestimmung* is a calling (vocation) to develop and express the rationality that is proper to our kind.

To understand Kant's claim that this vocation is itself sublime, it might help to consider the German term for the sublime, *das Erhabene*, which derives from the verb *erheben*, "to raise or lift up." Presumably, then, the vocation of the rational animal is "sublime" because it involves

---

[12] Strictly speaking, Kant distinguishes between the moral law as such from its formulation as an *imperative* binding categorically on all *finite* rational beings (G 4:414; CPrR 5:32–3). For present purposes, I speak of "the moral law" and "the categorical imperative" interchangeably. The categorical imperative is formulated as follows: "So act that the maxim of your will could always hold at the same time as a principle in a giving of universal law" (CPrR 5:30; see also G 4:402 and 421, with alternate formulations at 421, 429, and 438).

[13] *Anthropologie in pragmatischer Hinsicht*, KGS 7, *Anthropology from a Pragmatic Point of View*, trans. Robert B. Louden, in *Anthropology, History, and Education*, trans. and ed. Robert B. Louden and Günter Zöller (Cambridge: Cambridge University Press, 2007), 7:324 (Anth). To achieve consistency across Kant's texts when translating *Bestimmung* (and its cognates), I have modified the translation: Louden renders *Naturbestimmung* here as "natural destiny."

[14] See Reinhard Brandt, "The Guiding Idea of Kant's Anthropology and the Vocation of the Human Being," in *Essays on Kant's Anthropology*, ed. Brian Jacobs and Patrick Kain (Cambridge: Cambridge University Press, 2003), 85–104, pp. 96–7.

looking *up* to an ideal of perfect rationality and making the approximation of that ideal one's end. At the same time, we should now be able to make better sense of Kant's slightly different remarks, to the effect that the sublime is a state of mind that is distinguished by a certain attraction, or "feeling," for our "supersensible vocation" (CJ 5:257). The sublime is a state of mind in which we are uplifted, or oriented toward, what can only be conceived through reason alone, an ideal that must guide our conduct even though we could never recognize it (i.e., perfect virtue) in the flesh.[15] Hence the sublime is a reflective state of mind, one in which the subject is somehow attuned to her condition, or predicament, as a rational animal.

Indeed, even our enjoyment of the sublime in nature – in which we obviously engage with some object in the world – is a reflective state of mind. Our appreciation of the sublime in nature begins with a physical comparison, be it of might or size. Peering out into the Grand Canyon, seeing eons etched into the countless ridges in the stone and the depths forged by the unceasing movement of water, we are aware of our relative spatiotemporal insignificance. We are lost in the comparison. And yet we are aware of our capacity, and readiness, to make this comparison – to accept our physical insignificance. What in us accepts this? Surely not our "sensible" or "animal" nature. The experience of the sublime points to something that remains unthreatened by the physical comparison. The subject must be ready to suppose that something in her survives the ravage, or eludes estimation by any spatiotemporal measure. Her attraction – that she lingers as she looks out over the precipice – points to something supersensible: her "intelligible" or "rational" nature. At the same time there is the competing claim – that element of repulsion, registering as the subject's fear that she will "disappear" in the comparison. When the canyon's open abyss arouses these contrasting movements of attraction and aversion, the mind is uplifted – *sublime* – only to the extent that the attraction holds sway.

MORAL FEELING

As we saw at the end of the section on the sublime in nature, Kant links our feeling for the sublime in nature with "moral feeling"; this suggests that one's readiness to linger over an open abyss might correlate with the development of one's capacity for moral feeling. But Kant does not say much about moral feeling in the *Critique of the Power of Judgment*, except to gloss it as "the feeling for (practical) ideas" (CJ 5:265), or "the feeling of a vocation of the mind that entirely oversteps the domain of [nature]" (CJ 5:268). Later, I explain why our enjoyment of the sublime in nature cannot quite involve moral feeling directly, but only something akin to it. First, however, we must examine Kant's account of moral feeling.

Kant defines moral feeling as "practically effected feeling": it is feeling that depends on, and arises from, a subject's representation of the moral law (CPrR 5:75). It is thus distinguished from "pathologically effected" feeling: that is, a feeling that "underlies all of our inclinations" and is produced by an object of the senses. Kant explains moral feeling through a developmental story; the background to this story is as follows. To come into one's reason is to be able freely to adopt certain ends. It is to be in a position to recognize that one does *x* for the sake of *y* – and thus to conceive of oneself, however dimly, as an agent. The rational subject represents her actions under rules: to act is to endorse, at least tacitly, a maxim or subjective principle of action. Now, it follows from Kant's view that the moral law is constitutive of practical, or will-determining, reason that when a subject comes into her reason she also has some tacit grasp – again, however dim – of the moral law. So, on the one hand, a rational agent cannot help having some appreciation of what morality requires, and conceiving of the good in a way that answers to the moral law. On the other hand, a rational *animal* is affected by sensuous desire

---

[15] On perfect virtue as an unattainable ideal, see CPrR 5:84 and *Die Metaphysik der Sitten*, KGS 6, *The Metaphysics of Morals*, in *Practical Philosophy*, 6:409 (MM).

and inclination, so whatever promises to bring about or sustain her own well-being and comfort is liable to appear as something that ought to be pursued, or good. Thus a conflict is writ into human nature, expressed as competing conceptions of the good.

Moral feeling appears against the background of this conflict. Kant's story begins with "our pathologically determinable self," presuming that it is "our entire self" and thus trying "to make its claims primary and originally valid" (CPrR 5:74). The claim of the pathologically determinable self – the claim it takes to be "primary and originally valid" – is that some object of sensuous inclination ought to be pursued. Kant calls this "self-love." Self-love is perfectly natural, and even morally permissible: I may act out of self-love as long as it does not conflict with moral duty.[16] However, self-love tends to outrun these limitations, giving rise to a certain illusion. A subject is liable to take sensuous inclination to be indicative of what is objectively good, when in fact it is indicative only of what appeals on the basis of her individual constitution and beliefs about the conditions of her own well-being. Kant calls the illusion that stems from self-love run amuck "self-conceit": it "prescribes as laws" – that is, as universally binding sources of the determination of the will – "the subjective conditions of self-love" (CPrR 5:74).

We should recall Kant's claim that someone who has come into the use of reason unavoidably has some consciousness (however dim) of the moral law. This consciousness of the moral law "*strikes down* self-conceit" (CPrR 5:73), he claims, and "humiliates every human being when he compares it with the sensible propensity of his nature" (CPrR 5:74). Consciousness of a law binding on all rational beings as such "deprives self-love of its influence and self-conceit of its illusion"; it checks the tendency to treat subjective grounds of the determination of the will as objective and lawful. Moral feeling, or respect for the moral law, emerges as a reverential attraction to what makes us *able* to overcome the dominance of self-love, even though in point of fact it probably only momentarily "weakens" it (CPrR 5:73).

Kant takes moral feeling to be a natural endowment. This means that the rational animal who comes into the use of reason cannot help but enjoy some rudiment of moral feeling (MM 6:399). However, the capacity for moral feeling remains weak if left uncultivated, because the feeling itself is highly unstable: after all, it involves the subject's *attraction* to something that humiliates her, and humiliation is *painful*. Our capacity for moral feeling must be strengthened and made stable. To understand this point, let us consider how Kant recasts his claim about "respect for the moral law" in more concrete terms, namely, as respect for another human being. Kant writes:

Fontenelle says, "*I bow before an eminent man, but my spirit does not bow*." I can add: before a humble common man in whom I perceive uprightness of character in a higher degree than I am aware of in myself *my spirit bows*, whether I want it or whether I do not and hold my head ever so high, that he may not overlook my superior position. Why is this? His example holds before me a law that strikes down my self-conceit when I compare it with my conduct, and I see observance of that law and hence its *practicability* proved before me in fact. (CPR 5:76–7)

Let us suppose that I am aware of what morality requires of me, and, at least for the most part, I act accordingly – but occasionally I allow myself to suppose that my circumstances make this impossible. Now, in Kant's vignette, I am humiliated by a humble common man, someone of comparatively meager resources who, let us suppose, demonstrates the practicability of the duty of beneficence. His example affronts my attempt to excuse myself from its requirements. I am humbled by his example: "*my spirit bows*." Such humiliation is painful: I am averse to the example that this common man presents to me. As Kant notes, "we give way" to the feeling of respect "only reluctantly with regard to a human being" (CPrR 5:77). I will likely want to gratify my feeling of aversion, perhaps by magnifying some previously overlooked character flaw, or

---

[16] This is what Kant refers to as "rational self-love" (CPrR 5:73).

perhaps by projecting a false one onto his image. If I do this, I extinguish the feeling of respect. I must not recoil from this humiliation if I am to sustain the feeling of respect.

To see how the recoil might be avoided, let us examine Kant's vignette more closely. We should note that I am actually humiliated not by the man but rather by the moral law itself.[17] Kant is careful to present the vignette so that no *external* humiliation is involved; every social convention has been observed. So "*my spirit bows*" while my head remains high. The humiliation, rather, is *internal*.

The idea of an internal humiliation deserves further examination. We tend to think of humiliation as hitting from outside: I am humiliated by someone or something without. Humiliation is typically external, in other words. So we should press on this idea of an internal humiliation – that is, on the idea that the moral law "unavoidably humiliates every human being" (CPrR 5:74). Because Kant supposes that the moral law is constitutive of rational agency, or of what it is to be a rational being with a will, it does not seem correct that the moral law can humiliate a rational being, at least if we suppose that humiliation has an external origin. Kant's point, however, is that this humiliation rests on a moral illusion: it is how things look if the subject takes herself to be principally a "sensible," rather than a "rational," being. Recall that Kant's account of moral feeling began with the episode in which our "pathologically determinable self" supposes that it is "our entire self" (CPrR 5:74). A person who more readily identifies with her "pathologically determinable self" is more liable to gratify the aversion that springs from the pain of humiliation. Such a person cannot sustain moral feeling and in turn avoids comparing her conduct against the standard of the moral law. All of this follows from her self-conception, from the supposition that she *just is* her "pathologically determinable self."

According to Kant, even a person of sound moral disposition will experience resistance to the moral law. But the person of sound moral disposition does not gratify this aversion quite so readily, because the moral law does not seem to impinge on her *from outside*. This allows the attractive aspect of respect to dominate, so that it can be sustained: "[O]nce one has laid self-conceit aside and allowed practical influence to that respect, one can in turn never get enough of contemplating the majesty of this law, and the soul believes itself elevated in proportion as it sees the holy law elevated above itself and its frail nature" (CPrR 5:77, translation altered). To "lay self-conceit aside" is to give up supposing that one maintains *oneself* by acting from self-love as an unconditional maxim. Put in positive terms, it is to think of oneself as principally a rational being that is to be respected, rather than as principally a sensible being to be preserved. The individual who can sustain a feeling of respect has this self-conception, and this enables her to look up to the "majesty" of the moral law without experiencing it as an oppression raining down on her from without.[18]

Because Kant does not suppose that we can arrive at a state of character where we experience no resistance to moral duty, there is always an element of resistance in moral feeling. Aversion is a basic ingredient. And even though the capacity for moral feeling is a natural endowment of our species, such feeling cannot so much as register in one's consciousness if it is not sustained. The ability to sustain a feeling of respect requires that the attractive aspect effectively determine the subject's mental state. And this, in turn, rests on the subject's self-conception: she must conceive of herself, by essence and by calling, as a rational being. If this

---

[17] On this point, see Allen W. Wood, "Self-Love, Self-Benevolence, and Self-Conceit," in *Kant, Aristotle, and the Stoics*, ed. Stephen Engstrom and Jennifer Whiting (Cambridge: Cambridge University Press, 1996), 141–61.

[18] See Andrews Reath, "Kant's Theory of Moral Sensibility," *Kant Studien* 80 (1989), 284–302, who points out the danger of supposing that, for Kant, the attraction to the ideal represented in the moral law mechanically interacts with the attractions of happiness, so that the stronger of two affective forces wins out (as in a Humean philosophy of mind). "The appropriate metaphor," Reath writes, "is rather that of a struggle between two parties for something like legal authority or political legitimacy" (289n13; see also 296).

orientation toward her vocation as a rational being is firm, then the feeling of respect can be sustained. For only then will the subject take pleasure in recognizing that there is something in her that has the capacity to resist the claims of her sensible nature.

MORAL FEELING AND THE SUBLIME

Now that we have considered Kant's view of moral feeling, it is time to address its relation to the sublime. There is plenty of circumstantial evidence in the *Critique of Practical Reason* to support the claim that Kant saw a connection between moral feeling and the sublime. Once Kant concludes his account of respect in chapter III of the *Analytic of Pure Practical Reason* (around CPrR 5:81), the remainder of the chapter dances around the topic of the sublime in one way or another. First, Kant denies that morality is like beauty – something pleasant and gentle, which we would enter into without any feeling of aversion – and hints instead that it is like the sublime, in that there is always an element of aversion (CPrR 5:82–4; see also CJ 5:271). Then Kant follows with an encomium to the sublimity of duty – sublime due to its source in what "elevates a human being above himself (as a part of the sensible world)" (CPrR 5:86).

But we need to understand the connection between moral feeling and the sublime and not simply note Kant's hints about it. To address this issue, it will help to recognize that not every "uplifted" state of mind is genuinely sublime by Kant's lights. In the *Critique of the Power of Judgment*, Kant points to *enthusiasm* as an example, which he glosses as "the idea of the good with affect" (CJ 5:272). Affect is overwhelming feeling that renders the subject "incapable of engaging in free consideration of principles, in order to determine itself in accordance with them" (CJ 5:272).[19] Someone might, for example, be overcome during a political speech; this could be "uplifting" if she finds herself longing for certain ideals. But if we do not understand what we seek, and why it is good, then we are not freely aiming at anything at all: it is the sweep of affect that urges us on, and we are chasing an image.

For this reason, Kant takes enthusiasm to be a fraudulent mode of the sublime; he first says that it merely "seems to be sublime," before clarifying that it is "aesthetically sublime" (CPrR 5:272). This specification is somewhat jarring, because we are left wondering how it relates to the aesthetic judgment regarding the sublime in nature (which I consider in the following). But Kant's point presumably rests on a distinction he often draws between *aesthesis* and *logos*, that is, between what has its source in our receptivity versus what has its source in the spontaneity of our reason. Enthusiasm is aesthetically sublime in the sense that the mind is "uplifted" through *affect*, something that is brought on the subject from without and renders her momentarily incapable of rational reflection on principles. What is aesthetically sublime in this sense works us over, inducing an "agreeable exhaustion" that Kant likens to having one's muscles and joints worked over by a masseur (CJ 5:273–4). It does not exercise the freedom that is proper to a rational being.[20] The Kantian sublime – the sublime that Kant endorses and takes up under the banner of critical philosophy – can be distinguished as the "logical" sublime in the sense that it depends on the subject's consciousness of rational principles. Moral feeling is a mode of the Kantian sublime: it is an elevated state of mind, registering as the subject's attraction to an ideal

---

[19] Kant discusses *affect* (*Affekt*) at length and distinguishes it from *passion* (*Leidenschaft*); see CJ 5:272n; MM 6: 407–9; and Anth 7:251–65.

[20] For an opposing interpretation of the sense in which enthusiasm is "aesthetically sublime," see Robert R. Clewis, *The Kantian Sublime and the Revelation of Freedom* (Cambridge: Cambridge University Press, 2009). For a discussion of the problems with Clewis's interpretation, see Melissa McBay Merritt, review of Robert Clewis, *The Kantian Sublime and the Revelation of Freedom*, *British Journal for the History of Philosophy* 18, 3 (2010), 529–32.

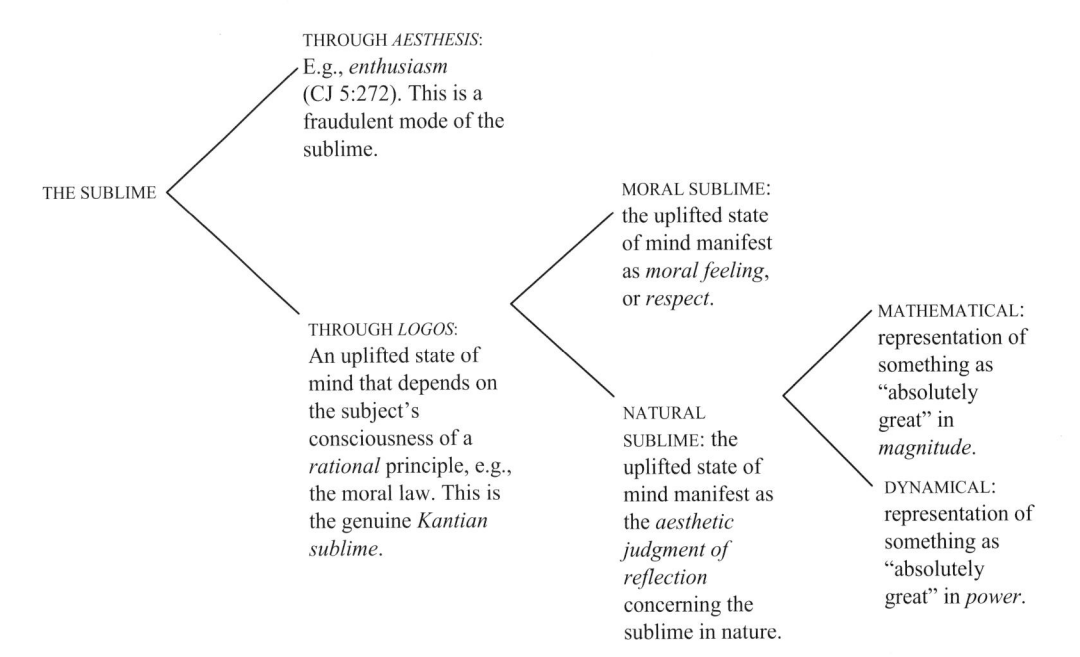

```
                                    THROUGH AESTHESIS:
                                    E.g., enthusiasm
                                    (CJ 5:272). This is a
                                    fraudulent mode of the
                                    sublime.

                                            MORAL SUBLIME:
                                            the uplifted state
                                            of mind manifest
                                            as moral feeling,
                                            or respect.                    MATHEMATICAL:
THE SUBLIME                                                                representation of
                                                                           something as
                                                                           "absolutely
                                    THROUGH LOGOS:                         great" in
                                    An uplifted state of                   magnitude.
                                    mind that depends on
                                    the subject's          NATURAL
                                    consciousness of a     SUBLIME: the
                                    rational principle, e.g.,  uplifted state of
                                    the moral law. This is   mind manifest as   DYNAMICAL:
                                    the genuine Kantian      the aesthetic      representation of
                                    sublime.                 judgment of        something as
                                                             reflection         "absolutely
                                                             concerning the     great" in power.
                                                             sublime in nature.
```

FIGURE 3.1. Modes of the sublime.

conceived through the moral law. As we will see in the next section, even one's enjoyment of the sublimity of the Grand Canyon is sublime in the "logical" sense that Kant endorses. Kant's taxonomy of terms can be summarized in Figure 3.1.

ADMIRATION AND RESPECT

In order to assess the relation between the moral and the natural sublime, it will help to distinguish them more clearly. We can do this by specifying the feeling operative in each. According to Kant, the sublime can be made manifest either through admiration (*Bewunderung*) or through respect (*Achtung*) (CJ 5:245). Kant distinguishes these feelings first by their proper objects: the proper object of respect is the moral law, or *persons* inasmuch as they may figure as "examples" of this law; the proper object of admiration, by contrast, is some *thing*, "for example, lofty mountains, the magnitude, number, and distance of the heavenly bodies, the strength and swiftness of many animals" (CPrR 5:76). Thus Kant implies that the moral sublime is experienced as respect, or moral feeling, whereas the natural sublime is experienced as admiration.

Kant claims that admiration is "analogous" to the feeling of respect (CPrR 5:78). Both feelings require the subject to conceive of an absolute standard, something against which everything else falls short. The difference is that the subject who feels *respect* conceives of a standard that she recognizes as holding *for herself*. Recall the respect I feel for the "humble common man" in our earlier example. The man's example enables me to represent the moral law in all of its "purity": I see that this law commands categorically, without granting an exception for me on the basis of my circumstances, which have been shown to be comparatively favorable at that. His example, or rather my respect for it, exhorts me to practice greater beneficence. Now consider the other feeling. I watch Olympic gymnastics in a state of astonished admiration. The athletes seem stronger, faster, and more dexterous than any I can imagine. Yet they do not serve as "examples" of a law, or a standard, that I give to myself. I do not share their end: I do not get up off the couch and begin to stretch or jump.[21] I admire their skill, but it would be delusional for me to respect it.

Admiration, then, is contemplative, whereas respect is exhortative. If, as I have argued, the natural sublime is enjoyed through admiration, whereas the moral sublime is enjoyed through respect, then it would follow that our appreciation of the sublime in nature is merely contemplative. And indeed, this conclusion is supported by Kant's view that we make a "pure aesthetic judgment" when we enjoy the sublime in nature. An *aesthetic* judgment is one that is determined by a feeling of pleasure or pain; by this it is distinguished from a *logical* judgment, which is determined by a concept or a rule. Hence the aesthetic judgment on the sublime in nature does not directly involve the concept of the moral good. Our enjoyment of the sublime in nature is morally indeterminate. It is, in this regard, merely contemplative: it does not directly exhort me to develop moral character, or cultivate my capacity for moral feeling.[22]

Still, Kant insists that our capacity to enjoy the sublime in nature "has its foundation in human nature," and, more specifically, in our propensity for moral feeling (CJ 5:262 and 265). The cultivation of this propensity "remains our responsibility" (CJ 5:262), and without it we would be unable to enjoy the sublime in nature (CJ 5:265). As I have argued, the requisite moral development turns on the subject's recognition that she is by nature and by calling a rational being. Only with this self-conception can the subject avoid being overwhelmed by the feeling of aversion that is an essential ingredient of the sublime. Thus the enjoyment of the sublime in nature depends not only on a background consciousness of the moral good but also on the particular power of one's attraction to it.

CONCLUSION

It is worth considering, in closing, how Kant's theory of the sublime develops from his 1764 *Observations on the Feeling of the Beautiful and the Sublime* to his mature view in the critical period. In the early work, Kant claims that the sublime "stretches the powers of the mind more forcefully" than the beautiful; it is exhausting and so must be sweetened by a certain measure of beauty in order to be endured by the subject.[23] To some extent, the mature Kant continues this theme, inasmuch as he conceives of the sublime in terms of an arousal of contrasting impulses of the mind: surely particular individuals will become quickly exhausted by such a state of mind. Thus it is all the more striking that, in one of the most memorable passages of Kant's critical philosophy, we find talk of a sublime state of mind that is not inherently exhausting:

Two things fill the mind with ever new and increasing admiration and reverence, the more often and more steadily one reflects upon them: *the starry heavens above me and the moral law within me*.... The first view of a countless multitude of worlds annihilates, as it were, my importance as an *animal creature*.... The second, on the contrary, infinitely raises my worth as an *intelligence* by my personality, in which the moral law reveals to me a life independent of animality and even of the whole sensible world. (CPrR 5:161–2)

---

[21] Kant makes the related point when he imagines a "true scholar" who *respects* Voltaire "at least with regard to his talents"; both share the end of learning, and so the scholar measures himself against the standard that Voltaire putatively exemplifies. But by contrast the "common" admirer (a dilettantish Enlightenment enthusiast, perhaps) "gives up all respect" for Voltaire with the belief that he has "somehow learned [his] badness of character" (CPrR 5:78).

[22] My point about the merely contemplative quality of the natural sublime could be strengthened by taking note of the "disinterested" quality of the pleasure that is proper to *pure* aesthetic judgment.

[23] *Beobachtungen über das Gefühl des Schönen und Erhabenen*, KGS 2, *Observations on the Feeling of the Beautiful and Sublime*, in *Observations on the Feeling of the Beautiful and Sublime and Other Writings*, ed. and trans. Patrick Frierson and Paul Guyer (Cambridge: Cambridge University Press, 2011), 2:211 (OBS). Cf. Anth 7:243.

Kant points here to a sublimity of mind that gathers strength the more it is sustained. Now, the crucial difference between Kant's early and mature theories of the sublime revolves around the issue of the moral source of sublimity. In the early work, the connection between morality and the sublime is drawn tenuously at best.[24] Kant's mature view, by contrast, is that our capacity to appreciate the sublime in nature is grounded in the development of sound moral disposition. Presumably, then, the sublime is not exhausting for someone of sound moral disposition. And if Kant takes the cultivation of sound moral disposition to be the proper end of a rational animal – its "natural vocation" – then we can be sure that the sublime and its connection to morality is not a peripheral curiosity for Kant. It runs, rather, to the very heart of his critical philosophy.

---

[24] Some commentators have tended to exaggerate the extent to which Kant draws a connection between the sublime and morality in the precritical *Observations*. See, for example, John Zammito *The Genesis of Kant's Critique of Judgment* (Chicago: University of Chicago Press, 1992), 31–32 and 276, and Clewis, *The Kantian Sublime*, 13. Kant is actually casual about the connection in the *Observations*: he singles out "true virtue" as the only "moral quality" that is properly called "sublime" but evinces greater interest in the idea (reminiscent of British moral sense theory) that sympathy is "beautiful and loveable" (OBS 2:215).

4

Imagination and Internal Sense
The Sublime in Shaftesbury, Reid, Addison, and Reynolds

Timothy M. Costelloe

INTRODUCTION

In addition to the associationism of Henry Home (Lord Kames), Alexander Gerard, Archibald Alison, and Dugald Stewart (considered by Rachel Zuckert in Chapter 5 of the current volume), the two other decipherable theoretical traditions in eighteenth-century aesthetics comprise thinkers who emphasize either internal sense or the faculty of imagination. The first approach is based on the premise that aesthetic value presupposes some foundation in human nature without which one could not speak of beauty or sublimity at all, and that this should be conceived as an internal counterpart to the external senses of sight, hearing, touch, and gustatory taste. The second, by contrast, although it does not necessarily exclude the idea of internal sense, focuses on the imagination to explain the active and passive features of artistic creativity and aesthetic receptivity. Various writers in the tradition as a whole might be ranged under these two headings, but with respect to the sublime, four figures stand out as having made significant contributions: on the side of internal sense stand Anthony Ashley Cooper, third Earl of Shaftesbury (1671–1713) and Thomas Reid (1719–1796), and on the side of imagination, Joseph Addison (1672–1719) and Joshua Reynolds (1723–1792).

THE SUBLIME AND INTERNAL SENSE

Anthony Ashley Cooper, Third Earl of Shaftesbury

Shaftesbury's contribution to aesthetic theory is found primarily in "The Moralists, a Philosophical Rhapsody," one of a series of lengthy essays composed 1705–1710 and brought together in three volumes as *Characteristicks of Men, Manners, Opinions, Times* in 1711.[1] Shaftesbury was educated under the direction of John Locke (whose patron was the first earl, Shaftesbury's grandfather), but although Lockean language pervades the *Characteristicks*, it is a gloss on a philosophical canvas indebted fundamentally to the rationalist lineage of neo-Platonism and reminiscent, in particular, of *Ennead* I.6 "On Beauty," in which Plotinus (himself echoing Plato's *Symposium*) argues that the beauty of physical objects is but a "trace" of some higher reality to which the philosophical mind ascends.[2] This school of thought was alive and well in Shaftesbury's own

---

[1] Anthony Ashley Cooper, third Earl of Shaftesbury, *Characteristicks of Men, Manners, Opinions, Times*, 3 vols. (Indianapolis, IN: Liberty Fund, 2001 [1711]). "The Moralists" is contained in vol. 2, 103–247 (M). All other references are to volume and page number of this edition.

[2] See *Ennead*, I.6, "On Beauty," in *Plotinus*, Greek text with English trans. by A. H. Armstrong, 7 vols. (Cambridge, MA: Harvard University Press, Loeb Classical Library, 1968–1988), vol. 1, and on disagreements between Shaftesbury

time through the influence of the late seventeenth-century group of philosophers known as the Cambridge Platonists, and Shaftesbury himself was responsible for publishing the posthumous edition of the *Select Sermons* of Benjamin Whichcote (1609–1683), generally considered the founding father of the movement.[3]

Surveying retrospectively the progression of eighteenth-century British aesthetics, Shaftesbury's approach seems increasingly anachronistic, a nod back to a tradition that, with the exception of isolated elements found in Reid, Reynolds, Archibald Alison, and the late Romantics,[4] his successors departed in favor of one that followed the empiricism of Addison and Francis Hutcheson, whose *Inquiry into the Original of Our Ideas of Beauty and Virtue* influenced a generation of writers that followed.[5] At the same time, Shaftesbury also addresses for the first time various themes that crystallize into the nascent discipline of philosophical aesthetics.[6] This is true of the sublime, and the only writer with any real claim to address the issue before Shaftesbury is John Dennis, whose concerns were primarily religious and lay not with sublimity as an aesthetic category in its own right.[7]

That being said, Shaftesbury's writing still bears the stamp of Augustan criticism and the Longinian tradition: he uses the *term* "sublime" sparingly, and when he does it refers primarily to the ecstatic effect of studied literary style on an audience irresistibly astounded or passionately compelled.[8] Shaftesbury captures Longinus's emphasis on both the authorial intent to produce these effects through rhetorical technique and the immediate, untutored nature of the emotions aroused, but he sounds an unmistakable note of derision, characterizing it as historically early and conceptually primitive. For Shaftesbury it denotes one among "several Styles and Manners of Discourse or Writing,... the *Miraculous*, the *Pompous*, or what we generally call the SUBLIME," and the particular emotion of "astonishment" it excites; "of all other Passions," he adds, it is "the easiest rais'd in raw and unexperienc'd Mankind" (1.149). For in this type of "Poetry, and study'd Prose," Shaftesbury continues, "the *astonishing* Part, or what commonly passes for *Sublime*, is form'd by the variety of Figures, the multiplicity of Metaphors, and by quitting as much as possible the natural and easy way of Expression, for that which is most unlike to Humanity, or ordinary Use" (1.150). The sublime is a style employed by the "earliest Poets" who valued metaphor and (as Locke had already dubbed it)[9] "figurative speeches" over the "*natural* and *simple*," a state of affairs remedied only by the genius of Homer, who extracted

---

and Locke, Daniel Carey, *Locke, Shaftesbury, and Hutcheson: Contesting Diversity in the Enlightenment and Beyond* (Cambridge: Cambridge University Press, 2006).

[3] Benjamin Whichcote, *Select Sermons*, with a preface by Anthony Ashley Cooper, third Earl of Shaftesbury (London, 1698).

[4] For a detailed account of this trajectory, see Timothy M. Costelloe, *The British Aesthetic Tradition: From Shaftesbury to Wittgenstein* (Cambridge: Cambridge University Press, forthcoming).

[5] See Francis Hutcheson, *An Inquiry into the Original of Our Ideas of Beauty and Virtue in Two Treatises*, 2nd ed. (Indianapolis, IN: Liberty Fund, 2004 [1726]). Hutcheson advertised the first edition of the work as an explanation and defense of "the principles of the late Earl of Shaftesbury," an homage omitted in later editions.

[6] For an informative discussion of the discipline's beginnings, see Paul Guyer, "The Origins of Modern Aesthetics: 1711–35," in *The Blackwell Guide to Aesthetics*, ed. Peter Kivy (Oxford: Blackwell, 2004), 15–44.

[7] See John Dennis, *The Advancement and Reformation of Modern Poetry* (1701) and *The Grounds of Criticism in Poetry* (1704), in *The Critical Work of John Dennis*, ed. Edward Niles Hooker, 2 vols. (Baltimore: Johns Hopkins Press, 1939), 1:197–278, and 325–73, respectively.

[8] See Malcolm Heath, "Longinus and the Ancient Sublime," chap. 1 of the current volume, and for the rise and fall of Longinus in the early modern period, Samuel Holt Monk, *The Sublime: A Study of Critical Theories in XVIII-Century England* (Ann Arbor: University of Michigan Press, 1935), chap. 1. See also Walter J. Hipple, Jr., *The Beautiful, the Sublime, and the Picturesque in Eighteenth-Century British Aesthetic Theory* (Carbondale: Southern Illinois University Press, 1957), 16–17.

[9] John Locke, *An Essay Concerning Human Understanding*, ed. Peter H. Nidditch (Oxford: Oxford University Press, 1975 [1689]), 3.10.34.

and retained what was "decent" in these "spurious" forbears by turning his "thoughts towards the real Beauty of Composition, the Unity of Design, the Truth of Characters, and the just Imitation of Nature in each particular" (1.150; see also 1.160).[10]

It would be a mistake, however, to confine Shaftesbury's treatment of sublimity to the context of Longinian criticism, because, although his aesthetics focuses ostensibly on the category of beauty, he at once articulates the *concept* later writers call the sublime. We might distinguish here between the Longinian sublime or *sublime style* to describe a mode of written or spoken discourse and the aesthetic sublime or *sublimity*, which isolates a particular kind of ecstatic experience or state involving feelings of elevation, transcendence, awe, fear, and shock, excited by being in the presence of something greater than oneself. As we shall see, this difference is articulated explicitly by Addison and echoed later in Reid and Reynolds, all of whom speak of the aesthetic sublime as "great" or "grand" and reserve "sublime" for the tradition of Longinus. In Shaftesbury, this distinction is still implicit – submerged, as it were, in the concept of beauty – but active nonetheless and emergent in his view that all aesthetic value has its ultimate source in a metaphysical principle, the discovery of which is inseparable from the experience the contemplative mind undergoes in ascending through the three levels or "orders" of beauty. In "The Moralists," this moment of *ekstasis* or – as the title of the essays has it – "rhapsody" is personified in the character of Theocles, an avatar of Shaftesbury himself, who, the reader might infer, has at least approached the experience in question.

The Sublime and the Three Orders of Beauty
Shaftesbury presents his view of beauty in "The Moralists" by delineating a metaphysical principle that operates above and beyond the immediate object of perception, namely, what he variously calls God, nature, or Universal Mind, and the order displayed in the relation of parts that combine and cooperate to form a perfect whole. Through contemplating nature the mind moves from the base elements and minerals that compose the lowest regions of the earth to the surface, populated by plants and animal bodies, reaching finally the highest level from which particular systems, previously and erroneously seen as complete in themselves, are revealed to have place only within "the WHOLE *a system* compleat, according to one *simple, consistent*, and *uniform* DESIGN" (M 162). Like a detail in a painting, the beauty of any part is apparent and depends on and receives its full meaning only in the context of the entire composition; properly speaking, then, the *whole itself* is beautiful and the part valuable only to the extent that it participates in it. The whole, moreover, becomes the *source* of beauty because it confers value on the particular. The philosophical mind can grasp this principle, Shaftesbury insists, due to an internal sense, something "imprinted on our Minds" and "closely interwoven with our Souls," namely, the "Idea or Sense of *Order* and *Proportion*" through which one can decipher harmony from discord, cadency from convulsion, orderly motion from its accidental counterpart, and design from randomness. This is not, he urges, a *feeling* from "Sense *alone*," which would grasp only apparent beauty, but an expression of reason through which the mind can "contemplate" Nature and receive thereby a higher "rational enjoyment" (M 221). Beauty is not *sensed* as a feature of the experienced world but *apprehended* as a mystery of the universe.

Through this principle, Shaftesbury explains, the mind grasps identity in terms of some underlying cause. The aesthetic value of a beautiful coin, for example, lies not in the metallic compound that constitutes its matter but through the workmanship displayed in the engraving that imposes a particular form on the material. "For that which is beautify'd, is beautiful," as Shaftesbury expresses the thought, "only by the accession of something beautifying: and by the recess or withdrawing of the same, it ceases to be beautiful" (M 226). The source of the beauty is the

---

[10] Shaftesbury also describes friendship as a "sublime heroick passion" (M 135) and uses the term as a verb ("to sublime") in its other sense of "change into a vapor" (see M 167).

power that imposes this form – the artist who created it – without which it would cease to have the feature that confers aesthetic value. Thus, Shaftesbury concludes, "*the Beautiful, the Fair, the Comely* were never in the *Matter*, but in the *Art* and *Design*; never in the *body* it-self, but in the *Form* or *forming Power*.... 'Tis *Mind* alone which forms. All which is void of *Mind* is horrid: and Matter formless is *Deformity it-self*" (M 226). On this basis arise "*Three* Degrees or Orders of Beauty" through which the mind moves to grasp in a moment of rhapsodic insight the origin of beauty itself. The first is the beauty of "*the dead forms*" – objects of art and craft, and natural phenomena – ".. which bear a Fashion, and are form'd whether by Man, or nature; but have no forming Power, no Action, or Intelligence" (M 227); the beauty lies in the form appreciated, but that contains no forming power itself. At the second degree of beauty, one grasps the power to which the dead forms refer, what Shaftesbury calls "*the Forming Forms*; that is, which have Intelligence, Action, and Operation." Here one finds the power of human mind that gives dead forms their shape, "such as the Palaces, the Coins, the Brazen or the Marble Figures of Men" (M 227). At this level, there is a "double beauty," that of the dead form that is formed *and* of "*Mind* itself," the forming power. At the third and highest order of beauty, finally, lies that "which forms not only such as we call mere Forms, but even *the Forms that form*" (M 227–8), that is, the source of the power of the human mind to give identity to what is dead. This, Shaftesbury concludes, is the "Principle, Source, and Fountain of all Beauty" (M 228) into which all lower forms resolve.

The Theoclean Sublime
In order to grasp this principle, however, the philosophical mind must ascend the three orders of beauty and itself *experience* the moment of rhapsody. Much like the initiate of Descartes's *Meditations* or the traveler through Hegel's *Phenomenology of Spirit*, philosophical understanding manifests itself in and through the process that constitutes it. In "The Moralists," Shaftesbury dramatizes this insight through the character of Theocles, a past conversation with whom the narrator Philocles relates in present time to his friend Palemon. The dialogue is set in various scenes of pastoral life, the interlocutors conversing at their ease over the course of two days spent walking, dining, and riding on a coach, echoing the ancient ideal of philosophy as a naturally occurring discursive practice. The setting allows Shaftesbury both to juxtapose wild untamed nature to the artifice of the domesticated garden and to present her as the philosopher's muse, the object of contemplation through which the mind discovers the original pattern for all things beyond the partial and derivative appearances given through sense. Nature is a source of inspiration, the channel through which Philocles travels to reach those "unsociable Places" that other thinkers later designate sublime: where precipices and cataracts "amaze," extremes of temperature "annoy," and our own voices are a source of fear (M 219). Philocles is a man at war with himself, a rational investigator tinged by a madness that carries him away in fits of enthusiasm and ecstasies of poetic expression, from which he struggles to withdraw and return, often embarrassed and apologetic. Shaftesbury thus dramatizes a profound paradox of his view, namely, that philosophy is like a painting, which represents and distorts nature in the very act of stripping away the veil of appearance that hides its real form: Philocles (and, by extension, Shaftesbury and his readers) can only move beyond the world to the source of phenomena through the very appearances he seeks to unveil. As Philocles describes it at one point, philosophy is a "magical glass" (M 203) that represents nature and, by imposing a conceptual scheme on her, breaks the "Uniformity, and destroy[s] that admirable Simplicity of Order, from whence the ONE infinite and perfect Principle is known" (M 189).

This rhapsodic experience is only possible through the attitude of "disinterestedness," a concept more often associated with Immanuel Kant and later Edward Bullough, but that has its first formulation in the *Characteristicks*.[11] For Shaftesbury, being disinterested means embracing the

---

[11] Immanuel Kant, *Kritik der Urteilskraft*, in *Kant's gesammelte Schriften*, Königlichen Preussischen (later Deutschen) Akademie der Wissenschaften, 29 vols. (Berlin: Reimer [later Walter de Gruyter], 1900–), 5:203–11 (CJ), and

stoic thought that involvement and enlightenment are mutually exclusive; the latter requires release from the desires that "interest" us in and bind us to the world of everyday life. This applies to sensuality, interest in objects for the sake of gratification, and to material possessions, interest in objects for the sake of ownership. The first, Shaftesbury urges, is overcome through rational contemplation, which frees the mind from the heavier elements demanded by the senses, and the second, through freedom from material possessions, which frees the mind from practical concerns, allowing the philosopher to ascend through the orders of beauty. I might enjoy the taste of the fruit that grows on the tree in my orchard, for example, but the aesthetic value of these things arises from contemplating nature, and when the mind turns to the liking of sense or consciousness of ownership, rational pleasure dissipates. For Shaftesbury, there is a fundamental difference between a mere appearance or indirect *representation* of beauty at the level of interest and the direct *presentation* of beauty through the original, the order and design of which appears regardless of practical concerns, personal involvement, or feelings of gratification. Indeed, only when these are left behind can the ordering principle in which aesthetic value originates be *apprehended* and *experienced* in a moment of sublime insight.

Thomas Reid

Thomas Reid (1719–1796) occupied a professorship at King's College, Aberdeen, before being called to succeed Adam Smith as professor of moral philosophy at Glasgow. He is best known for *An Inquiry into the Human Mind on the Principles of Common Sense* (1764) and as founder of the school of thought that bears its name. This work contains no reference to aesthetics at all, and although Reid apparently delivered lectures on the subject,[12] only some twenty years later did he publish "On Taste," the final essay of *Essays on the Intellectual Powers of Man* (1785), in which he applies his "principles of common sense" to beauty and the sublime. There is a distance of some seventy years between Shaftesbury's *Characteristicks* and Reid's *Essays*, but in the main – and despite obvious differences between the two approaches – they both revolve around the idea of an internal sense, contemplation, and the view that the sublime and, importantly for Reid, what we *call* sublime can be traced back originally to some power of mind.

Two features of Reid's philosophical approach more generally frame his aesthetics. First, he rejects the tendency of philosophers to reduce the complexity of their explananda to "fewer principles than the nature of the things will permit"; in aesthetics, in Reid's view, this has led many eighteenth-century writers to focus on "some particular kinds of beauty, while they overlooked others" (I.575.14–16).[13] For the term "beauty," as he points out, applies to a great variety of objects that are more different than they are similar – inter alia, poems, palaces, music, a "fine woman," animals, the body and mind of men, and God (I.575.5–8) – and this speaks persuasively against the temptation, born of a "love of simplicity," to reduce it to some univocal source: Shaftesbury's Universal Mind, Addison's pleasures of imagination, or, paradigmatically, Hutcheson's "uniformity amidst variety."[14]

Edward Bullough, "Psychical Distance," *British Journal of Psychology* 5 (1912), 87–117. For an appreciation of Shaftesbury's contribution, see Jerome Stolnitz, "On the Significance of Lord Shaftesbury in Modern Aesthetic Theory," *Philosophical Quarterly* 11, 43 (1961), 97–113, and "On the Origins of 'Aesthetic Disinterestedness,'" *Journal of Aesthetics and Art Criticism* 20, 2 (1961), 131–44.

[12] These lectures survive as a manuscript dated 1774, although not in Reid's hand, and add little to what is contained in the later published work. See *Thomas Reid's Lectures on the Fine Arts*, transcribed from the original manuscript with an introduction and notes by Peter Kivy (Den Haag: Martinus Nijhoff, 1973).

[13] Essay VIII, "Of Beauty," in Thomas Reid, *Essays on the Intellectual Powers of Man* (University Park: Pennsylvania State University Press, 2002 [1785]), 573–614. All references are to chapter, page, and line numbers of the essay as it appears in this edition.

[14] See Hutcheson, *Inquiry*, 1.3.3 passim.

Second, and more fundamentally, Reid undertakes a tireless campaign against "modern Philosophers" (III.584.11) who have flouted the "dictates of common sense" (III.584.16–17) and reduced the material world to a "phænomenon only" that "has no existence but in the mind" (III.584.5–6). The root of this evil Reid traces to the doctrine of primary and secondary qualities, which was inaugurated by the ancients, refined in Descartes and Locke, and perfected by Hume. This track has been "pursued to such an extreme," he intones, "as to resolve every thing into sensations, feelings, and ideas in the mind, and to leave nothing external at all" (III.583.28–30). Reid is the first to acknowledge that any aesthetic experience requires some affective *capacity* – "it is impossible to perceive the beauty of an object, without perceiving the object, or at least conceiving it" – but the moderns, he contends, have been misled by the fact that the sensation *and* the quality have the same name – taste – which has led them to place *both* in the mind. This contradicts common practice and natural language, in which we distinguish unproblematically between the "agreeable sensation we feel, and the quality in the object that occasions it," plain evidence in Reid's view that the sensation is really the effect or "sign" of the quality, which is a distinct cause of the thing "signified" (I.573.33–5). Indeed, the term "taste," he urges, does denote an internal sense or power of the mind necessary for aesthetic judgment, but it has this meaning only *metaphorically*, when "taste of the palate" is extended to the sphere of mental taste. This has "led men, in all ages," he observes, ".. to give the name of external sense to this power of discerning what is beautiful with pleasure, and what is ugly and faulty of its kind with disgust" (I.573.20–3).

This does not provide warrant in Reid's view, however, to denude the *object* of aesthetic value and assign it instead to some idea of the mind. On the contrary, "beauty or deformity in an object, results from its nature or structure," he writes. "To perceive the beauty therefore, we must perceive the nature or structure from which it results. In this the internal sense differs from the external. Our external senses may discover qualities which do not depend upon any antecedent perception" (I.578.15–19). Thus "when I hear an air in music that pleases me," Reid reports, by way of example,

I say, it is fine, it is excellent. This excellence is not in me; it is in the mussaic. But the pleasure it gives is not in the music; it is in me. Perhaps I cannot say what it is in the tune that pleases my ear, as I cannot say what it is in a sapid body that pleases my palate; but there is a quality in the sapid body that pleases my palate, and I call it a delicious taste; and there is a quality in the tune that pleases my taste, and I call it a fine or excellent air. (I.574.2–9)

Like Hutcheson and the "moderns" he derides, Reid still defines taste as a power of the mind, but he understands it as an "*intellectual* power," and, in a way reminiscent of Kant's distinction between the agreeable and a "judgment of taste," he distinguishes the *perception* of the quality that gives rise to a sensation from a *judgment* – "an affirmation or denial of one thing concerning another" (I.577.15–16) – that produces knowledge of something real and thus a belief or opinion that there is a quality in the object perceived. "I feel pain" describes a sensation without the existence of an object, whereas "I see a tree" is a judgment involving an object independent of the observer. When it comes to aesthetics, then, "when I say that VIRGIL's Georgics is a beautiful poem," Reid maintains, I report not on "myself and my feelings" but am committed to the fact "that there is something in the power, and not in me, which I call beauty" (I.577.23–9). To deny this, Reid insists, is to deny that an object *is* beautiful or sublime, a contravention of the "necessary rules of construction" and principles of common sense.

The "real quality," Reid then proposes, is an attribute of an object adapted to please a good taste because it contains "excellence" or "perfection"; he admits that sometimes the quality is unknown or "occult," although that is not to deny its existence, only to acknowledge our ignorance of its nature. Things "fit" for the nourishment of bodies, for example, are the most excellent of their kind (or are at least good for us), and this gives rise to the sensation of agreeableness. A depraved taste, conversely, is when we have a relish for something that has no nutritional value (eating dirt or ashes) – the result of bad habits, arbitrary association, and the negative effects of education. What is true of gustatory taste is true of aesthetic taste as well, and (adopting explicitly the triad coined by Addison some seventy years earlier),[15] Reid distinguishes "three objects of taste" (II.579.5–7) – novelty, grandeur or sublimity, and beauty, all three of which involve a "real relation" to some quality in the object itself, be it the novel, beautiful, or sublime. Thus novelty, Reid urges, involves "pleasing surprise" due to the "relation which the thing has to the knowledge of the person" (II.579.34–5), and all beauty, although differentiated in various objects, includes the sensation of agreeableness coupled with the belief (from a judgment) that the object has the excellence (in a clear reference to Edmund Burke)[16] of a love or liking (or, in the case of persons, benevolence), and the more we discover this excellence, the more beautiful the object appears.

Reid's treatment of the grand or sublime, to which we can now turn specifically, follows a similar pattern, although before seeing how this works, there are two aspects of his view that should be emphasized. First, as noted above, Reid retains the distinction – implicit in Shaftesbury and explicit in Addison – between sublime style and sublimity. He refers to the former as the "sublime in description" (III.586.1) and associates it with Longinus and literary composition (III.585.26–8), and he terms the latter the "grand," "truly grand," the "true sublime," or on one occasion simply "sublime" (III.591.5). The sublime in this sense – that is, sublimity – cannot arise from composition alone, he urges, but requires "grandeur in the subject" (III.586.11–12).

Second, Reid holds that, strictly speaking, the grand (or what we can also simply call the sublime) applies only to qualities of mind and not to inanimate or material objects of sense; or, at the very least, there should be a "different name" for each, he observes, to reflect that they are "very different in their nature, and produce very different emotions in the mind of the spectator" (III.591.16–17). Only people or depictions of people (historical or fictional) can be sublime, because they alone possess "intellectual" qualities. Inanimate objects, by contrast, are *nominally* sublime; the title is conferred on them because they "are the effects or signs" of "something intellectual" or "bear some relation or analogy" to it (III.588.24–6). When we say objects are sublime, it is a metaphorical use of the term when, often unwittingly, we connect in imagination otherwise different objects that are analogous, contrasting, resembling, or otherwise related; we thus extend the concept by *ascribing* qualities to "the one what properly belongs to the other" (III.589.1–2). Reid finds in this imaginative *transmutio* the origin of poetic language, and an explanation for why sublimity is routinely connected with magnitude or terror,[17] qualities of mind assigned to those of body (sweet, austere, simple, and duplicitous), and inanimate objects dignified with human qualities they obviously do not possess (the "raging" sea or "murmuring" rivulet).

With these two important clarifications in place, we can understand why Reid distinguishes the *emotion* that constitutes the experience of the sublime from what "grandeur in an object *is*" (III.582.29–30, emphasis added). The emotion aroused by grand objects is not pleasure (as in novelty) or agreeableness (as in beauty) but is "awful, solemn, and serious" (III.582.12), which – in a perfect description of the rhapsodic state of Shaftesbury's Theocles – "disposes to

---

[15] See the following and Joseph Addison and Richard Steel, *The Spectator*, ed. Donald F. Bond, 5 vols. (Oxford: Clarendon Press, 1965), 3:540 (no. 412). Here and elsewhere, all references are to the pagination in this volume of Bond's edition followed by the original essay number.

[16] See Edmund Burke, *A Philosophical Enquiry into the Origin of Our Ideas of the Sublime and Beautiful*, ed. James T. Boulton (London: Routledge and Kegan Paul, 1958 [1759, 1st ed. 1757]), 3.1.91. All references are to book, section, and page number.

[17] Reid suggests that the "similarity between dread and terror" explains Burke's equation of the sublime with what is terrible: both emotions are grave and solemn, he observes, but only admiration involves the "enthusiasm" requisite for sublimity. See III.590.30ff., and Burke, *Enquiry*, 2.1–2.57–8 passim.

seriousness, elevates the mind above its usual state, to a kind of enthusiasm, and inspires magnanimity, and a contempt of what is mean" (III.582.25–7). It comes, moreover, in degrees but finds highest expression in the face of that "most grand" of objects, the Supreme Being, whose defining characteristics of eternity, immensity, power, justice, rectitude, and wisdom raise "devotion: a serious recollected temper which inspires magnanimity, and disposes to the most heroic acts of virtue" (III.582.20–3).

Although this describes the emotion raised by contemplating grand objects, grandeur itself is a "degree of excellence, in one kind or another, as merits our admiration" (III.582.31–2). It is admired, moreover, because it is "intrinsically valuable and excellent" (III.582.37) and is so "from its own constitution, and not from ours" (III.584.21). This "real intrinsic excellence" – as we saw previously – refers primarily to qualities of mind and secondarily, by transference, to inanimate objects: power, knowledge, wisdom, virtue, and magnanimity are attributes of mind or excellences that are admired and, when they exist to an "uncommon degree" (III.582.35–6), raise in the spectator the awful, solemn, serious emotion that constitutes sublime experience. Thus, "true grandeur," as Reid defines it, "is such a degree of excellence as is fit to raise an enthusiastical admiration" (III.591.6–7). This accounts not only for the sublimity of God and biblical descriptions of his works, but also for the emotions that attend reflection on historical and literary figures: the great souls of Cato and Seneca, for example, noble, superior, and magnanimous in the face of terrible misfortune; the characters, actions, and events of the *Iliad*; the virtues of Aristides, Socrates, and Marcus Aurelius; and those poets, philosophers, lawgivers, and orators whose "extraordinary talents and genius" fill us with admiration and awe. Reid insists that in all these cases sublimity is found in qualities of mind: either in the "grand thoughts" of the author (such as Homer) who conceived the characters or, when the work is considered independent of the writer, in the qualities of the characters depicted (Hector and Achilles) (III.587.22ff.). Thus, as in the case of an object to which we attach the epithet due to some point of similarity, only by mistake do we call some *deed* sublime: the *person* is intrinsically excellent and raises admiration, whereas the action is the effect (or sign) of that cause (or signified) and is sublime by extension only. It is for this reason that Reid concludes his treatment of grandeur with an apt metaphor of light and life: grandeur is "discerned in objects of sense only by reflection, as the light we perceive in the moon and planets is truly the light of the sun; and that those who look for grandeur in mere matter, seek the living among the dead" (III.591.9–12).

THE SUBLIME AND THE IMAGINATION

Joseph Addison

In the June 19th, 1712, issue of *The Spectator*, Addison announced his intention to enter on "an Essay *on the Pleasures of the Imagination*, which though it shall consider that Subject at large, will perhaps suggest to the reader what it is that gives a Beauty to many Passages of the finest Writers both in Prose and Verse." It will prove "an Undertaking," he promises, "... entirely new" (3:530–1, no. 409).[18] The claim to complete originality is an exaggeration: Shaftesbury's *Characteristicks* had appeared the previous year (1711), and much of Addison's subject matter had been given voice already in the well-established tradition of literary criticism stretching from Horace through modern French, Italian, and English writers up to Dennis. Even the phrase "pleasures of the imagination," although popularized by Addison, was already in use.[19]

---

[18] "The Pleasures of the Imagination" comprises eleven essays published between June 21st and July 3rd, 1712, in *The Spectator* 3:535–82.
[19] The phrase had been used by Sir William Temple in his *Observations upon the United Provinces of the Netherlands* (1687) and appears in a letter written by Lady Mary Pierrepont of July 21st, 1709. See Bond's notes in *The Spectator* 3:536 and 538.

That the essays are not "entirely new," however, should not detract from their significance, because, Shaftesbury's *Characteristicks* notwithstanding, they represent the first sustained treatment of ideas and concepts destined to cast a long, deep shadow across the nascent discipline of aesthetics, beyond even the publication of Burke's *Enquiry* in the latter part of the century. This is true of the sublime, as it is of the other aesthetic categories Addison explores.

By "pleasures of the imagination" Addison conveys the idea – familiar from Locke and prominent later in Hutcheson – that aesthetic value arises through the interplay of an object with certain primary qualities, and with a faculty – the imagination – so constituted to receive those qualities and capable of being affected by them to produce a particular sort of pleasure. Pleasures are of "two kinds," depending on their origin. "Primary pleasures" arise from the "actual view and survey of outward Objects" (3:540, no. 412); we perceive *real* objects that are great, uncommon, or beautiful, ideas of which strike the imagination immediately and produce pleasure.[20] "Secondary pleasures," on the other hand, originate in the "action of the mind" we call *comparison*, a spontaneous mechanism of imagination rather than an act of understanding. In this case, we have the idea of an object, either a real one recalled by memory or a fictional one invented by the imagination, which we compare with the idea received from some other object that represents it, a "Statue, Picture, Description, or Sound" (3:559–60, no. 416). In both cases, Addison maintains – whether from an actual view or via comparison – pleasure is immediate and independent of cognition.

What appeals to Addison in particular is the way the imagination involves a kind of *seeing*, and he seems to regard imagination and sight as essentially of a piece. Addison observes that of the external senses, sight is the origin of the "largest Variety of Ideas" because it is free of the constraints involved in touch, smell, and hearing; in particular, sight overcomes distance and is not easily tired or satiated. It is a "more delicate and diffusive kind of Touch," he writes, "that spreads it self [sic] over an infinite Multitude of Bodies, comprehends the largest Figures, and brings into our reach some of the most remote Parts of the Universe" (3:536, no. 411). In a comparable way, the imagination involves a *mental* seeing; it is the eye by which the mind roams the world and discovers in material objects of art and nature, as well as in ideal objects of history and fable, an endless source of untold pleasure. Like the physical eye, the imagination moves outward and is pleased in proportion to the liberty it enjoys to expand and – in notable contrast to Shaftesbury's disinterestedness – possess and make objects its own, for an individual in whom the imagination is active "looks upon the World, as it were, in another Light, and discovers in it a Multitude of Charms" and makes a "kind of Property in everything he sees" (3:538, no. 411).

With this modified but distinctly Lockean view of the relation between mind and world, we can better appreciate Addison's treatment of the sublime: when this quality is apparent in some object, it gives rise to an emotion that strikes the imagination and constitutes a feeling that Addison categorizes as a primary pleasure. One should note straightaway that, like Shaftesbury, Addison uses the term "great" or "grand" rather than "sublime," reserving the latter – as in his discussions of Milton's *Paradise Lost*, for example – to invoke the Longinian tradition, with its focus on the use of language to produce a particular emotional state. This marks a decisive shift away from sublime style to sublimity and makes explicit what was intimated in Shaftesbury. "To write on the sublime style is to write on rhetoric," as Samuel Monk puts it succinctly, "to write on sublimity is to write on aesthetic."[21] As the century progressed, the phenomenon Addison calls "greatness" was increasingly designated by the term "sublime," and although Longinus remained a central figure in literary circles at least to midcentury, his influence on philosophical

---

[20] Although individually the three elements had long been in currency, there is no precise source for the triad as such, which appears to be original to Addison. See Bond's editorial comment in *The Spectator* 3:540n2.

[21] See Monk, *The Sublime*, 12.

speculation dimmed.[22] When the subject received it fullest and most famous treatments in Burke and Kant, Longinus and the Longinian sublime were but faint echoes.

By "great" – or what we can now without risk of ambiguity call sublime – Addison refers to the experience of some phenomenon striking as a whole, a totality, or a single entity that fills and surpasses the capacity of the imagination to contain. Objects are great or have grandeur not in view of their magnitude or size but in terms of "Largeness of a Whole View, considered as one entire Piece" (3:540, no. 412). "Such are the prospects of an open Champian Country," Addison writes at the head of a list of examples that become common coin in subsequent philosophical discussion, "a vast uncultivated Desart, of huge Heaps of Mountains, high Rocks and Precipices, or a wide Expanse of Waters, where we are not struck with the Novelty or Beauty of the Sight, but with that rude kind of Magnificence which appears on many of these stupendous works of Nature" (3:540, no. 412). We might expect to feel pain – terror, horror, or panic – in the face of such overwhelming phenomena, but Addison emphasizes how at such moments, as if in the eye of the storm, amid great danger we actually experience calm and clarity. This happens because when the imagination expands or is stretched, our emotional response is "astonishment" or "amazement" rather than fear, an idea employed already by Shaftesbury in his sublime style of discourse and borrowed and expanded later by Burke (*Enquiry* 2.2.57–8 and 4.7.136). These terms denote the experience of trying to grasp something barely comprehensible, as well as the singular pleasure to be found in the exultation and sense of freedom that rises when barriers collapse and limits are transgressed. "Our imagination loves to be filled with an Object," Addison observes, "or to graspe at any thing that is too big for its Capacity. We are flung into a pleasing Astonishment at such unbounded Views, and feel a delightful Stillness and Amazement in the Soul at the Apprehension of them" (3:540, no. 412). As the pleasure we take in great objects comes from an imagination expanded, so pain and desolation follow on the contraction of the same and the corresponding sense that one's liberty has been checked and freedom stifled. "The mind of Man naturally hates every thing that looks like a Restraint upon it," Addison writes, "and is apt to fancy it self under a sort of Confinement, when the Sight is pent up in a narrow Compass, and shortened on every side by the Neighbourhood of Walls or Mountains" (3:540–1, no. 412).

Sir Joshua Reynolds

At first sight, it might seem an oddity to consider Reynolds as a contributor to the philosophical history of the sublime. He is remembered not as a theorist or man of letters but is famous instead as one of the two great portrait painters of the eighteenth century, the other being Thomas Gainsborough, with whom he founded the Royal Academy of Arts under the patronage of George III in 1768. At the academy's inception Reynolds was appointed president, a position he held until his death and under the auspices of which he delivered the series of fifteen lectures (1769–90) later collected and published together as *Discourses on Art* (1797), although the central doctrines developed in the work were in place long before, in three letters dating from 1759.[23] The tone of the lectures is didactic, written as they were expressly for an audience

---

[22] Two notable exceptions to this rule are Reid, as we have seen, and Kames. On the latter, see Rachel Zuckert, "The Associative Sublime," chap. 5 in the current volume.

[23] Sir Joshua Reynolds, *Discourses on Art*, ed. Robert W. Wark (San Marino, CA: Huntington Library, 1959; reprint, New Haven, CT: Yale University Press, 1997 [1975]). All references are to discourse number followed by line and page numbers of this edition. The aforementioned letters were first published in the *Universal Chronicle*, September 29th, October 20th, and November 10th, 1759. All references are to the letters as they appear in Samuel Johnson, *The Yale Edition of the Works of Samuel Johnson*, 18 vols. (New Haven, CT: Yale University Press, 1958–2004), vol. 2, *The Idler and The Adventurer*, ed. W. J. Bate, John M. Bullitt, and L. F. Powell (1963), nos. 76, 79, and 82, pp. 235–9, 246–9, and 254–8, respectively (*Idler* followed by number and page).

of art students, but they should be read less narrowly as a great artist's prolonged reflection on his own creative activity – rivaled in the century only by William Hogarth's *Analysis of Beauty* (1753), of which Reynolds was highly critical – to yield a guide for fledgling artists framed as a practical manifestation of the sublime, what Reynolds calls the "great" or "grand style" in painting. Reynolds's persistent theme is how the artist can produce works of art that stretch or expand the imagination and move the viewer in the same way as the philosophical journey of Shaftesbury's Theocles, the qualities manifest in Reid's Supreme Being or the rocks and precipices of Addison. It is for this reason that Reynolds deserves a place in any discussion of the eighteenth-century sublime.

Philosophically, Reynolds stands very much in the tradition of Locke and Hutcheson (he speaks unselfconsciously of memory "stored" and "stocked" with ideas to be "combined and varied" [II 32 and 66, 26–7 passim]) and like Addison places great emphasis on the faculty of imagination. He identifies the faculty as the source of creativity on the side of the artist and as the seat of aesthetic affect on the part of the audience, but he goes further in emphasizing imagination as the sine qua non of good criticism. He dismisses the "frigid mind" of those who judge pedantically according to rules of art "instead of giving up the reigns of their imagination into their author's hands" (*Idler* 76, 236) and recommends that art students enter a "kind of competition" with great painters, by comparing them with their own efforts (II 96–8, 31).[24] Reynolds insists artists should aim at "captivating the imagination" of the spectator (III 27, 42) and emphasizes how the "great end of art is to strike the imagination" (IV 82, 59), to "make an impression on [it]" and so produce a "pleasing effect on the mind" (XIII 384–9, 241).

What is noteworthy about Reynolds's conception of imagination, however, is the way it recalls Addison's emphasis on the feeling of pleasure caused by "great" objects because the mind (to recall Addison's words) "naturally hates every thing that looks like a Restraint upon it" but loves to be "filled" by or "grasp" at objects "too big for its Capacity." The *Discourses* contain a few references to Burke's *Enquiry* – Reynolds knew and admired both the work and its author (see VIII 561n, 162) – but with the exception of acknowledging a "certain degree of obscurity" as "one source of the sublime" (VII 70–1, 119), its influence on him is minimal. He clearly rejects Burke's astonishment born of pain, danger, and terror in favor of Addison's "Stillness and Amazement in the Soul" – "*repose*," as Reynolds characterizes it at one point – that comes when the imagination is expanded, uplifted, and freed from "hurry and anxiety" (VIII 73–6, 147). Reynolds often speaks of "beauty," it is true, but he effectively collapses this category into "great" and "sublime," terms he uses synonymously (and without any hint of the Longinian tradition) to refer to a *style* of painting and the *effect* it has on an audience.

This Addisonian view of imagination is crucial, because it leads directly to the central doctrines of the *Discourses*: that the mind feels pleasure when filled by the "great and noble ideas" (*Idler* 79, 247) excited when an artist draws the viewer's attention to the whole, which the artist achieves, in turn, through "imitations" that capture general features of the subject over and above extraneous details; this expands the imagination rather than "retarding" its "progress" (*Idler* 79, 247). Reynolds expresses this idea through the philosophical trope of universal and particular, likely inspired by the work of his close friend Samuel Johnson, especially the *Preface to Shakespeare* (1765), in which he contrasts "just representations of general nature" with the "accidents of transient fashions or temporary opinions."[25] Reynolds takes over Johnson's language

---

[24] Reynolds's image is reminiscent of Hogarth's method of scooping out objects in imagination to reveal them as "thin shells" composed of lines circumscribing inner space. See William Hogarth, *The Analysis of Beauty*, ed. Ronald Paulson (New Haven, CT: Yale University Press, 1997 [1753]), 21. Hogarth in turn echoes Addison's discussion of the "concave and the convex" in "Pleasures of the Imagination" (3:556, no. 415).

[25] See Samuel Johnson, *Preface to Shakespeare, 1756*, in *The Yale Edition of the Works of Samuel Johnson*, vol. 8, *Johnson on Shakespeare*, ed. Arthur Sherbo (1968), 8:59–113, esp. 59–65 (the quotes are taken from pp. 61 and 62). For the theme of universal and particular in the *Discourses*, see Hipple, *The Beautiful, the Sublime, and the*

verbatim but fortifies it with a stiff dose of Platonic rationalism sufficiently potent at moments to recall the enthusiastic rhapsodies of Shaftesbury's Theocles. Reynolds then derives from experience rules for artistic practice that articulate a timeless pattern inscribed in "nature" – shorn, however, of the neo-Platonist metaphysics embraced by Shaftesbury – to which the enduring principles of art stand in the same relation as ideas to their instantiations, reality to its apparent manifestations: they transcend and explain it, even if the "great ideal perfection and beauty are not to be sought in the heavens, but upon the earth" (III 99–100, 44) – discovered, that is, in and through experience of their worldly expression and subsequently reduced to "precept."

The force of the argumentative strategy underlying the *Discourses* derives from the strength of the analogy between beauty in nature and beauty in art. Reynolds suggests that as the philosophical mind ascends from contemplating beautiful objects to beauty itself, so the empirical eye with the help of "observation" moves from sensing beautiful natural things to grasping the "general and invariable ideas of nature" (I 66–7, 16). Analogously, then, works of art can be studied to reach the general and invariable ideas of artistic composition, and as the former might be framed as principles that explain and constitute *natural* beauty, so the latter can be expressed as rules of art that explain and constitute *artistic* beauty. Reynolds insists that nature herself is "imperfect" and "deformed," so that the general and invariable ideas are really an ideal re-presentation of her in garments she would display were her timeless "central form" or "ideal beauty" made manifest. Given the argument by analogy that motivates his thinking, one would expect Reynolds to make the same point about art, namely, that the central form of composition is an ideal re-presentation of artistic practice that overcomes imperfections and deformities of extant works of art. Reynolds, however, skips a number of steps and substitutes principles of natural beauty for rules of composition, so that what artists come to enshrine in their work are not the general and invariable ideas of composition but the general and invariable ideas of nature.

The artist, on this view, looks to nature as the "model" and final arbiter of taste; nature is a book open to all – she "denies her instructions to none, who desire to become her pupils" (III.145–6.45) as Reynolds says – but the lesson (to extend the metaphor) must be inferred from her works and, to invoke Locke's famous metaphor, the empty cabinet of the artistic mind must be furnished with general ideas through the activity of abstraction and recombination.[26] The pupil can take instruction directly, by immediate contemplation of natural phenomena, or indirectly through studying the great masters who have done so already and, although their best efforts are "faint and feeble" in comparison to the "splendor" of the original, who successfully approximate ideal beauty in their work (II 175–7, 30). In this regard, Reynolds recommends works of "established reputation" (II 232–3, 32): Claude Lorrain, Nicolas Poussin, Eustache Le Sueur, and Charles Le Brun among the French and, from the schools of Italy, Raphael, Titian, and especially the "divine" Michelangelo – the "Homer of Painting" (*Idler* 79, 248).

Whether artists look to her directly or through other works, Reynolds urges that they "imitate" rather than copy nature, capturing her general features and in so doing perfecting her defects and deformities; Reynolds evokes language by this time long familiar: artists "conceive and represent their subjects in a poetical manner" (IV 95–5, 59), which in the "grand style of Painting" means that the artist "corrects nature by herself, her imperfect state by her more perfect" (III 116, 44), a process Reynolds compares to the method of the naturalist who extracts the "invariable" and "general form" of a species from a sample of particular specimens:

Thus among the blades of grass or leaves of the same tree, though no two can be found exactly alike, yet the general form is invariable: A Naturalist, before he choose one as a sample, would examine many,

---

Picturesque, 136–7, and for connections between Reynolds and Johnson, Sarah Howe, "General and Invariable Ideas of Nature: Joshua Reynolds and His Critical Descendants," *English* 54 (2005), 1–13.

[26] Locke, *Essay*, 1.2.15.

since if he took the first that occurred it might have, by accident or otherwise, such a form as that it would scarce be known to belong to that species; he selects as the Painter does, the most beautiful, that is, the most general form of nature. (*Idler* 82, 255)

In the same way, the perfect form of the human body is never exemplified in any actual human being, but it is possible to extract "all the characters which are beautiful in that species" and by combining them depict its "perfect beauty" (III 194–5, 47).

In the realm of aesthetic *practice* this reconstruction of nature is translated into artistic representations that capture the central form and excite the imagination to the feeling of sublimity. The "whole beauty and grandeur of art," as Reynolds writes, "consists … in being able to get above all singular forms, local customs, particularities, and details of every kind" (III 102–5, 44); great art does not so much pass the test of time as ignore the transient altogether by depicting what is changeless, for "works, whether of poets, painters, moralists, or historians, which are built upon general nature live for ever," Reynolds writes, "while those which depend for their existence on particular customs and habits, a partial view of nature, or the fluctuation of fashion, can only be coeval with that which first raised them from obscurity" (IV 506–11, 73). Reynolds acknowledges that it is difficult to specify exactly the "precise invariable rules" (III 89–90, 44) that encapsulate this demand, but he manages to discover and present, quite literally, a *book* of rules that direct almost every aspect of artist education and practice, and he recommends that the "grand style of history painting" be placed at the highest pinnacle of art.

First and foremost, artists should choose themes that address subjects of universal human appeal, instances of heroic action or suffering found in Greek and Roman fable, historical moments of great import, or iconic episodes from scripture. Subjects drawn from the vulgar details of ordinary life, by contrast, confine the artist and audience to a time and place, and although the works of David Teniers, Adriaen Brouwer, Antoine Watteau, and even Hogarth are excellent "in their kind," Reynolds admits, "as their genius has been employed on low and confined subjects, the praise which we give must be as limited as its object" (III 320–1, 51). Similar limitations restrict those working in Reynolds's own oeuvre, portrait painting, which is an inherently humble style because it focuses by necessity on a single individual. "An History-painter paints man in general," Reynolds remarks, "a Portrait-Painter, a particular man, and consequently a defective model" (IV 414–16, 70). The best portraits, however, are infused with elements of the grand style – iconically Reynolds's own *Mrs. Siddons as the Tragic Muse* – which the painter achieves by "taking the general air, [rather] than in observing the exact similitude of every feature" (IV 68–70, 59), and giving the sitter bodily posture and facial expressions that would suit *anyone* and represent to the viewer universal and instantly recognizable sentiments and passions (IV 126ff., 60–1).

Second, and in accord with the idea of perfecting nature, artists should depart from "matter of fact" when required to impart the requisite dignity and nobility to their subjects. St. Paul, Reynolds reports, was "*mean*" in "*bodily*" presence" as Alexander the Great was of "low stature," deformities that should be not copied but imitated and thus corrected in the process of artistic representation. The artist "cannot make his hero talk like a great man," Reynolds remarks, but "he must make him look like one" (IV 123–4, 60). There is, moreover, no question here of "falsifying any fact"; it is simply a matter of "taking an allowed poetical license" (IV 108–9, 60), "improving" nature through paint on canvas as the gardener "improves" a view by rearranging features of the landscape: in both cases the aim is to make nature look more like a reconstructed version of herself.

Third, even with the appropriate subject matter firmly impressed on the mind, artists should aim at "absolute unity" of composition (VIII 84, 147) – Peter Paul Rubens is Reynolds's model in this regard – and take care not to burden the picture and the viewer with unnecessary details that distract from the central image. An artist must remember that the "sublime impresses the mind at once with *one great idea*; it is a single blow," so, concomitantly, the composition should raise "that effect so indispensably necessary to grandeur, that of one complete whole" (IV 274–80, 65, emphasis added) whereby the viewer's attention is "entirely occupied by the subject itself" (IV 383–4, 69). "The sublime in Painting, as in Poetry," as Reynolds expresses the same requirement later, "so overpowers, and takes such a possession of the whole mind, that no room is left for attention to minute criticism" (XV 362–4, 276).

From this approach to painting various rules follow, all of which aim to maximize sublime effect by avoiding anything that breaks unity or particularizes the whole. Artists should guard against placing too many figures in their compositions, avoid excessive ornamentation (VIII 107–8, 148), curtail variety (VIII 73–6, 147), and resist resorting to "tricks," "trifles," and "petty effects" like the Dutch who represent candlelight as it appears during the day (red) rather than as it does at night (white) (IV 378–81, 69). The same principle directs the artist's choice and use of color, which must reflect a proper grandeur by being uniform and simple, and applied with appropriate breadth, as in the chiaroscuro of the Bolognese school (Carevaggio) and the distinct and forcible use of blue, red, and yellow in the schools of Rome (Michelangelo) and Florence (Raphael). An excessive blending and softening of colors of the sort found in Hendrik Jansen and Anthony Van Dyck, by contrast, undermines sublimity by blurring the definite outlines of objects, as does the use of color in Venetian painting, which aims to "dazzle" rather than "affect" the viewer (IV 205–6, 63).

Indeed, it is worth noting that Reynolds's remarks on color echo Shaftesbury's downgrading of the senses – a subject with which the current chapter began – and anticipate Kant's later claim that colors only "charm" and "gratify" (CJ 5:223–6). Unlike both these thinkers, however, Reynolds is willing to recognize the valid claims of two competing elements in aesthetic taste and the tension they create: a "kind of sensuality," on the one hand, *and* a "love of sublime," on the other (VIII 284–8, 153). The former refers to the "external form of things," he writes, whereas the latter is "addressed to the mind," that is, the "imagination and the passions" and the invariable principles that govern them (VII, 458–62, 131). In Reynolds's view they must be kept apart, for ultimately painting is not "merely a gratification of the sight" (IV 349–50, 68) but a contemplation of those general ideas of nature that constitute its eternal form and explain its aesthetic value. Although he may not have recognized it in such terms, Reynolds's distinction effectively draws a line between what others called the "objective" and "subjective" sides of the sublime, a choice, as William Wordsworth was to put it near the century's end, between fixing one's gaze "chiefly ... upon external objects & their powers, qualities, & properties," or "upon the mind itself, and the laws by which it is acted upon."[27] Wordsworth and the Romantics were concerned with the art of poetry rather than painting, but like Reynolds, they would also look to the imagination and passions to articulate the "sense sublime," as Wordsworth put it famously in "Lines Composed a Few Miles above Tintern Abbey." This too is part of the philosophical history of the sublime but is an episode for a separate chapter in the current volume.

---

[27] William Wordsworth, *The Sublime and the Beautiful* (1798), appendix III to *A Guide through the District of the Lakes in the North of England, with a Description of the Scenery, &c. for the Use of Tourists and Residents*, 5th ed., with *Considerable Additions* (Kendal and London, 1835), in *The Prose Works of William Wordsworth*, ed. W. J. B. Owen and Jane Worthington Smyser, 3 vols. (Oxford: Clarendon Press, 1974), 3, lines 257–8.

5

The Associative Sublime

Gerard, Kames, Alison, and Stewart

Rachel Zuckert

According to the two best-known accounts of the sublime in the eighteenth century – those of Burke and Kant – the sublime is an aesthetic experience markedly distinct from that of the beautiful: instead of pure pleasure in response to orderly, proportioned objects, the sublime is a mixed response involving fear and frustration as well as heightened energy and delight. The objects that arouse this response – in the first instance, large or powerful objects – inspire negative feelings because cognitively or (in imagination at least) physically they challenge the aesthetic spectator. Thus a chief philosophical problem concerning the sublime is to explain how the painful experience of such objects could nonetheless be a source of pleasure, a question similar to the "paradox of tragedy" (the question why we are attracted to tragic works, given that they arouse painful feelings), which also occupied many eighteenth-century thinkers.[1]

This conception of the sublime as mixed and challenging is often assumed in current discussions, as, for example, in those concerning the "postmodern" sublime.[2] It is, however, by and large not shared by the Scottish philosophers and contemporaries of Burke, whose accounts of the sublime are the subject of the present chapter: Alexander Gerard, Lord Kames (Henry Home), Archibald Alison, and Dugald Stewart. Although they do identify large objects as paradigmatic objects of the sublime, these thinkers often describe our response to such objects as

---

[1] This debate has its origins in Aristotle's *Poetics*, in which he speaks of the "tragic pleasure of pity and fear" that the poet has to "produce by a work of imitation." See Aristotle, *Poetics*, in *The Complete Works of Aristotle*, ed. Jonathan Barnes (Princeton, NJ: Princeton University Press, 1984), 2:1453b12–13. The best-known, but by no means only, formulation of the problem in the eighteenth century is that of Hume, who writes of the "unaccountable pleasure, which the spectators of a well-written tragedy receive from sorrow, terror, anxiety, and other passions, that are in themselves disagreeable and uneasy." David Hume, "Of Tragedy," in *Essays: Moral, Political, and Literary*, ed. Eugene F. Miller (Indianapolis, IN: Liberty Fund, 1987), 216–25, p. 216. Among the authors discussed here, Kames is the only one to discuss the paradox of tragedy in any detail; see his essay "Our Attachment to Objects of Distress" in *Essays on the Principles of Morality and Natural Religion*, ed. Mary Catherine Moran (Indianapolis, IN: Liberty Fund, 2005 [1779, 1st ed. 1758]), 11–22.

[2] For the origins of the postmodern sublime, see Jean-François Lyotard, "Presenting the Unpresentable: The Sublime," *Artforum* 20, 8 (1982), 64–9; and *Leçons sur l'analytique du sublime* (Paris: Galilée, 1991); *Lessons on the Analytic of the Sublime*, trans. Elizabeth Rottenberg (Stanford, CA: Stanford University Press, 1994). Guy Sircello's interest in the sublime as (purportedly) an experience transcending human understanding, and thus impossible to theorize, suggests a similar conception of the sublime, which is again also similar to the texts under discussion here. See Guy Sircello, "How Is a Theory of the Sublime Possible?," *Journal of Aesthetics and Art Criticism* 51, 4 (1993), 541–50.

In working on this chapter, I was much aided by an unpublished book chapter by Emily Brady on the eighteenth-century sublime. I am also grateful to Timothy Costelloe and Les Harris for comments, and to the participants in a graduate seminar on eighteenth-century aesthetics at Northwestern University – Casey Droseyn, Lee Goldsmith, Derek Green, David Johnson, Seth Mayer, Hung Nguyen, Daniel Tovar, and Tyler Zimmer – for stimulating discussions of the sublime and other aesthetic matters.

serene, pleasurable elevation. Thus their accounts tend not to raise, nor indeed do they attempt to solve, such a "problem" of the sublime. They are concerned instead with a logically prior question, namely, whether (or how) the sublime can be understood as a single, unified aesthetic category, a definite type of response to a specifiable class of objects. In answering this question, they attempt to be true to the plurality, richness, and complexity of the sublime as human beings experience it and to the way it is presented in the literary and philosophical tradition. They do so, in large part, by claiming that appreciation of the sublime is characterized by *imaginative association*. As a result of the centrality of association to the sublime in their accounts, I shall argue, Dugald Stewart's suggestion that the sublime is something like a family-resemblance concept represents the ultimate purport of their accounts. Although this position is not theoretically satisfying in the way at least some of them hope – Alison, for example, promises to provide a *definition* of the sublime as a single, unified category – it allows them to recognize, better than many other theorists, the sublimity of artworks (as opposed to the sublimity of nature), the ways in which artistic representation can be transformative of sublime experience, and the associative, figurative, plastic character of emotional and imaginative response in aesthetic experience. Before turning to these issues, however, I begin by outlining the basic contours of their accounts of the sublime.

PLEASURABLE ELEVATION

The works under consideration in this chapter were published over a range of fifty years, beginning with Alexander Gerard's treatment of the sublime in his *Essay on Taste* of 1759. Kames's *Elements of Criticism* was published soon after in 1762, whereas Archibald Alison's *Essays on the Nature and Principles of Taste* of 1790 and Dugald Stewart's discussion of aesthetics in his *Philosophical Essays* of 1810 are the last major works in the long eighteenth-century British tradition in aesthetics. Although written over the course of a relatively long period, these accounts of the sublime are in many ways similar (though they also disagree in significant ways). Like nearly all British aestheticians, they hold, in Kames's words, that "*grandeur* and *sublimity* have a double signification: they ... signify the quality or circumstance in objects by which the emotions of grandeur and sublimity are produced; sometimes the emotions themselves."[3] Such usage reflects the nature of the sublime on their view, namely that it is a (broadly) Lockean secondary quality: an object is sublime not independently of human beings but only insofar as it arouses human affective response.[4]

All four identify, moreover, similar objects of the sublime: as listed by Gerard, "the Alps, the Nile, the ocean, the wide expanse of heaven, or the immensity of space uniformly extended without limit or termination."[5] Storms, battles, architecture, and virtuous traits such as the ability to hold riches and power in contempt also figure in all these accounts as examples of sublime objects. As suggested by their use of "grandeur" as a synonym for "sublimity,"[6] they tend to identify great magnitude and elevation as characteristics of objects that render them sublime.

---

[3] Henry Home, Lord Kames, *Elements of Criticism*, ed. Peter Jones, 2 vols. (Indianapolis, IN: Liberty Fund, 2005 [1785, 1st ed. 1762]), 1:151 (EC).

[4] Archibald Alison, *Essays on the Nature and Principles of Taste* (Dublin, 1790), 195 (ENPT).

[5] Alexander Gerard, *An Essay on Taste*, 3rd ed. (Edinburgh, 1780 [1759]); reprint, ed. Walter J. Hipple, Jr. (Gainesville, FL: Scholars' Facsimiles and Reprints, 1963), 11 (ET).

[6] The one exception on this point is Kames, who treats grandeur and sublimity as two related but distinct aesthetic values: large objects are grand, whereas objects that are elevated are sublime. Kames takes these two qualities of objects to arouse very similar feelings, however, and treats them together in a single chapter.

As noted previously, these thinkers tend to characterize our responses to such objects as more straightforwardly pleasurable than Burke does.[7] All claim that the sublime is a "species" of agreeable feeling, a state of pleasurable wonder, admiration, a "pleasing awe," a "solemn sedateness," or "elevated" emotion.[8] Kames and Gerard endorse Longinus's description of the feeling of the sublime: "The mind is elevated by [the sublime], and so sensibly affected as to swell in transport and inward pride, as if what is only heard or read, were its own invention" (EC 159n).[9] Although both Gerard and Kames mention terror (in passing), the Burkean response of fear and pain is largely absent from their description of sublime experience. Writing at the end of the tradition, and in full cognizance of Burke's writing, Stewart and Alison discuss Burkean aspects of the sublime more extensively, for they aim to be comprehensive, incorporating aspects of all prior aesthetic theory (see, for example, ENPT 202–5).[10] Thus they both note that terror may be part of the experience of the sublime, but for them, unlike for Burke, terror is not the definitive moment of the sublime. Stewart, probably following Kames, holds that elevation – of objects and of feeling – is the central, defining characteristic of the sublime (both argue that this central meaning of the sublime is indicated by its etymology),[11] and he takes terror to be a secondary emotional response to the sublime. (Stewart criticizes Burke explicitly for making the category of the sublime too "narrow" by focusing only on terror [PE 277].) Alison holds that the sublime, like the beautiful, is a second-order pleasure, felt when we experience a train of associated ideas – a reverie – which is experienced as unified because the ideas therein share a common (first-order)[12] emotional tone. An object that occasions such an emotionally unified and thus pleasing train of ideas is beautiful or sublime. He appears to hold that terror – like wonder, awe, elevation, or admiration – might be one such first-order emotion in the case of the sublime[13] and is closest to Burke among our writers, often linking the sublime with desolation, melancholy, or danger, suggesting a Burkean connection between the sublime and mortality. Terror is merely one of the possible emotions we might feel for the sublime, however, and because all aesthetic emotions are experienced as part of a dreamlike reverie on Alison's account, neither they nor their objects seem to be threatening or disruptive to the aesthetic spectator. They do not, therefore, lead to a "problem" of the sublime: we can feel pure pleasure in perceiving such objects, feeling these emotions, and engaging in the trains of ideas they occasion.

The dominant conception of the sublime among these thinkers thus differs from the Burkean one, which is characterized by the centrality of pain and terror.[14] In emphasizing elevation and

---

[7] None of these authors appears to be familiar with Kant's work, whether the early *Observations on the Sublime and the Beautiful* or the *Critique of Judgment*, which appeared after most of them wrote; thus I shall refer to Burke, rather than Kant, as the main contrast case here.

[8] See EC 152; ET 11, 12, 34, and 303; and Dugald Stewart, *Philosophical Essays*, in *Collected Works*, ed. William Hamilton, 11 vols. (Edinburgh: Thomas Constable, 1855), 5:303 (PE).

[9] Scholars now refer to the author of *On the Sublime* as pseudo-Longinus (although see the contribution by Malcolm Heath in this volume). I shall use "Longinus," however, in concert with our thinkers' references.

[10] Kames and Gerard may not have known of Burke's work, as neither refers to it.

[11] On the etymology of the sublime, see Jan Cohn and Thomas H. Miles, "The Sublime: In Alchemy, Aesthetics and Psychoanalysis," *Modern Philology* 74, 3 (1977), 289–304.

[12] Alison himself distinguishes between "complex" and "simple" emotions, but I use (respectively) "second-order" and "first-order" emotions because this more clearly indicates their relationship: first-order emotions concern objects or ideas thereof, whereas second-order emotions arise from trains of those emotions or ideas.

[13] Alison does not explicitly discuss the difference between the sublime and the beautiful, nor does he provide a separate account of the sublime, and thus my claim here that particular first-order emotions are characteristic of the sublime is somewhat speculative.

[14] As Monk points out, these thinkers also tend to downplay wildness, rule breaking, the overwhelming, and the dramatically free as connotations of the sublime, all of which become prominent in later Romantic conceptions. See Samuel Holt Monk, *The Sublime: A Study of Critical Theories in XVIII-Century England* (Ann Arbor: University of Michigan Press, 1935), 130–5.

sedateness (or dreamlikeness) these accounts depict a milder, more straightforwardly uplifting response to large objects and take the experience of contemplating the Alps, the calm ocean, or the starry sky as emblematic of the sublime. Such experience strikes one not as markedly painful or frightening, but rather as calm and elevating. Thus (again contra Burke), these thinkers also hold that objects may be both beautiful and sublime: an object, like the starry heavens above, for example, may be ordered, proportionate, useful (characteristics of the beautiful, on some of their accounts), and *also* large and elevated; we may feel two corresponding pleasurable responses to it at once.[15]

These accounts thus do not raise, or attempt to answer, a special "problem" of the sublime, a puzzle about why a prima facie painful experience should (also) be pleasurable. Indeed, they perhaps raise questions concerning the phenomenological adequacy of the Burkean sort of account that occasions such a problem: such views may be "too narrow," as Stewart writes, leaving out or obscuring from recognition more straightforwardly pleasurable experiences of elevation in response to large and powerful objects. Although they are not concerned with this question, the thinkers under consideration here do ask *why* we find perceiving such objects pleasing (even if not in an especially puzzling way), and *what* defines the sublime, if it is not this distinctive sort of response. I turn now to their answers to these questions.

EXPLAINING OUR PLEASURE IN THE SUBLIME

Following Hutcheson, all of these thinkers deny that we feel pleasure in sublime objects on the basis of judging those objects to accord with rational principles of aesthetic or artistic value. Rather, the perception of an object occasions pleasure, which is in turn the basis for a judgment that the object is sublime. More specifically, they seem to hold, again following Hutcheson, that taste – in this case the appreciation of the sublime – consists in an "internal" or "reflex sense," an affective, involuntary, unreasoning response to an object presented to the mind by another sense or another mental faculty.[16] They take their philosophical task to be that of identifying which sorts of objects occasion such pleasure and why.

Kames and Stewart in fact restrict themselves largely to the first half of this task: Kames, content in the *Elements of Criticism* to describe different "natural" sources of pleasure, simply claims that we feel pleasure in perceiving large or elevated objects, without explaining it; Stewart explicitly eschews discussion on this point, claiming that he agrees with his predecessors' accounts, particularly Alison's. Alison and Gerard, by contrast, do attempt to explain why such perception is emotionally elevating. Gerard writes:

> When a large object is presented, the mind expands itself to the extent of that object, and is filled with one grand sensation, which totally possessing it, composes it into a solemn sedateness, and strikes it with deep silent wonder and admiration: it finds such a difficulty in spreading itself to the dimensions of its object, as enlivens and invigorates its frame: and having overcome the opposition which this occasions, it sometimes imagines itself present in every part of the scene which it contemplates; and from the sense of this immensity, feels a noble pride, and entertains a lofty conception of its own capacity. (ET 12)

Gerard suggests that our pleasure derives from our imaginative, perceptive activity: in attempting to perceive a large object, the mind is challenged and energized and, on its success, feels itself to be expanded and therefore feels pride. Thus, as Gerard claims about all "internal senses," we

---

[15] See, for example, ET 75–6; EC 153; PE 235–6.
[16] See Gerard, ET 147n. For a nuanced discussion of the relation between Hutcheson and these later thinkers, see Peter Kivy, *The Seventh Sense: Francis Hutcheson and Eighteenth-Century British Aesthetics*, 2nd ed. (Cambridge: Cambridge University Press, 2003 [1976]), 184–5, 189ff., and 234–5.

attribute the pleasure to the object's effect on us, but in fact we are taking pleasure in the mind's own activities (ET 3). Gerard also suggests that this mental activity is something like an identification with the object: the mind "imagines itself present in every part of the scene it contemplates." Furthermore, he prefaces the preceding passage by stating that "we always contemplate objects and ideas with a disposition similar to their nature" (ET 12; Kames appears to concur, suggesting that the spectator's body reflects such identification, that we expand the chest or stand taller while appreciating the sublime [EC 151]). Hence, perhaps, the purely pleasurable character of sublime feeling on Gerard's (and Kames's) account: the perceiver is not threatened by the object but rather imaginatively identifies with it and is thus expanded or elevated.

Like Gerard, Alison claims that the pleasure in the sublime results from the mind's own activity. Pleasure in the sublime arises both from the "exercise of our emotions" – from having first-order emotional responses to particular ideas – and from our dreamlike, imaginative, associative activity, pursuing the "train of [such emotionally charged] ideas" (ENPT 102–6). The imagination has a second, somewhat different function for Alison, however, in generating the experience of the sublime as well. Not satisfied (as is Kames) with the claim that large objects simply are moving or pleasing, Alison asks what *about* such large objects could be emotionally moving (how they can arouse the first-order emotions that comprise part of the "train of ideas" subsequently found sublime). We can and do perceive things that are large or elevated without being moved; for example (anachronistically), a large, high billboard seems unlikely to arouse much feeling, sublime or otherwise. But if these qualities were the causes of our emotional responses, Alison argues, we should have such responses to any object with such qualities (ENPT 112–13). Indeed Alison argues that *all* material, sensibly perceived qualities of objects fail, by themselves, to move us. Although he does not put it this way, he seems to believe that material, sensible qualities are, by themselves, "flat," merely factual, and meaningless to us and so cannot by themselves arouse emotional response. Therefore, he suggests, it is not the sensible qualities themselves but rather those qualities taken as expressive that move us: we respond to sensible qualities because we associate them with other, nonsensible qualities that *are* meaningful, moving.[17] Thus Alison suggests that great magnitude is moving (when it is) because it is taken as expressive of power or of the abilities of its maker, for example, and that loud sounds are moving because they convey danger (see, for example, ENPT 131–5). Stewart similarly suggests that we find elevated objects moving because of their associations – with upright posture, for example, or with the gods and the abode of the blessed – or because height is expressive of the object's surprising, unusual ability to resist gravity's pressure to move downward (PE 299–305; Gerard makes similar points at ET 17–20).[18]

Neither Alison nor Stewart explains why these further objects or qualities are moving; perhaps they hold, like Kames, that these are fundamental responses, part of human nature. Perhaps they hold, like Gerard, that such responses may be traced to yet more fundamental human mental activities: we may be moved by power (for example) because we imaginatively identify with the powerful object. Or perhaps we are moved by the sublime because the object is of a sort that would impinge on our practical activities, as suggested by some of their examples: weapons or the ocean are sublime because we sympathize with those who may be threatened by them (ENPT 207; PE 310). I use the subjunctive mood here (such an object "*would* impinge"), however, not only because they (like Burke) hold that one cannot appreciate an object as sublime

---

[17] One may well doubt that expression is the same as, or even a form of, association. This concern also holds, I note in anticipation, for the claim that representation (e.g., by words or their referents) is a form of association, a view also held by these thinkers. Such concerns about the overbroadness of their category of association and the naïveté of their view of forms of representation (whether expressive or referential) apply, of course, to the entire Lockean or, particularly, Humean British tradition and raise larger issues than can be treated here.

[18] Gerard cites Hume's *Treatise* as a source for this line of argument, and Hume would appear to be the ultimate, if unacknowledged, source on this point for Alison and, particularly, Stewart as well.

if one is in fact threatened by it, that is, if it *in fact* impinges on one's practical activity, but also because, for both Stewart and Alison, aesthetic appreciation is not direct practical interaction with an object but instead consists in finding that object meaningful and connecting it to other perceptions, memories, and ideas, including meanings derived from practical activity.

Whatever the explanation (and they may mean to endorse all of these and others), it is clear that on their accounts, as on Gerard's, our experience of the sublime is fundamentally active, brought about by our power of imagination.[19] The importance of imaginative association on these accounts of the sublime means that, unlike much of the tradition, these thinkers tend to take art objects to be equally or more sublime than natural objects. Thus for all of them architecture and poetry are prominent examples of sublime objects, which gain their sublimity from associations – with durability and strength, the wealth and prominence of the owner of the building, the skill of the architect or poet, the objects with which the words are associated[20] or the passions they express, or the kinds of people who use such words (see, for example, ET 19–26).

On Gerard's account, such objects are not paradigmatic of the sublime (as are large, natural objects such as the sky or ocean), but they seem nonetheless to count for him as fully (not weakly, or secondarily) sublime. Kames claims that art objects may be more sublime than natural objects because the artist can choose the elements of the work (whereas of course natural objects simply have all qualities that they do have); thus the artist may heighten the sublime effect of an artwork by concentrating on elements that promote sublime feeling and eliminating qualities that might be less moving (EC 165; cf. ENPT 75; PE 266–7 and 273). For Alison and Stewart, associative meaning is, as we have seen, itself a primary source of sublime experience, and thus art objects, which are sublime through such association (representation, expression, evocation) are paramount exemplars of sublimity. Indeed Alison and Stewart suggest, strikingly, that our experience of natural objects as sublime is itself at least strengthened, and possibly produced, by poetic or other artistic associations that we bring to the experience of those natural objects, endowing them with a wealth of evocative meaning (ENPT 18 and 38–40; PE 298). Thus both thinkers invert the common priority of natural over artistic objects in eighteenth-century treatments of the sublime, which frequently present artistic sublimity as consisting at most in the imitation of, and thus dependence on, natural sublimity. By contrast, Alison and Stewart suggest that art (or other cultural meanings) may have transformative powers in *rendering* natural objects sublime, through investing those objects with meaning. The Alps, for example, are more sublime if associated with Hannibal, Alison suggests, and a poem might render sublime grains of sand, pebbles, or sparrows – objects neither large nor powerful and therefore not typically sublime – through association with the endless passage of time, the grinding down of everything through powerful, impersonal forces, or the incalculable solicitude of God.

Thus these thinkers employ association to explain the powerful sublimity of art. Association is also crucial in their views concerning the nature and unity of the category of the sublime, to which issue I now turn.

THE ASSOCIATIVE CATEGORY OF THE SUBLIME

So far in my discussion I have moved loosely among various objects or qualities of objects that we might find sublime, such as size, power, and elevation. All of these qualities, as well

---

[19] Stewart distinguishes imagination, as a faculty responsible for generating fictional images, from the power of association (PE 194–5), but because it is standard in this period (as in Gerard and Alison) to attribute association to the imagination, I shall do so here as well, with the caveat that it is not accurate to Stewart's usage.

[20] As noted previously, on these thinkers' view, words are "associated" with the objects to which they refer, which is no doubt a problematic conception of linguistic representation.

as the objects Gerard, Kames, Alison, and Stewart mention as examples of the sublime – the ocean, the Nile, stoic virtues, eternity, and the like – are referred to in Longinus and the tradition sparked by Longinus's work. None of these thinkers has the intention of correcting this tradition; all four aim instead to explain and understand the category of the sublime on the accepted view.[21] Like other thinkers in the British tradition (such as Addison and Reid), they take their project to be consonant with, but also philosophically prior to, Longinus's (and some of his followers): they are not articulating rhetorical and literary strategies but rather, as we have seen, aim to identify and explain the character of the experience on which sublime rhetoric draws, the effects of which it aims to bring about.[22] Gerard, Kames, Alison, and Stewart are also quite occupied by a question that they believe is raised by the traditional discussion of the sublime: the objects frequently used as examples of the sublime do not seem to share any one common, sublime-making quality, but, as I have just noted, they exhibit an array of different qualities (such as magnitude or power).[23] Thus, they ask, in virtue of what are all of these objects sublime?

Stewart, Gerard, and Kames begin to answer this question by identifying core or paradigm cases: objects of great magnitude (Gerard, and Kames for grandeur) or objects that are elevated (Stewart, and Kames for the sublime).[24] Gerard and Kames add that such objects must be uniform or regular in order to give us the impression of *one* large object, as opposed to an array of different parts or objects stuck together, which we cannot take in as a whole (ET 12–13; EC 152).[25] These objects or qualities of objects (and the responses to them) are what Kames and Stewart call the "literal meaning" of "sublime" (or "grandeur"), a reference point for articulating the nature of this experience or the character of this aesthetic value.

Once this paradigm case has been identified, however, the theorists must explain why other things that do not seem to share that defining quality – armies, heroic virtues, eternity, and poetry – are nonetheless sublime. Our theorists attempt to respond to this question in three different ways: by analyzing the qualities of those objects, by pointing to the feeling of the sublime, and by pointing to association as a mental activity that constructs the extension of "sublime." I will treat these in turn.

In accord with his claim that all objects of an internal sense have some quality in common (ET 77), Gerard attempts to unify the category of the sublime by showing that all sublime objects are characterized by large quantity and thus do have something in common with large objects. He argues, for example, that the ancients are found sublime owing to the long period of time between them and us, and that armies are found so because they consist of a large number of men united to one common end (ET 14 and 19). These objects may, by virtue of such

---

[21] This respect for the Longinian tradition is subject to one proviso: Gerard (ET 27) criticizes Longinus for including all excellences of composition (such as the pathetic, the elegant, and the vehement) in the category of the sublime, and thus of using "sublime" in too broad a sense to mean greatness or excellence (see also EC 159n for a similar objection from Kames). Although the other two theorists do not explicitly make this argument, they seem to concur. All of them emphasize instead another strand in Longinus's thought concerning the sublime as an aesthetic category distinct from pathos, vehemence, or elegance.
[22] For a good statement (by an author who influenced Gerard) of this justification for the turn from the analysis of style to that of experience, see John Baillie, "An Essay on the Sublime," in *The Sublime: A Reader in British Eighteenth-Century Aesthetic Theory*, ed. Andrew Ashfield and Peter de Bolla (Cambridge: Cambridge University Press, 1996), 87–100, p. 87. On the transformations in the British discussion of the sublime more generally, see Monk, *The Sublime*.
[23] Alison and Stewart also wish to explain the fact that objects with contrary characteristics may be sublime – for example, loud noises and yet also the silence of the calm before a storm.
[24] As noted previously, Kames takes grandeur and sublimity to be two closely related aesthetic categories.
[25] Although Alison does not identify paradigm cases, he seems to take great quantity to be at least a frequent characteristic of sublime objects; against Gerard and Kames, he rejects uniformity as a defining characteristic of the sublime (ENPT 74–5 and 206–9).

quantity, arouse a similar feeling in us to that aroused by large objects, and for the same reasons: it is difficult and energizing to apprehend a lengthy temporal duration or a large number of men in an army, just as it is to apprehend an expansive spatial magnitude.

As Gerard acknowledges, pursuing this strategy becomes difficult with respect to passions, heroic virtues, and poetry, objects often identified as sublime in the tradition but that do not seem to have any relevantly quantifiable characteristic. One might find passions or virtues sublime because of their degree (ET 17), although it is unclear that such an intense passion is thereby more difficult to apprehend (and so whether it would fully fit Gerard's psychological explanation of the sublime is likewise unclear). More difficult to see is how stoic virtue or poetry is relevantly quantifiable (a poem's length seems unpromising as the source of its sublimity). Gerard argues, however, that the passions and virtues are nonetheless related to things of quantity as their objects, causes, or effects, and that they are thereby sublime: individuals with heroic virtue, for example, are conquerors of *many* men and countries; universal benevolence is sublime because it is oriented toward all (a large quantity of) human beings (ET 15–16). Works of poetry are sublime because their words are associated with (refer to) objects that are sublime because of their quantity.

These last claims of course weaken Gerard's case that all sublime objects have some sort of large quantity. They also fail in fact to account for all of the traditional examples of sublime objects. Could not a hero who fails to conquer others still have sublime virtues? What about the stoic virtue of being able to hold luck and misfortune in contempt? This virtue appears to have no relation to quantity (whether in itself or in its objects or effects).

Gerard might be aided by Kames's suggestion that we find such virtues sublime because of identification: we "accompany," Kames writes, the "sublimest sentiments and most hazardous exploits" of such virtuous persons "with a magnanimity equal to theirs" (EC 162). Such virtues might, then, be classed as sublime because our response to them is similar in structure and "feel" to our identificatory appreciation of large objects (on Gerard's account). But this too leads to a fragmentation of the (Gerardian) category of the sublime, as is perhaps suggested already in the passage quoted in the preceding section on our pleasure in the sublime (ET 12); is the sublime to be characterized as that which is pleasurable through identification or as that which is pleasurable through the accomplishment of difficult cognitive tasks?

Perhaps as a result of such worries, Gerard claims – and this is the second strategy for unifying the category of the sublime – that any object inspiring the same pleasurable sensation of elevation, expansion, and consequent pride in the mind may be classed as sublime (ET 16). Kames concurs: objects that are neither elevated nor of great magnitude may nonetheless be "figuratively" grand or sublime because they arouse the same feeling as those that are "literally" so (EC 158). Like all of these thinkers, he points to figurative expressions such as "high" social rank as evidence of the "figurative" sublimity of objects that are not in fact elevated, and he takes the commonality of feeling in response to such objects to explain such figurative use of language. Alison appears to agree (without making a literal vs. figurative distinction): he points to a distinctive pleasurable feeling of the sublime and claims that objects that give rise to this feeling are called sublime (or, more properly, these objects arouse the first-order emotions that, when presented in a "train," then arouse sublime feeling) (ENPT 150).

Stewart also endorses this second strategy, but he emphasizes (explicitly against Kames) that one must explain *why* other objects come to elicit such responses, or how they come to *count as* "figuratively" sublime (PE 279). He argues that the answer to this question is association (our third unificatory strategy). Here Stewart both follows Alison in emphasizing the importance of association and expands on Gerard's attenuated unifications. The basic idea is that there is no one quality in objects that arouses the feeling of the sublime, but this feeling may arise in response to many different qualities of objects and for different reasons. Thus, per Kames, we call all of these objects sublime because they arouse similar feelings, although not, at least necessarily, for the same reason, or because they share the same quality. In addition, Stewart claims, the further, different qualities of objects (that is, beyond the paradigm case) can come to arouse this feeling *because* those qualities are associated with other qualities that are (originally) sublime. Thus, as noted previously, Stewart takes it that elevated objects are the primary, original object of sublime feeling – paradigmatically, for him, the sky. Objects of course have many qualities beyond height; the sky is also wide, filled with light or darkness, and so on (see PE 295–7 and 306). Our emotional responses, including sublime feeling, are imprecise: they do not indicate which quality of an object in particular has aroused them. They may then be "transferred" (as Stewart puts it); they apply to the object overall (without precision) and so may slide from the quality of the object that originally aroused such a response (height) to a quality of that object that did not (breadth, light, or darkness) (PE 201 and 306).[26] So, Stewart suggests, thunder and lightning come to be found sublime – elevating – because they occur in the sky and are thereby also associated with the gods, and thus the emotional tone of our response to the heavens (as high, divine) is transferred to them as well (PE 295–7). Once these objects or qualities come to be invested with sublime feeling, moreover, they may arouse that feeling independently of the object or quality from which it was "transferred": we may find the wide ocean sublime (not just the wideness of the sky); we may find other terrible objects sublime, just as we do thunder and lightning; and so on.[27]

The details of Stewart's account seem a bit questionable; it is, for example, hard to believe that thunder and lightning do not occasion their own, intense response from human beings, prior to and independently of any association they might have with the heavens and our elevated feeling in response to them. But as I shall now suggest, this account – at least in its structure – seems correct concerning the character of the sublime on all of our theorists' accounts or can be seen as the "logical outcome" of their general approach: it renders the sublime, as Stewart himself suggests, something like a family-resemblance concept.

FAMILY RESEMBLANCE, OR SOMETHING LIKE IT

Stewart suggests that he understands the sublime as (what we would call, following Wittgenstein) a family-resemblance concept, that is, one wherein objects A, B, C, D, and E all fall under the concept (or are part of its extension), but not because they all have some property or properties in common. Rather, A has some property in common with B, whereas B has a different property in common with C, and C with D, and so on.[28] Strictly speaking, none of these thinkers, including Stewart, holds a family-resemblance view, because all claim that all sublime objects *do* have a necessary, sublime-making property in common, namely that they all arouse the same feeling.[29] But this claim in fact does not hold up in their actual treatments of the sublime, nor can it be retained, I would argue, given the importance of association (or "figurative meaning") on their accounts, as well as their aims to preserve and explain common usage.[30]

---

[26] Cf. Gerard, ET 157–8. Kames is similarly interested in such promiscuity of feeling, which he takes to be the source of figurative language.

[27] Such transference can happen through contiguity (as in this example) but also through resemblance, or other associative relations identified in this Humean tradition. Thus, works of fine art can be sublime because of their reference, often understood in terms of resemblance, to objects previously found sublime.

[28] PE 195–6 and 253–4. Stewart provides this account in the course of discussing the beautiful, but because he notes explicitly that his view of the sublime is similar to his view of the beautiful, I take it that this account applies to the sublime as well.

[29] I thank Derek Green, who pressed this point to me.

[30] These claims may not apply to Kames, who among these thinkers refers least to association and does not do so to unify the category of the sublime, relying instead on the identifiability of a particular feeling. One may wonder whether we can so identify that feeling (as I suggest in the text), as well as whether this proposal can characterize

As noted previously, none of these thinkers endorses the Burkean view of sublime feeling as fundamentally painful. But none of them, I would argue replaces the Burkean feeling by another, identifiable, single feeling, one that could, by itself identify a class. As noted previously, Gerard and Kames both endorse the Longinian description of sublime feeling as elevation or expansion and consequent pride, but they, like Alison and Stewart, also gloss the feeling of the sublime in different ways when describing responses to different objects – as wonder, astonishment, admiration, and (if less prominently than Burke) terror. These feelings are not obviously identical: astonishment and pride seem rather distant from one another, for example, in having (or not) a tinge of surprise or shock, and in having (or not) positive self-reference; certainly terror is distinct from elevation or "solemn sedateness."[31]

Unlike the others, Gerard recognizes this issue and attempts to assimilate terror to elevation via astonishment by saying that all of these emotional states "suspend" the mind's animation (ET 16). This claim is somewhat difficult to reconcile with his initial account of sublime feeling (as resulting from the mind's expansive activity in apprehending a large object), and if taken seriously as definitional of sublime feeling it would render objects that bore us (that is, "suspend" mental activity) sublime. The suggestion of Stewart's account (if not his own claim) seems more appropriate here: some experiences – of terrified energy in experiencing a storm, say – are associated (on one or another ground) under the concept of the sublime with others – say, of serene, elevated contemplation of the night sky – with which they do not have anything strictly in common, including the tonality and nature of the feeling in question.

Thus, I would suggest that although none of these thinkers in fact endorses a family-resemblance account (even Stewart, who develops this understanding of concepts), their accounts involve this sort of view in practice. Indeed, their accounts ultimately propose a conception of the extension of the sublime as even more weakly connected than on the family-resemblance view: thunder and lightning (and our responses to them) do not, on Stewart's portrayal anyway, have anything in common with the calm night sky (and our responses to it) but are associated because of contiguity (thunder and lightening occur *in* the sky), a different principle of association than resemblance. Thus neither do these two items in the extension of "sublime" have any relevant sublime-making feature in common, nor are they linked in virtue of a third item that has some relevant commonality with each of them (as on a class family-resemblance view); rather the two are simply, only, associated.

This consequence of their analysis is not, I believe, coincidental or based on confusion or on some sort of sloppy use of language concerning feelings. It may arise in part from the difficulty (perhaps not really recognized by these thinkers) of clearly identifying a single feeling that could define the category of the sublime: we have perhaps a less sure grasp on the complex phenomenology of our feelings than would be required for a classification of objects purely by a very specific feeling they might arouse. (One might also wonder whether, and to what degree of precision, feelings can be identified independently of the character of the objects to which they are responses, as this type of account would require them to be, in order for the feelings, by themselves, to constitute the commonality among the objects that arouse them.) But it also clearly stems from the role that association plays in their accounts. As we have seen, on their view association bestows sublime "meaning" on many objects that have different properties and that arouse a range of emotional responses. These objects, then, have no (set of) common properties in virtue of which they are sublime. As Stewart suggests, association also leads to the "transference" of feeling from one object to another, thereby constituting the category of the

---

a concept with as broad an extension as the sublime appears to have at this date – and this might be a reason to push Kames closer to the others. But Kames could also insist that "the sublime" refers properly only to objects that arouse a particular feeling of elevation, not terrifying objects or others far from his paradigm cases.
[31] See Monk, *The Sublime*, 142 and 161 on other thinkers of the period who grapple with this problem.

sublime itself by grouping objects and responses to them together *as* sublime.[32] Indeed "family resemblance" simply is one version of the structure of association, which works (on these theorists' view) precisely by linking one thing or idea to another and then to another, but not necessarily (indeed usually not) on the grounds of some commonality holding among all links in the chain, or even of (relevant) commonalities of one object to the next "link."

This result is also a consequence of these theorists' methodological choices. All of them attempt to incorporate into their accounts the whole range of feelings and objects that have been identified as sublime in the tradition. This implicit constraint on their accounts, together with the observational acuity they share with the rest of the British tradition, leads to the expansiveness and open-endedness, the family-resemblance-like character, of their accounts. The tradition identifies a wide range both of types of objects and of feelings as sublime. As Stewart suggests in his treatment of the myriad meanings that the ocean may have for us – as calm, stormy, mirroring the heavens, the locale of English national triumph, and so on (see PE 308–13) – observational attention to aesthetic experience of (traditionally identified) sublime objects will likely lead to a pluralistic conception of the sublime. Some cases of sublime experience may be identificatory (as on Gerard's and Kames's suggestion that our minds "expand" or are elevated along with a large or high object), whereas others may be sympathetic (as when, on Stewart's suggestion, we feel fear for sailors who might be threatened by the ocean and thus find the ocean sublime); some will be characterized by a "solemn sedateness," and others by a thrilling terror.

CONCLUDING REMARKS

I suggest, then, that Gerard, Kames, Alison, and Stewart do not, ultimately, provide an account of the sublime as a single, unified category but instead suggest a pluralist and open-ended associative account of the sublime. They account for the concept's unity (insofar as it has any) by referring to association and transferable feeling. This conception of the sublime allows them to achieve their goal of accommodating the range of feelings and types of objects that have been traditionally identified as sublime.

As in the case of many pluralist accounts, one may worry, however, that this achievement comes at a cost: the concept of the sublime threatens to become diffuse and uninformative, and the account of the sublime may come to be inaccurate to the experience it purports to describe and explain, precisely through its permissiveness. Anything or everything might count as sublime, and the sublime may be thereby rendered a vague, characterless concept, void of any determinate meaning: anything may have *something* in common with some object or feeling identified as sublime or might be associated or associable thereto. Thus Samuel Monk objects to this sort of account that poetry about sublime objects such as the Alps may not in fact succeed in being sublime (although on these accounts, it ought to, as it is associated with a sublime object).[33] Or, to take this worry in a somewhat different direction, why not say that the tradition has grouped together different sorts of experience that are not, in fact, all of one (natural) kind? Might it not be more productive to avoid grouping such diverse experiences or objects under one name (or trying to explain why they have been so grouped) but rather to analyze this category further, into (say) "the admirable" and "the terrifying-thrilling"?

---

[32] As discussed previously, Alison also claims that our *activity* of aesthetic appreciation consists in association (dreamlike reverie), which is the source of aesthetic pleasure. Thus for Alison engaging in association and receiving pleasure in it are definitive of (necessary conditions for) the sublime. As for the other thinkers and for similar reasons, however, it is not clear that Alison really can identify necessary and sufficient conditions for sublimity, as he claims to do.

[33] See Monk, *The Sublime*, 115–16.

Gerard, Kames, Alison, and Stewart do have some means at their disposal for addressing such concerns. As we have seen, they tend to characterize the sublime not only in terms of association but also by reference to paradigm cases (of objects and experiences); the "literal" sublime is the basis for the associative or "figurative" expansions of the category. Such a starting point, Stewart argues, is necessary in order to set the process of association going: we must first take pleasure in some sort of experience or object before this feeling can be "transferred" to something else associated with that object (PE 242).[34] As a result, they might argue, although the extension of the sublime might be extended indefinitely, a core meaning for the concept is nonetheless preserved. Thus, as suggested previously, their conception of the sublime is in one sense "weaker" than a standard family-resemblance understanding of concepts, because it can include objects or experiences that are simply associated with one another and share *no* relevant common property (even via a third member of the extension). At the same time, however, it is in another way "stronger" than a standard family-resemblance account, because it treats the extension of the concept of the sublime asymmetrically: some members of the class are paradigmatic or original, whereas others are not.

Gerard, Kames, Alison, and Stewart identify this core experience, in turn, as the natural one: human beings are naturally moved – elevated – by large or elevated objects (as Kames puts it) or by other nonsensible properties such as power (as on Alison's view). This emotional charge might then be transferred to other objects through associations or artistic transformations, but the natural pleasure is prior to and independent of these latter accretions and is a universal response based on human nature. Stewart and Alison also suggest that there might be natural, universal, human *associations*. Thus, although in principle there could be unlimited associations of objects or feelings to one another (and there may be unlimited "personal" or "accidental" associations), the category of the sublime is limited to those objects or experiences that will be in fact *naturally* and universally associated by all human beings with the original, paradigm cases or objects (ENPT 205; PE 201 and 291–2). There may, similarly, be constraints on which associations "stick" and which do not: perhaps some connections, analogies, or associations make more "natural" sense to human beings, flow better, or are more memorable and thus enter the common culture or tradition. (Some poems about the Alps may not "work" with such natural associative patterns and thus may not sustain the sublime association sufficiently to arouse feeling.)

They might argue as well that to differentiate the sublime into more specific, less associative categories is ultimately fruitless or untrue to the phenomena. For if the experience of the sublime – and/or the experiences in the subgenres of the sublime – is constituted by feeling (which is both imprecise and transferable) and imaginative association, then its objects and feelings will be linked to many other feelings and objects that are not necessarily similar to one another. Any such category will be, ineliminably, expandable through transference and associative mechanisms.

Whether these claims to identify natural pleasures and associations can be substantiated is a larger question than I can address here. I have suggested, however, that the key insights at their root – the "transference" logic of feeling and the imaginative endowment of objects and perceptions with associative meaning (expression, representation, evocation) – are rich

---

[34] This claim might not be true for Alison, who holds that we take pleasure in *having* emotions and in engaging in a "train of ideas," neither of which pleasures requires or is "transferred" from a prior pleasure. Alison's account would seem, however, to require that the explanation of first-order emotions "bottoms out" in identifying objects that simply do move us. Indeed this is part of his distinction between first-order emotions and the pleasures of taste: the latter, he claims, are not immediately aroused by objects but are aroused by associative reveries occasioned by objects. (This distinction requires some modification, however, because Alison also claims, as noted previously, that first-order emotions are aroused by material objects only when such material objects are associated with nonsensible properties.)

and plausible ones that would fruitfully bear further reflection. As Kames emphasizes, these proposals attempt to characterize the origins and power of figurative language, whether in dead metaphors (high social rank, for example) or in the living metaphors of artistic creation: feelings "spill over," or transfer themselves, to other, possibly quite dissimilar objects, leading to the possibility of figurative representation and explaining its emotionally moving character. As Alison suggests, imaginative associative activity endows objects with a richness of evocative significance that the bare perception of them lacks. As all of these thinkers suggest, these characteristic aesthetic responses are not only elicited by large or powerful natural objects but may also be enlisted, heightened, and even transformed by artistic representation. If such transference of feeling and imaginative association is a central feature of aesthetic experience, as these thinkers plausibly contend, it may indeed be no wonder that philosophers have had difficulty in providing definitions of aesthetic values.

6

The "Prehistory" of the Sublime in Early Modern France
An Interdisciplinary Perspective

Éva Madeleine Martin

INTRODUCTION

According to the story told until recently, the sublime first burst onto the French scene in 1674. This was the date that Nicholas Boileau Despréaux (1636–1711), "Lawmaker of the poets," published the *Traité du sublime ou du merveilleux dans le discours*, his French translation of the *Peri hupsous* περι ὕψους. Boileau claimed that, without it, the author he called Longinus would "only be known to a very few scholars."[1] Scholars since have treated at length the preeminence of Boileau's work in late seventeenth-century France, from its importance in the quarrel of the ancients and the moderns to the parallels with the *je ne sais quoi* of Dominique Bouhours (1671)[2] and from the *Réflexions* of René Rapin (1674) to the interpretations of Pierre Daniel Huet (1630–1721).[3]

Outside French studies, however, we are apt to find this assessment: Boileau led early modernity to identify "sublimity simply with excellence." The *Traité du sublime* thus offered a merely technical and rhetorical starting point for the sublime, which was not yet associated with aesthetics and the visual arts. Many critics have suggested that the truly fascinating sublime – the sublime of "overwhelming or transporting" – emerged later and elsewhere.[4] Jean-François Lyotard's thesis is well known: the sublime understood as a "mode of sensibility" is specific to modernity.[5]

Today, with the myth of a rule-bound French classicism dismantled, it is generally accepted that Boileau did not present a new school of thought but rather summarized traits of literature and criticism he admired.[6] In this light, some contemporary scholars have focused on

---

[1] This author will be called "Longinus" throughout. All translations are mine. Nicolas Boileau Despréaux, *Traité du sublime ou du merveilleux dans le discours*, in *Oeuvres complètes* (Paris: Firmin Didot Frères, 1837; Elibron Classics Replica, 2007), 316–48, p. 317 (B).

[2] See, for example, Louis Marin, "Le sublime dans les années 1670: Un je ne sais quoi?" *Papers on French Seventeenth Century Literature: Biblio 17*, 25 (1986), 185–201, and Richard Scholar, *The Je-Ne-Sais-Quoi in Early Modern Europe* (Oxford: Oxford University Press, 2005).

[3] See, for example, Anne T. Delehanty, "From Judgment to Sentiment: Changing Theories of the Sublime, 1674–1710," *Modern Language Quarterly* 66 (2005), 151–72; Anne-Marie Lecoq, ed., *La Querelle des Anciens et des Modernes, XVIIe–XVIIIe siècles*, prefaced by "Les abeilles et les araignées," by Marc Fumaroli (Paris: Gallimard, 2001); Théodore A. Litman, *Le sublime en France (1660–1714)* (Paris: Nizet, 1971); and Baldine Saint Girons, *Fiat lux: Une philosophie du sublime* (Paris: Quai Voltaire, 1993).

[4] The citations are from James Kirwan, *Sublimity: The Non-Rational and the Irrational in the History of Aesthetics* (New York: Routledge, 2005), vii. See also, for example, Samuel Holt Monk, *The Sublime: A Study of Critical Theories in XVIII-Century England* (Ann Arbor: University of Michigan Press).

[5] Jean-François Lyotard, "Le sublime et l'Avant-garde," in *L'inhumain: Causeries sur le temps* (Paris: Galilée, 1988), 101–18, p. 105.

[6] See E. B. O. Borgerhoff, *The Freedom of French Classicism* (Princeton, NJ: Princeton University Press, 1950), and Jules Brody, *Boileau and Longinus* (Geneva: Droz, 1958).

the reception of Longinus before Boileau.[7] The following pages, similar to the endeavor of Richard Scholar with regards to the *je ne sais quoi*, further explore the sublime's "sedimentation," and the lesser-discussed or unrecognized aspects of its cultural "prehistory" in early modern France.

This first part of this chapter surveys (1) the unorthodox trajectory of the French reception of Longinus until Boileau, (2) the "interdisciplinary" place of rhetoric and sublimity in early modern French culture, and (3) the "interdisciplinarity" of the first French translation of Longinus now known: a manuscript predating Boileau titled "De la sublimité du discours," discovered a few decades ago in a forgotten volume of manuscripts at the Bibliothèque Nationale (the codex MS Italian 2028).[8] The second part of the chapter presents the early modern semantic field of *sublīmis* as bound up in a new hermeneutics, which privileged the cognitive and emotional experience of the individual reader – or listener, or spectator – without whom the sublime would not be possible. Interpreted as an essence rather than a quality, the Longinian term *hupsos* (ὕψους) evoked the passion celebrated by poets, painters, philosophers, and mystics as *admiration*. Boileau's *Traité du sublime* and the French translation that preceded it had differing renditions of *hupsos*; their uses of *sublimité* or *magnificence*, on the one hand, and *sublime* or *merveilleux*, on the other, speak to their respective positions in the political and literary battles of their day. For both, and in early modern France in general, *sublīmis* existed in tension with *humīlis*: the experience of the finite faced with infinity.

THE PREHISTORY OF THE SUBLIME

The Unorthodox Trajectory of Longinus

The vogue for the sublime in late seventeenth-century France was as much a culmination as a beginning.[9] Marc Fumaroli is the eloquent herald of this interpretation; for him, Boileau's *Traité* represents "the end of a long process of indirect and careful disclosure on the frontiers of the *res literaria*, a process that began in 1554–55 with the appearance of the Greek text in the printed world," or perhaps, he suggests, even earlier, in manuscripts read in humanist circles at the end of the fifteenth century. Key to this development were the dozen or so published versions of the *Peri hupsous* that preceded Boileau's, beginning with Francesco Robortello's Greek edition in 1554.[10]

The rise of the vocabulary of the sublime in early modernity depended in large measure on relationships within the literate classes of Europe that indirectly transmitted Longinian concepts and expressions. For example, the *Peri hupsous* was an important source for Marc-Antoine de Muret, who translated it into Latin (c. 1550). Muret's encounter with Longinus can be glimpsed in the works of his students and friends, such as the poet Pierre Ronsard, the playwright Étienne Jodelle, the essayist Michel de Montaigne, and the historiographer Joseph Scaliger. Similarly, Torquato Tasso diffused Longinian ideas in his *Gerusalemme liberata* (1575)

---

[7] Many examples of scholarship that evokes the sublime before Boileau will be cited in the following pages. The place to start would be Marc Fumaroli, *L'age de l'éloquence* (Geneva: Droz, 1980).

[8] Bernard Weinberg, "Une traduction française du 'Sublime' de Longin vers 1645," *Modern Philology* 59, 3 (1962), 159–201 (W). See also Emma Gilby, ed., *Pseudo-Longin, "De la sublimité du discours"* (Chambéry: L'Act Mem, 2007).

[9] For an opposite view, see *Longin, Traité du sublime, trad. par Nicolas Boileau (1674)*, ed. Francis Goyet (Paris: LGF, Livre de Poche, 1995), 162–3nn14 and 17.

[10] See Marc Fumaroli, "Rhétorique d'école et rhétorique adulte," *Revue d'histoire littéraire de la France* 86, 1 (1986), 33–51, p. 40, and Bernard Weinberg, "Translations and Commentaries of Longinus, *On the Sublime*, to 1600: A Bibliography," *Modern Philology* 57, 3 (1950), 145–51.

and poetic discourses (1594) to an enthusiastic following in France, including the playwright Pierre Corneille and the painter Nicolas Poussin.

The celebrated epistler Guez de Balzac (1597–1654) also disseminated the vocabulary of Longinus.[11] Ironically criticized by his contemporaries as *trop sublime*, meaning he employed the "sublime style," Balzac used the term *sublimité* as a neologism as early as 1636, worked on a commentary on the *Peri hupsous* in 1644, and paraphrased the *Peri hupsous* explicitly in his widely read works (*Socrate chrétien*, 1652; *Entretiens*, 1657).[12] Balzac's *Peri hupsous* was likely Gabriel de Petra's edition, published by a Huguenot printer in 1612. At the height of Balzac's popularity, around 1645, an anonymous dignitary, apparently associated with the Chancel of France, used Petra's Greek and Latin text to write the first-known French translation of Longinus, titled "De la sublimité du discours." In 1663, the Huguenot Tanneguy Le Fèvre published a new Latin version of the *Peri hupsous*. His critical innovations later influenced Boileau.

The associations of these initial editions of Longinus with religious, stylistic, and political nonconformists are intriguing. What are we to make of the fact that with few exceptions, most of the early modern translators and publishers of the *Peri hupsous* known in France – Muret (1554), Andreas Dudith (1560), Gabriel de Petra (1612), Le Fèvre (1663) – had either been accused of Calvinism or had reputations for heresy? "It is likely," John Logan suggests, "that these early associations with heterodoxy made the treatise more appealing than it might have been otherwise to a later group of Augustinian dissidents, the Jansenists and their supporters, among whom Boileau figured prominently." In any case, the *Peri hupsous* was promoted by early modern French dissenters from the cultural status quo.[13] Their appeals were less to formal considerations (figures and characters of style) than to the literary models proposed in the treatise (Sappho, Homer, Moses).

Renaissance Lyon, a center of humanism, neo-Platonist poetry, and publishing, was particularly taken by Robortello's 1554 edition. As François Rigolot argues, the treatise responded to the desire of Lyonnais literati for a sensual voice to balance Platonism: they found it in Longinus's treatise, which made known for the first time one of Sappho's most stunning poems.[14] In 1555 Louise Labé published a sonnet that paraphrased this discovery:

> I live, I die: I burn and I drown.
> I am hot to the extreme while enduring the cold
> Life is too tender and too harsh for me.
> I feel great despair intermingled with joy.

By citing this "rendezvous of the passions" from a woman's pen, Labé became Lyon's "new Sappho," offering the first published French adaptation of the Longinian sublime. Labé's appropriation of Sappho's tension-filled lyric enabled her to maneuver successfully around long-standing relations between gender, power, and art and to gain legitimacy as an independent woman poet.[15]

---

[11] For more on Balzac and the sublime, see Emmanuel Bury, *Le classicisme* (Paris: Nathan, 1993), 33–4, and Sophie Hache, *La langue du ciel: Le sublime en France au XVIIe siècle*, ed. Philippe Sellier (Paris: Champion, 2000), 31–83.

[12] For Balzac's specific references to Longinus, see Guez de Balzac, "Lettre à Chapelain," in *Oeuvres*, 2 vols. (Paris: Augustin Courbé, 1665), 2:736 and 857 (GB).

[13] John Logan, "Longinus and the Sublime," in *The Cambridge History of Renaissance Criticism*, ed. Glyn P. Norton, 3 vols. (Cambridge: Cambridge University Press, 1999), 1:529–39, p. 533.

[14] François Rigolot, *Louise Labé Lyonnaise, ou La Renaissance au féminin* (Paris: Champion, 1997), 66.

[15] See Rigolot, *Louise Labé Lyonnaise*, 1–30. The Italian woman poet Gaspara Stampa perhaps preceded Louise Labé in citing Longinus's Sappho. Jane Tylus has recently intimated as much in her talk at Princeton University, "Gaspara Stampa and the Rediscovery of the Sublime in Early Modern Europe" (November 11, 2010). See Tylus's important new edition of Stampa in Troy Tower and Jane Tylus, eds., *Gaspara Stampa: The Complete Poems* (Chicago: University of Chicago Press, 2010).

At the end of the sixteenth century, Montaigne distanced himself from the demagoguery and cruelty of the religious wars, aided perhaps by an understanding of Longinus that Logan calls "unequalled and unsurpassed" in his time. In terms that echo the *Peri hupsous*, the essay "Of Cato the Younger" praises resistance against tyranny at the same time as "divine poetry." "One doesn't see it, not more than the splendor of a stroke of lightening ... it ravishes and ravages."[16] In the seventeenth century, the *Peri hupsous* provided a showground for debate – from the "Querelles de Balzac," which began in the 1620s; to the "Querelle des Anciens et des Modernes," which continued through the Enlightenment; and to the "Querelle du Quiétisme" at the end of the seventeenth century. Sophie Hache has shown how Balzac and his supporters used Longinus to bypass their day's rules for literature, and Milad Doueihi argues that Longinus's "poetics of simplicity" offered Boileau and his friends an escape from "the domination of the political in an age of monarchy."[17]

Sublimité: An Interdisciplinary Semantic Field

The clear-cut categories of modernity simply do not apply to early modern culture. The ideal of educating a *Homo universalis*, as outlined in Italy by Baldassare Castiglione's *The Book of the Courtier* (1528), quickly spread to France, where it would be central to theories of elite pedagogy for centuries. Practically speaking, rhetoric was inseparable from poetics and the fields that today we call aesthetics, politics, and ethics. As Brian Vickers has put it, "Renaissance readers did not regard literary works as autotelic; indeed, the concept that any work of art could be self-ended, without a function in human life, would have been foreign."[18] Of course, the term "interdisciplinary" is itself anachronistic with regards to the Renaissance, because the academic disciplines we refer to today were largely defined in the nineteenth century. I use this word nonetheless to stress the fluidity of the applications early modernity prepared for the sublime.

Leonardo's reinterpretation of Horace's simile, *ut pictura poesis*, encouraged theories of discourse to ramify into the visual arts. Via Tasso's transmission, the *Peri hupsous* infiltrated art treatises such as Raffaello Borghini's *Il riposo* (1584), in which the vocabulary of *hupsos* was applied to painting rather than literature.[19] Having used Tasso to elaborate on a theory of the sublime for the visual arts, Nicolas Poussin represents in his proto-Romantic landscapes the "*irreprésentable*, the sublimity of a tempest on earth" (Figure 6.1).[20]

Whereas scholars have often noted the sublime's relation to natural spectacles in Romanticism, they have neglected the central place of natural science in the early modern lexicon of *sublīmis*. In alchemy, so intertwined with spiritual and religious quests, the term *sublimatio* distinguished the heated metal object from what lifted away during vaporization and condensed again. The Renaissance polymath Ambroise Paré generalized this idea: "To distill is an art ... some call this *sublimer*, which signifies nothing more than to separate the pure from the impure."[21] Jacques

---

[16] Logan, "Longinus and the Sublime," 537; Michel de Montaigne, *Les essais*, ed. Pierre Villey, 3 vols. (Paris: Quadrige/Presses Universitaires de France), 1:231 (M).

[17] Hache, *La langue du ciel*, 32. Milad Doueihi, "The Politics of Simplicity," *Modern Language Notes* 107 (1992), 639–58, p. 658.

[18] Brian Vickers, "Rhetoric and Poetics," in *The Cambridge History of Renaissance Philosophy*, ed. Charles B. Schmitt and Quentin Skinner (Cambridge: Cambridge University Press, 1988), 715–45, p. 715.

[19] For the Renaissance parallel of the arts, see Rensslaer W. Lee, *Ut Pictura Poesis* (New York: Norton, 1967) and Jacqueline Lichtenstein, ed., *La peinture* (Paris: Larousse, 1995), 385–93. For a specific example of this parallel see Raffaello Borghini, *Il riposo*, trans. Lloyd H. Ellis Jr. (Toronto: University of Toronto Press, 2008), 45–6 (RB).

[20] Louis Marin, *Sublime Poussin*, ed. Alain Badiou and Barbara Cassin (Paris: Seuil, 1995), 75. Among the recent scholarship that has addressed Poussin's debt to Tasso, see, for example, Jonathan Unglaub, *Poussin and the Poetics of Painting* (Cambridge: Cambridge University Press, 2006).

[21] Ambroise Paré, *Oeuvres*, 26 vols. (Paris: Gabriel Buon, 1575), 26:1.

FIGURE 6.1. Nicolas Poussin, *L'hiver*, or *Le déluge* (*Winter*, or *The Flood*),
c. 1664, oil on canvas, 46½ x 63 in. Paris, France: Musée du Louvre.
Photo credit: Réunion des Musées Nationaux / Art Resource, NY.

Amyot took the alchemic image further, associating the verb *sublimer* with the powers of the mind and language. He wrote in 1587, "Wisdom is the perfection ... that illuminates, *sublimes*, and refines the discourse of reason by the knowledge of things." In the following generation, the alchemic ideal of *sublimer* was omnipresent: from the Counter-Reformation's obsession with the penitence and elevations of Saint Madeleine, to the moralist vogue for maxims, to Port-Royal's attempt to purify discourse (Arnauld and Nicole's *Logique*, 1662), and to the theater's distillation of complex intrigues from antiquity. In Pierre Richelet's *Dictionnaire françois* of 1680, half of the entries for words derived from the Latin *sublīmis* relate to alchemy: *sublime*, *sublimation*, *sublimer*.[22]

Amyot's association of *illumine* and *sublime* also evokes the relationship between astronomy and *sublīmis*, as in Pierre Gassendi's 1642 *De Apparente Magnitudine Solis Humilis atque Sublimis Epistolae Quatuor* (*On the Apparent Magnitude of the Sun on the Horizon and Overhead*). Just as Amyot's "wisdom" refines the mind through the mundane, Gassendi's impression of the sun in the heavens (*sublīmis*) is inextricable from how it is viewed below (*humīlis*). As we will see, the marriage of humility and sublimity is particularly striking in the early modern Christian sublime, both in Protestant-inspired visual arts such as still life and in the Catholic literary traditions.

---

[22] Jacques Amyot, "Épitre au roi," in *Les Œuvres Morales et Mêlées de Plutarque*, ed. and trans. J. Amyot (Paris: Barthélemy Macé, 1587), 2; César-Pierre Richelet, *Dictionnaire françois* (Geneva: Jean Herman Widerhold, 1680).

For Boileau, the preeminent dramaturge of the sublime among his contemporaries was Jean Racine, who had been educated in predestination by the Augustinians of Port-Royal. Like Labé a century before, Racine's *Phèdre* (1677), granddaughter of the sun, paraphrases the Longinian citation of Sappho's passions (act 1, scene 3). Evoking the alchemist's "oeuvre au rouge," the half-innocent heroine burns in her crimes – "et moi, je brûle encore!" (act 4, scene 6) – and, in a final tirade, emphasizes the "longer path" of her agony. In the end she sees only across a mist but suggests that although her soul may never reach paradise, her suicide will leave behind a *sublimatio*: "Et la mort, à mes yeux dérobant la clarté / Rend au jour qu'ils souillaient toute sa pureté" ("And death, in stealing from my eyes their clarity / gives back to the day that they sullied all its purity," act 4, scene 7). Now the alchemic image is melded with that of the realm just beneath the outer limits of the universe, where the unbaptized souls go as they wait at the doors of paradise, in the hopes of a final cleansing (*limbes*).

The term *sublimité* was a new word in seventeenth-century French, brought into the language by Guez de Balzac in 1636. In Richelet's 1680 *Dictionnaire*, the term *sublimité* inherits the heterogeneity of the Latin and Greek traditions, in which the qualifier *sublîmis* serves for evaluation and the substantive ὕψος indicates an essence.[23] In its association with early modern *hauteur*, *sublimité* goes beyond excellence to connote a general sense of depth and truth. Richelet's open-ended series of expressions reveal its multiple associations: "The sublimity of sacred things, the sublimity of thoughts, of style, of genius, of mind, etc." In early modernity, *sublimité* (like the Greek ὕψος) was not limited to one domain of experience.

Sublimité in Codex: Interdisciplinarity in Translation

The anonymous translator who preceded Boileau employed this new word, *sublimité*, to render Longinian *hupsos*. The choice is intriguing, especially because his translation relied on Petra's 1612 Greek and Latin edition, *De Grandi, Sive Svblimi genere Orationis* (W 167). The translator may have also known Niccolo Pinelli's 1639 Italian translation, *Dell'altezza del dire*. Yet he chose neither "style sublime" nor "élévation du discours" to render the title. Initially left blank, it only became "De la sublimité du discours" after the second version of the text had been corrected. Among other things, this use of *sublimité* begs the question: Was the translator in conversation with Balzac? The epistler wrote on style in 1652, "I aim for a higher *sublimité*.... I am in quest of the truth.... I want to learn the language of heaven" (GB 123–4).

Bernard Weinberg suggests that the codex or anthology of manuscripts he discovered (MS Italian 2028) represents the readings of someone at the French chancellery, someone with access to royal scribes (for the manuscripts were written in various hands) and papers with royal watermarks (W 174). Based on handwriting samples, the filigrees of royal papers, and stylistic clues including faulty grammar, Weinberg's argument is intriguing: the person responsible for this volume of manuscripts and the translator of "De la sublimité," he submits, was none other than the Italian Cardinal Jules Mazarin, chief minister and ruler of France during the childhood of Louis XIV (1643–1661). The cardinal was renowned for his passion for books and paintings, his devotion to the French state, and his imperfect French.

The debate over Weinberg's hypothesis continues. Emma Gilby points to a number of "fragilities" in his argument, which produce no conclusive evidence that Mazarin would have translated Longinus into French.[24] More important, Gilby concludes, this document proves that the reception of Longinus prior to Boileau was "more general and more interesting than has previously been acknowledged."[25] Let us take Gilby up on her evocative suggestion. Knowledge

---

[23] Baldine Saint Girons, "Sublime," in *Vocabulaire européen des philosophies*, ed. Barbara Cassin (Paris: Dictionnaires le Robert, Seuil, 2003).
[24] See, Gilby, *Pseudo-Longin*, 17–20.
[25] Gilby, *Pseudo-Longin*, 47.

of "De la sublimité" does make the French reception of Longinus more interesting to us from the standpoint of literary history. Whoever translated or commissioned this translation on royal papers, "De la sublimité" proposes a place for sublimity in the minds of France's elite, if not its most powerful leaders. Furthermore, on close examination, this translation points to the heretofore unrecognized interdisciplinarity of *sublīmis* in early modernity. Nineteenth of twenty and by far the longest manuscript excerpt included in MS Italian 2028, "De la sublimité" dominates its codex.[26] Here we find no other extracts on rhetoric as the moderns conceive it but several referencing Longinian ideas. Excerpted from prominent books published in Italian or Latin between 1584 and 1644, half pertain to the visual arts, perspective, and optics; seven deal with poetry; and four concern polemics in history, religion, and politics.

In Weinberg's defense, the *Homo universalis* Mazarin was known to have been passionately interested in all these subjects. An art collector and bibliophile extraordinaire, Mazarin established a public library in 1643 and the French Academy of Painting and Sculpture in 1648. In no small measure, Mazarin was the architect of the Grand Siècle's artistic and literary culture as well as its absolutist state.[27] One of his multiple roles was directing the education of the young Louis XIV (who only seized power after Mazarin's death). In this regard, the codex MS Italian 2028 includes a substantial selection from Jean Bodin's *Les six livres de la République* (1577), which propounds the theory of absolute sovereignty that Mazarin and Louis XIV would famously embrace.

Most of the selections in this codex pertain to recent innovations in the visual arts. These include Jacomo Vignola's 1583 influential book on perspective, François d'Aguilon's 1613 master treatise on optics and mathematics, and Pietro Accoliti's 1625 *Deception of the Eyes*, with a dedication to the academic painters that inspired the Académie Royale de Peinture et de Sculpture. We also find an excerpt from Borghini's *Il riposo* (1584), the first piece of art criticism on record specifically written for the connoisseur rather than the practitioner. Recalling Longinus, Borghini uses the term *bellisimo* to indicate not beauty but rather "something done with such facility or technical accomplishment as to provoke admiration or wonder" (RB 27).

Just as Borghini argues that *bellisimo* painting benefits the nobleman destined for war (RB 224), "De la sublimité du discours" suggests that literary sublimity can be "useful for a person in the employment and in the handling of world affairs" (W 185). Here the anonymous translator is roundabout in rendering the Greek ἀνδράσι πολιτιχοῖζ (Petra's Latin: *viris politicis*). In 1674, Boileau simply writes "orateurs" (B 319). The translator of midcentury, on the other hand, gives a more sympathetic portrait of the person who benefits from sublimity, bringing out his public service and his weighty, worldwide responsibilities.

The commissioner of the codex was drawn to controversies. Two extracts, for example, speak to polemics regarding Tasso, and a large section is devoted to Joseph Scaliger, who revolutionized ancient historiography. Even more contentious is the selection from Thomas Browne's 1644 bestseller, *Religio medici*, which was put on the papal index for embracing esoteric beliefs and alchemy. The codex also excerpts Paolo Sarpi's *Historia del Concilio Tridentino* (1621), popular with Protestants for unmasking the "reality" behind the Counter-Reformation. Such selections testify again to the connection between unconventional beliefs and Longinus, as well as to a time when the French elite was strategically acquainted with unorthodoxy. These were the years of an uneasy religious concubinage: the French state, allied with the German Protestant princes during the Thirty Years' War, promised compromise to Huguenots to delay their revolt.

By placing "De la sublimité du discours" in its codex (that is, in the volume of manuscripts in which it was found), we get the sense that what interests this unknown translator is a notion

---

[26] A codex is a volume of manuscripts and in this case can be thought of as an early modern anthology.
[27] See, for example, Isabelle de Conihout and Patrick Michel, *Mazarin, les lettres et les arts* (Paris: Monelle Hayot, 2006).

of *sublimité* that could apply to more than discourse. Consider for example how the translator renders the second sentence of the treatise (Greek: ἐπί πασῆς τεχνολογίας; Petra's Latin: *in omni artis tractatione*). Following Weinberg, the words in brackets are from the first version of the translation: "We seek two things in all kinds of arts [*toutes sortes d'arts*]: the first, to know in what consists [its] their perfection; the second according to order, (but certainly) the first and the principle (if one considers the importance), I mean the method by which one is able to perfectly master [it] them" (W 184).

The awkward language of this passage reveals hesitation between the first and second copy: was the subject of sublimity singular or plural? In the final version, the translator opted for the plural, as signaled by the change in pronouns: *leur* (their) instead of *sa* (its) and *les* (them) rather than *la* (it). Compare these solutions with Boileau's: "When one treats an art [*un art*], there are two things one must always study. The first is to explain fully one's subject; the second, which in the end I hold to be the most important, consists in showing how and by which means what we teach can be acquired" (B 319). For Boileau, the matter at hand is grammatically singular. What Longinus teaches is "an art," a singular reinforced with *sujet*, a choice close to Petra's *in demonstratione subjecti*. The earlier translator, however, goes back to the Greek (τό ὑποκείμενον) to find his term, *perfection*. Unlike *sujet*, *perfection* accommodates both singular and plural pronouns (*son* and *leur*) and carries connotations of ultimate achievement, more adequate to the focus of the passage: *toutes sortes d'arts*.

In emphasizing a plurality of arts, "De la sublimité du discours" suggests broad interests on the part of the person who commissioned the translation, in keeping with the universality of the Renaissance mind. MS Italian 2028 can be read as a compilation of the most groundbreaking writings in print in the mid-seventeenth century. If it cannot prove who initiated the codex, placing this anonymous translation in its surroundings points to the myriad associations of the *Peri hupsous* in early modernity and puts literary sublimity into conversation with the latest, most influential, and most controversial ideas in politics, painting, science, and religion.

THE READER'S SUBLIME: *Sublīmis-humīlis*

Hermeneutics of the Individual

As for the noun *sublime*, Richelet's *Dictionnaire* follows the tradition of *genus sublime dicendi*, defining it as at once the "the most pompous style" and the subject of Boileau's 1674 translation. In this, Richelet seems to have misunderstood Boileau. Boileau's *sublime* is far closer to *hupsos* and *sublimité* than its usage heretofore; his preface insists that "by sublime, Longinus does not mean what orators call the sublime style" (B 318). Contrary to popular critical opinion, the central distinction between the adjective (*style sublime*) and the substantive (*le sublime*) did not originate with Boileau – he borrowed it (although he does not directly acknowledge this debt) from Tanneguy Le Fèvre. Le Fèvre's great contribution to the story of the sublime is his Cartesian understanding of Longinus: in his preface to his 1663 Latin edition of the *Peri hupsous*, Le Fèvre links sublime style to the body and associates the noun *sublime* with the spirit.[28]

The proximity of Boileau's *sublime* to the neologism *sublimité* is evident in his preface, in a citation from a section of the *Peri hupsous* Boileau calls "De la sublimité des pensées." This passage – the famous *fiat lux* from Genesis – appears about a third of the way through the text. Almost an aside in Longinus, the citation is for Boileau "the most adequate to bring my thoughts to the light of day," hereby melding obedience, the sacred, mental effort, the

---

[28] On Boileau's debt to Le Fèvre, see Nicholas Cronk, *The Classical Sublime: French Neoclassicism and the Language of Literature* (Charlottesville, VA: Rockwood, 2002), 96–7.

idea of illumination, and the sun with *sublime* and *sublimité*: "*God said, let there be light and there was light*: this extraordinary expression, illustrating so well the creature's obedience to the orders of the Creator, is truly sublime and has something of the divine" (B 318). In some ways Boileau's preference follows his contemporaries; thanks to seventeenth-century theories of predication, the term *sublime* had become a synonym for the sacred in the broader literature.[29]

With "creature's obedience" Boileau also brings to the fore the one who reacts to the sublime, the reader otherwise left between the lines: "The sublime is … that extraordinary and that marvelous that strikes [you, the reader] in a discourse" (B 318). Here again, Boileau does not innovate. Blaise Pascal's *Pensées* associate the sublime with scripture, readers, and their learning: "The simplicity of the Gospel … elevates the just to the very participation in Divinity, teaching them that in this sublime state it still carries the source of all corruption."[30] Faithful student of the fourth book of Augustine of Hippo's *De Doctrina christiana*, Pascal maintains that *humĭlis* is the genre of sublime words; he reinforces the duality *sublīmis-humĭlis* by placing corruption subjacent to "participation in Divinity." The reading of scripture illuminates this "sublime state" within the soul, leading, as in Augustine, to the transformation and the comprehension of the self.

Pascal's reception of Augustine and his vocabulary of *sublīmis* was part of a new interest in how individuals received and reacted to the arts, what Terence Cave has described as a "new theory of reading." From the fifteenth century onward, the Renaissance promoted the individual's communion with the sacred, spurred on by *De imitatione Christi*, the printing revolution, and translations of Judeo-Christian scripture. Like editions of Longinus, vernacular versions of the Bible came from nonconformists – the evangelist Jacques Lefèvre d'Étaples (1509–1532), for example, and the Jansenist Lemaistre de Sacy (1613–1684). By the seventeenth century, the status of both reader and text had shifted considerably, a change that reached those who remained in the Catholic fold. François de Sales's *Introduction à la vie dévote* (1609), for example, addressed not just those in monasteries but any *Philothea* (Lover of God).[31]

Other cultural revolutions also fueled this preoccupation with reception, and the rise of the French sublime should be understood in their context. Advances in perspective, optics, and observational astronomy gave new priority to the onlooker's gaze. "*Read* the story and the painting," wrote Poussin, engaging his commissioner's judgment, and again, "there are two ways of seeing objects, one in merely seeing them [*aspect*], the other in considering them with attention [*prospect*]." Poussin's *prospect* depends on the eye's *savoir* – its recognition of its "distance to the object."[32] Such experience of artwork is a pendant to the duality *sublīmis-humĭlis* that so intrigued seventeenth-century thinkers. For the geometrician Pascal, human dignity amounts to the recognition of distance – the individual's smallness in the cosmos: "With space the universe envelopes me and engulfs me like a dot: with thought I understand this … man is great in that he recognizes himself as miserable" (P 114/397).

The young Pascal attended the "first Academy of Sciences" that gathered around Marin Mersenne (1588–1648), where he heard the debates of Galileo Galilei, Réne Descartes, and Pierre Gassendi. During these years Pascal wrote his groundbreaking treatise on the void in nature and began his forays into the infinite series and infinitesimal calculus. In the *Pensées*, Pascal interweaves his interests in nothingness, the infinite, the divine, and the human being's plight, "lost

---

[29] For the theological use of the term "sublime" in the French seventeenth century see Hache, *La langue du ciel*, 135–9.
[30] Blaise Pascal, *Pensées*, in *Oeuvres*, ed. Louis Lafuma (Paris: Seuil, Intégrale, 1963), 493–649, fragment 208/435 (P).
[31] See Terence Cave, "Mimesis of Reading in the Renaissance," in *Mimesis: From Mirror to Method*, ed. John D. Lyons (Aurora, CO: Davies Group, 2004), 143.
[32] Nicolas Poussin, *Lettres et propos sur l'art*, ed. Anthony Blunt (Paris: Hermann, 1964), 36 and 62–3, my emphasis.

FIGURE 6.2. Louis Le Nain, *Famille de paysans dans un intérieur* (*Peasant Family in an Interior*), c. 1642, oil on canvas, 44½ x 54¾ in. Paris, France: Musée du Louvre. Photo: Jean-Gilles Berizzi. Photo credit: Réunion des Musées Nationaux / Art Resource, NY.

in this corner of the universe" (P 198/693). Pascal's unbreachable chasm – *infini-rien* (P 418/233) – leads to the individual's terror before the cosmos ("les espaces infinis m'effrayent," P 201/206) and to his question, "What is a man in infinity?" (P 199/72).

Although Poussin's landscapes have rightly been associated with Longinus, many other seventeenth-century French paintings poignantly evoke the tension between *sublīmis* and *humīlis*. This was the "siècle des saints," and Calvinist- and Berullian-inspired arts such as still life and genre scenes infused the common person's daily experience with holy significance. Subjects such as Communion, once exclusively the domain of the high style of painting, now could be perceived in informal, familiar, and modest interiors (Figure 6.2).

Similarly, Georges de La Tour, finding his models on the streets of Paris, removed the Madeleine, beloved saint of the Counter-Reformation, from her traditional desert cave and brought her into the homes of everyone. If a mathematician's thoughts on the infinite and the void might not be accessible to all, each of us, with this poor penitent, can gaze into a candle's light (Figure 6.3).

Still-life painters, however, also imbued their kitchen scenes with nobility, a trend exemplified in Lubin Baugin's *Le dessert aux gaufrettes* (Figure 6.4). This painting, which on one level points to the Eucharist, is not bound to a religious reading. Like La Tour's *Madeleine* and Le Nain's *Famille de paysans*, the still life appeals directly to the individual onlooker, whose reaction alone instills the work with *sublīmis* and truth.[33]

---

[33] On sublimity in Baugin, see Éva Madeleine Martin, *Esthétiques de Port-Royal* (Paris: Nolin, 2012).

FIGURE 6.3. Georges de La Tour, *La Madeleine à la veilleuse* (*The Magdalen with the Nightlight*), c. 1644, oil on canvas, 50½ x 37 in. Paris, France: Musée du Louvre. Photo credit: Réunion des Musées Nationaux / Art Resource, NY.

Similarly, medieval codes of literature went by the wayside, and early modern hermeneutics encouraged eclectic personal interpretations. In the evangelist Marguerite de Navarre's *Heptaméron* (c. 1545), for example, the interlocutors tell stories and debate their judgments of them, allowing contradictory readings to coexist. Likewise, François Rabelais's Gargantuan texts, with their multiple and incoherent meanings, participated in what Michel Jeanneret calls the Renaissance "crisis of interpretation."[34]

The relation between reception and sublimity is nowhere more manifest than in Pascal, whose hermeneutics, as Pierre Force has shown, is closely related to the problems of translation and the sciences. In Pascal, reading is always a process of interpretation, in which the text itself is less important than the reader's relationship with it. The goal of reading is a new cognition – nothing less than transformation of the soul: "An understanding and a thoroughly

---

[34] This is Jeanneret's overriding thesis in Michel Jeanneret, *Le défi des signes* (Orléans: Paradigme, 1994).

FIGURE 6.4. Lubin Baugin, *Le dessert aux gaufrettes* (*Still Life with Wafers*), c. 1636, oil on wood, 51 x 20½ in. Paris, France: Musée du Louvre. Photo credit: Réunion des Musées Nationaux / Art Resource, NY.

extraordinary vision with which the soul considers objects and herself in an entirely new way."[35] Pascal's reading of Montaigne is striking in this regard: "It is not in Montaigne but in myself that I find all that I see there" (P 689/64).

The Passion Called Admiration

> Admiration: *Admirabilitas, Admiratio.*
> Chose digne d'admiration: *Miraculum*
> Avoir quelqu'un en grande admiration et estime: *stupere, suspicere.*
> – Jean Nicot, *Thresor de la langue françoyse* (1606)[36]

Although in early modernity sublimity and the sublime were not always divorced from cognition,[37] Lyotard might be questioned in his assertion that a sublime "mode of sensibility" is specific to modernity.[38] The verbs chosen by the two seventeenth-century French translators of Longinus – *frapper, enlever, ravir, transporter* – evoke communication, a quasi-physical contact between the minds of the author and the reader, and a passionate response in feeling. In early

---

[35] Pierre Force, *Le problème herméneutique chez Pascal* (Paris: Librairie Philosophique J. Vrin, 1989), 113–33; Pascal, "Sur la conversion du pécheur," in *Oeuvres*, 290–1, p. 290.
[36] Jean Nicot, *Thresor de la Langue Françoyse, tant Ancienne que Moderne* (Paris: David Douceur, 1606), np. The dictionary is transcribed without pagination and digitalized: http://artfl-project.uchicago.edu/content/dictionnaires-dautrefois.
[37] Emma Gilby, *Sublime Worlds: Early Modern French Literature* (Oxford: Legenda, 2006), 25.
[38] Lyotard, "Le sublime et l'Avant-garde," 105.

modern France, the *Peri hupsous* authorized the ravishment of the reader and the transport of overwhelming sentiment from the artist to the receiver.[39] It seems telling in this regard that Francis Robertello's edition of Longinus (1554) appeared just before his edition of the *Poetics* (1558), when Platonist poetry was the rage.[40] From its very emergence in the sixteenth century, the *Peri hupsous* promised a bridge between the frenzy of Ion's poet and the catharsis of Aristotle's spectator.

Montaigne references Plato and Aristotle with Longinus in "Of Cato the Younger," in which the lure of the sublime is the lightening bolt; great words are experienced in a ravishing flash: "la splendeur d'un esclair" (M 232). Montaigne paraphrases Socrates' metaphor of the rhapsode as a magnet transmitting the poet's emotions from the muse to the audience (*Ion* 535e–536d; M 232).[41] For Plato, this effect is ridiculous; for Montaigne, poetic rhapsody is a goal, and like Aristotle he associates it with pedagogy and childhood: "From my earliest childhood, poetry has had this effect, to transpierce me and to transport me" (M 233).

The unknown translator of "De la sublimité du discours" also draws on Plato: *sublimité* "makes the orator speak as though he were [taken by the fury that inspires enthusiasm in his mind] possessed by god, which gives to [these] his words a divine force" (W 190). Boileau too conflates Plato and Aristotle:[42] "Que tu sais bien, Racine, à l'aide d'un acteur, Émouvoir, étonner, ravir un spectateur!"[43] As for Montaigne, the art of poetry for Boileau is inextricable from three participants – the writer, the medium, and the experiencing subject – and the mounting scale of the latter's emotional experience – *émouvoir, étonner, ravir* – are hallmarks of the sublime.

In early modern France, those who evoked Longinus often had opposing practices of writing. If Boileau has been criticized for rigidity, he himself cruelly parodied Balzac's verbosity in 1674; Montaigne disdained "artifice," and his *Essays* are gleefully rambling, layered, and unfinished. Although there was disagreement on style, however, there was consensus on the effects of the sublime on the reader. As Montaigne put it, "He will clasp his hands in admiration ... he will be stunned and paralyzed" (M 231). Similarly, Balzac wrote to Corneille of his play *Cinna* (1639) in terms that recall Longinus: "I declare it a miracle.... Your *Cinna* heals the sick, makes the paralyzed applaud, gives voice to the mute."[44] For Balzac, as for Montaigne before him, an intense and conflicting physical response to art indicates its sublimity. Montaigne's spectator claps his hands while transfixed; Balzac's mute cries out although he is speechless.

Also in the 1640s, Descartes codified "Les passions de l'âme," relating each sentiment to physiological response. In *admiration*, that "sudden surprise of the soul," Descartes focuses on the immobility of the admirer,[45] calling it "the first and the foundation of all passions." Analogous to Boileau's later *émouvoir, étonner, ravir*, Descartes's *admiration* is followed by a series of derivatives: *surprise, étonnement*, and *veneration* (D 723). Some forty years later, Descartes's verbal descriptions inspired Charles Le Brun in his lecture on the representation of emotions at the Royal Academy of Painting and Sculpture (1668). Like Descartes, Le Brun's *admiration* "produces a suspension of movement to give time to the soul" so that it may

---

[39] See Lawrence Kerslake, *Essays on the Sublime: Analyses of French Writings on the Sublime from Boileau to La Harpe* (Berne: Peter Lang, 2000), 25–40.
[40] Fumaroli, "Rhétorique d'école," 40.
[41] Plato, *Early Socratic Dialogues*, ed. Trevor J. Saunders (London: Penguin, 1987) (*Ion*).
[42] See the discussion of Platonism in Boileau's time in Cronk, *The Classical Sublime*, 31–50.
[43] Boileau, "Épitres," in *Oeuvres complètes*, 219–40, p. 229.
[44] Guez de Balzac, "À Corneille," in *Pierre Corneille, Cinna*, ed. Dominique Rabaud-Gouillart (Paris: Classiques Larousse, 1990), 190–1.
[45] René Descartes, "Les passions de l'âme," in *Oeuvres*, ed. André Bridoux (Paris: Gallimard, La Pléiade, 1953), 695–802, pp. 729–30 (D).

FIGURE 6.5. Charles Le Brun, *Surprise et admiration* (*Admiration and Astonishment*), c. 1668, black chalk on paper, 10⅓ x 7½ in. Paris, France: Musée du Louvre. Photo credit: Réunion des Musées Nationaux / Art Resource, NY.

engender all other passions (Figure 6.5).[46] In addition, the illustrations that Le Brun made to accompany his lecture show a clear debt to Descartes' treatise on the passions.

Magnificence and the Political Use of Sublimity

In the first version of its first sentence, "De la sublimité du discours" renders Longinian *hupsos* as *magnificence*, which is changed to *sublimité* in the correction (W 168). *Magnificence* is maintained as a secondary translation for *hupsos* and synonym for *sublimité* throughout the corrected manuscript. For example, "La magnificence, disent-ils, naît avec nous" (W 186); "principe de la magnificence" (W 191); and "demeure dans sa magnificence" (W 196). In Renaissance France, *la magnificence* is the quality of royalty, with connotations of the glorious, the laudable, and, above all, the imposing. It is a term that relies on Césare Ripa's *Iconologia* (1603), in which

---

[46] Charles Le Brun, "Sur l'expression des passions (7 avril et 5 mai 1668)," in *Les conférences de l'Académie royale de peinture et de sculpture*, ed. Alain Mérot (Paris: ENSB, 1996), 145–62, p. 153 (LB).

FIGURE 6.6. Charles Poerson, *Louis XIV en Jupiter, vainqueur de la Fronde* (*Louis XIV as Jupiter, Conquerer of the Fronde*), c. 1654, oil on canvas, 65⅓ x 56⅓ in. Versailles, France: Musée des châteaux de Versailles et de Trianon. Photo credit: Réunion des Musées Nationaux / Art Resource, NY.

Magnificentia is a virtue rewarded with "the royal mantle" and symbolized by the lightning bolt: "When Apelles painted Alexander's portrait, he is said to have put a lightning bolt (also the symbol of Jupiter, the king of the gods) in his hand."[47]

Alexander the Great was a favorite subject for literature and painting in the construction of French absolutism. During the civil wars of the Frondes, which pitted royal power (under Mazarin's administration) against the uprising nobility, Mazarin encouraged the identification of the king with Alexander, Appollo, and Jupiter. In midcentury, however, Ripa's symbolism appears overly softened by the boy's tender face (Figure 6.6).

After Mazarin died and Louis XIV took sole power, more convincing images of the king's *magnificence* appeared, as in Le Brun's *La Franche-Comté conquise pour la seconde fois* (Figure 6.7). A clear source for Eichler the Younger's *Magnificentia* (Figure 6.8), Le Brun's *Louis XIV* is also the pictorial pendant to the notion of *magnificence* in the anonymous translation of

---

[47] Cesare Ripa, *Iconologia*, ed. Edward A. Maser (New York: Dover, 1971), unpaginated, plate 56.

FIGURE 6.7. Charles Le Brun, *La Franche-Comté conquise pour la seconde fois* (*The Second Conquest of the Franche-Comté*), ceiling panel, Hall of Mirrors, Versailles, 1680–1684, oil on canvas, laid down, 37 x 55 in. Versailles, France: Musée des châteaux de Versailles et de Trianon. Photo credit: Réunion des Musées Nationaux / Art Resource, NY.

Longinus, in which sublimity appears as a swirling maelstrom, seizing authority through irresistible force: "Magnificence ... moves everything else of the way and makes itself noticed everywhere, and like a cyclone it destroys and throws into disorder everything it meets" (W 185).

Here "De la sublimité" contrasts with *Traité du sublime*, suggesting that the two translators had diverging political beliefs. Compare for example the following versions of the same passage:

The sublime ... ravishes, it transports, and produces in *us* a certain admiration, mixed with astonishment and surprise ... it gives to discourse a certain noble vigor. (Boileau, 320)

Sublimity ... sometimes ravishes *them* [makes them revolt against reason] without their being able to defend themselves from becoming one of its party.... This authority and force that sublimity gives to discourse governs with sovereignty. (Anonymous, W 185)

Whereas Boileau, an independent humanist and friend to *anciens frondeurs*, emphasizes the noble impact of the sublime on the reader ("us"), his anonymous predecessor, who wrote during the Thirty Years' War and perhaps the Frondes, treats *sublimité* as a tool that allows "us" to control others ("them"). Like *révolter*, the expression *suivre son parti* had political connotations in the Renaissance. "Tenir le party de quelqu'un," for example, meant to be allied with; "estre en dur parti d'armes" signified a difficult military situation. The vocabulary of "De la sublimité

FIGURE 6.8. Jeremias Wachsmuth (after Gottfried Eichler the Younger), *Magnificentia*, c. 1760, copper engraving, 7⁹/₁₀ x 4⁹/₁₀ in. Johann Georg Hertel's edition of Cesare Ripa's *Iconologia*: plate 56.

du discours" thus suggests employing sublimity for political purposes, an aide in maintaining sovereignty.

This contrast offers a glimpse of the role Longinus played in a larger debate over ethical oratory.[48] For the writers of the French Grand Siècle as for Augustine and Longinus, the use of *sublīmis* was fundamentally ambivalent; there was danger in its power.[49] In 1648, for example, Guez de Balzac criticized the "violence" of preachers who "force themselves on the ears and eyes; either they steal, or they ravish our judgment; there is either trickery or violence in their methods" (GB 180). Although Balzac fearlessly attacked religious pundits who used *sublīmis*

---

[48] Hache, *La langue du ciel*, 135–254.
[49] On the dangers of oration see Marc Fumaroli, "Crépuscule de l'enthousiasme," in *Héros et orateurs: rhétorique et dramaturgie cornéliennes* (Geneva: Droz, 1990), 349–77.

to manipulate, he was wisely more diplomatic in treating the political eloquence of the ancients in 1644: "She ravishes the agreement of Princes and Republics, and brings to reason the most opinionated and strongest wills.... Sovereign Eloquence long governed the best part of the human race" (GB 181). Choosing vocabulary and phrasing similar to "De la sublimité," Balzac flatters the political orator, whose eloquence would lead to reason rather than revolt.

The ultimate acquisition of authority – apotheosis – is an idea shared by "De la sublimité" and *Traité du sublime*. The translator of midcentury praises writing with "divine force"; *sublimité* transforms those who use it into "something like the gods" (W 190). Corneille understood this already in *Cinna*, in which Auguste succinctly imposes his law, "Take a chair, Cinna" (*Cinna*, act 5, scene 1) and pronounces his absolute sovereignty, "I am master of myself as I am of the universe." Auguste's apotheosis occurs in the simple grandeur of statements that assert his will to power ("Je le suis, je veux l'être"; "I am it, I want to be it") and that strikingly assimilate him to the Christ: "Let us be friends.... As my enemy I have given you life" (act 5, scene 3).

In the Grand Siècle, politics followed theater, and scholars have shown how the French court utilized images, choreography, poetry, music, and architecture to deify Louis XIV.[50] Racine's 1665 *Alexandre le Grand*, for example, was the literary equivalent of Le Brun's *Entrée d'Alexandre dans Babylone* (Figure 6.9), a depiction of Louis XIV entering Versailles.[51] As the translator of "De la sublimité" writes, such "*magnificences* publicly display grandeur and pomp" (W 190).

Another "Merveilleux Chrétien": *Anéantissement*

In Boileau's Longinian lexicon, *merveilleux* is the term he returns to most frequently, deeming it equivalent to *sublime* with an "or" (*ou*): *Traité du sublime ou du merveilleux*. "The sublime in Longinus should be understood as the extraordinary, the surprising, and as I translated it, the marvelous in discourse" (B 318). At first reading, Boileau appears to be working within the critical framework of his predecessors. Tasso translated Aristotle's criterion for the epic poem *thaumaston* as *meraviglioso*, which subsequent French literary critics rendered as *merveilleux* or *admirable*.[52]

Let us propose here that Boileau's use of *merveilleux* was not in keeping with Tasso's but was rather particularly "quarrelsome." The dispute pitting the "merveilleux païen" against the "merveilleux chrétien" was central to the quarrel of the ancients and the moderns. Boileau, leader of the ancients, sanctioned Tasso's *Jérusalem délivrée* for abandoning classical mythology and mixing magic with Christian miracles. He was equally critical of the "merveilleux chrétien" in epics of his own generation, like Jean Desmarets de Saint-Sorlin's *Clovis* (1657). In the *Art poétique*, Boileau proscribes the "merveilleux chrétien" for impoverishing poetry and playing with blasphemy, giving a "fabulous air" to the highest truths.[53]

Just as Boileau chooses the noun *sublime* in opposition to the "style sublime," his use of *merveilleux* opposes the "merveilleux chrétien." With *merveilleux*, Boileau points beyond Tasso to the *thaumastos* of the Greek New Testament, which carries qualities including the "extraordinary, striking, and surprising," that which "passes human comprehension," and that which is "worthy of pious admiration."[54] For Boileau, the sublime elicits the reader's response to the *merveilleux* of scripture while eluding the dangers of the "merveilleux chrétien."

---

[50] See, for example, Louis Marin, *Politiques de la représentation*, ed. Alain Cantillon (Paris: Kime, 2005), and Peter Burke, *The Fabrication of Louis XIV* (New Haven, CT: Yale University Press, 1994).
[51] Burke, *The Fabrication of Louis XIV*, 28.
[52] Cronk, *The Classical Sublime*, 94.
[53] Boileau, *L'art poétique*, in *Oeuvres complètes*, 241–52, p. 248.
[54] J. H. Thayer, *A Greek-English Lexicon of the New Testament* (New York: American Book, 1889), 284. Thayer's dictionary is a translation, revision, and expansion of C. L. W. Grimm's *Clavis Novi Testamenti* (Leipzig: Libraria Arnoldiana, 1879).

FIGURE 6.9. Charles Le Brun, *Entrée d'Alexandre dans Babylone* (*Entrance of Alexander into Babylon*), detail, 1665, oil on canvas, 278 x 177 in. Paris, France: Musée du Louvre. Photo credit: Réunion des Musées Nationaux / Art Resource, NY.

If Boileau's *merveilleux* debated with the literary criticism of the "moderns," the experience of the sacred he evoked had always been at the center of *veneration*, the last of Descartes' derivatives of admiration. In early modernity, *thaumastos* inspired the raptures of the greatest generation of French mystics, who learned their *ravissement* from the works of Teresa of Avila (published in France in 1603). The oratorians of Pierre de Bérulle, for example, borrowed from both Teresa and Descartes: "Admiration: it is an act or a state of the soul, surprised by the view of the greatness of God that she contemplates; she stays in suspense ... she is completely outside herself ... she does not know what to say, she is so filled, troubled, dazzled."[55]

In rapture, says Le Brun, "the eyebrows lift high, and the pupil likewise" (LB 154), a movement suggested already by the entry in Jean Nicot's *Thresor* under *suspicere* ("to look upward with the mind"). Le Burn's pictorial code (Figure 6.10) melds Descartes with Poussin's archetypes, like Michel Natalis's circa 1660 engraving of Poussin's 1650 *Ravissement de saint Paul* (Figure 6.11).

[55] G. Letourneau, "La méthode d'oraison mentale" (Paris, 1903), 129–31, cited in Henri Bremond, *Histoire littéraire du sentiment religieux* (Paris: Bloud et Gay, 1926), 3:112–13.

FIGURE 6.10. Jean Audran, *Ravissement* (*Rapture*), after Charles Le Brun's drawing of the same title, eighteenth century, burin etching, 17 x 11 in. Paris: Musée du Louvre département des Arts graphiques. © 2004 Musée du Louvre / photo Martine Beck-Coppola.

Another likely source for Le Brun's *Ravissement* was Poussin's *L'inspiration du poète*, which had been acquired by Mazarin in 1653 (Figure 6.12). *Inspiration* is a striking evocation of Poussin's reception of Longinus and defends, with Aristotle, the artist's passion.[56]

In this regard, let us look for a moment at an early painting by Le Brun's colleague and sometimes rival, Philippe de Champaigne. Painted around 1645, at a moment when Champaigne was both decorating the queen mother's court and making his acquaintance with the Augustinians of the Port-Royal circle, *Saint Augustine* (Figure 6.13) brings an image of Augustine's poetic

[56] Marc Fumaroli, "L'inspiration du poète de Poussin et l'allégorie du Parnasse," *Revue du Louvre et des Musées de France* 3 (1989), 194.

FIGURE 6.11. Michel Natalis (1610–1668), *Le ravissement de saint Paul* (*The Ecstasy of Saint Paul*), after Nicolas Poussin's painting of the same title, detail, c. 1661, burin etching. Liège, Belgium: University of Liège, Collections Artistiques. © Collections Artistiques de l'Université de Liège.

inspiration (*De Doctrina Christiana*, IV, 32) together with aspects of both *la magnificence* and *le merveilleux*.

Here Augustine is caught quill in hand, midstream in writing, at the very instant he turns to look over his right shoulder and spots divine *Veritas*. The saint presents his forehead as he holds out the sacred heart; the encounter comes from behind, and, stupefied, the old man stares up at the dazzling light, awestruck, incapable of movement or utterance. Marin's words on Boileau are appropriate here: "The effect-affect sublime is ... marked by an alteration, a lapse in the subject's identity, a lack of appropriation of the subject to himself."[57] His mouth agape, his pen frozen, his forehead hairless and smooth, the saint is momentarily emptied of himself, an inner void that allows for a sacred passage. The fulguration of truth crosses from one side of the canvas to the other; striking Augustine's gaze with meteoric force, it sets his mind and the heart afire. Cognitive and emotional transports are one.

[57] Marin, "Le sublime dans les années 1670," 187–8.

FIGURE 6.12. Nicolas Poussin, *L'inspiration du poète* (*Inspiration of the Poet*), detail, c. 1627 or 1630, oil on canvas, 71⅔ × 83⅞ in. Paris, France: Musée du Louvre. Photo credit: Réunion des Musées Nationaux / Art Resource, NY.

So many traits of *magnificence* in this work – the opulent mantel of red and gold (in the original version of the work), the encumbered décor, the fantastic blazing symbol of divine love – seem distant from the austere and simple interiors Champaigne created for Port-Royal, the convent in which he placed his daughters after 1648. Different indeed is Champaigne's *Ex-voto* of 1662 (Figure 6.14), which presents a moment of prayer, that of Mother Angès Arnauld, and a *miraculum*, the healing from paralysis of Champaigne's daughter Catherine. Champaigne paints his subjects and their environment candidly. His debts to the naturalism of the *peintres de la réalité* are manifest in the uneven lines and tones of Agnès's face, the rugged details of the wooden floor, the cracks and splotches on the cell's concrete wall, and the simple precision of the straw-seated chair.

As in Baugin's still life, the palette of the *Ex-voto* is simple – dominated by neutrals of beige and brown and punctuated by the bright red of the cross on the nuns' habits, the pitch black of their hoods, a bit of ocher straw, and a sliver of light-blue cushion. In comparison with Champaigne's *Saint Augustin* and Poussin's models of *Ravissement*, the expressions of *vénération* are strikingly reduced. Only Catherine's eyes reveal her emotion, "lifted toward the heavens, where they seem to be attached as though in the attempt to discover what the soul can not conceive" (LB 154). For Le Brun, the movement of the eyes marks "the humiliation of the soul and its incapacity" (LB 154). The rest of the body is motionless, here literally paralyzed, but for the hands, "clasped together" as in Montaigne. Receiving and responding to the miracle – "a thing worthy of admiration: *miraculum*" (Nicot) – "the entire action" of the painting portrays "profound humility" (LB 161).

FIGURE 6.13. Philippe de Champaigne, *Saint Augustine*, c. 1645–1650, oil on canvas, 31⅛ x 24⅝ in. Gift of the Ahmanson Foundation. Los Angeles, U.S.: Los Angeles County Museum of Art. Digital Image © 2009 Museum Associates / LACMA / Art Resource, NY.

Here, the realms of *miraculum* and *sublîmis* encounter that of *anéantissement*, a term that had tremendous success in the religious vocabulary of early modernity. In the active sense, *anéantissement* (like its relatives *abnégation*, *mortification*, and *renonciation*) is a hyperbolic synonym for humility, the foundation of all virtue.[58] For François de Sales, this *anéantissement* also refers to the devout person's abandonment of his or her own will in order to unite with that of God. For the Berullian school, *anéantissement* evokes enthusiastic self-sacrifice, in imitation of the Christ.[59] Spiritual purification is the first stage of *anéantissement*, first sought by methodically emptying one's mind, in the purposeful nonconsideration of one's own existence. The Spanish Saint John of the Cross (1542–1591) would call this state "the active night of the senses," and his correspondent Teresa of Avila would speak of the "no pensar nada" that prepares the passage from active prayer to passive contemplation.

---

[58] Jeanne de Chantal, *Oeuvres* (Paris: Plon, 1875), 2:167.
[59] M. Viller, F. Cavallera, and J. de Guibert, eds., *Dictionnaire de spiritualité ascétique et mystique*, 17 vols. (Paris: Bauchesne, 1981), 11:560–2.

FIGURE 6.14. Philippe de Champaigne, *Portrait de mère Agnès Arnauld et de soeur Catherine de Sainte-Suzanne (Portrait of Mother Agnès Arnauld and Sister Catherine de Sainte-Suzanne)*, also known as *Ex-Voto*, 1662, oil on canvas, 65 x 90⅛ in. Paris: Musée du Louvre. Photo credit: Réunion des Musées Nationaux / Art Resource, NY.

At Port-Royal, Agnès Arnauld took Avila's teachings to their most polemical limits. In her "Secret Rosary" of 1626, Agnès wrote that the divine "must make every other being disappear, as the sun effaces all other lights by its very being and in order to be."[60] In Agnès's extreme Augustinian interpretation, worshippers can never know if they have fully emptied themselves of their thoughts and their selves, nor if their sacrifice is accepted or refused. She concludes her "Rosary," "Let souls not present themselves to him to be the object of his application, but rather to be rebuffed by the preference he owes to himself ... wanting rather to be exposed to his forgetfulness."[61] Here we read a slippage from the activity of those who willingly sacrifice themselves ("se présentent ... à lui") to a passivity ("être rebutées"; "être exposées") that culminates in the possibility of being forgotten in the eyes of God – the definitive annihilation of self.

Later in the century, a more famous friend of Port-Royal also sought and ultimately experienced the sublimity of *anéantissement* ("Renonciation totale ... Soumission totale"). For a few ecstatic night hours of 1654, the philosopher's gods (his reflections) were no longer necessary; Pascal knew oblivion and union with the Divine ("Oubli du monde et de tout, hormis Dieu"). He recorded the experience in the fragment known as "Le mémorial" and sewed it to his clothing, so that in perpetual rereading he could recognize religious certitude and remember the

---

[60] Agnès Arnauld, "Le chapelet secret du Saint-Sacrement" (1626), ed. Jean-Robert Armogathe, *XVIIe siècle* 170 (1991), 77–86, p. 86.
[61] Arnauld, "Le chapelet secret," 86.

moment of inspiration and passion: "Feu." In Pascal's era, *feu* referred not merely to fire but also to love's ardor and poetic inspiration in all its guises.[62] And so the *pensée* becomes poem, worthy pendant to Champaigne's *Saint Augustin*.

> Feu.
> Dieu d'Abraham, Dieu d'Isaac, Dieu de Jacob,
> Non des philosophes et des savants.
> Certitude, certitude, sentiment, joie, paix....
> Oubli du monde et de tout, hormis Dieu....
> Renonciation totale et douce.
> Soumission totale. (P 913)

> Fire.
> God of Abraham, God of Isaac, God of Jacob,
> Not of the philosophers and the scholars.
> Certitude, certitude, feeling, joy, peace....
> Oblivion of world and of everything, except God....
> Sweet and total renunciation.
> Total submission. (translation mine)

Pascal, the scientist who writes that thoughts are the consolation and grandeur of man, glorifies here the absence of all thought during an encounter with the sublime. Nowhere more than in such *anéantissement* do we see how *humīlis* and *sublīmis* were codependent in the *siècle de Saint Augustin*. Although Pascal never mentions Longinus, his sublime "mode of sensibility" emanates from at once religious rapture and cognitive genius, a combination that, in the final analysis, makes for the appeal of the sublime in early modern France.

As we have seen in the course of this chapter, in sixteenth- and seventeenth-century France the vocabulary of *sublīmis* and the Longinian treatise together fit into an array of preoccupations broader than technical questions of writing – spanning unorthodox religiosity, politics, the visual arts, and the sciences. Should we still maintain that Boileau "invented the sublime" and that ours is a "prehistory"? However we respond, it is clear that many vistas remain wide open in the study of *sublīmis* in early modernity, and that these entail the crossing of not only disciplines but also national and linguistic boundaries: all of Europe participated in the emergence of the sublime. Most urgently, the relations between *sublīmis* and early modern science – alchemy, astronomy, and mathematics – are terrains we should explore.

---

[62] For example, Oronte's "feux" in Molière's *Misanthrope*, act 5, scene 2, and the "feu de tant de saints prophètes" of Racine's *Esther*, act 1, scene 3.

7

The German Sublime After Kant

Paul Guyer

INTRODUCTION

Immanuel Kant's account of the sublime used the framework of earlier eighteenth-century theories, but it radically interiorized or, to use Hans-Georg Gadamer's term,[1] subjectivized them: whereas most theorists, whether German or British, characterized the experience of the sublime as our emotional response to the magnitude and power of nature and to exemplary cases of human morality, Kant explained the complex feeling of this experience as a response to the limits of our own imagination, and the power of our own theoretical and practical reason. Kant reduced the natural objects other theorists took as the proper object of the experience to mere triggers, the proper object of the experience being ourselves.

Friedrich von Schiller's influential essays on the sublime from the middle of the 1790s largely followed Kant, but after him the "absolute idealists" Friedrich Wilhelm Joseph Schelling and Georg Friedrich Wilhelm Hegel reverted to an objectivist approach that interpreted sublimity as the response to the magnitude or infinitude of realities beyond our own mental faculties. These philosophers interpreted both beauty and sublimity as sensible manifestations of reality and thus effaced the sharp line Kant had drawn between the beautiful and the sublime and, particularly in the case of Hegel, treated the sublime as an early stage in the two categories. They still considered reality to be inherently rational, however, and so maintained the general connection between sublimity and rationality that Kant had pioneered. Arthur Schopenhauer, by contrast, was convinced that reality was nonrational and, consequently, turned the sublime into an experience of natural beauty achieved in the face of nature's hostility to individual existence. Schopenhauer's reinterpretation of the sublime along these lines was subsequently turned back into a category of art by the young Friedrich Nietzsche, even though he based his conception of the relation between the Apollonian and the Dionysian in *The Birth of Tragedy* on Schopenhauer's view that individual rationality is a veneer placed over the underlying non-rationality of existence. In Nietzsche's hands the sublime becomes an experience of the transcendence of rationality rather than of transcendent rationality but remains, as it had for Kant, an affirmative experience: in what he would later call the "transvaluation of values,"[2] Nietzsche sees human redemption in transcending the limits of individual reason and identifying with the absurd and contradictory character of existence. Nietzsche, in effect, returns the sublime to the

---

[1] See Hans-Georg Gadamer, *Truth and Method*, trans. Joel Weinsheimer and Donald G. Marshall, 2nd ed. (London and New York: Continuum, 2004), 37–46.
[2] See, for example, Friedrich Nietzsche, *The Genealogy of Morals*, ed. Keith Ansell-Pearson; trans. Carol Diethe (Cambridge: Cambridge University Press, 2007), Third Essay, §§27–8, 118–20 (GM). For commentary, see Alexander Nehamas, *Nietzsche: Life as Literature* (Cambridge, MA: Harvard University Press, 1985), 135–7, and Christopher Janaway, *Beyond Selflessness: Reading Nietzsche's Genealogy* (Oxford: Oxford University Press, 2007), 252–4.

position of importance that it had enjoyed under Kant and Schiller but gradually lost in the work of Schelling, Hegel, and Schopenhauer.

THE KANTIAN SUBLIME

Our story must begin, however, with a brief review of the Kantian sublime and the background against which he developed it. Kant's *Critique of the Power of Judgment* is divided into the *Critique of the Aesthetic Power of Judgment* and the *Critique of the Teleological Power of Judgment*. The former, which contains Kant's aesthetics, is divided into an *Analytic of the Beautiful* and an *Analytic of the Sublime*, commonly understood to reflect Edmund Burke's *A Philosophical Enquiry into the Sublime and Beautiful* (1757). Kant dismissed Burke's account of both aesthetic categories as merely "psychological," referring in particular to Burke's explanation in part IV of the *Enquiry* of our experience of the sublime and the beautiful in terms of the tensing and relaxing of the "fibers of the body" that, he claimed, function as the "efficient causes" of these experiences.[3] Nevertheless, Burke's account of the negative pleasure or "delight" that characterizes the experience of the sublime, and the positive pleasure characteristic of the experience of beauty,[4] is mirrored in Kant's account of the difference between the straightforwardly pleasurable "quality" of the experience of the beautiful and the more complex "quality" of the experience of the sublime that includes elements of both pain and pleasure. In other respects, Kant's account is better compared to British and German predecessors who emphasized the typical objects of the sublime experience rather than its phenomenology. I have in mind the characterization of the sublime as a straightforward response of admiration to either the vastness or power of nature or the exceptional moral stature of human heroes that we find in many eighteenth-century writers.

One British text Kant surely knew, Alexander Gerard's *Essay on Taste* (1759), published only two years after Burke's *Enquiry*, stated that we do not "bestow the epithet *sublime*" on a "small rivulet, however transparent and beautifully winding" or "on a little valley, though clothed with the most delightful verdure," but "on the Alps, the Nile, the ocean, the wide expanse of heaven, or the immensity of space uniformly extended, without limit or termination." We do so because "when a large object is present, the mind expands itself to the extent of that object, and is filled with one grand sensation, which totally possessing it, composes it into a solemn sedateness." Gerard also adds that "we attribute grandeur and sublimity to some things, which are destitute of *quantity* of every kind," namely "heroism ... magnanimity ... contempt of honours, of riches, of power ... a noble superiority to things external ... patriotism ... universal benevolence."[5] In other words, Gerard recognizes that the expanding and uplifting sentiment that we call sublime can be produced either by the quantitative magnitude of natural objects and vistas or by the qualitative magnitude of human moral dispositions.

Alexander Gottlieb Baumgarten, who discussed the sublime in his unfinished *Aesthetica* (1750–1758) under the rubric of "aesthetic magnitude," likewise distinguishes between "natural" and "moral" magnitude as typical objects of this experience: "AESTHETIC MAGNITUDE," he writes, "absolute as well as relative, is further either NATURAL, which pertains to that which is not closely connected with freedom, or MORAL, which is to be attributed to things and thoughts insofar as they are more closely connected with freedom."[6] For Baumgarten,

---

[3] See Edmund Burke, *A Philosophical Enquiry into the Origin of Our Ideas of the Sublime and Beautiful*, ed. James T. Boulton (London: Routledge & Kegan Paul, 1958 [1759, 1st ed. 1757]).
[4] See Burke, *Enquiry*, part I, section IV, 35–6.
[5] Alexander Gerard, *An Essay on Taste* (London, 1759), part I, section II, 13–14 and 17.
[6] Alexander Gottlieb Baumgarten, *Ästhetik*, Latin text edited with facing German translation by Dagmar Mirbach, 2 vols. (Hamburg: Felix Meiner Verlag, 2007), 1:156–7, §181.

"natural magnitude" refers to what is vast or great in nature, whereas "moral magnitude" concerns the greatness of human actors and their intentions, what he also calls "aesthetic dignity."[7] This distinction between the sublime of natural magnitude and the sublime of moral quality, or between natural and moral magnitude, paves the way for Kant's own distinction between the "mathematical" and the "dynamical sublime." In contrast to Baumgarten, however, and even more than Gerard, Kant emphasizes that what we really respond to in the experience of the two forms of the sublime is the power of our own minds, and in particular the power of our own reason, theoretical in one case and practical in the other, in contrast to the limitations of our imagination; thus external objects trigger these experiences but are not the proper objects of such experience.

Turning from the objects that are the typical content of experiences of sublimity to our own faculties as the proper object of such experience also allows Kant silently to eliminate the characterization of the moral sublime as admiration of the moral power of *other* heroes, and to interpret it instead as admiration for *our own* potential for moral heroism in the face of nature: thus Kant characterizes his mathematical and dynamical sublimes as two different responses to the perception of nature, a response to the *magnitude* of nature that triggers a recognition of the power of our own theoretical reason and a response to the *might* of nature that triggers a recognition of the power of our own practical reason and will. The experience of the mathematical sublime is a complex mixture of displeasure at the inability of imagination to comprehend in a single grasp (*comprehensio aesthetica*)[8] the apparently infinite magnitude of a natural vista and of pleasure connected with the fact that the task of such a *comprehensio aesthetica* stems from our own power of theoretical reason (see CJ §27, 5:257).

Kant characterizes the dynamical sublime in similar terms, although in this case he speaks of a combination of a perception of fearfulness (not outright fear) with self-esteem triggered by the perception of mighty and potentially destructive forces in nature (hence the "dynamical") rather than of a complex of displeasure and pleasure. As long as we are not threatened with actual physical destruction by such forces – threatening cliffs, towering thunderclouds, and the like – then

> we gladly call these objects sublime because they elevate the strength of our soul above its usual level, and allow us to discover within ourselves a capacity for resistance of quite another kind, which gives us the courage to measure ourselves against the apparent all-powerfulness of nature ... the humanity in our person remains undemeaned even though the human being must submit to that domination. (CJ §29, 5:261–2)

The power of pure practical reason determines our will to do what is right regardless of the threats or blandishments of nature, which are presumably ultimately our own physical and psychological nature, for which the power of nature outside of us is a symbol (see CJ §28, 5:262). Although our physical safety is a condition for the possibility of this experience, it is not, as it is for Burke, the object of the experience; for Kant the object is the superiority of our moral faculties to all physical factors whatsoever.

In addition to the different ways Kant characterizes the experience of the mathematical and dynamical sublime (pleasure and displeasure, and fear and self-esteem, respectively), we should also note another important difference between the two. Discussing the mathematical sublime previously, I emphasized a connection between our ultimate pleasure in this experience and the fact that the task of *comprehensio aesthetica* is set by our own reason; Kant himself uses causal

---

[7] Baumgarten, *Ästhetik*, 1:158–9, §182.
[8] Immanuel Kant, *Kritik der Urteilskraft*, in *Kant's gesammelte Schriften*, Königlichen Preussischen (later Deutschen) Akademie der Wissenschaften, 29 vols. (Berlin: Reimer [later de Gruyter], 1900–), vol. 5; *Critique of the Power of Judgment*, ed. Paul Guyer; trans. Paul Guyer and Eric Matthews (Cambridge: Cambridge University Press, 2000), §26, 5:254 (CJ). All references are to section and page of the Akademie edition.

language – *erweckt* or "aroused" – to describe this relationship. Discussing the dynamical sublime, by contrast, he uses partially cognitive language: he speaks of "recognition" of physical powerlessness "revealing" our capacity for moral power, or of "presenting cases" that make this power "palpable" to us. The experience of the mathematical sublime seems to be a combination of perceptions and feelings that the philosopher can explain in terms of our faculties of imagination and reason, but the experience of the dynamical sublime includes the subject's own awareness of and thoughts about the relevant powers of his faculties of pure practical reason and will; concepts and judgments about these faculties are thus internal to the experience of the dynamical sublime in a way that they are not to the experience of the mathematical sublime. Kant's account of the sublime as a whole seems to include ambivalently elements of both a purely aesthetic and a more cognitivist approach.

There is nothing in Kant's explicit theoretical framework that would force him (or enable us) to resolve this ambivalence one way or the other. He states at the outset that "as a judgment of the aesthetic reflecting power of judgment, the satisfaction in the sublime, just like that in the beautiful, must be represented as universally valid in its **quantity**, as without interest in its **quality**, as subjective purposiveness in its **relation**, and the latter, as far as its **modality** is concerned, as necessary" (CJ §24, 5:247). In this comparison, however, he does not assert that the experience and the judgment of the sublime must be made, like those of the beautiful, *without a concept* (see CJ §9, 5:219), nor does he ever say that the experience or judgment on the sublime is *pure*, and independent of any concept. Thus Kant leaves open the possibility that the experience of and judgment about the sublime are *impure* aesthetic phenomena; this might be compared to the experience and judgment of adherent beauty or fine art in general that require concepts or conceptually-based judgments, also leaving room for the free play of our mental powers with such concepts or judgments and the feelings of pleasure (or displeasure and pleasure combined) that it produces. For this reason they are properly called aesthetic although not pure.[9] So Kant's ambivalence between his more purely aesthetic account of the dynamical sublime and his at least partially cognitivist account of the dynamical sublime might not prove an outright contradiction.

Nevertheless, this ambivalence might be seen as fateful for the history of the concept of the sublime, because one way of reading the history of aesthetics after Kant is to see his cognitivist approach to the dynamical sublime as spreading not only to the treatment of the sublime in general but also to the treatment of the beautiful, with the sublime ultimately being absorbed into a cognitive interpretation of the beautiful as merely one species of it or even just one stage on the way to the realization of beauty proper. Perhaps paradoxically, the example of Kant's more cognitivist approach to the dynamical sublime, which might in its own right be a more plausible approach to the sublime than a purely aesthetic approach, may also be what ultimately undermines the sublime's independent status.

SCHILLER

The move toward a cognitivist approach to the sublime in general is already evident in Schiller,[10] even though he hews close to Kant and does not subsume the sublime under the beautiful. In his 1793 essay "On the Sublime (Toward the Further Development of Some Kantian Ideas),"[11]

---

[9] For a general approach to Kant's aesthetic theory that leaves room for such a possibility, see Paul Guyer, "The Harmony of the Faculties Revisited," in *Values of Beauty: Historical Essays in Aesthetics* (Cambridge: Cambridge University Press, 2005), 77–109.

[10] Frederick Beiser emphasizes the cognitivist character of Schiller's account of the sublime in *Schiller as Philosopher: A Re-Examination* (Oxford: Clarendon Press, 2005), 257.

[11] Schiller published this essay in his periodical *Neue Thalia* (Leipzig: Göschen, 1793), vol. 3, parts 1–3, 320–66; trans. Daniel O. Dahlstrom, in Friedrich von Schiller, *Essays*, ed. Walter Hinderer and Daniel O. Dahlstrom (New York: Continuum, 1993), 22–44 (OS).

Schiller characterizes the sublime in a way that is clearly based on Kant's account of the dynamical sublime, beginning with an emphasis on feeling and then introducing an additional element of awareness that involves concepts. He begins with the general claim, applicable to both the mathematical and the dynamical sublime, that "we call an object *sublime* if, whenever the object is presented or represented, our sensuous nature feels its limit, but our rational nature feels its superiority, its freedom from limits," but he quickly turns this general statement in the direction of the dynamical sublime: "Thus, we come up short against a sublime object *physically*," he continues, "but we elevate ourselves above it *morally*, namely, through ideas." He follows this with a statement that clearly echoes Kant's account of the dynamical sublime: "A sublime subject matter gives us *in the first place* a feeling of our dependency as natural beings, because *in the second place* it makes us aware of the independence that, as rational beings, we assert over nature, as much *inside* as *outside* ourselves" (OS 22). This statement makes explicit what was only symbolic in Kant's account of the dynamical sublime, namely, that moral power really requires the superiority of our reason over *our own* nonrational nature rather than over nature outside us; it also starts by talking simply of a feeling of dependency – presumably an unpleasant feeling – but continues by talking of our awareness of our independence as rational beings over our own nature – presumably a pleasant awareness, but one that involves cognition as well as mere feeling.

Schiller next makes room for Kant's mathematical sublime as well, while continuing the move toward a cognitivist model: "With the help of reason, we maintain our *independence* from nature in two senses," he writes,

first, because (in a theoretical sense) we pass beyond natural conditions and can *think* more than we know; *second*, because (in a practical sense) we set ourselves above natural conditions and, by means of our will, can contradict our *desires*. When perception of some subject matter allows us to experience the former, it is *theoretically magnificent*, something cognitively sublime. A subject matter providing us with the feeling of the independence of our will is *practically magnificent*, a sublimeness of character [*der Gesinnung*]. (OS 23)

Although this passage obviously reproduces Kant's distinction between the two varieties of the sublime, it also subtly transforms his account: first, it explicitly calls its version of Kant's mathematical sublime – theoretical magnificence – "cognitively sublime," and second, it continues the project already begun of making explicit that the nature over which we are aware of being superior in the experience of the dynamical sublime – or practical magnificence – is our own nature (specifically our natural desires), and it links this to traditional accounts of the moral sublime by calling it a sublimeness of character.

Schiller explores the conditions for the experience of the two forms of the sublime in much more detail than does Kant, but what is particularly important for our larger story is that he also transforms the experience of the sublime *from a response to nature into a response to art*. Kant was adamant that "the sublime in nature is only improperly so called, and should properly be ascribed only to the manner of thinking, or rather to its foundation in human nature" (CJ §30, 5:280); he was also cautious about claiming that any art, even "colossal" art such as the ruins of ancient architecture, could really induce the experience of the sublime, suggesting that art could at most represent in limited ways the natural objects that can trigger the experience of the sublime (CJ §23, 5:245). Schiller, by contrast, emphasizes that art rather than nature triggers the experience of his version of the dynamical sublime: what he calls the "pathetically sublime" has "two main conditions ... *first*, a vivid image of *suffering*, in order to awaken the emotion of compassion with the proper strength, and *second*, an image of the resistance to the suffering, in order to call into consciousness the mind's inner freedom." He then claims that art, and in particular the art of tragedy, satisfies these two conditions: "From this basic principle flow the two fundamental laws of all tragic art. These are *first*: portrayal of the suffering nature; *second*, portrayal of moral independence in the suffering" (OS 44). Once the true character of the dynamical sublime is understood as the experience of the potential superiority of human moral character over the natural circumstances of human life, it follows that art is the only or at least the paradigmatic vehicle for triggering and communicating this experience.[12] This resolves the tension in Kant's account between a purely aesthetic and a cognitive account of the sublime, although in doing so, Schiller turns the sublime into a property of art rather than of nature. This is decisive for his successors, all of whom except Schopenhauer consider the sublime a quality of art, a move that might be responsible in part for its eventual absorption into the concept of beauty.

SCHELLING

Schelling considers the sublime briefly in his *System of Transcendental Idealism* (1800) and returns to it with almost equal brevity in his 1802–1803 lectures *The Philosophy of Art*, after his conversion to the so-called identity philosophy.[13] The *System of Transcendental Idealism* famously claims that art is the "universal organ of philosophy" (STI 219) because both artistic creation and aesthetic intuition (Schelling's term for the experience of art) most clearly instantiate the relationship between consciousness and reality that Schelling holds to be generally true. Schelling's approach to transcendental idealism is to reinterpret Kant's distinction between thing-in-itself and appearance into a relation between unconscious and conscious thought, in which the gap between the two can be overcome by the growth of consciousness. Drawing on Kant's conception of genius for an image of the artist as accomplishing more than he can consciously intend, Schelling writes that "it can only be the contradiction between conscious and unconscious in the free act which sets the artistic urge in motion; just as, conversely, it can be given to art alone to pacify our endless striving, and likewise to resolve the final and uttermost contradiction within us" (STI 222), between, that is, our unconscious urges and conscious intentions. The "testimony of all artists," Schelling asserts, demonstrates that "aesthetic production proceeds from the feeling of a seemingly irresoluble contradiction" but ends "in the feeling of an *infinite* harmony" (STI 223). So "the work of art reflects to us the identity of the conscious and the unconscious activities" (STI 225) of thought in general, and thus the most fundamental fact about reality itself. Recognition of the resolution is not confined to artists, however, because the "infinite tranquility" achieved by the artist in the course of production "must also pass over into the work of art itself," the "outward expression" of which is thus "one of calm, and silent grandeur."[14]

Within this framework, Schelling finds a place for "sublime works of art" by allowing that some works of art do not in fact contain the resolution of the ultimate metaphysical contradiction within themselves but nevertheless lead to the resolution of that contradiction in our experience of them. He writes:

There are, admittedly, sublime works of art, and beauty and sublimity in a certain respect are opposed to each other, in that a landscape, for example, can be beautiful without therefore being sublime, and *vice versa*. However, the opposition between beauty and sublimity is one which occurs only in regard

---

[12] See Beiser, *Schiller as Philosopher*, 257–62, who observes that Schiller's account of the sublime is also his account of tragedy, and that he emphasizes the dynamical sublime over the mathematical sublime for this reason.

[13] Friedrich Wilhelm Joseph Schelling, *System of Transcendental Idealism*, trans. Peter L. Heath (Charlottesville: University of Virginia Press, 1978) (STI), and *The Philosophy of Art*, trans. and ed. Douglas W. Stott (Minneapolis: University of Minnesota Press, 1989) (PA).

[14] Schelling effectively appropriates and provides a metaphysical foundation for Winckelmann's famous characterization of the "noble simplicity and sedate grandeur" (*edle Einfalt und stille Größe*) of Greek art and its imitation by modern art. See Johann Joachim Winckelmann, *Reflections on the Painting and Sculpture of the Greeks* (1755), trans. Henry Fuseli (London: A. Millar, 1765); reprinted in Winckelmann, *Essays on the Philosophy and History of Art*, ed. Curtis Bowman, 3 vols. (Bristol: Thoemmes Press, 2001), 1:30.

to the object, not in regard to the subject of intuition. For the difference between the beautiful and the sublime work of art consists simply in this, that where beauty is present, the infinite contradiction is eliminated in the object itself, whereas when sublimity is present, the conflict is not reconciled in the object itself, but merely uplifted to a point at which it is involuntarily eliminated in the intuition; and this, then, is much as if it were to be eliminated in the object. (STI 226)

Schelling does not illustrate this claim but is perhaps thinking that whereas a beautiful work of art is itself an image of something harmonious and communicates its resolution of the "infinite contradiction" by directly representing harmony, a sublime work of art, such as a tragedy, does not directly present the resolution of the conflict it portrays but nevertheless leads to a sense or thought of resolution on the part of the audience. If something like that is what Schelling has in mind, then his account would preserve some sense of Kant's view that sublimity really exists only in the mind of the aesthetic subject and is only "improperly" or at least indirectly ascribed to the object of aesthetic experience (which again for Kant is nature and not a work of art).

Schelling also preserves a trace of Kant's suggestion that the sublime has something to do with magnitude, although he does not make any mention either of Kant's distinction between the mathematical and dynamical sublime or of Schiller's version of it as the distinction between theoretical and practical grandeur. Schelling continues the passage just cited in the following way:

It can also be shown very easily that sublimity rests upon the same contradiction as that on which beauty rests. For whenever an object is spoken of as sublime, a magnitude is admitted by the unconscious activity which it is impossible to accept into the conscious one; whereupon the self is thrown into a conflict with itself which can end only in an aesthetic intuition, whereby both activities are brought into unexpected harmony; save only that the intuition, which here lies not in the artist, but in the intuiting subject himself, is a wholly involuntary one, in that the sublime ... sets all the forces of the mind in motion, in order to resolve a contradiction which threatens our whole intellectual existence. (STI 226)

Schelling speaks only of the unconscious and conscious, without differentiating the mind into separate faculties of sensibility, understanding, and reason, let alone distinguishing further between theoretical and practical applications. He thus has neither need nor resources to make the distinction between the mathematical and dynamical sublime, but instead he uses the two ideas, separated in Kant, of grasping magnitude and preserving what is significant about our existence (for Schelling, the "intellectual" and, for Kant, the moral) in a single characterization of the sublime.

This is not the most important difference between Schelling and Kant, however, and two others should be emphasized. First, Schelling completes and makes thoroughly metaphysical the move toward a cognitive account of the sublime that Kant had initiated with his dynamical sublime. He does this by interpreting the creation and experience of the sublime as the cognition of the infinite contradiction and by interpreting the possibility of its reconciliation as the most fundamental of truths about reality. Second, having placed the same cognitive and metaphysical interpretation on the creation and experience of artistic beauty, Schelling reduces the difference between beauty and sublimity to a matter of phenomenology: in the case of beauty, resolution is present in the object, and in the case of sublimity, in the subject, and whereas in the experience of sublimity there seems to be something involuntary about the realization of this resolution, there must presumably be something voluntary about it in the experience of beauty. This prepares the way for the lesser importance and almost complete disappearance of the sublime in aesthetic theory generally, and for Hegel's subsequent treatment of it as merely a stage in the development of beauty, in particular.

Before turning to the details of Hegel's account of the sublime, it is worth noting how Schelling follows Schiller in identifying sublime art specifically with tragedy. He does so by equating the finite with individual action and the infinite with suffering, characterizing the subject matter of sublime art as "the courageous person engaged in a struggle with misfortune, a struggle in which he neither wins a physical victory nor capitulates morally ... the symbol of the infinite, of that which *transcends all suffering*" (PA 89). The symbol of the infinite in the sublime work of art is the tragic hero, a finite being who struggles with the infinite power of the universe that works to inflict suffering. By this route Schelling actually returns to a pre-Kantian conception of the moral sublime, or of the sublimity of moral character:

> The genuinely tragic sublime depends for just this reason on two conditions, namely, that the moral person capitulate to the forces of nature and simultaneously be victorious through his *inner character*. It is essential that the hero be victorious only through that which is not an effect of nature or of chance, and hence only through inner character or disposition, as is always the case with Sophocles. (PA 89)

When Schelling turns the abstractions of his metaphysical characterization of the sublime into something more concrete, it transpires, what we admire in the sublime in art is moral courage in the face of great adversity. This, of course, is a thoroughly cognitive interpretation of the experience of the sublime in art.

Schelling's emphasis on the capacity of the universe to inflict suffering on the tragic hero may have been influential on the metaphysics of Schopenhauer, who was deeply influenced by Schelling, even if not by his treatment of the sublime specifically. Schopenhauer's metaphysics in turn would ultimately influence Nietzsche's conception of the sublime, as we will see. But what would be most significant immediately for the subsequent development of the conception of the sublime was neither Schelling's return to a pre-Kantian conception of its moral significance nor his influence on subsequent metaphysics, but his characterization of the finite work of art as only a *symbol* of the infinite. This was the conception of the sublime taken up by Hegel, although as we will see in the next section he took this idea in a different direction from Schelling and by presenting it as only a characteristic of an early stage of art diminished its importance further.

HEGEL

In his system, Hegel adopts Schelling's conception of the sublime as a symbol of the infinitude of the spirit, and in doing so transforms the sublime into one stage on the way to beauty.[15] Beauty, in turn, is only a stage on the way to philosophy within the developing self-consciousness of spirit, itself the realization that human thought is a manifestation of the intellectual nature of reality. This diminishes the importance of the sublime compared to the place it held for eighteenth-century thinkers culminating in Kant and Schiller, and for this reason Hegel's treatment of the sublime must be regarded as a major factor in the virtual disappearance of the category from aesthetics in the century or more following the posthumous publication of his *Lectures on Fine Art* in 1835. The work of the early Nietzsche is an exception, as we shall see, although Schopenhauer rather than Hegel influenced him.

Hegel's aesthetics is a theory of fine art, which largely dismisses the significance of aesthetic responses to nature. Hegel states this point at the start of his lectures, acknowledging that equating "aesthetics" with the "philosophy of fine art" effectively "exclude[s] the beauty of nature." Only the "beauty of art is beauty *born of the spirit and born again*," he writes, in which "spirit alone is the *true*, comprehending everything in itself, so that everything beautiful is truly

---

[15] See William Desmond, *Art and the Absolute: A Study of Hegel's Aesthetics* (Albany: State University of New York Press, 1986), 42 and 201–2n71, who alone among commentators emphasizes Hegel's association of the sublime with symbolic art, although he does not discuss the significance of this association for the larger history of the sublime. The sublime is not mentioned at all in Stephen Bungay, *Beauty and Truth: A Study of Hegel's Aesthetics* (Oxford: Oxford University Press, 1987), or in Annemarie Gethmann-Seifert's more recent *Einführung in Hegels Ästhetik* (Munich: Wilhelm Fink Verlag, 2005).

beautiful only as sharing in this higher sphere and generated by it."[16] Even before he reduces the sublime to a species and stage of beauty, Hegel thus rejects the Kantian conception of the sublime, which interpreted sublimity paradigmatically as a response to rather than a property of nature. Hegel's philosophy in general is based on the premise that "the truly actual is only that which has being in and for itself" (LFA 8), that is, consciousness, and his aesthetics in particular is based on the idea that art "only fulfils its supreme task when it has placed itself in the same sphere as religion and philosophy, and when it is simply one way of bringing to our minds and expressing the *Divine*, the deepest interest of mankind, and the most comprehensive truths of the spirit" (LFA 7). "In works of art the nations have deposited their richest inner intuitions and ideas," Hegel holds, and "art shares this vocation with religion and philosophy, but in a special way, namely by displaying even the highest [reality] sensuously, bringing it thereby nearer to the senses, to feeling, and to nature's mode of appearance" (LFA 7–8). With this premise Hegel establishes both the importance and limitation of art and a fortiori of the sublime: the importance of art is due to its intellectual content. Hegel does not share Kant's estimation of the equal importance of sense and intellect for human knowledge, however, and essentially reverts to a pre-Kantian, rationalist conception of the superiority of intellect over the senses. His view is that sensory cognition is ultimately inferior to purely intellectual cognition, so that art must give way to philosophy in the development of the self-consciousness of spirit.

This view leads Hegel to his thesis concerning "the death of art." This is obviously not a factual assertion that people have stopped or will stop singing and painting[17] but rather a claim that "art no longer affords that satisfaction of spiritual needs which earlier ages and nations sought in it, and found in it alone" such that "art, considered in its highest vocation, is and remains for us a thing of the past" that "has lost for us its genuine truth and life" (LFA 10–11); art, instead, "far removed ... from being the highest form of the spirit, acquires its real ratification only in philosophy" (LFA 13). Because the sublime is but a stage in the development of art, this general restriction on art reduces the importance of the sublime as well.

Hegel expands his initial criticism of the importance of beauty or other aesthetic qualities in nature by defining art and important aesthetic properties as a vehicle of human self-consciousness: "The universal need for art ... is man's rational need to lift the inner and outer world into his spiritual consciousness as an object in which he recognizes again his own self" (LFA 31), but his own self as an essentially spiritual rather than physical creature. Striking a tone that would later be taken up by some writers (including Benedetto Croce and R. G. Collingwood) and resisted by others (such as Samuel Alexander),[18] Hegel diminishes the importance of nature in general, as well as the physical medium of art. "This aspect – external existence – is not what makes a work into a product of fine art," he writes; "a work of art is such only because, originating from the spirit, it now belongs to the territory of the spirit; it has received the baptism of the spiritual and sets forth only what has been formed in harmony with the spirit." This leaves the possibility that the artistic *representation* of nature may be of significance: "For example," he writes, "owing to the feeling and insight whereby a landscape has been represented in a painting, this work of the spirit acquires a higher rank than the mere natural landscape. For everything spiritual is

---

[16] G. W. F. Hegel, *Aesthetics: Lectures on Fine Art*, trans. T. M. Knox, 2 vols. (Oxford: Clarendon Press, 1975), 1:1–2 (LFA).

[17] On this point, see Arthur C. Danto, "The End of Art," in *The Philosophical Disenfranchisement of Art* (New York: Columbia University Press, 1986), 111, and *After the End of Art: Contemporary Art and the Pale of History* (Princeton, NJ: Princeton University Press, 1997), xiii–xiv, 4, and 15.

[18] See Benedetto Croce, *The Aesthetic as the Science of Expression and of the Linguistic in General*, trans. Colin Lyas (Cambridge: Cambridge University Press, 1992), chap. VI, 56–7; R. G. Collingwood, *The Principles of Art* (Oxford: Oxford University Press, 1938), chap. II, 37, and chap. VII, 130–5 (but cf. chap. XIV, 302–8); and Samuel Alexander, *Art and the Material: The Adamson Lecture for 1925* (Manchester: Manchester University Press, 1925), and *Beauty and Other Forms of Value* (New York: Crowell, 1968), 22–5.

better than any product of nature" (LFA 29). It remains the case, however, that the aesthetic response to nature itself, such as the experience of the sublime as understood by Kant, is still of limited importance.

Hegel diminishes the importance of the sublime, however, not because he understands it as a response to the immensity or power of nature, but because he interprets it as the most preliminary and least adequate form that self-consciousness of spirit takes in artistic media. This is the import of Hegel's famous division of the "forms" of art into the three developmental stages: "symbolic," "classical," and "romantic." He ascribes to all art one and the same "vocation," namely, "to unveil the *truth* in the form of sensuous artistic configuration, to set forth the reconciled opposition just mentioned, and so to have its end and aim in itself, in this very setting forth and unveiling" (LFA 55). This takes place in different "forms of art," which are "nothing but the different relations of meaning and shape, relations which proceed from the Idea itself" – for present purposes, another term in Hegel's system for the self-understanding of spirit – "and therefore provide the true basis for the division of this sphere" (LFA 75). This conception does not lead to any version of relativism on Hegel's part – that is, the idea that different media and styles of art might be used equally well at different times and places to express the fundamental truth at which all art is supposed to aim – but to a theory in which the stages of art are seen to develop from the least to the most adequate expression of the truth about the spiritual nature of reality; this is the case, even though the whole series of forms is also limited by the fact that no art can be as adequate an expression of this truth as religion and philosophy are destined to be.

The first, defective, form of art Hegel calls the "*symbolic* form of art" (LFA 76), in which "the Idea is presented to consciousness only as indeterminate or determined *abstractly*" and "for this reason the correspondence of meaning in shape is always defective and must itself remain purely abstract" (LFA 77). That is, in the symbolic stage both the understanding of spirit and the spiritual character of reality are vague, the selection of artistic means to represent it is only vaguely understood, and its truth is arbitrary. In "*classical* art," the second form, "the double defect of the symbolic form is extinguished" because "it is the free and adequate embodiment of the Idea in the shape peculiarly appropriate to the Idea itself in its essential nature" (LFA 77). This might sound as if the classical stage should be the culmination of art, but this is not the case, because what makes possible the happy correspondence between content and art is that spirit is understood in restrictively human form (the anthropomorphic gods of Greece), and thus it can be represented (above all in Greek sculpture) only because the self-understanding of spirit in this stage of artistic development remains inadequate to the true nature of spirit. Classical art does represent a culmination of art in one sense, because "in so far as art's task is to bring the spiritual before our eyes in a sensuous manner," the "anthropomorphism" of the classical conception of spirit is particularly well-suited to the potential of artistic media; this is also a mark of the limitation of art as such: classical art is successful artistically but not philosophically because in it "the spirit is at once determined as particular and human, not as purely absolute and eternal" (LFA 79).

This leads to the supersession of classical art by the third form of art, "the *romantic*," the hallmark of which is its attempt to realize as its content "no longer the sensuous immediate existence of the spiritual in the bodily form of man, but instead the *inwardness of self-consciousness*" (LFA 80). Paradigmatically, in literary forms such as the novel, romantic art attempts to portray "the attainment, and the transcendence of the ideal as the true Idea of beauty"; precisely because of this "higher perfection, it is not susceptible of an adequate union with the external, since its true reality and manifestation it can seek and achieve only within itself." In other words, no artistic medium is fully capable of expressing the spiritual nature of reality, so rather than constituting the perfection of art, romantic art is "the self-transcendence of art" (LFA 80), which prepares the way for the supersession of art by religion – a halfway house between art and philosophy – and finally by philosophy itself.

Within this scheme Hegel's conception of the sublime emerges: relying tacitly on Kant's original characterization of the experience of the sublime as a response to the inadequacy of imagination to capture ideas formed by reason, Hegel equates the sublime with the first and most inadequate stage, the experience of *symbolic* art. For Kant, however, experiencing the superiority of reason over imagination in response to the immensity or power of nature is ultimately satisfying, an experience of transcendence not itself to be transcended. For Hegel, by contrast, sublime art only hints at the true nature of spirit and is something to be superseded, first within the history of art itself and then by the supersession of all art by religion and philosophy.

Hegel expands on this introductory characterization in the section of his lectures entitled "The Symbolic Form of Art," in which he explicitly associates the sublime with the dual defects of symbolic art, the inadequacy of its conception of the spirit, and the ensuing indeterminacy of its means of expressing its inadequate grasp of the truth. The experience of sublimity consists merely in a vague sense of the spiritual nature of reality and an awareness of the inadequacy of any physical medium to express this nature. In sublime art, "the meaning, as spiritual explicit universality, is separated for the first time from the concrete existent, and makes that existent known as its negative, external to it, and its servant. In order to express *itself* therein, the meaning cannot allow this existent to subsist independently, but must posit it as the inherently deficient, something to be superseded" (LFA 318). Hegel adds to this characterization some of the other terminology of his own system, but throughout, his message about the sublime remains the same: the experience of sublimity is the experience of the inadequacy of any physical medium to express the spiritual nature of reality, which at the stage of symbolic and sublime art is itself understood only inadequately. Whether considering the Indian myths of the endless transformations of the gods or the crudities of Egyptian architecture, Hegel always emphasizes both the inadequacy of the understanding of spirit that these arts express and the poverty of their means of expression.

SCHOPENHAUER

Given Schopenhauer's views that the ultimate character of reality is nonrational, neither the Kantian understanding of the sublime as an expression of our own rationality nor the Hegelian conception of it as an expression of the rational character of reality is open to him. This does not mean, however, that Schopenhauer interprets the sublime as an *experience* of the nonrationality of reality. He has a cognitivist interpretation of the experience of beauty in terms of characteristic forms – what he calls "Platonic Ideas" – that are "objectifications" in the form of appearances of the nonrational will. Schopenhauer then interprets the sublime as consisting of insight into the Platonic Ideas, wrung out of experience with difficulty rather than with the ease that characterizes the experience of beauty. Thus, the beautiful and the sublime have the same cognitive content for Schopenhauer and differ only subjectively.

Schopenhauer's account of aesthetic experience is a variation of Kant's transcendental idealism, which he regarded as having its only proper reconstruction in his own philosophical system, expressed and developed in *The World as Will and Representation*.[19] Schopenhauer understands the world as we experience it to be the mere appearance of an underlying reality, structured by the subjectively valid forms of space, time, and causality. All of this is close enough to Kant, but Schopenhauer departs company from him when he depicts the insatiable character of human desire as an intimation of the nature of underlying reality itself, an irrational force that can be called "will" by analogy with the apparent character of human willing. On Schopenhauer's view, the ethical task for human beings is to escape this circle of desire, first

---

[19] See Arthur Schopenhauer, *The World as Will and Representation*, trans. E. F. J. Payne, 2 vols. (Indian Springs, CO: Falcon's Wing Press, 1958), 1:xxiii (WWR).

by losing oneself in the contemplation of the timeless and impersonal forms of appearance or objectifications of the will, and then, more adequately, by identifying oneself with the single and all-pervasive will that underlies reality, rather than with one's own particular will at the level of appearance. Aesthetic experience, which for Schopenhauer begins with the experience of natural beauty, provides the first of these stages of escape from the demands of desire. In this regard, Schopenhauer too sees aesthetic experience – including the experience of the sublime – as only a stage to something greater, although in his case it concerns achieving a moral condition rather than gaining theoretical insight, as it had for Hegel.

Schopenhauer's account of the beneficial effect of aesthetic experience is predicated on the distinction he draws between the fully individuated particulars of ordinary experience and the essential forms of such experience, or the determinate ways in which the underlying will can manifest itself in appearance. His key assumption is that contemplation of the essential forms of experience affords release from preoccupation with one's own insatiable desires, even before identification with the underlying will that affords more permanent release from the frustrations of ordinary selfhood. Schopenhauer works with the distinction between "the will [as] the *thing-in-itself*, and the *Idea* [as] the immediate objectivity of that will at a definite grade" (WWR §31, 170) or as a characteristic way in which individuals can appear. He identifies the former with Kant's thing-in-itself, plausibly enough allowing for his conception of this will as essentially nonrational, and the latter with Plato's Ideas, somewhat implausibly, because for Plato the Ideas are the essential forms of reality that are only imperfectly reflected in the characteristic forms of sensible appearance that "participate" in them. Whatever the justice of his invocation of Plato, Schopenhauer claims that contemplation of the Ideas transforms the individual who contemplates them into a "pure subject of knowing" and releases him, at least as long as such contemplation is sustained, from the circle of desire and frustration characteristic of ordinary selfhood. If we "devote the whole power of our mind to perception, sink ourselves completely therein, and let our whole consciousness be filled by the calm contemplation of the natural object actually present ... we *lose* ourselves entirely in this object ... we forget our individuality, our will, and continue to exist as pure subject" (WWR §34, 178). In this (paradoxically) desirable state, the individual is released from the frustration of desires that cannot be satisfied simply by putting them out of mind through contemplating an Idea.

Schopenhauer then argues that beautiful objects in nature are those that strike us with their own inherent Ideas without any special effort on our part, and that induce in us the state of being a pure subject, whereas works of art present such Ideas in virtue of artistic creativity, which subsequently induces the state of contemplation in the rest of us. "*Art*, the work of genius ... repeats the eternal Ideas apprehended through pure contemplation, the essential and abiding element in all the phenomena of the world.... Its only source is knowledge of the Ideas; its sole aim is communication of this knowledge" (WWR §36, 184–5). Contemplation of the Ideas thus communicated produces the same state as does contemplation of the Ideas inherent in natural beauty. Artistic genius, the power to produce art, "consists precisely in the preeminent ability for such contemplation," a "power of knowledge ... far exceeding that required for the service of an individual will" (WWR §36, 185–6) and that allows the artistic genius to perceive such Ideas where ordinary individuals could not but then also to express them in forms that communicate them to more ordinary minds.

Finally, Schopenhauer, like Kant, treats the experience of the sublime primarily as a response to nature, an experience in which Ideas are successfully presented for contemplation even when we are aware of the threat posed by objects to our bodily security or existence. On such occasions we are aware of an effort to tear ourselves away from those threatening objects whose Ideas afford us the benefits of pure contemplation. Schopenhauer writes:

These very objects, whose significant forms invite us to a pure contemplation of them, may have a hostile relation to the human will in general, as manifested in its objectivity, the human body. They may be opposed to it, they may threaten it by their might that eliminates all resistance, or their immeasurable greatness may reduce it to naught. Nevertheless, the beholder may not direct his attention to this relation to his will which is so pressing and hostile, but, although he perceives and acknowledges it, he may consciously turn away from it, forcibly tear himself from his will and its relations, and, giving himself up entirely to knowledge, may quietly contemplate, as pure, will-less subject of knowing, those very objects so terrible to his will. (WWR §39, 201)

Or, as he also remarks, "with the sublime, that state of pure knowing is obtained first of all by a conscious and violent tearing away from the relations of the same object to the will which are recognized as unfavourable, by a free exaltation, accompanied by consciousness, beyond the will and the knowledge related to it," and thus the "feeling of the sublime is distinguished from that of the beautiful only by the addition, namely the exaltation beyond the known hostile relation of the contemplated object to the will in general" (WWR §39, 202). The content and effect of the experiences of the beautiful and the sublime are thus the same – in both cases, the content of the experience is a Platonic Idea of some essential form of appearance and the effect of the contemplation of such an Idea is the state of painless will-lessness. In the case of the sublime, however, content and effect are also connected, or preceded, with consciousness of the threat presented by the object and the effort to tear oneself away from fear of that threat in order to contemplate the Idea. Thus the beautiful and the sublime differ only on this point of phenomenology, and the sublime can be regarded as a variant of the beautiful.

As mentioned previously, Schopenhauer regards the experience of sublimity primarily as a response to nature. The only examples of human artistry capable of inducing the experience of the sublime that he explicitly mentions are the conventional ones of colossal architecture, the Egyptian pyramids and St. Peter's in Rome (already mentioned by Kant and many before him), and the dome of St. Paul's in London, an addition to the traditional catalog. These he adduces specifically as inducing the experience of the mathematical rather than dynamical sublime, a distinction he adopts from Kant (CJ §39, 205–6). Although he does not do so explicitly, there is no reason why Schopenhauer could not assimilate his account of the sublime with that of artistic genius: sublime art would be when an artistic genius has to wrest his Idea out of his own experience of a threatening or terrifying object and manages to communicate both the Idea thus wrested from this struggle and the sense of struggle itself. This could be accomplished in many artistic media other than architecture or colossal sculpture and could be done perhaps better than those, because they do not reveal any record of the artistic process that produced them. Schopenhauer, however, does not explicitly associate the sublime either with an early stage of art, as does Hegel, or with a specific form of art such as tragedy, as do Schiller and Schelling.

NIETZSCHE

Nietzsche's most famous contribution to aesthetics is his first book, *The Birth of Tragedy out of the Spirit of Music* (1872), based, as he acknowledges with regret in the later "Attempt at Self-Criticism" (added to the second edition) on Schopenhauer's metaphysics.[20] Despite this acknowledgement, neither in this book nor in the extended essay "Schopenhauer as Educator" published two years later[21] does Nietzsche addresses Schopenhauer's aesthetics and a fortiori his account of the sublime. In *The Birth of Tragedy*, Nietzsche creates an aesthetic version

---

[20] Friedrich Nietzsche, *The Birth of Tragedy and Other Writings*, ed. Raymond Geuss and Ronald Speirs; trans. Ronald Speirs (Cambridge: Cambridge University Press, 1999), 10 (BT).
[21] Friedrich Nietzsche, "Schopenhauer as Educator," in *Untimely Meditations*, trans. R. J. Hollingdale (Cambridge: Cambridge University Press, 1983), 125–94. The standard commentary on *The Birth of Tragedy*, M. S. Silk and J. P. Stern, *Nietzsche on Tragedy* (Cambridge: Cambridge University Press, 1981), does not discuss Nietzsche's account of the sublime.

of Schopenhauer's metaphysics, but with a subtle twist. He does not explicitly contrast the beautiful and the sublime but instead contrasts "Apollonian" and "Dionysian" art, or aspects of art in Greek tragedy, equating Apollonian art with the representation of the superficial rationality of existence and Dionysian art with the recognition of the radical irrationality of underlying reality. The Dionysian differs from the Apollonian not merely in the subjective dimension of ease or difficulty but in its objective content, and if we take the Dionysian as Nietzsche's version of the sublime, then Nietzsche has radically reconceived the experience of the sublime as an intimation of the fundamental nonrationality of existence, rather than its rationality, whether our own (as in Kant) or that of reality in general (as in Hegel). Nietzsche also finds redemption in the identification of the individual with transindividual reality, and thus in the affirmation of the Dionysian in and through art, and in this regard revives Kant's positive conception of the sublime against the Hegelian move that reduces it to a mere stage in the development of beauty.

As we have seen, Schopenhauer presents the experience of the sublime primarily as a response to nature, and thus as an experience of the general aesthetic subject rather than the artist in particular. Given Nietzsche's later dismissal of Schopenhauer's aesthetics as one of the spectator rather than the artist (GM §6, 73–5), we should not expect him to be drawn to Schopenhauer's account of the sublime. Nietzsche uses the term "sublime" (*erhaben, das Erhabene*) adjectivally and nominally a number of times in *The Birth of Tragedy*, but he does not reserve it exclusively for topics associated with the traditional conception of sublimity; indeed, on several occasions he employs it to characterize a high or exalted degree of beauty (see BT §1, 17 and §3, 25). Yet it is clear that Nietzsche primarily associates the sublime as traditionally understood with his own concept of the Dionysian in art, and, therefore, with the artistic experience and representation of the underlying nonindividuated, nonrational reality of life in contrast to the beautiful, individuated, and apparently rational forms of imagery captured by Apollonian art. Only when Apollonian art itself represents the Dionysian can it too be called sublime. In Nietzsche, the conception of the sublime is decisively transformed from its original significance as an aesthetic intimation of rationality in Kant, Schiller, and even Hegel to an aesthetic intimation of the transcendence of individual rationality; at the same time the category of the sublime is thereby restored to the prominent place it had for Kant but lost in the philosophy of Schelling, Hegel, and Schopenhauer.

On the one occasion in *The Birth of Tragedy* in which Nietzsche explicitly treats the sublime as a concept of aesthetics, he contrasts it not to the beautiful but to the comic. Having characterized the "ecstasy of the Dionysiac state, in which the usual barriers and limits of existence are destroyed" and identified it with Bacchic rites and the chorus of Greek tragedy, he writes the following:

Here, at this moment of supreme danger for the will, *art* approaches as a saving sorceress with the power to heal. Art alone can re-direct those repulsive thoughts about the terrible or absurd nature of existence into representations with which man can live; these representations are the *sublime*, whereby the terrible is tamed by artistic means, and the *comical*, whereby disgust at absurdity is discharged by artistic means. (BT §7, 40)[22]

Crucially, Nietzsche here associates both the sublime and the comic, in implicit contrast to the beautiful, with the artistic treatment of "repulsive thoughts about the terrible or absurd nature of existence"; the sublime "tames" these terrible thoughts while the comic "discharges" them, a distinction Nietzsche does not explain, but he suggests that sublime art retains the terror and absurdity that the comic, fully discharging these, does not.

---

[22] Nietzsche also contrasts the sublime and the comic in the 1870 essay "The Dionysiac World-View," in *The Birth of Tragedy and Other Writings*, 117–38, pp. 130–1.

The other passages, by contrast, where Nietzsche uses the term "sublime" (in connection with the Dionysian and without reference to the comic) do not suggest that the artistic sublime even tames the experience of terror and absurdity. Instead, Nietzsche takes the sublime simply to present the Dionysian – or the presentation of the Dionysian is sublime – and sees the experience of the Dionysian itself as an experience of reconciliation in which the individual is subsumed into a larger reality and the cares of individual existence, the ordinary focus of our vaunted rationality, are lost in the absorption of the individual into the underlying oneness. This is, of course, Nietzsche's metaphorical version of Schopenhauer's philosophy. This passage at the end of the first section of *The Birth of Tragedy* presents the essentials of Nietzsche's conception of the sublime:

> Not only is the bond between human beings renewed by the magic of the Dionysiac, but nature, alienated, inimical, or subjugated, celebrates once more her festival of reconciliation with her lost son, humankind.... If one were to transform Beethoven's jubilant "Hymn to Joy" into a painting and place no constraints on one's imagination as the millions sink into the dusty, shivering in awe, then one could begin to approach the Dionysiac.... Now, hearing this gospel of universal harmony, each person feels himself to be not simply united, reconciled or merged with his neighbour, but quite literally one with him, as if the veil of maya had been torn apart.... Singing and dancing, man expresses his sense of belonging to a higher community; he has forgotten how to walk and talk and is on the brink of flying and dancing, up and away into the air above ... he feels himself to be a god, he himself now moves in such ecstasy and sublimity as once he saw the gods move in his dreams. Man is no longer an artist, he has become a work of art: all nature's artistic power reveals itself here, amidst shivers of intoxication, to the highest, most blissful satisfaction of the primordial unity. (BT §1, 18)

Here, the Dionysian and sublime art are identified primarily with the arts of performance (music and dance) but can be imagined in a visual art form such as painting as well. The distinctions of ordinary life are dissolved and reconciled – between one person and others, human beings and nature more generally, ordinary persons and artists, and artists and works of art. Of course this dissolution of all distinctions is also the dissolution of ordinary reason itself, and thus for Nietzsche the sublime becomes the experience of the dissolution of rationality, not its affirmation. Terrifying as that idea may seem, for Nietzsche it is ultimately the source of joy rather than terror, and although it stands opposed to the apotheosis of individual reason found in Kant, his account of the sublime shares with the latter an ultimately affirmative character.

In a second passage on the sublime, Nietzsche reveals that Apollonian and Dionysian are not two separate and alternative forms of art but, at least in the most perfect works of art, are fully combined, the clarity of imagery typical of the Apollonian being employed to present the Dionysian reality and its redemptive potential. Nietzsche begins this passage with the first-person assertion that

> the more I become aware of those all-powerful artistic drives in nature, and of a fervent longing in them for semblance [*Schein*], for their redemption and release in semblance, the more I feel myself driven to the metaphysical assumption that that which truly exists, the eternally suffering and contradictory, primordial unity, simultaneously needs, for its constant release and redemption, the ecstatic vision, intensely pleasurable semblance. (BT §4, 25–6)

Here the Apollonian drive for "semblance" or distinct, individuated imagery, although deceptive in its very distinctness and individuation, is driven by the Dionysian, suffering, and "contradictory" nature of reality and our need for release therefrom. But, Nietzsche argues, using a supreme work of visual rather than literary art – Raphael's final painting, the *Transfiguration* (1516) – what Apollonian imagery must show is precisely that redemption is possible only by acceptance of the Dionysian character of the human condition:

> Here, in the highest symbolism of art, we see before us the Apolline world of beauty and the ground on which it rests, that terrible wisdom of Silenus, and we grasp, intuitively, the reciprocal necessity of these

two things. At the same time, however, we encounter Apollo as the deification of the *principium individuationis* in which alone the eternally attained goal of the primordial unity, its release and redemption through semblance, comes about; with sublime gestures he shows us that the whole world of agony is needed in order to compel the individual to generate the releasing and redemptive vision and then, lost in contemplation [*Anschauen*] of that vision, to sit calmly in his rocking boat in the midst of the sea. (BT §4, 26)

Nietzsche here suggests that the release from suffering through the transcendence of individuality, which Schopenhauer regarded as a temporary effect of aesthetic experience and only permanently realized in the ethical attitude of compassion, is in fact fully achieved in the highest instances of the aesthetic: this is what Nietzsche means by his provocative statement that "only as an *aesthetic phenomenon* is existence and the world eternally *justified*" (BT §5, 33). The passage also shows that the idea of the sublime can transcend the distinction between the Apollonian and Dionysian, but only insofar as the Apollonian use of beautiful imagery is put in service of expressing the Dionysian insight into the transcendence of individuality; with due caution the association of the sublime with the Dionysian can be accepted after all. It may be misleading of Nietzsche to identify the sublime exclusively with the Dionysian (see BT §8, 41), but he clearly thinks the revelation and acceptance of the Dionysian is necessary if there is to be any sublimity at all.

It is worth noting, in conclusion, that after Nietzsche, the category of the sublime largely disappeared from academic aesthetics, perhaps to be replaced by the category of "difficult" art in such aestheticians as Bernard Bosanquet and Croce. More recently, Nietzsche's characterization of the sublime and Dionysian art as a means of offering insight into the nonrational character of reality have been taken up by writers such as Jean-François Lyotard, albeit without Nietzsche's strongly affirmative and thus Kantian valuation of the experience involved. The fate of the idea of the sublime after Nietzsche is beyond the scope of this chapter but is taken up by other contributors to the present volume.

8

The Postmodern Sublime

Presentation and Its Limits

David B. Johnson

In the last three decades of the twentieth century, the philosophical concept of the sublime underwent a renaissance among a number of "continental" philosophers, after having fallen largely out of favor around the end of the preceding century. Many thinkers who turned to the concept of the sublime at this time were associated in one way or another with the then-nascent and fiercely debated categories of "postmodern theory" and "postmodernism" in general;[1] accordingly, this trend in continental thought quickly became identified by the name "postmodern sublime."[2] In this chapter, we examine the work of four influential thinkers of this postmodern incarnation of the sublime: Jean-François Lyotard, Julia Kristeva, Gilles Deleuze, and Fredric Jameson. Other writers also contributed to this discourse, but the work of these four encapsulates effectively its central themes and issues, while at the same time illustrating the wide range of its elaboration and use.[3]

Common to these thinkers' work is a more or less explicit but fundamental engagement with Kant's "Analytic of the Sublime."[4] For each of them, the contemporary importance of the experience of sublimity, as well as the central problematic of its concept, concerns the issue of what Kant in the *Critique of the Power of Judgment* calls *Darstellung*: the process through which the imagination presents sensible intuition to rational thought. In the aesthetic experience of the sublime, on their interpretation, the imagination tries to present an intuition of some object that is strictly and intrinsically unpresentable, thereby running up against its own limit. This means, in these thinkers' view, that the experience of the sublime involves a crisis for the faculty of

---

[1] Not all late twentieth-century continental philosophers of the sublime can be associated with postmodernism, however one might construe the term. Theodor Adorno, for example, is not generally considered a postmodernist but wrote on the sublime at the end of the 1960s. See Theodor W. Adorno, *Ästhetische Theorie*, ed. Gretel Adorno and Rolf Tiedemann (Frankfurt am Main: Suhrkamp Verlag, 1970); *Aesthetic Theory*, trans. Robert Hullot-Kentor (New York: Continuum, 1997).

[2] We must note here that the term "postmodern sublime" denotes not only a philosophical discourse on the sublime but also a trend in art, architecture, and literary criticism and practice. The present chapter focuses on the philosophical and not the more specifically art-, architecture-, or literary-critical uses of the sublime in postmodernism.

[3] For some articulations of the postmodern sublime that are not considered directly in the present chapter, see Jean-Luc Nancy, "L'Offrande sublime," in *Du sublime*, ed. Jean-François Courtine et al. (Paris: Belin, 1988); "The Sublime Offering," in *Of the Sublime: Presence in Question*, ed. Jean-François Courtine et al.; trans. Jeffrey S. Librett (Albany: State University of New York Press, 1993), 25–54; Jacques Derrida, *La Vérité en peinture* (Paris: Flammarion, 1978); *The Truth in Painting*, trans. Geoffrey Bennington and Ian McLeod (Chicago: University of Chicago Press, 1987); and Paul de Man, "Phenomenality and Materiality in Kant" and "Hegel on the Sublime," in *Aesthetic Ideology*, ed. Andrzej Warminski (Minneapolis: University of Minnesota Press, 1996), 70–90 and 105–18.

[4] *Kritik der Urteilskraft*, *Kant's gesammelte Schriften*, Königlichen Preussischen (later Deutschen) Akademie der Wissenschaften, 29 vols. (Berlin: Reimer [later de Gruyter], 1900–), vol. 5 (KGS); *Critique of the Power of Judgment*, ed. Paul Guyer; trans. Paul Guyer and Eric Matthews (Cambridge: Cambridge University Press, 2000), §23–9, 5:244–78 (CJ). All references are to volume and page of the Akademie edition.

presentation in the form of an irresolvable conflict between it and a set of objects that remain fundamentally inaccessible to it, but that it strives to present nonetheless. This issue of irresolvability, which is central to the way these thinkers conceptualize the sublime, was first and most rigorously analyzed by Kant in the third *Critique*. For this reason, the thinkers of the postmodern sublime focus almost exclusively on Kant's interpretation and reject both pre-Kantian and German Idealist and Romantic discourses of the sublime; the latter tend to resolve the conflict between presentation and what cannot be presented, whereas the former ignore the issue altogether. On the postmodern view, this conflict, although irresolvable, takes on an affirmative role, generating a profound and violent affective response, and reveals a mode of thinking or sensing that is radically different from our usual ways of thinking and sensing. In the experience of the sublime, these thinkers believe, we find resources for new forms of intellectual and aesthetic endeavor.

Although their conceptions of the sublime come directly from their readings of Kant, these philosophers also critique, invert, or undermine Kant's analysis. They do so in four ways. First, each of them conceptualizes the nature of the unpresentable object in the sublime differently than Kant, who had identified this object as the rational idea of absolute magnitude or power (CJ 5:251–64): Lyotard conceives of the unpresentable in terms of the absolute in general; Deleuze, in terms of pure sensation; Kristeva, in terms of a very early stage of an individual's psychosexual development; and Jameson, in terms of the vastness of contemporary capitalism. Second, they all contest Kant's downplaying of the importance of the sublime for philosophy – his assertion that the "Analytic of the Sublime" constitutes a "mere appendix" to the project of the third *Critique* (CJ 5:246) – insisting instead that the experience of the sublime is indispensable for thought to reflect on its own conditions or the conditions of contemporary cultural life. Third, each of them moves away from the association, still operative in Kant's account, between the experience of the sublime and emotions like awe and respect, instead relating sublimity to more subversive, corporeal, or even base affective and ethical registers. Fourth and finally, each rejects Kant's insistence that the sublime is primarily germane to our experience of nature and only secondarily and weakly relevant to our judgments of art; they deploy the concept of the sublime expressly as a means to think about art and literature.

In spite of the several important commonalities just enumerated, however, each of these postmodern thinkers of the sublime approaches his or her analysis in a highly singular way and comes to quite different conclusions than the others. Accordingly, we treat each thinker singly, beginning with Lyotard, the archetypal postmodern theorist of the sublime. Of the four thinkers under consideration, he alone forges an explicit and thoroughgoing notion of the postmodern sublime as both an aesthetic tendency and an analytic object. By contrast, Jameson develops an explicit but much less fully theorized concept of the postmodern sublime, whereas neither Deleuze nor Kristeva links the experience of sublimity to a notion of the postmodern at all. Lyotard's account of the sublime is also the most faithfully Kantian of the four. From him, we will turn to Deleuze and then to Kristeva, both of whom push the concept of the sublime quite far from its Kantian articulation, while still maintaining Kant's critical notion of a crisis occurring at the limit of the transcendental faculty of presentation. Deleuze displaces Kant's concept of the sublime toward a theory of pure sensation, whereas Kristeva converts it into a psychoanalytic-semiotic concept of abjection. We conclude with the critic of postmodernism, Jameson, who identifies the postmodern sublime as a symptom of the postmodern acquiescence to late capitalism.

JEAN-FRANÇOIS LYOTARD

Lyotard's engagement with the concept of the sublime is the most focused, thematic, and sustained of any of his peers. Through this concept, Lyotard addresses a set of interlinked questions concerning the function and significance of modern art and the artistic avant-gardes that produced it, the metaphysics of "the event," and the nature of postmodernism itself. More broadly, the concept of the sublime enables Lyotard to carry out what he calls "an *anamnesis* of criticism itself (in Kant's sense)."[5] By this, he means that the concept of the sublime makes possible a renewal of Kant's critical project: it directs us toward and allows us to reflect on the limits and conditions of our experience. In so doing, it shows us how those limits can be forced, effecting a kind of negative but unfettered aesthetic process, which enables us to reconceive how we orient our thought and our action in the world, and in particular, how we do so through art.

Lyotard's longest and most concerted discussion of sublimity is found in his *Lessons on the Analytic of the Sublime* (1991),[6] an extended close reading of Kant's theorization of the sublime in the third *Critique*. Following Kant very closely, Lyotard identifies the experience of sublimity as the simultaneous feeling of pleasure and pain that accompanies the imagination's inevitably failed attempt to present to thought an intuition that would adequately correspond to an idea of the absolute generated by the faculty of reason. Through this failure, thought is made to feel the unintuitable presence of this idea of the absolute, as well as the superiority of the faculty of reason over both the imagination and the phenomena of nature the latter presents. For Lyotard, the essential mechanism of this experience can thus be summarized in one short formula: the *presentation of the unpresentable*. Importantly, the failure of the imagination in the experience of sublimity is not merely contingent; the imagination is barred a priori from presenting an intuition corresponding to an idea of the absolute, because it is constitutively capable only of presenting phenomena that are by definition conditioned, limited, and finite. It is this humbling failure of the imagination before reason, in spite of the former's greatest efforts, that gives rise to the painful component of the feeling engendered in the sublime; it is the awareness of the limitlessness and absolute power of ideas that subsequently "awakens the feeling of a supersensible faculty in us," that generates the feeling of pleasure we take in the sublime (CJ 5:250).

This experience of sublimity, Lyotard argues, shows us something surprising and unsettling about Kant's critical thought generally. The sublime rests, he says, on a principle of "thinking's getting carried away ..., as if fascinated by its own excessiveness" (LAS 55). The sublime, in other words, is the aesthetic manifestation of thought's inexorable attraction to transcendental illusions: in sublime experience, thought tantalizes itself, as it were, with the possibility of discovering the absolute in phenomenal intuition by transgressing its own boundaries, boundaries that it, itself, establishes through critical reflection. In the *Critique of Pure Reason*, Kant had acknowledged that the impetus toward such illusions – the desire to cognize the absolute – is an essential motivation of thought, despite the errors that it frequently causes.[7] Lyotard turns this observation back to reflect on Kant's critical project itself, arguing, in a passage worth quoting at length, that critical philosophy depends crucially on this "deaf desire for limitlessness":

What critical thought does, in short, is to look for the *a priori* conditions of the possibility of judging the true, the just, or the beautiful in the realms of knowledge, of morality, and in the territory of the aesthetic. The project seems modest and reasonable. However, it is motivated by the same principle of fury that the critique restrains.... Reflection pushes the analysis of its own conditions as far as it can, in accordance with the demand of the critique itself. Reflection thus touches on the absolute of its conditions.... All thought is a being put into relation – a "synthesis," in the language of Kant. Thus when thinking reaches the absolute, the relation reaches the without-relation, for the absolute is without

---

[5] Jean-François Lyotard, "Complexity and the Sublime," trans. Geoffrey Bennington, in *Postmodernism*, ed. Lisa Appignanesi (London: Institute of Contemporary Arts, 1986), 11.

[6] Jean-François Lyotard, *Leçons sur l'analytique du sublime* (Paris: Galilée, 1991); *Lessons on the Analytic of the Sublime*, trans. Elizabeth Rottenberg (Stanford, CA: Stanford University Press, 1994) (LAS).

[7] *Kritik der reinen Vernunft*, KGS 3 and 4; *Critique of Pure Reason*, trans. Paul Guyer and Allen W. Wood (Cambridge: Cambridge University Press, 1999), A321/B378–A338/B396. All references are to the pagination of the first (1781) and second (1787) Akademie editions, abbreviated CPR A/B.

relation. How can the without-relation be "present" to relation? It can only be "present" as disavowed (as metaphysical entity), forbidden (as illusion).... The consequence for thought is a kind of spasm. And the Analytic of the Sublime is a hint of this spasm.... It exposes the "state" of critical thought when it reaches its extreme limit – a spasmodic state. (LAS 56)

On Lyotard's view, then, by taking us to the limit of what can be presented, attempting in vain to surpass that limit, and thereby raising us to an awareness of the power of the supersensible that lies beyond that limit within us – in short, by presenting the unpresentable – the Kantian sublime recapitulates and brings us to feel, aestheticizes, the essential movement of critical thought in general: the "spasm" entailed by thought's fascination with what it forbids itself.

Importantly, for Lyotard, the mode in which the sublime achieves this presentation of the unpresentable is one of "negative presentation." In spite of – in fact, because of – the incapacity of the imagination to render a presentation adequate to the unpresentable idea of the absolute, we are brought to feel the presence and the power of the content of that idea in the experience of the sublime. This bringing-to-feel, this presentation of the absolute, is achieved not positively by the imagination but negatively in that faculty's failure. This does not merely mean, however, that the absolute is presented simply by virtue of its not being presented. Rather, Lyotard points out, in its being forced to its limit by reason, the imagination discovers a kind of paradoxical limitlessness; it "feels itself to be unbounded" as Kant writes (CJ 5:274). Unable to discover anything sensible that would enable it to fulfill its sublime task, brought before the abyss, as it were, of its failure to present the absolute, the imagination feels itself become unlimited, infinite. It presents properly and positively nothing; reason's idea of the absolute is left without a sensible datum it could subsume. At the same time, in the feeling of unboundedness that it experiences in this discovery of its inadequacy, the imagination evokes the absolute by "mak[ing] a sign of" its failure-induced limitlessness – a limitlessness that negatively signifies the absolute in the form of "the trace of a retreat ... an almost insane mirage" (LAS 152).

In this procedure of negative presentation, we find the ultimate expression of the irresolvable relationship between presentation and the unpresentable in the sublime – an irresolvability Lyotard calls "differend" (LAS 147–53).[8] The faculty of presentation can never properly and positively present the absolute, and yet the faculty of reason demands that it do so. Rather than resulting in a kind of stultified impasse, however, the irresolvability of this situation itself becomes generative: it produces a negative presentation of what exceeds presentation, "a sign of the presence of the absolute" (LAS 152). In particular, for Lyotard, this generative irresolvability of presentation in the sublime effects a turning point in the history of art: "The shock of the thought of the absolute for the thinking of forms expresses and sanctions a major shift in the stakes of art and literature.... Its stakes can be formulated simply: is it possible, and how would it be possible, to testify to the absolute by means of artistic and literary presentations, which are always dependent on forms?" (LAS 153). Lyotard had already addressed this question of the role of the sublime in artistic and literary endeavor almost ten years before *Lessons on the Analytic of the Sublime* was first published. In an essay entitled "Answering the Question: What Is Postmodernism?" (1982),[9] Lyotard employs his concept of the sublime to articulate and defend the idea of avant-garde modernism in the arts. The essential project of the avant-garde, Lyotard argues, is to ask "the question of reality implicated in that of art" (AQ 75). The modern avant-garde, then, interrogates the rules of art making; it experiments with

---

[8] For Lyotard's theoretical articulation of this concept, see Jean-François Lyotard, *Le Différend* (Paris: Éditions de Minuit, 1983); *The Differend*, trans. Georges Van Den Abbeele (Minneapolis: University of Minnesota Press, 1988).

[9] Jean-François Lyotard, "Réponse à la question: qu'est-ce que le postmoderne?" *Critique* 419 (1982); "Answering the Question: What Is Postmodernism?" trans. Régis Durand, in *The Postmodern Condition*, trans. Geoffrey Bennington and Brian Massumi (Minneapolis: University of Minnesota Press, 1984), 71–82 (AQ).

presuppositions about what art is and can be. In so doing, it questions dominant assumptions about creative endeavor and communication more broadly, assumptions that entail demands for clear identity, liquidation of ambiguity, stability, and easy recognizability in signifying processes – in short, the crystallization and consolidation of existing "reality." In opposing such demands, avant-garde modernism effects a "shattering of belief and ... discovery of the 'lack of reality' of reality, together with the invention of other realities" (AQ 77).

In refusing the "reality" of both traditional art and contemporary mass communication and capitalism, Lyotard argues, avant-garde art undertakes precisely the task that the imagination is compelled to perform in the experience of the sublime. It attempts "to present the fact that the unpresentable exists" – a fact that the discourse of reality must expunge at all cost, because this discourse relies on the assumption of a stable, easily determinable concordance between thought and referent, between idea and presentation, and because, in other words, it assumes the world to be merely beautiful (AQ 78). A work of *properly* modern art, then, will initiate a sublime experience. It will, Lyotard writes, "'present' something though negatively; it will therefore avoid figuration or representation. It will be 'white' like one of Malevitch's squares; it will enable us to see only by making it impossible to see; it will please only by causing pain" (AQ 78). The project of the modern avant-garde, then, according to Lyotard, is essentially sublime in character.

In another text from about the same period, Lyotard frames this link between the avant-garde and sublimity in terms of the temporality of "the event" – a notion, derived from Martin Heidegger's concept of *Ereignis*, which describes the relationship between an emergent phenomenon and the thought that tries to think this phenomenon simply in its happening, rather than identifying it as a "what" that has happened. We experience modern, avant-garde art, Lyotard says, in the radical present of the event – a "*now* that is no more than *now*," as he puts it.[10] In this present of the event, the work of art absents itself from determinant or even determinable experience and "happens as a question mark 'before' happening as a question" (SAG 90). Thus, modern art "attempts combinations allowing the event" (SAG 101), in which allowing the event is tantamount to "bearing pictorial or otherwise expressive witness to the inexpressible" – tantamount, that is, to the sublime (SAG 93). Again, then, Lyotard shows the sine qua non of modern art to be the experience of sublimity.

By identifying the sublime as essential to artistic modernism in this way, Lyotard establishes a principle of distinction within modern aesthetics, a principle that enables him to answer his titular question: what is postmodernism? He argues that one must distinguish between a form of sublime modernism that places greater emphasis on the failure of the imagination and the absence of the absolute from presentation, and a form that privileges the becoming-unbounded of the imagination and its negative presentation of the absolute. There are, accordingly, two modes of avant-garde art: one that emphasizes the failure of presentation and evokes the unpresentable merely as a kind of missing content, while indulging in pleasurable, nostalgic forms through which to convey that absence (Lyotard invokes Marcel Proust here), and another that avails itself of the bewildering movement of negative presentation and relentlessly seeks out new and unfamiliar forms through which to evoke the unpresentable in its presence to form, and not merely its absence from content (Lyotard points to Joyce). The former Lyotard calls "aesthetic modernism," and the latter, "postmodernism" (AQ 81).

Postmodernism, then, is that form of modern, avant-garde aesthetics that deploys the sublime in full and that seeks out the irresolvability of the unpresentable for presentation in every corner of aesthetic activity. For Lyotard, postmodernism does not come after the end of modernism

---

[10] Jean-François Lyotard, "Le Sublime et l'Avant-garde," in *L'Inhumain: Causeries sur le temps* (Paris: Galilée, 1988); "The Sublime and the Avant-Garde," in *The Inhuman: Reflections on Time*, trans. Geoffrey Bennington and Rachel Bowlby (Cambridge: Polity Press, 1991), 90 (SAG).

but is that aspect within modernism that is always suspicious of what has come before, of what has been firmly established – even what has been firmly established by modernism itself. Thus, far from constituting the end or the successor of modernism, postmodernism is modernism "in the nascent state, and this state is constant" (AQ 79). In other words, postmodernism is the engine of permanent revolution within the modern; it is the modern impulse that harnesses the full power of the sublime in its attempt to break with reality. In this way, Lyotard rediscovers in postmodern art the violent and aporetic but affirmative movement of critical thought that he found in the *Analytic of the Sublime*: avant-garde postmodernism is the "spasm" that art undergoes as it runs up against its own limits and, in presenting nothing, negatively presents the idea of a reality absolutely different from our own.

GILLES DELEUZE

In the late 1970s and early 1980s, Deleuze developed an account of the sublime that diverged strongly from the strictly Kantian formulation given by Lyotard, while still retaining its transcendental framework.[11] In Deleuze's account, the experience of the sublime is no longer located in the conflict between the faculty of presentation and a present but unpresentable rational idea of the absolute. Rather, in an almost opposite fashion, the sublime testifies to the primacy of sensation itself, to the constant functioning of a kind of trans-sensible aesthetic rhythm that underlies all experience and that invests sensation with an immense power that exceeds and disrupts presentation. Deleuze thus takes up the sublime as a critical (in Kant's sense) anti-Kantian, finding in the resources of a transcendental philosophy of sublimity the means to account for an experience of sensation that short-circuits presentation and reveals a purely sensible encounter with forces and intensities.

Of the several works by Deleuze from the 1970s and 1980s dealing with the sublime, we will focus on two: a seminar he gave on Kant on March 28, 1978, at the University of Paris VIII[12] and *Francis Bacon: The Logic of Sensation* (1981).[13] The latter contains his most central and most focused treatment of the concept of the sublime from this period, even though the term "sublime" appears nowhere in the work (Daniel Smith uses it in his translator's introduction [FB xix–xxiii]). The Kant seminar, by contrast, contains an explicit although occasionally elliptical discussion of the concept of sublimity toward which Deleuze is working during this period. For

---

[11] Deleuze's interest in the sublime dates to the early 1960s, although his work from that period falls outside the purview of the current discussion. See Gilles Deleuze, *La Philosophie critique de Kant* (Paris: Presses Universitaires de France, 1963); *Kant's Critical Philosophy*, trans. Hugh Tomlinson and Barbara Habberjam (London: Athlone Press, 1984); Gilles Deleuze, "L'Idée de genèse dans l'esthétique de Kant," in *Revue d'esthétique* XVI, 2 (1963); "The Idea of Genesis in Kant's Esthetics," trans. Michael Taormina, in *Desert Islands and Other Texts*, ed. David Lapoujade (New York: Semiotext(e), 2002), 56–71; and Gilles Deleuze, *Différence et Répétition* (Paris: Presses Universitaires de France, 1968); *Difference and Repetition*, trans. Paul Patton (New York: Columbia University Press, 1994). For brief but helpful discussions of Deleuze's use of the sublime in these early works, see Paul Patton's introduction to *Deleuze: A Critical Reader* and Daniel W. Smith's "Deleuze's Theory of Sensation: Overcoming the Kantian Duality," in *Deleuze: A Critical Reader*, ed. Paul Patton (Malden, MA: Blackwell, 1996), 1–17 and 29–56.

[12] This seminar has not been officially published, but it is available online at http://www.webdeleuze.com/php/texte.php?cle=68&groupe=Kant&langue=2, trans. Melissa McMahon (accessed June 18, 2011) (CGD).

[13] Gilles Deleuze, *Francis Bacon: Logique de la sensation* (Paris: Éditions de la Différence, 1981), 2 vols.; *Francis Bacon: The Logic of Sensation*, trans. Daniel W. Smith (Minneapolis: University of Minnesota Press, 2003) (FB). For other examples of Deleuze's use of the concept of the sublime from this period, see Gilles Deleuze and Félix Guattari, *Mille Plateaux* (Paris: Éditions de Minuit, 1980); *A Thousand Plateaus*, trans. Brian Massumi (Minneapolis: University of Minnesota Press, 1987), 310–50; and Gilles Deleuze, *Cinéma 1: L'Image-mouvement* (Paris: Éditions de Minuit, 1983); *Cinema 1: The Movement-Image*, trans. Hugh Tomlinson and Barbara Habberjam (Minneapolis: University of Minnesota Press, 1986), 40–55.

this reason, we must begin from the seminar. By gleaning what we can from it and then turning back to *Francis Bacon*, we will gain a robust and complex picture of Deleuze's later thinking on the sublime.

In the seminar, Deleuze argues that to understand the experience of the sublime one must begin from Kant's discussion of the transcendental syntheses of perception in the first edition of the *Critique of Pure Reason*. There, Kant had identified three synthetic operations that are crucial for all experience: apprehension, reproduction, and recognition (CPR A98–111; see also B160–2). Together, these transcendental syntheses enable the subject to integrate and represent the sensible manifold so as to form a properly spatiotemporal object capable of being subsumed under concepts of the understanding and thereby of being cognized as experience. The first of these syntheses, apprehension, is carried out by the imagination as it unifies the successive parts that an intuition comprises, "determining the parts of a space and a time," as Deleuze expresses it (CGD). Beneath this synthesis, however, lies an even more fundamental operation: for apprehension to unify the parts of an intuition, a determination must first be made as to what constitutes a part in the first place – "something like a lived evaluation of a unit of measure" (CGD). Deleuze follows Kant in calling this spontaneous evaluation on which the synthesis of apprehension rests "aesthetic comprehension" (CJ 5:251–2). Because the content and the scale of our intuitions vary constantly, the unit of measure "chosen" by aesthetic comprehension must vary in kind:

When I see a tree, for example, ... I say that this tree must be as big as ten men.... I choose a kind of sensible unit to carry out my successive apprehension of parts. And then, behind the tree, there is a mountain, and I say ... it must be ten trees tall. And then I look at the sun and I wonder how many mountains it is. (CGD)

Deleuze characterizes the continuous and variable determination of this fundamental aesthetic measure as the "exploration" of a rhythm. Deleuze is clear that by "rhythm" he does not mean a regular, homogenous beat or meter but rather an essentially variable repetition or pulsation. Thus a constantly fluctuating sensible rhythm constitutes the foundation of all aesthetic comprehension and, transitively, all perceptual synthesis – a rhythm that we may call "trans-sensible," insofar as it traverses sensation in its entirety, allowing it to be synthesized by the imagination. Rhythm thus emerges as a fundamental condition of the possibility of all experience.

Deleuze assigns a source to this trans-sensible rhythm of aesthetic comprehension: it "comes out of chaos" (CGD). The nature of this chaos and the manner in which rhythm "comes out of" it are issues that Deleuze leaves unexplained in this seminar; they will become clearer in *Francis Bacon*. The important point to note here is that in the relationship between rhythm and chaos, Deleuze discovers the possibility of a "catastrophe": the catastrophe of rhythm's returning back to chaos, a catastrophe that is tantamount, for Deleuze, to the ignition of the sublime. In the experience of sublimity, Deleuze says, "I can no longer apprehend parts, I can no longer reproduce parts, I can no longer recognize something.... This is because my aesthetic comprehension is itself compromised, which is to say: instead of rhythm, I find myself in chaos" (CGD). On Deleuze's interpretation, then, the experience of the sublime consists in a disorientation or deranging of the syntheses through which the imagination presents sensation to thought. This disorientation is caused by a disruption of the aesthetic comprehension on which those syntheses rest, as it falls into a kind of chaotic arrhythmia, unable to find a unit of perceptual measure. Deleuze does not clarify in the seminar how this sublime disorientation comes about, but, again, this becomes clearer in *Francis Bacon*, to which we can now turn.

In *Francis Bacon*, Deleuze attempts to develop a "logic of sensation" by examining the work of the Irish painter Francis Bacon. Bacon is almost peerless in the history of art, Deleuze believes, because he paints sensation and the forces that give rise to it, rather than, like most painters, painting either objects that are supposed to represent things or abstractions that tend toward a kind of "cerebrality" (FB 46). Bacon achieves this painterly communication of sensation by painting images of figures, but without allowing them to become *figurative* – that is, without allowing them to tell stories or represent models.[14] Instead, the type of figure that appears in Bacon's painting – Deleuze calls it "the Figure" – functions as a kind of recording surface through which variations in sensation are transmitted. "The Figure is the sensible form related to a sensation" (FB 31), Deleuze says, "an 'accumulated' or 'coagulated' sensation" (FB 33). In order to produce the Figure, in order to make paint into the medium of sensation, Bacon becomes a rhythmicist, in precisely the sense of rhythm discussed previously: "This operation [of painting the Figure] is possible only if the sensation of a particular domain (here, the visual sensation) is in direct contact with a vital power that exceeds every domain and traverses them all. This power is Rhythm, which is more profound than vision, hearing, etc." (FB 37).

As we have seen already, there is a chaos churning just beneath rhythm, a chaos that rhythm both "comes out of" and, in the experience of the sublime, returns to. Here in *Francis Bacon*, Deleuze argues that the artist can only discover the rhythm of sensation by seeking this chaos, by finding "the point where rhythm itself plunges into chaos" (FB 39). It follows that the painter of the Figure – the painter who, as a rhythmicist, paints sensation itself and not merely its representation – must go through the experience of the sublime. Despite not invoking the concept of sublimity explicitly, Deleuze is here more forthcoming about the nature of the relationship between rhythm and chaos in the sublime than he was in the Kant seminar. To go to the point at which rhythm becomes chaos, Deleuze explains, is to go "beyond the organism," beyond the "paltry thing" that phenomenology calls the "lived body," and toward the "almost unlivable Power" contained in what he famously names the "body without organs" (FB 39). This concept of a body without organs designates the intensive reality of the sensing body, a body engulfed by a chaotic profusion of sensations at different levels and intensities. Lacking "that organization of organs we call an organism," this body contingently generates temporary and multifunctional "organs," or sites of reception, consumption, and expulsion, in response to the chaos that permeates it (FB 39). Near-constant sensory fluctuation and interminable polymorphousness fundamentally characterize this body. As Deleuze writes,

A wave with a variable amplitude flows through the body without organs; it traces zones and levels on this body according to the variations of its amplitude. When the wave encounters external forces at a particular level, a sensation appears. An organ will be determined by this encounter, but it is a provisional organ that endures only as long as the passage of the wave and the action of the force, and which will be displaced in order to be posited elsewhere. (FB 41)

The body without organs is activated in Bacon's work through what Deleuze calls "the diagram." This is a compositional element found in each of Bacon's canvases, which he uses to disrupt his conscious intentions for the painting and, with them, the possibility of conventional figuration. It consists in a localized zone of indeterminacy in the pictorial structure, an area of the composition that has been scrambled and deformed via a series of aleatory or uncontrolled marks – "a catastrophe," Deleuze says, echoing his Kant seminar (FB 83). The diagram intervenes in the representational order of the picture, vitiating the figurative qualities of figural form and engendering the Figure as a transmitter or modulator of pure sensation.

In these related discussions of the body without organs and the diagram, we discover the meaning, left unarticulated in the Kant seminar, of the relation between chaos and the rhythm that comes out of it. This rhythm is nothing other than the movement of interminable disorganization and reorganization performed by the body without organs as it reacts to the chaotic and

---

[14] Deleuze takes this notion of a nonfigurative figure from Lyotard. See Jean-François Lyotard, *Discours, figure* (Paris: Klincksieck, 1971); *Discourse, Figure*, trans. Antony Hudeck and Mary Lydon (Minneapolis: University of Minnesota Press, 2011).

manifold sensory stimuli it encounters in the forces exerted on it. "Chaos becomes rhythm," Deleuze says;[15] the latter is like a modification or mutation of the former, produced when the "perpetually and violently mixed" intensities of the body without organs are temporarily organized through the generation of transitory and protean organs (FB 39). Rhythm, then, is *chaos ordering itself* through the constant mutation of the body without organs. The deranging of this rhythm and ignition of the sublime are caused when certain disordered and disordering phenomena – violent, "catastrophic" phenomena that function, like the diagram in Bacon's paintings, to "break up the sovereign ... organization" of perception (FB 82) – produce sensations that are so confused, so intensely deformed, that they momentarily forestall any possibility of sensory organization in the body without organs, sending rhythm back into chaos and rendering aesthetic comprehension and perceptual synthesis inoperable. At the same time, such a violent disruption of perception is also "a germ of order or rhythm" – the order, in Bacon's paintings, of the Figure (FB 83): "A new figuration," Deleuze writes, "that of the Figure, should emerge from the diagram and make the sensation clear and precise" (FB 89). With this engendering of the Figure through the chaotic ordeal of the sublime, we rediscover the rhythm running through sensation, because, as we saw previously, this rhythm is fundamental to the figuration of the Figure. This means that what emerges from the experience of the Deleuzian sublime, what comes out of the passage through the chaos of the body without organs, is *rhythm itself*.

Initially, this may seem circular and rather uninteresting: the upshot of the experience of the sublime is nothing but the return of the very rhythm whose dysfunction initiated the process in the first place – as if the Deleuzian sublime amounted to no more than losing rhythm only to find it again. For Deleuze, however, the rediscovery of rhythm in the sublime is more complex than this. We lose rhythm and then find it again – but we find it in a new state, having undergone a transformation. In addition to making possible the cognition-supporting syntheses of apprehension, reproduction, and recognition, rhythm now makes possible the noncognitive figuration of the Figure, which was impossible before the adventure of the sublime; it now testifies to the presence and the power of the "non-organic life" of a body without organs that is "felt *under* the [organic] body," and whose transformations constitute rhythm itself (FB 43). This renewed rhythm thus shows itself to be of such a power as to organize, even if only in a provisional and temporary way, the chaos of the body without organs as it is deformed by and responds to the forces that affect it. Thus we discover in the experience of sublimity a more profound rhythm, one that we sense as such in its emergence from and harnessing of the chaos that seemed to sweep it away. With it, we also discover a more profound sensation: not sensation synthesized by the imagination, represented to the understanding, and placed in the service of the cognition of objects, but, beneath these processes, sensation as "encountered," as Smith puts it,[16] sensation as an immediate and uncognized response to forces registered on the body and impressed "directly onto the nervous system" (FB 32).

Thus, for Deleuze, as for Lyotard, the sublime is an aestheticization of the fundamental irresolvability in the relation between presentation and a domain that exceeds it. But whereas Lyotard takes this irresolvability to subsist in the relation of presentation to a supersensible idea, Deleuze locates it in the relation between presentation and a sensation whose violence and power to deform stymie the imagination's synthetic operations. Moreover, Lyotard and Deleuze conceive of the culmination of this irresolvability in the sublime quite differently. For Lyotard, the presence of the supersensible idea is felt in the movement of negative presentation, in the imagination's attaining a kind of negative infinitude as it is forced to its limit by reason. In the Deleuzian sublime, by contrast, there is no negative presentation; the failure of

---

[15] Deleuze and Guattari, *A Thousand Plateaus*, 313.
[16] Smith, "Deleuze's Theory of Sensation," 23. Smith's article contains an excellent account of the theory of sensation within which the Deleuzian sublime functions.

imagination does not make itself a sign of the trans-sensible rhythm of sensation. Rather, the failure of imagination makes possible the fully positive realization of this rhythm; it allows sensation to be felt as an immediate, unsynthesized, and wildly rhythmic force exerted on the body, capable of harnessing the power of chaos in the service, as Deleuze says, of "an increasingly powerful Figure of life" (FB 53).

JULIA KRISTEVA

Here and there in *Francis Bacon*, Deleuze characterizes Bacon's painting as "abject," at one point saying of it, "Abjection becomes splendor; the horror of life becomes a very pure and very intense life" (FB 45). This idea of abjection, which hovers at the edge of the Deleuzian sublime, becomes central in the work of Julia Kristeva, in which it colonizes and supplants the concept of sublimity. Kristeva is not an explicit theorist of the sublime, but she deserves inclusion here on the basis of *Powers of Horror* (1980),[17] in which her articulation of the concept of abjection reinterprets the Kantian sublime within a framework of Freudian and Lacanian psychoanalysis and structuralist semiotics. Accordingly, as we will see, each of the key components of the Kantian sublime is recast through the concept of abjection: the pleasure and pain felt simultaneously in sublimity become *jouissance* and revulsion in abjection; the idea of the absolute for which no presentation is available becomes the memory of an archaic psychic state that is strictly unpresentable in the mature subject's psyche; the negative presentation of the idea of the absolute becomes the affective eruption of a long-obliterated past; the evocative intuition of an object of immensity or overpowering force becomes an intuition of an object of filth or disgust; and the power of the faculty of reason becomes the ambivalent, explosive power of the immediate, the nonsymbolic, the prerational, and the maternal as they appear within language. In short, Kristeva, in an almost point-by-point fashion, inverts and undermines the Kantian sublime, transmuting its difficult exaltation of the rational into a shameful and disgusted joy in the revolting, all the while retaining much of the Kantian sublime's dynamic structure.

Like the sublime, the experience of abjection is one most people have felt. It is embodied – literally – in an overwhelming sense of revulsion in the squalid or horrific presence of such intolerable things as filth, excrement, vomit, blood, contamination, decay, or, what Kristeva identifies as the epitome of the abject, a corpse. In addition to disgust, however, the experience of the abject includes an illicit pleasure or joy, which Kristeva associates with Jacques Lacan's notion of *jouissance* – an excessive, transgressive pleasure that one experiences as a kind of suffering. A central task of *Powers of Horror* is to explain the mechanism behind this deeply unsettling affect, thereby explaining, on Kristeva's view, the origin of subjectivity.

Kristeva's account of the genesis of abjection contains two interrelated moments: one diachronic, exploring the evolution of the abject emotion in the psychic development of the child, and the other synchronic, examining the psychic structures through which abject affects manifest in the consciousness and language of fully formed, mature subjects. Beginning with the diachronic, Kristeva hypothesizes that prior to what Lacan terms the "mirror stage" of psychosexual development – roughly, the stage at which a child recognizes her own reflection in the mirror as such – the infant inhabits a psychic space utterly unlike anything experienced by the mature subject. In this state, the infant, under the full sway of biological-psychic drives, has yet to distinguish between subject and object. The infant thus experiences itself as undifferentiated from those things nearest to it and, in particular, from its mother, who is the most intimate and involved element of its world. Borrowing from Plato's *Timaeus*, Kristeva calls this state *chora*.

---

[17] Julia Kristeva, *Pouvoirs de l'horreur* (Paris: Éditions du Seuil, 1980); *Powers of Horror: An Essay on Abjection*, trans. Leon S. Roudiez (New York: Columbia University Press, 1982) (PH).

The infant, of course, does not remain in this state for long; the drives affecting it begin almost immediately to orient its developing psyche in such a way that it soon separates itself from its environment, thereby taking the first, crucial step toward the formation of an ego. This elementary process of separation is carried out through the mechanism of abjection – that is, through a casting-off of the other as "radically excluded" (PH 2) – and the first thing abjected is the thing closest to the infant: the body of the mother. "The abject confronts us," Kristeva writes, "... with our earliest attempts to release the hold of *maternal* entity even before ex-isting outside of her" (PH 13). With this abjection of the maternal, an inchoate subject begins to emerge, but it is as yet lacking the well-defined, or at least definable, objects necessary for its full and proper functioning as a subject; at this point it has only the archaic mother, which, as abjected, is not a proper object. The infant begins to obtain objects, thereby finally developing into a full subject, only when it acquires the symbolic and linguistic resources of human culture, which Kristeva, following Lacan, relates to the figures of the father and the law.

Importantly, this transition to subjecthood does not result in the abject's being relegated to an archaic and elementary mechanism buried under the symbolic order's proliferation of subjects, objects, and their signs. Quite to the contrary, the subject's immersion in the symbolic order is founded on and *structured by* the abject; the subject ensures its existence as such only by violently casting away everything that might blur the boundary between it and its objects, that might transgress the codes and injunctions of symbolic exchange, thereby threatening the coherence and stability of its ego. In this way, the "archaic economy [of the abjected *chora*-state] is brought into full light of day, signified, verbalized. Its strategies (rejecting, separating, repeating/abjecting) hence find a symbolic existence, and the very logic of the symbolic – arguments, demonstrations, proofs, etc. – must conform to it" (PH 15). Moreover, it is only now, when the consolidation of the subject and its symbolic installation are accomplished, that the abject begins to appear as such, as repulsive and loathsome. As the subject develops and becomes more fully integrated into the symbolic order, encountering new threats to its stability and integrity, the ranks of the abject swell beyond the abjected maternal to encompass those materials mentioned earlier: inter alia filth, decay, and death.

At this point, we arrive at the synchronic account of the abject, its outlines clearly visible and bearing a striking resemblance to the Kantian sublime as interpreted by Lyotard. Through the representational resources of the symbolic order, those things we call abject affectively testify to – or negatively present – the inexorable presence and power of a memory that lies beyond that order and is rigorously unpresentable. The content of this memory, which conditions every experience of the subject, lies at the limit of thought, where thought shades into "spasmodic" affect. Thus we find in the synchronic concept of the abject something of the transcendental notion of limit origins discussed by both Lyotard and Deleuze: just as the sublime shows us the condition for the possibility of critical thought in the supersensible or the origin of rhythm in chaos, the abject "takes the ego back to its source on the abominable limits from which, in order to be, the ego has broken away – it assigns it a source in the non-ego, drive, and death" (PH 15). Like the sublime, moreover, in which something alien to the order of imaginative presentation intrudes on and disrupts the functioning of that order, the appearance of the abject "shatters the wall of representation and its judgments," despite the fact that its occurrence is possible only through the representative structures of the symbolic (PH 15). The experience of this process of negative presentation generates the simultaneous feelings of pain and pleasure characteristic of abjection. The symbolically ordered psyche's structural and necessary inadequacy to the appearance of the unpresentable memory evoked by the abject engenders a feeling of revulsion in the subject, an overwhelming emotion of disgust and terror. At the same time, this negatively sensed memory is discovered to possess an unexpected power: it offers the possibility of a form of expression that momentarily transgresses the narrow strictures of the symbolic, resulting in the frenzied pleasure of *jouissance*.

Despite these substantial similarities between the sublime and the abject, however, the nature of the unpresentable in the latter could not be more different from that belonging to the former. Rather than the exalted rational idea of the absolute, or even the unprecedented power of the rhythm of the trans-sensible, in the abject we encounter the discomfiting but undeniable trace of a form of organic existence in the subject's prehistory, long ago overwritten and prohibited. The abject thus testifies not to the power of a living or renovated capacity, as in the sublime, but to the inexorable return of a long-forgotten event.

Insofar as the entry of the infant into the symbolic order constitutes the moment when abjection becomes the foundation for social and psychic organization, language, as the fundamental expression of the symbolic, has a special place in the analysis of abjection. Accordingly, Kristeva finds in the language of what she calls the "speaking subject" a host of abject traces, for example, Freud's "parapraxes," jokes, obscenities, and laughter. For Kristeva, it follows that literature is one of the privileged artistic forms for the expression of the abject. In particular, she sees in modernist literature an especially strong gravitation toward the experience of abjection. Referring to the increasing disappearance of religious authority in modern Western societies (whose relation to abjection she spends a good bit of the book exploring), Kristeva writes:

In a world in which the Other has collapsed, the aesthetic task – a descent into the foundations of the symbolic construct – amounts to retracing the fragile limits of the speaking being, closest to its dawn, to the bottomless "primacy" constituted by primal repression. Through that experience, ... "subject" and "object" push each other away, confront each other, collapse, and start again – inseparable, contaminated, condemned, at the boundary of what is assimilable, thinkable; abject. Great modern literature unfolds over that terrain: Dostoyevsky, Lautréamont, Proust, Artaud, Kafka, Céline. (PH 18)

Like the sublime of Lyotard and Deleuze, then, Kristeva's abject finds a special expression in modern art. Whereas Lyotard and Deleuze, however, see the sublime in modern art to possess an almost unequivocally affirmative power, Kristeva finds in the modern literary use of the abject a more ambivalent, pessimistic, and menacing gift: not the joy of a "very intense life" but the *jouissance* of an eminently fragile and blasted existence, "a ridiculous little infinite," as Kristeva writes, quoting the French author Louis-Ferdinand Céline (PH 134). Through its language, prosody, and style, the literature of abjection gives us the power – the power, as her title suggests, of horror – to laugh in the face of what disgusts and terrifies us – "a piercing laughter" (PH 133), "the laughter of the apocalypse" (PH 204). But this laughter overcomes nothing, neither the strictures of symbolic discourse (it only points, flashingly and transgressively, to their instability) nor the frailty of the human animal (it only remarks its absurdity). Thus Kristeva's abject, a perversion of the sublime, places the subject starkly before the fragility of the organism – the "paltry thing" that Deleuze's trans-sensible rhythm seeks to surpass – laughing, almost deliriously joyful, but without hope of transcendence, "bare, anguished, and as fascinated as it is frightened" (PH 206).

FREDRIC JAMESON

We conclude our treatment of the postmodern sublime with Fredric Jameson, whose approach to the issue is very different from that of Lyotard, Deleuze, or Kristeva. Unlike them, Jameson is not so much a postmodern theorist of the sublime as a critic of postmodernism and the aesthetic of sublimity it has engendered – an aesthetic that, in his view, is little more than a symptom of the postmodern inability to marshal a critique of what he calls "late capitalism." He does not put forward his own conceptualization of the sublime but deploys the concept, ready-made, in his analysis of postmodernism. Nonetheless, his conception of the sublime, as articulated in his influential essay "Postmodernism, or the Cultural Logic of Late Capitalism,"[18] shares with

---

[18] Fredric Jameson, "The Cultural Logic of Late Capitalism," in *Postmodernism, or the Cultural Logic of Late Capitalism* (Durham: Duke University Press, 1991) (PCL).

those of our other three thinkers a foregrounding, à la Kant, of an irresolvable but forced heterogeneity between the capacity of presentation and a set of unpresentable objects – in this case, the networks and flows of advanced capitalism.

For Jameson, postmodernism is not a component of modernism, as it is for Lyotard. Rather, Jameson understands postmodernism as a radically new development in the cultural history of the West, a general trend in culture that manifests itself in a number of diverse ways, but that can be traced in every instance to the transformations undergone by capitalism in the second half of the twentieth century. "What has happened," he writes, "is that aesthetic production today has become integrated into commodity production generally" (PCL 4). As a result, the long-standing and fundamentally modern distinction between "high" cultural forms and commercial production has disappeared, effaced by capitalism's demand for ever-new commodities. This postmodern mutation of culture, moreover, "does more than merely replicate the logic of late capitalism; it reinforces and intensifies it" (PCL 46). This is because, Jameson argues, the expropriation of cultural production by commodity capitalism and the concomitant disappearance of the autonomy of the cultural sphere lead to the foreclosure of all "critical distance" from which to mount any sort of critique (in the Marxist sense of a "critical theory"): "Distance in general (including 'critical distance' in particular) has very precisely been abolished in the new space of postmodernism" (PCL 48). The result for culture is the entire symptomatology of the postmodern: "A new depthlessness … ; a consequent weakening of historicity … ; a whole new type of emotional ground tone … which can best be grasped by a return to older theories of the sublime" (PCL 6).

Why this return to the sublime? Jameson argues that in response to the "depthless," "simulacral" aesthetics of the postmodern, we come increasingly to experience the world in such a way that it "momentarily loses its depth and threatens to become a glossy skin," an experience in which we suffer a kind of mixed emotion of exhilaration and terror (PCL 34). This experience of a "camp or 'hysterical' sublime" often explicitly evokes, Jameson claims, the unpresentable complexity of contemporary technologies – technologies, he observes, that have more to do with reproduction, representation, communication, and computation than with traditional production. Beneath this preoccupation with technology, however, lies a more fundamental concern: the "whole new decentered global network of … capital itself" (PCL 38). Thus the postmodern resurrection of the aesthetics of the sublime is ultimately an attempt to represent, in a displaced or disguised way, the properly unimaginable complexity of advanced, multinational capitalism. In fact, Jameson sees the postmodern sublime as the figure in which "this whole extraordinarily demoralizing and depressing original new global space … has become most explicit, has moved the closest to the surface of consciousness, as a coherent new type of space in its own right" (PCL 49). The postmodern sublime, in other words, is the most acute symptom of late capitalism's thorough saturation of culture and concomitant vitiation of critical distance from which forms of resistance may originate.[19]

Yet for all the "demoralizing and depressing" conclusions he draws, Jameson does not believe that late capitalism and the rise of postmodern culture exclude the possibility of any politically interventionary aesthetics. Specifically, he holds out the promise of an aesthetics of "cognitive mapping" as a form of "pedagogical political culture" strong enough to counter the disorienting and disempowering effects of postmodernism. This "new political art," he says, "will have to hold to the truth of postmodernism, that is, … the world space of multinational capital … at the same time at which it achieves a breakthrough to some as yet unimaginable new mode of representing this last" (PCL 54). Because, however, the "world space of multinational capital"

---

[19] For a more recent and thoroughgoing critique of the theories of the postmodern sublime, see Jacques Rancière, *Le Destin des images* (Paris: La Fabrique, 2003); *The Future of the Image*, trans. Gregory Elliott (New York: Verso, 2007), esp. chap. 5, "Are Some Things Unrepresentable?" 109–38.

is, as Jameson says, an "impossible totality ... only dimly perceivable" (PCL 38) – an "unrepresentable" but not unknowable "global world system" (PCL 53) – the aesthetic practice through which that space is conceptually mapped will have to participate in the very attempt to present the unpresentable that characterizes the postmodern sublime as conceptualized by Lyotard. Thus, despite Jameson's dissatisfaction with postmodern artistic expressions of the aesthetic of sublimity, he presupposes as the exigent task of aesthetics today precisely the same function of the sublime proposed, in one way or another, by the theorists of the "postmodern sublime" considered here: the evocation through presentational means of an "object" that is inherently and irresolvably heterogeneous to the order of presentation.

PART TWO

DISCIPLINARY AND OTHER PERSPECTIVES

9

The "Subtler" Sublime in Modern Dutch Aesthetics

John R. J. Eyck

INTRODUCTION

In *Observations on the Beautiful and the Sublime* (1764), Kant comments disparagingly on the taste of the Dutch nation. "Among the types of people of our part of the world," he writes, "in my opinion the Italians and the French are those who distinguish themselves most from all the rest by the feeling for the beautiful, but the Germans, English, and Spanish by the feeling for the sublime. Holland can be considered as the land where this finer taste becomes rather unnoticeable."[1] Given the worldwide renown Dutch art enjoys today, this judgment from the sage of Königsberg rings hollow to contemporary ears. In that respect, ironically enough, a current English edition of the *Observations* bears an image by the seventeenth-century Dutch Gouden Eeuw (Golden Age) artist Aelbert Cuyp, a painter known primarily for his portraits of cows.[2] Whether Kant would have appreciated such barnyard pastorals, his observation on the lack of "finer taste" in Holland raises an interesting question regarding what the Dutch themselves considered sublime. Namely, with regard to the more prevalent (French, English, or German) definitions of the concept found in the present collection, how might developments in Dutch aesthetics cast a different light on the sublime in the face of those more dominant artistic or cultural developments?

This question regarding what we might call the "Dutch sublime" has only recently been taken up by scholars, and even then almost exclusively by literary historians in the Low Countries. Among these studies, the research undertaken by Christophe Madelein stands out. In his dissertation, "Juichen in den adel der menschlijke natuur: Het verhevene in de Nederlanden (1770–1830)" ("Jubilance in the Nobility of Human Nature: The Sublime in the Low Countries [1770–1830]"), Madelein pursues philosophical debates over the concept of the sublime written in Dutch and framed within the classic contexts of Longinus, Boileau, Burke, Kant, and Schiller.[3] According to Madelein, between 1770 and 1830 these contributions consisted, first,

---

[1] *Beobachtungen über das Gefühl des Schönen und Erhabenen*, in *Kant's gesammelte Schriften*, Königlichen Preussischen (later Deutschen) Akademie der Wissenschaften, 29 vols. (Berlin: Reimer [later de Gruyter], 1900–) (KGS), 20:243. References are to pagination of the Akademie edition. All translations from the German and Dutch are my own.

[2] Immanuel Kant, *Observations on the Feeling of the Beautiful and Sublime*, trans. John T. Goldthwait, 2nd ed. (Berkeley: University of California Press, 2003 [1969]). The painting reproduced is not of a cow, but Cuyp's more genteel *Lady and Gentleman on Horseback* (c. 1660), from the National Gallery of Art, Washington, DC.

[3] Christophe Madelein, "Juichen in den adel der menschlijke natuur: Het verhevene in de Nederlanden (1770–1830)," PhD dissertation, Vakgroep Nederlandse literatuur, University of Ghent, 2008. More generally, Madelein's investigations have led to the trade publication of three largely ignored texts: P. van Hemert's *De Redevoering over het verhevene* (1804), Willem Bilderdijk's *Gedachten over het verhevene* (1821), and Johannes Kinker's *Iets over het schoone* (1823). See Christophe Madelein and Jürgen Pieters, eds., *Bilderdijk, Kinker & Van Hemert: Als van hooger bestemming en aart* (Groningen: Historische Uitgeverij, 2008).

of translations into Dutch from German and English (of Mendelssohn, Riedel, Beattie, and Blair); second, in subsequent attempts at popularizing Kant's philosophy in the Netherlands (by P. van Hemert, T. van Swinderen, and J. F. L. Schröder); and, finally, in specific treatments of the beautiful and the sublime (by Johannes Kinker and Willem Bilderdijk). Given their limited domestic influence, Madelein's argument maintains that our full comprehension of these Dutch contributions "must be based on a comparison with the contemporary conceptions of the sublime in the wider European context."[4] Madelein's otherwise plausible thesis presumes improbably, however, that the early translations from English and German, although carried out well before Kant's influential *Critique of the Power of Judgment* (1790), themselves brought nothing new to Dutch intellectual interaction with their originals; that original Dutch thought on the place of the sublime in art came primarily after Kant; and that Dutch classicists before 1770 essentially made little or no contribution to the European discussion in Western aesthetics continuing since Longinus.

Although I appreciate the scholarly dividends derived from Madelein's recovery of otherwise obscure works, in this chapter I propose to investigate the Dutch sublime against the background of Kant's statement in his *Observations*, with the express aim of revealing how the Dutch themselves understood and developed the concept. My discussion is organized in terms of three questions, which characterize the philosophical tenor of three time periods – the late seventeenth and early eighteenth century, the latter part of the eighteenth century, and the early nineteenth century – and correspond to three generations of Dutch thought. First, given the strong, even dominating, influence of Dutch classical scholars on seventeenth-century Europe, is there a decipherable notion of the sublime evident in the Dutch approach to the arts? Second, to what degree can the homegrown eighteenth-century tradition of aesthetics in the Netherlands be understood as a reaction to Kant and his influence? Third, and finally, how did Dutch intellectuals develop their own response to their continental colleagues in the early nineteenth century, when nearly all had become Kantians of one stripe or another after the appearance of Kant's mature critical aesthetics in the *Critique of the Power of Judgment*?

In order to answer these questions, I consider the writings of three exemplary Dutch authors, each of which represents the eras and generations adumbrated previously. I turn first to the work of Balthazar Huydecoper (1695–1778), whose programmatic *Proeve van Taal- en Dichtkunde* (*Essay on Language and Poetry*, 1730) set the literary-theoretical tone for subsequent generations, and whose work for and about the stage protracted the "high" heroic tragedy of Neoclassicism. I turn next to *Het Ideaal in de kunst* (*The Ideal in Art*, completed 1821) by Rhijnvis Feith (1753–1824), who emphasizes both a moral and a creative role for genius if art is to achieve beauty and sublimity. Finally, taking this idea of a moral position further, I consider *Gesprek op den Drachenfels* (*Talk atop the Drachenfels*, 1835), in which Jacob Geel (1789–1862) subjects the sublime of post-Kantian classicist and Romantic thinkers alike to a Socratic investigation that finds them both wanting.

There are indeed other Dutch works that might be considered, as Madelein has shown; however, the ones under current consideration share the feature of encompassing a much larger circle for the arts in the Netherlands. These three works entered the critical canon well before the contemporaneous works recovered more recently – those cited previously by Kinker and Bilderdijk, for example – but all three are connected by a dedication to Dutch aesthetic endeavors. As the following examination of their writings shows, Huydecoper, Feith, and Geel were both aesthetic theorists and practitioners, all offering a vision of the sublime that proves, however paradoxically, to be both lofty and grounded: what I shall refer to as the "subtler" sublime in the Low Countries.

---

[4] "Kant in de fout? Het verhevene in de Nederlanden," *De Achttiende Eeuw* 39, 1 (2007), 77–93, p. 77.

BALTHAZAR HUYDECOPER (1695–1778): HONORING THE (NEW) DUTCH "ANCIENTS"

It is difficult to overestimate the influence of Balthazar Huydecoper on how the Dutch thought about art and artistic endeavors. By the end of his century, he had long been a household name for Dutch writers and artists, and the popularity of his Neoclassical plays extended well into the 1800s, as did praise for his poetry and prose, which he composed in both Latin and Dutch. Huydecoper was required reading for any would-be literator, and subscribers to the second edition of his four-volume *Proeve van Taal- en Dichtkunde*[5] (*Essay on Language and Poetry*) ran into the hundreds (small by current international standards but a major publication in the Netherlands, even to this day) and included then-celebrated names like Van Hemert, Bilderdijk, and Feith (who alone ordered four copies). Balthazar Huydecoper was born into a long-established family of the Amsterdam patriciate and enjoyed an upbringing befitting his regent class, beginning with a classical education at Amsterdam's Latin academy and completing his studies with a degree in law at Utrecht University.[6] On graduating he returned to Amsterdam and held a series of civic appointments; among them was a position on the board of regents overseeing the municipal theater in 1723. For nearly a decade, Huydecoper was intimately involved in that capacity with theatrical production and practice, eventually taking up residence next door to the Schouwburg, Amsterdam's leading theater.

Such training points out a principal, even distinct, feature of Dutch society in Huydecoper's era: the pervasive nature of classicism in the Low Countries, familiarity with which was de rigueur for anyone, burghers included, who wanted to be thought well educated; indeed, the general assumption was that ancient authors were indispensable for becoming a civilized Dutchman. To appreciate the dominance of this brand of Dutch learning, one need only note the preeminence of Leiden University, established in 1575 by William the Silent during the Dutch revolt from Spain (1568–1648), after which it attracted liberal-minded scholars from across the continent through to the early eighteenth century. The influence of antiquity extended to other areas of social and cultural life, including individual adoption of Latinized Dutch names and taste in literature – until the mid-1600s, neo-Latin texts accounted for half of all Dutch publications.

Coming only a few generations after that *aurea aetas*, Huydecoper and his peers were steeped in this tradition; this was manifest throughout his works and in his view of the sublime, albeit with a notable twist. Huydecoper's work for the theater, in particular, attests to the turn he gave to the wisdom of the ancients, taking the classicist model from the French and expanding it further for Dutch dramatists. Although fully conversant in antiquity's artistic tenets, he drew on his own experience to conceptualize an art form different from its neighboring continental interlocutors. Ultimately, he made an aesthetic choice for his "high" tragedy, which runs closer to Longinus than Aristotle in what it regards as elevated or sublime.

Huydecoper's modern engagement with the ancients is exemplified in *Essay on Language and Poetry*, which was begun in the period when he worked for the theater and published finally in 1730. The *Essay* stands as a foundational text of Dutch linguistics, prescribing a grammar for language use, which has since been regarded by some as despotic.[7] Its philological concerns notwithstanding,

---

[5] Balthazar Huydecoper, *Proeve van taal- en dichtkunde, in vrijmoedige aanmerkingen op Vondels vertaalde Herscheppingen van Ovidius* (*Essay on Language and Poetry* ...), ed. Frans van Lelyveld and Nicolaas Hinlópen, 2nd ed. (Leiden: A. en J. Honkoop, 1782–1794) (*Proeve*). For the full list of subscribers to the work, see pp. vii–xvi.

[6] For fuller biographical information on Huydecoper, Feith, and Geel, see A. J. van der Aa, *Biographisch woordenboek der Nederlanden* (Haarlem: J. J. van Brederode, 1852–1878); G. J. van Bork and P. J. Verkruijsse, eds., *De Nederlandse en Vlaamse auteurs van middeleeuwen tot heden* (Weesp: De Haan, 1985); and G. Kalff, *Geschiedenis der Nederlandsche letterkunde*, 7 vols. (Groningen: J. B. Wolters, 1906–1912).

[7] This view originated in R. A. Kollewijn, "Een taaldespoot uit de pruiketijd," *Taal en Letteren* 16 (1906), 1–29. For a dissenting view, see R. J. G. de Bonth, *De Aristarch van 't Y: De "grammatica" uit Balthazar Huydecopers Proeve van Taal- en Dichtkunde (1730)* (Maastricht: Shaker, 1998).

the work is equally concerned with a poetics arising from Huydecoper's expertise in classics. Even the frontispiece engraving in the posthumous edition from 1782 instructs its audience: the image depicts a shining classical monument to the author, placed under an oak tree; personifications of the liberal arts are shown giving homage to the author, and lying before them are works by literary luminaries of previous centuries, taken from a vault in near ruin behind them, which bears the inscription "Thesaurus Antiquitatum Teutonicarum" (Treasury of Teutonic Antiquity). The image leaves little doubt as to the author's intention of putting new Dutch works on par with the ancients, and with their own Dutch "ancients" as well: as a classicist, that is, Huydecoper sought to trace a line of aesthetic authority and in the process compile a compendium of sources both old and new for the modern Dutch practitioners who would excel in the arts.

To achieve this effect, Huydecoper took as exemplary the versifications of arguably the greatest playwright from the Dutch Golden Age, Joost van den Vondel (1587–1679). Huydecoper annotated Vondel's 1671 translation of Ovid's *Metamorphoses* with a commentary that allowed him to enter into dialogue with his Golden Age forebears and their desire to equal, if not surpass, the ancients. In the main, Huydecoper criticizes Vondel for both his misuse and overuse of Latinate constructions and devices, which he finds generally unsuitable for a modern Dutch nation. Reflecting his training in the mores of Dutch scholarship, Huydecoper compares the language of Vondel's verse with other wordsmiths. Accordingly, as he embarks on his scrutiny of Vondel, Huydecoper covers more than fifteen pages and includes easily more than a hundred citations in the examination of only two turns of phrase; this effluence was possible thanks to continuous investigations into such topics as well as previous, personal insights gained from searching for such lineages: "Although formerly we had other thoughts [on the matter], instead we finally have been taught by experience, that not only the dead languages, like Greek and Latin, but also the living ones, like our Dutch, need to be clarified through examples of eminent Authors, whether they are New or Old" (*Proeve* xxix). The "experience" is no doubt an allusion, in part, to Huydecoper's own day-to-day dealings with theatrical practices at the time. The inclusion of rather low-brow farces (*kluchten*) amid the more high-brow tragedies of his day likely instigated initial investigations into medieval Dutch writing, from which the more popular comic sketches demanded by contemporary audiences had derived. After coming into possession of or developing access to these oldest extant manuscripts in Dutch – which, after ending his work for the Schouwburgh, he continued to analyze, annotate, and index – Huydecoper acquired a unique erudition in, and an almost singular appreciation for, medieval Dutch writing. In consequence, Huydecoper encouraged modern practitioners to look as much to earliest authors in Dutch literature as they would to the classics. By including such extensive references in his *Essay* to ancient and modern Dutch authors in addition to the classics, Huydecoper departed definitively from any codifying conventions esteemed by his European peers, such as the classical criteria praised by Boileau in his *L'Art poëtique* (1674).

Indeed, despite the fact that his European predecessors were quite taken with the classical delineation for the sublime – besides Boileau, his international references included, for example, Philip Sidney's *Apologie for Poetrie* (1595) – Huydecoper avoided prescribing the concept outright for would-be artists in the Low Countries. The classical source for conceiving of a modern notion of the sublime, Longinus, merits but one mention in Huydecoper's *Essay*. Yet this citation comes at a telling moment, namely, when Huydecoper again invokes his aesthetic imperative that Dutch poets even in adhering to the writerly conventions of antiquity nevertheless retain the character of their language. In his treatise's anthology of authoritative annotations, Huydecoper cites a response to Karel van Mander (1548–1606), who had translated Virgil's eclogues and georgics (1597), given by Van Mander's critical coeval Cornelis Taemssoon (1567–1600).[8] Referring to Van Mander's efforts toward classical cultural transfer, Taemssoon

---

[8] Karel Van Mander's *Schilder-Boeck* (1604) on classical, Italian, and Dutch artists made him one of the first Dutch art theoreticians and historians. He translated Virgil's verses as *Ossen-stal en Landt-werck* (*Oxen-Stall and*

declaims, "Yet once this mania has quit them, / And the Dutchman again becomes a Dutchman, / Then a flood of honor shall pour upon you Netherlands" (*Proeve* 166). Huydecoper continues with his own commentary, remarking:

This expression [of Taemssoon] has something sublime about it, and the Greek writer, whose work on the Sublimity of Style we still possess, namely, LONGINUS, shows that he too understood his material, when, speaking of HOMER – who in his old age had not as much fire and power as before – Longinus expresses himself in this way: For although there is senescence in Homer, it is still the senescence of Homer. (*Proeve* 167)

Analogously, given the connections made here, Huydecoper maintains that, even if Dutch authors seldom manifest the fury and force of their classical predecessors, their strengths are nevertheless Dutch, and they ought to foster them.

Longinus's treatise, intended as a vade mecum for public servants who would ascend to higher office, stressed the significant position of the sublime in rhetorical practice as a superior style that could be achieved through technique, assuming one possessed the requisite degree of innate ability. It is on this discursive or textual level that Boileau, who translated Longinus into French in 1674, sees the sublime inspiring awe in an audience, and, in a similar sense, this is also the point Huydecoper makes as an adapter of Boileau's classicism for the Netherlands. Indeed, Huydecoper makes clear that "poetry is truly a sublime art. Where it is handled properly, it proclaims praise for the Creator, or instructs creation in innumerable ways" (*Proeve* xxxiv). As Huydecoper further states in the foreword to the *Essay* – although in a much more homegrown manner – the work aims to inspire all writers to aspire to such heights of creativity:

What else is there to be done than to weed our common garden together, to make our special gifts one, by conveying them to each other mutually again and again? Only doing this will we be in a position, with combined strengths, to bring Art a step closer to Perfection, which always escapes us, yet striving for which is always laudable, however impossible it is for us to achieve the same. (*Proeve* xxxvii)

Although Huydecoper's work is now seen as being primarily of linguistic interest, it also represents two major achievements: it envisioned the same practice for the sublime as Longinus and set a precedent for establishing and esteeming a domestic Dutch aesthetics.

It is worth noting how Huydecoper further distilled his classicist program for the general public with the prefaces he furnished for his plays, as in the comprehensive foreword to his tragedy *Arzases* (first published 1722).[9] In reworking an obscure reference from ancient history, he departs from perceived French classicist strictures, a move he defends in the preface to the work and the authority for which he finds in antiquity. On the topic of verisimilitude, for example, he notes Aristotle's support for Agatho's proposition, "namely, *that it is probable that many things happen contrary to probability*" (*Arzases* 4 [facing]). In the play, Huydecoper's Parthian hero, Arzases, places his uncle Varanes within his privy council, even though Varanes had previously usurped his nephew's rightful claim to the crown. Although contravening neo-Aristotelian rules of tragedy, Huydecoper pleads his position by claiming his particular understanding of Aristotle: "In this [character] Varanes, my intention was to put to the test whether I had understood the meaning of Aristotle sufficiently, so as to bring powerfully enough to the stage the terror and compassion just as these are required by him in a well-regulated Tragedy" (*Arzases* 4 [facing]). To excuse his nonconformity to dramatic unities in *Arzases*, moreover, Huydecoper notes the current fashion among Dutch audiences, familiar to him

---

Country-Work). In the *Schilder-Boeck* he included a dedicatory poem to Taemssoon, praising him for his efforts to compose elevated poetry in the vernacular, i.e., in Dutch rather than Latin.
[9] Citations here from Balthazar Huydecoper, *Arsazes, of 't edelmoedig verraad*, 3rd ed. (Amsterdam: Izaak Duim, 1743).

both through successful staging of his own compositions and through his administrative role at the municipal theater:

> I know well that this [design] will not be accounted to me as a fault, since no one finds any offensiveness in it any longer, being accustomed to such even in the finest French pieces. Just the same, I have tried to improve it inasmuch as feasible, and to give it an appearance, which can make such a thing more acceptable. (*Arzases* 7 [unnumbered in text])

That is, Huydecoper takes both the letter and the spirit of French classicism to heart, thereby recognizing the character of Dutch thought for its language and its impact on Dutch writing. Huydecoper thus intends to formalize Dutch writing practice to match – if not best, then certainly not imitate – the ancients. He not only integrates but also increases the scope of Dutch classical scholarship by applying that schooling to contemporary artistic practice. In this way he breaks new ground for the modern Dutch aesthetic that would develop over the next one hundred years.

RHIJNVIS FEITH (1753–1824): FINDING A "NEW TESTAMENT" FOR ANTIQUITY

Despite its contemporaneity with Kant, Rhijnvis Feith's *Het Ideaal in de kunst* (*The Ideal in Art*)[10] reveals the degree to which self-directed Dutch aesthetic thought since Huydecoper had become thoroughly domesticated. It also represents a further stage in the development of an independent Dutch response in dealing with the sublime. The essay epitomizes Feith's ideas on art and artistic creativity, acquired over a lifetime of observation and practice. Feith was involved in a number of learned and literary societies since his student days at Leiden, where he studied law, and he first achieved continental fame with his sentimental epistolary novel *Julia* (1783), which was translated into French, German, and Russian. Success, however, brought with it a degree of infamy, as domestic Dutch critics satirized his efforts to bring Dutch literature into the European mainstream to a greater degree. His remaining days, moreover, saw his literary practice divided by the demands of public office he held in his hometown of Zwolle. Retiring finally to the peace and quiet of his country estate, Boschwijk, one of his last accomplishments involved translating psalms for inclusion in the Dutch Reformed psalter (many of which are still in use today).

By then, Feith had expounded his accumulated views in a number of treatises composed for both artistic and scholarly societies, on the one hand, and for a wider reading public, on the other. He frequently participated in poetry and essay contests and won gold medallions with submissions such as *Heil van den Vrede* (*The Salvation of Peace*, 1779) and *Verhandeling over het Heldendicht* (*Treatise on the Epic*, 1781), and he addressed similar topics to the general public with his six-volume *Brieven over verscheide onderwerpen* (*Letters on Divers Subjects*, 1784–1793) and (with J. Kantelaar) the three-part *Bijdragen ter bevordering der schoone kunsten en wetenschappen* (*Contributions for the Promotion of Fine Arts and Sciences*, 1793–1796).

Feith's essay *The Ideal in Art* intersects both these audiences as a medium intended to inform and instruct his fellow countrymen in general. The work itself was written in 1821 in response to a competition sponsored by the Hollandsche Maatschappij van fraaije Kunsten en Wetenschappen (Holland Society of Fine Arts and Sciences) on the question, as Feith phrased it, "What do we understand by Ideal in the realm of the Arts, and to what degree must the practitioner of the same be directed by it?" (*Ideaal* 73). As P. J. Buijnsters has shown in his edition of the work,[11] Feith's response to the society incorporated a large portion of writing

---

[10] Rhijnvis Feith, *Het Ideaal in de kunst* (*The Ideal in Art*), ed. P. J. Buijnsters, 2nd rev. ed. (Den Haag: Martinus Nijhoff, 1979) (*Ideaal*).

[11] Buijnsters's introduction details the origins of Feith's manuscript, paying particular attention to its relation to Feith's other theoretical texts. See *Ideaal* 53–69.

later posthumously published as *Verhandeling over de oorspronkelijkheid in de werken der Dichtkunde, vooral met betrekking tot de Nederlanders* (*Treatise on the Originality in Works of Poetry, Especially in Relation to the Dutch*, 1828). Feith was determined, it would appear, that his dedication to the arts would survive his death.

From the very beginning of his essay, he addresses the popularity of contemporaneous aesthetic debate as well as the dangers implicit in the fashionability of such discussion. Nobody, he declares, appears to know exactly what anyone else is talking about, the terms of discussion having become either too generic or too divergent to achieve any mutual understanding. In response, Feith goes back to original sources, as had Huydecoper, in attempting to resolve the disparity. Following a logic invoked since antiquity, Feith builds his argument by considering first the origin of the ideal for the painter and sculptor and then, by extension, as well as by power of his own experience, for the writer. In a move that is significant for a sentimentalist writer such as Feith, his piece starts and ends by repeating the declaration Ovid himself rephrased for his *Ars amandi* and *Fasti*: "Est Deus in nobis, agitante calescimus illo."[12] For Feith, there is a divinity in art that impassions the artist to higher realms. Even as he invokes the authority of classical works, however, Feith sets out to debunk classical attitudes toward modern ideals. Like Huydecoper's efforts before him, Feith's subsequent endeavor to determine the ideal in art only touches on the sublime, although his investigation into the highest order of aesthetic expression necessarily acknowledges the concept. As Feith himself indicates, such an ideal is, sublimely put, perhaps the only true one "because it puts no bounds to art, is elevated above time and, just like our soul itself, continues to work and compel us into eternity, inasmuch as its nature allows the sublime artist to be urged to work for the same" (*Ideaal* 74).

With his *Ideal in Art* thus aiming to spread light "over the most sublime that is in humanity" (*Ideaal* 88), Feith's return to original inspirations can dispose with, for instance, the fine classicist distinctions between *imitatio* and *emulatio*. In fact, Feith even qualifies the modern notion of genius in no uncertain terms, asserting that "never has anyone borne the Ideal of the highest possible beauty in himself, without first having borne the highest morality inside, or, in other words, that it is impossible to be a great Genius, without at the same time being a noble human" (*Ideaal* 96). Although he relies on the force of his conviction to prove his point, in a telling footnote Feith addresses any criticism for such a break with old and new conventions:

I know very well that to play the well-grounded Poet there is nothing more fitting than to begin by finding Homer to be unsurpassable everywhere, and after him, for us, Vondel. Once one has foregrounded this *ad captandum benevolentiam*, one is protected and so reasonably safe from all critique. Now, if one does this from the depth of his heart, it is all well and good. Both [i.e., Homer and Vondel] are excellent Poets, even if truly not everywhere. But I cannot stand that so many take up this signboard, or rather shield, before the Public, when among themselves they have spoken so wholly differently. (*Ideaal* 114–15n2)

With this subtle aside, Feith engages two prominent adversaries, Willem Bilderdijk (1756–1831) and Johannes Kinker (1764–1845), who espoused what Feith saw as a mistakenly fashionable aesthetic stance that failed to issue from their hearts and, for that matter, their souls. Feith had tangled with both of them prior to penning his *Ideal*, and he had doubtless been made aware of their more explicit, albeit esoteric, expositions on the sublime. Over the same years, Kinker's essay *Iets over het schoone* (*Something about the Beautiful*, 1823) had sought to synthesize the beautiful and the sublime into an ideal beauty, based on his reading of Kant, albeit via Schiller. In point of fact, Feith had already countered Kinker's Kantian leanings in a series of open epistolary, admonitory exchanges to the Dutch public entitled *Brieven aan Sophie* (*Letters to Sophia*, 1806). Feith's *Ideal* here incorporates much of the insight he derived during that earlier

---

[12] "[If] god is in us, [then] we glow whenever he stirs [the embers]." For more on this point, see Buijnsters's introduction, in *Ideaal* 117n2 and 128–9n2.

dialogue with Kinker, much as it also aims at the pseudophilological, quasi-mystical writing of Bilderdijk. Never inclined to Enlightened thought, Bilderdijk – who was a monarchist, in contrast to the Republican Feith – composed *Gedachten over het verhevene* (*Thoughts about the Sublime*, 1821) by construing a mostly random association of concepts back to Longinus, while working that perceived sublimity up into his own peculiar variety of religious feeling.[13] Neither derivative view came close to what Feith had in mind or had experienced with inspired artistic practice.

Thus, having established himself as clearly and consistently opposed to the thinking of his fellow literati Bilderdijk and Kinker, with the *Ideal in Art* Feith put forth a more circumspect approach to the sublime. He argues "that the true Artist ... never represents according to his senses, which causes him rather to come closer to the beautiful, even if he never achieves it" – for the genuinely beautiful constitutes nothing less, according to Feith, "than the Ideal of the beautiful, standing before the eyes of his spirit, which he truly sees, but cannot reach" (*Ideaal* 89). Given the spiritual, if not religious, foundation for his zeal, Feith's search takes him to older sources outside the classical canon, barely glossing even the "new" Dutch ancients so prized by Huydecoper. Referencing instead a much older source, he wonders whether "the same Jupiter hurling his lightning bolts turns into a marionette at Jehova's side, on his wagons thundering through the wasteland, just as the Hebrew Poets in countless images have painted; and where is there something of that nature in the Greeks that can stand next to the majestic Psalm 29?" (*Ideaal* 115). Inevitably, then, for all antiquity's theorizing and philosophizing about the arts – much less modernity's grappling with such concepts – Feith asserts here that there is a spirituality to each aesthetic undertaking. Feith avows with his *Ideal in Art* that, once such testimony from the Old and New Testaments is brought to bear on artistic creativity, "then and only then, is the thorough practice of those [old and new] excellent masters more than somewhat appropriate to inflame the genius in us, to awaken the most splendid images in our spirit, and to perfect the Ideal of the beautiful in us" (*Ideaal* 123). Feith foregoes the Kantian concerns of his compatriots altogether, invoking instead the homegrown artistic practices he had admired in his predecessor Huydecoper. Thereby stressing the difference between aesthetic theory and praxis, Feith opened new ground for abandoning antiquity and its notion of a sublime altogether, wedding sublimity with morality and the humility demanded by the presence of the awe-inspiring, all-powerful divine.

JACOB GEEL (1789–1862): MAKING A CLASSIC(AL) EXIT FOR MODERNITY

Although he was a good century removed from the classicism of Huydecoper's age, by the time Jacob (officially Jacobus) Geel published his *Gesprek op den Drachenfels* (*Talk atop the Drachenfels*),[14] he had become a consummate classical scholar. His formal education began, as had Huydecoper's, at the Latin academy in Amsterdam, where Geel's instruction was directed by D. J. van Lennep, whose studies of ancient Greek had influenced, among others, Bilderdijk. Van Lennep saw to Geel's continued education at the Amsterdam Athenaeum and further helped Geel make well-placed connections in intellectual and social circles, leading ultimately to his appointment as head librarian at Leiden University in 1833. In that position Geel adeptly fulfilled what he, like Feith, viewed as his mission to transmit the world of ideas to the public at large. Although eventually awarded an honorary doctorate and named *Professor extraordinarius*

---

[13] It was one of Bilderdijk's cohorts, Mathijs Siegenbeek (1774–1854), who made the first translation of Longinus into Dutch (1811).

[14] Jacob Geel, *Gesprek op den Drachenfels: Een dialoog uit 1835 over de literatuur in de negentiende eeuw* (*Talk atop the Drachenfels: A Dialogue from 1835 about Literature in the Nineteenth Century*), ed. J. C. Brandt Corstius (Amsterdam: Atheneum-Polak & Van Gennep, 1968) (*Gesprek*).

at Leiden, he held no formal classes, extending his intellectual influence instead through collegial contacts with both scholars and students. Geel was invited to membership in learned societies nationally (notably the Dutch then-premier Koninklijk Instituut van Wetenschappen, Letterkunde en Schoone Kunsten [Royal Institute of Sciences, Literature, and Fine Arts]) as well as internationally (especially in Germany). Students under Geel's tutelage went on to raise literary awareness in the Low Countries and included the founders of a new journal, *De Gids* (*The Guide*), which became the forum for revitalizing cultural commentary throughout most of the nineteenth century.

Geel's scholarly lectures and publications (all written in Latin) and his editions of ancient Greek and Roman authors (e.g., Euripides [1846]) earned him an international reputation. Along with his numerous translations and original studies of the classics in Dutch, Geel enormously advanced national scholarship in Latin and Greek. In addition to being celebrated today for accomplishments in these areas, Geel is remembered equally for his interest in contemporary Dutch literature. His undertakings in that regard showed an abiding concern for the relationship between the sciences and the arts, particularly in the correlation of prose to poetry. Geel's critical surveillance of the interaction between reason and emotion is evident especially in the collection entitled, appropriately, *Onderzoek en Phantasie* (*Investigation and Imagination*, 1838). However, it is Geel's *Talk* that has long represented for Dutch scholars his most trenchant literary and philosophical insights. The work was originally delivered as a lecture in 1834 – a year before its publication – to the Leiden branch of the Hollandsche Maatschappij van Fraaije Kunsten en Wetenschappen (Holland Society of Fine Arts and Sciences, also one of Feith's former forums). In the piece one sees again the Dutch view through the door Kant opened on aesthetic thought that would continue into the nineteenth century. It also marks a final perspective on aesthetics that informs the distinctive approach to the subtler Dutch sublime.

Accompanied by an interloping – presumably Dutch – narrator, the *Talk* features two German academicians discussing various points of aesthetic contention, in which the one, Diocles, unvaryingly mouths the conventional classicist viewpoint, whereas the other, Charinus, as adamantly apes the latest Romantic antics. Small wonder that Geel situated this *Talk* of theirs on a rugged, winding path up the Drachenfels, a summit celebrated for its sweeping vistas across the Rhine Valley, that culturally liminal space between Germany and France, where the terms "classic" and "romantic" were being hotly contested among artists. For Geel, though, there was scarcely anything subliminal, much less sublime, behind this post-Kantian squabble. Like Feith in his desire to determine how to arrive at the ideal in art, Geel bemoans the conflicting (mis)understandings of the aesthetic term "romantic." However, unlike his compatriot sentimentalist – or "pre-Romantic" – trailblazer, Geel finds little connection for the sublime along the path he delineates as the classicist–Romanticist divide.

Indeed, as the scholars and their companion work their way uphill, caught in an argument over the meaning of "romantic," they come upon a site well suited for their confabulations: the once-supposed entrance to a cave that, as Charinus points out, local legend had said to contain the dragon's lair for which the mountain was named. Yet this locus, notes Diocles, next to which is a huge rock, is also where the ancient Greeks would have sought an oracle. Whereupon their young companion proposes that he and Charinus put questions to the oracle about the meaning of "romantic," if Diocles, sitting on the boulder outside the cave, will serve as that oracular medium. After a series of unsatisfying queries without coming any closer to an understanding of the term, the narrator loses himself in a contemplative digression. It includes one of the very few observations made regarding the sublime in this canonical work by Geel. Thinking to himself, the narrator opines that "the Northerner never [will become] a Greek, in spite of Winckelmann and Goethe – no matter how boldly or correctly written, no matter how roaring or sublime!" (*Gesprek* 36). This passage, shrouded in both Germanic legend and Delphic oracle, proves a critical juncture for the two antagonists representing Romanticism and classicism, with neither arriving at any greater level of clarity than when they started their climb, much to the despair of their fellow traveler. This passage also shows Geel's own skepticism as to the suitability of the sublime for his time and place.

The discussion becomes increasingly confused as the characters near the summit and survey the sundry forms artistic expression may take. Their observations progress to the highest literary genre, tragedy, at which point Diocles declares, "If one had permission in the theater to cry, 'Stop! We're tired of the beautiful!' then the scrim would fall until one had recovered." "You know art *so* well," Charinus responds, "but still look at our question from the wrong angle. Historical and aesthetic truth must go hand in hand; without these truths, art floats in emptiness" (*Gesprek* 56–7). Placing these rather classicist terms into the mouth of the Romanticist Charinus might at first glance seem contradictory to Geel's purpose. Yet in response to Charinus's absolutist declaration, Diocles retorts that

the ancient tragedians wanted to effect, to target the emotions, to express the nobility in suffering, to exhaust the entire depth of that sensation: a wrestling match between will and fate, which elevates the soul and which, even if the sufferer succumbs, leaves with it the awareness of a power that triumphs over the material world. The heart of the spectator is shocked, if you will, but not tormented or tortured as with the hands of an executioner. That's what your romantic drama does. Away with your truth, if it must destroy the nobility of the ideal! (*Gesprek* 57)

With the "truths" of both scholars here at their incompatible end, Geel has ironically made his point: that the validity of neither movement stands up to systematic scrutiny. All three descend the Drachenfels in silence.

In *Talk*, then, Geel supersedes the poetics of both classicism and Romanticism, having found their taste aesthetically to be at bottom little more than old classicist wine in a new Romantic cask.[15] In this respect, the epigraphs with which he begins the dialogue between Diocles and Charinus could just as well serve as epitaphs to end his transcript of their debate.

The question of the difference between the romantic school and the classic has been merely that of forms. What, in the name of common sense, signify disputes about the unities and such stuff, – the ceremonies of the Muses? The *Medea* would have been equally Greek, if all the unities had been disregarded; the *Faust* equally romantic, if all the unities had been preserved. It is among the poems of Homer and Pindar, of Aeschylus and Hesiod, that you must look for the spirit of Antiquity; but these gentlemen look to the rules of Aristotle: it is as if a sculptor, instead of studying the statue of Apollo, should study the yard measure that takes its proportions. – Bulwer

But those other Gentlemen, because they did not know much more of Antiquity than the measuring stick of Aristotle, said: it is disgusting, and there is completely no need for any measure. – Anonymous (*Gesprek* 20)[16]

By marking his work with these mutually equivocating mottos, Geel attempts to bring the arts out of the rift running between ancients and moderns, which was widened in no small measure by the reading of Schiller reading Kant given by German Idealists. In that post-Kantian nineteenth-century mindset, greatness and grandeur were limited to the heights of the Drachenfels, to the absolute if not supernatural, as encountered at times in nature yet only very rarely happened upon in art.

Geel thus looks instead to prose – even with its concomitant sense of the prosaic – as the most relevant and viable literary genre for a modern world in which the empirical and practical

---

[15] Kinker, Feith's antagonist mentioned previously, also stakes out a similar position, but without the foresight for revitalization that Geel ultimately advocates in his *Gesprek*. See, Johannes Kinker, "Iets over het romantische: Eene voorlezing," in *De recensent, ook der recensenten* 2 (1836), 329–50.

[16] The first citation, given in English by Geel, comes from E. Bulwer-Lytton's *England and the English* (1833); the second, in Dutch, remains anonymous.

are constantly increasing in significance, much as science and technology were in his era, and in sharp contrast to the fantasies of classicism and Romanticism alike. Considering that nearly all his continental contemporaries thought themselves to be Kantians, Geel's work demonstrates again how Dutch intellectuals developed a different response to the critical aesthetic derived from Kant's *Critique of the Power of Judgment*. That is, despite his frequently intellectual subject matter, Geel's writings diverge from those continental Kantians – not to mention Kant himself – by showing how one needs to write as workably as one speaks. As had Feith, Geel thus follows lines similar to Huydecoper, yet he extends his prosaic point with more contemporaneous references – namely, to Laurence Sterne, whose *Sentimental Journey* (1768) Geel translated and published anonymously in 1837, the tragicomic character of which nearly all Geel's work reflects. That ludic yet lofty nature, Geel gives his fellow writers to understand, would help retain the place of the arts in the Netherlands, if not regain their firm standing in world culture.

CONCLUSION

To bring this chapter to both its apex and close, we can conclude that although recent literary-historical research has unearthed several important accommodations for the cultural and philosophical discussion of the sublime among Dutch philosophers and creative thinkers, examining writings by authors who were also committed to being practitioners in the arts reveals a seemingly corollary if not contradictory face of Dutch aesthetics to the Western rest. It draws on a distinct domestic tradition derived from the classics yet features traits quite different from those moderns in Europe who would follow Kant (much less Burke), and it countenances instead a rather subtler sublime.

Indeed, thanks to their practical experience in their domestic economies, Huydecoper, Feith, and Geel all understood the ill effects of misbegotten and misunderstood imitation of ancient models, a trend that was, in Feith's words, analogous to "bringing over Greek fruits to northern ground, where they will never be anything but artificial plants" (*Ideaal* 109). Or, expressed another way, although a given cultural notion may play out well against an international backdrop in the abstract, the degree of actual intercultural interplay will depend on the adaptability of that notion to local sociocultural ends. Here one might observe how virtually all works created by Dutch masters in their Golden Age included some reference to daily life, as illustrated by either the two little girls caught in the middle of Rembrandt van Rijn's *Night Watch* (1642) or the farmers working the fields under ominously towering clouds in Jan van Goyen's *View of Haarlem and the Haarlemmer Meer* (1646): the mundane almost always enters into what we call sublime.[17] In this regard, the young Kant may have characterized it correctly when, in the *Observations*, he goes on to say that "the Dutchman is of an orderly and assiduous type of temperament and, as he looks solely to the useful, he has little feeling for that which in the finer understanding is beautiful or sublime" (KGS 20:248). Yet, some twenty-five years later, the older, wiser Kant who composed the third *Critique* would surely have conceded the relativity of a comparative term like "finer." The prevalence here in these Dutch writings of an identifiable alternative for understanding the sublime thus articulates another, less apparent contribution to the development of aesthetics in Western thought.

To be sure, these Dutch conditions imposed on creativity could be seen as anticipating the less Romantic, more realist concept of a modern sublime, including the extreme hyperrealism of the surrealists after Duchamp, the readymades of Fluxus, and the soup cans produced by

---

[17] My thanks to Robert L. Fucci of the Department of Art History and Archaeology at Columbia University for corroborating this observation, which has informed his own historical research on art from the Dutch Gouden Eeuw. See also *Gesprek* 53, in which Geel, albeit implicitly, also praises this aspect of seventeenth-century Dutch art.

Warhol's factory. From its divergent aesthetic, Dutch art puts forth a far more literal reading of the sublime than usually interpreted, carrying our ideas about art over the threshold into another reality, yet a reality nonetheless. That is to say, although the Dutch recognized the "sublime" and the "beautiful" to comprise "aesthetics" as developed over the course of the eighteenth century, they nonetheless came to subdue that particular aesthetic notion, emphasizing instead a more practical side to artistic creation and production. This perspective can explain, perhaps, the transition from seventeenth-century Dutch masterpieces to late twentieth-century *droog* (i.e., "dry") design (not to mention the kitsch craze for tulips, cows, and windmills) in the Netherlands. Yet although the Dutch seemingly failed to incorporate the then-dominant trends, there still remains for us something compelling and valuable in the aesthetic they employed and employ still today (many around the world from age to age have found themselves fanatical for all things Dutch).[18]

So how do we answer for this peculiar Dutch response to a concept otherwise embraced by the rest of the Western world? In point of fact, the Dutch do not add to an understanding of the sublime as a concept, particularly if one takes the notion as was defined historically by thinkers in France, Britain, and Germany. The Dutch had indeed read their Corneille, Burke, and Kant – in addition to the classics – as exemplified by each of the writers (Huydecoper, Feith, and Geel) featured in this essay. Still, they could not match that later line of European thought to their own particular sensibilities. As Geel puts it: "The more the storyteller or singer or describer refines everything, making all of it sublime or majestic, the more unnatural his representation becomes. He wearies the reader or the spectator, whose awe must always remain taut; sooner or later, that tension will result in their indifference, and ultimately perhaps even their ennui" (*Gesprek* 54). Eliciting that level of disaffection from their beholders could hardly encourage artists, in any time or place, to depict expressions of what conventionally is held to be sublime.

In the wake of prevailing (post-)Kantian paradigms, the Dutch alternative outlined here – filtered through a moral inclination toward modesty before the omnipotent – offers a counterpoint to predominant cultural tendencies, casting those notions of sublime into relief. In the end, these three Dutch aestheticians provided a subtlety for artistic practice that finds that grandeur on a smaller scale can be as great: not so much an antisublime, perhaps, as a semi-, quasi-, or even minisublime. In that vein, the turn-of-the-century Dutch poet Hendrik Tollens (1780–1856), a protégé of Feith as well as peer of and prototype for Geel,[19] declaimed, "Follow the Greeks? I would be ashamed.... / What does their elegance matter to me? / Nature teaches me how to pluck the lyre's strings."[20] What came naturally to a Dutch artist, then, living in a culture with fewer shock-and-awe designs on the world, necessarily departs from conventions established by greater or grander cultures with, as history has shown, more supremely imperial ambitions. In the end, the Dutch take on the sublime (grounding it instead of flying into wondrous fancies) offers us something distinctly original, and at least as magnificent in its gentler genius.

---

[18] See, for example, Annette Stott, *Holland Mania: The Unknown Dutch Period in American Art and Culture* (Woodstock, NY: Overlook Press, 1998).

[19] Tollens was Geel's model for his naïve interlocutor in the "Tafelgesprek over zaken van groot gewicht" ("Table Talk over Matters of Great Import" [c. 1831]), collected in Jacob Geel, *Onderzoek en Phantasie* (Leiden: Van der Hoek, 1838).

[20] Cited in G. Kalff, *Geschiedenis der Nederlandsche letterkunde* (*History of Dutch Literature*), 7 vols. (Groningen: J. B. Wolters, 1906–1912), 7:44.

10

The First American Sublime

Chandos Michael Brown

INTRODUCTION

Intellectuals on the far side of the world looked eagerly to English and continental savants to help them make sense of their place, even as they inhabited a landscape that few across the Atlantic could imagine. The provincial inhabitants of the British colonies in North America confronted nature in its most primal setting, and perhaps the great cultural work of the Anglophonic migration was to render *terra incognita* into vernacular terms. For two centuries this was largely an empirical undertaking, but the American Revolution and the subsequent invention of the American state compelled Americans to expand their imagined geography to encompass both a physical environment – North America – and an emergent community conceived in revolution – the United States. Place and ideology commanded a uniform explanation, and the Enlightenment authorized a totalizing narrative that intimately conjoined what Samuel Stanhope Smith, president of the College of New Jersey, loosely referred to as "climate" with the character of society, and, indeed, with the individual as well. The varieties of complexions among the American Indians, Smith observes, are "nothing more than the known effects of climate, of food, of culture, or of other natural causes, operating on animal bodies ... here they are seen in lower stature, and there of taller and more noble port."[1] His emphasis on the somatic is characteristic of a society obsessed with racial difference, and this firm belief that the peculiar "climate" of North America literally stamps its impression on the "animal bodies" of its inhabitants is a powerful cultural trope. The kindred conviction that nature thus animated might in turn shape thought informed a multitude of intellectual, social, and political dialogues during the era of revolution and the formation of the early American republic.

Anglo-Americans of the eighteenth century were as widely read as many of their English counterparts and engaged the same philosophical, political, belletristic, and scientific literature, much of which was reasonably well represented in colonial bookstores and college curricula. Jonathan Edwards, the influential American divine, encountered Locke's *Essay Concerning the Human Understanding* at Yale in 1717 as a fourteen-year-old undergraduate, with consequences that we shall see. As did the more thoughtful of his contemporaries, he found in Locke a hard-headed emphasis on experience, on the primacy of the senses as the conduit for knowledge about nature and, ultimately, about civil society's relation to the natural world. Mind and identity are the sum of one's "sensations" of the natural world and of

---

[1] Samuel Stanhope Smith, *An Essay on the Causes of the Variety of Complexion and Figure in the Human Species*, 2nd ed. (New Brunswick, 1810), 149.

I should like to acknowledge that this chapter profited much from the careful reading and critical commentary of several colleagues, most notably Timothy Costelloe, Mel Ely, Grey Gundaker, Adam Potkay, and Alan Wallach. I am grateful for their tremendous support and enthusiasm.

one's "reflections" on it and on the more complex associations that such mediated experience affords.[2] From such thoughtful observation derives the basis of good judgment and virtue, and these, in turn, direct our behavior in the world of men. God smiles on a society that conforms to his purposes, although those purposes often remain obscure. Yet the observable properties of the universe suggested an immanent order governed by laws susceptible to human understanding. The American founders would eventually translate this understanding of natural law into a federal constitution conceived as a "machine that would go of itself."[3] Edwards's transcendent evangelism drove him toward a far more interventionist God than Locke's and a radically different view both of the transparency of the natural world and of the power of the unregenerate mind to make sense of it at all.

I shall here consider the American sublime within this matrix of imperial expansion, revolution, the pursuit of knowledge, and the contested meaning of natural and national history. I undertake to explore some of these conversations – to recapture some of the richness of the intellectual discourse that framed what I shall call consecutively the "ideological sublime," the "nationalist sublime," and the "first American sublime." These terms constellate, of course, around the concept of the "sublime" as the intellectuals of the Anglophonic Atlantic understood and epitomized in their receptiveness to Edmund Burke. They also periodize an extended chronology that precedes Burke's popularization of the idea at midcentury and that extends virtually to the middle of the nineteenth century in its American context. The ideological sublime roughly corresponds to the provincial era of North American settlement (post-1700); the nationalist sublime comprehends the revolutionary decades between the middle of the eighteenth century and the opening decades of the early American republic (1760–1820); and the first American sublime, although subsuming the earlier periods, extends to the late 1840s.

THE IDEOLOGICAL SUBLIME I

Two epistemological traditions converged on the reception and application in North America of Burke's systematic exposition of the sublime as a category of experience.[4] The second tradition I shall take up in the following section in my discussion of North American Protestantism. The first is perhaps the one that most directly explains Burke himself – the long descent of English empiricism that found early voice in the writings of Francis Bacon and Isaac Newton and that was institutionalized in the charter of the Royal Society of London for the Improvement of Natural Knowledge in 1660 (Locke was elected a member in 1668). By the middle of the

---

[2] See Jerome Huyler, *Locke in America: The Moral Philosophy of the Founding Era* (Lawrence: University Press of Kansas, 1995).

[3] James Russell Lowell actually penned the phrase in 1888, as quoted in Michael Kammen, *A Machine that Would Go of Itself: The Constitution in American Culture*, 2nd ed. (New York: St. Martin's Press, 2006), 125. On science, system, nature, and constitutionalism in post-Revolutionary America, see I. Bernard Cohen, *Science and the Founding Fathers: Science in the Political Thought of Thomas Jefferson, Benjamin Franklin, John Adams, and James Madison* (New York: W. W. Norton, 1995).

[4] Most educated North Americans knew Longinus intimately and modeled their rhetorical pursuits accordingly, and "sublime" was thus a term much in currency throughout the eighteenth century. Burke's *Enquiry* evidently circulated widely enough to appear in a Philadelphia book auction in 1769 (see *Catalogue of Books, to be Sold, by Public Auction, at the City Vendue-Store, in Front-Street* [Philadelphia, 1769]) and in the catalog of Ebenezer Hazard and Garrat Noel's bookstore in New York two years later (see *Catalogue of Books, Sold by Noel and Hazard, at Their Book and Stationary Store, Next Door to the Merchants Coffee-House, Where the Public May Be Furnished with All Sorts of Books and Paper* [New York, 1772]). It appears regularly in catalogs after this date. Burke appeared actually to crystallize in the American imagination at century's end, when writers and thinkers confronted the country's sovereign landscape most directly. For a concise overview of the place of the sublime in North American oratory, see Adam Potkay, "Theorizing Civic Eloquence in the Early Republic: The Road from David Hume to John Quincy Adams," *Early American Literature* 34, 2 (1999), 147–70.

eighteenth century, when Burke published *A Philosophical Enquiry into the Origin of Our Ideas of the Sublime and Beautiful* (1757), the impulse to catalog nature (and all manner of natural processes, including human behavior) was simply reflexive in the English imagination. The first English empire required an epistemology that reckoned the value of things as an end in itself – knowledge was power only as it advanced the ambitions of the emergent English state and as it aided in the discovery and often ruthless exploitation of the contents of the globe. It also required considering the nature of the English as a people distinct from any other.[5] The *natural* history of the world, then, at least as the early English Atlantic understood it, was preeminently the history of conquest and the improvement of the English nation. The legitimacy of the *translatio studii et imperii* from England to North American rested on the superiority both of English institutions and of the English themselves, who were uniquely prepared by the physical conditions of their Atlantic archipelago to command both knowledge and empire in hostile domains.

For Burke, the problem was to describe the mechanism that accounted for the direct correspondence between things perceived and one's cognitive and emotional response to them. The experience of the sublime described a psychological reaction to a material stimulus, one that impressed itself forcibly on the reflective mind. The *Enquiry* is a taxonomy of sorts. It catalogs the various "ideas" of pain, beauty, ambition, and fear. Burke is careful, however, to describe the limits of his investigation, and indeed of any investigation into the imponderable interiority of the self. Burke hesitates to peer much below the surface of nature, or too deeply into the mind itself, for this transgressive scrutiny violates the sanctified realm of final causes. He confines himself to things as they are – because how they came to be and to what end are not manifest in their disposition on earth: "That great chain of causes, which linking one to another even to throne of God himself," he writes, "can never be unraveled by an industry of ours. When we go but one step beyond the immediately sensible qualities of things, we go out of our depth."[6] Burke virtually echoes the preface to *The Great Instauration* (1620), in which Bacon had written: "My first admonition (which was also my prayer) is that men confine the sense within the limits of duty in respect of things divine: for sense is like the sun, which reveals the face of the earth, but seals and shuts up the face of heaven."[7] Or, in a yet more pointed form, take Bacon's expansion of the theme in *The New Organon* (1620): "And in general every student of nature must hold in suspicion whatever most captures and holds his understanding; and this warning needs to be all the more applied in issues of this kind ["*the idols of the cave*"], to keep the understanding clear and balanced."[8]

In the realm of the known, in which states must live, a nation merely imagined was an exercise in hubris. To *discover* a new nation, however, and, more important, to *discover* the new people who inhabited it, was a different matter altogether.[9] In North America, the stakes were inordinately high, especially for the intellectuals and ideologues of the immediate

---

[5] See Joyce Chaplin, *Subject Matter: Technology, the Body, and Science on the Anglo-American Frontier, 1500–1676* (Cambridge, MA: Harvard University Press, 2001), esp. chap. 4, 116–56, and Susan Scott Parrish, *American Curiosity: Cultures of Natural History in the Colonial British Atlantic World* (Chapel Hill: Published for the Omohundro Institute of Early American History and Culture, Williamsburg, VA, by the University of North Carolina Press, 2006), esp. chap. 2, 77–102.

[6] Edmund Burke, *A Philosophical Enquiry into the Origin of Our Ideas of the Sublime and Beautiful*, ed. James T. Boulton (London: Routledge and Kegan Paul, 1958 [1759, 1st ed. 1757]), 4.1.129–30. All references are to part, section, and page number.

[7] Francis Bacon, "The Great Instauration," in *The Works of Francis Bacon*, collected and edited by James Spedding, Robert Leslie Ellis, and Douglas Denon Heath, 14 vols. (London: Longman, 1861–1879), vol. 4 (1861), 20.

[8] Francis Bacon, *The New Organon*, ed. Lisa Jardine and Michael Silverthorne (Cambridge: Cambridge University Press, 2000), 48.

[9] I am influenced here by Paolo Rossi, *The Dark Abyss of Time: The History of the Earth and the History of Nations from Hooke to Vico*, trans. Lydia G. Cochrane (Chicago: Chicago University Press, 1984), esp. chap. 22, 158–67.

post-Revolutionary period, who confronted, as had their Elizabethan forebears, the problem of creating a national identity as the sine qua non of the formation of the state itself, for they believed that nations must have a "natural history," else they are simple inventions of the human intellect – mere ropes of sand.

In July 1806, Dr. John Gorham of Cambridge, Massachusetts, wrote to his friend, the Yale mineralogist Benjamin Silliman. Gorham was en route to Niagara Falls, a stage in his scenic tour of New England and New York: "The predominating stone around here is argillaceous schistus. On my return I shall endeavor to send you specimens of the different stones I have seen. I hope you will make allowances for this very imperfect account. I am quite a tyro you know in mineralogy, do not therefore anticipate much from my letters." The soon-to-be Irving Professor of Chemistry at Harvard College could not resist an accompanying observation:

I cannot command the pen of Mrs. Radcliffe and therefore you must not anticipate any regular long-drawn description of their beauties. How often have I wish'd that some of the narrow minded prejudiced Europeans we have both met with might be suddenly transported to some of the spots over which we passed. Were they ignorant of the country in which they were placed they would probably imagine themselves sometimes among the wild romantic scenery of Switzerland; at others, surrounded by the rich and harmonious scenes of Italy. We live in a charming country.[10]

Gorham here invokes Ann Radcliffe, whose *The Mysteries of Udolpho* (1794) introduced American readers to the horror of the gothic sublime in the form of the terrifyingly mountainous landscape of the Swiss Alps and the contrastingly picturesque and beautiful landscapes of Italy. Gorham here engages in a subtle appropriation. In a scant few days he had traversed a landscape that rivals the most distinctive features of three nations, such is the abundance of *this* "charming country." The first paragraph possesses perhaps the greater gravity, for Gorham departs from the conventions of the picturesque travel narrative and *geologizes* the scene.

Both Gorham and Silliman, as was common among the American professoriate of their generation, graduated from Harvard and Yale respectively and completed their professional educations at the University in Edinburgh, which at the turn of the nineteenth century was a fruitful environment for the study of natural history. Attending classes in 1805 and 1806, they confronted competing theories that purported to explain the history of the earth. The first, dominant in Edinburgh, was founded on the work of Abraham Gottlob Werner of Freiberg, Saxony. Werner believed that water – a primeval ocean – encompassed the whole of the globe on its creation. From this ocean precipitated, as salt or sugar crystals form in a solution, all the current features of the globe. The highest peaks, composed of the most durable and heavy elements, emerged first. The successive visible structures of the earth deposited themselves, according to the weight and chemical structure of their mass. The competing theory, advanced by Edinburgh native James Hutton, held that volcanism was the agent of terrestrial formation. Strata were the result of alluvial action, so water did figure as a transforming mechanism, but the principal features of the earth came about through the violent heat and pressure created by volcanoes. The earth was a vast, bubbling cauldron, its features constantly cast down, constantly thrust up anew; the earth, Hutton proposed, was a "beautiful machine."[11]

These systems offer radically divergent perspectives on natural history, and Gorham and Silliman were hardly disinterested consumers. Neptunism (after Werner) postulated that the features of the earth emerged from a terraqueous globe, from a deluge, as it were. Over time it became dry, at which point natural forces of vastly inferior magnitude began to work on it.

---

[10] John Gorham to Benjamin Silliman, July 5, 1806, Silliman Family Papers, Yale University Library; quoted in Chandos Michael Brown, *Benjamin Silliman: A Life in the Young Republic* (Princeton, NJ: Princeton University Press, 1989), 199–200.

[11] Martin Rudwick, *Bursting the Limits of Time: The Reconstruction of Geohistory in the Age of Revolution* (Chicago: Chicago University Press, 2005), 162–3.

The face of the earth remained, in essence, as God had created it. The Plutonists (after Hutton) envisioned something altogether different. Transformation was the rule of history. The agencies that had shaped the world still operated on it. One can observe the activity of volcanoes – many English at the end of the eighteenth century flocked to Mount Aetna, in Italy, for this very purpose – and one can derive some pretty definite conclusions from these observations. The world is old, older even than the biblical chronology, strictly interpreted, permitted. If Werner offered a natural history comforting to the standing order of society, then Hutton by all rights should have stoked the ardor of the post-Revolutionary generation, for geology itself bespoke change as *natural* and by implication *ordained*. Yet Silliman and Gorham faltered, and herein the history of American geology and of the American sublime converges with the legacy of North American Puritanism, and here I return to the second of the epistemological traditions I mention previously.

THE IDEOLOGICAL SUBLIME II

Bacon's *Novum Organum* and *The Great Instauration* appeared in the year of the settlement of Massachusetts Bay, although the settlers hardly needed reminding that the human imagination was a licentious thing. One hesitates to totalize the experience of the many, but the Winthrop fleet did in broad measure agree on a few salient points. In its fallen estate, humanity was ill equipped to make sense of the world. The attributes of the Creator could not be derived from the study of nature – for divinity did not manifest itself in the material world – and even when God chose to express his will through providential means, his intent was often obscure. Original sin constituted an epistemological crisis; whereas Eve and Adam once knew the names of all the beasts, their descendants could merely gaze on nature "as through a glass, darkly." Yet enough remained of the sensibility with which humanity was once endowed to allow for a certain latitude of discovery. God had entered a covenant, so far as the Puritans were concerned, and although he could have created a universe over which chaos reigned (the grand agenda of Milton's Satan), he did not. Whatever regular processes appeared in nature were merely *emblematic* of God's design. The beautifully ordered solar system as described by Copernicus pointed toward the perfection of the creator – but did not instantiate it. The sublunary globe was consumable. English Protestants, unlike the Catholics they despised, denied the doctrine of transubstantiation; the separation between the deity and the material world was absolute. The Puritans sought utility in nature and conceived of it in utilitarian terms, but we must reflect that *use* is, of course, measured by *want*, one of the stigmata of the Fall. Thus the discovery of utility, the fulfillment of desire, simultaneously attested to humanity's disgrace. Cotton Mather, the third-generation prodigy of a New England ministerial dynasty, writes of minerals in *The Christian Philosopher* (1721):

There are above a dozen several sorts of *Stones*, that are found in *larger* Masses.

What *Vessels*, what *Buildings*, what *Ornaments* do these afford us; especially the *Slate*, the *Marble*, the *Free-stone*, and the *Lime-stone*?

How helpful the *Warming-stone*?

How needful the *Grind-stone* and the *Mill-stone*?

To the *Service* of our maker we have so many calls from the *Stones* themselves, [for if *Men* should be silent at proclaiming the Glory of God, the very *Stones* would speak] that a learned and pious *German* so addresses us: *Audis tibi, loquentes Lapides; tu ne sis Lapis in hac parte, sed ipsorum Vocem audi, & in illis Vocem Dei.*[12]

---

[12] Cotton Mather, *The Christian Philosopher*, ed. Winton L. Solberg (Urbana-Champaign: University of Illinois Press, 1994), 124. Solberg translates the Latin thus: "You hear the stones speaking to you; do not be a rock in this matter, but hear their voice and in them the voice of God" (124n12).

For the Puritans, revelation alone provided insight into the meaning of history; all else was chronology. Nature revealed little beyond a certain predictable regularity. Cotton's father, Increase Mather, speaks to the inscrutability of God's design in a sermon delivered in Boston in 1697:

> *God has appointed Lights in the Heaven to be for Signs and Seasons.* Gen. I. 14. These move regularly and unfailably according to that Order which the Creator has established. Therefore man may know infallibly how many hours or minutes such a day or night will be long before the Time comes; He may know when there will be an *Eclipse* of the Sun or of the Moon, twenty, or an hundred years before it comes to pass: but for Contingent Things; which have no necessary dependence on the constituted Order of nature, but upon the meer Pleasure and Providence of God, they are not known except unto God, or to them unto whom he shall reveal them.[13]

Unilluminated by grace, the significance of "contingent things" remains dark, their contours only dimly visible through the clotted skein of the senses.

In 1802, when Silliman made a public confession of his faith during a revival at Yale College, the formula was transformed, but the terms remained familiar. The New England Protestantism to which he pledged himself insisted on a strict separation of God from nature, for if divinity were to manifest itself in natural forms, then humanity too must perforce embody the Godhead, which was unthinkable. But the great eighteenth-century leavening of North American Protestantism, activated by the ideological dramas of the Revolutionary era, joined with a strident early American nationalism to yield a heady brew. The attributes of the Creator may well be discernible in nature. The "natural" order was the end of creation made manifest. Nature was a second scripture, a repository of ethical values, and nature predicted the republican enterprise.

"Do you know *Bartram's Travels*?" Thomas Carlyle asked the American philosopher Ralph Waldo Emerson long after the two had met, "Treats of *Florida* chiefly, has a wonderful kind of floundering eloquence in it; and has grown immeasurably *old*. All American libraries ought to provide themselves with that kind of book; and keep them as a future *biblical* article."[14] William Bartram undertook his journey to the Carolinas, Georgia, Florida, and the Southwest in the early 1770s – on the eve of the Revolution (in fact, he returned to Philadelphia during the winter 1776–1777) – and after some time in manuscript circulation, the *Travels* appeared in Philadelphia in 1791. Carlyle looked back from a vantage of some sixty years (his letter to Emerson dates from 1851) on a peculiar form of enthusiasm that possessed American writers of the Young Republic, of whom Bartram was among the first.[15]

Carlyle responds, I think, to the subjectivity of the *Travels*, and to Bartram's attempt to articulate it – the revelation of a sensibility – which for the most part tends to the vividly descriptive, scientific in its own way, but frequently gives way to the remarkable "floundering elegance" that so intrigues him. He gives us no examples, but one might venture at what struck the Englishman. Consider a passage near the opening of part II, chapter VII. Bartram prepares for a jaunt to a trading post on the Gulf of Mexico. He writes: "My mind yet elate with the various scenes of rural nature, which as a lively animated picture had been presented to my view; the deeply engraven impression, a pleasing flattering contemplation, gave strength and agility

---

[13] Increase Mather, *A Discourse Concerning the Uncertainty of the Times of Men and the Necessity of Being Prepared for Sudden Changes and Death. Delivered in a Sermon Preached at Cambridge in New England. Decemb. 6. 1696. On Occasion of the Sudden Death of Two Scholars Belonging to Harvard Colledge* (Boston, 1697), 15.

[14] Thomas Carlyle to Ralph Waldo Emerson, July 8, 1851, in Charles Eliot Norton, ed., *Correspondence of Thomas Carlyle and R. W. Emerson 1834–1872*, 2 vols. (Boston, 1884), 1:197–8.

[15] The material here regarding Jefferson and Bartram draws with much revision on Chandos Michael Brown, "Scientific Inquiry: The British Colonies," in *Encyclopedia of the North American Colonies*, ed. Jacob Ernest Cooke, 3 vols. (New York: Scribner, 1993), 3:165–75.

to my steps, anxiously to press forward to the delightful fields and groves of Apalatche."[16] This sentence rings with a wonderful resonance and exoticism, the latter of which would have caught Carlyle's eye, and exposes the sensations of the narrator, even as he hurries into the mosquito-infested Florida wetlands. Bartram, merely by describing his reaction to nature, unconsciously uncovers the hidden correspondence between external nature and the psyche. "Fair seed-time had my soul, and I grew up / Foster'd alike by beauty and by fear," William Wordsworth wrote in the *Prelude* of 1805. Bartram much earlier embraced the invigorating and shaping force of the American environment on the European mind.[17]

Bartram encounters a special sort of nature in his travels, one that is surprisingly talkative. Riding through a pine barrens, a "most dreary, solitary, desert waste," he nevertheless finds a remarkable expression of harmonious life: "The symphony of the western breeze, through the bristly pine leaves, or solitary crickets screech, or at best the more social converse of the frogs, in solemn charus [sic] with the swift breezes, brought from distant fens and forests." Everywhere he turns, Bartram finds community and coherence, an ordered nature that in its forms of mutual cooperation provides a model for human social interaction. After a good dinner of crane soup, he regrets the killing of the bird, which has a higher use: "We had this fowl dressed for supper and it made excellent soup; nevertheless as long as I can get any other necessary food I shall prefer his seraphic music in the etherial skies, and my eyes and understanding gratified in observing their economy and social communities, in the expansive green savannas of Florida."[18]

Bartram is not so far from Jonathan Edwards in a passage like this. Edwards records in his "Personal Narrative" similar moments of contentment and delight as he viewed his God "in the sun, moon and stars; in the clouds, and blue sky; in the grass, flowers, trees; in the water and all nature."[19] The evangelical Edwards sought types and antitypes in nature that would sustain his millennial aspirations, which were related to those of his Puritan forbears and to that of his grandfather, Solomon Stoddard: to "gather" Christians into a commonwealth of saints, to purify society, and to erect on the unspoiled plains of the Connecticut River valley a community of regenerate souls in an anticipation of the second advent of Christ and the fulfillment of history. Edwards here ushers in a way of viewing nature, although he could never see it as anything more than an "image and shadow" of divine truths, that is, as an irradiated expression of divine presence in the world.

Bartram's vision is at once more secular – even the terms "economy" and "social community" are drawn from the political rhetoric of the 1760s and 1770s – and more material, for he sees in nature not a simulacrum of divine form but a version of regulated polity that is connected by degree to similar, human organizations. The *Travels* promises that the American environment, correctly observed, projects the organic shape of an ideal republic: cooperative, harmonious, and enlightened. American intellectuals of the post-Revolutionary era soon reached similar conclusions. For the geologist Silliman, the study of American nature was an interpretive act akin to reading scripture. It revealed the vista both of a benign future and of an apocalyptic past. Burke never presumed to read the will of God in nature, either in the past or future. Other Americans were quite certain they could, and that the prospect was sublime.

---

[16] William Bartram, *Travels Through North and South Carolina, Georgia, East and West Florida, the Cherokee Country, the Extensive Territories of the Muscogulges, or Creek Confederacy, and the Country of the Chactaws; Containing an Account of the Soil and Natural Productions of Those Regions, Together with Observations on the Manners of the Indians* (Philadelphia: James & Johnson, 1791), 215.

[17] *The Prelude: 1799, 1805, 1850*, ed. Jonathan Wordsworth, M. H. Abrams, and Stephen Gill (New York: W. W. Norton, 1979), 1805 text, I:305.

[18] Bartram, *Travels*, 221.

[19] [Samuel Hopkins], *The Life and Character of the Late Reverend, Learned, and Pious Mr. Jonathan Edwards, President of the College of New-Jersey Together with Extracts from His Private Writings and Diary and Also Seventeen Select Sermons on Various Important Subjects* (Northampton, MA, 1804), 29.

The natural history of the Wernerian globe commenced with Creation and ended, in the American version at least, with the millennium.[20] Thomas Jefferson captured something of this spirit in *Notes on the State of Virginia*. The *Notes*, like his Declaration of Independence, attempted to set America apart from Europe even as he was keen to establish parity – against the assertions of George-Louis Leclerc, Comte de Buffon, that the New World was home to creatures inferior in size and variety to the old. Jefferson quite persuasively demonstrates that the opposite is true. Aside from the catalog of resources and animal and vegetable productions that the *Notes* afforded the curious European reader, Jefferson included sharp and well-wrought glimpses into a landscape that few Europeans had encountered, as in his famous description of the natural bridge in Rockbridge County, Virginia (see Figure 10.1), or in the carefully contrived description of the falls of the Shenandoah and Potomac rivers through the Blue Ridge Mountains at Harpers Ferry (see Figure 10.2).

The falls at Harpers Ferry, wrote Jefferson, is "perhaps one of the most stupendous scenes in nature":

You stand on a very high point of land. On your right comes up the Shenandoah, having ranged along the foot of the mountain an hundred miles to seek a vent. On your left approaches the Potomac, in quest of a passage also. In the moment of their juncture, they rush together against the mountain, rend it asunder, and pass off to the sea. The first glance of this scene hurries our senses into the opinion, that the earth has been created in time, that the mountains were formed first, that the rivers began to flow afterwards, that in this place, particularly, they have been damned up by the Blue Ridge of mountains, and have formed an ocean which filled the whole valley; that continuing to rise they have at length broken over this spot, and have torn the mountain down from its summit to its base.... But the distant finishing which nature has given to the picture, is of a very different character. It is in true contrast to the foreground. It is as placid and delightful as that is wild and tremendous. For the mountain being cloven asunder, she presents to your eye, through the cleft, a small catch of smooth blue horizon, at an infinite distance in the plain country, inviting you, as it were, from the riot and tumult roaring around, to pass through the breach and participate of the calm below.[21]

Invited to respond to a series of enquiries regarding the state of Virginia, Jefferson published the *Notes* first in a limited Paris edition, translated into French, in 1781 and then in London, in English, in 1787; both editions were clearly directed to a European audience.

These circumstances direct the strategy of his presentation. Jefferson adopts a direct address – "you" – placing the viewer (emphatically not an American) directly in the scene. He invokes the commonplace association of nature with a psychological state ("hurries our senses into the opinion") and moves on to suggest a theory of geology. The earth is old and was not necessarily created of a piece.[22] Natural forces conspired to alter it to the forms we now apprehend, and Jefferson imbued these forces with a peculiar teleology, at least as they operated in North America, for here one witnessed a progressive development that, in turn, determined the social and civic character of a nation. Nature and history combined into the most sublime of vistas. More subtle is the reorientation of the *translatio studii* from west to east for the immediate purposes of his allegory. In contrast to the sublime ruggedness and disarray of the foreground – the physical record of great natural forces in historical conflict – is the placid

---

[20] See Ruth H. Bloch, *Visionary Republic: Millennial Themes in American Thought, 1756–1800* (Cambridge: Cambridge University Press, 1985).

[21] Thomas Jefferson, *Notes on the State of Virginia*, ed. William D. Peden (New York: W. W. Norton, 1972), 18.

[22] At this point in his life, Jefferson, as did most of his Atlantic contemporaries, confronted competing schools of thought regarding the age of the earth. The "short chronology," which adhered closely to biblical sources, held that the earth was a scant several thousand years old. The "long chronology," which attempted to reconcile the evidence of erosion and other observable forces with the received short chronology and thus extend the age of the earth, was still a comparatively novel idea at the time of Jefferson's composition of the *Notes*.

FIGURE 10.1. Frederick Edwin Church, *The Natural Bridge, Virginia*, 1852, oil on canvas, 28 x 23 in. Charlottesville, VA: Collection of the University of Virginia Art Museum, Gift of Thomas Fortune Ryan, 1912.

background: the "smooth blue horizon" and the "plain country." The eye is naturally drawn by this "inviting" prospect, just as the flow of the river draws one irresistibly to the sea.[23] But *Notes* is a revolutionary document. Jefferson addressed it to a European audience from whom he evidently anticipated a skeptical reaction, and he employed a rhetorical strategy calculated to compel such readers to view the Virginia landscape in a particular way; Jefferson advances in this seemingly neutral description of a geological phenomenon a theory of history as well, one that is revolutionary and progressive, and, above all, *natural*. This is an allegorical representation of colonial history as Jefferson understood it, in which the Shenandoah and the Potomac

---

[23] Jefferson, perhaps more readily than many of his contemporaries (for reasons I shall discuss later), appears to embrace what Burke described as the "infinite" sublime, believing, as he did, that the North American continent was an inexhaustible reserve of land and treasure. See Burke, *Enquiry*, 2.8.73–4.

FIGURE 10.2. *Great Falls of the Potomac*, drawn by G. Beck, Philadelphia; engraved by J. Cartwright, London (London: Atkins & Nightingale, 1802). Washington, DC: Library of Congress Prints and Photographs Division.

rivers stand for the grand movement of English and European peoples westward through the Allegheny Mountains into the Shenandoah Valley and beyond. As the pressure of migration increased, as indeed it had through the middle decades of the eighteenth century, these boundaries (especially the geographical one imposed by the Proclamation of 1763, which prohibited settlement west of the Appalachian Mountains) became permeable. The Proclamation of 1763 attempted to restrain European settlement of Indian lands west of the Appalachian Mountains and to consolidate and further regulate the British colonies in North America at the conclusion of the Seven Years War. Finally, in the great "riot and tumult" of revolution, settlement expanded precipitously into the valleys below.[24]

Jefferson locates the event within a natural frame of reference; material circumstance (hydraulic force) dictates the outcome, and the inevitable consequence of free expansion is a landscape at once domestic and productive, "placid and delightful." Nature, in short, exhibits a process analogous to the social progress of humankind. The natural sublimity of the scene *and* its ideological significance for Jefferson, despite his expressing elsewhere a variety of cautious doubts, energizes his enthusiastic and triumphal utterance in the face of the spectacle of

---

[24] Most of Jefferson's contemporaries would have immediately grasped the association between "riot and tumult" and the Revolution. See, for instance, Thomas Pownell, *The Speech of Th-m-s P-wn-ll, Esq; Late G-v-rn-r of This Province, in the H – se of C-m – ns, in Favor of America* (Boston, 1769), 4.

the falls: "This scene is worth a voyage across the Atlantic." The important thing to emphasize in these examples of Silliman and Gorham and Bartram and Jefferson is how the American landscape acquired an urgent sublimity that the instincts of these men licensed and the power of their God ordained. This impulse to discover, rather than to create or invent, such reassuring messages of transcendent approval guided the work of American nationalism early in the nineteenth century. Many who engaged in the task would soon be disappointed by what they encountered.

GEOLOGY AND THE NATIONALIST SUBLIME

Although British by birth, Thomas Cole (1801–1848) quickly succumbed to the atmospheric allure of the nationalist sublime and became one of its most accomplished spokesmen. Cole possessed an almost uncanny grasp of the simultaneity of forces, which he taxonomizes in a paean to American exceptionality entitled "Essay on American Scenery" (1836). The face of nature was beautiful and picturesque, a delight to the senses and a source of joyous rejuvenation. God's good design ordered the placid landscape and even the built environment of the city:

He who looks on nature with a "loving eye," cannot move from his dwelling without the salutation of beauty; even in the city the deep blue sky and the drifting clouds appeal to him. And if to escape its turmoil – if only to obtain a free horizon, land and water in the play of light and shadow yields delight – let him be transported to those favored regions, where the features of the earth are more varied ... but in gazing on the pure creations of the Almighty, he feels a calm religious tone steal through his mind, and when he has turned to mingle with his fellow men, the chords which have been struck in that sweet communion cease not to vibrate.[25]

If here swells the soundtrack to Disney's *Bambi*, elsewhere resounds a darker score. At Franconia Notch, in New Hampshire, the American landscape uncloaks its potent sublimity, provoking a terror that approaches very near to the afflatus of worship:

Shut in by stupendous mountains which rest on crags that tower more than a thousand feet above the water, whose rugged brows and shadowy breaks are clothed by dark and tangled woods, they have such an aspect of deep seclusion, of utter and unbroken solitude, that, when standing on their brink a lonely traveller, I was overwhelmed with an emotion of the sublime, such as I have rarely felt. It was not that the jagged precipices were lofty, that the encircling woods were of the dimmest shade, or that the waters were profoundly deep; but that over all, rocks, wood, and water, brooded the spirit of repose, and the silent energy of nature stirred the soul to its inmost depths. (*Essay* 7)

The marvelous ubiquity of such sublime sights ordained Americans as a special people, but the very success of the republican enterprise had already compromised their exceptionality.

As it had for Silliman, Gorham, and Jefferson, geology provided Cole a medium through which he could negotiate the essential tension of the American sublime.[26] A favorite Puritan

---

[25] Thomas Cole, "Essay on American Scenery," *American Magazine*, New Series, Vol. I, January 1836 (Boston and New York, 1836), 3 (*Essay*).

[26] Cole and Silliman possessed a closer affinity than this juxtaposition suggests. Among Cole's staunchest patrons was Daniel Wadsworth of Hartford, Connecticut, whose mountaintop estate, Montevideo, provided Cole both a subject and a vantage point for his painting. For Cole's knowledge of contemporary geology, which was impressive, see Rebecca Bedell, "Thomas Cole and the Fashionable Science," *Huntington Library Quarterly* 59, 2–3 (1996), 349–78. See also Elwood C. Parry II, "Acts of God, Acts of Man: Geological Ideas and the Imaginary Landscapes of Thomas Cole," in *Two Hundred Years of Geology in America: Proceedings of the New Hampshire Conference on the History of Geology*, ed. Cecil J. Schneer (Hanover, NH: University Press of New England, 1979), 60–1. Parry addresses Cole's affinity for geology and his friendship with Silliman in *Nature and Culture: American Landscape Painting 1825–1875*, 3rd ed. (Oxford: Oxford University Press, 2007), 50–4.

figure for the regenerate soul was that she treads like a lamb, invoking the image of the bifurcated hoof intimately familiar to a people who crossed its track daily. Christians lived simultaneously in this world and the next, attended to animal needs, and partook of a grace that defied human expression. For Cole, the American landscape itself reinforced this duality. In Europe, he writes, the "primitive features of scenery have long since been destroyed or modified ... rugged mountains have been smoothed ... the once tangled wood is now a grassy lawn ... crags that could not be removed have been crowned with towers, and the rudest valleys tamed by the plough." In extinguishing its sublime landscape, Europe diminished its soul. Although it was "fast approaching" a similar state, in America by contrast "nature is still predominant":

and there are those who regret that with the improvements of cultivation the sublimity of the wilderness should pass away: for those scenes of solitude from which the hand of nature has never been lifted, affect the mind with a more deep toned emotion than aught which the hand of man has touched. Amid them the consequent associations are of God the creator – they are his undefiled works and the mind is cast into the contemplation of eternal things. (*Essay* 5)

Geology is the most historical of the earth sciences, but American Protestants in the first quarter of the nineteenth century dismissed the question of origin out of hand, because, as Silliman writes in his preface to Bakewell's text, "the only proper answer to the question, *How was the world made?* is briefly this – 'By the almighty power of its Creator.'"[27] Still, Cole evokes "the silent energy of nature" in the preceding passage, which posed as a dramatic counterbalance to the sharply uttered *logos* of Creation. Americans consumed the English Romantics, and their own tradition of belle lettres soon acquired its peculiar complexion, yet American intellectuals were eclectic to a fault; it was the nature of the democratic mind to pick and choose rather than to subscribe to any one school. The *Naturphilosphie*, too, engaged them, although perhaps none more so than the sage of Concord, Ralph Waldo Emerson, who preached its insights to often-baffled although enthusiastic audiences throughout the cis-Mississippi east. Cole was doubtless aware of the literature of English geology, and there is evidence that he was familiar with Charles Lyell's *Principles of Geology*, which appeared in three volumes from 1830–1833.[28] Lyell painstakingly demonstrated that one could, by observing the quotidian effects of volcano and quake, flood and wind, measured over historical time, extrapolate the age of notable features of the landscape – and this age was almost unimaginably vast. Lyell effectively epitomized the work of other English and European practitioners, many of whom were known to American intellectuals, and he established a working paradigm for the concept of uniformitarianism and "deep time" that was essential to Charles Darwin's *On the Origin of Species* (1859).[29]

Cole's intellectual milieu was expansive, but neither he nor it could easily embrace the notion of an eternal earth or of a planet ancient beyond reckoning, or, conversely, young beyond comprehension. Scripture, however liberally interpreted, promoted a distinctly millennial eschatology. In 1803, Connecticut minister William F. Miller predicted that the year 2000 would witness the "papal government of Rome ... entirely and forever destroyed, the city of Rome burnt with fire, and eternally looted."[30] The "pope" of Connecticut, President Timothy Dwight, of Yale,

---

[27] Robert Bakewell, *An Introduction to Geology: Intended to Convey a Practical Knowledge of the Science, and Comprising the Most Important Recent Discoveries; with Explanations of the Facts and Phenomena which Serve to Confirm or Invalidate Various Geological Theories*, ed. Benjamin Silliman (New Haven, CT: Second American from the Fourth London Edition, 1833), 2.
[28] Bedell, "Thomas Cole and the Fashionable Science," 350.
[29] See Rudwick, *Bursting the Limits of Time*.
[30] William F. Miller, *Signs of the Times, or the Sure Word of Prophecy: A Dissertation on the Prophecies of the Sixth and Seventh Vials, and on the Subsequent Great Day of Battle, Immediately Preceding the Millennium* (Hartford, CT, 1803), 45–6. See also Bloch, *Visionary Republic*, 217. Miller shares his name with the better-known William Miller, who early in the 1830s inspired the eponymous sect of Millerites, which held, until the "Great Disappointment," that the second advent of Christ would occur sometime in 1842 or 1843.

saw in the surge of Illuminism and Jacobinism at the end of the eighteenth century the opening of the Sixth Vial: "So alarming a state has not existed since the deluge ... the advent of Christ is at least at our doors.... Think what convulsion, what calamities, are portended by that great Voice out of the temple of Heaven from the Throne. – 'It is done!'"[31] The accuracy of Dwight's prediction is not at issue; rather we marvel at how intimate is his frame of temporal reference. The Reformation, Dwight believed, signaled the opening of the Fifth Vial; the end times were now upon us. The landscape of the present was, save human development, substantially as God had created it and would remain so until Armageddon.[32] In the twenties and thirties, liberal American Protestants began to grant that scriptural chronology, so far as it bore on the Creation, was more metaphorical than literal, but they stubbornly persisted in the belief that time remained somehow human scaled. The entirety of humanity's history might ultimately host the rise and fall of many great civilizations, but surely not an infinitude of them.

In 1810, Charles Jared Ingersoll explained simply that the "American Republic is the natural fruit of the American soil."[33] Modern geology unrelentingly undercut any simple understanding even of natal "soil" and complicated incalculably many of the "correspondences" that were so essential to the composition of the nationalist sublime. At the most extreme range resided the horrific tableau that confronted Henry David Thoreau on the summit of Ktaadn, in Maine, which he ascended in fall 1846. Struggling through low-lying clouds, he emerges above the tree line:

The mountain seemed a vast aggregation of loose rocks, as if some time it had rained rocks, and they lay as they fell on the mountain sides, nowhere fairly at rest, but leaning on each other, all rocking-stones, with cavities between, but scarcely any soil or smoother shelf. They were the raw materials of a planet dropped from an unseen quarry, which the vast chemistry of nature would anon work up, or work down, into the smiling and verdant plains and valleys of earth. This was an undone extremity of the globe; as in lignite, we see coal in the process of formation.[34]

The English actress Fanny Kemble, who was just beginning a tour that would eventuate in her marriage to an American and long residence in the United States, anticipated Thoreau's reaction, but shared its source, when she described Niagara Falls (already an icon of the American sublime) in August 1832:

There are but three places I have ever visited that produced upon me the appalling impression of being accursed, and empty of the presence of the God of nature, the Divine Creator, the All-loving Father: this whirlpool of Niagara, that fiery, sulphurous, vile smelling wound in the earth's bosom, the crater of Vesuvius, and the upper part of the Mer de Glace at Chamouni [Chamonix]. These places impressed me with horror, and the impression is always renewed in my mind when I remember them: God-forsaken is what they looked to me.[35]

---

[31] Timothy Dwight, *The Duty of Americans: At the Present Crisis, Illustrated in a Discourse, Preached on the Fourth of July, 1798* (New Haven, CT, 1798), 31. See, in this context, Chandos Michael Brown, "Mary Wollstonecraft, or, the Female Illuminati: The Campaign Against Women and the 'Modern Philosophy' in the Early Republic," *Journal of the Early Republic*, Special Issue on Gender in the Early Republic, 15, 3 (1995), 389–424.

[32] Dwight, *Duty*, 8.

[33] [Charles Jared Ingersoll], *Inchiquin, the Jesuit's Letters, During a Late Residence in the United States of America ... Containing a Favourable View of the Manners, Literature, and State of Society, of the United States, and a Refutation of Many of the Aspersions Cast upon This Country by Former Residents and Tourists* (New York, 1810), 111.

[34] Henry David Thoreau, "Ktaadn," in *The Maine Woods*, ed. Joseph J. Moldenhauer (Princeton, NJ: Princeton University Press, 1972), 63.

[35] Frances Ann Kemble, *Records of a Girlhood*, 2nd ed. (New York, 1879), 584. A polymath in her own right, Kemble significantly alludes to geological sites that were instrumental to the development of theories sustaining the theory of deep time – in the case of Niagara, the operation of erosion. Vesuvius also provided Lyell, in his *Principles of Geology*, the opportunity to reconstruct the sequence of the deposition of lava and its likely chronology. *La*

Thoreau's vision of the world "undone," a mere aggregate of "raw material," and of time measured by the slow, remorseless compression of vegetable matter into coal and of a landscape "vast, Titanic, and such as man never inhabits" would hardly have astonished readers in 1864, the year it appeared posthumously in print. Thoreau was merely terrified by the prospect of the infinite – in contrast to Jefferson's delight in it. What had once been sublime was now an object of unredeeming terror. The Civil War would soon introduce Americans to human desolation on a scale that would have beggared the imagination of Cole's generation; neither would Kemble's evocation of a nature forsaken by God have shocked them, for the same reason.[36] Thoreau did not speak to the sixties; instead he neatly pathologized the jitters of the thirties and forties, which nevertheless anticipated the anomie of the war years. He wrote from within the period during which Cole and his largely conservative cohort had to reconcile their own faith in God and their image of themselves and their nation, not merely with the troubling rise of an appallingly anarchic democracy but with a nature grown vast, deep, and, perhaps, utterly unsympathetic to their very existence.[37]

The paintings reproduced here, *Sunny Morning on the Hudson* (1827) (Figure 10.3) and *A View of the Mountain Pass* (1839) (Figure 10.4) are narratives, not of redemption but of limitless time and its latent ravages.

Jefferson's vertiginous epiphany atop the natural bridge, where in the thrall of a near-blinding migraine he uttered a uniquely American testimony – this is "the most sublime of Nature's works" – defined, in a sense, the American nationalist.[38] Gorham noted at the beginning of the century that America contained multitudes of landscapes, which Cole, assiduous as any botanist, classified in *An Essay on American Scenery*. The prospects that Cole visually represents are not especially unique – the nation possesses them in abundance – nor are they especially remote; many of them became sites of pilgrimage for travelers eager to experience the equivalent of Jefferson's éclaircissement. Yet the images are nonetheless disturbing, for they depict a landscape in a state of transient equilibrium. *Sunny Morning on the Hudson* mimics Jefferson's account of the juncture of the Potomac and the Shenandoah rivers, even to the "smooth blue horizon" of the oxbow, with its miniature sailing vessels sedate on the waters. This much is conventional: the *translatio studii* realized; onward the course of the American empire. Still, civilization is a small thing in this grand vista, which figures in the foreground and in illustrative detail a wind-carved spire of sedimentary rock, outcrops of granite exposed by the elements, and in the background a river meandering in its ancient floodplain. Visible everywhere are vestiges and portents of transforming forces. Cole's blasted trees and streaming foliage indicate prevailing gales. The sediment is a record of alluvial deposit, the signature of time, but the clouds promise the deluge that the thickening froth of mist in the valley bottoms apparently foretells. *A View of the Mountain Pass* is yet a darker representation of the same theme. Amid

---

Mer de Glace, is, of course, echoed in the title of Caspar David Friedrich's well-known *Das Eismeer* (1823–1824). The Swiss naturalists Louis Agassiz (soon to emigrate to the United States) and Jean de Charpentier would discover in the glacial ice evidence of a previous *eiszeit*, the existence of which Agassiz fully demonstrated in his two-volume *Etudes sur les glaciers* (1840). For an overview of the transmission and reception of English aesthetic theory in early national America and a subtle treatment of Niagara Falls' emblematic character through the period, see Elizabeth R. McKinsey, *Niagara Falls: Icon of the American Sublime* (Cambridge: Cambridge University Press, 1985).

[36] Thoreau, "Ktaadn," 64.
[37] Cf. Alan Wallach, "Thomas Cole: Landscape and the Course of American Empire," in *Thomas Cole: Landscape into History*, ed. William H. Truettner and Alan Wallach (New Haven, CT: Yale University Press, 1994), 23–111, and Angela Miller, *The Empire of the Eye: Landscape Representation and American Cultural Politics, 1825–1875* (Ithaca, NY: Cornell University Press, 1993), and "Thomas Cole and Jacksonian America: *The Course of Empire* as Political Allegory," *Prospects* 14 (1990), 65–92. Both Wallach and Miller emphasize how the production of Cole's art was embedded in the social, political, and commercial circumstances of his age.
[38] Jefferson, *Notes*, 19.

FIGURE 10.3. Thomas Cole, *View of the Round-Top in the Catskill Mountains (Sunny Morning on the Hudson)*, 1827, oil on canvas, 18⅝ x 25⅜ in. Boston: Museum of Fine Arts. Gift of Martha C. Karolik for the M. and M. Karolik Collection of American Paintings, 1815–1865. Photograph © 2010 Museum of Fine Arts, Boston.

the autumnal glow, the "one season when the American forest surpasses the entire world in gorgeousness," the settler's cabin is dwarfed by the surrounding mountains, as the horseman is virtually indistinguishable in the scene. Again, the blasted trees attest to previous catastrophe, and again the elements are ominous: the clouds on the left of the canvas curve as inexorably as surf; the mist above the falls in the center middle ground congeals into a mass of water poised to inundate the clearing below. This is the world imminently undone and the world, potentially, done over.

THE FIRST AMERICAN SUBLIME

"The history of the world affords no instance of a great nation retaining the form of a republican government for a long series of years," wrote Alexis de Tocqueville in *Democracy in America* (1835). De Tocqueville temporizes in the case of America but sounds this note of caution: "But it may be advance with confidence that the existence of a great republic will always be exposed to far greater perils than that of a small one."[39] Jefferson, too, had earlier succumbed to the melancholy reflection that the grand republican experiment might not outlive its makers:

But is the spirit of the people an infallible, a permanent reliance? Is it government? Is this the kind of protection we receive in return for the rights we give up? Besides, the spirit of the times may alter, will

---

[39] Alexis de Tocqueville, *Democracy in America*, trans. Henry Reeve (New York, 1838), 140.

FIGURE 10.4. Thomas Cole, *View of the Mountain Pass Called the Notch of the White Mountains (Crawford Notch)*, 1839, oil on canvas, 40 3/16 x 61 5/16 in. Washington, DC: National Gallery of Art, Andrew W. Mellon Fund.

alter. Our rulers will become corrupt, our people careless ... from the conclusion of this war we shall be going down hill.[40]

It is not so much that Americans feared history; American intellectuals of the early Republic still largely held that providence and history were compatible, and geology initially appeared to sustain scriptural accounts of creation, which concomitantly preserved the integrity of long-held millennial aspirations.[41] Geology had once revealed the signature of God in his creation, and this script was writ large across the American landscape, a special sign of his providential resettling of a people and of his high expectations for them. This was the telos of American exceptionality. To contemplate this tremendous landscape was to grasp God's design for a great nation, and the vision was wondrous and terrible, blinding almost in Jefferson's case, and

---

[40] Jefferson, *Notes*, 161.
[41] See Bloch, *Visionary Republic*, especially part III, 119–231. Samuel Hopkins, in *A Treatise on the Millennium. Showing from Scripture Prophecy, That It Is Yet to Come; When It Will Come; in What It Will Consist; and the Events which Are First to Take Place, Introductory to It. By Samuel Hopkins, D.D. Pastor of the First Congregational Church in Newport, Rhode Island* (Boston, 1793), remarked, following Edwards, that "it has been observed, that the natural world is evidently a designed type or shadow on the moral world" (p. 36). That the United States was in a hopeful way to serve as the site from which the universal redemption of the world would proceed seemed perfectly evident to followers of his "New Divinity." See especially [Stephen West, D. D.], ed., *Sketches of the Life of the Late Rev. Samuel Hopkins, D. D., Pastor of the First Congregational Church in Newport Written by Himself, Interspersed with Marginal Notes Extracted from His Private Diary to which Is Added, a Dialogue, by the Same Hand, on the Nature and Extent of the Christian Submission Also, a Serious Address to Professing Christians, Closed by Dr. Hart's Sermon at His Funeral with an Introduction to the Whole by the Editor* (Hartford, CT, 1805), 190–3.

sublime. Yet natural history rapidly transformed into a suspect terrain during these crucial early years of national self-definition, and the once-self-evident correspondences between nature and human society that had been so essential a component of the nationalist sublime became steadily more obscure.

In 1832, even as they opened to the oxen-drawn plows of white settlers, William Cullen Bryant memorialized the interior plains of North America and their vanished ancient inhabitants:

> These are the gardens of the Desert, these
> The unshorn fields, boundless and beautiful,
> For which the speech of England has no name –
> The Prairies.[42]

The prairies were a uniquely American phenomenon. They existed outside even the linguistic pale of English. For Americans, who, like Bryant, saw in the west the beckoning hand of agriculture and enterprise, they were yet another marvelous providence. Already God had prepared the land for Euro-American settlement.

Jefferson once imagined that humanity could divert the historical *ricorso* – the inevitable rise and fall of an American civilization, indeed, of *any* civilization – if not actually defeat it. Space competed with time as the primary dimension of the early American republic. The infinite resources of the continent, so the Jeffersonians believed, would diminish the forces of centralization, of urbanization, of the large-scale market commerce that ultimately nurtured corruption and its attendant civic maladies.[43] Bryant writes from this belief (although he was no especial friend to Jefferson himself). The "chosen people of God," as Jefferson portrayed them, would soon till an earth that had lain fallow for centuries and thereby establish a new Arcadia, where a benevolent nature would nourish a virtuous race, secure in the permanence of their appointed habitation:

> ... I hear
> The sound of that advancing multitude
> Which soon shall fill these deserts. From the ground
> Comes up the laugh of children, the soft voice
> Of maidens, and the sweet and solemn hymn
> Of Sabbath worshippers. The low of herds
> Blends with the rustling of the heavy grain
> Over the dark-brown furrows.[44]

Bryant laments the passing of the Mound Builders – the prehistoric inhabitants of the Mississippi and Ohio valleys – who figure largely in his poem, yet he tempers the terrors of their extinction with a distinctly picturesque vision of toiling yeomanry. Bryant invokes the sublime as an historical moment – the awful destruction of a civilization – but it is more than comfortably remote, for the arrival of white Christian settlers among the former lands of the Mound Builders represents the perfection of the landscape as the cradle of the "white man's republic." Bryant was reactionary by instinct and inclination, although the poem is nonetheless optimistic; still there lingers a certain hollowness of tone, of despair, even.

Bryant draws directly on a trope (the extinction of the Mound Builders) that gained currency in the early republic and that had already attracted the attention of James Fenimore Cooper, who explored it in *The Prairie: A Tale*, which he published in 1827, five years before

---

[42] William Cullen Bryant, "The Prairies," in *Poems*, 5th ed. (New York, 1840), 51.
[43] See Drew McCoy, *The Elusive Republic: Political Economy in Jeffersonian America* (Chapel Hill: Published for the Institute of Early American History and Culture, Williamsburg, VA, by the University of North Carolina Press, 1980), esp. chap. 1.
[44] Bryant, "The Prairies," 54.

Bryant's poem appeared in print.[45] Notable here, I think, is that Cooper revised this text for a London edition in 1832 and added a substantial introduction, which commences with a lesson in geology:

> There is much reason to believe that the territory which now composes Ohio, Illinois, Indiana, Michigan, and a large portion of the country west of the Mississippi, lay formerly under water. The soil of all the former states has the appearance of an alluvial deposit; and isolated rocks have been found, of a nature and in situations which render it difficult to refute the opinion that they have been transferred to their present beds by floating ice.[46]

Agassiz soon settled the question of glacial erratics, and Cooper's vast interior lake became an *eismeer*, or, more properly, a glacier, but this new introduction amplifies the scale of the prairie itself; the actions of the novel's human protagonists are dwarfed not only by the seemingly limitless space of the trans-Mississippi west but, increasingly, by the dark abyss of time. Cooper, as had Jefferson in the *Notes* before him, directed this edition to a foreign reader, which had the double effect of compelling him to explain the meaning of the tale more fully – which he accomplished through the addition of the introduction and seventeen footnotes – and to draw out one of its central themes. Cooper may not have known of Cole's adoption of the *Last of the Mohicans* as the subject of several small canvases in the late 1820s (Cooper and his family embarked on a several years' residence in Europe in the spring of 1826), but his reaction to the five canvases of Cole's *Course of Empire*, which was exhibited in New York in the fall of 1836 shortly after his return, was emphatic: it was "the work of the highest genius this country has ever produced," and "one of the noblest works of art that has ever been wrought."[47] Cooper's fascination with Cole's paintings is best understood within the context both of the new introduction and of the visible and impending radical recalibration of the earth's history, of which Cooper was evidently aware.

The cultural work of the first American sublime achieved several ends during the decades following the American Revolution. It helped to make sense of a variety of converging ideas and opinions. It yoked together evangelical millennialism and revolutionary republicanism and situated them in a specific environment. It characterized this environment as exceptional, both in providential terms (as in the "errand into the wilderness") and in material terms (it was unremittingly sublime). It incorporated Enlightenment psychology, borrowing freely (and not always consistently) from Shaftsbury, Locke, Hume, and Burke, and their many English and Scottish contemporaries, but it emphasized above all the power of environment in shaping not only the somatic self but the collective character of a people. The conditions of the North American environment; its varied terrains, climates, prospects, and geological features; its mysterious flora and fauna; its aboriginal inhabitants, both present and extinct; and the near-perpetual spectacle of the natural world in unfettered operation – all of these worked on the plastic stuff of the European mind and made it, well, American.[48]

The Prairie aggregates many of the features of the first American sublime and exposes the contradictions that would eventually render it obsolete as an ideological system. Cooper opens the tale in the autumn of 1804, as Lewis and Clark ascend the Missouri River "some hundreds

---

[45] *The Prairie*, although the final novel in the series, was not composed last. Cooper later published *The Pathfinder* (1841) and *The Deerslayer* (1842), both of which are set previous to the events depicted in the novel. For the "myth" of the Mound Builders, see Angela Miller, "The Soil of an Unknown America: New World Lost Empires and the Debate over Cultural Origins," *American Art* 8, 3–4 (1994), 8–27.

[46] James Fenimore Cooper, *The Prairie: A Tale*, ed. James P. Elliott (Albany: State University of New York Press, 1985), 3 (*The Prairie*).

[47] Wallach, "Thomas Cole," 79. See also Louis Legrand Nobel, *The Life and Works of Thomas Cole, N.A.*, 3rd ed. (New York, 1856), 225–6.

[48] See Angela Miller, *Empire of the Eye*, who makes a similar set of points.

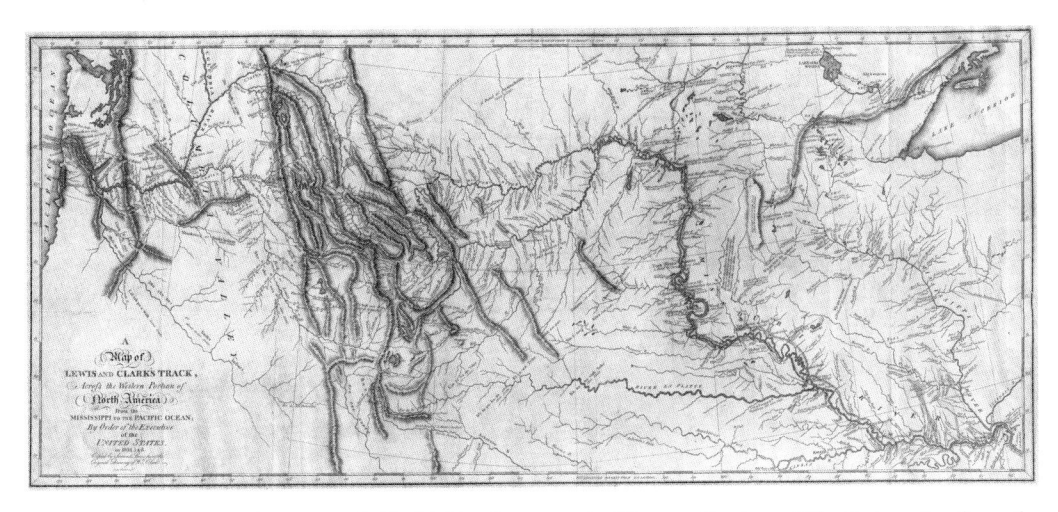

FIGURE 10.5. *A Map of Lewis and Clark's Track, across the Western Portion of North America from the Mississippi to the Pacific Ocean: By Order of the Executive of the United States in 1804, 5 & 6 / Copied by Samuel Lewis from the Original Drawing of Wm. Clark; Saml. Harrison, fct.*, 1814. Philadelphia, PA: (Philadelphia, 1814). Library of Congress.

of miles" northwest of the scene of the novel, which takes place within the largely indeterminate space of the trans-Mississippi west – Cooper plays fast and loose with the geography (*The Prairie* 117). The moment is pivotal, for in the spring of 1805, the Corps of Discovery crossed the Rocky Mountains and descended the Columbia River to the Pacific Ocean, which they reached in November. The map they subsequently produced (Figure 10.5) effectively delimits the westward extent of the nation.

The map would continue throughout the antebellum period to acquire new territories and dispute boundaries; still, the continental dimensions of the United States were effectively knowable, and indeed, one transcontinental corridor was well mapped, at least by the standards of the era.[49] This redaction of an *ideal* republic, limitless in space, to a map, cramped within an oblong sheet 23 by 14 centimeters in dimension, starkly contrasts with the geological scale of time that Cooper imposed on the novel with the introduction of 1832.[50] The tension between these two modes of reckoning surfaces elsewhere in the novel, for example, in the depiction of a United States grown small and a nature grown large, caught between a sublime prospect reduced to a black-and-white engraving and the unnerving contemplation of an ice-flecked sea, on whose bed its characters now trod. When Captain Duncan Uncas Middleton enters the camp occupied by Natty Bumppo (no longer the hale Leatherstocking of his youth and middle age, he is at this point in the story an octogenarian trapper), the naturalist Dr. Obed Bat demands evidence of his identity. "It is customary to be provided with such a document," explains the doctor, "and on all suitable occasions to produce it, in order that congenial and friendly minds, may at once, reject unworthy suspicions" (*The Prairie* 111). Men and women of Cooper's class and generation were raised among people who valued "transparency" of person above all; one's countenance

---

[49] For a fascinating account of Lewis and Clark's attempts to impose narrative order on a progressively intractable western geography and its native inhabitants, see Martin Brückner, *The Geographical Revolution in Early America: Maps, Literacy, and National Identity* (Chapel Hill: Published for the Omohndro Institute of Early American History and Culture, Williamsburg, VA, by the University of North Carolina Press, 2006), 210–37.
[50] Cooper apparently studied the reports of Lewis and Clark with some care; see E. Soteris Muszynska-Wallace, "The Sources of *The Prairie*," *American Literature* 21, 2 (1949), 193–4.

and behavior were sufficient to attest the character within.[51] Dr. Obed Bat, otherwise known as "Battius," speaks for the modern within *The Prairie*. He is obsessed with taxonomy, with the artificial, with the surface value of things. He rapturously reads aloud the commission that Middleton produces: "Why, this is the sign manual of the Philosopher Jefferson! The seal of State! Countersigned, by the Minister of War!" (*The Prairie* 111). That Battius should require documentary evidence of Middleton's character, and that Middleton should acquiesce to the request, represents a redaction of sorts. As the sublime American landscape submits to the tyranny of map engravers, so the sublime American character, too, diminishes in scale to mere "sign[s] manual" on a page.

Cooper's evocation of the Mound Builders finally situates *The Prairie* within the realm that I characterize here as the first American sublime. Natty and Battius view the world, and each other, across the abyss of time. Natty, as he repeatedly emphasizes, is a "man without a cross," which is to say that he is Caucasian without admixture of Indian blood. He is nonetheless a creature of the American landscape, perhaps as much so as any European can be. Moreover, he is a professing Christian, whose views on nature and nature's God are inextricably entangled in the Protestant traditions that I have described previously. Whether his views reflect those of Cooper we can only surmise, although the evidence suggests that they did.[52] As they chat deeply into the night, Battius attempts to explain his own pursuit of truth. His "problem," it appears, is to understand how best to reconcile geology and morality. The prairies, he proposes, represent the "exhaustion" of nature, as do the deserts of Egypt. They will never, he suggests, sustain the condition of "second child hood," this most necessary component of the historical *ricorso*; they are, Battius exclaims, "the works of man! The glories of Thebes and Balbec. Columns, catacombs, and Pyramids, standing amid the sands of the East, like wrecks on a rocky shore, to testify to the storms of ages!" (*The Prairie*, 238–9). Natty swiftly rebuts:

They are gone. Time has lasted too long for them. For why? time was made by the Lord, and they were made by man. This very spot of reeds and grass, on which you now sit, may once have been the garden of some mighty King. It is the fate of all things to ripen, and then to decay.... Tell me not of your worlds that are old, it is blasphemous to set bounds and season in this manner, to the works of the Almighty, like a woman counting the ages of her young. (*The Prairie*, 240–41)

In fact, Natty had first to interrogate Middleton at significant length to establish that he was, in truth, the grandson of his youthful companion Major Duncan Heywood, so his once-vaunted perspicacity may have dimmed with age. Or he perhaps senses that Middleton *will* marry the Spanish Inez de Certavalis, daughter of a wealthy Louisiana plantation owner (the object of *his* errand into the wilderness) and follow her into the Catholicism that she so piously professes, thus to become both literally and figuratively the "man with a cross" from whom Natty perpetually distances himself. Natty returns to the faith of Jonathan Edwards, who upheld the absolute distinction between works of God and works of man. Cooper appears here simply to turn his back on the vexing correspondence between nature and nation, for, whereas the former remains unsullied and as opaque to human inquiry as the mind of God, the latter is invariably corrupt, as befits its human origins. Where for Bryant the fall of the Mound Builders predicted a "second" and perhaps prolonged American national childhood, Cooper imagined something far grimmer. Long after Natty's death, Middleton returns to the remote site of his grave with a marker, on which he has had engraved the line "*May no wanton hand ever disturb his remains*," also the last line of the novel (*The Prairie* 386).

[51] See Karen Halttunen, *Confidence Men and Painted Women: A Study of Middle-Class Culture in America, 1830–1870* (New Haven, CT: Yale University Press, 1982), esp. chap. 2. Halttunen suggests that this sentimental convention eroded substantially in the 1830s and 1840s, which also provides some context for Cooper's concern with the subject here.

[52] Wayne Franklin, *James Fenimore Cooper: The Early Years* (New Haven, CT: Yale University Press, 2007), 52–3.

FIGURE 10.6. Thomas Cole, *The Course of Empire: Destruction*, 1836, oil on canvas, 39¼ x 63½ in. Accession #1858.4. New York: Collection of The New-York Historical Society.

CONCLUSION: NATTY'S GRAVE

Disturb his remains they did, although in symbolic rather than actual terms of course. Cooper's reaction to the *Course of Empire*, I propose, here signals the end of the first American sublime as a coherent and unifying national trope. The contemplation of the nationalist sublime requires a secure vantage, and for many American intellectuals of the late eighteenth and early nineteenth centuries, the Enlightenment conviction that the close study of nature would ensure the perfection of civilization, and the near-certain proximity of the final epoch of human history, which would fulfill itself at the millennium, offered such a platform. A Protestantism grown profligate and unruly; a litigious culture driven by commerce, greed, and competition; and a feckless democracy hell-bent on its own destruction instead greeted Cooper on his return from Europe in 1834. Doubtless he was moved by Cole's magnificent canvases, possibly the more so because two of the five represented destruction and desolation (Figures 10.6 and 10.7), which *The Prairie* poignantly anticipates in its dark reflections on the fundamental separation between nature and *human* nature.

Gone is any pretense that anything about the American experiment is exceptional. Cooper would never join arms with Thoreau, who shuddered in the presence of a land "such as no man ever inhabited," nor could he have ever willingly acknowledged the cabin boy Pip's sublime antibaptism while briefly cast away in the currents of the southern Pacific, as Herman Melville told it in 1851, the year of Cooper's death: "So man's insanity is heaven's sense; and wondering from all mortal reason; man comes to that celestial thought, which to reason, is absurd, and frantic; and weal or woe, feels then uncompromised, indifferent as his God."[53] Still, Cole's

---

[53] Herman Melville, *Moby Dick; or the Whale* (Berkeley: University of California Press, 1979), 425. Melville first published *Moby Dick* in England as *The Whale* (London: Richard Bentley, 1851), 3 vols.

FIGURE 10.7. Thomas Cole, *The Course of Empire: Desolation*, 1836, oil on canvas, 39¼ x 63 in. Accession #1858.5. New York: Collection of The New-York Historical Society.

Course of Empire was pinned at the apex of many gazes, among them Cooper's, and its allegory was not lost on him. The Mound Builders and the Americans were one and the same. Absent the sustaining framework of the ideological sublime and the faith that sustained it, Cole allows little range for the "loving eye." Instead the prospect was bleak. Civilizations whirred and buzzed, like the reciprocating arm of a Cornish engine, through endless cycles of corruption and regeneration, on the face of a near-eternal globe, which periodically erupted into a scourging violence. God's promise to his plantations, if, indeed, he had ever made one, seemed now dishearteningly in abeyance.

In an irony that should appeal to our contemporary sensibilities as perfectly sublime, the Smithsonian Institution, newly established in the city of Washington on the bequest of an Englishman, John Smithson, undertook to publish the first of its "Contributions to Human Knowledge." Such publications, so reasoned its secretary Joseph Henry, would best fulfill the injunction in Smithson's will to increase and diffuse "Knowledge among men."[54] Thus appeared in 1848 Squier and Davis's *Ancient Monuments of the Mississippi Valley*. The authors' fascination with the topic appears to derive from their understanding of the Mound Builders as "stationary and agricultural ... conditions indispensable to large population, to fixedness of institutions and to any considerable advance in the economic or ennobling arts" (*Ancient Monuments* 301). The authors dwell on this characterization: "If they were a numerous, stationary, and an agricultural people, it follows of necessity that their customs, laws, and religion, had assumed a well defined form" (*Ancient Monuments* 303). That Squier and Davis might have been describing the early

---

[54] E[phraim] G[eorge] Squier and E[dwin] H[amilton] Davis, *Ancient Monuments of the Mississippi Valley* (New York: Bartlett & Welford; Cincinnati: J. A. & U. P. James, 1848), [iii]. The volume is exquisitely produced and illustrated, representing, as it does, the institution's first intellectual offering to the Atlantic world (*Ancient Monuments*).

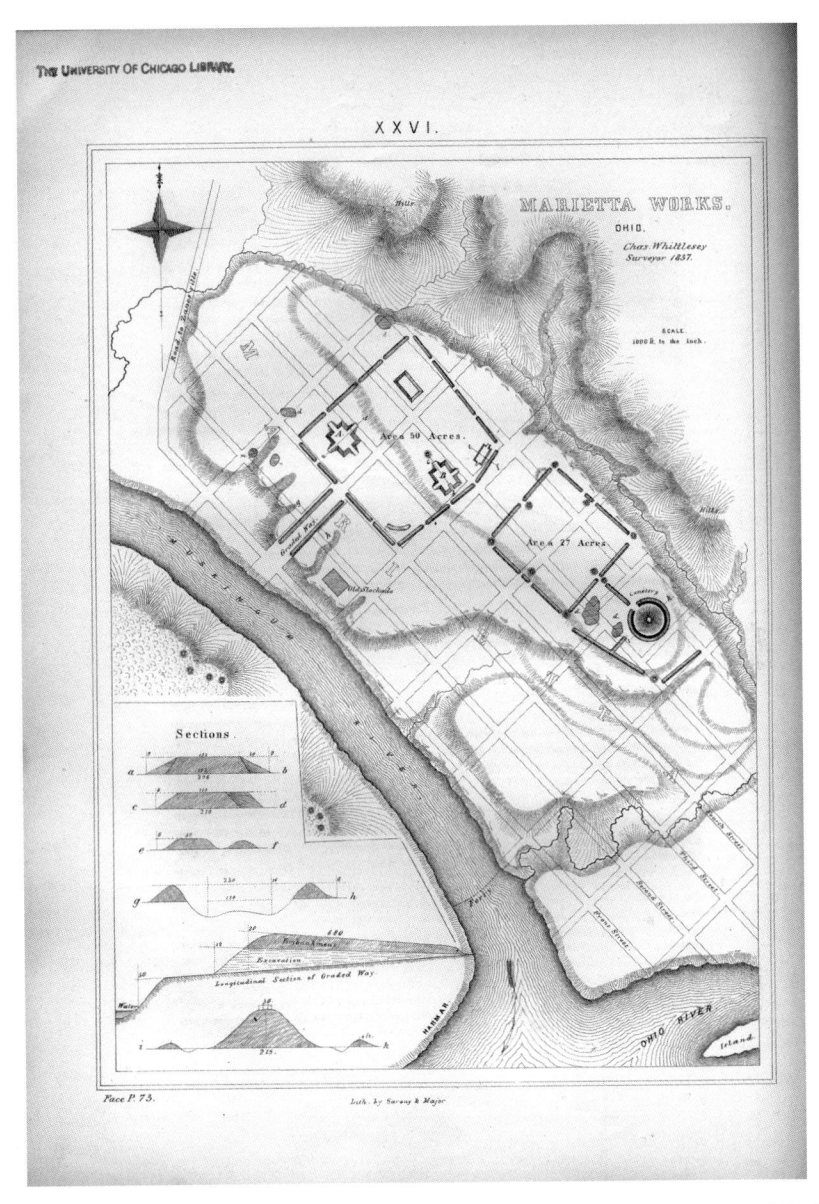

FIGURE 10.8. Plate XXVI, *Marietta Works*, in Squier and Davis, *Ancient Monuments of the Mississippi Valley* (New York, 1848). Special Collections Research Center, University of Chicago Library. Note that the street plan of Marietta, Ohio, overlays the archeological remnants of the "works."

American republic seems never to have occurred to them, but it must to us. Their uneasy displacement of the builder's "final disappearance" into the category of "the archeological and ethnological point of view" does not altogether ring true (*Ancient Monuments* 301). Their evocation of "dense commercial and manufacturing communities" and their literal superimposition of the modern social order on a culture that, by their own calculation, has been extinct for "centuries" (Figure 10.8) suggest a deep, if inarticulate, need for correspondence, although one cannot set aside the racism that regarded ancient Indians as only semicivilized (*Ancient Monuments* 302 and 306).

Here was an anxiety rightly placed, it appears. In the preface, Squier and Davis allude simultaneously to the timing of the work and to its significance:

> The importance of a complete and speedy examination of the whole field cannot be over-estimated. The operation of the elements, the shifting channels of the streams, the leveling hand of public improvement, and most efficient of all, the slow, but constant encroachment of agriculture, are fast destroying these monuments of ancient labor, breaking in upon their symmetry and obliterating their outlines. (*Ancient Monuments* xxx)

This, of course, is the fate of Natty's grave. Here, in a publication intended to impress the world, American scholars anticipated, at least faintly, the archeological excavation of their own ruined society.

11

The Environmental Sublime

Emily Brady

WHY THE SUBLIME, NOW?

Academic study of the sublime has been broad, crossing disciplines such as philosophy, literary theory, critical and cultural theory, art theory, landscape studies, and architecture. However, sublimity has been neglected in contemporary aesthetics, where one might expect it to be discussed; any attention it has received is mainly confined to Immanuel Kant's aesthetic theory or to discussions in the history of philosophy.[1] More generally, analytic philosophy has largely ignored the topic, and although continental philosophy has shown an interest, the focus tends to be on the artistic sublime, rather than the natural sublime, despite the legacy of the natural sublime bequeathed by the eighteenth century. This collection will certainly help to fill these gaps in the literature, and a key aim of this essay is to carve out a contemporary home for the sublime.

Why is discussion of the sublime neglected in these ways? It could be that the concept is considered of little relevance to current debates. Mary Mothersill's *Beauty Restored* is usually credited with reviving discussions of another concept, beauty, which, historically, was central to aesthetic theory and was usually set in contrast to the sublime.[2] Beauty is now very much back on the philosophical agenda – and on other agendas too. Is such a future possible for the sublime? Here I shall argue that the sublime is indeed relevant and that its relevance is tied to environmental thought and, in particular, to debates in environmental aesthetics. Making progress toward an environmental sublime begins by trying to understand various arguments for why the concept has been neglected. To this end, I examine and reply to three different arguments for its neglect, which I describe as follows: (1) the historical argument; (2) the metaphysical argument; and (3) the anthropocentric argument.

---

[1] Recent extended work on the sublime in philosophy includes Paul Crowther, *The Kantian Sublime: From Morality to Art* (Oxford: Clarendon Press, 1989); Andrew Ashfield and Peter de Bolla, eds., *The Sublime: A Reader in British Eighteenth-Century Aesthetic Theory* (Cambridge: Cambridge University Press, 1996); Kirk Pillow, *Sublime Understanding: Aesthetic Reflection in Kant and Hegel* (Cambridge, MA: MIT Press, 2000); James Kirwan, *Sublimity: The Non-Rational and the Irrational in the History of Aesthetics* (New York: Routledge, 2005); Christine Battersby, *The Sublime, Terror and Human Difference* (London: Routledge, 2007); and Robert R. Clewis, *The Kantian Sublime and the Revelation of Freedom* (Cambridge: Cambridge University Press, 2009). There has always been interest in the sublime in literary studies and criticism, reaching as far back as Longinus's *On the Sublime*, which was probably written in the first century but only rediscovered in the sixteenth century. See Philip Shaw, *The Sublime* (New York: Routledge, 2006), and chaps. 1 and 6 of the current volume.

[2] Mary Mothersill, *Beauty Restored* (Oxford: Oxford University Press, 1986).

THE HISTORICAL ARGUMENT

The historical argument draws on historical reasons for why the sublime has been neglected, using these to argue that it is essentially an outmoded concept. Before addressing some of these reasons, let me first provide a very brief history of the concept to establish some context. The first treatise on the sublime, *On the Sublime*, is now generally attributed to Longinus, the first-century Greek critic. Influenced by classical discussions of rhetoric, including Aristotle's, Longinus articulated the sublime as a literary style. The treatise was apparently rediscovered in the sixteenth century, and its translation into English and French in the seventeenth century was pivotal to its reception by eighteenth-century literary criticism and aesthetic theory.

Philosophical discussion of the sublime reached a pinnacle in eighteenth-century aesthetic theory, when it was unusual not to include it within discussions of taste. Contemporary debates engage mainly with Edmund Burke's and Kant's theories of the sublime, but (as the chapters in the current volume show) there is significant work on the topic by other writers during that period.

In Burke's empirical approach, the sublime is attributed to objects that are great, powerful, vast, infinite, massive, rugged, dark, and gloomy, as well as to loud sounds, bitter tastes, and stenches. The sublime involves an immediate feeling of delight mixed with terror in response to something distant enough not to be painful in a strong sense. We are completely overwhelmed by sublime objects: "The mind is so entirely filled with its object, that it cannot entertain any other, nor by consequence reason on that object which employs it."[3] Burke and, later, Kant argue that the sublime response occurs only if the spectator experiences the sublime object firsthand, and when situated in a safe position relative to it.

Although Kant's mature theory of the sublime, as it appears in the *Critique of the Power of Judgment* (1790), was influenced by Burke and earlier theories, he develops the concept through his own critical and transcendental philosophy.[4] Kant's approach is also distinctive for its almost exclusive focus on nature. Following other writers, he distinguishes between the "mathematically sublime," in which the senses and imagination are overwhelmed when confronted by the seemingly infinite magnitude of nature – such as a vast ocean – and the "dynamically sublime," in which the awesome power of nature – such as a raging sea – evokes anxious pleasure and calls forth an awareness of our distinctive capacities as moral beings, namely, freedom and the power of reason. We feel insignificant and powerless in comparison to the mightiness of nature, yet ultimately we judge ourselves, rather than objects, sublime as we discover a capacity to measure ourselves in relation to nature.

Although the sublime was then taken up in Romantic poetry and literature and in some later philosophical discussions, it has since not featured as a major category of aesthetic value. The historical reasons for this are no doubt myriad and complex, and I shall address only a few of them here. These reasons are tied to shifts in both the empirical and theoretical bases of the sublime. Empirical considerations are certainly relevant, because shifts in aesthetic taste and in theoretical discussion of aesthetic judgments can influence each other. On this point, it is useful to make a distinction between (1) experience of the sublime or sublime experiences, that is, the phenomenological experience of the sublime: for example, William Wordsworth's actual experience of Mt. Snowdon; (2) sublime discourse, or language that is immediately descriptive or expressive of such experiences and proceeds directly from them, for example, Wordsworth's

---

[3] Edmund Burke, *A Philosophical Enquiry into the Origin of Our Ideas of the Sublime and Beautiful*, ed. James T. Boulton (London: Routledge and Kegan Paul, 1958 [1759, 1st ed. 1757]), 2.1.57.

[4] Immanuel Kant, *Kritik der Urteilskraft*, in *Kant's gesammelte Schriften*, Königlichen Preussischen (later Deutschen) Akademie der Wissenschaften, 29 vols. (Berlin: Reimer [later de Gruyter], 1900–), vol. 5; *Critique of the Power of Judgment*, ed. Paul Guyer; trans. Paul Guyer and Eric Matthews (Cambridge: Cambridge University Press, 2000) (CJ).

poetic expression of this experience in *The Prelude*; and (3) talk about the sublime, that is, the "reflective or analytic discourse" on the topic, as we find in Burke, Kant, and other theories.[5] These three categories tend to run together in practice and are often difficult to separate, which in itself speaks to the strong relationship between them. Still, it is worth trying to keep the distinction in mind for clarity's sake and when teasing out some of the reasons behind the neglect of the sublime.

The early development of the sublime from its literary to natural treatment, and subsequent celebration by the Romantics, meant that it became deeply associated with natural objects and phenomena. In art history and theory, moves away from representational art and toward the expressive and avant-garde are responsible to some extent for diminishing philosophical interest in aesthetics of nature until very recently. Apart from eighteenth- and nineteenth-century Romantic conceptions of the sublime in painting and music, the sublime has also been of less interest in art until recently, when it has enjoyed resurgence among artists and postmodern theorists such as Barnett Newman and Jean-François Lyotard. Although these accounts have their own merits, I am not persuaded that the sublime, as it is originally and best understood, applies in important ways to art. We can find support for this claim in a range of eighteenth-century writers who argue that nature is the original sublime, and that art can only express sublimity through representation, and therefore only indirectly. Paintings, for example, do not possess the key qualities of vastness and overwhelming power required to evoke sublime feeling. Indeed, on many interpretations of Kant, artifacts are simply not candidates for the sublime response.[6] There may be cases of artifacts – art as well as technology – that we would want to call sublime, in which sublimity is being expressed metaphorically.[7] The limits of space do not allow me to provide a more thorough defense of this view, but it is a question worth pursuing in any new reflections on the sublime.

Alongside shifts in aesthetic theory and the arts lie significant changes in landscape tastes. Much has been written about how changes in European and North American landscape tastes made appreciation of the sublime possible in the first place, where fear and hatred of mountains, deserts, and other wild places became tempered by admiration and reverence.[8] This new landscape taste was made possible by a number of economic, social, religious, and technological factors that enabled many people to have direct, relatively safe access to such places. Theories of the sublime emerged in line with these changes, as more people – typically the elite, but also the middle classes – were in a position to appreciate sublime nature rather than simply fear it.[9]

Does the current neglect in *discourse* on the sublime reflect changes in taste and experience away from sublime objects? Has there been a decline in "taste" for the sublime? It could be argued that opportunities to appreciate the natural sublime have declined, presumably because

---

[5] Guy Sircello, "How Is a Theory of the Sublime Possible?" *Journal of Aesthetics and Art Criticism* 51, 4 (1993), 541–50, p. 542.

[6] I follow Guyer's view that the two artifacts mentioned by Kant, St. Peter's basilica and the pyramids in Egypt, are not true examples of the sublime because they are too "finite to induce a genuine experience of the sublime." See Paul Guyer, *Values of Beauty: Historical Essays in Aesthetics* (Cambridge: Cambridge University Press, 2005), 158n16. Kant does not dismiss the possibility of artistic sublimity outright, but if there are cases of it in the *Critique of the Power of Judgment*, they are likely to be of a different type (e.g., impure rather than pure judgments). See Uygar Abaci, "Kant's Justified Dismissal of Artistic Sublimity," *Journal of Aesthetics and Art Criticism* 66, 3 (2008), 237–51, and Robert R. Clewis, "A Case for Kantian Artistic Sublimity: A Response to Abaci," *Journal of Aesthetics and Art Criticism* 68, 2 (2010), 167–70.

[7] The massive scale of some earthworks projects and other forms of environmental art, as well as of some pieces of music, are possible candidates for sublimity. The "technological sublime" also offers a new area of potentially sublime artifacts, e.g., the turbines of wind farms.

[8] See Marjorie Hope Nicolson, *Mountain Gloom and Mountain Glory: The Development of the Aesthetics of the Infinite* (Seattle: University of Washington Press, 1997 [1959]).

[9] Denis Cosgrove, *Social Formation and Symbolic Landscape* (London: Croom Helm, 1984), 223.

many cultures and societies are now even less awed by nature. We appear to be less fearful, having developed technological means to control and exercise power over much of nature. For many people, great mountains and the vast sea may no longer evoke that edgy feeling of the sublime, and the anxious pleasure it involves. In other words, the relationship for many societies has become much less troubled. There may still be room for neighboring categories of response, such as awe, majesty, and wonder, but not really (it might be claimed) for the complex experience of the sublime, at least if we rely on an understanding of the concept as it was put forward in the eighteenth century. So, the main conclusion of the historical argument is that the sublime is no longer relevant theoretically because those very experiences so prevalent in the past just no longer exist, or if they exist they are, in fact, uncommon.

This conclusion is too quick, however. Our access to natural environments makes many of our experiences, thankfully, safe, and technology has also allowed us to access places that are still wild to a great extent – huge waterfalls, raging rivers, volcanic eruptions, the vast sea, space, deserts, and the like – in ways that still leave room for the sublime response. Although the concept of wilderness is highly contested, we still have experiences of more or less extreme wild places that offer possibilities for the sublime. In his essay "The Unhandselled Globe," Nick Entrikin's reflections suggest the possibility of a contemporary sublime: "As places on the margin, high places are invested with varied and often contradictory meanings, from landscapes of fear to morally valued 'pure' and natural landscapes. They have offered people sites of escape, reverence, physical challenge, discovery and learning, but at the same time have been sources of evil, human failure and death."[10] The emergence of extreme sports provides another example of ways people find risk where it may no longer exist, and some small degree of risk (if only fear "incurred in imagination," as Kant put it) is crucial to any experience of the sublime. Extreme sports are not in themselves experiences of the sublime, but they offer opportunities for aesthetic experiences of this kind because of the ways in which they situate people in the environment. There are cases, though, in which technology itself cannot match nature's power, even if it can deliver us to sublime places. Consider the eruptions of Iceland's Eyjajallajoekull volcano in 2010, which caused severe disruption to flight travel across the United Kingdom and several other European countries. We also face catastrophic changes to the earth and its landscapes from climate change taking place now and predicted for the future, changes that are unmanageable through technological fixes. Models predicting changes on a huge scale provide a kind of indirect, representational picture of a great, sublime event on a huge temporal and spatial scale.

Present-day experiences of the sublime need not be limited to extreme or remote situations. On a clear night, away from light pollution, we can gaze at that very expanse celebrated in Kant's theory: "The starry heavens above." Granted, the vast earth can now be examined at our fingertips through Google Earth and the like, but there are many opportunities for direct experience of the natural sublime. It is also possible to argue that less technologically developed societies retain a greater sense of the sublime, although this is speculative, and proof would need to be found in empirical studies. In general, however, these points support the view that opportunities remain for experiencing phenomena commonly associated with the sublime, thus making our use of the concept still relevant today. But the problem doesn't end there. The concept itself is not without its problems, and a better grasp may help us to understand whether it can indeed be legitimately associated with actual experiences of the sublime in nature.

THE METAPHYSICAL ARGUMENT

A major obstacle for the relevance of the sublime in contemporary thought, generally, has been its association with issues of a transcendental and metaphysical sort, stemming in large part

---

[10] Nicholas Entrikin, "Afterword: The Unhandselled Globe," in *High Places: Geographies of Mountains, Ice and Science*, ed. Denis Cosgrove and Veronica Della Dora (London: I.B. Tauris, 2009), 216–25, p. 222.

from the influence of Kant's theory and its development in Romantic thought and literature.[11] The metaphysical argument gathers together objections to the metaphysical dimension of the sublime, whether understood in theological or nontheological terms. Such an argument might be characterized as a type of *aesthetic eliminativism*, an attempt, that is, to theorize away the metaphysical dimension of aesthetic responses. I am not convinced that we need to shy away from the metaphysical aspect of sublime experience, however, even when an obvious alternative would be to favor an empirical account over a metaphysical one, such as those offered by Burke or Johann Gottfried Herder.[12] My worry is that such a choice would throw the baby out with the bathwater. Although I have not worked this out fully, what seems to distinguish the sublime from awe, wonder, and other neighboring concepts is (at least) its very metaphysical quality. To help support my views here, I turn to the late philosopher Ronald Hepburn, whose writings on the aesthetics of nature support the role of more speculative, metaphysical components of aesthetic experience, in addition to more particular or concrete ones.[13]

Hepburn offers careful reflections on what he calls "metaphysical imagination" in the aesthetic appreciation of nature:

Why should metaphysical imagination be under-acknowledged today? I suspect that some of the undervaluers may wish to keep their own account of aesthetic engagement with nature well free of the embarrassment of what they see as the paradigm case of metaphysics in landscape. I mean Wordsworthian romanticism.... Embarrassment, because this is taken to express a religious experience whose object is very indeterminate, whose description virtually fails of distinct reference, and which may lack adequate rational support.... But my response to that is not to urge an aesthetic experience of nature *free* of metaphysics, for that would be grossly self-impoverishing, but rather, to encourage its endless variety. What comes to replace a theistic or pantheist vision of nature may well itself have the status of metaphysics – naturalistic, materialistic, or whatever: and may have its own metaphysical imaginative correlatives.[14]

Hepburn makes a substantive point that the metaphysical dimension of aesthetic experience of nature – especially as he ties it to metaphysical imagination – cannot be ignored. The problem is the abstract quality of the experience, the actual content of which can be difficult to pin down. But this is not in itself a reason to set the metaphysical aspect aside, for the claim does not entail that the experience cannot be analyzed or critically treated. It is not the metaphysical or transcendental aspect of the sublime that is the problem but rather the way this aspect has been associated with religious or mystical experiences and discourse on nature. Some eighteenth-century theories of the sublime associate it with God's power as symbolized in nature, but in Kant we find a more secular sublime, one better suited to understanding aesthetic appreciation of nature in contemporary times. I am not marginalizing spiritual, mystical, or religious experiences, for these can provide a significant basis for valuing nature; however, it is important to understand distinctions between aesthetic and religious modes of experience.

---

[11] The metaphysical dimension in Romanticism is, arguably, pantheistic, whereas in Kant it is a metaphysical aspect associated with the autonomous self.

[12] See, for example, Rachel Zuckert, "Awe or Envy: Herder Contra Kant on the Sublime," *Journal of Aesthetics and Art Criticism* 61, 3 (2003), 217–32. Zuckert argues that Herder offers a more plausible theory of the sublime in the form of a naïve naturalism that combines the best aspects of the sublime in Burke and Kant. Herder agrees with Kant that the sublime is ultimately an elevated feeling in response to awe-inspiring objects but is critical of Kant's transcendental, a priori method and pursues instead an empirical approach, which recenters the sublime object and provides a more realist understanding of sublime feeling. In setting aside the metaphysical framework, Herder does not abandon the moral import of the sublime, but he does remove from it awareness of the ideas of reason and felt freedom that characterize the Kantian sublime.

[13] For his earlier views on the issue, see Ronald W. Hepburn, "Contemporary Aesthetics and the Neglect of Natural Beauty," in *Wonder and Other Essays: Eight Studies in Aesthetics and Neighbouring Fields* (Edinburgh: Edinburgh University Press, 1984), 9–35.

[14] Ronald W. Hepburn, "Landscape and Metaphysical Imagination," *Environmental Values* 5 (1996), 191–204, pp. 193–4.

What role might the metaphysical imagination have in aesthetic valuing of nature, and how is this relevant to my defense of the sublime? Let me begin with the first part of the question, which will lead to the second. Appreciation may be metaphysically thin or thick (my terminology) for Hepburn: "Aesthetic experience of nature can include great diversity of constituents: from the most particular ... rocks, stones, leaves, clouds, shadows – to the most abstract and general ways we apprehend the world – the world as a whole."[15] He defines metaphysical imagination as

> an element of interpretation that helps to determine the overall experience of a scene in nature. It will be construed as "seeing as ..." or "interpreting as ..." that has metaphysical character, in the sense of relevance to the whole of experience and not only to what is experienced at the present moment. Metaphysical imagination connects with, looks to, the "spelled out" systematic metaphysical theorizing which is its support and ultimate justification. But also it is no less an element of the concrete present landscape experience: it is fused with the sensory components, not a meditation aroused by these.[16]

This last point is especially important, because it clearly links the metaphysical aspect to perceptual qualities of environment, where the stimulus for aesthetic experience begins. This is a key point for environmental aesthetics, which in recent debates has wholeheartedly embraced the importance of developing theories that value nature on its own terms, or "nature as it really is" – as far as we can understand it.[17] We ought not confuse metaphysical imagination with mere fancy or reverie. Functioning in a nonfanciful mode, in response to natural objects and phenomena, metaphysical imagination, Hepburn says, "interprets nature as revealing metaphysical insights: insights about things such as the meaning of life, the human condition, or our place in the cosmos."[18]

The metaphysical dimension of aesthetic appreciation of nature is captured by Hepburn in the contemporary context of environmental aesthetics, in which it is contrasted with models that emphasize the role of science. He argues against a "one-sidedly science-dominated appreciation of nature" on various grounds, the discussion of which is beyond the scope of this chapter. But let me at least point out by way of emphasis that Hepburn again, in this context, defends metaphysical experience: "Science does not oust metaphysics: the questions of metaphysics arise on and beyond the boundary of science."[19] Essentially, we see here a celebration of a dimension of aesthetic experience that is ineliminable.

Hepburn's metaphysical imagination provides a reply to the skepticism of aesthetic eliminativism, but how might we more precisely apply this to the sublime? It helps us to explain a puzzling, difficult, yet crucial component of the sublime response, at least as characterized by Kant. In Kant's theory, the sublime involves an essential mix of negative and positive feeling. Negative feeling is associated with our capacities being overwhelmed by vast or powerful natural phenomena, whereas positive feeling is associated with an apprehension or felt awareness of freedom and our power of reason, through which we transcend awareness of the phenomenal realm and find ourselves able to measure up to nature.[20] The sublime involves an appreciation

---

[15] Hepburn, "Landscape and Metaphysical Imagination," 192.
[16] Hepburn, "Landscape and Metaphysical Imagination," 192.
[17] See Yuriko Saito, "Appreciating Nature on Its Own Terms," *Environmental Ethics* 20 (1998), 135–49; Ronald W. Hepburn, "Trivial and Serious in Aesthetic Appreciation of Nature," in *Landscape, Natural Beauty and the Arts*, ed. Salim Kemal and Ivan Gaskell (Cambridge: Cambridge University Press, 1993), 65–80; Hepburn, "Landscape and Metaphysical Imagination," 192; and Malcolm Budd, *The Aesthetic Appreciation of Nature* (Oxford: Oxford University Press, 2002).
[18] Allen Carlson, "Environmental Aesthetics," *Stanford Encyclopedia of Philosophy* (2007), http://plato.stanford.edu/entries/environmental-aesthetics (accessed June 30, 2010)
[19] Hepburn, "Landscape and Metaphysical Imagination," 194.
[20] On this point, see Paul Guyer, *Kant and the Experience of Freedom: Essays on Aesthetics and Morality* (Cambridge: Cambridge University Press, 1996), 203–5, 208–9, and 210–14, who discusses the different and sometimes inconsistent ways Kant describes the relationship between pleasure and displeasure in the sublime, and Rudolf Makkreel,

of natural qualities that precipitate a new, felt awareness of our place in the world. Metaphysical imagination helps to articulate that apprehension – an opening out of the felt experience that the anxious exhilaration of the sublime affords. If we want to keep hold of the transcendental thread in the sublime, we might speak of a type of aesthetic transcendence occurring through metaphysical imagination.

This type of metaphysical imaginative expansion complements the very distinctive role played by imagination in the Kantian sublime.[21] Imagination is, on Kant's account, "outraged" by nature.[22] Although it makes a great effort, imagination ultimately fails to present the aesthetic object to the mind. Most commentators simply leave the role of imagination at that: it fails. But we ought to recognize that imagination functions in vital ways in that very experience of failure. Briefly, in the mathematically sublime, imagination is expanded through the attempt to take in the apparently infinite, yet that activity in itself reveals a distinctive way imagination operates in the aesthetic response. The power of the imagination is opened out in relation to seemingly boundless objects – a vast glacier spread before us. In the dynamically sublime, imagination functions to present an imagined, distanced fear that is essential to the negative feeling associated with sublime qualities.[23] These crucial functions relate to an expansion of the mind and suggest an intensity absent in other types of aesthetic experience.

THE ANTHROPOCENTRIC ARGUMENT

So far, I have argued that the natural sublime, even in its metaphysical expression, is relevant for contemporary debates. It is not an outmoded concept tied to eighteenth-century experience or taste, and even its metaphysical aspect should not be a reason for suspicion. There is, however, another obstacle that must be overcome if the sublime is to be revalued in environmental thought and beyond, namely, the anthropocentric argument. This argument holds that the sublime is inherently anthropocentric, especially given the hierarchical relationship, it is claimed, that sublime aesthetic experience sets up between humans and nature.

The first thread of this argument claims that it is humanity that is valued rather than nature, such that the sublime becomes both *self-regarding* and *human regarding*. Many accounts of the sublime in poetry – going as far back as Longinus – point to how the human mind is elevated in its response. John Dennis, for example, wrote in 1696 that the "soul is transported upon it, by the consciousness of its own excellence, and it is exalted, there being nothing so proper to work on its vanity … if the hint be very extraordinary, the soul amazed by the unexpected view of its own surpassing power."[24] This elevation of the mind is brought into the context of responses to the natural sublime, in which we see in many eighteenth-century writers the idea that it is the human mind that is found to be sublime, as well as nature, in its capacity to find itself a measure to nature's might. In Kant's influential account, it is humanity (as moral personhood), reason, and freedom that is sublime and not, strictly speaking, nature itself. Kant writes that this is at least because sublimity is formless and so cannot be contained:

We express ourselves on the whole incorrectly if we call some object of nature sublime, although we can quite correctly call very many of them beautiful; for how can we designate with an expression of approval that which is apprehended in itself as contrapurposive? We can say no more than that the

---

Imagination and Understanding in Kant (Chicago: Chicago University Press, 1994), 310, who maintains that the feelings of pleasure and displeasure are simultaneous. Budd, *The Aesthetic Appreciation of Nature*, 85, interprets the sublime as a state that oscillates between feelings of repulsion and attraction.

[21] Emily Brady, "Reassessing Aesthetic Appreciation of Nature in the Kantian Sublime," *Journal of Aesthetic Education* 46, 1 (2012), 91–109.

[22] Ronald W. Hepburn, *The Reach of the Aesthetic* (Aldershot: Ashgate, 2001), 80.

[23] This point invites further discussion concerning similarities between how imagination functions in our responses to the sublime and in our responses to fiction in the arts.

[24] John Dennis, *Remarks of a Book Entitled, Prince Arthur* (1696), in Ashfield and de Bolla, *The Sublime*, 30–1, p. 30.

object serves for the presentation of a sublimity that can be found in the mind; for what is properly sublime cannot be contained in any sensible form, but concerns only ideas of reason.[25]

Kant's view is carried into the humanist sublime of Romanticism, and it was John Keats who described Wordsworth's *Prelude* as the "egotistical sublime."[26] These ideas suggest that nature becomes the means to our own self-discovery, a way through which we realize our place in the world – a place that is viewed as greater than nature in many ways. Hepburn writes that Kant's theory downgrades "*nature's* contribution in favor of the one-sided exalting of the rational subject-self"[27] and that "the natural, external world may come to be seen as of value in the sublime experience, *only* because it can make a person feel the capaciousness of his soul. Intensity of experience may become the solely prized value."[28] The sublime could be seen as a type of aesthetic experience that both distorts and humanizes nature, "degrading nature to our measure."[29]

Leading from this, a second thread of the argument is that the experience of and discourse about the sublime posits nature as an "other," different and separate from ourselves, and over which we have power. In William Cronon's well-known critique of the concept of wilderness, he argues that the sublime only serves to deepen the separation of humans and nature.[30] There are other objections that relate to the anthropocentric argument, but they lie beyond the scope of this chapter. Suffice to say they emerge from a range of positions including feminist, postcolonial, Marxist, and sociological thought.[31]

Confronting the sublime's historical legacy is a first step in replying to the anthropocentric argument. We can retain some of the most interesting features of the concept of the sublime, especially its strong association with appreciation of nature, while at the same time decoupling it from problematic connections to elitist notions of taste. Some of my earlier remarks against the historical argument have shown that there is something we can call a contemporary experience of the sublime, in which we are confronted not with some social construction but with a material experience of a natural world that "surprises and resists human desires and ambitions."[32] That is, there is something vital about the sublime that outruns criticisms of its theoretical and cultural underpinnings in eighteenth-century discussions of taste. It is worth remembering, too, that those discussions were not just about identifying appropriate categories of aesthetic taste for a particular kind of subject but were also concerned with investigating a distinctive kind of experience of the world, expressed as beauty, novelty, tragedy, sublimity, ugliness, and so on. Many eighteenth-century accounts speak to the centrality of nature as the original material of the sublime. James Beattie, a student of Alexander Gerard, sums up this point:

The most perfect models of sublimity are seen in the works of nature. Pyramids, palaces, fireworks, temples, artificial lakes and canals, ships of war, fortification, hills levelled and caves hollowed by human industry, are mighty efforts, no doubt, and awaken in every beholder a pleasing admiration; but appear as nothing, when we compare them, in respect of magnificence, with mountains, volcanoes,

---

[25] Kant, CJ 5:245. Kant uses the term "subreption" for the "substitution of a respect for the object instead of for the idea of humanity in our subject" (CJ 5:257).
[26] See Christopher Hitt, "Toward an Ecological Sublime," *New Literary History* 30, 3 (1999), 603–23, p. 604.
[27] Hepburn, "Landscape and Metaphysical Imagination," 201.
[28] Ronald W. Hepburn, "The Concept of the Sublime: Has It Any Relevance for Philosophy Today?" *Dialectics and Humanism* 15 (1988), 137–55, p. 143.
[29] Ronald W. Hepburn, "Nature Humanised: Nature Respected," *Environmental Values* 7 (1998), 267–79, p. 277.
[30] William Cronon, "The Trouble with Wilderness; or, Getting Back to the Wrong Kind of Nature," in *Uncommon Ground: Rethinking the Human Place in Nature,* ed. William Cronon (New York: W. W. Norton, 1996), 69–90.
[31] See, for example, Kate Soper, "Looking at Landscape," *Capitalism, Nature, Socialism* 12, 2 (June 2001), 132–8, p. 134; Hitt, "Toward an Ecological Sublime," 603; and Battersby, *The Sublime, Terror and Human Difference.*
[32] Entrikin, "Afterword: The Unhandselled Globe," 222.

rivers, cataracts, oceans, the expanse of heaven, clouds and storms, thunder and lightning, the sun, moon, and stars. So that, without the study of nature, a true taste in the sublime is absolutely unattainable.[33]

Kant's theory of the sublime was influenced by theories in this tradition and thus reflects an emphasis on nature, although, as we have seen, his ideas are expressed through the contours of his own philosophical system.[34]

I have argued elsewhere that the Kantian sublime is not anthropocentric in the ways various criticisms suggest, and although that argument is too complex to repeat here, a brief sketch will give some indication of its main claims.[35] Rather than reducing sublime appreciation to awareness of our moral vocation, I argue that we cannot overlook Kant's insistence that judgments of the sublime fall squarely within the aesthetic domain, and as such, natural objects, on his own disinterested notion of aesthetic judgment, cannot serve as mere triggers to grasping human sublimity. High mountains, thunderclouds and lightning, vast deserts, and starry skies are also valued for themselves. This is shown through an understanding of imagination's functioning and the direct attention given to nature in sublime appreciation. Furthermore, Kant's theory characterizes a form of aesthetic appreciation, which provides the outline of a distinctive aesthetic-moral relationship between humans and nature.[36] Various commentators on Kant have tried to draw out a connection between aesthetic appreciation of nature and a duty not to harm nature.[37] Specifically, Robert Clewis's interpretation of the sublime as a type of disinterested aesthetic judgment reveals sublime experience as preparing us for an attitude of respect for nature, even if that respect takes the form of an indirect duty.[38]

I have not shown conclusively (here, at least) how Kant's account escapes the objections of the anthropocentric argument, but I have pointed to how it is possible to recognize the element of humility running through reflections on the sublime in nature, through which we feel insignificant in the face of powers that exceed us. My aim has been to defend the more difficult, metaphysical Kantian concept of the natural sublime because it is truer to the concept in terms of its development and influence. In any case, and for the sake of moving my overall aims forward, let me show why we ought to be interested in sublime, non-anthropocentric valuing of nature.

How might we characterize appreciation of the natural sublime? I address this question by articulating how a distinctive aesthetic-moral relationship between humans and nature develops. This relationship can be seen as involving elements of both humility and self-reflection,[39] and rather than being cozy or easy it is characterized by agitation. Many contemporary theories in environmental aesthetics stress the deep engagement afforded by environmental appreciation as contrasted with scenic or picturesque appreciation, and with some forms of artistic appreciation.[40] I agree with these views, and I do think the sublime offers a type of

---

[33] James Beattie, *Dissertations Moral and Critical* (1783), in Ashfield and de Bolla, *The Sublime*, 180–94, p. 186.

[34] See Paul Guyer, "Eighteenth Century German Aesthetics," *Stanford Encyclopedia of Philosophy* (2007), http://plato.stanford.edu/entires/aesthetics-18th-german (accessed July 3, 2010).

[35] Brady, "Reassessing Aesthetic Appreciation of Nature in the Kantian Sublime."

[36] There is some dispute whether the Kantian sublime falls within the aesthetic or moral domain. In "Reassessing Aesthetic Appreciation of Nature in the Kantian Sublime," I defend an aesthetic interpretation of his theory. Cf. the contribution by Melissa McBay Merritt in this volume.

[37] See, for example, Jane Kneller, "Beauty, Autonomy, and Respect for Nature," in *Kant's Aesthetics*, ed. Herman Parret (Berlin: Walter de Gruyter, 1998), 403–14, and for a less anthropocentric reading of Kant's ethics, Onora O'Neill, "Kant on Duties Regarding Nonrational Nature," *Proceedings of the Aristotelian Society: Supplementary Volume* 72, 1 (2003), 211–28.

[38] Clewis, *The Kantian Sublime and the Revelation of Freedom*, 143–4.

[39] Other writers note this dual respect. See Arnold Berleant, "The Aesthetics of Art and Nature," in *Landscape, Natural Beauty and the Arts,* ed. Salim Kemal and Ivan Gaskell (Cambridge: Cambridge University Press, 1993), 228–43, and Hitt, "Toward an Ecological Sublime."

[40] See Arnold Berleant, *Aesthetics of Environment* (Philadelphia: Temple University Press, 1992); Allen Carlson, *Aesthetics and the Environment* (New York: Routledge, 2000); Hepburn, "Contemporary Aesthetics and the

environmental – environing – aesthetic experience, but it is not one of the intimate kind. The sublime is typified by feeling overwhelmed, anxious, and insignificant amid crashing waves, towering cliffs, great storms, and the like. This is not a delightful or contemplative experience of nature, as we might find in varieties of the beautiful. In this respect, the sublime does not define a relationship of loving nature, or even a friendly relationship with nature.[41] Rather, it is uncomfortable, even difficult – an imposition of environmental events. Returning to Entrikin, his reflections echo these ideas of humility, "extreme latitudes and elevations of the globe, vividly illuminate natural resistance to human projects ... some aspects of nature remain external to the weave of place-making and often function as barriers to such efforts."[42]

What sense can be made of the overwhelming quality of the sublime, and the sense of "otherness" often associated with it? It is an aesthetic response of nature as something much greater than ourselves, and as we have seen, this gives way to metaphysical imagination. But how are we to articulate this sense of otherness without falling foul of criticisms that otherness is simply an empty term?[43] One way around this is to adopt the concept of *mystery*, and to argue that it is the quality of mystery that characterizes this puzzling aspect of sublime experience, that is, some feature of a particular natural environment or phenomenon that cannot be known. This strategy is promising as a reply to the anthropocentric objection because it suggests that although we may appreciate a set of qualities associated with the sublime, some natural phenomena are certainly not completely within our grasp. Appreciating nature as having the quality of mystery underpins a kind of regard for nature where nature cannot be fully known or appropriated, which supports an attitude of humility.

Lyotard's philosophy enhances our understanding of how the self relates to environment in sublime experience. Although mainly directed at the sublime and art, Lyotard shows us how the subject of sublime feeling is decentered through encounters with the "inexpressible," "unpresentable," and "indeterminate." Discussing the sublime in Barnett Newman's artworks and ideas, Lyotard writes that "with the occurrence, the will is defeated."[44] In the context of nature, we might synthesize Lyotard's ideas to interpret the sublime as an overwhelming of the subject, in which the self is dislocated through a sense of nature as mysterious, and neither fully known nor appropriated by human reason. Lyotard interprets Kant to show this movement beyond a subject who "feels in the object the presence of something that transcends the object. The mountain peak is a phenomenon that indicates that it is also more than a phenomenon."[45] Against the anthropocentric argument, then, Lyotard shows how the sublime signifies a "dehumanizing" of aesthetic experience, and how it also renders a complex relationship between humans and nature arising out of an experience of great affect.

In a 2003 manuscript, "Mystery in an Aesthetic Context," Hepburn offers some interesting ways to understand mystery in aesthetic appreciation of both art and nature.[46] Although he

---

Neglect of Natural Beauty"; and Emily Brady, *Aesthetics of the Natural Environment* (Edinburgh: Edinburgh University Press, 2003).

[41] Interestingly, Kant suggests something similar, not explicitly in terms of an aesthetic relationship but as a preparation for morality: "The beautiful prepares us to love something, even nature, without interest; the sublime, to esteem it, even contrary to our (sensible) interest." (CJ 5:267).

[42] Entrikin, "Afterword: The Unhandselled Globe," 223.

[43] For a defense of the concept of otherness in the environmental context, see Simon Hailwood, "The Value of Nature's Otherness," *Environmental Values* 9 (2000), 353–72.

[44] Jean-François Lyotard, "The Sublime and the Avant-Garde," in *The Lyotard Reader*, ed. Andrew Benjamin (Oxford: Blackwell, 1989), 196–211, p. 199.

[45] See Jean-François Lyotard, "The Communication of Sublime Feeling," in *Lyotard Reader and Guide*, ed. Keith Crome and James Williams (Edinburgh: Edinburgh University Press, 2006), 254–65, p. 260.

[46] Ronald W. Hepburn, "Mystery in an Aesthetic Context," manuscript read to the Philosophy Department Research Seminar, University of Durham, 2003. See also David E. Cooper, *The Measure of Things: Humanism, Humility and Mystery* (Oxford: Clarendon Press, 2002).

does not align it explicitly with the sublime, some of his remarks on mystery in Romanticism are helpful here. Hepburn adopts the category of "indeterminate mystery" to describe that feature of Romanticism, which Isaiah Berlin described as "the absence of a structure of the world to which one must adjust oneself."[47] The sublime overwhelms through its qualities, but depending on the specific nature of those qualities, they express the infinite, the unknowable, or the nonsensual.[48]

Stan Godlovitch has adopted the idea of mystery to characterize his "acentric theory" of aesthetic appreciation of environment, which commentators have dubbed the "aloofness" or "mystery model."[49] The acentric perspective places the aesthetic subject in a position of radical desubjectivity, in which all cultural and even scientific interpretation is removed. In a position of being acutely aware of both nature's independence from us and that nature lies beyond our knowledge, our only appropriate aesthetic response is a sense of mystery.[50] Although Godlovitch in fact distinguishes mystery from the sublime because he views the latter concept as too culturally laden, his line of thought does help to express a quality associated with the sublime response. He pins down why the quality of mystery relates to the unknowable in nature, and how this may be connected to, or may even aesthetically ground, a moral attitude toward nature. I should add here, though, that I do not agree with Godlovitch's acentric aesthetic as such. A major objection is the apparent emptiness of the aesthetic subject it involves: what is left of aesthetic appreciation if it becomes *only* a sense of mystery, shorn of any layers or elements commonly associated with the aesthetic response? Mystery, as I see it, may helpfully characterize one aspect of sublime experience rather than aesthetic appreciation of nature more generally.

Turning back to the self, what sense can we make of the self-reflective component in the sublime? Hepburn indicates another useful direction by pointing to how aesthetic appreciation of nature offers opportunities for reflexivity that artistic experience (often) does not. That is, we are "involved in the natural situation itself ... both actor and spectator, ingredient in the landscape ... playing actively with nature, and letting nature, as it were, play with me and my sense of self." This type of involvement means that we may be able to experience ourselves in "an unusual and vivid way; and this difference is not merely noted, but dwelt upon aesthetically ... we are in nature and a part of nature; we do not stand over against it as over against a painting on a wall."[51] Applied to the sublime, we become a mere ingredient in the landscape, but we are at the same time aware of ourselves as overwhelmed, humbled by particular qualities in nature. This is a kind of self-reflection that need not be understood as anthropocentric, given its context.[52]

These aspects of appreciation function to fill out or in some sense articulate – at least in theoretical terms, but perhaps phenomenologically too – the metaphysical dimension of the sublime. First, mystery helps to articulate the aesthetic terms on which the sublime is overwhelming: what is literally supersensible, beyond our ken, profound, and ineliminable. Second, mystery can express a dimension of the aesthetic response that feeds into an ethical attitude, at least in terms of articulating the sublime in terms of that which cannot be overhumanized

---

[47] Isaiah Berlin, *The Roots of Romanticism* (London: Chatto and Windus, 1999), quoted in Hepburn, "Mystery in an Aesthetic Context."
[48] Hepburn, "Mystery in an Aesthetic Context."
[49] As described by Budd, *The Aesthetic Appreciation of Nature*, and Carlson, *Aesthetics and the Environment*, respectively.
[50] Stan Godlovitch, "Icebreakers: Environmentalism and Natural Aesthetics," *Journal of Applied Philosophy* 11, 1 (1994), 15–30, p. 26.
[51] Hepburn, "Contemporary Aesthetics and the Neglect of Natural Beauty," 13.
[52] Again, I have tried to interpret Kant in a way that does not commit him to this view. See Brady, "Reassessing Aesthetic Appreciation of Nature in the Kantian Sublime."

and overpowered. To this, add self-reflection understood in terms of reflexivity, and we have, arguably, a clearer understanding of the sublime as a distinctive aesthetic experience.[53] We also arrive at a kind of aesthetic interaction with nature. As we are affected by sublime qualities, we are forced into a position of admiration for nature, feeling both insignificant *and* aware of ourselves in relation to the power and magnitude of elements of the natural environment. Sublime experience could thus be said to constitute a type of meaningful relationship between humans and other parts of nature.

THE SUBLIME AND NEGATIVE QUALITIES

To conclude, I would like to make a final point about the relevance of the natural sublime. Quite apart from its metaphysical tone, it is important not to overlook the concrete phenomena and qualities that generate the sublime response in the first place. This feature of the sublime should be of great interest to aesthetics and beyond, especially given recent discussions concerning more difficult forms of aesthetic appreciation. Sublimity involves a range of qualities linked to vastness, enormous size, and power, such as the mysterious, dark, obscure, great, huge, powerful, towering, dizzying, blasting, raging, disordered, dynamic, tumultuous, shapeless, formless, boundless, frameless, and so on. These qualities are commonly contrasted with beauty, in which natural beauty is associated with harmony, for example, or smoothness, order, tranquility, and gracefulness. In an effort to support appreciation of nature on its own terms, some philosophers in environmental aesthetics have argued for the importance of recognizing the "unscenic."[54] The sublime is not the same as the unscenic, although there is overlap between some varieties of the sublime and scenic landscapes. The sublime is closer, although not equivalent, to what has been described as "terrible beauty." Just as the sublime operated when it was first applied to so-called raw nature some three hundred years ago, it now contributes to understanding aesthetic qualities that can be characterized as more negative.

The natural sublime enables us to consider forms of appreciation in relation to more threatening or overwhelming natural qualities in nature and articulates, I believe, the unsentimental and complex side of environmental experience. The sublime potentially affords aesthetic responses that throw up epistemic value too, in which we grasp nature as something that cannot be appropriated and something that, after all, deserves respect. If the sublime is to have a place in current environmental thought, its value will lie in the relatively neglected qualities it identifies, the way it characterizes a distinctive type of aesthetic engagement with environment, and the particular aesthetic-moral relationship that emerges through that engagement.

---

[53] See also Berleant, "The Aesthetics of Art and Nature," 234–8, for a reconstruction of the sublime, although one that is critical of Kant's theory.

[54] See Yuriko Saito, "The Aesthetics of Unscenic Nature," *Journal of Aesthetics and Art Criticism* 56, 2 (1998), 101–11.

12

Religion and the Sublime

Andrew Chignell and Matthew C. Halteman

And the LORD said, "Go out and stand on the mountain in the presence of the LORD, for the LORD is about to pass by."

Then a great and powerful wind tore the mountains apart and shattered the rocks before the LORD, but the LORD was not in the wind. After the wind there was an earthquake, but the LORD was not in the earthquake. After the earthquake came a fire, but the LORD was not in the fire. And after the fire came a gentle whisper.

When Elijah heard the whisper, he pulled his cloak over his face and went out and stood at the mouth of the cave.

1 Kings 19:11–13[1]

Saying this, Krishna
the great lord of discipline
revealed to Arjuna
the true majesty of his form.

It was a multiform, wondrous vision,
with countless mouths and eyes
and celestial ornaments,
brandishing many divine weapons.

Everywhere was boundless divinity
containing all astonishing things,
wearing divine garlands and garments,
anointed with divine perfume.

If the light of a thousand suns
were to rise in the sky at once
it would be like the light
of that great spirit.

Arjuna saw all the universe in its many ways and parts,
standing as one in the body
of the god of gods.
Then filled with astonishment,

---

[1] *The Holy Bible, New International Version* (London: Hodder & Stoughton, 2008).

Our thanks are owed to participants in discussions at Calvin College and the University of Notre Dame. Timothy Costelloe, Paul S. DePindican, Paul Draper, Richard Etlin, Rick Anthony Furtak, Kristen Inglis, Ryan Nichols, Alvin Plantinga, and Patrick Todd provided additional very helpful feedback. Work on this paper was supported by a generous grant from the Center for Philosophy of Religion at Notre Dame.

> his hair bristling on his flesh,
> Arjuna bowed his head to the god.
>
> *Bhagavad-Gita* 11.12–14[2]

INTRODUCTION

The relationship between the religious and aesthetic domains in human life is deep, complicated, and hard to describe in philosophical prose. Characterizing it is all the more challenging when the proposed point of intersection is the sublime, which by its very definition runs up to ("sub") the limit ("limen") of conceptual analysis and phenomenological description.[3] As a result of the elusiveness of the topic – as well as the vastness of the historical territory here – scholarly work on the relationship between religion and the sublime has tended to focus on a specific period or set of figures, with few attempts to provide a theoretical template for the whole.[4] Our goal here, however, is to do precisely that. We begin with some conceptual ground clearing before briefly highlighting some undernoticed connections between religion and the sublime in two central eighteenth-century authors, Edmund Burke and Immanuel Kant. We then devote the bulk of the chapter to a fourfold taxonomy of what we call the *theistic* sublime, the *spiritualistic* sublime, the *dymythologistic* sublime, and the *nontheistic* sublime. These models depict four main ways in which sublime experience relates to central features of religious life – that is, to what Rudolf Otto calls experience of the "numinous," to the acceptance of religious doctrine, and to the behaviors and affections that often characterize religious practice.[5] We conclude with a survey of what we regard as the main prospects for and obstacles to theoretical attempts to bring the domains of the religious and the sublime together in this way.

THE SUBLIME: DISCURSIVE PRELIMINARIES

It is worth noting right away that we do not take ourselves to be characterizing *the* concept of the sublime, largely because (as the various chapters of this volume indicate) there is more than one concept that goes by the name. In contemporary parlance, "sublime" functions as a term of general approbation: a highbrow version of "awesome" that can be ascribed without irony to almost any object, person, or quality that produces pleasure (thus it doesn't sound odd to speak of a politician's "sublime speech," a chef's "sublime cake," or a philosopher's "sublime beard"). This everyday concept is thus distinct from – or at most an extremely watered-down descendent of – the more technical eighteenth-century concept, which makes essential reference to *sensory* experience of art or nature. The authors who established the contours of the latter concept (Baillie, Addison, Burke, and Kant) also construe genuine sublime experience as requiring two distinct moments: first, a feeling of being dazzled and even terrified in the face of something vast, violent, threatening, or incomprehensible, and, second, a feeling of reassurance accompanied by a reflective epiphany or realization. Moreover, a certain logic is supposed to connect the two moments: whereas the first tears apart, bursts, and threatens to

---

[2] *Bhagavad-Gita*, trans. Barbara Stoler-Miller (New York: Columbia University Press, 1987).
[3] Cf. editor's introduction to the current volume.
[4] David B. Morris, *The Religious Sublime: Christian Poetry and Critical Tradition in Eighteenth-Century England* (Lexington: University Press of Kentucky, 1972), focuses on a particular century in British literature; Henry Hart, "Robert Lowell and the Religious Sublime," *New England Review* 14, 1 (1991), 24–47, on a single poet; Jan Rosiek, *Maintaining the Sublime: Heidegger and Adorno* (Bern: Peter Lang, 2000), on two twentieth-century philosophers; and Clayton Crockett, *A Theology of the Sublime* (New York: Routledge, 2001), primarily on Kant and his legacy in twentieth-century continental philosophy.
[5] See Rudolf Otto, *The Idea of the Holy*, trans. John W. Harvey, 2nd ed. (Oxford: Oxford University Press, 1950), chap. 2. The term derives from the Latin *numen*, which literally means "nodding" but has been used since Roman times to refer to divine presence and will.

annihilate, the second pieces back together, repairs, and reconstructs, although often in new and unexpected ways.[6]

Although our account takes its cues from this historical tradition and is thus about a restricted, technical concept of the sublime, we do not toe the Enlightenment line unthinkingly. Instead we propose to divide the traditional two "moments" into *three* distinct phases or stages. The first stage remains that of bedazzlement, terror, and transfixedness, but there is also a second, distinct stage at which the subject's conceptual or linguistic faculties are felt to be transcended or surpassed: she has a vertiginous sense of encountering something whose salient features outstrip her intellectual grasp, and her mind is thus "raised" over or at least beyond its typical cognitive transactions with objects (this aspect of the experience is reflected in the German for "the sublime" – *das Erhabene* – literally, "the elevating"). The sense of outstripping or transcendence can persist well beyond the point at which the initial bedazzlement or fright has subsided. Finally, third, there is a more explicit epiphany – a eureka stage at which the subject's affections or beliefs are changed, existing states are in some way strengthened, or familiar commitments are transformed. These three stages are conceptually distinct, and in what follows we will characterize paradigmatic sublime experience as involving all three. We refer to them as the stages of *bedazzlement, outstripping,* and *epiphany*, respectively.

Before proceeding, a few additional comments are in order. First, although exemplifying all three stages is certainly sufficient for an experience to count as sublime, we do not mean to suggest that every such experience exemplifies each stage in a discrete way. There will be at least a family resemblance between such episodes, however, and thus we think the sublime can be usefully articulated in terms of the three-stage heuristic proposed.

Second, each stage comes in degrees. Being dazzled is clearly a gradable property, as is being outstripped: one's conceptual and linguistic faculties can seem (and be) inadequate to a given task to a greater or lesser degree. Perhaps having an epiphany is an all-or-nothing affair: either one's affections or beliefs are altered in some way, or they are not. Once the threshold has been crossed, however, there will be more or less dramatic epiphanies, depending on the number of states that change, the degree to which they change, and the logical relationships they bear to prior states of the subject. Thus someone whose epiphany involves adopting the belief that the physical universe is a mere phenomenal sheen draped across ultimate reality by the senses (Arjuna in the *Bhagavad-Gita*, for instance) clearly has a more dramatic epiphany than someone who forms a new belief about, say, the vastness of space. Other things being equal, the first person's experience will also be that much more sublime.

Third, despite the etymology, "epiphany" here is not meant as an alethic or truth-guaranteeing term. Epiphanies, at least as we are thinking of them, may be false or misleading.

Fourth, temporal relations between these three stages can vary. In some cases all three may overlap, whereas in others the epiphany stage will be achieved gradually and much later than the first two. From a psychological point of view it seems that the first two – bedazzlement and outstripping – will almost always occur in close succession: the initial, hair-raising sight leads naturally to the "raising" of the mind as well. Still, a large temporal gap is possible; perhaps the original fright occurred last week, but my memory of the episode today is what leads to the sense of transport to the "beyond."

This point about memory raises the related, fifth, issue of whether sublimity can be ascribed to nonsensory as well as sensory experiences. Thomas Aquinas and Blaise Pascal famously reported visions followed by the epiphanic realization that certain philosophical conceptions were inadequate to what they had "seen."[7] Although such visions are not sensory experiences

---

[6] This is the traditional logic of the sublime, but as we will see in discussing the nontheistic sublime in the following, some contemporary theorists are less sanguine about the prospects for repair and reconstruction.

[7] Aquinas is supposed to have had a mystical experience while saying Mass on December 6th, 1273. On being asked to resume his scholarly writing after this experience, he allegedly replied that "all I have written seems like straw to me compared to what I have seen." See Brian Davies, *The Thought of Thomas Aquinas* (Oxford: Clarendon Press, 1993), 9.

strictly speaking, they often have a quasi-sensory component (consider Pascal's "*Fire!*"[8]) and exemplify the three-stage pattern discussed previously. Thus it is natural to view these and other such illusionary, dreaming, or even bare thinking episodes as borderline cases of the sublime. Even so, the eighteenth-century sources of the conception of the sublime at issue typically insist on its explicitly *aesthetic* character. In an effort to restrict our discussion to aesthetics and avoid embarking on a discussion of religious experience in general, we too will focus on episodes involving the *sense-perceptual* apprehension of vistas, natural objects, and artifacts, as well as the memory of such, and will make this restriction clear by using "bedazzlement" rather than the more general "overwhelmedness" to refer to the characteristic feeling of the first stage. It is important to note, however, that inner awareness of perceptual content that has been *self-consciously* reconfigured by imagination may also figure into sublime experience, even though it is not directly sense perceptual. This is presumably the sort of creative-memorial apprehension of sense-content one has while reading literature and poetry. By contrast, un-self-consciously produced dreams and visions, as well as all nonsensory mystical experiences, fall outside the scope of our discussion here.

Finally, eighteenth-century writers often assume that reference to the beholder's subjective experience is essential to the sublime, religious or otherwise. Kant even argues that sublimity is a property of the mind rather than of the external object, although we quite naturally (albeit "subreptively") ascribe sublimity to the latter. Here we will adopt a more irenic view, according to which saying that "X is sublime" is short for saying that a certain *relation* holds between X and a perceiver. "That mountainscape is sublime!" for instance, is shorthand for the claim that the vista in question evokes an instance of the three-stage experiential episode (bedazzlement, outstripping, and epiphany) in a suitably situated and well-functioning subject. We remain neutral about whether there is in addition some "objective" property of sublimity in the world, and about related issues such as whether everything, in principle, could be an object of sublime experience if beheld in the right way. We also won't say much about the characteristics that make someone a "suitably situated" and "well-functioning" subject, and we will use "sublime experience" and "experience of the sublime" as synonyms.

BURKE AND KANT: INTIMATIONS OF RELIGION IN THE SUBLIME

With these preliminary remarks in the background, we can now turn to an analysis of the ways in which certain experiences of the sublime might be considered religious. As already noted, one of the main challenges for any account of the sublime is that the first two stages do not lend themselves to easy analysis. The vertigo involved in perceiving a volcanic eruption at night or an angry sea from a sheer overlook makes a deep impression on those who experience it, but adequate description of the episode eludes philosophical prose. Perhaps this is why Kant, rarely at a loss for words, turns to his faculty psychology for an abstract, albeit curiously anthropomorphic, account of these stages. Certain vistas in nature, he says, are an "abyss" for the imagination "in which it fears to lose itself"; an encounter with them is "repulsive to mere sensibility" and even "does violence to inner sense."[9] Presumably the same could be said for various art objects or literary or imaginative descriptions; Kant himself adduces "Milton's depiction of

---

[8] Pascal's vision of November 23, 1654, led him to write on a scrap of paper, "Fire! God of Abraham, God of Isaac, God of Jacob, not of the philosophers and the scholars." Pascal kept this scrap of paper on his person until his death. See Blaise Pascal, *Oeuvres complètes*, ed. Louis Lafuma (Paris: Seuil, Intégrale, 1963 [1654]), 493–649, p. 618.

[9] Kant, *Kritik der Urteilskraft*, in *Kant's gesammelte Schriften*, Königlichen Preussischen (later Deutschen) Akademie der Wissenschaften, 29 vols. (Berlin: Reimer [later de Gruyter], 1900–), vol. 5 (KGS); *Critique of the Power of Judgment*, ed. Paul Guyer; trans. Paul Guyer and Eric Matthews (Cambridge: Cambridge University Press, 2000), 5:258–9 (CJ). All references to Kant's works are to the pagination of the Akademie edition.

the kingdom of hell" as a paradigmatic example of the sublime in literature.[10] In this he follows Burke, who says that in Milton's description of Death in book II "all is dark, uncertain, confused, terrible, and sublime to the last degree."[11] Burke cites (and slightly misquotes) the following passage (from *Paradise Lost* II, 666–73):

> The other shape,
> If shape it might be called that shape had none
> Distinguishable in member, joint or limb;
> Or substance might be called that shadow seemed,
> For each seemed either; black he stood as night;
> Fierce as ten furies; terrible as hell;
> And shook a deadly dart. What seemed his head
> The likeness of a kingly crown had on.
> Satan was now at hand; and from his seat
> The monster, moving onward, came as fast
> With horrid strides; Hell trembled as he strode.

The narrator here appears to experience not just the first but also the second stage of the sublime. "Death" is depicted as outstripping our normal categories: it has a shape without a real shape, it has no distinguishable member, it is both substance and "shadow" or perhaps neither, and so forth. This awareness or sense of being transported, in the second stage, may have a figurative direction to it: upward toward God and perfection; horizontally in the direction of previously unimagined discursive possibilities; or, as here in *Paradise Lost*, downward into abjection, privation, or nothingness. Apart from that very minimal phenomenological movement, however, it can be difficult to find nontrivial content – religious or otherwise – in the second, concept-transcending stage (although this too, however, is surely a matter of degree).

In the epiphanic third stage, by contrast, the religious dimension becomes more explicit, and thus more accessible to philosophical analysis. For Burke, the epiphany often involves contemplation of the divine power that is shadowed or symbolized by the terrifying power and vastness of nature (*Enquiry* 2.5.68–70). Indeed, absolute divine power is the implicit referent of so much of Burke's theory that God himself might be seen as "the occluded hero of the sublime, for Burke."[12] According to Kant, the third stage involves the recognition of the superiority of mind to natural phenomena, a superiority grounded in reason's participation in an ultimate moral or religious reality that is itself governed by an omnipotent, omniscient, and wholly good God (CJ 5:244–78).

For two of the main historical sources of the technical concept of the sublime, then, the aesthetic experience in question is not a traditional "religious experience" precisely, but it is still integrally bound up with substantive religion as they conceived of it. Other early attempts to articulate the content of the third stage share this Burkean-Kantian tendency to understand the sensuously dazzling by appealing to ways in which the subject relates to even more fundamental, supersensuous realities. Nineteenth- and twentieth-century heirs of this conception, by contrast, retained the bedazzlement aspect of the first stage, as well as the ability of the

---

[10] Kant, *Beobachtungen über das Gefühl des Schönen und Erhabenen*, in KGS 20:208; cf. *Observations on the Feeling of the Beautiful and Sublime and Other Writings*, ed. and trans. Patrick Frierson and Paul Guyer (Cambridge: Cambridge University Press, 2011).

[11] Edmund Burke, *A Philosophical Enquiry into the Origin of Our Ideas of the Sublime and Beautiful*, ed. James T. Boulton (London: Routledge and Kegan Paul, 1958 [1759, 1st ed. 1757]), 2.3.55 (*Enquiry*). References are to part, section, and page number.

[12] Vijay Mishra, *The Gothic Sublime* (Albany: State University of New York Press, 1994), 31–2. Mishra also suggests that for Burke, in what we are calling the first stage of the sublime, "the object of astonishment remains the unnameable presence of God."

sublime to lead the mind, in Longinus's words, "to rise above what is mortal,"[13] but they also tended to excise or flatten the theological content such that sublime experience came to offer at most an inchoate sense of something transcending experience and categorization. The transcendent thing *might* be interpreted, in a Schleiermachian vein, as divinity manifesting itself to us in nature and art.[14] But as we will see, it became commonplace to interpret the sublime in a completely nontheological way and thus as consistent with a fully secular outlook. Beginning with the most explicitly theistic model, the taxonomy to which we now turn lays out these competing conceptions and seeks to highlight some of the theoretical costs and benefits involved in each of them.

TAXONOMY OF RELATIONS BETWEEN RELIGION AND THE SUBLIME

The Theistic Sublime

Let "theistic sublime" stand for episodes whose epiphanic content includes some affirmative theistic doctrine or other: "Yahweh is both just and merciful," for example, or "reality is at bottom personal," "Allah has the property of omnipotence," "God loves me unconditionally," "Jesus wants me to commit my life to him," "Shiva will destroy the universe," and the like. Although the contents of these propositions differ radically, they each entail the existence of some deity or other. In what follows, we distinguish three distinct species of the theistic sublime: the *conversional*, the *corroborative*, and the *transformative*.

The Conversional Theistic Sublime
It seems at least possible for sublime experience to lead someone who is not at all religious, and not even consciously disposed toward religion, to adopt a robust theistic belief. Such a person may also come to believe that God is the cause and/or object of the experience, although that is not required in order for the episode to fall into this category. During his now-famous grand tour of continental Europe with Horace Walpole, for instance, the eighteenth-century British poet Thomas Gray noted that he was not moved by the art objects he encountered, but that

> those of nature have astonished me beyond expression. In our little journey up to the Grande Chartreuse I do not remember to have gone ten paces without an exclamation that there was no restraining; not *a precipice, not a torrent, not a cliff, but is pregnant with religion and poetry*. There are certain scenes that would awe an atheist into belief, without the help of other argument. One need not have a very fantastic imagination to see spirits there at noon-day. You have Death perpetually before your eyes, only so far removed as to compose the mind without frighting it.[15]

Gray's claim here is that an atheist (and presumably an agnostic too) would be "awed" into theistic belief "without the use of any argument," simply on confronting the torrents and cliffs of the French Alps. Perhaps this is just literary flourish on Gray's part, but supposing that it is not: what would constitute the connection between the first two stages of the experience and the explicitly theistic third stage? In other words, what is it about the experience that would make the atheist suddenly believe?

---

[13] Longinus, *On the Sublime*, trans. W. Rhys Roberts (Cambridge: Cambridge University Press, 1899), 36.1.
[14] See Friedrich Schleiermacher, *On Religion: Speeches to Its Cultured Despisers*, ed. and trans. R. Crouter (Cambridge: Cambridge University Press, 1988 [1799]).
[15] From Gray's correspondence with his friend Richard West in late 1734, just after he and his touring party reached Turin. Quoted in Edmund Gosse, *Gray* (London: Macmillan, 1902 [1882]), 33. The emphasis appears to be original to Gray. For other accounts of conversions on the basis of what might be called sublime experience, see William James, *The Varieties of Religious Experience* (New York: Touchstone, 1997 [1902]), passim.

Reflection on this question reveals that the conversional theistic sublime can be conceived in two importantly different ways. On the one hand, sublime experience might produce theistic epiphanies in someone who satisfies no other nontrivial conditions that incline him toward such episodes. On the other hand, sublime experience might lead to a change in belief or affect only for those in whom a specific and nontrivial "subjective condition" is present, a condition whose description is itself a matter of contention.

Genuine instances of the first conception are hard to identify, because the presence of the subjective condition will presumably be hard to detect, even for the subject involved. A possible example, however, is that of the Roman centurion who was on duty at Golgotha when Jesus of Nazareth was crucified.[16] As the Synoptic Gospels relate the story, soon after piercing Christ's side, the centurion witnessed a series of stupendous events in nature – the blackening of the sky at noon, an earthquake, the splitting of rocks, and the spontaneous opening of tombs. His response was to be "terrified" and then to exclaim (and presumably form the belief that), "Truly, this man was the Son of God!" (Matthew 27:50–54; compare Mark 15:39). According to the Lucan author, the centurion's response was actually to "worship God" and then exclaim, "Surely this was a righteous man!" (Luke 23:47).

Note that this example involves sensory perception of natural objects (sky, rocks, earth, and tombs) whose irregular and terrifying behaviors were apparently witnessed by everyone present. This makes the episode importantly different from, say, Saul's theophany on the road to Damascus, which was not available to others in his party. The example also involves a subject who is not, at least as far as we are told, predisposed toward the belief that he endorses in the third stage. Indeed, if the centurion had had any inkling that the man he was ordered to beat, strip, torture, and execute was in fact *divine* – even in the polytheistic Roman sense, much less in the monotheistic Jewish sense – it is likely that he would have sabotaged the operation or at the least expressed some reservations. The fact that he is depicted as participating in the whole ordeal – including personally piercing Christ's side with a lance – provides strong circumstantial evidence that he had no inclination to believe that the victim was divine.

But then comes the sublime experience in its three stages: the centurion is "terrified" at the strange events in nature, events whose ultimate significance fully outstrip his understanding, and he then falls down in awe and worship while endorsing (and exclamatorily uttering) a proposition about God's existence in the form of Christ. The sublime episode is pictured in a particularly effective fashion in Lucas Cranach the Elder's sixteenth-century piece *The Crucifixion with the Converted Centurion* (Figure 12.1). The centurion clings to his rearing horse in the foreground, exclaiming his epiphanic realization (note the words emitting from his mouth), even as the black sky above him roils and the rest of the earth takes on the appearance of an arid, inhospitable wasteland. Church tradition declares that the centurion's conversion was so complete that he subsequently assisted Joseph of Arimathea and the Marys in bringing the body down from Golgotha, cleansing it, and laying it to rest in the tomb.[17]

The other main variety of the conversional theistic sublime involves preexisting subjective conditions that are "non-doxastic" in that they do not involve any particular beliefs (*doxa*) on the part of the subject. These conditions are thus still consistent with the complete absence of theistic belief. In the Augustinian or Kierkegaardian tradition, the idea here is typically expressed in terms of cognitive "grace": God unilaterally imparts the ability to apprehend his

---

[16] See Tsang Lap-chuen, *The Sublime: Groundwork towards a Theory* (Rochester, NY: University of Rochester, 1998), who uses the Crucifixion as the paradigmatic instance of the sublime *simpliciter* rather than of the religious sublime in particular.

[17] Incredibly, at least for scholars of the sublime, this very centurion was later canonized as "Saint Longinus" on account of his having been the one who lanced Christ's side (Greek for "lance" is "*longche*"). That he shares his Christian name with the author of the famous treatise makes it all the more fitting that St. Longinus's conversion experience would count as a paradigm case of the religious sublime.

FIGURE 12.1. Lucas Cranach the Elder, *The Crucifixion with the Converted Centurion*, 1538, oil on panel, 24¼ x 16⅝ in. New Haven, CT: Yale University Art Gallery. Gift of Hannah D. and Louis M. Rabinowitz.

existence and features through experience of finite nature and art, and this condition need not be either doxastic or conscious. It does involve something more than the mere possession of concepts, however: for reasons inscrutable to us, God enables, inclines, or (in a more Calvinist spirit) positively determines certain minds to interpret sublime experience as having a religious content or even a divine relatum. This gift of grace leads, in the epiphanic stage, to full-blown theistic belief.

Clearly in the second variety of the conversional theistic sublime, the subjective condition itself is what underwrites the move from the phenomenology of the first two stages to the explicit commitments of the third. That is not to say that the subject's interpretation of the experience is *justified* in some strong internalist sense – by an introspective appeal to the presence of the subjective condition, for example. Again, in most cases the subject will be unaware of the condition and unable to be aware of it. This doesn't preclude the interpretation from being justified in some other sense, however.

In the first variety of the conversional theistic sublime, by contrast, there is by hypothesis no special subjective condition. The experience of noonday darkness, earthquakes, splitting rocks, and the like would be terrifying to almost anyone, and very likely to occasion a sense of understanding outstripped. But it is hard to see why anyone should associate such an occurrence per se with the existence of divinity, much less the divinity of someone in particular. So there must be something else about the experience, the subject, or both together that motivates the endorsement of theistic content in the epiphanic stage. The centurion experiences terrifying events in nature while facilitating the crucifixion of a self-proclaimed messiah; he then makes what looks like an *inference* from the occurrence of these events to the veracity (and innocence) of the man he had executed. Our suspicion is that this sort of inference-to-best-explanation process from the subject's background beliefs will be at work in many or even most cases of the conversional theistic sublime.

The Corroborative Theistic Sublime
The corroborative theistic sublime involves the strengthening of preexisting theistic belief and/or affection. Occurrently or not, the subject already believes in God and has certain religious affections but then finds these states corroborated in the experience of the sublime. Talk of "corroboration" here is not meant to suggest that sublime experience, on its own, somehow raises the objective *probability* that God exists. In other words, the idea is *not* that one can simply read off of the experience of the vast night sky or the Himalayan peaks the information that there is a divine creator. Rather, what happens is presumably more of a reading *into* than a reading *off*: background beliefs are involved, and the kind of corroboration in question is importantly subjective. In other words, the sublime experience, given a theist's prior commitments, makes it rational for her to raise credence levels with respect to various doctrinal propositions. The important role played by background beliefs explains why people in different traditions take similar sorts of experience to corroborate very different religious doctrines, and also why rational apologists have not found much probative force in appeals to the sublime.

John Henry Newman's distinction between "real" and merely "notional" assent offers a different way of thinking about the epiphanic upshot here. Newman argues that propositions can be held "notionally," in the way that a docile member of a congregation might assent to the proposition that God is love, and that this is quite different from the "real" way in which a subject of an intense religious experience of divine love holds the same proposition. It may be that the content and even strength of the assent is the same in both cases, but the experience so transforms the latter subject's associations and affections that the assent somehow becomes "real" for her in a way that a "notional" assent just isn't. For our purposes, this still counts, broadly speaking, as a corroborative effect.[18] The same sort of thing can happen, presumably, as the result of a sublime experience.

For an account of how the corroborative theistic sublime might go with respect to religious affections rather than beliefs, consider the following passage from Ann Radcliffe's eighteenth-century novel *A Sicilian Romance*, which describes the experience of a nun as she takes her vows:

The high importance of the moment, the solemnity of the ceremony, the sacred glooms which surrounded me, and the chilling silence that prevailed when I uttered the irrevocable vow – all conspired to impress my imagination, and to raise my views to heaven. When I knelt at the altar, the sacred flame

---

[18] John Henry Newman, *Essay in Aid of a Grammar of Assent*, 9th ed. (London: Longmans and Green, 1903 [1870]), 10ff. Thanks to Steve Wykstra for pointing us to Newman here.

of pure devotion glowed in my heart, and elevated my soul to sublimity. The world and all its recollections faded from my mind, and left it to the influence of a serene and holy enthusiasm which no words can describe.[19]

Although fictional, the passage is instructive: the context of the experience – in a church, at the altar, taking holy vows – coupled with the nun's background beliefs makes it natural for her to feel a strengthened religious affection (a "serene and holy enthusiasm"). Her degree of belief in God's existence, presence, and concern needn't be raised in such a case; indeed, we can suppose that she already believes these things to the highest degree. The affections alone are strengthened by the experience, given the subject's interpretation of it. This is consistent, in our view, with the episode being, broadly speaking, an instance of the corroborative theistic sublime.[20]

The Transformative Theistic Sublime
The third species of the theistic sublime also involves a doxastic subjective condition – at the very least some kind of preexisting theistic belief – but the experience has a transformative rather than merely corroborative effect. The experience may lead the subject, in the epiphanic stage, to *realize* something and thus to *change* her conception of the divine, of the self, of the relation between the two, and so on. It may also, or alternatively, cause a transformation of her affections: the subject of the sublime may develop a new love, or a new commitment to her karmic duty. In many cases, the subject presumably regards this change not just as the causal upshot of the experience but as a way of taking account of or being true to it. William James quotes testimony from a clergyman in this connection:

I have on a number of occasions felt that I had enjoyed a period of intimate communion with the divine.... Once it was when from the summit of a high mountain I looked over a gashed and corrugated landscape extending to a long convex of ocean that ascended to the horizon, and again from the same point when I could see nothing beneath me but a boundless expanse of white cloud, on the blown surface of which a few high peaks, including the one I was on, seemed plunging about as if they were dragging their anchors. What I felt on these occasions was a temporary loss of my own identity, *accompanied by an illumination which revealed to me a deeper significance than I had been wont to attach to life*. It is in this that I find my justification for saying that I have enjoyed communication with God.[21]

The transformation involved in this species of the theistic sublime often, although certainly not always, moves in the direction of expanding concepts and loosening dogmatic commitments. David Morris writes that in eighteenth-century Britain

a taste developed among almost all classes of society for the qualities of wildness, grandeur, and overwhelming power which, in a flash of intensity, could ravish the soul with a sudden transport of thought or feeling.... Sublimity lifted men above the daily world of prudence; in an age of reason, it temporarily teased men out of thought-constricting systems of belief.[22]

What Morris does not emphasize here is that sublime experience makes it difficult to return to those putatively "thought-constricting systems" unchanged. Relaxation of doctrinal commitment, or even a general skepticism about a doctrine's ability to get numinous things precisely right, is a natural if not inevitable response to the sense of having one's understanding outstripped or transcended. In other words, sublime experience in its category-busting aspect

---

[19] Ann Radcliffe, *A Sicilian Romance* (London: Hookham and Carpenter, 1792), quoted in James Kirwan, *Sublimity: The Non-Rational and the Irrational in the History of Aesthetics* (New York: Routledge, 2005), 28.
[20] For the canonical discussion of religious affections and the ways they can be changed by such experience, see Jonathan Edwards, *A Treatise Concerning Religious Affections*, ed. John E. Smith, in *The Works of Jonathan Edwards*, 26 vols. (New Haven, CT: Yale University Press, 1959 [1746]), vol. 2.
[21] James, *The Varieties of Religious Experience*, 71, our emphasis.
[22] Morris, *The Religious Sublime*, 1.

occasions the suspicion that there is more in heaven and earth than is dreamt of in our philosophy (or theology for that matter).

One of the main problems involved in analyzing the corroborative theistic sublime arises again in this transformational context. How can the content of a sublime experience be sufficiently determinate to transform a subject's beliefs in anything but the most trivial manner? Should a doxastic transformation be conceived as occurring by way of an inference? If so, then why is it that subjects of such experience have a hard time identifying the aspect of the experience that made their prior beliefs seem so inadequate to what they have seen? If not, then why does the belief revision take the precise form that it does, and why does the subject often view the transformation as an effort to be true to the experience?[23]

A full answer to these questions is beyond the scope of our efforts here. One thing to say, however, is that even what seems like a trivial doxastic change may lead, together with the right set of background beliefs, to a substantive transformation. Consider the simple reflective belief that "That was sublime!" or, less technically, "That was mortally terrifying!" or even less technically still, "That scared the bejeezus out of me and I have no idea what it means!" Such beliefs may operate as premises in an implicit argument for conclusions such as "I am deeply vulnerable," or "I am absolutely dependent," or "there is a source of value that outstrips my current conceptual scheme," and the like. In such cases the subject does not glean determinate content from the sublime experience itself; rather, she infers a substantive and broadly religious conclusion simply from the reflective awareness of having *had* such an experience.[24] Or, if talk of inference seems out of place in this context, perhaps we can say, with Otto, that the feeling of "creatureliness" before a transcendent other is part of the content of the experience of the sublime itself – the subjective "shadow" of what is primarily an outward-directed awareness.[25]

The Spiritualistic Sublime

It should be clear that there is a trajectory in our account of the religious sublime thus far. Conversional theistic experiences *produce* religious beliefs and affections, corroborative experiences *strengthen* them somehow, and transformative experiences *change* them. For better or worse, the change involved in the latter often involves revision or expansion of traditional conceptions of God in order to accommodate the outstripping aspect of the experience. As we move into the second main species of the religious sublime, the expansion of traditional theistic conceptions plays an increasingly central role.

The spiritualistic sublime bears affective similarities to the theistic sublime and often has similar effects on behavior to such a degree that traditional believers often regard it as friendly to their general outlook. Doxastically, however, the experiences in question tend to lead away from personal monotheisms and toward a kind of collectivism of a pantheistic or panentheistic sort. The epiphanic content here will thus involve or entail propositions like "the universe is a harmonious and interrelated whole," or "I am united with everything else," or "Atman is Brahman." Like its theistic counterpart, the spiritualistic sublime has, at the very least, *conversional*, *corroborative*, and *transformative* species, and we will discuss them in that

---

[23] Analogous questions regarding how experience of the numinous can lead to transformed beliefs about the "holy" or the good have been forcefully pressed by Otto's critics. See, for example, John Reeder, "The Relation of the Moral and the Numinous in Otto's Notion of the Holy," in *Religion and Morality*, ed. G. Outka and J. Reeder (Garden City, NJ: Doubleday, 1973), 255–92.

[24] See Friedrich Schleiermacher, *On the Christian Faith*, ed. and trans. H. R. Mackintosh and J. S. Stewart (London: T & T Clark, 1999 [1821–1822]), 33.

[25] See Otto, *The Idea of the Holy*, 10: "The 'creature-feeling' is itself a first subjective concomitant and effect of another feeling-element, which casts it like a shadow, but which in itself indubitably has immediate and primary reference to an object outside the self."

order. Because there is close structural resemblance to the theistic cases, however, these can be treated at less length.

The Conversional Spiritualistic Sublime

Sublime experience may lead to the adoption of new spiritualistic beliefs and/or affections, some of which can affect behavior. As mentioned earlier, the line between this category and the transformative theistic sublime is blurry. It seems possible for a traditional theist to have sublime experiences that lead initially to an expansion of doctrinal commitments and an openness to other forms of theistic expression. Later, however, the same person might cite those same sublime experiences as motivating the relinquishment of classical theism altogether in favor of a broader, spiritualistic credo. A prominent example is Ralph Waldo Emerson, who came out of traditional Christianity (he was pastor of Boston's Second Church for a time), through something like the transformative theistic sublime, and ultimately to a departure from traditional theistic commitment, although he did not abandon transcendent metaphysics entirely.

It seems equally possible, however, for an atheist or agnostic to undergo the conversional spiritualistic sublime. Such a person would presumably experience the bedazzlement-outstripping-epiphany trio as leading directly to a spiritualistic vision of the world, bypassing theism altogether. An example of the second sort of conversional movement might be Emerson's protégé, Henry David Thoreau, who from an early age claimed to have experiences that produced various "transcendentalist" beliefs about being and "the world-soul," as well as an ethical outlook that emphasized tolerance, unity, and collective consciousness.[26]

The Corroborative Spiritualistic Sublime

The corroborative spiritualistic sublime is the species of experience that Emerson went on to have – and encourage in others – during the later years of his life as an essayist and public intellectual. His interactions with nature and art led to increased confidence that

> within man is the soul of the whole; the wise silence; the universal beauty, to which every part and particle is equally related, the eternal ONE. And this deep power in which we exist and whose beatitude is all accessible to us, is not only self-sufficing and perfect in every hour, but the act of seeing and the thing seen, the seer and the spectacle, the subject and the object, are one. We see the world piece by piece, as the sun, the moon, the animal, the tree; but the whole, of which these are shining parts, is the soul.[27]

It is worth noting that what spiritualists in both Western and Eastern traditions call "cosmic consciousness" comprises not so much a set of propositional attitudes as a general stance toward the world: an awareness of the connection between one's own flourishing and that of the whole, and a commitment to living in harmony with others and the natural environment without divisions. Still, such cosmic consciousness may be susceptible to corroboration by an experience of being dazzled (by the vastness of the whole), outstripped (vis-à-vis one's understanding of the situation), and then epiphanically convinced that one's previous inklings about connectedness with what Emerson calls "the ONE" correspond to the ultimate fact of the matter.

For example, in his immensely popular book, *Autobiography of a Yogi*, Sri Yogananda describes a specific experience that he had in his student days. Despite a lot of hard work, he had been unable to approximate anything like the sort of cosmic consciousness reported by others, and he finally decided to express his frustration to his guru. In response, the guru approached him and punched him lightly in the chest, just above his heart. Suddenly, Yogananda writes,

---

[26] For some evidence of this, see Alan D. Hodder, *Thoreau's Ecstatic Witness* (New Haven, CT: Yale University Press, 2001). Even if it is not correct to say that Thoreau himself took precisely this path, however, there are presumably others who have, especially in South and East Asia, where traditional monotheism was rarely if ever dominant.

[27] Ralph Waldo Emerson, "Over-Soul," in *Essays: First Series* (Boston: James Munroe, 1850 [1841]), 245.

my body became immovably rooted; breath was drawn out of my lungs as if by some huge magnet. Soul and mind instantly lost their physical bondage, and streamed out like a fluid piercing light from my every pore.... My sense of identity was no longer narrowly confined to a body, but embraced the circumambient atoms.... All objects within my panoramic gaze trembled and vibrated like quick motion pictures. My body, Master's, the pillared courtyard, the furniture and floor, the trees and sunshine, occasionally became violently agitated, until all melted into a luminescent sea; even as sugar crystals, thrown into a glass of water, dissolve after being shaken. The unifying light alternated with materializations of form, the metamorphoses revealing the law of cause and effect in creation. An oceanic joy broke upon calm endless shores of my soul. The Spirit of God, I realized, is exhaustless Bliss; His body is countless tissues of light. A swelling glory within me began to envelop towns, continents, the earth, solar and stellar systems, tenuous nebulae, and floating universes. The entire cosmos, gently luminous, like a city seen afar at night, glimmered within the infinitude of my being.... I cognized the center of the empyrean as a point of intuitive perception in my heart.[28]

The context of this passage indicates that Yogananda's "realization" didn't involve a serious change in any of his (nontrivial) beliefs; he was already a committed spiritualist-monist. But the beliefs were very much strengthened or corroborated by his experience. The really important change occurred at the level of Yogananda's affections: the experience produced a renewed enthusiasm for his religious duties, as well as overwhelming gratitude to his teacher for (apparently) occasioning this sublime encounter.[29]

The Transformative Spiritualistic Sublime
The spiritualist's beliefs are typically so inclusive and expansive that it is hard to see what a really *transformative* version of the spiritualist sublime would amount to. Perhaps there can be migrations from one broadly pantheistic or panentheistic outlook to another. Much more common, however, will be transformations of *affections*, some of which have powerful effects on character and behavior.

Pop culture sources provide interesting examples in this context: entering "sublime" and "spiritual" into a search engine delivers inter alia a Web site called Cold Weather Nude Hiking. The main contributor to the site claims that "hiking with the least amount of covering possible (a hat, hiking shoes and a fanny pack slung over the shoulder ... sometimes absolutely nothing at all)" can lead, even in someone who is already a committed spiritualist, to a feeling of tactile bedazzlement (if you will), and to a sense of having one's normal grasp of what is appropriate and required outstripped (so to speak), before ultimately achieving the "epiphany" that makes him a "newly converted nudist." The contributor concludes a long discussion of the group's activities by making explicit references to both the sublime and the spiritual:

While I enjoy endless roaming around the mountains nude in the balmier months, taking off my clothes in a wide-open and pristine snowfield and hiking free is a unique and almost *spiritual experience*. Also, while I consider hiking nude in the snow a personal challenge, I temper it with the realization that I have to be aware of how my body is responding. But what else is a nudist good for than being aware of his or her body's interaction with the environment? We nude hikers know how *sublime the experience is* ...[30]

Lest these sentiments seem unusual, note that the idea that prolonged nudity can occasion an experience of the sublime, as well as a kind of spiritual transformation, is by no means new. The author of the apocryphal Gospel of Thomas appears to sanction the idea in the following

---

[28] See Paramhansa Yogananda, *Autobiography of a Yogi* (Los Angeles, CA: Self-Realization Fellowship Press, 1946), chap. 14, para. 15–21.
[29] See Yogananda, *Autobiography of a Yogi*, chap. 14.
[30] http://www.scribd.com/doc/11040895/Cold-Weather-Nude-Hiking (accessed September 23, 2010), emphasis added.

FIGURE 12.2. *Doukhobors Looking for Christ in Canada in Winter*, c. 1904–1909, from *The Alienist and Neurologist Journal* 35, ed. Charles Hughes (St. Louis, MO: Carreras Publishers, 1914).

pericope: "And Jesus said, 'When you strip without being ashamed, and you take your clothes and put them under your feet like little children and trample them, then you will see the Son of the Living One and not be afraid'" (Gospel of Thomas, verse 37).[31] Similarly, the "Sons of Freedom" or "Freedomites" in Canada (an anarchist offshoot of the Doukhobor sect of Christian spiritualists) regularly engaged in collective nude marches and even large-scale nude burnings of their own clothing, homes, and money (Figure 12.2). Their motive was the belief that a simple Edenic condition could be recovered by achieving liberation from clothes and property (they also set their domestic animals free). Accounts of Freedomite activities suggest that something like the transformative sublime was at work: the intentional relinquishment of all of their possessions led, apparently, to a kind of terror and transport in some of them, but ultimately to a new attitude toward value, property, and the divine.[32]

The Demythologistic Sublime

We turn now to a third main model of how the domains of the religious and the sublime intersect. Although it would be possible to continue with the general pattern used previously – examining conversional, corroborative, and transformational variations on the model – it seems more efficient simply to highlight the unique aspects of the model as a whole.

"Demythologistic" in this context refers to the absence of both the robust "mythology" of traditional religion and the broadly spiritualistic "mythology" discussed in the last section. The term is taken from the existentialist tradition in twentieth-century theology – associated

---

[31] *The Gospel of Thomas: The Hidden Sayings of Jesus*, trans. and ed. Marvin Meyer (San Francisco: Harper, 1992).
[32] J. C. Yerbury, "The 'Sons of Freedom' Doukhobors and the Canadian State," *Canadian Ethnic Studies* 16, 2 (1984), 47–70. Thanks to Del Ratzsch for directing us to the Freedomites on this issue.

primarily with Rudolf Bultmann – according to which the general stance and attitude assumed by the religious person is valuable and worth retaining, even if mythological religious beliefs – theistic or collectivist – are no longer possible for us "moderns."[33]

Demythologizing modes of biblical interpretation seek to salvage what is ethically and religiously valuable in those texts despite the untruth of various nonscientific or full-blooded mythological doctrines. In the same spirit, proponents of the demythologistic model of the sublime argue that sublime experience is a valuable analogue of religious experience – that it is an experience *as of* transcendence that neither presupposes, causes, nor corroborates beliefs about transcendent items. Sublime experience is thus not a species of bona fide religious experience on this view; rather, it's always just an analogue. As a result, the sublime becomes a space where hard-bitten Western intellectuals can, as James Edwards put it, "be religious when we can't really believe any of that glorious stuff ... we used to believe."[34] Indeed, some theorists explicitly claim that a lack of genuine religious commitment is a precondition for experience of the sublime: "Talking about the sublime," says James Elkins, "is a way of addressing something that can no longer be called by any of its traditional names." Thus "the sublime has come to be the place where thoughts about religious truth, revelation, and other more or less unusable concepts have congregated."[35]

This last claim overreaches, however, or is at least not entailed by any of the claims about analogy per se. Rudolf Otto, for instance, finds in the sublime a demythologized analogue of religious experience, but he explicitly refuses to regard it as an ersatz *replacement* for the latter. In his neo-Kantian terminology, sublime experience is a "schema" of experience of the numinous – "something more than a merely accidental analogy" holds between the two – and thus the first may function as a stage along the way to the second.[36] In the same spirit, Thomas Weiskel begins his influential book *The Romantic Sublime* with the claim that "without some notion of the beyond, some credible discourse of the superhuman, the sublime founders."[37]

Let us call these two competing conceptions of the demythologistic sublime *ersatzist* and *non-ersatzist*. Again, both conceptions portray the appeal to certain broadly religious categories (transcendence, the other, the "beyond") in aesthetic experience as part of an extended analogy that is fully available in a secular context. Non-ersatzists follow Otto, however, in thinking that such episodes simply play the traditional informative role of an analogy: just as certain metaphors can acquaint us, by analogy, with the properties of a really existent God, so sublime experience acquaints us, by analogy, with the structure of genuine, religious experience. Ersatzists, by contrast, assume that the kind of full-blown religious experience described by Otto is unavailable. Art historian Randall Van Schepen reports that

> according to ... modernist principles ... the only form of transcendence possible is through the tradition of modern epiphanic aesthetic experience. Therefore, the spiritual heritage of Western aesthetics enters in through the side door of formalist criticism as form, autonomy, manifestness and other pseudo-religious notions in order to claim the only realm of experience that has (perhaps) not yet been subsumed by positivist materiality.[38]

---

[33] Rudolf Bultmann, *New Testament and Mythology and Other Basic Writings*, ed. and trans. Schubert M. Ogden (Philadelphia: Fortress Press, 1984 [1941]), 5.

[34] James Edwards, *The Plain Sense of Things* (University Park: Pennsylvania State University Press, 1997), 195. Thanks to Gordon Graham for this reference.

[35] James Elkins, "Against the Sublime," in *Beyond the Finite: The Sublime in Art and Science*, ed. Roald Hoffmann and Iain Boyd White (Oxford: Oxford University Press, 2011), 75–90, p. 84.

[36] Otto, *The Idea of the Holy*, 47.

[37] Thomas Weiskel, *The Romantic Sublime: Studies in the Structure and Psychology of Transcendence* (Baltimore, MD: Johns Hopkins University Press, 1976), 3.

[38] Randall K. Van Schepen, "From the Form of Spirit to the Spirit of Form," in *Re-Enchantment*, ed. James Elkins and David Morgan (New York: Routledge, 2008), 47–68, p. 62.

Sublime experiences are thus sought and celebrated by ersatzists as able to fill the ugly gulch left behind when the tide of faith withdrew: they offer many of the benefits of the religious experiences they replace, while also being more authentic, "scientific," and acceptable across traditions.

In order properly to evaluate either of these conceptions of the demythologistic sublime, we would need to know more about the various features in which the analogy is supposed to consist. Which natural objects can be the analogues of the numinous object, and which natural feelings are analogous to the (for Otto, sui generis) sense of the holy?[39] The difficulties involved in working this out might lead a religious theorist to suspect that the best explanation of at least some sublime experiences is that they are not merely analogous to religious experience after all but rather inchoate, *de re* experiences of a genuine transcendent thing (of God, the soul, the ONE, and so on). Thus there might be metaphysical commitments on the part of some third-person theorists of sublime experience, even if the subject of the experience construes it demythologistically. Committed demythologizers, however, will share the subject's evaluation of the situation in such a case, and the ersatzists among them will celebrate the fact that such experiences are still possible even after the death of God. What demythologizers give up in metaphysical transcendence, they regain in authenticity.

The Nontheistic Sublime

There are limit cases of the religious sublime that also appear to belong in our taxonomy – namely, cases that result in the abandonment of religious belief, or the adoption of belief in a kind of nondivine metaphysical principle or entity. Experience of horrendous evils – or even just learning about such evils – seems to be the most common context or source of such episodes. Again, it is hard to be precise here, because the content of the first two stages of the experience will often lack the structure required for the latter to ground a premise in an argument, or to defeat some preexisting belief. Even so, there does often appear to be something like an inferential connection between, say, the experience of overwhelming incomprehension at the horrendous suffering of a child and the subsequent epiphanic thought that God does not exist. Background beliefs regarding what a perfect being would allow are thus almost certainly involved in many of these cases, just as they were in the conversional theistic sublime discussed previously.

The Nontheistic Sublime: Evil as Privation
The first main species of the nontheistic sublime is negative in the sense that it involves relinquishing or rejecting theistic belief. Liberators of concentration camps at the end of World War II were often presented with scenes of human degradation that defied normal modes of comprehension; indeed, first-person reports suggest that many of them were initially both terrified and transfixed in a manner characteristic of the first stage of the sublime. This initial response was followed by a sense of incapacity to understand such evil using normal cognitive resources and, finally, by an epiphanic endorsement of atheistic claims such as that the universe is empty of sacred purpose, justice, and goodness.[40]

Evils on the scale of Auschwitz are not required for this sort of experience, however. Witnessing a terrible accident involving the violent death of a friend or a child – or, worse, being

---

[39] See Otto's discussion of "analogies and associated feelings," *The Idea of the Holy*, chap. 7.
[40] For discussion of Holocaust reports in this connection, see Gilles Deleuze, *Coldness and Cruelty* (New York: Zone, 1991), and Peter Haidu, "The Dialectics of Unspeakability" in *Probing the Limits of Representation*, ed. Saul Friedlander (Cambridge, MA: Harvard University Press, 1992), 277–99.

the inadvertent cause of such a death – are events that seem equally capable of producing the relevant sort of episode.

The Nontheistic Sublime: Evil as Abjection
The second species of the nontheistic sublime is more positive than the first in that the epiphany involves forming a belief in something like radical evil or a dark but metaphysically robust force, or perhaps even fully evil beings (demons and the like). It is also consistent, in the way the first species is not, with positive belief in the existence of the traditional God or the spiritualist's One. In itself, however, it is nontheistic: its objects are not the metaphysically good beings of traditional or spiritualistic religion but rather something like their evil counterparts.

Clear examples of this species of the sublime are hard to identify. Richard Kearney borrows Kant's term "the monstrous" (*das Ungeheure*) to describe this kind of metaphysical evil as it presents itself aesthetically in nature and even art.[41] Julia Kristeva describes the sight of pits of bodies, body parts, mud, and excrement jumbled chaotically together – or an artwork representing such a scene – as capable of eliciting a kind of terror, fascination, confusion, and sense of outstripped understanding that, taken together, sound very much like the first two stages of the sublime.[42] More speculatively, the theologian William Abraham suggests (in conversation) that experience of an exorcism, if such a thing were possible, would also do the trick. Such encounters with art and nature (broadly speaking) are at once so riveting and horrifying that our power to understand their salient features is simply overwhelmed, at least for a time; when it is all over, we are left with the sense that there is a metaphysical "abjectness" in the universe that is not merely privative but palpable. Contemporary photographic work by Sarah-Jane Lynagh aims to elicit something like this response by juxtaposing classical objects of beauty (the pale, naked female torso) with vile objects of disgust (dismembered, bloody animal parts, such as a cow tongue) (Figure 12.3). The epiphany resulting from such an experience (if "epiphany" is the right word) is not that the universe is empty of transcendent goodness; rather, it is that the universe is perhaps even *worse* than that. The abjectness in our treatment of other beings (including in this case animals) stands over and against us as a genuine metaphysical entity, a kind of inscrutable evil force that threatens to overwhelm or swallow the regular, predictable benignity of ordinary things and ordinary explanations. In figurative biblical terms, the sublime experience of the monstrous, the horrible, or the abject may reveal the unspeakable reality of the *tohubohu* of Genesis 1:2 – the primordial, formless, and yet still very present void that gapes beneath the apparent order and regularity of our phenomenal universe.[43]

PROSPECTS AND PROBLEMS

Given the various ways in which the sublime relates to the religious, it is no surprise that some people will regard one or more of these models as having exciting theoretical and practical consequences, whereas others will view that same model with skepticism, suspicion, or even alarm. The main *philosophical* prospects and problems in this area, as we see them, can be brought under four main headings.

(1) For the religious and nonreligious alike, the glimpse of the "beyond" that is found in sublime experience may provide at least one part of the value that human beings have traditionally

---

[41] Richard Kearney, "Evil, Monstrosity, and the Sublime," in *Revista Portuguesa de Filosofia* 57, 3 (2001), 485–502.
[42] Julia Kristeva, *Powers of Horror: An Essay in Abjection*, trans. Leon S. Roudiez (New York: Columbia University Press, 1982).
[43] Kearney, "Evil, Monstrosity, and the Sublime," 489.

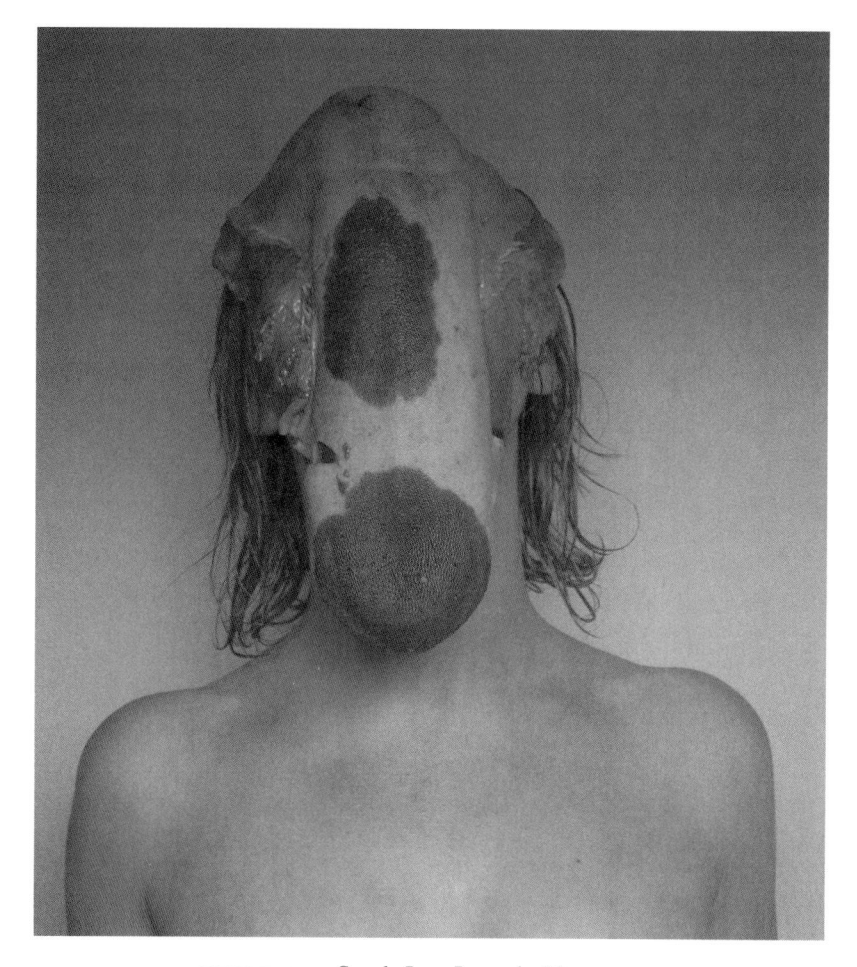

FIGURE 12.3. Sarah-Jane Lynagh, *Mute*, 2007.

sought in the religious life. The religious person can go on to interpret her experience as having some relation to the numinous, whereas the nonreligious person can regard it purely naturalistically. (There is presumably a fact of the matter about which of them is correct, although that cannot be settled here.) The positive prospect is that, on either of these interpretations, precisely what this value amounts to or consists in is something that philosophers of art and philosophers of religion might seek to discover and articulate.

The other side of this coin, however, is that the experience of the sublime may too easily be assimilated to whatever religious sensibilities are already in place. The theist's interpretation of it as a sensory encounter with aspects of the living God will strike the atheist as an exercise in self-delusion and wish fulfillment. The spiritualist's interpretation of the sublime as an experience of our union with the whole will look to the traditional theist like the predictable result of pernicious New Age sentimentality – opening the gates of authentic religion to anyone who reports even the vaguest sense of transcendence. In effect, because the first two stages of the sublime typically have so little content, they become wax noses in the hands of our background beliefs – able to be twisted into innumerable different shapes at the epiphanic third stage.

(2) A second prospect-problem pair has to do with the ethical implications of the last point. Otto suggests that the "expansion of the soul" or "openness to mystery" resulting from religious

experience can help to undermine overly abstract or doctrinally rigid accounts of the divine by, on the one hand, presenting the numinous directly or indirectly to the subject and, on the other hand, defying strict categorization and thus returning the subject's focus to the ethical aspects of her relationships with others.[44] Perhaps this is true of some sublime experience as well: champions of one or more of our models might argue that such experience – given the category-busting aspect of the second stage – can lead to deepened awareness of commonality between religious traditions and greater enthusiasm for interreligious dialogue.

On the other hand, sublime experience may also lead to a dangerous kind of fanaticism, to the perception that God or the One has intervened from outside the phenomenal world of sense-perceptual experience to instruct *me* to do something. As we have seen, because there is so little content to particular sublime episodes – apart from the sense of having quotidian understanding outstripped in some way – the resulting epiphany is almost inevitably guided by background beliefs. The subject will take herself to have "seen" the things that she had previously just heard or taken on faith, and her religious affections will be significantly strengthened as a result. This is likely to make her less sensitive to defeaters for her epiphanic belief and to rational criticism generally.

(3) A third prospect is that the sublime may provide a site at which the divine or the ultimate can be experienced as somehow beyond traditional categories of male, patriarch, warrior, and domination. A transformative sublime experience, for instance, might lead to the expansion of our concept of God or ultimate reality to include other qualities (not more or less mythologistic, in this case, but just different). This would be analogous to what reportedly happened in some of the medieval mystics' experiences of God as nurturing mother or erotic lover. On the other hand, the fact that the sublime is said to begin with terror and lead to a feeling of being stripped of the ability to understand, or ravished discursively by an incomprehensible object, may make it hard for feminist philosophers and theologians to embrace it as a means of religious transformation.[45]

(4) Fourth and finally, although we have seen that sublime experience can play some of the roles that religious experience does in human life, it also throws down some of the same obstacles as an object of theory. Again, both kinds of experience have difficult-to-describe effects on the subjects who have them: as we have seen with respect to the sublime, the first two stages – and their connection to the epiphany stage – often seem to be too empty or inchoate to be of general theoretical use. For this reason, art historian James Elkins – once a great theoretical proponent of the sublime – contends in a recent recantation (called "Against the Sublime") that the notion is too vague to be useful:

In brief: saying something is sublime does not make it art or provide a judgment that can do much philosophical work or result in much understanding. I think the sublime needs to be abandoned as an interpretive tool, except in the cases of romantic and belated romantic art. Contemporary writers who use the word can always find synonyms to express what they mean, and those synonyms are apt to be more telling, and more useful, than the word "sublime."[46]

Because no one has a firm grasp on the concept, Elkins adds, references to the sublime allow a vestigial and unwelcome religiosity to sneak in through the aesthetic back door: "in contemporary critical writing, the sublime is used principally as a way to smuggle covert religious meaning into texts that are putatively secular," because the concept "cannot be fully excavated from

---

[44] Otto, *The Idea of the Holy*, 1–4.

[45] For an account of Emily Dickinson's alleged critique of the Christian sublime as submission to "an alienating, overpowering force," see Shawn Alfrey, "Against Calvary: Emily Dickinson and the Sublime," in *Emily Dickinson Journal* 7, 2 (1998), 48–64, especially pp. 48–9.

[46] Elkins, "Against the Sublime," 75.

its crypto-religious contexts."[47] Theorists and philosophers who are not in principle opposed to religious talk clearly will not view this as reason to dispatch all talk of sublimity. Still, the underlying concern about untheorizability, dispensability, and mere fabrication (i.e., that there's really no *there* there with respect to the sublime) needs to be more directly confronted by aestheticians and philosophers of religion who propose to retain the concept.

---

[47] Elkins, "Against the Sublime," 75 and 86.

13

The British Romantic Sublime

Adam Potkay

RETHINKING THE ROMANTIC SUBLIME

How did the Romantics conceive of the sublime? This question, to which I will return, is less easily answered than a related one: how have critics conceived of the Romantic sublime? In the critical literature, "the Romantic sublime" refers to the mind's transcendence of a natural and/or social world that finally cannot fulfill its desire. Revealed in the moment of the sublime is that the mind is not wholly of the world, but this revelation may be triggered by a particular setting in the world. The lonely grandeur of lakes and mountains, or the solemn interior of a cathedral, invite sublime musings. And these musings are typically conveyed in a heightened style that may itself be described as sublime or awe inspiring. Often cited as the epitome of the Romantic sublime is a passage from book 6 of William Wordsworth's 1805 *Prelude*:

> Our destiny, our nature, and our home,
> Is with infinitude – and only there;
> With hope it is, hope that can never die,
> Effort, and expectation, and desire,
> And something evermore about to be.
> The mind beneath such banners militant
> Thinks not of spoils or trophies, nor of aught
> That may attest its prowess, blest in thoughts
> That are their own perfection and reward –
> Strong in itself, and in the access of joy
> Which hides it like the overflowing Nile.[1]

At this point in his narrative, Wordsworth has just crossed the Alps unwittingly, failing en route to achieve the grand prospect view he earlier imagined. He turns from his disappointment to praise the imagination as a power superior to any actual experience and to celebrate, in these lines, the soul as fundamentally alien to the world of the senses. Wordsworth expresses a yearning for the infinite, the unbounded, the supersensible; he expresses, as though it were a natural or intuitive aspect of our being, the desire to transcend the limitations imposed on us as finite, historically situated beings. Although this yearning evidently has religious roots (particularly neo-Platonic and Augustinian ones), its quasi-secular or at least nonsectarian expression comprises what we now think of as the Romantic sublime. Whether or not this yearning aptly or

---

[1] *The Prelude: 1799, 1805, 1850*, ed. Jonathan Wordsworth, M. H. Abrams, and Stephen Gill (New York: W. W. Norton, 1979), 1805 text, 6:538–48 (P). Samuel Monk calls this passage the "apotheosis" of the eighteenth-century sublime. See Samuel Holt Monk, *The Sublime: A Study of Critical Theories in XVIII-Century England* (Ann Arbor: University of Michigan Press, 1935), 6.

sufficiently characterizes what authors of the Romantic era actually took to be sublime is a question I shall address in this chapter.

Before I set forth my own argument, however, let me first concede that the desire for transcendence, as an aspect if not necessarily the essence of the Romantic sublime, received widespread expression in, and well beyond, the British Romantic era (an era that spans from the 1780s into the 1830s). Indeed, the frequency with which authors of the Romantic era invoke the sublime of transcendence has led us to label it "Romantic" – although its ultimate provenance is in Longinus.[2] Romantic poets address the sublime in a correspondingly sublime or awe-inspiring style, again following the lead of Longinus, who (as Boileau famously quipped) "in talking of the sublime, is himself sublime."[3] Thus the "repetitions and asyndeta" that Longinus identifies as components of the sublime style (section 20) feature in William Blake's praise of the unbounded: "The bounded is loathed by its possessor.... The desire of Man being Infinite, the possession is Infinite, & himself Infinite."[4] Thirty years later, Samuel Taylor Coleridge wrote in one of his lectures, "The Gothic art is sublime. On entering a cathedral, I am filled with devotion and awe; I am lost to the actualities that surround me, and my whole being expands into the infinite."[5] Lord Byron garnered a much larger audience for such musings in his celebrated *Childe Harold's Pilgrimage*, which sings in part, "the feeling infinite, so felt / In solitude, where we are *least* alone" (canto 3, stanza 90).[6] Examples of such flights could be multiplied, and by the mid-nineteenth century some sensitive readers thought them more than enough. George Eliot's character Felix Holt characterizes the "Byronic-bilious" set as "gentlemen ... who have no particular talent for the finite, but a general sense that the infinite is the right thing for them."[7] Still, the quest for transcendence persisted, finding pure expression as late as D. H. Lawrence's *The Rainbow* (1915), whose narrator muses, "The human soul at its maximum wants a sense of the infinite."[8]

This yearning for transcendence has been, for twentieth-century literary criticism, the defining aspect of the Romantic sublime, the key to what is particularly Romantic about it – especially in the writings of Wordsworth, the touchstone figure for writing on the Romantic sublime. The criticism I shall shortly survey analyzes the ideal and artistry of individual transcendence, limning its structure, plumbing its psychological depths, and, most recently, revealing its unconscious

---

[2] In Longinus we find the germ of everything the Romantics have to say about the sublime, including the inability of the physical universe to satisfy the yearnings of men, into whose heart nature (*phusis*) has implanted "an unconquerable passion [*erōta*, the accusative case of *erōs*] for whatever is great and more divine than ourselves. Thus the whole universe is not enough to satisfy the speculative intelligence of human thought; our ideas often pass beyond the limits that confine us" (section 35). Unless otherwise noted, quotations from Longinus *On the Sublime* (cited by section number) are from the W. H. Fyfe translation, revised by Donald Russell, in *Aristotle: Poetics. Longinus: On the Sublime. Demetrius: On Style*, ed. Stephen Halliwell, Donald A. Russell, and Doreen C. Innes, Loeb Classical Library (Cambridge, MA: Harvard University Press, 1995).

[3] Nicholas Boileau Despréaux offered this much-quoted assessment in the preface to his 1674 French translation of Longinus. See Scott Elledge and Donald Schier, eds., *The Continental Model: Selected French Critical Essays of the Seventeenth Century, in English Translation* (Ithaca, NY: Cornell University Press, 1970), 270. Compare Alexander Pope's *An Essay on Criticism* (1711) on Longinus, "Whose own Example strengthens all his Laws, / And Is himself the great Sublime he draws" (ll. 679–80). Alexander Pope, *An Essay on Criticism*, in *The Twickenham Edition of the Poems of Alexander Pope*, 6 vols. (London: Methuen, 1961), vol. 1, *Pastoral Poetry and An Essay on Criticism*, ed. E. Audra and Aubrey Williams, 1:316.

[4] William Blake, "There Is No Natural Religion" (1788), in *Blake's Poetry and Designs*, ed. Mary Lynn Johnson and John E. Grant (New York: W. W. Norton, 1979), 15.

[5] From Coleridge's 1818 Lectures on European Literature, in *On the Sublime*, ed. David Vallins (Houndsmill, Hampshire: Palgrave Macmillan, 2003), vol. 5, *Coleridge's Writings*, 87.

[6] Quoted from *Byron's Poetical Works*, ed. Frederick Page; rev. John Jump (Oxford: Oxford University Press, 1970), 222.

[7] George Eliot, *Felix Holt, the Radical* (1866), ed. Fred C. Thomson (Oxford: Oxford University Press, 1980), 3:221, chap. 27.

[8] D. H. Lawrence, *The Rainbow* (Harmondsworth: Penguin, 1976), 301.

or repressed politics. But for all its virtues, this criticism uniformly ignores the morality that the Romantics sought to advance, albeit not always simply or clearly, in their sublime writing as in theoretical writing on the sublime.

In the British Romantics, I shall argue, the sublime of transcendence is related and finally subservient to the *moral sublime*. That is, one transcends one's immediate environment and one's self-interested relations in order to emerge a fully moral being, recognizing that the most awe-inspiring thing is either great virtue, pervading love, or the category of morality itself. Conceptions of a moral sublime, although strangely absent from recent literary-critical work on the sublime, were vital to the intellectual world the Romantics inhabited. Joseph Priestley, the scientist, Unitarian preacher, and political radical admired by the first-generation Romantics (Blake, Wordsworth, and Coleridge), wrote that sublimity is not confined "to the ideas of objects which have sensible and *corporeal* magnitude":

> *Sentiments* and *passions* are equally capable of it, if they relate to great objects, suppose extensive views of things, require a great effort of the mind to conceive them, and produce great effects. Fortitude, magnanimity, generosity, patriotism, and universal benevolence, strike the mind with the idea of the sublime. We are conscious that it requires great effort to exert them; and in all cases when the mind is conscious of a similar exertion of its faculties, it refers its sensations to the same class.[9]

Alternatively, for Kant, whose thinking on ethics and aesthetics would also come to influence Coleridge and Wordsworth, moral activity rises to sublimity not through the exertion it requires or the consequences it produces but rather by its transcendence of "the inconstancy of external things." For Kant, the most sublime thing is to act according to fixed principles:

> But what if the secret tongue of the heart speaks in this manner: "I must come to the aid of that man, for he suffers; not that he were perhaps my friend or companion, nor that I hold him amenable to repaying the good deed with gratitude later on. There is now no time to reason and delay with questions; he is a man, and whatever befalls men, that also concerns me." Then his conduct sustains itself on the highest ground of benevolence in human nature, and is extremely sublime, because of its unchangeability as well as of the universality of its application.[10]

The moral sublime admitted competing analyses in the eighteenth century, but no one questioned its reality in experience or its fundamental importance to culture. In the Romantic canon, examples of the moral sublime span from Michael's patient endurance through "the strength of love" in Wordsworth's pastoral poem[11] to the Marshallin's noble sacrifice of young Octavian, her *cavalier servente*, at the end of Strauss and Hofmannsthal's opera *Der Rosenkavalier*.

Let me illustrate the moral sublime with examples from Blake and from Wordsworth, two otherwise quite divergent authors. Blake, in his well-known pronouncements on perceiving infinity,[12] does not actually call this perception "sublime." Where he explicitly finds the sublime is, rather, the realm of morality: "The most sublime act is to set another before you." This proverb comes from the ironically titled "Proverbs of Hell," a litany of praise for action and exuberance over prudence and repression – but within which the "most sublime act" is the moral

---

[9] Joseph Priestley, *A Course of Lectures on Oratory and Criticism*, ed. Vincent M. Bevilacqua and Richard Murphy (Carbondale: Southern Illinois University Press, 1965 [1777]), Lecture 20, "Of the Sublime," 151–63, p. 154.

[10] Immanuel Kant, *Beobachtungen über das Gefühl des Schönen und Erhabenen,* in *Kant's gesammelte Schriften*, Königlichen Preussischen (later Deutschen) Akademie der Wissenschaften, 29 vols. (Berlin: Reimer [later de Gruyter], 1900–), vol. 20 (KGS); *Observations on the Feeling of the Beautiful and Sublime* [1763], trans. John T. Goldthwait (Berkeley: University of California Press, (2003 [1960]), 65.

[11] Wordsworth, *Michael: A Pastoral Poem* (l. 457), in *Lyrical Ballads 1798 and 1800*, ed. Michael Gamer and Dahlia Porter (Peterborough, ON: Broadview, 2008).

[12] In addition to "There Is No Natural Religion," quoted previously, see *The Marriage of Heaven and Hell*, plate 14, and "Auguries of Innocence," ll. 1–4: "To see a World in a grain of sand / And a Heaven in a Wild Flower: / Hold Infinity in the Palm of your hand / And Eternity in an Hour."

recognition of the other, whether (as it here seems) as an end in himself, an autonomous agent, or, as we might infer from a later plate in *The Marriage of Heaven and Hell*, for his superiority or "greatness" ("The Worship of God is: Honouring his gifts in other men, each according to his genius, and loving the greatest men best," plates 22–3).[13] These two alternatives may involve different conceptions of morality, but both comprise the moral sublime.

Wordsworth offers us another route to the moral sublime in his account of ascending Mount Snowdon (P bk.13). Atop this Welsh mountain, Wordsworth sees the "huge sea of mist" (l. 42) that covers all but a glimpse of the expansive sea below as an image or symbol of the creative or divine mind that transforms the world it perceives and "feeds upon infinity" (l. 70). Critics since Geoffrey Hartman have found in this image a partial reconciliation of the transcendent mind and the natural world it inhabits and transforms.[14] But for Wordsworth, the aim and end of the mind made aware of its "powers" is not simply contemplative but somehow moral, involving "truth in moral judgments; and delight / That fails not, in the external universe" (ll. 118–19). The philosophical reader may wish that Wordsworth had elaborated on what composes a "true moral judgment," but Wordsworth is never so analytic. As a moralist he prefers to echo with a generality itself sublime the Christian love ethic announced in Paul's first epistle to the Corinthians (13:1), which begins, "Though I speak with the tongues of men and of angels, and have not charity [love], I am become as sounding brass, or a tinkling cymbal."[15] Thus his further meditation on his moral apprenticeship under "sublime and lovely forms" ends with his learning to love, and with loving as the most sublime act:

> From love, for here
> Do we begin and end, all grandeur comes.
> All truth and beauty – from pervading love –
> That gone, we are as dust. (P 13:146–52)

The sublime and beautiful in nature lead beyond themselves to a moral sentiment, "pervading love," that is itself the final cause of the sublime: "From love ... all grandeur comes, / All truth and beauty." Thus, for Wordsworth, morality turns out to be a necessary condition of the sublime (as well as for all aesthetic and veridical judgment), even as the experience of sublimity awakens us to our moral being. Here in *The Prelude* Wordsworth is recasting an intuition earlier expressed in "Tintern Abbey," in which Wordsworth similarly casts his "sense sublime / Of something far more deeply interfused" (ll. 96–7) as guaranteeing his moral being, defined by its capacity for love:

> Therefore am I still
> A lover of the meadows and the woods,
> And mountains; and of all that we behold
> From this green earth; of all the mighty world
> Of eye and ear, both what they half-create,
> And what perceive; well pleased to recognize
> In nature and the language of the sense,
> The anchor of my purest thoughts, the nurse,
> The guide, the guardian of my heart, and soul
> Of all my moral being. (ll. 103–12)[16]

---

[13] *Blake's Poetry and Designs*, 99.
[14] Geoffrey Hartman, *Wordsworth's Poetry 1787–1814* (New Haven, CT: Yale University Press, 1964), 60–9.
[15] I quote from the King James Bible, which uses "charity" (from the Latin *caritas*, "love") in place of the "love" found in both earlier and later English translations of this Pauline passage. The term for love in Paul's original Greek is *agapē*. See *The Bible, Authorized King James Version with Apocrypha*, ed. Robert Carroll and Stephen Prickett (Oxford: Oxford University Press, 1997).
[16] Quoted from Wordsworth and Coleridge, *Lyrical Ballads 1798 and 1800*.

Intuitions of transcendent or immanent order are never for the Romantics ends in themselves but are rather instrumental to morality – be that morality Unitarian, as in Anna Barbauld and Coleridge; quasi-Christian, as in Wordsworth and Percy Bysshe Shelley; or heroic, as in Blake and Byron, at least in their "diabolic" moods. Either way, the Romantic sublime is in the final analysis a moral sublime.

That it is not widely recognized as such lies partly in the Romantics themselves: they invoke infinity more memorably than they do morality. But the problem lies as well with the critical orientation of Romantic studies over the past forty years. In the 1970s and 1980s, the rigorous exclusion of ethics – or, as Thomas Weiskel designated that which was to be avoided, "edification"[17] – from the advanced discussion of Romantic texts signaled a salutary break from a lingering Victorian mode of moral criticism. In the 1990s and into the first decade of the twenty-first century, moral criticism snuck back under the guise of a "political" criticism (as the word "moral," redolent of universal standards, remained suspect) that judged authors of the past according to their notions of race, class, and especially gender: according to these criteria, the male Romantics were judged and were often found wanting.

But surely by now the air has been cleared; by now we can move beyond both the Victorians' moral elevation of the Romantics and, its antithesis, their vilification by some new historicist and feminist critics. What I propose is that we attempt to come to terms with morality – and here, specifically, the moral sublime – as the Romantics themselves variously understood it; indeed, I propose that in an ethical sense we "set them before us." In doing so, we will see that the Romantics were closer than previously noticed to eighteenth-century British writing on the sublime, with its civic as well as ethical and theological concerns, as well as to Kant's writings on the sublime, which are closely related to his writings on morals. Up until now, criticism on the British Romantic sublime has neglected, in its numerous glances and side-glances at the Kantian sublime, the degree to which the sublime and morality are intertwined in Kant's *Critiques*.[18] Although I address this connection below (p. 215), it suffices here to quote from the conclusion of Kant's *Critique of Practical Reason* an eloquent passage on the infinitely great without and within: "Two things fill the mind with ever new and increasing admiration and reverence, the more often and more steadily one reflects on them: *the starry heavens above me and the moral law within me.*"[19]

THE CRITICAL TRADITION, AND WHAT MIGHT HAVE BEEN LEARNED FROM LONGINUS

The seminal work on the Romantic sublime was Thomas Weiskel's *The Romantic Sublime: Studies in the Structure and Psychology of Transcendence* (1976, reissued 1986). Subsequent criticism on the Romantic and post-Romantic sublime has drawn heavily on it, more often than not accepting its main points uncritically.[20] Although it is a brilliant work, the time has come to

---

[17] Thomas Weiskel, *The Romantic Sublime: Studies in the Structure and Psychology of Transcendence* (Baltimore: Johns Hopkins University Press, 1976), 37 (RS).

[18] The broader ethical concerns of Kant's third *Critique* are addressed in neither Weiskel's *The Romantic Sublime*, which includes a synopsis of the Kantian sublime (pp. 38–44) on which many literary critics have relied for their knowledge of Kant, nor Frances Ferguson's otherwise bracing *Solitude and the Sublime: Romanticism and the Aesthetics of Individuation* (New York: Routledge, 1992), which is framed as a defense of Kantian against empiricist and deconstructive aesthetics.

[19] Immanuel Kant, *Kritik der pracktischen Vernunft*, KGS 5; *Critique of Practical Reason*, in *Practical Philosophy*, trans. and ed. Mary Gregor (Cambridge: Cambridge University Press, 1997), 5:161.

[20] On the dangers of such uncritical acceptance, see Peter de Bolla, *The Discourse of the Sublime: Readings in History, Aesthetics, and the Subject* (Oxford: Blackwell, 1989), who claims that there is a radical break between the Romantic sublime (based wholly on Weiskel's view of what this is) and earlier eighteenth-century discourses on the sublime. The relation between the two seems to me far more fluid. For a more critical and creative engagement with the terms of Weiskel's argument, see Neil Hertz, "The Notion of Blockage in the Literature of the

look beyond it, toward elements of the sublime that it has obscured: first, the sublime's relation to ethics and, second, its deep roots in Longinus and his reception over time. Weiskel dismisses the "ethic of sublimity" as total alienation from the world, a suicidal posture (RS 44–8) – which involves a curious flattening of his main source for this "ethic," Friedrich von Schiller's essay "On the Sublime." Schiller, developing Kant's notion of moral autonomy, takes freedom from external determination to a metaphoric extreme in writing that when confronted by death a man can "by a free renunciation of all sensuous interest ... *kill himself morally* before some physical force does it." Schiller's emphasis, however, is not on suicide but on morality's pre-eminence over individual life. Indeed, his larger argument is that the sublime is properly a feature of morality, "the absolute moral capacity which is not bound to any natural condition."[21] Longinus also, in his own way, insists on the morality of the sublime: as Malcolm Heath writes in this volume, for Longinus "achieving sublimity requires not merely mastery of technique but also the ethical development of our nature."[22] Weiskel neglects the moral dimension of the sublime in both Longinus and Schiller.

Another aspect of Longinus's sublime that Weiskel overlooks, even as he reproduces it, is its antinomy between self-aggrandizement and self-effacement, or what Weiskel calls the "positive" and the "negative" sublime. For Weiskel, Wordsworth embodies the mainstream of the Romantic sublime, which he calls (after John Keats) the "egotistical sublime"[23] or, alternatively, the "positive sublime." This facet of the sublime involves perceiving all things as an extension of, or subservient to, the self. Its psychoanalytic equivalent, according to Weiskel, is primary narcissism. By contrast, there is a "negative" sublime that involves losing one's unique self, either in reason (Kant's mathematical sublime) or in attempted empathy with an external object (Keats's effort to merge with the nightingale of his great ode). Psychoanalytically, the negative sublime mimics the child's response to Oedipal anxiety, turning away from its attachment to sensible objects and toward an (paternal) ideal of totality and power that it then internalizes (RS 83).

Although one might question the usefulness of Weiskel's psychoanalytic model, his antinomy between a positive and negative sublime holds up quite well. This is so, in part, because the sublime has always been constituted by antinomies. Longinus presents the sublime as both a rhetorical mode and a feature of the natural world – the grandeur and danger embodied, for example, in the ocean and in volcanoes (section 35). In another antinomy, the rhetorical sublime derives from inspiration (the sublime speaker possessed by a god) but also from craft (the sublime is a skill that may be acquired). But we have yet to appreciate the antinomy in Longinus between – we may preliminarily use Weiskel's categories here – a positive and a negative sublime. Longinus holds, on the one hand, that the sublime "lifts [great writers] near the mighty mind of God" (section 36) – the sublime as apotheosis. And yet he implies, on the other hand, that the sublime involves – in Sappho's poem, *phainetai moi*, quoted and preserved for us by Longinus (section 10) – an entire loss of self, a loss that begins by standing *apart* from one who seems a god (it is the man who sits by the speaker's beloved that "seems to me equal to the gods" in the poem's opening line [my translation]) and that ends in the speaker's ecstasy,

---

Sublime," in Neil Hertz, *The End of the Line: Essays on Psychoanalysis and the Sublime* (New York: Columbia University Press, 1985), 40–60.

[21] Friedrich von Schiller, "On the Sublime," in *Naïve and Sentimental Poetry and On the Sublime: Two Essays*, trans. Julius A. Elias (New York: Frederick Ungar, 1966), 193–212, pp. 201 and 208 (emphasis added).

[22] Malcolm Heath, "Longinus and the Ancient Sublime," in this volume, chap. 1, within the section "The Ethics of Sublimity."

[23] Keats coined the phrase "egotistical sublime" and defended his own poetic practice in contradistinction to Wordsworth's in a letter of October 1818: "As to the poetical Character itself, (I mean that sort of which, if I am any thing, I am a Member; that sort distinguished from the wordsworthian or egotistical sublime; which is a thing per se and stands alone) it is not itself – it has no self – it is every thing and nothing.... It has as much delight in conceiving [the villainous] Iago as an Imogen [a virtuous heroine]. What shocks the virtuous philosopher, delights the camelion [sic] Poet." See *Letters of John Keats*, ed. Robert Gittings (Oxford: Oxford University Press, 1970), 157.

"near to death," inspired by the sound of her beloved's voice. Sappho's speaker, led beyond the senses ("I see nothing with my eyes, and my ears thunder"), unites with a dehumanized current of organic life, turning *chlōrotera* – the Greek comparative adjective here is variously translated as "paler" or "greener" than grass.

What, then, is the Longinian sublime – aggrandizement or negation of the self? The paradox may be real or merely apparent; there are no easy answers here, or no answer at all. It may suffice to say that Longinus exhibits a talent for dualism, one bequeathed to later aesthetics. This particular antinomy, however, is registered as a problem in eighteenth-century British aesthetics. For if the sublime *must* display the power of a godlike mind – as in the line from Genesis that Longinus adduces, "God said, let there be light; and there was light" (section 9) – then "he seems to me equal to the gods" cannot (at least in its content) be a sublime poem. Longinus may have erred in calling it one. According to this logic, the influential rhetorician Hugh Blair labels Sappho's poem not sublime but "merely elegant," whereas Lord Kames calls it "beautiful" – a term, after Burke, designating the antithesis of the sublime. "Beautiful it is undoubtedly," writes Kames, "but it cannot be sublime, because it really depresses the mind instead of raising it."[24]

This theoretical problem identified in eighteenth-century aesthetics was resolved in practice by the British Romantics, who develop what Weiskel calls the positive and negative sublime from a conceptual antinomy already apparent in Longinus. Following Longinus, the Romantics recognize not only a sublime of self-elevation but also one of self-loss. And the label "Sapphic sublime" is more apt for a good many Romantic lyrics than Weiskel's capacious "negative sublime" (able to fit both Kant and Keats). Consider, for example, Shelley's "To Constantia," which, like Sappho's poem, concerns a loss of self in response to hearing a beloved voice (here accompanied by music):

> Thy voice, slow rising like a Spirit, lingers
> O'ershadowing me with soft and lulling wings;
> The blood and life within thy snowy fingers
> Teach witchcraft to the instrumental strings.
> My brain is wild, my breath comes quick,
> The blood is listening in my frame,
> And thronging shadows fast and thick
> Fall on my overflowing eyes,
> My heart is quivering like a flame;
> As morning dew, that in the sunbeam dies,
> I am dissolved in these consuming extacies.[25]

Work remains to be done on the Romantics' relation to Longinus and the history of his reception in Europe – a point to which I return later in this section.

In calling for us to historicize the antinomy of the sublime, I am doing something different from what the "new historicism" in literary studies sought to accomplish with regard to the Romantic sublime. Tracing the critical tradition as it developed after Weiskel, we turn to the 1980s, when new historicist critics deconstructed the opposition between individual transcendence and the historical and political conditions the individual seeks to transcend. For new historicists, political and economic events are what are truly awesome; the attempted flight

---

[24] Hugh Blair, *Lectures on Rhetoric and Belles Lettres*, ed. Harold F. Harding, 2 vols. (Carbondale: Southern Illinois University Press, 1965), Lecture 4, "The Sublime in Writing," 1:57–79, p. 59; Henry Home, Lord Kames, *Elements of Criticism*, ed. Peter Jones, 2 vols. (Indianapolis, IN: Liberty Fund, 2005 [1785; 1st ed. 1762]), 1:150–78, chap. 4, "Grandeur and Sublimity," p. 159.

[25] Quoted from *Shelley's Poetry and Prose*, ed. Donald H. Reiman and Neil Fraistat, 2nd ed. (New York: Norton, 2002), 108. Further quotations from Shelley refer to this volume.

from them is illusory. Thus David Simpson grounds the Romantic sublime of transcendence on the industrialism and territorial conquest of the early nineteenth century: "The connection between an aesthetics of infinitude and an historical experience founded in expansion (coded positively as 'progress') is so obvious as to seem trite, but we have hardly begun to follow through its implications."[26]

As crucially as the new historicism has revised our understanding of the Romantics, it has left one of Weiskel's earlier assumptions unshaken: the ethical is structurally unnecessary to any discussion of the Romantic sublime. In deconstructing the opposition between the individual and the political, new historicist critics established a new opposition between the political (the privileged term) and the (parasitic) ethical; with political and/or economic causes in the ascendant, the ethical – the realm of moral value as it relates to oneself and one's relations to others – is reduced to a superstructural illusion or ideological screen. Fredric Jameson did much to set the agenda for the new historicism when in *The Political Unconscious* (1981) he opposed history and "collective life" to "the purely individualizing categories of ethics."[27] Jameson argues "that only the [Marxist] dialectic provides a way for 'decentering' the subject concretely, and for transcending the 'ethical' in the direction of the political and the collective" (60). Seeing Christian eschatology as a sign or "type" of secular historical process, Jameson imagines an apocalyptic future in which "the collective" will be free from all necessity, be it natural, material, or ethical (281–99). I would argue, however, that Jameson's is an irreducibly ethical vision, oriented toward (as he sees it) a future good; history can no more be uprooted from ethics than ethics can be uprooted from history. But in the absence of such an argument, the new historicist demotion of ethics has largely gone unchallenged in the post-1980s discussion of the Romantic sublime.[28]

Politics and ethics are similarly linked, as critics of the sublime might have learned, and as readers from the seventeenth century onward did learn, from Longinus. *On the Sublime*, as we currently have it, ends with a dialogue on whether political or ethical conditions are most important for sublime eloquence (section 44). Longinus (as we call the shadowy author of this text) argues for ethics, and his interlocutor for politics, but the debate is hardly conclusive; the lack of resolution may point to the fruitlessness of any attempt to extricate political from ethical conditions. The problem the dialogue addresses is the decay of sublime eloquence "in this age of ours" (the Roman Empire under Augustus and his successors – the text may date from the first century AD).[29] Longinus first allows a "certain philosopher" to argue that this decay has a political cause: the loss of republican liberty under the Caesars. Genius and great literature flourish under democracies and republics, with their "mutual rivalry and eager competition," "but in these days," the philosopher maintains, "we seem to be schooled from childhood in an equitable slavery" (*On the Sublime*, section 44). This argument, also found in Tacitus's *Dialogue on Orators*, was widely revived in mid-eighteenth-century Britain, particularly by those who, in opposition to the Court Whigs, decried Robert Walpole, the first "prime

---

[26] David Simpson, "Commentary: Updating the Sublime," *Studies in Romanticism* 26, 2 (1987), 245–58, p. 246. For new historical criticism of the sublime in *The Prelude*, see Ronald Paulson, *Representations of Revolution (1789–1820)* (New Haven, CT: Yale University Press, 1983), 248–75, and Alan Liu, "Wordsworth: The History in 'Imagination,'" *ELH* 51, 3 (1984), 505–48.

[27] Fredric Jameson, *The Political Unconscious: Narrative as a Socially Symbolic Act* (Ithaca: Cornell University Press, 1981), 116.

[28] One exception is Laurence Lockridge, *The Ethics of Romanticism* (Cambridge: Cambridge University Press, 1989), who argues against a Marxist dismissal of ethics (pp. 22–33) and touches on the ethical function of the sublime in Wordsworth and the "antisublime" in Shelley (pp. 232–4 and 291–6).

[29] Recent scholarship on the dating of *On the Sublime* is assessed in the 1995 Loeb introduction to the text, pp. 145–8, although for a dissenting voice see Heath, "Longinus and the Ancient Sublime," chap. 1 of the present volume.

minister" (the term began as one of derogation), as the foe of political liberty.[30] But those who invoked the political causes of sublimity's decline also concurred with the counterargument propounded by Longinus in propria persona: the corruption of literature is caused by the moral failure of individuals. "Perhaps it is not the world's peace that corrupts great natures but much rather this endless warfare which besets our hearts" – an inner turmoil originating in the private vices of "the love of money" and "the love of pleasure" (section 44). Of course, the competing arguments offered by Longinus and by his philosopher-acquaintance are not mutually exclusive. Nor were they received as such on their joint revival in Britain: Walpole had corrupted the country, according to his opponents, precisely through parliamentary bribery, his manipulation of the love of money. And indeed, a knotty sentence at the end of Longinus's ethical argument for sublimity's decline shows that ethics and politics are inextricable: the only proper motive of action, Longinus concludes, is "an eager and honorable desire to serve our fellows."[31] Here, as later in Blake, the most sublime act is to set another before you – but here the arena of action seems as civic as it does ethical.

Before considering the legacy of the Longinian sublime in the Romantics themselves, I turn to one more critical approach to the Romantic sublime, originating in the feminist reevaluation of the literary canon. This feminist approach is itself an ethical one, although its practitioners do not explicitly challenge the priority given to political and economic causes by a regnant new historicism. Rather, the new historicism is sidestepped (which is to say, ignored). Anne Mellor's 1993 *Romanticism and Gender* ushered into Romantic studies the concept of a "feminine sublime." Mellor opposes the sublime of Kant and Wordsworth, which she associates with "masculine empowerment,"[32] a feminine sublime in which nature is not transcended but rather salvaged as a space for joy in God and the other, adducing this latter mode in works by Ann Radcliffe, Helen Maria Williams, Susan Ferrier, and Sydney Owenson. In the last two authors Mellor loosely associates the feminine sublime with a Celtic sublime and associates both with "human morality.... For Ferrier, as for Morgan, the experience of a sublime landscape should produce a sense of participation in a human community" (RG 103). Although I approve Mellor's impulse to reconcile ethics and aesthetics – an impulse Mellor shares with other canny advocates of a feminine sublime[33] – I cannot endorse a simple antinomy between an immoral masculine and a moral feminine sublime.[34] My own interest lies in demonstrating the fundamental ethical concerns of the major male Romantic poets – concerns that do not always prove "masculine" in a simple or antique way.

---

[30] On the reception of Longinus and his hero Demosthenes in mid-eighteenth-century Britain, see Adam Potkay, *The Fate of Eloquence in the Age of Hume* (Ithaca, NY: Cornell University Press, 1994), chap. 1, "Ancient Eloquence and the Revival of Virtue," 24–58.

[31] This translation, my preferred one, is by T. S. Dorsch in *Aristotle/Horace/Longinus, Classical Literary Criticism* (Harmondsworth: Penguin, 1965), 158; the looser Loeb translation reads, "the honorable and admirable motive of doing good to the world," 307. A literal translation of the sublimely difficult Greek is "the beneficial activity [or service] that is worthy of emulation and honor" (with thanks to my colleague William Hutton).

[32] Anne K. Mellor, *Romanticism and Gender* (New York: Routledge, 1993), 85 (RG).

[33] Cf. Barbara Claire Freeman, *The Feminine Sublime: Gender and Excess in Women's Fiction* (Berkeley: University of California Press, 1995): "Unlike the masculinist sublime that seeks to master, appropriate, or colonize the other, I propose that the politics of the feminine sublime involves taking up a position of respect in response to an incalculable otherness" (p. 11). See also Patricia Yeager's groundbreaking essay "Toward a Female Sublime," in *Gender and Theory: Dialogues on Feminist Criticism*, ed. Linda Kauffman (Oxford: Blackwell, 1989), 191–212.

[34] The instability of the opposition of masculine vs. feminine sublime is addressed by Markus Poetzsch, *"Visionary Dreariness": Readings in Romanticism's Quotidian Sublime* (New York: Routledge, 2006), 6–16, whose study of the "quotidian sublime" – i.e., the Romantic sensitivity to the wonders of everyday life – cuts across the boundaries of gender, in reading, for example, Dorothy alongside William Wordsworth and Joanna Baillie alongside Robert Burns.

NOTES ON THE ROMANTIC OR MORAL SUBLIME

I start, however, with Lord Byron, the most masculine and classicizing of Romantics, in part to correct a shortcoming of the critical literature on the Romantic sublime, in which Byron is almost uniformly overlooked, and in part because of Byron's overt continuities with the Longinian tradition we have been examining. Byron invokes the sublime in a variety of ways in his poetic corpus, finding it, among other places, both in the grandeur and in the transcendence of nature. But it is in culture, and in self-culture, that Byron finds the sublime that animates him most vividly, and most often: we may call this his Greek sublime. Greece itself, in both its ancient glory and its Ottoman slavery, is apostrophized in the opening of Byron's swashbuckling verse narrative *The Giaour* (or "Infidel").[35] The narrator alternately praises sites associated with "Freedom's home" (l. 105) – Thermopylae, Salamis – and satirizes, with Longinian echoes, the Greeks of his own day, whose ills are both ethical ("There Passion riots in her pride, / And Lust and Rapine wildly reign" [ll. 59–60]) and political ("Self-abasement paved the way / To villain-bonds and despot sway" [ll. 140–1]). Byron offers the faintest hope, and that by way of implication, that Greece might once again regain its patriot fire:

> The hearts within thy valleys bred,
> The fiery souls that might have led
> Thy sons to deeds sublime,
> Now crawl from cradle to the Grave,
> Slaves – nay, the bondsmen of a Slave ... (ll. 147–51)

In that "now," there is at least the possibility that Greek slavery has a horizon.

Byron's Greek sublime draws on an ideal of moral and civic heroism ("deeds sublime") that derives, of course, from antiquity but that is mediated by the eighteenth-century authors who revived the moral sublime – a sublime found not in or in relation to external nature but in relation to others and to oneself. That the moral sublime is the highest sublime is a lesson of the blank verse poet Mark Akenside, follower of Shaftesbury and Addison, who exerted, in turn, considerable influence on the early Romantics. For Akenside, humanity's impatience with limits shows us that it is our destiny not to be limited by nature but to act as unconditioned moral beings, and so fulfill our divinely appointed telos. His moral emphasis, if not always his theology, echoes through Romantic writing:

> Say, why was man so eminently rais'd
> Amid the vast creation; why ordain'd
> Thro' life and death to dart his piercing eye,
> With thoughts beyond the limit of his frame:
> But that th' Omnipotent might send him forth
> In sight of mortal and immortal pow'rs,
> As on a boundless theatre, to run
> The great career of justice; to exalt
> His gen'rous aim to all diviner deeds;
> To chase each partial[36] purpose from his breast;
> And thro' the mists of passion and of sense,

---

[35] *The Giaour* (or "The Infidel"), in *Byron's Poetical Works*, ed. Frederick Page; rev. John Jump (Oxford: Oxford University Press, 1970), 252–64.

[36] The first two definitions of "partial" given by Samuel Johnson are "inclined antecedently to favor one party in a cause, or one side of the question more than the other," and "Inclined to favour without reason." See Samuel Johnson, *A Dictionary of the English Language; in Which the Words Are Deduced from Their Originals and Illustrated in Their Different Significations by Examples from the Best Writers. To Which Are Prefixed, a History of the Language, and an English Grammar. By Samuel Johnson, A. M. In Two Volumes* (London, 1755).

> And thro' the tossing tide of chance and pain,
> To hold his course unfalt'ring, while the voice
> Of truth and virtue, up the steep ascent
> Of nature, calls him to his high reward,
> Th' applauding smile of heav'n?[37]

Akenside concludes his poetic expatiation on "the sublime, / The wonderful, the fair" (ll. 145–6) with an apostrophe to the "Genius of ancient Greece!" the "nurse divine / Of all heroic deeds and fair desires!" (ll. 565–70).

Byron is in the Hellenizing line of Akenside – but only partly so. In one light, Akenside may seem closer to Kant; it is possible to imagine Kant writing Akenside's lines on humanity's impartial truth and virtue (should Kant have written verse, and in English). In both there is a universalizing abstraction, a debt to the philosophical style of the stoics. (Wordsworth by middle age inclined toward moral writing in this manner: for example, "Duty exists; – immutably survive, / For our support, the measures and the forms / Which an abstract Intelligence supplies; / Whose kingdom is, where Time and Space are not.")[38] Like Kant, Akenside praises actions rather than actors, and for both authors those actions appear more or less inaccessible: Akenside is inclined to relocate the moral actions he praises to a classical past, whereas Kant admits the empirical possibility that no truly virtuous (i.e., morally motivated) action has ever been performed.

Byron sets himself apart from this abstract moral sublime in two ways. First, he has a greater investment in individual heroes, including more or less contemporary ones, as models of the civic sublime. He is alert to the sublime in history. In *The Age of Bronze* (*Byron's Poetical Works*, 169–78), Byron casts America's founding fathers as a new Longinian pantheon, with Patrick Henry as "the forest-born Demosthenes, / Whose thunder shook the Philip of the seas" (ll. 384–5). This is monumentalizing in an antique vein. But in analyzing soi-disant heroes closer to home – Napoleon and his own heroic alter egos, Harold and Manfred – Byron admits impediments to the moral sublime or indeed renders flawed greatness sublime: this is his second and most distinctive contribution to the history of the Longinian sublime. His verse portrait of Napoleon, justly famous (*Childe Harold's Pilgrimage*, canto 3, stanzas 36–45), begins with an assessment of the world hero who had recently faced defeat at Waterloo; its first line is arresting and, its difficulty overcome, sublime: "There sunk the greatest, nor the worst of men." "Nor" comes as a surprise (unanticipated by a "neither"), shifting the elements of what might have been a balanced antithesis of superlatives ("greatest" and "worst") into a subtle asymmetry: he *is* the greatest (heroically) but not the worst (according to a nonheroic moral standard), implying that he was bad or evil but not exceptionally so, and perhaps implying too that the monarchs who triumphed over him are among the worst men. "Greatness," at the root of the sublime (of sublime ingredients, writes Longinus, "greatness plays a greater part than all the others" [section 9]), at once retains its connection to morality – the two are still assessed together – but is also unmoored from it: one can, in Byron's purview, be both great and bad, or great and evil. Indeed, as Byron's stanzas unfold, we find that greatness requires the lowness of a petty disposition, and it does not seem that either is being censured (as they would in a philosophic or Christian satire on worldly vanity):

> There sunk the greatest, nor the worst of men,
> Whose spirit, antithetically mixed,

---

[37] Mark Akenside, *The Pleasures of the Imagination*, book 1, ll. 151–66, in *The Poetical Works of Mark Akenside*, ed. Robin Dix (Madison, WI: Fairleigh Dickinson University Press, 1996). Subsequent quotations are also from book 1 of Akenside's poem.

[38] Wordsworth, *The Excursion* (1814), book 4, lines 73–6, quoted from *The Excursion*, ed. Sally Bushell et al. (Ithaca, NY: Cornell University Press, 2007).

> One moment of the mightiest, and again
> On little objects with like firmness fixed:
> Extreme in all things! hadst thou been betwixt,
> Thy throne had still been thine, or never been:
> For Daring made thy rise as fall: thou seek'st
> Even now to re-assume the imperial mien,
> And shake again the world, the Thunderer of the scene! (stanza 36)

The "little objects" of this stanza, which may appear morally neutral, reappear as "petty passions," and "in" Napoleon's spirit – that is, ethical flaws of the type that Longinus thought precluded greatness of soul and expression:

> An Empire thou couldst crush, command, rebuild,
> But govern not thy pettiest passion, nor,
> However deeply in men's spirits skilled,
> Look through thine own, nor curb the lust of War,
> Nor learn that tempted Fate will leave the loftiest Star. (stanza 38)

In this, Byron's most innovative conception of the sublime, soaring is inextricable from sinking, greatness from badness. His remains a moral vision, but a binocular one, composed of incommensurable standards of moral judgment, the great and the good. Byron glamorizes a greatness that is dependent on a lack of the goodness he also endorses.

Longinus, a clear proponent of "greatness," illustrates his postulate that "sublimity is the echo of a noble mind" with the example of Ajax in book 11 of Homer's *Odyssey*: "How grand … is the silence of Ajax in the Summoning of the Ghosts, more sublime than any speech!" (Longinus, section 9).[39] In the scene to which Longinus alludes, Ajax, summoned from Hades, proudly refuses to speak to Odysseus because he is still angry with him for having been awarded the armor of Achilles, armor he considers his own due. The scene concerns, in short, the sublime of the grudge. We can contrast this with Shelley and the anti-Longinian sublime of *forgiveness* central to his verse drama *Prometheus Unbound* – although once again the Romantic text is indebted to the rhetorical theory of the eighteenth century. Whereas Longinus praised a heroic pride that would neither remit nor complain, Joseph Priestley in "Of the Sublime" praises as the most sublime sentiment of all "the prayer of our Saviour upon the cross, in behalf of his persecutors, *Father, forgive them, for they know not what they do*" (Luke 23:34).[40] Priestley has shifted allegiance, within the discourse of the sublime, from heroic greatness to Christian goodness.

In *Prometheus Unbound*, cosmic rejuvenation stems from Prometheus, still bound, forgiving his prosecutor, Jupiter, whom he had earlier cursed: "For I hate no more, / As then, ere misery had made me wise. – The Curse / Once breathed on thee I would recall" (act 1, ll. 57–9).[41] Hearing once again the words of his earlier curse, Prometheus responds – sublimely – "It doth repent me: words are quick and vain; / Grief for a while is blind, and so was mine. / I wish no living thing to suffer pain" (1.303–5). The gospel verse Priestley ushered into the canon of the sublime – "Father, forgive them; for they know not what they do" – is later evoked by the Furies who tempt Prometheus to despair. According to the last Fury, "Many are strong and rich, – and would be just, – / But live among their suffering fellow men / As if none felt – they know not what they do" (1.629–31). Christ's act of forgiveness, evoked here under erasure – the line

---

[39] See Homer, *The Odyssey*, trans. A. T. Murray; rev. George E. Dimock, Loeb Classical Library, 2 vols. (Cambridge, MA: Harvard University Press, 1995), ll. 543–67.

[40] Priestley, *Lectures on Oratory and Criticism*, 155. On Shelley's (and Blake's) post-Christian adoption of the central Christian virtue of unconditional forgiveness, see Adam Potkay, *The Story of Joy from the Bible to Late Romanticism* (Cambridge: Cambridge University Press, 2007), 162–86.

[41] *Prometheus Unbound*, in *Shelley's Poetry and Prose*, 202–86.

"Father, forgive them" is precisely what the Fury omits – is for Shelley the essence of his teaching and the key to the possible perfection of man and his environment. Only pity for those who act unreflectively according to a chain of causal necessity ("they know not what they do") can inaugurate change within that chain; only forgiveness can open up a horizon of possible virtue beyond the calculation of probable evil. Prometheus responds to the final Fury: "Thy words are like a cloud of winged snakes / And yet, I pity those they torture not." These are the words that make the Fury vanish: "Thou pitiest them? I speak no more!" (1.634). Prometheus and the cosmos are unbound from their respective fetters by the virtues of pity and forgiveness, virtues that prove sublime in effect as well as in motive and exertion.

Moving in conclusion from Romantic practice to its theory of the moral sublime, I turn to Wordsworth's essay "The Sublime and the Beautiful" (probably written between 1806 and 1812), and its relation to Kant's mature aesthetic in his *Critique of the Power of Judgment*. Wordsworth's debt to Kant (via Coleridge) has been aptly analyzed by Raimonda Modiano, who traces the movement of Wordsworth's essay away from the sublime of natural form and toward the Kantian sublime of supersensible reason. Modiano recognizes that for Kant sublimity belongs exclusively to the mind, in its ability to think a supersensible totality, although the mind comes to recognize its powers only after an unsuccessful imaginative effort "to encompass nature's magnitude ('the mathematical sublime') or to resist its might ('the dynamical sublime')."[42] But one Kantian note that Modiano misses in Wordsworth is his relation of reason to morality. For Wordsworth, sublimity requires that the fears produced by absolute power "terminate in repose ... & that this sense of repose is the result of reason & the moral law." Wordsworth, although characteristically vague, seems in context to imply that without the assurance that reason and law govern God as well as the world, there could be pleasure in neither the idea of God as power nor those worldly prospects commonly deemed sublime ("a precipice, a conflagration, a torrent").[43]

For Wordsworth, here as in the poems we examined previously ("Tintern Abbey," *The Prelude*, book 13), the moral law appears to be a necessary condition of the sublime, or at least of the theological sublime. I do not venture to say whether or not Kant would agree. Conversely, however, for Kant beauty and sublimity can contribute to the necessary conditions for morality: "The beautiful prepares us for loving something, even nature, without interest; the sublime, for esteeming it even against our interest (of sense)."[44] That which is to be esteemed – the moral law – cannot technically, in Kant's system, be the object of an aesthetic judgment (because such judgment involves indeterminate, not determinate, concepts). Nevertheless, Kant treats our response to the moral law as analogous to our response to the sublime: once we recognize the moral law as the source of the good and the guide to our duty, we are filled with an awe (of "the moral law within") comparable to our awe in response to the natural world without ("the starry skies above"). Kant writes, "If we judge aesthetically the good that is intellectual and morally purposive (the moral good), we must present it not so much as beautiful but rather as sublime" (CJ 5:271).

Much remains to be said about re-envisioning the Romantic sublime as, at least in part, the moral sublime: we need, first of all, a more thorough and variegated understanding of the relation between morality and transcendence in the period. There is work to be done on the Romantics in relation to the perceived sublimity, in style and content, of the King James

---

[42] Raimonda Modiano, "The Kantian Seduction: Wordsworth on the Sublime," in *Deutsche Romantik and English Romanticism*, ed. Theodore G. Gish and Sandra G. Frieden (Munich: Fink, 1984), 17–26, p. 17.

[43] Wordsworth, "The Sublime and the Beautiful," in *The Prose Works of William Wordsworth*, ed. W. J. B. Owen and Jane Worthington Smyser (Oxford: Clarendon Press, 1974), 2:349–60, pp. 354–5.

[44] Immanuel Kant, *Kritik der Urteilskraft*, KGS 5; *Critique of Judgment*, trans. Werner S. Pluhar (Indianapolis: Hackett, 1987), 5:267 (CJ). On the aesthetic and the conditions for morality, see Robert R. Clewis, *The Kantian Sublime and the Revelation of Freedom* (Cambridge: Cambridge University Press, 2009), 9–12.

Bible, Milton, and other earlier authors praised and analyzed in terms of sublimity.[45] We need a more detailed and thorough analysis of the sublime, as a concept and as a practice, in the male Romantics as well as in their female counterparts; if Mellor is correct that the feminine sublime is, in the Romantic era, a moral sublime, then the differences between male and female writers are likely to prove differences of degree more than of kind. We need, in short, to move beyond the way the Romantic sublime has been thought of in the past: as transcendence for the sake of transcendence, as an ethos of alienation, as a bad faith attempt to escape politics and history, or as a ruse for masculine and imperialist forms of domination. Just as we needed the new historicism to show us much of what we had been missing in earlier ethical appreciations of Wordsworth and company – and feminist criticism to show us that "the big six" male Romantics were not the only or even the characteristic voices of their era – so we could now use a revitalized ethical criticism to remind us of what we have been missing in Romantic poets, male and female both, since historicism and political criticism hardened into orthodoxies that are only now crumbling. Without a way of talking about literature and ethics, and in particular the moral sublime, we run the risk of losing touch with a crucial component of what draws us to reading in the first place.

---

[45] I touch on this topic in Adam Potkay, "Romantic Transformations of the King James Bible: Wordsworth, Shelley, Blake," in *The King James Bible after Four Hundred Years: Literary, Linguistic, and Cultural Influences*, ed. Hannibal Hamlin and Norman W. Jones (Cambridge: Cambridge University Press, 2011), 219–32.

14

The Sublime and the Fine Arts

Theodore Gracyk

> The sublime, by its solemnity, takes off from the loveliness of beauty.
> Uvedale Price (1796)[1]

INTRODUCTION

Concluding a recent visit to the Tate Britain to view Mark Rothko's later paintings, the Seagram Murals, I found that my path of departure sent me through one of the museum's shops. Walking through racks of merchandise on my way to the street entrance at the shop's far end, I could not help but notice a display of postcards, for one of them struck me as a travesty. It reproduced one of the paintings I had just visited, Rothko's *Black on Maroon* (1959). The postcard reduced Rothko's complex wash of maroon shades to a blotchy yet otherwise uniform dark red as background to a central, black rectangle. Rothko's subtlety was lost, replaced by an image more akin to Kasimir Malevich's geometric suprematism than Rothko's true antecedent, J. M. W. Turner's nuanced studies of clouds and light. Moments before, I'd been impressed by the museum's display of Turner's *Three Seascapes* (c. 1827) in close proximity to the Seagram Murals. Now, faced with crude color reproduction and with Rothko's 15 feet reduced to 6 inches, the Rothko-Turner comparison was visually inexplicable. As Robert Motherwell observed when eulogizing Rothko, his "cooler or darker pictures (those with ... earth colors and blacks)" feature "a luminescent glow from within ... on a sublime scale."[2] Motherwell was the not the first to remark on Rothko's combination of luminosity and sublime scale; he likely knew that his description of Rothko echoes a celebrated 1961 essay by art critic Robert Rosenblum – which, incidentally, includes an illustration of the Rothko-Turner parallel.[3] Rothko had himself praised Rosenblum's analysis, particularly its astute reliance on Edmund Burke's observation, "Greatness of dimension, is a powerful cause of the sublime."[4]

---

[1] Uvedale Price, *Essays on the Picturesque, as Compared with the Sublime and the Beautiful, and on the Use of Studying Pictures, for the Purpose of Improving Real Landscape* (London: J. Robson, 1796), 104.
[2] Robert Motherwell, "28 January 1971," in *The Collected Writings of Robert Motherwell*, ed. Stephanie Terenzio (Oxford: Oxford University Press, 1992), 198.
[3] Robert Rosenblum, "The Abstract Sublime," *Art News* (February 1961), 38–41 and 56–67. For criticism of Rosenblum's reliance on pre-Romantic sources, see Edward M. Levine, "Abstract Expressionism: The Mystical Experience," *Art Journal* 31 (1971), 22–5. These criticisms are largely put to rest by the expanded analysis in Robert Rosenblum, *Modern Painting and the Northern Romantic Tradition: Friedrich to Rothko* (New York: Harper & Row, 1975).
[4] Edmund Burke, *Philosophical Enquiry into the Origin of Our Ideas of the Sublime and Beautiful*, ed. James T. Bolton (London: Routledge and Kegan Paul, 1958), 2.7.72 (SB; unless indicated all references are to part, section, and page number); quoted in Rosenblum, "Abstract Sublime," 41. Rothko's endorsement of Rosenblum's analysis is documented in Anna C. Chave, *Mark Rothko: Subjects in Abstraction* (New Haven, CT: Yale University Press, 1989), 201n42, drawing on Irving Sandler, *Mark Rothko: Paintings, 1948–69* (New York: Pace Gallery, 1983), 6 and 13n20.

Consistent with Burke's remark, the postcard's problem goes beyond the loss of physical scale. The drastic reduction strips the image of visual nuance and so, too, of luminescence. As a representational vehicle, a postcard cannot provide the perceptual base that supports these aesthetic effects. Together, these alterations conspire to rob the representation of any hint of the sublimity of Rothko's painting. The process of representation drains the experience of its central rationale in providing visual access to the particular work of art.

The trivializing effect of reducing Rothko to a postcard encapsulates a central problem for the sublime and the fine arts. The postcard has a mimetic relationship to its subject matter, the painting *Black on Maroon*. The subject – the content, in the sense of an object represented – is sublime. However, the representation of it is not. Conversely, the sublimity of Rothko's painting derives, in part, from its failure to represent any definite subject. As a vehicle for presenting content, can art successfully convey the sublimity of sublime subject matter? Or, in order to convey the sublime, is it necessary for an artwork to possess sublimity in its own right, supplementing the aesthetic character of the subject matter? Both positions have adherents.

This issue concerning the presence of sublimity in fine art rises to the level of a serious problem only if it is endemic in the broad range of practices that characterize the fine arts. In other words, there is no general problem of how sublimity enters fine art if different arts are problematic for distinct reasons. What is true of a particular art form may or may not reflect on the fine arts qua fine art. For example, a case can be made that the literary sublime never extends to limericks and the visual sublime is never present in silhouette portraiture. Yet this may be due to peculiarities of those two species of art, so they do not support the inference that there is a general issue concerning art and sublimity. Something similar may be true of abstract expressionist painting. To appreciate why the postcard reproduction of Rothko's *Black on Maroon* encapsulates a general problem regarding subject matter in relation to its representational embodiment, let us backtrack to the formative stages of theorizing the fine arts in the eighteenth-century ideal of "les beaux arts."

ENLIGHTENMENT DEFINITIONS OF FINE ART

The individual arts of painting and music date back to the inceptions of human culture. However, the same is not true of the idea that they are siblings within a family of activity called "the fine arts." The unification of disparate practices and objects under the headings of "les beaux arts," "die schöne Kunst," and, initially, in English, "the polite" and "the finer" arts was an eighteenth-century innovation. It sprung from the marriage of an Enlightenment love of taxonomic systemization with a long-standing tradition of philosophical reflection on art and aesthetic experience. However, eighteenth-century texts on aesthetics and fine art reveal an important tension. Seminal discussions of aesthetic experience generally discuss both the beautiful and the sublime, and they generally contrast these two species of aesthetic experience by identifying examples in both art and nature. In contrast, early definitions of fine art generally ignore the sublime. What explains this asymmetry? There seem to be two reasons. First, aesthetic constraints on the presentation of any subject matter in a successful artwork preclude sublimity as an aesthetic feature of that artwork. Second, analyses of natural sublimity pose problems for its selection as artistic subject matter. Nonetheless, artistic practice offered prominent examples of sublime art. Hence, the aesthetic standards informing initial definitions of fine art inaugurated an ongoing tension between philosophy of art, art practice, and critical reception. This tension was exacerbated by the puzzle of how to understand the achievement of instrumental music.

These obstacles arise, in nascent form, at the very start of explicit theorizing about fine art. Historians generally locate the first definition of fine art in *Les beaux arts réduits à un même principe* (*The Fine Arts Reduced to a Single Principle*, 1746) by the abbé Charles Batteux

(1713–1780): the fine arts are imitative semblances "whose first object is to please."[5] The definition reflects a long tradition of recognizing the special status of the arts of imitation.[6] Batteux's originality rests on his proposal that the imitative arts reflect an overarching principle of division, located in a distinction between extrinsic and intrinsic values: utility (*l'utilité*) versus pleasure.[7] Batteux locates the fine arts within the broader family of human "art" by distinguishing them from two other genera of art, which are always undertaken as a means to some further end. Each species of art has extrinsic value, intrinsic value, or a mixture of both. The straightforwardly mechanical arts, such as engineering, are of extrinsic value, for they are only undertaken and developed to satisfy our basic needs. So are the nearer cousins of fine art, architecture and rhetoric, which are utilitarian arts that achieve their goals, at least in part, by pleasing their audience. In contrast, the fine arts of music, dance, poetry, painting, and sculpture are differentiated as the arts of leisure. Furnished as pleasing amusement to occupy the idle time that remains to people after they have satisfied life's necessities (and thus especially as the amusement of the upper classes), the fine arts lack utility, for their end lies in their consumption.

Batteux's next move is to argue that fine art is fundamentally imitative or representational. He thus arrives at his full definition of fine art as the pleasing imitation of beautiful nature (PA 9/9). However, he denies that fine art pleases by presenting us with representations of beautiful things as they are: "Nature should not be imitated such as she [ordinarily] is" (PA 9/9). Citing Aristotle's well-known distinction between poetry and history, Batteux generalizes from a few paradigmatic examples of art and concludes that the pleasure of art rests not in accuracy and truth but rather in the effect of the artist's "choice of the most beautiful parts of nature, to form one exquisite whole which should be more perfect than mere nature, without ceasing, however, to be natural" (PA 8/8).[8] The exploitation of perceptual design provides the audience with "an imaginary thing, a feigned being" (PA 14/16). So the fine arts do not merely please the senses. Instead, they operate on both sense perception and imagination, in which the pleasure involves both content recognition and a comparison of imagined, idealized objects with inferior models in nature.

As a template for subsequent theorizing about fine art, Batteux's analysis generates three obvious difficulties. First, sublimity has little or no place in fine art. In keeping with the phrase "les beaux arts," it has been ruled out by definition. Batteux signals as much when he pauses to consider the poet's handling of ugliness, particularly ugliness of character. The thing imitated

---

[5] Charles Batteux, *The Polite Arts, or, a Dissertation on Poetry, Painting, Music, Architecture, and Eloquence*, ed. and trans. anonymous (London: J. Osborn, 1749), 7, and *Les beaux arts réduits à un même principe* (Paris: Chez Durand, 1746), 7. Subsequent citations of this translation are given in the text as PA followed by pagination in the French. A modern critical edition is Batteux, *Les beaux arts réduits à un même principe*, vol. 2 of *Collection Théorie et critique à l'âge classique*, ed. Jean-Rémy Mantion (Paris: Aux Amateurs de livres, 1989). German translations quickly appeared: *Die Schöne Kunst aus einem Grunde Hergeleitet*, trans. anonymous (Gotha: J.P. Mervius, 1751), and *Batteux' Einschränkung der Schöne Kunst aus einen einzigen Grundsatz*, trans. J. A. Schlegel (Leipzig: Weidmann, 1751). The received wisdom that Batteux signals a genuine conceptual shift is debated in a recent exchange between James Porter and Larry Shiner. See James I. Porter, "Is Art Modern? Kristeller's 'Modern System of the Arts' Reconsidered," *British Journal of Aesthetics* 49, 1 (2009), 1–24; Larry Shiner, "Continuity and Discontinuity in the Concept of Art," *British Journal of Aesthetics* 49, 2 (2009), 159–78, and James I. Porter, "Reply to Shiner," *British Journal of Aesthetics* 49, 2 (2009), 171–8.

[6] A superior introduction to this complex history is Stephen Halliwell, *The Aesthetics of Mimesis: Ancient Texts and Modern Problems* (Princeton, NJ: Princeton University Press, 2002).

[7] See Larry Shiner, *The Invention of Art: A Cultural History* (Chicago: University of Chicago Press, 2001), 82.

[8] This sentence, and the later warning that pleasure vanishes when the theatrical spectator becomes conscious of unnatural artifice (93 [214]), points toward Immanuel Kant's doctrine that "fine art must have the *look* of nature even though we are conscious of it as art." Immanuel Kant, *Kritik der Urteilskraft*, in *Kant's gesammelte Schriften*, Königlichen Preussischen (later Deutschen) Akademie der Wissenschaften, 29 vols. (Berlin: Reimer [later de Gruyter], 1900–), vol. 5 (KGS); *Critique of Judgment*, trans. Werner S. Pluhar (Indianapolis, IN: Hackett, 1987), 5:174 (CJ). All subsequent references are to the pagination of the Akademie edition.

need not be beautiful in its natural state: "It matters not whether it be the furies or the graces," he argues (PA 20/27n). Any nonveridical imitation challenges the artist to combine the assembled parts with care. Taste must "guide" the imitation of nature (PA 15/23).[9] The representation must "form one exquisite whole," and its disparate source materials must "be so elegantly mix[ed] ... as to form one whole of the same nature" (PA 8/8 and 22/28). In an argument that presages David Hume's solution to the problem of the pleasurable effects of tragic theater, Batteux proceeds from the premise that the fine arts provide pleasure to the conclusion that any unpleasantness of subject matter must be mitigated by the beauty of the artistic achievement.[10] Sublimity should not dominate an artwork.

The second problem concerns instrumental music. To incorporate music into the fine arts, Batteux holds that music imitates the human passions: "A piece of music without words is still music. It expresses complaint or joy independently of words, which help it indeed; but neither give or take away anything that alters its nature" (PA 31/39–40). Yet, as Peter Kivy persuasively argues, developments in music were increasingly at odds with this strategy for uniting music with the other fine arts. The imitation thesis leaves subsequent theorists groping to explain the appeal of instrumental music that is of limited interest and therefore of dubious pleasure when approached as imitation.[11] (We might note that when Batteux published his theory, J. S. Bach had just published the first edition of *The Art of the Fugue*, Kivy's paradigm of absolute music.) With the publication of Immanuel Kant's *Critique of Aesthetic Judgment* (1790), nonimitative instrumental music's precarious status as a fine art had become suspect enough to warrant direct comment. Kant worries that nonvocal music seems no more than a species of agreeable design. Its appeal and value are akin to those of a well-designed carpet, rather than of poetry or sculpture.[12] By extension, post-Kantian aesthetics faces an obstacle in valuing sublimity in instrumental music, for there is no call for sublimity when the goal is mere agreeable design.

A third problem was highlighted after Jean le Rond d'Alembert incorporated a simplified version of Batteux's definition into the *Encyclopédie*'s "Preliminary Discourse of the Editors."[13] Although d'Alembert drops dance from the list of fine arts, adds architecture, and identifies poetry as the paradigm art, he reiterates three pillars of Batteux's analysis. Fine art's end is pleasure, its means is imitation, and thus it necessarily appeals to both the senses and imagination. Expanding on d'Alembert, J. G. Sulzer's essay on "beaux-arts" for the 1776 *Supplément à L'Encyclopédie* highlights the implication that the appeal of the fine arts is fundamentally irrational. It therefore requires supplementary justification through explicit consideration of art's effects on the character of its audience.[14] Although Batteux offers less context than Sulzer

---

[9] Kant's doctrine that taste should limit and guide genius provides another echo of Batteux in Kant (see CJ 5:188).

[10] David Hume, "Of Tragedy," in *Essays: Moral, Political, and Literary*, ed. Eugene F. Miller (Indianapolis, IN: Liberty Classics, 1987), 219.

[11] "During the early period of theorizing, from Dubos (say) to Batteux, the relative unimportance of instrumental music made it impotent as a challenge to the representational theory of art. It could simply be ignored as a peripheral case, indeed ignored without mention or explanation." Peter Kivy, *Philosophies of Arts: An Essay on Difference* (Cambridge: Cambridge University Press, 1997), 7. However, the material just reviewed shows that it is incorrect to accuse Batteux of passing over the issue of instrumental music without mention or explanation.

[12] Kant, CJ 5:76–7. On the difficulties of determining what Kant says about music, see Peter Kivy, *Antithetical Arts: On the Ancient Quarrel between Literature and Music* (Oxford: Clarendon Press, 2009), 41–52. Kant may have been familiar with Pluche's argument that instrumental music lacks true mimesis and so is no more significant than "beautiful Hungarian embroidery" (Noël-Antoine Pluche, "From *The Spectacle of Nature* (1746)," in *Music and Culture in Eighteenth-Century Europe: A Source Book*, ed. Enrico Fubini; trans. Wolfgang Freis [Chicago: University of Chicago Press, 1994], 82).

[13] Jean le Rond d'Alembert, "Discours préliminaire," in *Encyclopédie, ou dictionnaire raisonné des sciences, des arts et des métiers*, ed. Denis Diderot and Jean le Rond d'Alembert (Paris: Briasson, David, Le Breton, Durand, 1751), I:i–xlv.

[14] Johann Georg Sulzer, "Art, Beaux-arts," in *Supplément à l'Encyclopédie*, ed. Jean-Baptiste Robinet (Amsterdam: Marc-Michel Rey, 1776), 1:587–96.

for doing so, he likewise argues that the fine arts have the indirect value of improving taste and thus character. Batteux appeals to Plutarch's observation that a proper taste in music generates a love of order and design that translates into a general character of "decency, moderation, and order" (PA 3/119n).[15] No matter which passion is imitated, art's reliance on pleasing order and harmonious design must be the predominant effect. Disturbing passions and disreputable characters must be "delicately expressed" and so will have an improving effect on even the least virtuous members of the audience (PA 2/118). In the absence of sufficient mitigating delicacy, the strong passions associated with sublimity are a threat to the moral order.

As defining features of fine art during the Enlightenment, the intertwined requirements of representation, beautification, and pleasure create theoretical obstacles to the possibility and desirability of sublime art. Gradual recognition of these obstacles goes some way toward explaining why subsequent theorists on the sublime, such as Burke, James Beattie, and most notably Kant, emphasize sublimity in nature, where the sublime can be examined without the entanglements of the purposes – and consequent constraints – of art and taste.[16]

STYLE AND CONTENT

In 1948, just as his friend and associate Rothko arrived at the beginnings of his mature style, Motherwell published a short essay arguing that modern art is antithetical to the sublime. There is no reason to find irony in Motherwell's lack of prescience, for none of Rothko's paintings at that time point to a subsequent embrace of the sublime. If there is irony in Motherwell's description of sublimity, it is that he refers solely to *Peri hupsous*, attributed to Longinus, a treatise on language use.[17] Sublimity is an aesthetic effect in which the audience encounters "the exalted, the noble, the lofty," reflecting a great soul. But, Motherwell opines, this is not the stuff of *modern* art.[18]

Motherwell draws on a long-standing tradition in which sublimity is the Longinian rhetorical sublime. Seventeenth-century editions of *Peri hupsous* brought the topic into intellectual fashion just before the advent of modern aesthetics. Significantly, *Peri hupsous* rejects the doctrine that artworks should beautify their subject matter. A single moment of sublimity justifies otherwise failed writing (OS 48). Hence, given that beauty and sublimity are generally thought to interfere with one another, the beaux-arts tradition generates a prima facie conflict between beautifying one's subject and adopting a sublime style. No such issue arises if beauty is not art's raison d'être, but that possibility requires a radical rethinking of aesthetics and fine art as traditionally understood – a project of redefinition that characterizes Romanticism. However, the Romantic's embrace of sublime art followed considerable stage setting by eighteenth-century theorists who explored the problem of reconciling the Longinian sublime with the defining features of fine art as articulated by Batteux, popularized by d'Alembert, and, eventually, reconfigured by Kant. Let us explore the basic tension between the Longinian sublime and the beaux arts tradition.

The Longinian, rhetorical sublime is a function of style. As an effect of the activity of writing, it is an original aesthetic feature of an artwork. The desired "elevation" is contributed by the author's personality and command of language.[19] When it occurs, it operates "like a

---

[15] This issue is thought so important by Batteux's anonymous English translator that he reorders the text, replacing Batteux's own introduction with this discussion.

[16] See Kant, CJ 5:109.

[17] Motherwell draws on chapter 9 of *Peri hupsous* (Longinus, *On Great Writing [On the Sublime]*, trans. G. M. A. Grube [New York: Bobbs-Merrill, 1957], 12) (OS followed by page number).

[18] Robert Motherwell, "A Tour of the Sublime," in *Collected Writings*, 52; originally titled "Against the Sublime" and published in *Tiger's Eye* 6 (December 1948).

[19] To be precise, three of five contributing elements of the Longinian sublime are learned "art," whereas two, boldness of thought and passion for one's subject, are nonrhetorical "gifts of nature" (OS 10).

thunderbolt." However, *Peri hupsous* does not propose or imply that thunder and lightning are sublime (OS 4). Sublimity does not enter the literary work by dint of the sublimity of its subject matter. Its presence reflects the efforts of artistic genius.[20]

Like Longinus, Batteux's primary concern is the artist's power to control a particular aesthetic effect. Like Motherwell two centuries later, Batteux construes sublimity through the lens of *Peri hupsous*, as an author's power to impress, rather than to please, the audience. As such, the sublime is a desirable tool for securing the agreement of the hearer or reader. But this locates its value in its rhetorical utility, which conflicts with Batteux's normative expectation that fine art has no specific utility beyond pleasing the audience. This conflict becomes more apparent when subsequent theorists embrace the "utilitarian" arts of rhetoric and architecture as fine arts (i.e., as arts of pleasure) and construe the sublime as generally unpleasant and threatening.

The core difficulty is that the beaux arts tradition distinguishes between the beauty of subject matter and its beautification by the artist. Thus, the aesthetic properties of the work can obscure or omit aesthetic features of the work's subject matter. If there were no such distinction between the aesthetic properties of the work and of its subject, it would make no sense for Batteux and other eighteenth-century fine art theorists, such as Sir Joshua Reynolds, to invoke both genius and training to explain how a beautiful imitation of nature exceeds the beauty of nature (i.e., of subject matter).[21] Nor, failing this recognition, would it make sense for Batteux to recognize and endorse a species of literary harmony in which the work's "sound" is made to agree "with the object of the thought" (PA 74/171).[22] This category of harmony clearly presupposes the possibility of a discordant mismatch of vehicle and subject. (Unfortunately, Batteux does not elaborate on the conditions for parallel discords and harmonies in the other arts.)

As Batteux understood, a literary description of a beautiful face is not necessarily beautiful. The aesthetic properties of an artist's style – beautiful or sublime – are independent of the presence (or absence) of those same properties in the work's subject. However, an important consequence of grouping poetry and painting together as fine arts is that it sometimes encourages the view that they work in parallel ways, downplaying differences between literary and pictorial imitation.[23] An inept, ugly piece of writing can succeed in communicating that a face is beautiful by merely using the word. In contrast, an ugly painting of a face cannot communicate the degree of beauty possessed by its subject matter. Who can determine, looking at Pablo Picasso's *Les Demoiselles d'Avignon* or Willem de Kooning's *Woman, I*, whether the models had beautiful faces? Conversely, a beautiful painting will obscure the sublimity of its subject matter, a result encouraged by the doctrine that art should beautify and perfect its content.

Compounding their definitional obstacles to endorsing sublime art, early theorists of fine art faced the additional problem that they had not inherited any models for reconciling beauty and sublimity in the same artwork. The author of *Peri hupsous* recognizes a conflict between beautiful and sublime style but resolves it by prioritizing sublimity over beauty. No such path is open to the beaux arts tradition. Its emphasis on mimesis draws on the Renaissance tradition of

---

[20] *Peri hupsous* recognizes an innate human tendency to admire nature's most astounding displays, such as volcanic eruptions, but the sublime is restricted to rhetorical exploitation of this natural tendency (OS 47–8).

[21] See, for example, Joshua Reynolds, *Discourses on Art*, ed. Robert W. Wark (San Marino, CA: Huntington Library, 1959; reprint, New Haven, CT: Yale University Press, 1997 [1975]), 41 and 234. Reynolds's position that genius is necessary but not sufficient for fine art and must be constrained by educated taste is similar to Kant. See CJ 5:174–88.

[22] Harmonization of language and object is desirable, but it is not offered as an artistic necessity, for art sometimes addresses subject matter that is not in any way beautiful, as illustrated by Batteux's example of Molière's imaginative "genius" producing a successful (and, by implication, beautiful) representation of a misanthrope (PA 18/25–6).

[23] See Reynolds, *Discourses*, 133, 145–6, and 229.

mimetic accuracy but also, consequently, on an attendant neglect of the sublime.[24] In Batteux's case, the problem is temporarily defused by denying that rhetoric is a fine art. *Rhetorical* sublimity is a legitimate option provided it does not interfere with the overriding need for beauty.[25]

Ironically, a dawning recognition of the problem and an attempt at reconciliation predates Batteux, in Joseph Addison's essays on the arts and the pleasures of the imagination. Addison famously claims that beauty pleases the imagination, but then he makes the surprising move of extending this principle to the sublime, in which "greatness" flings us into "pleasing astonishment."[26] In proposing that visual beauty and greatness are distinct species of pleasure, Addison sets the stage for Burke's stricter dichotomization, in which "qualities ... ranged under the head of the Sublime be all found consistent with each other, and all different from those ... under the head of Beauty" (SB, preface to 2nd ed., 5).

More to the point, Addison foreshadows Batteux's harmonization problem by recognizing that our admiration of "what is Great" is frequently a function of both subject matter and artistic style. Again setting the stage for Burke, Addison proposes that artistic mediation permits the terrible and threatening aspects of nature to appear simultaneously "Dreadful and Harmless." The pleasure arises through "reflection" on the "safety" that we obtain in viewing a representation in place of the real thing.[27] In this respect Addison hews close to the Longinian tradition, for the sublime is more reliably encountered in artistic representation than in nature itself.[28] Yet Addison allows that a single aesthetic property, greatness, can be found in nature (as subject matter) and as an artifact of artistic representation. Initially, artworks are not included among his candidates for sublimity, for "greatness" is primarily a matter of "wide and undetermined Prospects."[29] Turning explicitly to the topic of arts that please the imagination, he immediately abandons the suggestion that greatness is not a property of individual objects by allowing that a building can be sublime either for itself or deceptively, in its manner.[30]

To confuse matters slightly, Addison is not consistent with his aesthetic categories. Following the Longinian tradition, he distinguishes between greatness and literary sublimity. Exploring the issue of how to classify and evaluate John Milton's *Paradise Lost*, Addison emphasizes that it succeeds as epic poetry because it combines stylistic elevation (here explicitly called "sublime") with greatness of subject matter.[31] He then departs from tradition by defending the sublime aspects of *Paradise Lost* against its critics by reclassifying sublimity as a species of beauty, rather than as beauty's competitor.[32] In keeping with the dominant view of fine art, Addison requires poets to both "mend" and "perfect" their representational content.[33] Unpleasant subject matter, such as the hordes of Satan in *Paradise Lost*, becomes pleasing through the proper design

---

[24] On mimesis as visual accuracy and on lack of discussion of the sublime, see Agnes Heller, *Renaissance Man* (Boston: Routledge & Kegan Paul, 1984), 408–10 and 246, respectively. See also Halliwell, *Aesthetics of Mimesis*, chap. 12. I do not discount the degree to which some Renaissance theorists advocated selection and perfection, among them Leon Battista Alberti and Sir Philip Sidney.

[25] Batteux does not mention sublimity when confronting this topic, but rather a "grandeur" that incites admiration (PA 37/46).

[26] Joseph Addison and Richard Steele, *The Spectator*, ed. Donald F. Bond, 5 vols. (Oxford: Clarendon Press, 1965), 3:540 (no. 412).

[27] Addison and Steele, *Spectator*, 3:568 (no. 418).

[28] Based on his multiple references to *Peri hupsous*, Addison was well acquainted with it. For an overview of Addison on "greatness" in nature, see Richard W. Bevis, *The Road to Egdon Heath: The Aesthetics of the Great in Nature* (Quebec: McGill-Queen's Press, 1999), 44–8.

[29] Addison and Steele, *Spectator*, 3:541 (no. 412).

[30] Addison and Steele, *Spectator*, 3:553–5 (no. 415).

[31] Addison and Steele, *Spectator*, 3:9–10 (no. 285); on greatness of topic, see 2:541 (no. 267). Addison articulates a third requirement, perspicuity of language (*Spectator*, 3:10 [285]).

[32] Addison and Steele, *Spectator*, 2:539 (no. 267). Addison's discussion of Milton predates that of the pleasures of imagination by six months.

[33] Addison and Steele, *Spectator*, 3:566 and 569 (no. 418).

of the artwork. Addison appears to hold that whatever is disturbing in its sublimity retains its greatness as subject matter – in what it summons up in (visual) imagination – despite its beautification through artistic transformation. Art contributes two additional pleasures in recognizing "the Aptness of the Description to excite the Image" (Batteux's category of harmony) and in making us aware of our own safety in meeting threatening material through the mediation of representation.[34]

In contrast to Addison, Burke is far less interested in fine art than in the types and sources of aesthetic response. Consistently opposing the beautiful and the sublime, Burke roots his inquiry in the natural rather than the rhetorical sublime. Beauty, but not sublimity, is essentially pleasing. It is difficult, therefore, to encounter the true sublime as the dominant character of a work of art, for "the ideas of the sublime and the beautiful stand on foundations so different, that it is hard, I had almost said impossible, to think of reconciling them in the same subject, without considerably lessening the effect of the one or the other upon the passions" (SB 3.13.113–14).

How then, for Burke, can an artwork be both beautiful and sublime? Not intending to write a treatise on art, he never explicitly addresses this question. However, he offers hints enough of an answer. To be sublime, art must create fear and horror that is simultaneously alleviated by pleasure. This requirement is secured, in typical eighteenth-century fashion, by appeal to "the pleasure resulting from the effects of imitation" (SB 1.15.47). Thus, Burke recognizes not wholly sublime works of art but rather "passages" of sublimity within a work through proper handling of sublime, tragic, or otherwise threatening subject matter (SB 1.17.51). In one example, Burke endorses a variation of the rhetorical sublime, in which unpleasant subject matter is "moderated ... in a description" and so is transformed from the painful (that is, painful if actually encountered in nature) to the sublime (when encountered imaginatively in a representation) (SB 2.21.85). This strategy informs other examples, as when Burke allows that some passages of *Paradise Lost* are "sublime to the last degree" (SB 2.3.59). In this case, he proposes that sublimity is present in a high degree because the subject matter retains its capacity to cause terror by Milton's deliberate obscurity in its presentation (and so, although Burke does not say so, Milton avoids perfecting and beautifying the subject matter).[35] As with the Longinian sublime, artistic style contributes the sublimity. However, unpleasant or horrific subject matter is corequired.

Burke's sole exception to that rule is, of course, established in Addison's discussion of architecture. Buildings can *be* sublime without possessing sublime subject matter. Possessing little or no reference or imitation, the scale and design of a building will sometimes satisfy the same sensory conditions that produce the sublime in nature (SB 2.10.76; see also 2.17.82). In Burke's wake, Kant also offers architectural works as his only specific examples of genuine sublimity in fine art, delegating them to the mathematical sublime, in which "imagination is inadequate for exhibiting the idea of a whole, [a feeling] in which imagination reaches its maximum, and ... sinks back into itself, but consequently comes to feel a liking."[36] Kant then observes that sublimity in art, by which he seems to mean sublimity as subject matter, is impurely mixed up with our awareness of human design in light of human purposes. He thus appears to be the first writer on aesthetic theory to state explicitly that the sublime is inherently problematic in fine art. Operating under the standard assumption that fine art requires both imitation and beauty, Kant believes that even when sublimity is present in the subject matter of a work of art, beauty

---

[34] Addison and Steele, *Spectator*, 3:567 (no. 418).

[35] Because the visual arts of his day required representational clarity, Burke argues that literature and instrumental music have a greater capacity for sublimity than do the visual arts (Burke, SB 2.4.60). Replacing Addison's requirement for perspicuity with obscurity, Burke's conditions for sublime literature reverse one of Addison's requirements.

[36] Kant, CJ 5:109. See Paul Crowther, *The Kantian Sublime: From Morality to Art* (Oxford: Clarendon Press, 1989), 152–61.

"can and should" be its dominant aesthetic modality, for otherwise it is "coarse, barbaric, and in bad taste."[37]

Historically, Kant's reservations are swept aside by the nineteenth-century fascination with the sublime. The consequences can be seen by considering a passage in Thomas Hardy's *The Return of the Native*. Hardy takes care to situate characters both socially and geographically. This novel begins with an extended description of the landscape in which he sets his story, and it includes Hardy's explicit tie between character types and aesthetic qualities of landscape. Interrupting his extended scene setting with a brief philosophical rumination, Hardy opines that we may be entering a time when the sublime in nature will be more satisfying than either natural beauty or architectural splendor:

Twilight combined with the scenery of Egdon Heath to evolve a thing majestic without severity, impressive without showiness, emphatic in its admonitions, grand in its simplicity. The qualifications which frequently invest the facade of a prison with far more dignity than is found in the facade of a palace double its size lent to this heath a sublimity in which spots renowned for beauty of the accepted kind are utterly wanting.... The time seems near, if it has not actually arrived, when the chastened sublimity of a moor, a sea, or a mountain will be all of nature that is absolutely in keeping with the moods of the more thinking among mankind. And ultimately, to the commonest tourist, spots like Iceland may become what the vineyards and myrtle gardens of South Europe are to him now; and Heidelberg and Baden be passed unheeded as he hastens from the Alps to the sand dunes of Scheveningen.[38]

Hardy's contemporaries often took offense at his pessimism, but in the wake of Burke and Kant they had no problem with the proposal that a desolate heath possesses sublimity.[39] We have come a very long way from Addison's Longinian position that Hardy's *prose* might contain flashes of the sublime, but Egdon Heath, the *place*, displays greatness rather than sublimity. Another point of departure is that nineteenth-century realism deprives the plot of *The Return of the Native* of greatness as understood by Addison.[40] Here again, the natural sublime is expected to supply the desired aesthetic effect in a literary work. In the course of theorizing that takes us from Addison to Kant, only Kant is likely to have been pleased with Hardy's proposal that humanity would soon reject beautiful art in favor of natural sublimity. Yet, a century after Kant, no one heeds his warning that this sublimity of subject matter poses a problem for taste.

THE NINETEENTH CENTURY

The Burkean sublime decisively opposes beauty and sublimity, leaving it to Kant to spell out the implication that the mimetic tradition of fine art interferes with the presentation of sublimity. As nineteenth-century artists increasingly explored emotive extremes through sublime subject matter, sympathetic theorists took up the task of redefining both fine art and sublimity. However, this embrace of sublimity was frequently contested. One way to grasp this post-Kantian phase of aesthetics and art history is to consider a few selected examples of critical discourse on the sublime in the nineteenth century. Let us consider painting, then music, and then finally the romantic denial of the necessity of mimesis.

---

[37] Immanuel Kant, *Anthropologie in pragmatischer Hinsicht*, KGS 7; *Anthropology from a Pragmatic Point of View*, trans. Mary J. Gregor (Den Haag: Martinus Nijhoff, 1974), 7:241. For a detailed discussion of this point and its implications, see Kirk Pillow, *Sublime Understanding: Aesthetic Reflection in Kant and Hegel* (Cambridge, MA: MIT Press, 2000), 67–77.

[38] Thomas Hardy, "The Return of the Native," *Belgravia Magazine* 34 (January 1878), 258. Concerning Hardy's thesis that the appeal of the sublime reflects modernism, see Bevis, *The Road to Egdon Heath*, 3–4.

[39] Concerning Hardy's direct debt to Burke, see S. F. Johnson, "Hardy and Burke's 'Sublime,'" in *Style in Prose Fiction: English Institute Essays*, ed. Harold C. Martin (New York: Columbia University Press, 1958), 55–86.

[40] Addison and Steele, *Spectator*, 2:539–43 (no. 267).

Romanticism is closely associated with the sublime in art. However, a romantic aesthetic does not necessarily support sublime handling of sublime topics. In the post-Kantian aesthetic most closely associated with Friedrich von Schiller, beauty remains opposed to the sublime, encouraging criticism of sublimity where it reduces beauty.[41] Consequently, nineteenth-century visual explorations of the sublime could be – and often were – challenged by critics who continued to prioritize compositional beauty. One notable case is the negative critical reception of Caspar David Friedrich's early masterpiece, *Cross in the Mountains* (1808). Judged by prevailing standards of optical clarity and fidelity, Friedrich's painting fails miserably. It provides excessive detail of distant objects, it apparently sets the viewer floating in the air parallel to a mountaintop, and the sky and the diffusion of light present conflicting signals as to time of day.

Friedrich's critics dismissed many of his paintings for their unsettling lack of differentiation between background and foreground. Viewers were disoriented by their inability to grasp the geographic space portrayed in the paintings.[42] Johann Wolfgang von Goethe, one of Friedrich's early champions, rejects *Monk by the Sea* (1809–1810) for obscuring basic spatial relationships.[43] Another critic turns Schiller's theory of aesthetic play against Friedrich's efforts.[44] Although Friedrich's novel visual effects and emphasis on greatness in nature can be praised as methods for incorporating sublime subject matter into visual representation (and, adapting Burke's advice about literature, for appropriately obscuring them!), the continued expectation for beautiful representation counted against Friedrich's acceptance by his contemporaries with an educated taste for fine art.

J. M. W. Turner is another nineteenth-century paradigm of sublime painting, employing "a veritable catalogue of the sublime" in his subject matter.[45] Yet his mature style, which blurs forms into indistinctness in order to intensify content,[46] was so controversial that he was routinely embarrassed in being passed over as lesser contemporaries received knighthoods. Turner's great champion, John Ruskin, defends his work by questioning the independence of sublimity: "The sublime is not distinct from what is beautiful, nor from other sources of pleasure in art, but is only a particular mode and manifestation of them."[47] Ruskin attacks the Burkean tradition as mistaken to think that sublime pleasure is associated with fear and terror. Consequently, the Burkean tradition misunderstands the "ideal in art."[48] Treating the sublime as a species of beauty, and so never in conflict with the standards of fine art, Ruskin argues that Turner displays a superior achievement of "truth and beauty."[49] Ruskin thus permits the natural sublime to enter art as a property of accurately rendered subject matter, especially fidelity in coloring, not as an independent stylistic achievement that Turner contributes through his controversial techniques.

[41] A summary of their essential tension is offered by Philip J. Kain, *Schiller, Hegel, and Marx: State, Society, and the Aesthetic Ideal of Ancient Greece* (Quebec: McGill-Queen's Press, 1982), 15–19.
[42] These criticisms are detailed in Brad Prager, *Aesthetic Vision and German Romanticism: Writing Images* (Rochester: Camden House, 2007), 94–100. *Monk by the Sea* is another nineteenth-century work that Rosenblum juxtaposes with Rothko ("The Abstract Sublime," 39).
[43] Quoted in Boris Asvarishch, "Friedrich's Russian Patrons," in *The Romantic Vision of Caspar David Friedrich: Paintings and Drawings from the U.S.S.R.*, ed. Sabine Rewald (New York: Metropolitan Museum of Art, 1990), 32.
[44] Prager calls it a "loosely Kantian approach" (*Aesthetic Vision*, 101), but the details point more directly back to Schiller.
[45] James Kirwan, *Sublimity: The Non-Rational and the Irrational in the History of Aesthetics* (New York: Routledge, 2005), 127.
[46] Andrew Wilton, *Turner and the Sublime* (London: British Museum, 1980), 72.
[47] John Ruskin, *Modern Painters*, vol. I, in *The Complete Works of John Ruskin (Library Edition)*, ed. E. T. Cook and Alexander Wedderburn, 39 vols. (London: George Allen, 1903–1912), 3:130. Ruskin subsequently admitted that there are some valuable cases of sublimity or greatness that are not a species of beauty.
[48] Ruskin, *Modern Painters* I, 3:129. Ruskin knew Kantian aesthetics secondhand, as filtered through Samuel Taylor Coleridge.
[49] Ruskin, *Modern Painters* I, 3:4; see also p. 52.

Ruskin's strategy for valorizing Turner echoes an approach that had already arisen in the philosophy of music. (Forget, for a moment, E. T. A. Hoffmann's celebrated defense of Beethoven.) Four decades before Kant questioned instrumental music's status as fine art, one of Burke's contemporaries argued that fine art's requirement of beauty limits the permissible range of sublimity in music. In 1752, Charles Avison argued that a pleasing combination of melody and harmony is the sine qua non of music, hence "it is their peculiar and essential property, to divest the soul of every unquiet passion ... and to fix the heart in ... tranquility."[50] He allows that music requires a "rough" style when imitating battles, storms, and other violent content, and he employs the familiar idea that only "the sense of our *security*" makes such content agreeable.[51] However, Avison introduces the subtle point that musical imitation is quite distinct from the "expressive" beauty essential to the musical art.[52] The sublime, then, enters music through representation and thus only by deviating from the true art of music. There appears to be no *musical* sublime, as James Beattie concurs.[53]

Avison's position has the unfortunate effect of excluding any harmonization of content and genuine musical expression, yet it mattered very much to religious music that such success was possible. Thus, to justify the sublime achievements of Handel and Haydn in their oratorios and religious music, William Crotch cites Reynolds's lectures on painting. Quoting Reynolds's assertion that all arts operate with an "affinity" in their principles, Crotch takes the existence of sublime painting as proof that music can be sublime.[54] More importantly, the affinity principle encourages a distinction between sublime style and sublime subject matter. Given that architecture can achieve sublimity without representing sublime content, there must be a musical sublime that can generate awe apart from subject matter.[55] Although Crotch does not limit the musical sublime to sacred music, he regards it as "peculiarly suited to the church service," and, based on the decline of the oratorio and the increasing fashion for beauty in sacred music, he concludes that the general art of music is on the decline.[56] The rise of the secular concert and the demand for beautiful art is music's loss.

Taken literally, Crotch's reservations about the expressive power of instrumental music put him at odds with enthusiasts for symphonic music, such as E. T. A. Hoffmann. Yet Crotch's account of the sublimity of instrumental music inadvertently provides them with a philosophical justification for their taste. Addressing unsympathetic critics who attack Beethoven's music as difficult and ugly, Hoffmann emphasizes the opposition of beauty and sublimity. The symphonies lack beauty for a good reason: they prioritize sublimity. Although it is relatively clear that Hoffmann regards Beethoven's fifth symphony as an inducement to feel the passions traditionally identified as sublime, it is by no means clear whether he thinks the music accomplishes this effect by incorporating sublime subject matter. In labeling Beethoven "Romantic" for exploring "the realm of the monstrous and the immeasurable" by providing disquieting experience of (and yearning for) infinity, Hoffmann concentrates on the Kantian mathematical sublime.[57] Strictly, Hoffmann seems to think that a *lack* of mimetic content generates the feeling of the

---

[50] Charles Avison, *Charles Avison's Essay on Musical Expression*, ed. Pierre Dubois (Aldershot: Ashgate, 2004), 5.
[51] Avison, *Essay*, 13n6.
[52] Avison, *Essay*, 24.
[53] James Beattie, *Essays on Poetry and Music as They Affect the Mind* (London: Dilly, 1776), 155.
[54] William Crotch, *Substance of Several Courses of Lectures on Music* (London: Longman, Rees, Orme, Brown, and Green, 1831); reprint, ed. Bernarr Rainbow (Clarabricken: Boethius Press, 1986), 27; Crotch quotes Reynolds, *Discourses*, 133.
[55] Crotch, *Lectures*, 28 and 45.
[56] Crotch, *Lectures*, 73.
[57] E. T. A. Hoffmann, "Beethoven's Instrumental Music," in *Source Readings in Music History*, ed. William Oliver Strunk and Leo Treitler; trans. William Oliver Strunk, 2nd ed. (New York: W. W. Norton, 1998), 1194.

sublime.[58] An awareness of the mathematical sublime appears to arise from nothing but musical *dynamics*. Burke's recommendation to obscure content is taken to the extreme of purging representation. Sublime handling of sublime content is replaced with sublime handling of nothing. With the nineteenth century's acceptance of instrumental music that achieves sublimity in the absence of beauty, music's lack of mimesis ceases to be an impediment to its status as fine art. After Hoffmann, music's lack of content is a positive asset. The path is open for the abstract sublime in painting.

CONCLUSION: AN ISSUE UNRESOLVED

"What should we say of a painter," Batteux asks, "who would be content to throw on the canvas bold strokes and masses of vivid colors, with no resemblance to a known object?" Surely it would be unfit for aesthetic judgment. But, luckily, music is not this way, for it naturally resembles the passions.[59] Batteux supposes that musical imitation of the basic emotions is natural and obvious rather than a matter of convention. Characteristically, he treats music as the special case, as the fine art that does not reflect the standard distinction of style and content.

Transposing the doctrine that music has a unique relationship to the passions, Barnett Newman's manifesto on the sublime proposes a direct relationship between abstract emotion and abstract visual design. Newman naively supposes that Americans have not inherited European views of fine art, permitting his generation of Americans (including his friends Motherwell and Rothko) to ignore traditional constraints on composition and beauty, thus freeing them to capture sublimity through a "self-evident" visual exploration of their own emotions.[60] Newman's polemic sounds remarkably like Richard Wagner's declaration that Beethoven has jettisoned the beautiful in favor of the sublime, producing art "released from all constraint of traditional or conventional forms."[61] A tradition stretching from Hoffmann to Wagner had defended the sublimity of nonrepresentational, "absolute" music. Shorn of its nineteenth-century metaphysical justifications, the aesthetic of the proponents of this tradition is applied to painting. Appropriating and simplifying a European philosophical and artistic tradition, Newman proclaims the utter originality of American abstract expressionism.

Rothko, I have suggested, is a paradigm of this visual tradition. Above all, take for example the massive dark canvases that he executed for Houston's Rothko Chapel. Rothko's and Newman's shared understanding of the coherence of this enterprise hinges on their willingness to pursue emotional effects without concern for the beauty of the painting or for the beautification of their subject matter. As in Hoffman's defense of Beethoven, their aesthetic embraces fine art shorn of all of the original requirements of "les beaux arts."

Sublime art requires, as Jean-Luc Nancy puts it, "a break within or from aesthetics."[62] Nonetheless, many art critics and historians continue to impose an ideal of a unifying affinity among the arts and so resist calling Rothko's large canvases "sublime." Dore Ashton, an art critic closely associated with abstract expressionism, has written extensively and influentially on Rothko's late paintings. Their design, she says, "challenged not only the eyes of the beholder but

---

[58] Hoffmann argues that vocal music is too definite about the emotions represented and so "excludes the character of infinite longing" ("Beethoven," 1195).
[59] Batteux, *Les beaux arts*, 263, my translation.
[60] Barnett Newman, "The Sublime Is Now," in *Art in Theory, 1900–2000: An Anthology of Changing Ideas*, ed. Charles Harrison and Paul Wood, 2nd ed. (Malden, MA: Wiley-Blackwell, 2003), 580–2, p. 582; originally published in *Tiger's Eye* (December 1948).
[61] Richard Wagner, *Beethoven*, trans. Albert R. Parsons (Indianapolis, IN: Benham Brothers, 1873), 99.
[62] Jean-Luc Nancy, "The Sublime Offering," in *Of the Sublime: Presence in Question*, ed. Jean-François Courtine et al.; trans. Jeffrey S. Librett (Albany: State University of New York Press, 1993), 25.

his entire psychological and motor being."[63] Yet Ashton never identifies these works as sublime and says that it does not matter that Rothko used that term.[64] Echoing Addison's defense of Milton and Ruskin's defense of Turner, she proposes that Rothko pursues a species of beauty.[65] Rothko pursues sublimity, whereas the apologist denies that sublimity is present. After three centuries of debate, we have not achieved cultural consensus on how and when sublimity is present in fine art.

---

[63] Dore Ashton, *About Rothko*, 2nd ed. (New York: Da Capo, 2003), 195.
[64] Dore Ashton, *Out of the Whirlwind: Three Decades of Art Commentary* (Ann Arbor: UMI Research Press, 1987), 190.
[65] Dore Ashton, *The Unknown Shore: A View of Contemporary Art* (Boston: Little, Brown, 1962), 73–4.

15

Architecture and the Sublime

Richard A. Etlin

When Immanuel Kant observed in the *Critique of the Power of Judgment* (1790) that the view of the starry heavens provoked the sentiment of the sublime, he was gazing into the epicenter of the potential relationship of architecture to the sublime.[1] Indeed, several years before, in 1784, the French architect Étienne-Louis Boullée had sought to honor Sir Isaac Newton for having discovered the single principle that regulated the workings of the universe – gravity – by burying him, or more properly speaking, his *manes* (spirit) "within his discovery," that is, within an architectural rendition of the cosmos (Figure 15.1).[2] Boullée wanted to place Newton's sarcophagus at the bottom of a vast spherical cavity whose dome was to have been punctured with small holes so as to allow the sun to shine through in the guise of twinkling stars, such that the viewer would experience an artificial rendition of the most quintessential of sublime scenes in the presence of Newton's *manes*.

Both Kant's observation and Boullée's project anticipate Charles Blanc's later insight that would relate the sublime to infinity and the absolute: "Issuing from the depths of nature, emanating from the divine, the sublime is absolute, imperishable.... The sublime is like a sudden glimpse of infinity."[3] Blanc, in turn, was paraphrasing Longinus, who, in similar words, conveys another aspect of the sublime: the immediate and intense feeling that it produces or that characterizes it. The sublime, he writes, is a feeling in response to some stimulus: "That ... is grand and lofty, which the more we consider, the greater Ideas we conceive of it; whose Force we cannot possibly withstand; which immediately sinks deep, and makes such Impressions on the Mind as

---

[1] Immanuel Kant, *Kritik der Urteilskraft*, in *Kant's gesammelte Schriften*, Königlichen Preussischen (later Deutschen) Akademie der Wissenschaften, 29 vols. (Berlin: Reimer [later de Gruyter], 1900–), vol. 5; *Critique of the Power of Judgment*, ed. Paul Guyer; trans. Paul Guyer and Eric Matthews (Cambridge: Cambridge University Press, 2000 [1790]), 5:270 (CJ). For Kant's earlier texts on this theme, see note 6.

[2] Étienne-Louis Boullée, *Architecture: Essai sur l'art*, ed. Jean-Marie Pérouse de Montclos (Paris: Hermann, 1968), 137 (*Architecture*). All translations from this text are my own.

[3] Charles Blanc, *Grammaire des arts du dessin* (Paris: Veuve Jules Renouard, 1867), 8.

For assistance, I thank Walter Cahn, Yassana Croizat-Glazer, Deborah Mauskopf Deliyannis, Paul Guyer, Mark Johnson, Lynne Lancaster, Deborah Parker, Giancarla Periti, Debra Pincus, James Saslow, Christine Smith, Marvin Trachtenberg, William Wallace, Ian Wardropper, and Roger Wieck. Joseph Solodow has been especially generous in clarifying the finer points of Greek and Latin. I am greatly indebted to Beatrice Rehl for constructive comments about this essay. I express particular gratitude to Timothy Costelloe and Rabun Taylor, who spent considerable time helping me to clarify my ideas and my writing in several drafts of this chapter. I also offer special thanks to Jean de Yturbe, proprietor of the Château d'Anet, who permitted me to study thoroughly the public spaces, and to Jean-Marie Pérouse de Montclos and Étienne Jollet, for having facilitated my visits. Michael Waters kindly took specific photos of the Pantheon at my request.

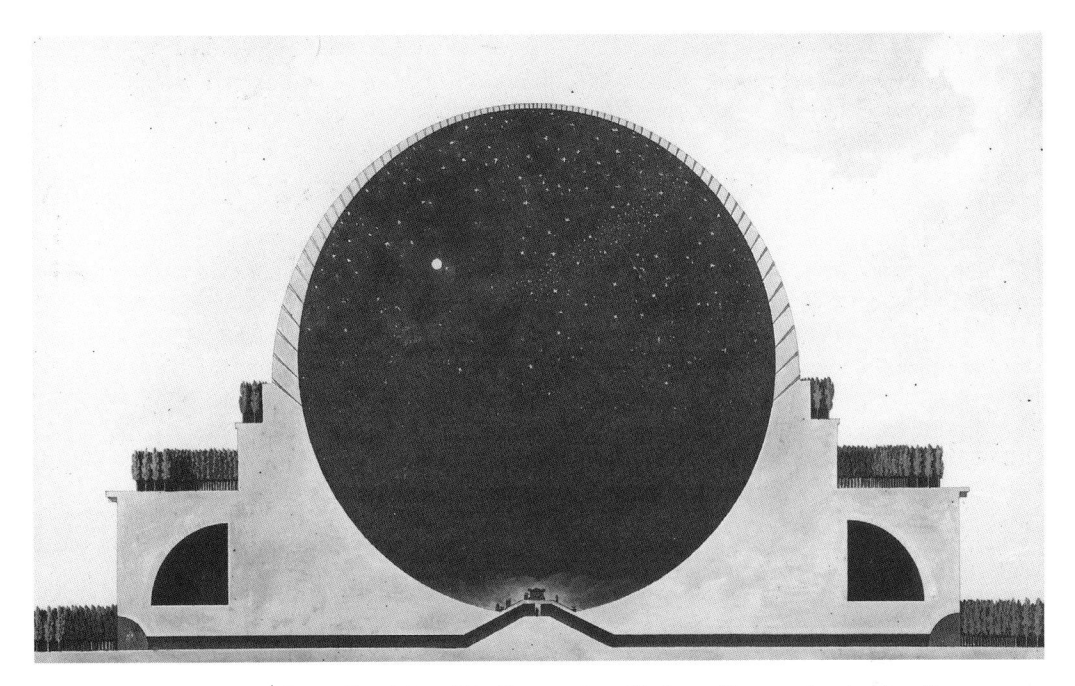

FIGURE 15.1. Étienne-Louis Boullée, Cenotaph to Sir Isaac Newton (project), 1784. Photo credit: Bibliothèque nationale de France.

cannot be easily worn out or effaced."[4] In the *Critique of the Power of Judgment* (1790), Kant repeatedly emphasizes that the sublime involves a feeling rather than an idea and that it resides not in the object but in a "disposition of the mind" (CJ 5:265).[5] Hence, in order for the starry sky to be sublime, one

> must not ground such a judging of it on concepts of worlds inhabited by rational beings, taking the bright points with which we see the space above us to be filled as their suns, about which they move in their purposively appointed orbits, but must take it, as we see it, merely as a broad, all-embracing vault; and it must be merely under this representation that we posit the sublimity that a pure aesthetic judgment attributes to this object. (CJ 5:270)[6]

---

[4] Dionysius Longinus, *On the Sublime*, trans. William Smith, 2nd rev. ed. (London: B. Dod, 1743 [1739]), 7.15 (OS). All references are to section and page. All references to the *Iliad* are to lines cited by Longinus as given in Smith's text, which uses Alexander Pope's translation of the *Iliad* throughout. For references to sources of texts quoted by Longinus but not given in Smith's edition, I have used D. A. Russell's translation: Longinus, *On Sublimity*, trans. D. A. Russell, in D. A. Russell and M. Winterbottom, eds., *Ancient Literary Criticism* (Oxford: Clarendon Press, 1972), 460–503. This passage is also quoted in Samuel Holt Monk, *The Sublime: A Study of Critical Theories in XVIII-Century England* (Ann Arbor: University of Michigan Press, 1935), 13.

[5] See also Monk, *The Sublime*, 8–9.

[6] Here Kant appears to be clarifying – possibly even critiquing – his earlier reference to the sublime found in the "starry heavens" in the short conclusion to the *Critique of Practical Reason* (1788), in which he passed immediately from "admiration and reverence" (*Ehrfrucht*) to musing about "worlds upon worlds and systems of systems" and so forth. In 1790, in a more extended discussion of the sublime, he explicitly separates the feeling of the sublime from such reflections. Here Kant is developing further his fundamental emphasis on "the feeling of the sublime," introduced in his earlier work on aesthetics, *Observations on the Feeling of the Beautiful and Sublime* (1764, reissued in 1766 and 1771), in which he had briefly included the view of the starry sky. Immanuel Kant, *Critique of Practical Reason*, in *Practical Philosophy*, trans. and ed. Mary Gregor (Cambridge: Cambridge University Press, 1997), 5:161–2; *Observations on the Feeling of the Beautiful and Sublime*, trans. John T. Goldthwait (Berkeley: University of California Press, 1960), 47.

Both nature and the divine have provided the subject matter for the architectural rendition of the sublime: either cosmic scenes, such as the starry night rendered as the dome of heaven, or the Heavenly Jerusalem as depicted in church architecture according to its consecration ceremony.[7] Feelings associated with the sublime have a psychospatial, hence phenomenological, character. As John Baillie points out in *An Essay on the Sublime*, "the *Sublime* dilates and elevates the Soul, *Fear* sinks and contracts it; yet *both* are felt upon viewing what is great and awful."[8] In architecture the sublime essentially falls into two categories. One involves wonder, awe, and even terror. This grouping of responses appears to belong to what Rudolf Otto defines as the experience of "primal numinous awe" in words that recall both Longinus and Blanc: "This experience of eerie shuddering and awe breaks out from depths of the soul."[9] Thus a chronicler describes the effect of the Gothic Cathedral of Notre-Dame in Paris in these terms: "quae mole sua terrorem incutit spectantibus" ("which by its mass inspires terror in onlookers").[10] The other involves a response to breadth, width, or height, spatial characteristics that Longinus adduces in literature when offering examples of the sublime. One instance presents an image of vertical expansiveness as a metaphor for Homer's genius:

So the Space between Heaven and Earth marks out the vast Reach and Capacity of *Homer*'s Ideas, when he says,

> While scarce the Skies her horrid Head can bound,
> She stalks on Earth.... (*Iliad* 4.443; OS 9.19)

In the notes to his 1739 translation of Longinus, William Smith remarks that Zachary Pearce, who published a Greek edition of the text in 1724,[11] associated this passage with a line from the *Wisdom of Solomon*: "Thy almighty word leaped down – it touched the heaven, but it stood upon the earth" (18.15–16; OS 9.121). Another example, also with the planet earth as its basis, extends space horizontally around the globe, with a bound that begins on an eminence:

> Far as a Shepherd from some Point on high
> O'er the wide Main extends his boundless Eye,
> Thro' such a space of Air, with thund'ring Sound,
> At one long Leap th'immortel Coursers bound. (*Iliad* 5.770; OS 9.20)

Then Longinus comments: "He measures the Leap of the Horses by the extent of the World. And who is there, that considering the superlative Magnificence of this Thought, would not with good reason cry out, that if the Steeds of the Deity were to take a second Leap, the World itself would want room for it" (OS 9.20). The three primary spatial qualities of height, breadth, and depth, as the psychiatrist and phenomenologist Eugène Minkowski has emphasized, belong to a primal psychophysical experience that is more immediate than their rational counterparts as coordinates of measurable distance. They belong to the realm of what Minkowski terms alternatively "primitive space" or "spiritual space," which has an "a priori spatial dynamism," as well

---

[7] On the Heavenly Jerusalem and the consecration ceremony, see Otto von Simson, *The Gothic Cathedral: Origins of Gothic Architecture and the Medieval Concept of Order*, 2nd rev. ed. (New York: Harper & Row/The Bollingen Library, 1962) esp. 8–11, and Laurence Hull Stookey, "The Gothic Cathedral as the Heavenly Jerusalem: Liturgical and Theological Sources," *Gesta* 8, 1 (1969), 35–41.

[8] John Baillie, *An Essay on the Sublime* (London: R. Dodsley, 1747), 32.

[9] Rudolf Otto, *The Idea of the Holy*, trans. John W. Harvey (Oxford: Oxford University Press, 1923), 125–6. Compare this with Shaftesbury's explanation that the sublime excites "of all other Passions, the easiest rais'd in raw and unexperienc'd Mankind," as quoted and discussed in Timothy M. Costelloe, "Imagination and Internal Sense: The Sublime in Shaftesbury, Reid, Addison, and Reynolds," chap. 4 of the current volume.

[10] Jacques Du Breul, *Le Théâtre des antiquités de Paris* (1612), 6, as quoted in Victor Hugo, *Notre-Dame de Paris 1482* (Paris: Garnier Frères, 1961 [1832]), 126.

[11] See Monk, *The Sublime*, 21.

as a qualitative significance, as revealed by phrases such as "the breadth of our knowledge" or "the depth of our feelings."[12]

The architectural sublime combines in various manners the spatial sublime – as illustrated by the spatial images collected by Longinus – with the cosmological sublime – as found either in response to the vast and awe-inspiring scenes of nature or in the theological renditions of the cosmos, such as the Christian church conceived as the Heavenly City of Jerusalem constructed here on earth. Because architecture, like all physical things, involves mass and weight subject to gravity, and because architecture by its nature is stationary, the architectural sublime will either employ these qualities to awe the spectator or will subvert them by seeming to deny them their customary earthbound and stationary nature. Hence, the great mass and height of the Cathedral of Notre-Dame inspired terror in the observer. On the other hand, the Cenotaph to Newton would have abolished fixed form, as well as gravity, to place the viewer within a spherical cavity whose rendition of the starry night would have presented an image of infinite extension. One particular virtue of Edmund Burke's epoch-making book, *A Philosophical Enquiry into the Origin of Our Ideas of the Sublime and Beautiful* (1757, 2nd ed. 1759), is that the author provides a rudimentary explanation of the mechanism by which the spatial sublime in architecture works on the psyche as a psychophysical experience. This account occurs in his two treatments of what he terms "the artificial infinite," to which we now turn to begin a consideration of the architectural sublime.

THE ARTIFICIAL INFINITE AND *EINFÜHLUNG*

Burke introduces the concept of the artificial infinite in part II of his treatise, after first considering vastness and infinity. He returns to the subject, devoting a section to it in part IV. To Burke, vastness is "a powerful cause of the sublime." Infinity, moreover, is not only a source of the sublime but possibly an inherent attribute: "Another source of the sublime, is *infinity*; if it does not rather belong to the last." In architecture, "greatness of dimension" corresponds to the general category of vastness. Infinity in architecture could be achieved through the artificial infinite, which offers two possibilities. One involves a succession of identical vertical elements, as in a quincunx of trees, a line of freestanding columns in an ancient temple, or a row of piers in a Gothic cathedral. The other arises from a hemispherical dome or "rotunda." In both types of architecture, Burke explains the operant principle as the succession of "frequent impulses on the sense to impress the imagination with an idea of their progress beyond their actual limits."[13] As is often the case with writers on the sublime, Burke is perceptive in identifying the type of image or scene that could prompt feelings of the sublime but is only partially successful in explaining the psychophysiological mechanism, what Richard Shusterman terms "somaesthetics," a philosophical notion adapted from neurophysiology, in which the word "somesthetic" refers to "sensory perception through the body itself rather than its particular sense organs."[14]

Because the sublime is not an idea but rather a feeling, Burke is actually discussing the psychophysical sensation of expanding when the eye follows the uninterrupted surface of a vast

---

[12] Eugène Minkowski, *Vers une Cosmologie: fragments philosophiques,* 2nd rev. ed. (Paris: Aubier-Montaigne, 1936), 63–6 ("La Triade psychologique") and 75–7 ("L'Espace primitif").

[13] Edmund Burke, *A Philosophical Enquiry into the Origin of Our Ideas of the Sublime and Beautiful*, ed. James T. Boulton (London: Routledge and Kegan Paul, 1958 [1759, 1st ed. 1757]), 2.9.74. All references are to part, section, and page number. This section of the current chapter develops further ideas that I have been discussing since 1984. See Richard A. Etlin, "Aesthetics and the Spatial Sense of Self," *Journal of Aesthetics and Art Criticism* 56, 1 (1998), 1–19.

[14] Richard Shusterman, *Body Consciousness: A Philosophy of Mindfulness and Somaesthetics* (Cambridge: Cambridge University Press, 2008), 1–2. See also Shusterman's "Somaesthetics and Burke's Sublime," *British Journal of Aesthetics* 45, 4 (2005), 323–41.

dome or the long line of piers or columns. Burke, however, errs in the literalness of his account, in which he imagines that the goal is to impart "an idea of their progress beyond their [that of a row of columns] actual limits." The goal, rather, to adopt Baillie's terminology, is to "dilate" the soul. Here, then, Burke's discussion of what he terms the uninterrupted, cumulative effect of successive "impulses" actually addresses the experience of sublimity. In other words, the primary cause of a feeling of the sublime derives not from imagining that columns extend beyond their actual limit but from the experience of expanding existential space.

Burke, unfortunately, did not have access to a terminology that would convey successfully this difficult notion of the commingling of physical with existential space. Aesthetic theory would have to await the advent of the late nineteenth-century philosophical school of *Einfühlung* (empathy), which addressed the relationship of aesthetics to the spatial sense of self. This movement extended the work of Johann Georg Sulzer, who, in his *General Theory of the Fine Arts* (1771–1774), emphasizes the origins of the term "aesthetics" in the Greek *aistheses*, what he takes to mean "the science of feelings," which serves as a tool for understanding the very "nature of the soul." For Sulzer, "aesthetics" refers to the nature of *Empfindungen* (sentiments) prompted by works of art so that the "soul becomes, in essence, all feeling" and "knows of nothing outside, but only of what is inside itself."[15] Burke's discussion of the artificial infinite belongs to the realm of *Empfindungen*; this experiential topography was later charted more fully by the philosophers of *Einfühlung*.

According to the *Einfühlung* school, the most general feature of aesthetic experience as it relates to *Empfindungen* can be expressed through one of two words, either *Lebensgefühl* or *Vitalgefühl*, both terms referring to the feeling of the life force.[16] In Burke's time, Jean-Jacques Rousseau had termed this feeling "le sentiment de l'existence" ("the sentiment of existence," that is, sentience) and had charted its existentially spatial aspects, especially as they relate to a feeling of expansiveness in the presence of nature.[17] The particular contribution of the *Einfühlung* philosophers resides in the articulation of other terms that specify more explicitly the nature of such feelings: *Körpergefühl*, to refer to that aspect of sentience that involves sentiment permeating the body; *Formgefühl*, to explain aesthetic response in the body to qualities of line or mass in artistic or natural forms; and *Raumgefühl*, to designate the feeling of sentience as it relates to circumambient space. This last term, *Raumgefühl*, involves what August Schmarsow explains to be the "intuited form of space, which surrounds us wherever we may be and which we then always erect around ourselves." As Schmarsow observes, *Raumgefühl* always involves a psychological, experiential central axis within the self that then emanates outward: "We all carry the dominant coordinate of the axial system within ourselves in the vertical line that runs from head to toe. This means that as long as we desire an enclosure for ourselves, the meridian of our body need not be visibly defined; we ourselves, in person, are its visual manifestation." As Schmarsow explains, existential space, through *Raumgefühl*, constitutes a primary way of experiencing architecture:

As the creatress of space, architecture creates, in a way that no other art can, enclosures for us in which the vertical middle axis is not physically present but remains empty.... The spatial construct is, so to

---

[15] Johann Georg Sulzer, *General Theory of the Fine Arts* (1771–74), in *Aesthetics and the Art of Musical Composition in the German Enlightenment: Selected Writings of Johann Georg Sulzer and Heinrich Christoph Koch*, ed. and trans. Nancy Kovaleff Baker and Thomas Christensen (Cambridge: Cambridge University Press, 1995), 25–6. For Sulzer's debt to Alexander Baumgarten, who, as Sulzer explains, "coined the name 'aesthetics,'" and their shared obligation to Christian Wolff's insight that – in Thomas Christensen's words – "our experience of beauty is sentient, not cognitive," see 11–12 and 26.

[16] On the *Einfühlung* school, see Harry Francis Mallgrave and Eleftherios Ikonomou, eds. and trans., *Empathy, Form, and Space: Problems in German Aesthetics, 1873–1893* (Santa Monica: Getty Center for the History of Art and the Humanities, 1994).

[17] See Jean-Jacques Rousseau, *Les Rêveries du promeneur solitaire*, passim; *Confessions*, 1:642 and 644; and "Troisième Lettre à Malesherbes," 1:1141, in *Œuvres complètes* (Paris: Gallimard/Bibliothèque de la Pléiade, 1959), 5 vols.

FIGURE 15.2. Étienne-Louis Boullée, Metropolitan Church (project), 1782.
Photo credit: RIBA Library Drawings and Archives Collection.

speak, an emanation of the human being present, a projection from within the subject, irrespective of whether we physically place ourselves inside the space or mentally project ourselves into it.[18]

Burke's account of the two ways of achieving the artificial infinite becomes clearer when understood in terms of the *Einfühlung* account of aesthetic experience in general, and of the essential nature of *Raumgefühl* to architecture.

BOULLÉE'S ARCHITECTURAL SUBLIME

Boullée appears to have addressed the challenge posed by Burke's treatise, because his project for the Metropolitan Church (c. 1781–1782, Figure 15.2) and his Cenotaph to Newton (1784, Figure 15.1) respond to the two types of the artificial infinite. He conceived the former as a temple that would convey the experience of the immensity of nature through the experience of long rows of freestanding columns, whereas the latter employed a vast rotunda, which was further extended as a continuous form through its mirror image to become a spherical cavity. Both buildings involve a sense of an expanding existential space such that the spectator would feel the immensity of nature, which Boullée saw as a pantheistic or deistic manifestation of divinity, the Supreme Being.

Boullée conceived his designs for both buildings and explained their aesthetic effect with reference to what he imagined was the exhilarating but also dangerous feeling that balloonists, who had begun to explore the skies in 1783, might encounter as they ascend far away from the surface of the earth:

Let us imagine man in the middle of the ocean, seeing only sky and water: this scene is truly that of immensity. In this position, everything is beyond our grasp. There is no way to make comparisons. It is the same for the balloonist who, floating through the sky and having lost sight of the objects on the

---

[18] August Schmarsow, "The Essence of Architectural Creation" (1893), in Mallgrave and Ikonomou, eds., *Empathy*, 288–9.

earth, sees in all of nature only the sky. Wandering so within immensity, in this abyss of extension, man is annihilated by this extraordinary spectacle of inconceivable space. (*Architecture* 85)[19]

To avoid this psychic annihilation while affording the spectator the opportunity to experience the immensity of nature through architecture would require some means to anchor the sense of spatial self while expanding outward. This was readily achieved in the Metropolitan Church project through the endless rows of columns, which serve as psychic anchors, as viewers feel themselves expanding outward from column to column. Boullée even went so far as to imagine that, as we feel ourselves expanding, we impart life to the columns themselves: "Thus, through a felicitous effect that is caused by our movement and that we can attribute to the objects themselves, it seems that they walk along with us and that we have given them life" (*Architecture* 83).

At the Cenotaph to Newton, Boullée takes his spectators to the razor's edge of psychic annihilation. Entering the space at the bottom of the spherical cavity, visitors would be frozen, so to speak, at the building's "center of gravity," which is occupied by the classical sarcophagus dedicated to Newton's *manes*. Responding experientially to the curvature of the walls, spectators would be "obliged, as if by innumerable forces" to remain at the center, where the "tomb is the sole material object" in the building. This tomb becomes the psychic anchor that permits visitors to expand outward to become one with the immensity of the space. In contemplating the vast, spherical cavity, the spectator "sees only a continuous surface with neither beginning nor end" and hence "would find himself transported into the sky as if by enchantment and carried on the clouds into the immensity of space." Expanding experientially to become one with the immensity of nature in a never-ending succession of impressions (or an ever-expanding spatial feeling), spectators are saved from the psychic annihilation of the balloonist through the anchor of the tomb, with which they identify. At the moment of epiphany, the viewer becomes one with nature through the endless circumference of the spherical cavity or with the impression of boundless space that the vast interior conveys, especially in darkness; at the same time the viewer becomes one with Newton through the tomb, thereby participating in the "sublimity of [Newton's] genius," which had risen to the height of divine intelligence (*Architecture* 137–9).[20] Through this existential encounter with architectural space, Boullée gave new meaning to the often-repeated notion "Deus est sphaera cujus centrum ubique, circumferentia nusquam" ("God is the sphere whose center is everywhere and whose circumference is nowhere").[21]

In these two projects, Boullée also addressed the issue of mass, weight, and gravity. In the church, whose size was intended to convey the immensity of nature, the placement of the columns, along with their projecting cornice, would give the illusion that the vast barrel vaults, as well as the central dome, were floating miraculously overhead. This was an application of an illusionistic arrangement in Jules Hardouin-Mansart's Dome of the Invalides (1679–1691), a building that Boullée criticized for its failure to exploit fully its sublime potential. Hardouin-Mansart had designed his centralized church with a triple dome: a tall exterior dome to convey

---

[19] Boullée uses the word *anéanti*. For a discussion of *anéantissement* as a desirable experience in late fifteenth- and early sixteenth-century religious meditation, as well as of Pascal's religious reflection on the experience of the infinity of space, see Éva Madeleine Martin, "The 'Prehistory' of the Sublime in Early Modern France: An Interdisciplinary Perspective," chap. 6 of the current volume.

[20] See also Boullée's comparable explanation of the experience in the Cenotaph to Newton related in a letter of 19 Prairial Year II (June 7, 1794) by Anne-Louise Brongniart, to her husband Alexandre-Théodore, a former student, after a visit during which the sixty-six-year-old architect "electrified" her by his graphic account (*Architecture* 184), thereby giving her what Shaftesbury had termed a "rhapsody." On Shaftesbury, see Costelloe, "Imagination and Internal Sense."

[21] This quotation constitutes the subject and furnishes the point of departure for the introduction in Georges Poulet, *Les Métamorphoses du cercle* (Paris: Plon, 1961), iii–xxiv (my translation). For a somaesthetic explanation comparable to Boullée's in Alexander Gerard's *An Essay on Taste*, 3rd ed. (1780 [1759]), see Rachel Zuckert, "The Associative Sublime: Gerard, Kames, Alison, and Stewart," chap. 5 of the current volume.

the desired height to the building's external massing and a double interior dome, the lower one with a broad oculus that permits a view to the heavenly scene painted on the middle dome, placed closely above and lit by windows hidden from view. Worshippers would have the impression that there was only one interior dome with a central picture of an illusionistic heavenly scene hovering weightlessly above and emanating from within a holy glow. While applauding this arrangement, Boullée observed that the windows in the drum below the dome admitted light that detracted from the effect of the central scene, a defect that he eliminated in his own proposed church. The cloud-filled scene of Boullée's dome would have made it seem weightless, whereas the barrel vaults of the four arms of his church retain mass and weight, seeming to float miraculously high above, thanks to the placement of the freestanding columns and the projecting cornice, which also hides natural lighting at the base of the vaults. Both the vaults and the dome would convey "the lightest and most aerial effect possible" (*Architecture* 91–6).

Boullée's two projects belong to a long architectural tradition in the West that extends back to ancient Rome and continues through every succeeding architectural period and then beyond, reaching into our own times. In the remainder of this chapter I turn to the main features of this historical sequence, concentrating on buildings most pertinent to the development of Boullée's ideas.[22]

LITERATURE AND THE ARCHITECTURAL SUBLIME

Before surveying the history of the architectural sublime from ancient Rome to Boullée, one might note the constant interchange between architecture and literature in creating either descriptions or architectural forms capable of imparting a feeling of the sublime, considerations already discussed by Longinus. We have already seen how Longinus adduces spatial descriptions from Homer involving vast length, height, and depth as exemplars of the sublime, but these, we should now note, relate to two other types of images that involve *dynamism*. One is spatial and the other emotional, although the two are often conjoined. Emotional dynamism conveys what Longinus identifies as "force, precipitation, strength, and vehemence" (OS 12.34). In the history of the architectural sublime that follows, accounts of the Gigantomachy between Zeus (Jupiter) and the Titans (Giants) will emerge as a favored theme in both its pagan and Christian form, the latter in the battle between God and the Fallen Angels.

This type of energetic movement finds its complement in Longinus – and in the architecture that follows – in plunges into the abyss, whether straight or spiraling, or spiraling upward into the sky. Longinus cites two passages from Euripides that will echo through time. One involves a straight plunge downward in the depths. Orestes exclaims:

> Loose me, thou Fury, let me go, Torment'ress:
> Close your embrace, to plunge me headlong down
> Into th' Abyss of Tartarus – (*Orestes*, 5.264; OS 15.44)

The other involves a spiraling descent through the vastness of space, as recounted through two fragments by Euripides, which Smith speculates come from his lost play *Phaeton* (OS 15.148), in the tragic hero's fatal chariot flight through the skies, as he is followed by his father, the sun god:

> He starts; the Coursers, whom the lashing Whip
> Excites, outstrip the Winds, and whirl the Car

---

[22] For brief treatments of the sublime in later periods, see Richard A. Etlin, "The Parthenon in the Modern Era," in *The Parthenon: From Antiquity to the Present*, ed. Jenifer Neils (Cambridge: Cambridge University Press, 2005), 362–95; "St. Peter's in the Modern Era: The Paradoxical Colossus," in *St. Peter's in the Vatican*, ed. William Tronzo (Cambridge: Cambridge University Press, 2005), 270–304, and "The Pantheon in the Modern Era," in *The Pantheon*, ed. Todd Marder and Mark Wilson Jones (Cambridge: Cambridge University Press, 2013).

> High thro' the airy Void. Behind[,] the Sire,
> Borne on his Planetary Steed, pursues
> With Eye intent, and warns him with his Voice,
> Drive there! – now here! – here! turn the Chariot
> here! (OS 15.41–2; fr. 779 Nauck)

Longinus's commentary is particularly precious for my account, because he explains that such passages engage the empathetic participation of the author and, by implication, of the reader: "Who would not say, that the Soul of the Poet mounted the Chariot along with the Rider, that it shar'd as well in Danger, as in Rapidity of Flight with the Horses?" (OS 15.41–2). Here then, we have a combination of spatial dynamism and emotional dynamism, both felt empathetically.

Longinus's understanding of the nature of empathetic response extends to a discussion of how far the author might – and should – take the reader to the razor's edge of terror. The issue that he raises may possibly have had important repercussions for Boullée, as discussed previously, and for various other writers and architects, including those considered throughout the remainder of the chapter. The passage concerns a ship wrecked by a tempest at sea, Homer's simile for Hector's furious onslaught against the Greeks:

> – He bursts upon them all:
> Bursts as a Wave that from the Cloud impends,
> And swell'd with Tempests on the Ship descends;
> ... the Winds aloud
> Howl o'er the Masts, and sing thro' ev'ry Shroud:
> Pale, trembling, tir'd the Sailors freeze with Fears,
> And instant Death on ev'ry Wave appears. (*Iliad* 15.624; OS 10.30)

Longinus disapproves of the attempt by the poet Aratus to improve on this text by adding the line "A slender Plank preserves them from their Fate" for, "instead of increasing the Terror, he only lessens and refines it away; and besides, he sets a Bound to the impending Danger, by saying, 'a Plank preserves them,' thus banishing their Despair" (OS 10.30; Aratus, *Phaenomena*, 299).

Repeatedly in the passages discussed by Longinus, architectural forms, especially the roof – readily transformed in Smith's translation into a dome – come to a poet's mind when inventing dynamic images of the sublime. One quotation, this time from an incomplete fragment of Longinus's book quoting Aeschylus, presents a complex image of Boreas, god of the cold winter wind, "Spewing against Heaven," with a spatial image of an ascending spiral of fire, in which heaven is likened to an architectural dome:

> Let them the Chimney's flashing flames repel.
> Could but these Eyes one lurking Wretch arrest,
> I'd whirl aloft one streaming Curl of Flame,
> And into Embers turn his crackling Dome. (OS 3.6; fr. 281 Nauck)

This dynamic spatial imagery, with its complex metaphors, is too excessive for Longinus and earns his criticism, as does the passage from Aeschylus when "the Palace of Lycurgus is surprisingly affected by the sudden Appearance of Bacchus":

> The frantic Dome and roaring Roofs convuls'd,
> Reel to and fro', instinct with Rage divine. (OS 15.43; fr. 58 Nauck)

All these passages, whether approved or condemned, were conveyed to future generations. Readers will hear their echo throughout the material considered in the remainder of this chapter, either through direct influence or by independent discovery, for all involve archetypes of human consciousness.

THE ROMAN SUBLIME

Two important Roman buildings appear to have addressed the challenge of the architectural sublime and became models for emulation in succeeding centuries down to Boullée's cenotaph: the Domus Aurea (Golden House) constructed by Nero circa 64–68 and the Pantheon, probably begun by Trajan circa 114 and completed by Hadrian circa 128.[23] The Golden House was partially destroyed by later emperors, its remains gradually filled with earth and then fully buried, but it lived on through literary accounts. Beginning with the underground visits that started in the 1480s, it was the object of careful archaeological study by Renaissance architects and painters who were inspired by its forms and décor.[24]

In the words of Suetonius, "there was nothing however in which [Nero] was more prodigal than in building." Of the Golden House he writes:

> Its size and splendour will be sufficiently indicated by the following details. Its vestibule was large enough to contain a colossal statue of the emperor a hundred and twenty feet high; and it was so extensive that it had a triple colonnade a mile long.... In the rest of the house all parts were overlaid with gold and adorned with gems and mother-of-pearl. There were dining-rooms with fretted ceilings of ivory, whose panels could turn and shower down flowers and were fitted with pipes for sprinkling the guests with perfumes. The main banquet hall was circular and constantly revolved day and night, like the heavens.

As J. C. Rolfe has remarked on this last sentence, "Suetonius' brevity is here inexact; it was evidently the spherical ceiling which revolved."[25] The suggestion of a suspended, revolving ceiling is also reinforced by the description of the turning panels in the ceilings of the dining rooms.

Nero used his Golden House to sustain the two major mythological associations of his persona with the Olympian gods: Jupiter and the sun god, Phoebus Apollo.[26] In each case he allied the architectural sublime with the literary sublime and, more particularly, with the cosmological sublime from Homer's account of Jupiter and the combined cosmological and spatial sublime in Ovid's story of Phoebus and Phaeton. "Even though he was never to see an army in peace or in war," explains Edward Champlin, "triumphalism marked Nero's life as a prince in Rome." Champlin reports that toward the year 65 "Nero was saluted as Imperator for the tenth time, an honor normally marking a claim to military success" but bestowed repeatedly on Nero despite his lack of military achievements. Not only was the triumphator in the ceremonial spectacle associated with Jupiter, but the triumphal arch decreed in 58 "was topped by a statue of Nero in triumphal toga and carrying his eagle-tipped scepter, as he drove four prancing horses in his triumphal chariot," and was erected "next to the Temple of Jupiter Optimus Maximus" on the Capitoline Hill, the traditional endpoint of a triumphal procession and site of "sacrifice to the god who had brought ... victory."[27] The colossal statue and the suspended dome on which Suetonius focuses his account of the Golden House appear, in this context, as an architectural ekphrasis of the towering Jupiter suspending the world from a golden chain, as recounted in the opening verses of book 8 of the *Iliad*, which describe the counsel of the gods "upon the topmost peak of many-ridged Olympus," where Zeus (Jupiter) announces his intention to end the

---

[23] On the Trajanic origin of the Pantheon, see the highly respected, recent article by Lisa M. Hetland, "Dating the Pantheon," *Journal of Roman Archaeology* 20 (2007), 95–112.

[24] On the Golden House of Nero in Renaissance architecture, see Charles L. Stinger, *The Renaissance in Rome* (Bloomington: Indiana University Press, 1985), passim.

[25] Suetonius, *Lives of the Caesars* in *Suetonius,* trans. J. C. Rolfe, 2 vols. (Cambridge, MA: Harvard University Press; London: William Heinemann, 1979), 2:135–7.

[26] On the association in the early empire of Apollo with Helios (Greek)/Sol (Roman) in the combined name of Phoebus Apollo, see Edward Champlin, *Nero* (Cambridge, MA: Harvard University Press, 2003), 114.

[27] Champlin, *Nero*, 212–17.

Trojan War and warns his fellow deities of the dire consequences should they attempt to thwart his project. To remind them of his unassailable strength, he asks them to imagine hanging "a chain of gold" down from the heavens all the way to the earth, where their assembled number would attempt, in vain, to pull him down; he, Zeus, by contrast, could easily lift them all, globe included: "But whenso I were minded to draw of a ready heart, then with earth itself should I draw you and with sea withal; and the rope should I thereafter bind about a peak of Olympus and all those things should hang in space."[28]

Nero's suspended, revolving dome was probably decorated with heavenly symbolism[29] and constituted an important aspect of the theatrical presentation of his persona in the guise of a sun god, sustained through depictions of him on coins as the Hellenistic Apollo.[30] As Champlin explains, "Nero's association with Sol/Helios in the Domus Aurea is so much a part of his public solar ideology,"[31] which featured prominently on what was called the Golden Day in late 66, marked by two important ceremonies. At dawn, as Cassius Dio relates, Nero entered the Forum "cloath'd in a purple Robe that was fit for the Ceremony of a Triumph,"[32] where he was paid homage by Tiridates, the Parthian prince, who prostrated himself before Nero while the emperor sat on an elevated throne. Champlin comments that as Tiridates likened Nero to his Zoroastrian god Mithra, also called the Sun, the actual sun shone fully over Nero's face.[33] The ceremony was followed by "a great Assembly at the Theatre of *Pompey* by order of the Senate," where the covering stretched over the Theater of Pompey was "adorn'd with a rich Stuff, of the colour of Purple, which represented Heav'n full of [golden] Stars, in the midst of which *Nero* appear'd driving a Chariot." The conceit of Nero as the sun god was extended to the entire theater, for "not only the Scene, but all the inside of the Theatre, and every body that came into it were cover'd with Gold, which made that Day, be call'd the Golden Day."[34] This temporary golden décor echoed the permanent one that covered significant portions of the Golden House.[35]

The literate audience of both related spectacles would readily have thought of the principal text linking Apollo with the sun god, Ovid's *Metamorphoses*, a text that had been closely associated with Augustus and his solar imagery as Phoebus Apollo and that is replete with dramatic chariot rides through the sky by Phoebus and his son Phaeton.[36] Indeed, a lost fresco originally in the Golden House depicted the scene in which Phaeton is asking to ride his father's chariot.[37] Ovid's dual account presents a powerful kinesthetic experience of the spatial sublime, centered on a spiraling theme. As Phoebus the sun god explains,

> The road starts off so steeply that my steeds
> must struggle hard, though they are fresh from sleep;

---

[28] Homer, *The Iliad*, trans. A. T. Murray, Loeb Classical Library, 2 vols. (London: William Heinemann/New York: G. P. Putnam's Sons, 1928), 2:8.19–26.338–41.

[29] Helmut Prückner and Sebastian Storz, "Beobachtungen im Oktogon der Domus Aurea," *Mitteilungen des Deutschen Archaeologischen Instituts, Roemische* 81 (1974), 323–39, pp. 333–5.

[30] E. Baldwin Smith, *Architectural Symbolism of Imperial Rome and the Middle Ages* (Princeton, NJ: Princeton University Press, 1956), 124.

[31] Champlin, *Nero*, 209.

[32] Cassius Dio Cocceianus, *The History of Dion Cassius. Abridg'd by Xiphilin. Containing the Most Remarkable Passages under the Roman Emperors, from the Time of Pompey the Great, to the Reign of Alexander Severus*, trans. Francis Manning, 2 vols. (London: A. and J. Churchill, 1704), 1:380 (62.4.3).

[33] Champlin, *Nero*, 226–9.

[34] Cassius Dio Cocceianus, *The History of Dion Cassius*, 1:382 (62.6.1–2).

[35] On the Golden House, see Elisabetta Segala and Ida Sciortino, *Domus Aurea*, trans. Colin Swift (Milan: Electa/Soprintendenza Archaeologica di Roma, 1999), 10 and 14.

[36] On Ovid's *Metamorphoses* as providing the principal text linking Apollo with the sun god, see Champlin, *Nero*, 114.

[37] See Smith, *Architectural Symbolism*, 124–5 and fig. 117.

> midway, it runs so high across the sky,
> that even I am often terrified –
> my heart is rocked with terror and dismay
> as I see earth and sea far, far below;
> and in descent, the course needs firm control –
> it plunges, sheer: then even Tethys, she
> who, at my journey's end, always receives me
> into her waves, is anxious lest I fall
> headlong. And add to this the heavens' own
> unending, wheeling round that draws along
> the steep stars on its dizzying, swift course.
> My path runs counter to the skies' rotation;
> I am the only one who can resist
> its impetus, a thrust that overcomes
> all else.[38]

With this description of Phoebus's ride across the heavens, Ovid provides an imaginatively kinesthetic account that engages the reader's *Körpergefühl*, translating a contemplation of movement through the sky into a bodily sentiment. Not content with a summary account of falling through space, as was Homer when he had Hephaestus remind his mother Hera how his father Zeus (Jupiter) had thrown him off Olympus (see *Iliad* 1.590–3), Ovid extends his story to provide the verbal equivalent to the succession of impulses that Burke would later explain as the psychophysiological basis of the experience of the sublime. Here Ovid is applying the rhetorical device of amplification, which constitutes the primary literary strategy to offer an experience comparable to the artificial infinite through architecture. Longinus devotes three sections of his treatise to the discussion of the use of amplification to achieve the sublime (OS 10–12.27–35).[39]

The reader retains this sentiment as it receives an additional coloring of feeling through the subsequent account of Phaeton's journey, when, in mid-flight, the sun god's son experiences a dizzying view that renders him faint and nearly unconscious:

> Sad Phaeton looked down from heaven's heights
> at earth, which lay so far, so far below,
> He paled; his knees were seized by sudden fright;
> and there, within the overwhelming light,
> a veil of darkness fell upon his eyes.[40]

Unable to control his horses, Phaeton careens through space like a storm-swept ship, upsetting cosmic order and harmony, as heavenly bodies are knocked off course and the earth is visited with cataclysmic fire and drought. Jupiter is obliged to end this destruction by striking Phaeton with his thunderbolts and lightning, sending him tumbling from his chariot into the void, his body aflame as it "plummets down" in a spiraling descent. Ovid here follows Lucretius's account of the fall of the birds over the volcanic Lake of Avernus in *On the Nature of Things*, filtered through Virgil's reworking of this geography in the *Aeneid* to recount the tale of the fall of

---

[38] Ovid, *The Metamorphoses of Ovid*, trans. Allen Mandelbaum, 2 vols. (New York: Harvest/Harcourt, 1993), 2.63–73. All quotations are from this translation.

[39] Although Longinus treats amplification directly in sections 11 and 12 of *On the Sublime*, he explains that the discussion of section 10 is intimately related to this rhetorical device. He also returns to this theme elsewhere, albeit without using the term, as in 32.73–7. On amplification in classical and English Renaissance treatises on rhetoric, see Quentin Skinner, *Reason and Rhetoric in the Philosophy of Hobbes* (Cambridge: Cambridge University Press, 1996), 136–7 and 148–9. See also Malcolm Heath's discussion in "Longinus and the Ancient Sublime," chap. 1 of the current volume.

[40] Ovid, *The Metamorphoses*, 2.178–81.

FIGURE 15.3. Stuccoed dome (lost), Domus Aurea (Golden House), Rome. From Giovanni Pietro Bellori, *Picturae antiquae cryptarum Romanarum* (Rome: Lazarinos, 1791).

Icarus.[41] One would not have to await Smith's observation in 1739 to recognize "the Sublimity, which Ovid here borrowed from Euripides," quoted above in Longinus, to connect these passages with the Greek playwright's now-lost *Phaeton* (OS 15.148–9). These falls through space ultimately lead back to Hesiod's *Theogony*, in which the Titans are consigned to the underworld of Tartarus. In this account, the image of the rapidly accelerating bronze anvil and buffeting gales depicts this punishment through one of the deepest and most vertiginous falls into the abyss in literature. Thus, architecture, scenography, and literature were mutually related and sustained each other in giving fuller mental coloring to the experience of each.

Like Hesiod's earlier Gigantomachy, Ovid's story of Phoebus's flight and Phaeton's fall presents a literary account of what might be termed the *vertiginous sublime*. Both engage the phenomenological experience of looking downward from a great height, what David Quint has called the "fear of falling," whose literary tradition he has charted. A lost stucco on a dome (Figure 15.3), most probably from Nero's Golden House, presents the pictorial pendant to vertigo from above through instilling vertigo from below.[42] At the center of the dome, Jupiter sits

---

[41] David Quint, "Fear of Falling: Icarus, Phaethon, and Lucretius in *Paradise Lost*," *Renaissance Quarterly* 57, 3 (2004), 847–81, pp. 848–51.
[42] See Karl Lehmann, "The Dome of Heaven," *Art Bulletin* 27, 1 (1945), 1–27, p. 17 and fig. 27.

enthroned on the clouds, thunderbolts raised in his right hand and his eagle astride a globe to his side, the entire composition hovering precipitously over the viewer's head. Everything about the accompanying features sustains this sense of the vertiginous sublime from below, especially the contrasted feeling prompted by the dissolving of the solid surface of the dome through the illusion of a tentlike canopy stretched around the central ring, miraculously hovering upward in its unsupported center, and by the emphasis on the solid materiality of the dome through the four illusionistically pierced oculi with views to a cloud-filled sky. The angled presentation of these oculi creates a phenomenological equivalent to the acceleration of a fluid when forced through a constricted opening.

One can easily imagine a visitor to Nero's house conjuring up an image of this hovering Jupiter – or rather, Nero as Jupiter – when looking upward through the oculus of the dome covering the great Octagonal Hall. In effect, the Octagonal Hall, as Larry Ball explains, is provided with a suite of adjacent rooms that open directly onto its centralized space and flood it with soft light from hidden windows, thereby contributing to the illusion of a dome hovering overhead. "The visual effect of a feather-light dome," he concludes, "appearing to hover in a sea of light all around it, is almost mystical." This scenographic arrangement of space and light in the Octagonal Hall finds its parallel in the eight openings around the tentlike canopy in the stuccoed scene. The "architectural revolution" that Ball studies in his book is not confined to the development of a new means of construction – Roman concrete – to fashion vast domes and vaults but involves the development of forms that "appeal to the viewer emotionally, viscerally." After Nero, Ball argues, "Roman concrete architecture would always retain a component of emotional awe,"[43] in other words, of the sublime. As we have seen, this architectural sublime can be accompanied by literary and pictorial renditions of a spatial or a cosmological sublime that contribute to a complex aesthetic response.

Nero's solar imagery was followed by Domitian's arrangement of his Domus Augustana as a cosmic temple of the sun god[44] and then by the Pantheon (Figure 15.4), which featured the largest dome until the Industrial Revolution. Its interior consists of a hemispherical cupola some 44 meters in diameter with a central oculus open to the sky, raised above a cylindrical base of virtually the same height, such that an entire sphere could be inscribed inside it. The dome, once containing metaphorical stars in the form of a gleaming gilt bronze rosette in each coffer, represented, as Cassius Dio conjectures, the heavens.[45] Despite being largely bereft of its original décor, today visitors can still experience the awesome sublimity of the dome, which, I believe, issues principally from the relationship between size and shape to the phenomenon of *Raumgefühl* later described by Schmarsow.

The possible meanings of the Pantheon are numerous, for it continues the association of the Roman emperor with solar and cosmic imagery and probably has important dynastic significance as well.[46] For the purposes of this chapter, I point to the religious interpretation postulated by William Loerke, whereby the Pantheon's dome is intended to be understood

---

[43] Larry F. Ball, *The Domus Aurea and the Roman Architectural Revolution* (Cambridge: Cambridge University Press, 2003), 219 and 26. In applying the phrase – the Roman architectural revolution – Ball is following the earlier work first of J. B. Ward-Perkins and then of William L. MacDonald.

[44] See Lehmann, "The Dome of Heaven," 22, and Smith, *Architectural Symbolism*, 126. See also E. Baldwin Smith, *The Dome: A Study in the History of Ideas* (Princeton, NJ: Princeton University Press, 1971 [1950]), who writes that "after the construction of the Golden House of Nero, where the kosmokrator dined and gave audiences beneath a revolving and astronomically decorated cupola of wood, the dome became an essential element in imperial palace architecture" (p. 53).

[45] See William L. MacDonald, *The Pantheon: Design, Meaning, and Progeny* (Cambridge, MA: Harvard University Press, 1976), 38 and 76.

[46] On this latter theme, see Mark Wilson Jones, *Principles of Roman Architecture* (New Haven, CT: Yale University Press, 2000), 177–82.

FIGURE 15.4. Pantheon, Rome, c. 114–c. 128. Photo: Courtesy Michael J. Waters.

as belonging not to this world but rather to the Roman *templum mundi*, a widespread idea that "the cosmos [is] a celestial temple."[47] To convey this meaning, the Pantheon continues the theme of the floating dome and the rotating building established in Nero's Golden House, albeit by illusionism and in a much larger building. As both J. B. Ward-Perkins and Loerke have observed, in its original form, before a significant eighteenth-century alteration to the attic zone (Figure 15.5), the massive, coffered dome of the Pantheon appeared to float above the modest attic, which was decorated with a continuous band of diminutive porphyry pilasters of colored marble, quite incapable of offering even a semblance of support. "Instead of a serious statement of weight and support at this critical juncture," explains Loerke, "the architect goes out

[47] William Loerke, "A Rereading of the Interior Elevation of Hadrian's Rotunda," *Journal of the Society of Architectural Historians* 49, 1 (1990), 22–43, p. 43.

Architecture and the Sublime 245

FIGURE 15.5. Pantheon, Rome, detail of attic zone with alteration of 1746–1748 and partial restoration of the original in 1929–1934. Photo: Courtesy Michael J. Waters.

of his way to emphasize that his attic cannot support the dome," an effect that, in the words of Ward-Perkins, contributes to its "magical, soaring quality."[48] This illusion conveyed the sense of a cosmic zone outside of the earthly realm. If Christiane Joost-Gaugier is correct in her interpretation that the Pantheon was a Pythagorean temple where the sixty-four pilasters that ring the attic represent "the great unifying number," then we can understand how this zone was able to support the massive dome through a cosmic numerology without need of a structure that obeyed the earthbound laws of physics.[49]

The floating appearance of the dome, as Loerke notes, is amplified by the asymmetrical and tilted arrangement of the stepped surfaces within the coffers, such that the receding forms appear to detach themselves from the surface grid of the dome and, one might add, even accelerate in movement away from the viewer below. The angling of these surfaces, moreover, enables the lower portion to capture sunlight while placing the upper and deeper recess in deep shadow, thereby enhancing these illusionistic effects of expansion outward and of acceleration.[50] Hence, in place of the turning panels in the ceiling of the Golden House, the architect of the Pantheon created illusionistic openings that enhance the sense of the floating dome. Instead of perfume and flowers raining downward, space appears to expand outward as each metaphorical star – that is, the rosette in the center of each coffer – is visually isolated from tangible support.

---

[48] J. B. Ward-Perkins, *Roman Imperial Architecture* (Harmondsworth: Penguin, 1981), 114, and Loerke, "Rereading," 31 (see also 33).
[49] Christiane L. Joost-Gaugier, *Measuring Heaven: Pythagoras and His Influence on Thought and Art in Antiquity and the Middle Ages* (Ithaca, NY: Cornell University Press, 2006), 172.
[50] Loerke, "Rereading," 42–3.

Finally, the rotational effect of Nero's dome, executed literally in the Golden House, is achieved illusionistically in the Pantheon as the viewer moves through the interior. This occurs both in the dome and on the floor. William MacDonald has observed that, from a position not at the center of the building and under certain conditions of light, "often a pattern is formed [on the surface of the dome] by the fuller illumination of the triangular portions of the coffers below their diagonals, intimating a sweeping curve of expanding lines like those formed by the sparks spun out from a pinwheel." MacDonald compares the effect to that of contemporary Roman floor mosaics:

> One is reminded of the mosaic pavements, popular in Hadrianic times, of Medusa heads enframed by a swirl of curves. In these, the head appears in a central, comparatively small circle, around which ever larger circles are set. These circles are traversed by curved lines running from the central medallion to the periphery of the whole, creating a powerful illusion of looking into a deep whirling space toward its vortex.

MacDonald also charts the movement of the intense disk of light at the summer solstice, as it travels across the northern half of the Pantheon's interior, beginning in the attic zone and then descending to the floor, before rising back to the attic and then onto the coffers of the dome. When dusk approaches, "with increasing speed [the disk of light] moves along the last, smooth portion of the dome [above the coffers], and then suddenly it disappears, as if it had been drawn abruptly out through the oculus."[51] As for the visitor standing at the center of the building, the original "tread" pattern around the drum and the radial "spokes" of the dome inspire one literally to rotate in place, creating a dizzying and disorienting experience consonant with the sublime.[52]

A participatory movement also creates a metamorphosis of the marble floor. When viewed diagonally to the main axis, the decorative pattern presents alternating rows of diamonds, one row's diamonds boldly outlined with hollow interiors and the other's solid but containing a central, colored circle.[53] As the visitor turns to align with the orthogonal axis of the building itself, the pattern morphs into an alternative configuration of aligned squares, each row presenting an alternating sequence that now mixes together the formerly separated shapes of the hollow center and the colored interior with the central circle. Colored circles, squares, and rectangles cover not only the floor but also the ground zone of the interior cylinder, as well as the original (pre-eighteenth-century) attic above, thereby unifying the entire space under the dome and in a manner that makes it seem as if the wall has wrapped around the floor or, conversely, as if the floor has turned upward to wrap around the lower zone of the wall, up to the base of the dome. Visitors are thus surrounded by two independent levels of space that rotate at different speeds: the hovering, coffered dome, whose movement depends on the pattern of the sunlight, and, when the spectator turns, the rotation of either drum and dome when looking upward or of floor when looking downward caused by the turning of the spectator. The moving shaft of sunlight pierces diagonally through these spaces so as to create its own sweeping effects.

The power of the illusion of the floating dome can be gauged by the vehemence of the reaction in later times when notions of propriety required buildings not only to be well constructed but also to appear to be solidly planted on the ground. The visual discrepancy between the dome and the attic deeply disturbed architects beginning in the fifteenth century. Although they apparently commented only on the lack of alignment between the pilasters and the meridional ribs of the dome, when each architect redrew the Pantheon to correct its purported mistakes, he took care in one way or another to provide visually robust supports in place of the

---

[51] MacDonald, *The Pantheon*, 74–5.
[52] I thank Rabun Taylor for this observation.
[53] See the computerized illustrations in Jones, *Principles*, 197 (figs. 9.28–9.29).

inadequate, diminutive pilasters.[54] When it became necessary to repair the attic zone in the eighteenth century, the offending décor was simply removed in favor of what was deemed a more suitable treatment. Only a small portion of the original was restored in 1929–1934. We know the original décor from Giovanni Paolo Pannini's paintings executed toward 1734, hence before the alteration of 1746–1748, as well as from Palladio's earlier black-and-white drawing of the elevation.[55]

FROM ROME TO BYZANTIUM

The history of architecture has been written primarily as a succession of different *styles* – Roman, early Christian, Byzantine, Romanesque, Gothic, Renaissance, Baroque, Neoclassical, and so forth – but this obscures the ongoing and uninterrupted tradition that cuts across all of these different eras with its attention to the sublime, primarily through the floating dome or vault, whether stationary or rotating. In what follows, I shall focus on the domed tradition, leaving the subject of the basilica church for another occasion.

The spiraling, swirling ascent of light at the summer solstice in the Pantheon, as well as the floating aspect of the dome at all times, may well have inspired a comparable effect within the domed chamber of the Mausoleum of Diocletian (Figure 15.6), believed to have been completed before the emperor's death in about 312.[56] Everything in this interior seems arranged to convey the sense of an unearthly presence, of the realm of immortality according to the strictures of the architectural sublime. The upper range of relatively diminutive columns, for example, appears to float, because the deeply projecting cornice over the lower range of colossal columns obscures the bottoms of their shafts. The upper cornice also protrudes deeply outward to obscure the base of the dome, such that the dome appears to float, an effect heightened by the sense of an unseen, flat, annular picture plane above the projecting tops of the smaller columns, which covers the base of the dome in the manner of a repoussoir, thereby accentuating the lack of connection between this imagined flat base and the actual surface of the dome itself, distinctly removed from this lower part.[57] This discrepancy between the projecting forms on top of the capitals and the curved surface of the dome heightens the tension between the two, in much the same way as Boullée later emphasized how the curved surface of the interior of the Cenotaph to Newton would freeze the visitor at the central point at the base of the cavity. All of this is merely a prelude to the surface pattern of the dome itself, constructed of interlocking, scalloped ascending semicircles of brick; if

---

[54] See T. Buddensieg, "Criticism and Praise of the Pantheon in the Middle Ages and the Renaissance," in *Classical Influences on European Culture, A.D. 500–1500*, ed. R. R. Bolgar (Cambridge: Cambridge University Press, 1971), 259–67, pp. 263–6, and "Criticism of Ancient Architecture in the Sixteenth and Seventeenth Centuries," in *Classical Influences on European Culture, A.D. 1500–1700*, ed. R. R. Bolgar (Cambridge: Cambridge University Press, 1976), 335–48, pp. 343–4. Aspects of Buddensieg's argument have been taken up by Loerke, "Rereading," 26–8; Tod Marder, "Bernini and Alexander VII: Criticism and Praise of the Pantheon in the Seventeenth Century," *Art Bulletin* 71, 4 (1989), 628–45, pp. 635–41, and Jones, *Principles*, 188–91. These scholars focus on how architects, in either writing and/or with illustrations, addressed the discrepancy in alignment between the pilasters and the vertical ribs of the dome. The architects' concern with the visual inadequacy of the diminutive pilasters to provide a satisfying "support" to the dome is my interpretation and suggests that they were responding to the perceptual qualities later identified by Ward-Perkins and Loerke.

[55] On the successive changes to the attic, see Loerke, "Rereading," 22–3 and 30–1.

[56] On dating, see Mark Joseph Johnson, *The Roman Imperial Mausoleum in Late Antiquity* (Cambridge: Cambridge University Press, 2009), 59.

[57] Goran Nikšić points out that the bottom section of the brick shell is a cylinder that avoids a "visual shortening of the dome by the deeply protruding cornice, which covers its springing" as well as provides the requisite height for a golden section proportion "between the diameter of the cella" and the total interior height. See "The Restoration of Diocletian's Palace – Mausoleum, Temple, and Porta Aurea (with the Analysis of the Original Architectural Design)," in *Diokletian und die Tetrarchie: Aspekte einer Zeitenwende*, ed. Alexander Demandt et al. (Berlin: Walter de Gruyter, 2004), 163–71, p. 165 and 170 (section).

248   *Richard A. Etlin*

FIGURE 15.6. Mausoleum of Diocletian, split. Photo: © Andrija Carli. From Antun Travirka, *Split: History, Culture, Art Heritage* (Zadar: Forum, 2000).

gilded – or covered with mosaics according to the same pattern – and viewed under the light of candles and torches, these would have shimmered so as to dematerialize the entire surface with the accelerating effect of a rapid ascent of the soul into the heavens.[58]

Various centralized buildings dating from the Byzantine period continue this tradition, such as the Orthodox Baptistery in Ravenna (Figure 15.7), enlarged and redecorated in the 450s by Bishop Neon. In closing her study of the building, Deborah Mauskopf Deliyannis concludes, "As the setting for the religious pageant of baptism, the interior of the Orthodox Baptistery overwhelms the viewer with color, texture, and imagery, creating, as [Spiro] Kostof noted, a visionary realm removed from ordinary space and time." Octagonal in shape to symbolize the Resurrection as the eighth day of the Creation and, through reference to octagonal Roman mausolea, death and rebirth,[59] the Orthodox Baptistery is crowned by a hemispherical dome 9.6 meters wide whose center presents a heavenly scene against a gold background: a glass mosaic image of St. John baptizing Christ in the River Jordan. This circular vision is placed directly over the baptismal font in the center of the building, 14.6 meters below. As Deliyannis notes, "the central scene is set off from the apostle register by the mosaic representation of a circular marble cornice with egg-and-dart molding, which creates the effect that one is looking

---

[58] The original intention for the decoration, as well as the actual surface treatment first executed, remains speculative.
[59] Deborah Mauskopf Deliyannis, *Ravenna in Late Antiquity* (Cambridge: Cambridge University Press, 2010), 88–100.

Architecture and the Sublime

FIGURE 15.7. Orthodox Baptistery, Ravenna, remodeled 450s. Photo credit: Scala / Art Resource, NY.

through a hole in the center of the dome straight up into heaven," an effect seconded by the gold background that places the scene in a "divine space."[60] Here the cosmic finger of the sun god shining through the oculus of the Pantheon has been replaced by its Christian equivalent.

Below this baptismal scene and occupying most of the surface of the dome, the twelve apostles walk in procession against a blue mosaic background of heavenly space. Viewed at night when the ceremony of baptism took place, under the light of hanging lamps, both zones of mosaic scenes would have glittered with an unearthly glow. Clementina Rizzardi has pointed out that the "alternation of colors in the depiction of the apostles creates a sense of rotation"[61]

---

[60] Deliyannis, *Ravenna*, 99. She is paraphrasing Spiro Kostof, *The Orthodox Baptistery of Ravenna* (New Haven, CT: Yale University Press, 1965), 105–6.
[61] Clementina Rizzardi, "I mosaici parietiali di Ravenna da Galla Placidia a Giustiniano," in *Venezia e Bisanzio. Aspetti della cultura artistica bizantina da Ravenna a Venezia (V–XIV secolo)*, ed. Clementina Rizzardi

FIGURE 15.8. Mausoleum of Theodoric, Ravenna, c. 526. Photo: Courtesy Seymour Mauskopf.

in this zone of the dome, such that, in the words of Deliyannis, the visitor looks up "into the ever-rotating heavenly realm of the dome."[62] Thus, in place of the metaphorical stars that floated within the dome of the heavens in the Pantheon, we now encounter the apostles moving in rotation like the dome of the Golden House.

Continuing the attention to the sublime in Ravenna, the mausoleum that the Ostrogothic king Theodoric had constructed there before his death in 526 (Figure 15.8), a stone decagon with an upper cylindrical chamber crowned by a massive monolithic domical cap, presents still another Christian variation on the Pantheon's theme of the cosmic temple, with its floating dome and rotating features. In a city of brick, this exceptional stone edifice was constructed of large blocks of limestone ashlar conveyed across the Adriatic Sea from Istria, assembled through the sophisticated technique of stereotomic vaulting. The mausoleum thus presents a striking image of wondrous accomplishment, celebrated, as Deliyannis explains, from Theodoric's time onward. "The *Anonymous Valesianus*," she observes, "points out the features that are still considered worthy of notice today: '... a monument of blocks of stone, a work of marvelous size, and he sought out a huge rock to place on the top.'" The very feat of erecting this domical cap, nearly 11 meters in diameter and "estimated to weigh over 300 tons," belongs to the realm of the technological sublime.[63]

(Venice: Istituto veneto di scienze, lettere ed arti, 2005), 231–73, p. 241, as summarized approvingly in Deliyannis, Ravenna, 338n320.
[62] Deliyannis, *Ravenna*, 94.
[63] Deliyannis, *Ravenna*, 124.

Architecture and the Sublime

The Mausoleum of Theodoric, through its fabric, applies the lessons of the Pantheon in a novel manner to present a Christian message of eternity. Above the decagonal chamber, the monolithic domed cap features twelve evenly spaced spurs that were presumably used to hoist it into place. Each spur is carved on the outer surface with the name of an apostle or an evangelist.[64] Here we find a creative application of the sublime to the common Christian metaphor, as expressed in Galatians 2.9, Ephesians 2.20, and Revelation 21.14, that the apostles are the columns or the foundations of the church or of the Heavenly Jerusalem; this, in turn, is a Christian appropriation of a concept found in Virgil's *Aeneid* (2.352) that the gods, as Saint Augustine reminds his readers, had been considered "pillars of the empire."[65] "These last two [biblical] texts," explains John Onians, "seemed to have captured the imagination of Constantine," who "erected groups of twelve columns or pedestals round the most important churches in the four religious and political centres of the empire," with an echo, as Onians notes, found later on the dome of the Mausoleum of Theodoric.[66]

The message in the Mausoleum of Theodoric is twofold: that the stone cap was erected not by mere men but rather by the apostles and the evangelists, who are miraculously elevating the heavy dome into heaven and maintaining it there.[67] The apostles walk in procession in the mosaic of the Orthodox Baptistery, and their appearance gives the impression that the dome is rotating. One wonders whether in Theodoric's time viewers would have imagined a similar rotation at his tomb. The inner surface of the dome would have probably presented a mosaic surface with a heavenly scene, possibly like the interior of the so-called Mausoleum of Galla Placida (Ravenna, c. 425), sister of Emperor Honorius, where "against a dark blue background, 567 gold eight-pointed stars swirl in concentric circles" around a central cross, while toward the corners in the pendentives "gold winged figures of the four living creatures of the apocalypse" – probably the four evangelists – hover in space as theological "supports" for the celestial dome.[68] In this manner, the interior mosaic and the exterior spurs of the Mausoleum of Theodoric would have presented complementary messages.

Our final example of Byzantine architecture, Hagia Sophia (Figure 15.9), constructed in Constantinople in 532–537 by Anthemius of Tralles and Isidorus of Miletus, continues the tradition of the Roman sublime while returning to a giant scale that suggests emulation of the Pantheon. As William Addis has emphasized, the vastness of the interior space was unprecedented. The central 30-meter dome rises "about 55 meters above the floor, which is rather higher than that of the Pantheon (44 meters) and the Basilica of Maxentius (about 36 meters)." "At about 76 meters," continues Addis, "the total length of the main, column-free space is a little larger than the basilica (about 70 meters)."[69]

Size was not the only factor: the dome was made to float even more dramatically than in the Pantheon. Rather than sitting on a massive cylindrical drum, the dome at Hagia Sophia appears to soar above the void over a concatenation of partial domes to the east and west sides, while touching or hovering lightly to the north and south over what appears to be a thin, recessed wall perforated with windows. Both the partial domes and the side walls, in turn, sit on two levels of walls fully opened with colonnades, such that the vast expanse of air and light obscures the solidity of the few supporting piers, which are, in turn, dissolved by veined marble veneer. The dome itself is lightened visually through division into a radiating sequence of thin bands, articulated

---

[64] Deliyannis, *Ravenna*, 127–8 and 134.
[65] Saint Augustine, *The City of God*, trans. Gerald G. Walsh et al., abridged ed. (New York: Image Books/Doubleday, 1958), 3.3, p. 80. The translators also note the reference to the passage in the *Aeneid*.
[66] John Onians, *Bearers of Meaning: The Classical Orders in Antiquity, the Middle Ages, and the Renaissance* (Cambridge: Cambridge University Press, 1988), 70–1.
[67] I owe this latter observation to Beatrice Rehl.
[68] Deliyannis, *Ravenna*, 80–1 (fig. 19).
[69] William Addis, *Building: 3000 Years of Design Engineering and Construction* (London: Phaidon, 2007), 66.

FIGURE 15.9. Hagia Sophia, Constantinople (Istanbul), 532–537.
Photo: Courtesy Marvin Trachtenberg © 1975.

in low relief on the inner surface. Justinian's court historian Procopius comments both on the "precipitous height" of each of the interior elements as well as the "terrifying [aspect of] the apparent precariousness" of this concatenation of partial domes, which seem "somehow not to be raised in a firm manner, but to soar aloft to the peril of those who are there."[70] Procopius comments on how the eastern and western semidomes "are suspended over empty air," just as Paulus Silentiarius marvels at how, one after the other, the eastern semidomes strike the viewer as "a never-ceasing wonder" as if "borne on air."[71] The latter even marvels at how the walls

---

[70] Procopius, *De aedif.*, in Cyril Mango, *The Art of the Byzantine Empire 312–1453: Sources and Documents* (Englewood Cliffs, NJ: Prentice-Hall, 1972), 74.

[71] Procopius, *De aedif.*, and Paulus Silentiarius, *Descr. S. Sophiae* [AD 563], in Mango, *Sources and Documents*, 74 and 82.

participate in this wondrous contradiction of the customary sense of stability, for the architects have opened them with voids, daringly placing six columns over two in the exedrae under the east and west semidomes, such that the upper range sits "over empty air."[72]

The crowning feature of these visual sleights of hand is the ring of windows at the base of the dome, which imparts the illusion that it floats miraculously above a golden necklace of divine light. Paulus Silentiarius explains that nocturnal illumination repeated this effect through a "revolving circle of lights" at the base of the projecting cornice beneath the dome, which the author likens to a necklace "glowing like fire with rubies set in gold."[73] With multiple shafts of light streaming in from all directions, filling the space and enhancing the surfaces covered with gilding, mosaics, or veined marble, the interior certainly seemed miraculous. On viewing his completed masterpiece, Justinian is said to have proclaimed, "Solomon, I have surpassed you."[74]

Whereas the massive stone dome of the Mausoleum of Theodoric is carried into heaven by the twelve apostles and the evangelists holding up its spurlike handles, the dome of Hagia Sophia is suspended by the grace of the holy relics embedded into its fabric after the laying of every twelve courses.[75] As Procopius explains, "whenever one enters this church to pray, he understands at once that it is not by any human power or skill, but by the influence of God, that this work has been so finely turned."[76] As Spiro Kostof notes, "we are now in the realm of what modern philosophers will call the *sublime*."[77] Indeed, the wonder of Hagia Sophia is that the entire complex of concatenating domes and arches gives the structure the appearance of being suspended; this prompted Procopius to compare this miraculous achievement not only to his Christian God but also to the earliest and most impressive pagan image of the cosmological sublime as recounted by Homer in the *Iliad* (8.19), discussed previously, in which Zeus (Jupiter) talks about suspending the world from a golden chain. The "enormous spherical dome," Procopius thus remarks, "seems not to be founded on solid masonry, but to be suspended from heaven by that golden chain and so cover the space. All of these elements, marvellously fitted together in mid-air, suspended from one another and reposing only on the parts adjacent to them, produce a unified and most remarkable harmony in the work."[78] Procopius's admiration is still appropriate today when the contemporary viewer sees the Hagia Sophia with its second dome. As Rabun Taylor points out, however, Procopius was praising the original dome of the building, before it partially collapsed in an earthquake of May 558. This first dome, Taylor stresses, was seated on a drum perforated with windows similar to Constantine's fourth-century Church of the Holy Apostles, as rebuilt by Justinian toward 550. Thus, remarkable as Hagia Sophia appears today, as the sixth-century historian Agathias attests, the original dome had excited an even more profound experience of sublimity. For the new dome, as Agathias writes, "was narrower and steeper so that it did not strike spectators with as much amazement as before, but it was far more securely set up."[79]

---

[72] Paulus Silentiarius, *Descr. S. Sophiae*, in Mango, *Sources and Documents*, 81.
[73] Paulus Silentiarius, *Descr. S. Sophiae*, in Mango, *Sources and Documents*, 91.
[74] Carolyn L. Connor, "The Epigram in the Church of Hagios Polyeuktos in Constantinople and Its Byzantine Response," *Byzantion* 69 (1999), 479–527, p. 480.
[75] The source for this information about the embedded relics is the later, semi-legendary *Narratio de S. Sophia*, in Mango, *Sources and Documents*, 98.
[76] As quoted in Spiro Kostof, *A History of Architecture: Settings and Rituals* (Oxford: Oxford University Press, 1985), 264.
[77] Kostof, *A History of Architecture*, 264.
[78] Procopius, *De aedif.*, in Mango, *Sources and Documents*, 75. Mango also notes the reference to the passage in the *Iliad*.
[79] Rabun M. Taylor, "A Literary and Structural Analysis of the First Dome on Justinian's Hagia Sophia," *Journal of the Society of Architectural Historians* 55, 1 (1996), 66–78, p. 69. See also Ahmet Ş. Çakmak, Rabun M. Taylor, and Eser Durukal, "The Structural Configuration of the First Dome of Justinian's Hagia Sophia (A.D. 537–558): An

Procopius describes the original dome of Hagia Sophia as rising above a drum and compares it to the rebuilt dome of the Church of the Holy Apostles, describing the latter as seeming "somehow to hover in air and not rest upon the solid structure."[80] If the first dome, with its lower profile, as Agathias observes, was more amazing than the second dome, with a higher and, therefore, seemingly more impressive aspect, one wonders whether the effect issued from the advantageous arrangement that had been found in Diocletian's mausoleum, with its analogous configuration of a dome rising above a low cylindrical drum whose seat was obscured by a projecting cornice. Was the first dome of Hagia Sophia modeled on this Roman mausoleum so that its hidden base made it seem to hover even more magically than the dome that we see today? Certainly the windows in the drum would have contributed to a hovering effect, and one wonders if windows may have been partially hidden so that light emanated as from a magical source. These speculations are prompted by Procopius's observation that the dome of the Church of the Holy Apostles, like that of Hagia Sophia, appears "not [to] rest upon the solid structure." Why else would Agathias find the aesthetic effect of the current dome, with its higher profile and its base perforated by a chain of closely set windows that make it seem to float in the air, inferior to the original?

THE RENAISSANCE SUBLIME

When considering the floating dome and the sublime in Renaissance architecture – especially in reference to the Golden House and the Pantheon – two buildings stand out: Giulio Romano's Palazzo del Te (1525–1532), built for Federico II Gonzaga, Duke of Mantua, and Philibert Delorme's Château d'Anet (1547–1555), constructed for Diane de Poitiers, Duchess of Valentinois, and, by extension, through her romantic connection, for Henri II (married since 1533 to Catherine de' Medici); Anet was both the lovers' private retreat and an unofficial semipublic setting for court life. Both buildings have special value for the current study, because they reintroduce the literary theme adumbrated previously through the quotations from Longinus and Ovid. Further, both involve the type of experience that Burke would describe as the artificial infinite, for which we have contemporary, or nearly contemporary, accounts. And both may well have informed Boullée's sublime projects.

The artistic context for these two examples of the architectural sublime can be found in the pictorial development of dynamic depictions of the spatial sublime in painted domes and ceilings that emerged in the first half – and especially the second quarter – of the sixteenth century, with hovering figures of God or Christ and the phenomenological sensation of space moving, even rushing, upward toward heaven. The most important – because it was the most dramatic and most influential for works such as Te and Anet – was Correggio's painted *Assumption of the Virgin* (begun 1526) in the octagonal cupola of the Cathedral of Parma, where the Virgin is lifted on a ring of clouds upward into an inverted funnel of space in which a floating Christ beckons her toward him. John Shearman emphasizes the importance of the active engagement of the spectator in making the vision possible. The asymmetrically painted scene in the dome only aligns properly when the viewer stands at the base of the steps toward the end of the nave that led up to the choir at the crossing. This perspectival arrangement is complemented pictorially by the depiction of the four patron saints of Parma and their angels at the base of the cupola, who gesture to invite our participation in the scene.[81]

Investigation Based on Structural Analysis and Literary Analysis," *Soil Dynamics and Earthquake Engineering* 29 (2009), 693–8.
[80] As recounted and quoted in Taylor, "A Literary and Structural Analysis," 72.
[81] John K. G. Shearman, *Funzione e illusione: Raffaello, Pontormo, Correggio*, ed. Alessandro Nova (Milan: Il Saggiatore, 1983), 178–81, and *Only Connect: Art and Spectator in the Italian Renaissance* (Princeton, NJ: Princeton University Press, 1992), 177–88.

FIGURE 15.10. Giulio Romano, Hall of Giants, Palazzo del Te, Mantua (1530–1532).
Photo credit: Scala / Art Resource, NY.

In the *Lives of the Most Eminent Painters, Sculptors, and Architects*, Giorgio Vasari recounts his visit of 1541 to the recently completed Hall of Giants (Figures 15.10 and 15.11) in the Palazzo del Te in the company of the architect who designed it.[82] This room rises as a rectangle and, following Correggio's example at Parma,[83] gradually changes shape to become a domed hall, without any dividing cornice between walls and cupola. It is decorated with illusionistic painting depicting the gods assembled in the clouds under a Pantheon-like dome, while Jupiter hurls thunderbolts and lightning down at the giants who are attempting to scale the heavens. The effect is of a room that appears to be crashing down on giants and admiring visitors alike. Originally the floor consisted of "smooth riverbed stones"[84] and continued up onto the lower

---

[82] See David Mayernik, "The Winds in the Corners: Giulio Romano, the Elements, and the Palazzo Te's *Fall of the Giants*," in *Aeolian Winds and the Spirit in Renaissance Architecture: Academia Eolia Revisited*, ed. Barbara Kenda (New York: Routledge, 2006), 125–49, p. 125. Mayernik situates the Hall of Giants within the realm of the sublime (see p. 143).

[83] Shearman, *Only Connect*, 188–90.

[84] Kurt W. Forster and Richard J. Tuttle, "The Palazzo del Te," *Journal of the Society of Architectural Historians* 30, 4 (1971), 267–93, p. 285.

FIGURE 15.11. Giulio Romano, Hall of Giants, Palazzo del Te, Mantua (1530–1532). Photo credit: Scala / Art Resource, NY.

part of the walls, thus extending the illusionary effect by enveloping the visitor. It is possible that the floor had a swirling or labyrinthian pattern in the spirit of the later stone refinishing.[85] Vasari was appropriately overwhelmed by this all-encompassing setting and the dizzying experience of the architectural sublime it conveyed:

Wherefore let no one ever think to see any work of the brush more horrible and terrifying, or more natural than this one; and whoever enters that room and sees the windows, doors, and other suchlike things all awry and, as it were, on the point of falling, and the mountains and building hurtling down, cannot but fear that everything will fall upon him, and, above all, as he sees the Gods in the Heaven rushing,

---

[85] On the new floor of the 1780s by Paolo Pozzo, as well as his alternative labyrinthian pattern, considered in connection with a sixteenth-century drawing of a labyrinthian pavement created in or intended for the central courtyard, see Forster and Tuttle, "The Palazzo del Te," 272 and 285–7.

some here, some there, and all in flight. And what is most marvelous in the work is to see that the whole of the painting has neither beginning nor end.[86]

The experience of the hovering and rotating domes of the Golden House and the Pantheon have been recreated here through a specific pictorial scene, achieved by the use of various techniques: the shape of the domed room "round after the manner of an oven" enveloped the spectator;[87] the architectural framing around the doors, windows, and the original fireplace was made of "rustic stones rough-hewn as if by chance ... disjointed and awry ... appeared to be really hanging over to one side and falling down";[88] and the fire, which warmed the room, was extended pictorially onto the wall above where the giant Typhoeus – "mythical source of Mount Aetna's eruptions" – "belches his last flames as he is crushed under boulders," thereby suggesting that the fireplace below be seen as the "great volcano of Sicily."[89] Even sound was part of the effect, for, as David Mayernik points out, the ball court adjacent to the Hall of Giants "would have provided an appropriately resonant racket to stand for Jupiter's thunder,"[90] for any noise would have been amplified by the double-shelled dome, which made the room into a resonating chamber.[91] Finally, as Kurt Forster and Richard Tuttle suggest, "the stone floor added the qualities of touch, and may even have affected the mobility and equilibrium of the viewer," thereby providing a fitting complement to the disorientating experience of "this totally enveloping visual panorama."[92]

Nor was the sublime effect of the Hall of Giants limited to this room. Mayernik has suggested that the famous partial ruination of the façades of the central courtyard extends the conceit of the dynamic architectural destruction caused by the interior Gigantomachy to the exterior. The shock of the thunderbolts and lightning and of the crashing stone inside appears to have caused several triglyphs and corresponding sections of the architrave to have slipped downward out of place from the entablature, keystones to have been thrust upward to break apart their pediments, and stone courses to have been jostled to the extent that they no longer rest on each other, whereas several large blank spaces on the wall suggest that several stones have even been knocked out of place.[93]

One can extend this observation to the garden façade, which backs up against the fireplace of the Hall of Giants. Flickering reflections of light bouncing off the fish ponds along the length of this façade provide the illusion of the entire exterior wall covered in flames, as if the fire inside the building, first spreading illusionistically through painting from the fireplace onto the interior wall around it, has penetrated the building's fabric to engulf the entire façade with a destructive fury intensified from within by the figures of the winds blowing vigorously from the corners of the room. This conceit recalls the image from Aeschylus quoted previously by

---

[86] Giorgio Vasari, *Lives of the Painters, Sculptors, and Architects*, trans. Gaston du C. de Vere, 2 vols. (New York: Alfred A. Knopf, 1996 [1912]), 2:132.

[87] Vasari, *Lives*, 2:130.

[88] Vasari, *Lives*, 2:130.

[89] Mayernik, "The Winds in the Corners," 140.

[90] Mayernik, "The Winds in the Corners," 136.

[91] See Vasari, *Lives*, 2:130, who recounts that the cupola was constructed as "a double vault." The room has already been recognized as a "whispering gallery." See, for example, Forster and Tuttle, "The Palazzo del Te," 285.

[92] Forster and Tuttle, "The Palazzo del Te," 285.

[93] Mayernik, "The Winds in the Corners," 144–5: "[I]t is remarkable that the cortile has mostly been seen as an autonomous exercise in architectural humor and not instead as directly impacted by the serious, thunderous drama of the Fall [of the Giants]." Here, and in the description of the garden façade that follows, I am extending Mayernik's insightful observation, which, however, he limits only to the "slipping triglyphs," found exclusively on the east and west courtyard façades, before arguing that the north and south courtyard façades are exempt from the interior "drama" of the Hall of Giants. Yet all four courtyard façades exhibit the other features that I list here.

Longinus, in which Boreas, "Spewing against Heaven," reduces a palace "to embers" with a "streaming Curl" of "flashing flames."

In establishing the iconographical theme for the Hall of Giants, Giulio was likening his patron the duke to Jupiter,[94] while creating a fully sensory pictorial and architectural ekphrasis of the Gigantomachy found in the texts of Hesiod and Ovid and in the more recent, anonymous dream romance *Hypnerotomachia Poliphili* (1499). Giulio achieved the same effect presented in these literary accounts through the use of extreme foreshortening when looking upward, which was pioneered by Andrea Mantegna and developed by the likes of Raphael and Correggio. Giulio used this technique throughout the frescoed ceilings of the Palazzo del Te, so that like the Octagonal Hall of the Golden House, the Hall of Giants stands as the centerpiece of a building ensemble that extends its effect beyond the confines of the room.

This foreshortening was a further development of the vertiginous sublime found in the stuccoed dome of the Golden House, where Jupiter hovers overhead (Figure 15.3). The parallel between the illusionism of the Roman prototype and the Hall of Giants is striking. Giulio even included a billowing, tentlike canopy with Jupiter's eagle below on a throne, much like the stuccoed dome in the Golden House, where Jupiter strikes a similar pose. Not only had Nero associated himself with Jupiter through a variety of visual allusions, direct and indirect, but Domitian had followed in his stead, as was well known through written accounts of the dining hall of his Domus Augustana, where he feasted, as E. Baldwin Smith explains, "under a symbolic heaven," which Statius likened to "resting with Jupiter in the midst of the stars"[95] and which Martial would assimilate to the sun god.[96] Forster and Tuttle have explained how Gulio appears to have modeled the Palazzo del Te on Theodoric's imperial palace in nearby Ravenna, whose name, *palatium*, also "refers to the imperial residences on the Palatine Hill at Rome" and thus has its patron participate in the ancient "Roman idea that the Palace of the Emperors was a divine place," where they could be "visited by the gods, and later, with ... deification, could join the gods in their *palatium coeli*, Mount Olympus." "Federigo's possession of the famous *impresa* of Mount Olympus," they continue, "bestowed on him after the Battle of Pavia by Charles V in 1525, can thus be seen as an heraldic key to the palace of the pagan gods."[97]

Thus Giulio's assimilation of the Duke of Mantua to Jupiter by way of the cosmic domed room of the Hall of Giants reestablishes the ancient Roman tradition of the palace used for religious rites that associate the ruler with Olympian gods, whether Jupiter or Phoebus Apollo; it would be continued by Delorme at the Château d'Anet, where Henri II was assimilated to Phoebus Apollo after the manner of the Golden House, and in a manner so extensive that one might see Delorme combining the Roman tradition of the palace as *templum* with the medieval tradition of the *univeralis machina mundi*, that is, explaining the universe as a vast and complex cosmic machine.[98] As the Château d'Anet is not only the culminating example of the sublime to be discussed in this chapter but also the building that presents the most complex set

---

[94] On the extensive association of Federico II Gonzaga with Jupiter at the Palazzo del Te, see Eugenio Battisti, "Conformismo ed eccentricità in Giulio Romano come artista di corte," in *Giulio Romano. Atti del Convegno Internazionale di Studi su "Giulio Romano e l'espansione europea del Rinascimento." Mantova, Palazzo Ducale, Teatro scientifico del Bibiena, 1–5 ottobre 1989* (Mantua: Accademia Nazionale Virgiliana, 1989), 21–43, p. 28, and for Federico's association with Mount Olympus, Rodolfo Signorini, *Il Palazzo del Te e la Camera di Psiche: Miti e altre fantasie e storie antiche nella villa di Federico II Gonzaga ideata da Giulio Romano a Mantova* (Mantua: Sometti, 2001), 19.
[95] Smith, *Architectural Symbolism*, 148. See also p. 111.
[96] Lehmann, "The Dome of Heaven," 22.
[97] Forster and Tuttle, "The Palazzo del Te," 279–80.
[98] On the medieval *univeralis machina mundi* and its antecedent in Lucretius, see Robert Bartlett, *The Natural and the Supernatural in the Middle Ages* (Cambridge: Cambridge University Press, 2008), chap. 2.

FIGURE 15.12. Philibert Delorme, chapel, Château d'Anet, dome (c. 1548–1552).
Photo: Richard A. Etlin.

of associations and multiple, reinforcing meanings, it requires a preamble to set the stage for an account of its sublimity.

The link between Giulio's Hall of Giants and Delorme's Château d'Anet were strong and numerous. Not only were there close ties between the French and Mantuan courts, but also, at the end of 1531, the Duke of Mantua sent Francesco Primaticcio, one of Giulio's principal assistants at Te, to work in France for François I, who in 1540 promoted him to head the works at the royal Château de Fontainebleau.[99] As Sylvie Béguin has shown, Giulio's dizzying manner of illusionistic painting, specifically including the Hall of Giants, was well known to artists at the French court who favored this type of dramatically foreshortened, upward views.[100] In addition, it is highly likely that Delorme had personal knowledge of the Palazzo del Te during his Italian sojourn from circa 1528–1529 to 1536. There are numerous signs throughout the Château d'Anet and in Delorme's early architecture that he repeatedly emulated the Mantuan prototype.[101] Delorme's principal parallel to the Hall of Giants was the château's chapel (Figures 15.12 and 15.13).

[99] Sylvie Béguin et al., *La Galerie d'Ulysse à Fontainebleau* (Paris: Presses universitaires de France, 1985), 1–2.
[100] Sylvie Béguin, "Giulio Romano et l'École de Fontainebleau," in *Giulio Romano*, 45–74.
[101] On Delorme using the Palazzo del Te as the prototype for his first major commission in France, the Château de St.-Maur-lès-Fossés (begun c. 1541), see Anthony Blunt, *Philibert Delorme* (London: A. Zwemmer, 1958), 22. Other scholars have agreed with this conclusion.

FIGURE 15.13. Philibert Delorme, chapel, Château d'Anet, floor (c. 1548–1552). Photo: Richard A. Etlin.

Not only does the Château d'Anet follow the example of the Palazzo del Te in its approach to the sublime, but it also appears to make direct reference to Nero's Golden House. In 1558 Gabriello Simeoni, an Italian antiquarian and poet living in Lyon, published a brief account of a recent visit to the Château d'Anet, which he compared favorably to Nero's Golden House.[102] Simeoni had been a supplicant at the French court since at least 1550 when he visited the château;[103] and because he had written earlier about Anet,[104] the seemingly innocent mention of his visit several years later, as if it were the first occasion, signaled to informed contemporaries that the comparison with the Golden House was hardly accidental. In effect, this "stupendous" French palace presented not merely a generic example of splendor and beauty comparable to the Roman prototype but also a chapel, whose sublime effect was intended to surpass that of the main banquet hall of Nero's mansion.

Having postulated these specific connections with antecedent models, we can now turn to the Château d'Anet itself and specifically to its chapel, where we find the architectural equivalent

[102] Gabriello Simeoni, *Les illustres Observations antiques du seigneur Gabriel Symeon florentin en son dernier voyage d'Italie l'an 1557* (Lyon: Jan de Tournes, 1558), fol. 95v.
[103] Maurice Jusselin, *Gabriel Syméon à Anet au temps de Diane de Poitiers* (Chartres: Lainé and Tantet, 1935), 4–5; Françoise Bardon, *Diane de Poitiers et le mythe de Diane* (Paris: Presses universitaires de France, 1963), 57.
[104] Gabriello Simeoni, *Épitomé de l'origine et succession de la Duché de Ferrare, composé en langue Toscane par le seigneur Gabriel Symeon et traduict en François par luy mesme. Avec certaines Epistres à divers personnages, et aucuns Epigrammes sur la proprieté de la Lune par les douze signes du Ciel. Pour madame la Duchesse de Valentinois* (Paris: Gilles Corrozet, 1553), fols. 44–5v.

to what David Quint, in a study of literary history, has termed "a typical Renaissance practice of *contaminatio*, the imitation of several models at once."[105] The references to Roman architecture in the Anet chapel were multiple. To begin, scholars have repeatedly noted that Delorme apparently modeled the diamond coffering of the dome after the two half-domes of the Temple of Venus and Rome, which he would have known from his Roman sojourn.[106] Yet from the late Middle Ages onward and throughout the sixteenth century, this building, with its east-west orientation, was known by another name, that is, as Temple of the Sun and the Moon.[107] Because this temple was erected by Hadrian on the site of the vestibule of the Golden House, it may even have become considered as a successor to Nero's house, because it prolonged in time the Golden House's cosmological themes.[108]

With its mirrored cellas each terminated in a partially domed apse, the so-called Temple of the Sun and the Moon presented an architectural palindrome. In his *Libro d'architettura* (1559), Antonio Labacco would imaginatively restore the Temple of the Sun and the Moon with a statue under each half-domed niche: Phoebus Apollo, holding a lyre, thus also god of the Muses, and Diana, with bow and arrow, as goddess of the hunt and the moon.[109] This appropriation of the building is apt, for a marble plaque over the doorway to the main entrance pavilion to Anet announces it metaphorically in Latin as the dwelling of the sister and brother Olympian gods Phoebus Apollo and Diana, ostensibly disguising the love between Henri II and Diane de Poitiers through the fiction of a Platonic admiration.[110] Throughout the château, symbols of Henri as Apollo and of Diane as Diana mark virtually every surface – the décor, furnishings, and even larger architectural features such as the crescent-shaped stair that once descended from the rear terrace to the enclosed garden directly behind the château. Nowhere is the symbolism more complex than in the chapel. At Anet, Delorme reoriented the mirror images of the Roman prototype in a vertical arrangement so as to present the sun god

---

[105] Quint, "Fear of Falling," 853.

[106] Blunt, *Philibert Delorme*, 42; Volker Hoffmann, "Philibert Delorme und das Schloss Anet," *Architectura* 2 (1973), 131–52, p. 141; Jean-Marie Pérouse de Montclos, *Philibert De l'Orme: Architecte du roi (1514–1570)* (Paris: Mengès, 2000), 118; Giuseppe Fallacara, "Philibert Delorme e l'*invenzione*," in Philibert Delorme, *Nouvelles inventions pour bien bastir et à petits fraiz*, ed. and trans. Maria Rita Campa (Bari: Poliba, 2009), 129–45, p. 141.

[107] Stefano Borsi, *Giuliano da Sangallo: i disegni di architettura e dell'antico* (Rome: Officina, 1985), 239. See also, for example, the designation "Solis et Lunae" in the plan in Giovanni Bartolomeo Marliani, *Urbis Romae topographia* (1544), in Philip Jacks, *The Antiquarian and the Myth of Antiquity: The Origins of Rome in Renaissance Thought* (Cambridge: Cambridge University Press, 1993), 210.

[108] The *Historia Augusta* (SHA *Hadr.* 19.12–13), believed to have been written in the late fourth century, records that Hadrian built this temple, which it calls by its alternative name Templum Urbis (Temple of City), after moving the colossal statue of Nero from the vestibule of the Golden House to a location near the Flavian Amphitheater, thereby freeing the site for new construction. The text erroneously attributes to Hadrian the transformation of the Colossus into the statue of the sun, a change undertaken previously by Vespasian, who had altered the face and added a crown of rays (Martial 1.70.7–8). According to the *Historia Augusta*, Hadrian had also commissioned as its pendant a statue of the moon, which may never have been executed. This literary reference associating Hadrian with paired statues of the sun and moon at the time when he erected the Templum Urbis may have been the origin of the misnaming of this edifice.

[109] Antonio Labacco, *Libro d'Antonio Labacco appartenante a l'architettura ...* (Rome: Casa Nostra, 1559), plates 2–3. In contrast, as Jacks explains, the Temple of Venus and Rome (Templum Veneris et Romae) originally had a "statue of Roma, progenitor of the Romulides" in one apse and a statue of Venus, mother of Aeneas, in the other, thereby uniting in one cult "the two putative ancestries of the Roman people" (Jacks, *The Antiquarian*, 16). The temple's architectural palindrome thus presents a built ekphrasis of the palindrome of the names ROMA and AMOR, the latter standing for Venus. According to Lawrence Richardson, Jr., Maxentius vaulted the temple and added the domed apses in his restoration after the fire of AD 307. See *A New Topographical Dictionary of Ancient Rome* (Baltimore: Johns Hopkins University Press, 1992), 409–10.

[110] "PHOEBO SACRATA EST ALMAE DOMUS AMPLA DIANAE / VERUM ACCEPTA CUI CUNCTA DIANA REFERT" ("The vast house of nourishing Diana has been dedicated to Phoebus [Apollo] / To whom Diana returns all that she has received").

Phoebus Apollo through the gilt dome and Diana as goddess of the moon and the underworld through the black-and-white spiraling pattern of the floor below it.[111]

The geometry of the dome of the chapel at the Château d'Anet combines with the similar floor pattern below as the culmination of an entire sequence of astonishing vaults and illusionistic geometric patterns found throughout the château.[112] In the chapel, the diamond coffering in the dome creates the illusion of swirling spirals. As Michel Gallet has observed, the "lanterned dome [is] decorated ... in a curious way: curves borrowed from the crescent, symbolic of Diane de Poitiers, overlap in a pattern that seems to be caught up in an endless gyration and that is repeated below in the pattern of the paved floor."[113] This movement introduces a cosmological theme, recalling the cycles of the sun and moon and reminding the visitor that the entire château is not merely a residence but a combination of Roman palace as *templum* and the medieval *univeralis machina mundi*. This idea found complex expression in the Renaissance, through, for example, the famous card set by Mantegna known as *Tarocchi*, which furnished the perfect model for conceiving a château for Diane de Poitiers and the king, because Apollo and the Muses (both associated with Henri II)[114] mediate between the planets and humans. "Apollo," explains Jean Seznec in his study of the influence of the *Tarocchi* on Renaissance thought, "in his double role of leader of the Muses and ruler of the Planets, is the soul of the Cosmos," an idea derived from Ambrosius Theodorius Macrobius's *Somnium Scipionis* (2.3), "where the Muses have become the movers of the Spheres."[115]

Both the chapel and the entrance pavilion of the château develop this cosmological theme. The weather vanes that rise atop the obelisks flanking the chapel's dome originally had a mechanism to register the direction of the wind on a wind rose below,[116] to which the swirling spirals of the dome and the floor may allude. In addition, the stellar pattern of the floor recalls the type of medieval cosmological patterns that James Ackerman has termed "a class of medieval *schemata* in circular form used to coordinate the lunar cycle with other astronomical inferences ... such as the Hours and Zodiac," a figure that, Ackerman suggests, Michelangelo evokes in his design for the contemporaneous plaza of the Capitoline Hill in Rome.[117]

All of these cosmological references are linked to the main entrance pavilion of Anet, which originally featured an astrological clock after the manner of the famous clock on the civic tower of Mantua, whose concentric rings could be adjusted to register the movement of the planets, stars, sun, and moon; at Anet, the black-and-white spirals at opposite sides of one of the dials link the clock to the black-and-white schema on the chapel's floor.[118] Two different gnomons for

---

[111] Giulio Romano had used the diamond motif from the Temple of the Sun and the Moon to decorate the cloister vault of the Room of the Sun and the Moon in the Palazzo del Te, which features a vertiginously foreshortened fresco in the center showing Phoebus Apollo driving his chariot out of the scene as Diana enters from the other side to usher in the night. On the triple role of the goddess Diana (hunt, moon, and underworld), see Bardon, *Diane de Poitiers*, 4–5.

[112] See Richard A. Etlin, "Death in the Enchanted Palace: Philibert Delorme's Château d'Anet," archived webcast lecture, Bernard and Anne Spitzer School of Architecture, City College of New York, March 17, 2011, http://www.totalwebcasting.com/view/?id=ccnyssa.

[113] Michel Gallet, "L'Orme, Philibert de," in *Praeger Encyclopedia of Art*, 5 vols. (New York: Praeger, 1971), 3:1208–9, p. 1209.

[114] On the association of Henri II with the Muses, see Ian Wardropper, "Le mécénat des Guise: Art, religion et politique au milieu du XVIe siècle," *Revue de l'art* 94 (1991), 27–44, p. 40.

[115] Jean Seznec, *The Survival of the Pagan Gods*, trans. Barbara F. Sessions (Princeton, NJ: Princeton University Press, 1972 [1953]), 140.

[116] Pierre Désiré Roussel, *Histoire et description du Château d'Anet...* (Paris: D. Jouaust, 1875), 45.

[117] James S. Ackerman, *The Architecture of Michelangelo* (Harmondsworth: Penguin, 1970 [1961]), 170–1, with illustration from Isidor of Seville.

[118] On the astrological clock at Anet, see [Le Marquant], *Description du Château d'Anet* (Paris: G. Desprez, 1789), 15–17.

studying solar movement flanked the astrological clock, each fashioned according to Diane's symbol of the moon's crescent, a form also placed sculpturally atop the terrace to dominate the central court and, along this central axis, a form that was used for the central exterior stair that led from the rear terrace directly behind the château into the enclosed garden.

Just as Michel Gallet's account of the rotating dome stimulates the thought of this cosmological imagery, an anonymous account from 1640 reminds us that there is an experiential dimension to the chapel comparable, through its abstract, geometrical forms, to that in the Hall of Giants:

The dome is extremely bright, and well vaulted, entirely gilt and azured as is the rest of the chapel. The floor is a marvel of beauty, composed of small pieces of marble ... delicately assembled ... and presenting (when one steps back a little to better appreciate the perspective) the appearance of an infinity of interlaced crescents ... diminishing progressively from large to small, such that the smallest seem to shrink to nothing toward the center of the composition.... And in the same manner the vault is industriously shaped with similar, gilded crescents interlaced analogously, one with the other, such that they seem to expand and contract, the way a stone thrown vigorously into a pool of water produces numerous [concentric] circles that multiply themselves until the act of expansion leads them suddenly to disappear.[119]

Here Delorme applies in an original manner the lessons of the swirling dome and floor of the Pantheon and recalls the rotating dome of the Golden House, while providing approximate mirror images with dome and floor that make the experience even more dramatic.[120] A projecting cornice at the base of the dome hides the origin of the swirling diamond coffers in a way that heightens the swirling dynamism by making them seem to emerge from behind this ring rather than sit firmly on it.

As the anonymous visitor realized, this powerful experience of watching the floor and the dome expand illusionistically before one's very eyes presents an architectural ekphrasis of Henri II's motto, DONEC TOTUM IMPLEAT ORBEM (until it/he fills the entire world),[121] which, as Volker Hoffmann has shown, was assigned the meaning of world peace through French imperial rule under Henri II, a message conveyed in festival architecture, as well as at the Château d'Anet, through cosmological symbolism.[122]

The psychophysical experience – or somaesthetics, to apply Shusterman's term – is even stronger than either Gallet or the seventeenth-century visitor recorded. On entering the chapel, a visitor is not merely confronted with a rotating swirl of forms in the dome and on the floor but undergoes a more powerful, visceral experience of being aspirated upward into the dome, while simultaneously being sucked downward into an abyss. The architect's intention to create this effect is revealed by the shape of the diamonds in the floor, which are elongated in comparison with those of the dome, and by the exaggerated curvature of the floor's diamonds so as to intensify the sense of a swirling downward suction. Only the stable central medallion of colored marble, set within the black-and-white marble swirling floor, offers a psychological anchor to ward off total vertigo, thereby anticipating Boullée's later discussion of the need to provide a stable point of focus and rest for the experience of the architectural sublime.

---

[119] "Description de la belle maison d'Anet, veu le mardy seconde feste de la Pentecoste 29 mai 1640," Bibliothèque Nationale de France, Manuscripts, Fonds Dupuy 550, fols. 198–202, fol. 200v. Most of this text has been reproduced in Bardon, *Diane de Poitiers*, 65 (my translation).

[120] As Pérouse de Montclos has noted, Delorme refers repeatedly to the Pantheon in his *Premier Tome de l'architecture* (1567) and includes this building in the list of Roman antiquities of which he says that he had made measured drawings. See *Philibert De l'Orme*, 32.

[121] "Description," fol. 200v; Bardon, *Diane de Poitiers*, 65.

[122] On the imperial theme, see Volker Hoffmann, "Donec Totum Impleat Orbem: Symbolisme impérial au temps de Henri II," *Bulletin de la Société de l'Histoire de l'art français*, année 1978 (1980), 29–42.

This experience might readily have prompted a series of reminiscences in a sixteenth-century visitor, not only of the Pantheon, Nero's Golden House, and the Hall of Giants but also of the entire literary tradition of the sublime, once again, through the practice of *contaminatio*. In addition, the contemporary viewer would have in mind Primaticcio's project for the round, central panel in the long Gallery of Ulysses at the royal Château de Fontainebleau, which was commissioned by François I and continued by his son Henri II in the years immediately preceding the design of Anet and was completed, after an interruption, in the years immediately following.[123] This fresco, with its dramatically foreshortened perspective from below, has traditionally been called *The Ring Dance of the Hours* and shows a three-tiered dance in which each successive ring rises higher and moves faster – the bottom female figures dancing on a platform of clouds, the next ring floating in air, and the final top figures twirling rapidly in isolation. Although the Hours, or Horai, can be found in the *Iliad* and the *Odyssey*, as well as other classical sources,[124] the composition is fully Dantesque.

In effect, the dominant images that come to mind when experiencing the upward and downward vortexes in the chapel at the Château d'Anet are the eschatological topography and the ring dances of Dante's *La Divina Commedia* (*The Divine Comedy*), a work that, as I explain elsewhere, was repeatedly used in commissions by Diane de Poitiers.[125] As the reader learns at the end of the last canto of *Inferno*, the stepped, inverted funnel of the abyss of hell and its mirror image in the stepped mountain of purgatory were both created as the result of Lucifer's fall when he was thrown out of heaven: the earth pulled back in horror at the approach of the falling Lucifer to create the void of hell, while the displaced mass "rushed upwards" as it emerged from the other side of the planet as the mountain of purgatory.[126] The near mirror images of the dome and the floor evoke the stepped, funneling rings of hell and purgatory and the spiraling experience of voyaging through both domains; in addition, the stable disk of colored marble at the center of the floor corresponds to the light-filled lantern, symbolic of paradise, which crowns the dome directly above it and in turn is crowned with a cross. The dome also presents a second reading as the rings or spheres of paradise. Most coffers contain a stuccoed winged head of an angel, arranged much like the vision of the nine orders of angels in the 1463 manuscript illumination for the French translation of Vincent de Beauvais's *Bibliotheca mundi*, a cosmological arrangement that Beatrice explains to Dante in canto 28 of *Paradiso*.[127]

Over the course of nearly three hundred years, from the time of its completion in the early fourteenth century until the beginning of the seventeenth century, the popularity of Dante's *Divine Comedy* can be likened to the ever-expanding circles in the patterns of the Anet chapel. Only in 1554 did it acquire its qualifying adjective "divine" as part of the title.[128] In Italy, the *Divine Comedy* was the most widely copied manuscript in the fourteenth century after the Bible and in the fifteenth century was the most extensively printed book. Responding to the petition of its citizens, the Florentine government instituted public readings and commentaries beginning in 1373. The *Divine Comedy* became so popular with ordinary people that the elites told humorous stories about its success.[129]

---

[123] Béguin et al., *La Galerie d'Ulysse*, 62 and 92–3. The work is thought to have stopped in circa 1550 and, in the case of this central panel, begun again in 1557.

[124] Béguin et al., *La Galerie d'Ulysse*, 166. On the Horai, see http://www.theoi.com/Ouranios.html.

[125] Etlin, "Death in the Enchanted Palace."

[126] Dante Alighieri, *The Divine Comedy. I. Inferno*, trans. John D. Sinclair (New York: Oxford Press, 1961), 427. All subsequent quotations from Dante are from *The Divine Comedy*, trans. Allen Mandelbaum (New York: Alfred A. Knopf, 1995), given as cantica (*Inferno, Purgatorio,* or *Paradiso*) followed by canto and line number(s). On Dante's eschatological geography, see Richard A. Etlin, *Modernism in Italian Architecture, 1890–1940* (Cambridge, MA: MIT Press, 1991), chap. 14.

[127] For the illustration, see Bartlett, *The Natural and the Supernatural*, 74 (fig. 7).

[128] Werner P. Friederich, *Dante's Fame Abroad, 1350–1850* (Rome: Edizioni di Storia e Letteratura, 1950), 79.

[129] Anne Dunlop, "'El Vostro Poeta': The First Florentine Printing of Dante's *Commedia*," *RACAR* 20, 1–2 (1993), 29–42, pp. 31–2. See also Michael Caesar, ed., *Dante: The Critical Heritage: 1314(?)–1870* (London: Routledge, 1989), 6.

With the rise of printed books, as the new technology of printing began in the 1460s to extend into "urban centers beyond the Rhineland,"[130] came the "heyday of infernal cartography," to apply a phrase from John Kleiner, which took place between circa 1460 and 1600[131] and hence coincided with the Renaissance. Between 1472 and 1596 there were at least fifty printed copies of the Italian-language *La Divina Commedia*. In France, *La Divina Commedia*, in its original language, first appeared in the early sixteenth century in Delorme's Italophile city of Lyon, which was establishing itself as a major center for book publishing, through counterfeits of the Aldine edition of 1502, later followed by three legitimate printings in 1547, 1551, and 1552.[132] Many of these maps accompanied the printed texts.

During this period, cartographers vied with one another to represent the abyss of *Inferno*. Vasari even reported that a friend of the painter Filippino Lippi made a three-dimensional model of hell, "which was held to be something marvelous."[133] The Florentine architects Filippo Brunelleschi and Antonio Manetti had been keenly interested in the shape and measurements of Dante's hell, the latter's calculations serving, for example, as the basis for Girolamo Benivieni's map – or rather, topographical portrait – of 1506 and the map in the 1515 pirated Aldine edition of the *Inferno*,[134] both of which present marked similarities to the illusionistic abyss of the Anet chapel's floor.

The topical interest in Dante during this period is reflected in the painting in the Florentine Cathedral by Domenico di Michelino, dating from the two-hundredth anniversary of Dante's birth, 1465, which depicts him standing in front of an anachronistically contemporary scene of the city. Holding open the *Divine Comedy* such that the first lines can be read by the viewer, Dante gestures with his right hand as if to invite spectators to voyage into the otherworld of his book, shown with an entrance into the spiraling abyss of hell immediately to his right; the stepped mountain of purgatory has been placed centrally in the background, and the entire painting is crowned by the concentric rings of paradise.[135] This scene was widely disseminated through a fifteenth-century print.[136] In the next decade, Lorenzo de' Medici, in the words of Debra Pincus, engaged in a campaign "to catapult Dante into a figure of heroic proportions," transforming the exiled Florentine poet, who had died in Ravenna, into "an emblem for the cultural hegemony of Florence." Illustrations for all three cantos – ninety-three in all – were commissioned from Botticelli, and Cristoforo Landino's popular public lectures were collected into "the influential and long-lived" Italian-language commentary on Dante, published in 1481 as part of a fully annotated edition of the *Divine Comedy*, which had its own ambitious program of illustrations. The humanist Bernardo Bembo then commissioned an elaborate tomb for Dante in Ravenna.[137]

---

[130] Elizabeth L. Eisenstein, *The Printing Revolution in Early Modern Europe* (Cambridge: Cambridge University Press, 1983), 3 and 13.

[131] John Kleiner, *Mismapping the Underworld: Daring and Error in Dante's "Comedy"* (Stanford, CA: Stanford University Press, 1994), 23–4.

[132] Caesar, *Dante*, 29; Deborah Parker, *Commentary and Ideology: Dante in the Renaissance* (Durham, NC: Duke University Press, 1993), 132–4 (table 1) and 146. On Delorme's ongoing connection to Lyon and more generally on the tendency of artists and writers to identify with their native city, see Pérouse de Montclos, *Philibert De l'Orme*, 24–6. According to Parker, the Lyonnais Italophile Jean de Tournes's 1547 edition of *La Divina Commedia* – dedicated to the Lyonnais Italophile poet Maurice de Scève – was "known for [its] beautiful types and elegant arrangement" (p. 146).

[133] As quoted in Giovanni Morello, "Sandro Botticelli's *Chart of Hell*," in Hein-Th. Schulze Altcappenberg, ed., *Sandro Botticelli: The Drawings for Dante's "Divine Comedy"* (London: Royal Academy of Arts, 2000), 318–25, p. 323.

[134] Kleiner, *Mismapping the Underworld*, 24 and 27–9 (figs. 2–3), and Parker, *Commentary and Ideology*, 141–3.

[135] Richard Thayer Holbrook, *Portraits of Dante from Giotto to Raffael: A Critical Study, with a Concise Iconography* (London: Philip Lee Warner, 1911), 173–5; Rudolph Altrocchi, "Michelino's Dante," *Speculum* 6, 1 (January 1931), 15–59, especially pp. 21, 24, and 26–8.

[136] See Altrocchi, "Michelino's Dante," plate 3.

[137] Debra Pincus, "The Humanist and the Poet: Bernardo Bembo's Portrait of Dante," in *Patronage and Italian Renaissance Sculpture*, ed. Kathleen Wren Christian and David J. Drogin (Farnham [Surrey]: Ashgate, 2010), 61–94.

Dante's writings acquired new importance in the first three decades of the sixteenth century, as Pietro Bembo's *Prose della volgar lingua* (1524) helped to raise the status of literature in the vernacular tongue, including classical texts, as Michael Caesar explains, to a level comparable to Latin. In addition, the *Divine Comedy* was now accorded "the same kind of philological care that had been developed in the reestablishment of ancient texts." At the French court, Luigi Alamanni, a connoisseur of Dante, read from the *Divine Comedy* to François I, whose sister, Marguerite de Navarre, has been adjudged by scholars as the poet whose work most closely approaches Dante's in the entire history of French literature. Her great work, *Les Prisons* (1548), reaching nearly six thousand lines, is modeled on the *Divine Comedy* and demonstrates familiarity with Landino's commentary. Toward 1550 the *Divine Comedy* was translated into French in a manuscript edition probably commissioned by the king or somebody close to the crown, thereby adding to the number of French- and Italian-language copies of the poem in the libraries in royal châteaux. This latest edition of Dante was tailored specifically to flatter royal sensibilities by adjusting the text in *Purgatorio* 20.52, because François I had been angered by Dante making his ancestor Hugh Capet declare his lowly origins as the son of a Parisian butcher.[138]

The pulse of this Renaissance engagement with Dante can also be ascertained from the passion for the *Divine Comedy* shown by eminent artists. A few examples other than Brunelleschi and Manetti will suffice. Giuliano da Sangallo drew a topographic map of *Inferno*, which he kept inside his copy of Landino's edition of the *Divine Comedy*.[139] Vasari reports that Dante was Michelangelo's "best-beloved poet."[140] As a young man Michelangelo read from the *Divine Comedy* to his host, the Bolognese nobleman Giovan Francesco Aldovrandi, just as the mature Bramante did for Pope Julius II. And the sculptor Benvenuto Cellini, who worked at the French court of François I between 1540 and 1545, was known for his deep knowledge of Dante.[141] In his autobiographical *Vita*, believed to have been written in Italy between 1558 and 1566, Cellini becomes the Dante pilgrim of the *Divine Comedy*, in which, as Margaret Gallucci explains, "he journeys to the Otherworld with a boy-angel as his guide, first to Hell where he sees an infinite number of suffering souls, and then to Heaven, where he envisions the Godhead" through a mystical vision of a blazing sun – "a bath of the purest liquid gold" – that metamorphoses first into a "Christ on the Cross, made out of the very stuff of the sun," which then becomes a radiant image of a beautiful Madonna with Child.[142] In sum, Dante's writings constituted an integral part of Renaissance artistic, aristocratic, and curial culture. This is the cultural matrix for which Delorme was designing and in which he had been formed.[143] Moreover, Dantesque cartography, Cellini's *Vita*, and several of Marguerite de Navarre's works[144] demonstrate contemporary enthusiasm for a participatory engagement with the *Divine Comedy*, an experience

---

[138] "Inventaire de la librairie royale de Blois, lors de son transfert au château de Fontainebleau en 1544," in Henri Omont, *Anciens Inventaires et catalogues de la Bibliothèque nationale*, 4 vols. (Paris: E. Leroux, 1908–1921), vol. 1, nos. 1468–9 and 1623–8; Robert J. Clements, "Marguerite de Navarre and Dante," *Italica* 18, 2 (1941), 37–50, p. 38; Friederich, *Dante's Fame Abroad*, 63–70; Caesar, *Dante*, 23–5 and 29–30.

[139] Morello, "Sandro Botticelli's *Chart of Hell*," 318 (fig. 62) and 323.

[140] Vasari, *Lives*, 2:694.

[141] William E. Wallace, *Michelangelo: The Artist, the Man, and His Times* (Cambridge: Cambridge University Press, 2010), 55; Ingrid D. Rowland, *The Culture of the High Renaissance: Ancients and Moderns in Sixteenth-Century Rome* (Cambridge: Cambridge University Press, 1998), 171; Michael W. Cole, *Cellini and the Principles of Sculpture* (Cambridge: Cambridge University Press, 2002), 7; Margaret A. Gallucci, *Benvenuto Cellini: Sexuality, Masculinity, and Artistic Identity in Renaissance Italy* (New York: Palgrave Macmillan, 2003), 8 and passim.

[142] Gallucci, *Benvenuto Cellini*, 65–6 and 92–4.

[143] Pérouse de Montclos, *Philibert De l'Orme*, 37–8. During Delorme's Roman sojourn in the 1530s, he had been welcomed into the humanist circle of Marcello Cervini (future Pope Marcellus II), who also served Pope Paul III as director of archaeological excavation at Hadrian's villa outside Rome in Tivoli. Delorme himself was also in the service of Paul III before being taken into the fold of the French ambassador Cardinal Jean Du Bellay.

[144] Clements, "Marguerite de Navarre and Dante," 50.

that Delorme offered to his patron and visitors to the Anet chapel through a vicarious journey through hell, purgatory, and paradise by means of a vertiginous application of the somaesthetics of the sublime.

At the Anet chapel, the apparent reference to Dante also provides a Christian meaning to the palindrome of upper and lower worlds associated with the pagan gods Diana and Phoebus Apollo. As Georg Rabuse and Luzius Keller have noted, Dante's eschatological geography may well derive from Macrobius's *Somnium Scipionis*, where both universe and soul have fallen from the perfect state of the sphere into the degenerate form of a cone.[145] We have already seen the importance of Macrobius for the Renaissance concept of the universe as a machine of the world and for Henri II's dual role as Apollo, ruler of the universe and guide of the Muses.

Once a visitor thinks of Dante, an entire chain of literary associations involving the spatial sublime follows. As Dante descends into the eighth circle of hell on the back of the giant flying beast Geryon, whom Virgil, his guide, had counseled to "take care/to keep your circles wide, your landing slow," his mind turns readily to the tales of Phaeton and Icarus:

> I do not think there was greater fear
> in Phaeton when he let his reins go free –
> for which the sky, as one still sees, was scorched –
> nor in poor Icarus when he could feel
> his sides unwinged because the wax was melting,
> his father shouting to him, "That way's wrong!"

Like the architectural tradition of the sublime, the literary tradition presents a parallel sequence of texts that convey the reader into the floating and swirling space of the sublime. Dante the narrator, as he flies off into space with Phaeton and Icarus in mind, uses amplification to achieve a literary effect of the sublime, with language reminiscent of Hesiod's Gigantomachy and Ovid's story of Phoebus and Phaeton:

> ... on all sides, I saw
> that I was in the air, and everything
> had faded from my sight – except the beast.
>   Slowly, slowly, swimming, he moves on;
> he wheels and he descends, but I feel only
> the wind upon my face and the wind rising.
>   Already, on our right, I heard the torrent
> resounding, there beneath us, horribly,
> so that I stretched my neck and looked below.
>   Then I was more afraid of falling off,
> for I saw fires and heard laments,
> at which I tremble, crouching, and hold fast.
> ...
>   Just as a falcon long upon the wing –
> who, seeing neither lure nor bird, compels
> the falconer to cry, "Ah me, you fall!" –
> descends, exhausted, in a hundred circles. (*Inferno* 17.106–23, 17.127–30)

With this description of the descent into hell, Dante provides an imaginatively kinesthetic account that engages the reader's *Körpergefühl*, translating a contemplation of movement through space into a bodily sentiment. The reference to Phaeton then reminds one of Ovid's

---

[145] Luzius Keller, *Piranèse et les romantiques français: le mythe des escaliers en spirale* (Paris: José Corti, 1966), 15–16. Keller refers to Georg Rabuse, *Der kosmische Aufbau der Jenseitsreiche Dantes* (Graz and Cologne: Böhlau, 1958), 66–7.

Metamorphoses and the account of Phoebus the sun god's successfully vertiginous flight, with Phoebus here assimilated to Henri II, followed by Phaeton's vertiginous fall.

The chain of associations that the spiraling experience in the Anet chapel might have prompted was not necessarily limited to literature. In addition to creating an experience of the sublime at the Palazzo del Te in the Hall of Giants, where the Duke of Mantua was presented in the guise of Jupiter assuring cosmic order though the chaos of the battle with the giants, Giulio Romano repeated the same political allegory in the Room of the Eagle, also know as the Room of Phaeton, where the central octagonal compartment of the ceiling presents a fresco dating from 1527 with a dramatic portrayal of Ovid's account of Jupiter hurling thunderbolts and lightning at Phaeton, who hurtles out of his father's chariot to plunge into space.[146] Five years later, Michelangelo was so struck by a marble relief on an ancient Roman sarcophagus depicting Phaeton's disastrous flight that he immediately made a preliminary sketch. When he sent the completed work from Florence to the eminent Roman aristocrat Tommaso de' Cavalieri in September 1533, this event, as William Wallace recounts, "caused a sensation in Rome." Awed by the widespread enthusiasm for Michelangelo's *Fall of Phaeton*, Cavalieri "reported that 'everybody wanted to see it,'" including Cardinal Ippolito de' Medici and Pope Clement VII.[147] Delorme, active in Roman humanist culture at this time, was one of several Frenchmen who could have reported this news back to France at the appropriate moment. These images came directly to the French court when Primaticcio was decorating the ceilings of the royal Château de Fontainebleau in the years just preceding the design of the Château d'Anet, for he consecrated one panel to the fall of Phaeton, with a dramatically foreshortened and chaotic scene that combines features from both Giulio's and Michelangelo's recent views.[148]

For Dante, the tale of Phaeton's disastrous ride and subsequent fall is not merely a felicitous occasion to convey the sense of the spatial sublime; it also serves as a foil to the astronomical and hence spiritual order of the universe and is invoked in this context both in *Purgatorio* 4.71–5 and *Paradiso* 31.124–9. Similarly, Phaeton's failure provides a mirrored obverse to Dante's successful ascent, such that Dante the narrator is presented, in the words of Kevin Brownlee, as "a 'corrected' Phaeton,"[149] a pairing effectively captured by Delorme's architectural palindrome.

Dante's ascent in the *Divine Comedy* is closely associated with the figure of the ring dance, which becomes a metaphor of the cosmic order. In *Inferno*, the dance is appropriately abortive; in *Paradiso*, it conveys cosmological harmony and divine love. All references are readily experienced in the illusionistic setting of the Anet chapel. Through reference to Scylla and Charybdis in *Inferno* 7.22-4, Dante provides a Christian meaning of eternal punishment by means of a round dance:

> Even as waves that break above Charybdis,
> each shattering the other when they meet,
> so must the spirits here dance their round dance.

Howling, the avaricious and the prodigal spirits wheel enormous weights in opposite directions, only to crash into the opposite stream of movement and then turn around in their punishing, stillborn dance. Because Dante's guide here is Virgil, a reader would readily recall the comparable passage from the *Aeneid*, which finds its echo in the feeling of being sucked down into the

---

[146] On the association of Ovid with this scene, see Signorini, *Il Palazzo del Te*, 33.
[147] Wallace, *Michelangelo*, 179–80. The reference to Paul III should read Clement VII and will be corrected in the forthcoming paperback edition of this book. E-mail communication of January 7, 2011, with the author.
[148] Dominique Cordellier, "L'Appartement sous la Galerie François Ier et les bains, avant 1540(?)–1543," and Laura Aldovini, "La Chute de Phaéton," in D. Cordellier et al., *Primatice: Maître de Fontainebleau*, ed. D. Cordellier, Exhibition catalog, Paris: Musée du Louvre, September 22, 2004–January 3, 2005 (Paris: Réunion des Musées Nationaux, 2004), 186–92 and 193.
[149] Kevin Brownlee, "Phaeton's Fall and Dante's Ascent," *Dante Studies* 102 (1984), 135–44, p. 137.

abyss by the spiraling pattern of the floor of the Anet chapel, while the dome above allows for the completion of the scene:

> On the right side Scylla, on the left implacable Charybdis
> threatens and three times into the deep whirl of the abyss
> it suddenly sucks a giant flood and again into the air
> spews it forth, and the wave lashes the stars. (*Aeneid* 3.420–3)[150]

Canto 12 of *Paradiso* begins with an extended simile of a ring dance of the planets that is readily accommodated by the spiraling pattern of the dome in the Anet chapel:

> No sooner had the blessed flame begun
> to speak its final word than the millstone
> of holy lights began to turn, but it
>   was not yet done with one full revolution
> before another ring surrounded it,
> and motion matched with motion, song with song – (*Paradiso* 12.1–6)

In Primaticcio's *Round Dance of the Hours*, the top three dancers are presented upside down, that is, in the pose of the falling Phaeton, but reversed into a movement upward toward the divine light. Instead of devastating the earth with fire and drought, these figures bestow abundance, as signaled by the cornucopia that each carries. Primaticcio presents here a pictorial anticipation of the more abstract experience that Delorme would convey with his dome. Both Primaticcio's painting and Delorme's architecture correspond to the heavenly vision of Dante's ring dance, while placing the French monarchy at the center of the cosmic order through the experience of the spatial and cosmological sublime and, at the same time, permitting the viewer to participate vicariously in the dance.

Finally, Delorme spoke the language of the sublime. In a study of the influence of modern publications about the sublime in France, beginning with Greek and Latin versions in the 1550s, Éva Madeleine Martin explains that the use of the words *émouvoir*, *étonner*, and *ravir* (to move, to astonish, and to ravish) furnish a "mounting scale of ... emotional experience," which are "hallmarks of the sublime."[151] In *Le Premier Tome de l'architecture* (1567), Delorme uses comparable terms in his discussion of the *trompe* (trumpet vault) at the Château d'Anet that carries the king's study, a small room called a *cabinet*, which seems miraculously "suspended in air." Like the pattern of the floor in the chapel, the shape of the trumpet vault is strongly warped; Delorme writes proudly of "this warping that is so strange," as well as lamenting that the weakness of the bracing walls did not permit him to "astonish" the spectator even more greatly (*beaucoup plus esbahy*) by making the form seem "the strangest and most difficult that I could have imagined." Imagining a vault carrying a spiraling stair constructed with the form of a *vis de Saint-Gilles* (twisting barrel vault), the surface of which would be finished with "coffers and moldings that are all rampant and thus offering a nonpareil image," Delorme explains the effect in terms that would also apply to the dome and the floor of the Anet chapel: watching the spectacle of the "entire work turn and warp would have shown it to be truly superb and very difficult to achieve." Such accomplishments in architecture are possible only to those who have mastered geometry, "the subtlest, the most ingenious, and the most inventive of all the disciplines," which permits the imagination to conceive "the most incredible things, so difficult to comprehend."[152]

---

[150] For this passage from Virgil, see Dante Alighieri, *The Divine Comedy. Volume 1. Inferno*, ed. and trans. Robert M. Durling, intro. and notes by Ronald L. Martinez and Robert M. Durling (New York: Oxford University Press, 1996), 121.

[151] See Martin, "The 'Prehistory' of the Sublime in Early Modern France," and Monk, *The Sublime*, 32.

[152] Philibert Delorme, *Le premier Tome de l'architecture* (Paris: Federic Morel, 1567), fols. 86–90v and 124–124v. Here Delorme anticipates the eighteenth-century use of "astonishment" and "amazement," terms that denote

MILTON AND BURKE

The story that began with Burke's definition of the artificial infinite comes full circle with Milton's literary sublime. We have seen how Ovid and Dante use the rhetorical strategy of amplification to convey the effect of the sublime through literary means; Hesiod and the anonymous author of the *Hypnerotomachia Poliphili* could supply similar examples. Ovid and Dante apply amplification to descriptions of moving through vast spaces; the *Theogony* and the *Hypnerotomachia Poliphili*, to the tumult of battle. In all cases, whether the movement is rushed or slow, the poet lingers over the tumult or the spatial expanse, amplifying his theme with ever-increasing images and lines. The result of this literary tour de force is analogous to the cumulative effect of succession in architecture explained later by Burke. Perhaps no poet excelled in this mode more than Milton, who, in *Paradise Lost*, extends amplification to book after book. In 1734 Jonathan Richardson identified this manner of lingering as Milton's particular accomplishment: "Then he goes not On Directly, but Lingers; giving an Idea of *Chaos* before he Enters into it. 'tis very Artfull!"[153]

Although Burke describes Milton in the *Enquiry* as "our great poet" (2.14.80) – he appears only briefly in the *Enquiry* – one wonders the degree to which the theory of the artificial infinite is a response to *Paradise Lost*, a poem, as Samuel Johnson remarks, whose "characteristic quality is sublimity," or, as Francesco Algarotti puts it more aptly, a gigantesque sublimity unique to Milton ("gigantesca sublimità Miltoniana"). Johnson understood that the expansiveness of what contemporaries termed "episodes" within the epic genre – which was a departure from the accepted notion that action should not be unduly interrupted[154] – constituted the source of Milton's sublimity:

> He seems to have been well acquainted with his own genius, and to know what it was that Nature had bestowed upon him more bountifully than upon others: the power of displaying the vast, illuminating the splendid, enforcing the awful, darkening the gloomy, and aggravating the dreadful: he therefore chose a subject on which too much could not be said, on which he might tire his fancy without the censure of extravagance.[155]

Here Johnson was explaining the nature of Milton's lingering, an achievement that did not escape the eye – and ear – of later critics. As T. S. Eliot would observe, "it is only in the period that the wave-length of Milton's verse is to be found.... The peculiar feeling, almost a physical sensation of a breathless leap, communicated by Milton's long periods, and by his alone, is impossible to procure from rhymed verse."[156] Note the psychophysiological aspect of the experience – "almost a physical sensation of a breathless leap" – that Eliot, with his sensitivity as a poet, perceives in Milton's verse without rhyme, which readily links it to the spatial and the architectural sublime.

In the very first book of *Paradise Lost*, Milton combines all three modes of the sublime: the spatial, cosmological, and architectural. "Hurl'd headlong from th'ethereal sky," Milton's Satan first contemplates his new abode, lingering through thirty-three lines of description, before

---

the experience of trying to grasp something barely comprehensible, and pleasure derived from the exultation of success. See Costelloe, "Imagination and Internal Sense."

[153] As quoted in Leslie Moore, *Beautiful Sublime: The Making of* Paradise Lost, *1701–1734* (Stanford, CA: Stanford University Press, 1990), 28.

[154] Here I am following Moore's discussion of episodes in *Beautiful Sublime*, 114–18, 130ff.

[155] For Algarotti and Johnson, see Samuel Johnson, *Lives of the English Poets* (1779), in John Milton, *Paradise Lost. Authoritative Text. Sources and Backgrounds. Criticism*, ed. Gordon Teskey (New York: W. W. Norton, 2005), 385.

[156] T. S. Eliot, "Milton II," *On Poetry and Poets* (1957), 157–8, as quoted in Christopher B. Ricks, *Milton's Grand Style* (Oxford: Clarendon Press, 1978 [1963]), 28. See also in Ricks the comment by Matthew Arnold.

Beelzebub will address him.[157] The passage recalls the fall of the Titans in Hesiod's *Theogony* but with an additional Ovidian flavor of place description, in which each myth is tied to a specific place:[158]

> Him the Almighty power
> Hurl'd headlong from th'ethereal sky,
> With hideous ruin and combustion down
> To bottomless perdition, there to dwell
> In adamantine chains and penal fire,
> ...
> Nine times the space that measures day and night
> To mortal men, he with his horrid crew
> Lay vanquish'd rolling in the fiery gulf
> ... he views
> The dismal situation waste and wild:
> A dungeon horrible, on all sides round,
> As one great furnace, flam'd: yet from those flames
> No light, but rather darkness visible,
> Serv'd only to discover sights of woe.
> ...
> As far removed from God and light of heaven
> As from the centre thrice to th'utmost pole.
> O how unlike the place from which they fell!
> There the companions of his fall, o'whelm'd
> With floods and whirlwinds of tempestuous fire (*Paradise Lost* 1.44–77)

After this exchange and before Satan calls his minions, Milton supplies another landscape account, lasting more than thirty lines (1.296–330). Satan's troops then assemble over a vast landscape, also fully described (1.340–55). The prodigious assembly of fallen angels – "a horrid front / Of dreadful length" (1.563–4) – is described in a way that suggests expansive space, and so forth.

Not only does Milton apply the rhetorical device of amplification extensively and effectively, but he also invokes the Golden House and, by implication, the Pantheon as part of his account of Satan establishing his abode in hell. Throughout sixty lines (1.670–730), Mammon opens "a spacious wound" in a hill, where he mines gold that Mulciber uses to construct Satan's palace; the architect enjoys his own twenty-one lines of temporal flashback, which ends in his being sent "headlong" out of heaven just as Hephaestus had been "thrown out of heaven by Zeus in Homer's *Iliad* 1.590–93"[159] and as had the Titans in Hesiod's Gigantomachy. At the end of the period, Mulciber lands just in time "with his industrious crew to build in hell" the palace. Called Pandemonium, this palace "rises, suddenly out of the deep" to afford a place for the council of "the infernal peers." Pandemonium's name indicates that it is not the Pantheon, the grand and sublime Roman temple to all the gods with the world's largest dome, but rather the "place of all demons," hence the obverse of the Pantheon, which in 609 had been consecrated as a Christian church and dedicated to the Virgin Mary and all martyrs, and whose dome was famously covered with gilt bronze tiles.[160] By prompting the reader to think of the Pantheon,

---

[157] John Milton, *Paradise Lost*, ed. David Hawkes (New York: Barnes and Noble Classics, 2004), 1.46–77 (*Paradiso*).
[158] On the link between myth and place in Ovid, see Stephen Hinds, "Landscape with Figures: Aesthetics of Place in the *Metamorphoses* and Its Tradition," in *The Cambridge Companion to Ovid*, ed. Philip Hardie (Cambridge: Cambridge University Press, 2002), 122–49.
[159] For the association with the *Iliad*, see John Milton, *Paradise Lost*, ed. Hawkes, 36, note to line 740.
[160] On the Pantheon, see Joost-Gaugier, *Measuring Heaven*, 167 and 310n6: Whereas the tiles were removed in 663, their existence was immortalized in the late twelfth-century *Mirabilia Urbis Romae*.

Milton effectively contrasts Satan's palace with Christ's temple. Like the Pantheon that it is not, Pandemonium is also vaulted:

> Anon out of the earth a huge fabric
> Rose like an exhalation, with the sound
> Of dulcet symphonies, and voices sweet,
> Built like a temple, where pilasters round
> Were set, and Doric pillars, overlaid
> With golden architrave: nor did there want
> Cornice, or frieze, with bossy sculptures graven;
> The roof was fretted gold.
> …Th'ascending pile
> Stood fixt her stately height: and straight the doors
> Op'ning their brazen folds, discover wide
> Within her ample space o'er the smooth
> And level pavement: *from the arched roof,*
> *Pendent by subtle magic*, many a row
> Of starry lamps, and blazing cressets, fed
> With Naptha and Asphaltus, yielded light,
> *As from a sky*. (1.710–30, my emphasis)

Built of gold, expansive in size, and furnished with a vast dome suspended in air "by subtle magic," Pandemonium evokes the Golden House of ancient Rome's wicked emperor, now appropriately associated with Satan. Milton's evocation of the Golden House is doubly significant, not only because it allows him to associate Satan with both Mammon and Nero – through a palace fitting in size for Satan's vast legions – but also because he understood that in architecture, the visual equivalent to the expansive spaces and falling angels of his verbal accounts of the spatial sublime could best be found in the floating dome of the architectural sublime.

CONCLUSION

The road, then, from Longinus to Burke and Boullée is richly paved with an unbroken development of the architectural sublime and with a literary tradition of amplification applied to both a cosmological and a spatial sublime. Boullée's efforts at the sublime owe much to this history, and the introduction to his treatise demonstrates that he considers the sublime as the highest end of art. His remark on the "intoxicating" writing of Lucretius reveals a familiarity with the literary tradition of the sublime (*Architecture* 55),[161] and his reference to Raphael's "sublime image of the Creator separating [light from] chaos" in the Vatican and repeated invocation of *fiat lux*[162] show his attentiveness to the painterly renditions of this quintessential theme in the sublime and the importance he attached to Longinus (*Architecture* 35, 55, and 91; see OS 9.22–3). In the Cenotaph to Newton, the spherical cavity might be understood as a Pantheistic rendition of the spherical volume that can be inscribed within the Pantheon, while allowing for an alternative experience of the sublime afforded by the Pantheon's dome. Boullée's use of the sarcophagus as the psychological anchor, as we have seen, may well have been inspired by Delorme's stable, central, colored marble disk placed amid the swirling black-and-white pattern on the floor of the chapel at the Château d'Anet. Although medieval architecture lies beyond the bounds of the present discussion, it should be noted that the floating effects of the vaults

---

[161] See Quint, "Fear of Falling," 847–81, who shows Milton's engagement with Lucretius, as well as with the vertiginous literary falls of Icarus and Phaeton.

[162] For a discussion of Boileau's elaboration on this passage in his 1674 French translation of Longinus, see Martin, "The 'Prehistory' of the Sublime in Early Modern France," chap. 6 of the current volume.

and dome in the Metropolitan Church project were inspired, as Boullée explains, by the floating effect of Gothic architecture, which gives the impression "that these buildings appear to support themselves miraculously," as if "by a supernatural power" (*Architecture* 91–2).[163] Indeed, Boullée's terminology of an "aerial" architecture derives as much from the lessons of Gothic cathedrals as it does from Delorme, who also spoke repeatedly of an architecture "suspended in air."[164]

In closing, we might apply Boullée's admiration for the Gothic to the entire tradition of the architectural sublime, for in all cases it was achieved through the "magic of art," thereby reflecting a "philosophical" approach to this field (*Architecture* 89, 95–6, and 185). Moreover, the experiential effect that Boullée hoped to achieve was what the architect Julien-David Leroy termed the "metaphysical" dimension of architecture.[165] In this way, these two Enlightenment artists situated the architectural sublime at the intersection of philosophy and, more particularly, of metaphysics and the bodily experience of aesthetics.

---

[163] For similar accounts by Boullée's contemporaries in preceding years, see Richard A. Etlin, *Symbolic Space: French Enlightenment Architecture and Its Legacy* (Chicago: University of Chicago Press, 1994), 116–18. The classic study of this theme is Robin D. Middleton, "The Abbé de Cordemoy and the Graeco-Gothic Ideal: A Prelude to Romantic Classicism," *Journal of the Warburg and Courtauld Institutes* 25, 3–4 (1962), 278–320, and 26, 1–2 (1963), 90–123.

[164] Delorme, *Le premier Tome de l'architecture*, fols. 88–90v.

[165] Julien-David Leroy, *Histoire de la disposition et des formes différentes que les Chrétiens ont données à leurs temples, depuis le règne de Constantin le Grand, jusqu'à nous* (Paris: Desaint and Saillant, 1764), 71, discussed in Etlin, *Symbolic Space*, 118–21.

Bibliography

Aa, A. J. van der. *Biographisch woordenboek der Nederlanden*. (Haarlem: J. J. van Brederode, 1852–1878).
Abaci, Uygar. "Kant's Justified Dismissal of Artistic Sublimity." *Journal of Aesthetics and Art Criticism* 66, 3 (2008), 237–51.
Abrams, Meyer H. *The Mirror and the Lamp: Romantic Theory and Critical Theory*. (Oxford: Oxford University Press, 1953).
Ackerman, James S. *The Architecture of Michelangelo*. (Harmondsworth: Penguin, 1970 [1961]).
Addis, William. *Building: 3000 Years of Design Engineering and Construction*. (London: Phaidon, 2007).
Addison, Joseph, and Richard Steele. *The Spectator*, ed. Donald F. Bond, 5 vols. (Oxford: Clarendon Press, 1965).
Adorno, Theodor W. *Aesthetic Theory*, trans. Robert Hullot-Kentor. (New York: Continuum, 1997).
  Ästhetische Theorie, ed. Gretel Adorno and Rolf Tiedemann. (Frankfurt am Main: Suhrkamp Verlag, 1970).
Akenside, Mark. *The Poetical Works of Mark Akenside*, ed. Robin Dix. (Madison, WI: Fairleigh Dickinson University Press, 1996).
Alexander, Samuel. *Art and the Material: The Adamson Lecture for 1925*. (Manchester: Manchester University Press, 1925).
  Beauty and Other Forms of Value. (New York: Crowell, 1968).
Alfrey, Shawn. "Against Calvary: Emily Dickinson and the Sublime." *Emily Dickinson Journal* 7, 2 (1998), 48–64.
Alison, Archibald. *Essays on the Nature and Principles of Taste*. (Dublin, 1790).
Altrocchi, Rudolph. "Michelino's Dante." *Speculum* 6, 1 (January 1931), 15–59.
Amyot, Jacques. "Épitre au roi." In *Les Œuvres Morales et Mêlées de Plutarque*, ed. and trans. J. Amyot. (Paris: Barthélemy Macé, 1587).
Aristotle. *Poetics*. In *The Complete Works of Aristotle*, ed. Jonathan Barnes. (Princeton, NJ: Princeton University Press, 1984), vol. 2.
Armstrong, A. H., ed. *Porphyry: Life of Plotinus*, Greek and English. In *Plotinus*, ed. A. H. Armstrong (Cambridge, MA: Harvard University Press, 1966), vol. 1.
Arnauld, Agnès. "Le chapelet secret du Saint-Sacrement" (1626), ed. Jean-Robert Armogathe. *XVIIe siècle* 170 (1991), 77–86.
Ashfield, Andrew, and Peter de Bolla, eds. *The Sublime: A Reader in British Eighteenth-Century Aesthetic Theory*. (Cambridge: Cambridge University Press, 1996).
Ashton, Dore. *About Rothko*, 2nd ed. (New York: Da Capo, 2003).
  Out of the Whirlwind: Three Decades of Art Commentary. (Ann Arbor, MI: UMI Research Press, 1987).
  The Unknown Shore: A View of Contemporary Art. (Boston: Little, Brown, 1962).
Asvarishch, Boris. "Friedrich's Russian Patrons." In *The Romantic Vision of Caspar David Friedrich: Paintings and Drawings from the U.S.S.R.*, ed. Sabine Rewald. (New York: Metropolitan Museum of Art, 1990), 19–40.

Avison, Charles. *Charles Avison's Essay on Musical Expression*, ed. Pierre Dubois. (Aldershot: Ashgate, 2004).
Axelsson, Karl. *The Sublime: Precursors and British Eighteenth Century Conceptions*. (Oxford: Peter Lang, 2007).
Bacon, Francis. "The Great Instauration." In *The Works of Francis Bacon*, collected and edited by James Spedding, Robert Leslie Ellis, and Douglas Denon Heath, 14 vols. (London: Longman, 1861–1879), vol. 4 (1861).
    The New Organon, ed. Lisa Jardine and Michael Silverthorne. (Cambridge: Cambridge University Press, 2000).
Baillie, John. *An Essay on the Sublime*. (London: R. Dodsley, 1747).
    "An Essay on the Sublime." In *The Sublime: A Reader in British Eighteenth-Century Aesthetic Theory*, ed. Andrew Ashfield and Peter de Bolla. (Cambridge: Cambridge University Press, 1996), 87–100.
Bakewell, Robert. *An Introduction to Geology: Intended to Convey a Practical Knowledge of the Science, and Comprising the Most Important Recent Discoveries; with Explanations of the Facts and Phenomena which Serve to Confirm or Invalidate Various Geological Theories*, ed. Benjamin Silliman. (New Haven, CT: Second American from the Fourth London Edition, 1833).
Ball, Larry F. *The Domus Aurea and the Roman Architectural Revolution*. (Cambridge: Cambridge University Press, 2003).
Balzac, Guez de. "À Corneille." In *Pierre Corneille, Cinna*, ed. Dominique Rabaud-Gouillart. (Paris: Classiques Larousse, 1990), 190–1.
    "Lettre à Chapelain." In *Oeuvres*, 2 vols. (Paris: Augustin Courbé, 1665), 2:736 and 857.
Bardon, Françoise. *Diane de Poitiers et le mythe de Diane*. (Paris: Presses universitaires de France, 1963).
Bartlett, Robert. *The Natural and the Supernatural in the Middle Ages*. (Cambridge: Cambridge University Press, 2008).
Bartram, William. *Travels Through North & South Carolina, Georgia, East & West Florida, the Cherokee Country, the Extensive Territories of the Muscogulges, or Creek Confederacy, and the Country of the Chactaws; Containing an Account of the Soil and Natural Productions of Those Regions, Together with Observations on the Manners of the Indians*. (Philadelphia: James & Johnson, 1791).
Battersby, Christine. *The Sublime, Terror and Human Difference*. (London: Routledge, 2007).
Batteux, Charles. *Batteux' Einschränkung der Schöne Kunst aus einen einzigen Grundsatz*, trans. J. A. Schlegel. (Leipzig: Weidmann, 1751).
    Die Schöne Kunst aus einem Grunde Hergeleitet, trans. anonymous. (Gotha: J. P. Mervius, 1751).
    Les beaux arts réduits à un même principe. (Paris: Chez Durand, 1746).
    Les beaux arts réduits à un même principe: Collection Théorie et critique à l'âge classique, ed. Jean-Rémy Mantion (Paris: Aux Amateurs de livres, 1989), vol. 2.
    The Polite Arts, or, A Dissertation on Poetry, Painting, Music, Architecture, and Eloquence, ed. and trans. anonymous. (London: J. Osborn, 1749).
Battisti, Eugenio. "Conformismo ed eccentricità in Giulio Romano come artista di corte." In *Giulio Romano. Atti del Convegno Internazionale di Studi su "Giulio Romano e l'espansione europea del Rinascimento." Mantova, Palazzo Ducale, Teatro scientifico del Bibiena, 1–5 ottobre 1989*. (Mantua: Accademia Nazionale Virgiliana, 1989), 21–43.
Baumgarten, Alexander Gottlieb. *Aesthetica/Ästhetik*, Latin text edited with facing German translation by Dagmar Mirbach, 2 vols. (Hamburg: Felix Meiner Verlag, 2007 [1750/1758]).
    Meditationes philosophicae de nonnullis ad poema pertinentibus/Philosophische Betrachtungen über einige Bedingungen des Gedichtes, ed. Heinz Paetzold. (Hamburg: Felix Meiner Verlag, 1983 [1735]).
    Reflections on Poetry: Alexander Gottlieb Baumgarten's Meditationes philosophicae de nonnullis ad poema pertinentibus, trans. Karl Aschenbrenner and William B. Holther. (Berkeley: University of California Press, 1954).
Beattie, James. *Dissertations Moral and Critical* (1783). In *The Sublime: A Reader in Eighteenth-Century Aesthetic Theory*, ed. Andrew Ashfield and Peter de Bolla. (Cambridge: Cambridge University Press, 1996), 180–94.
    Essays on Poetry and Music as They Affect the Mind. (London: Dilly, 1776).
Bedell, Rebecca. "Thomas Cole and the Fashionable Science." *Huntington Library Quarterly* 59, 2–3 (1996), 349–78.

Béguin, Sylvie. "Giulio Romano et l'École de Fontainebleau." In *Giulio Romano. Atti del Convegno Internazionale di Studi su "Giulio Romano e l'espansione europea del Rinascimento." Mantova, Palazzo Ducale, Teatro scientifico del Bibiena, 1–5 ottobre 1989*. (Mantua: Accademia Nazionale Virgiliana, 1989), 45–74.

Béguin, Sylvie, et al. *La Galerie d'Ulysse à Fontainebleau*. (Paris: Presses universitaires de France, 1985).

Beiser, Frederick. *Schiller as Philosopher: A Re-Examination*. (Oxford: Clarendon Press, 2005).

Berleant, Arnold. "The Aesthetics of Art and Nature." In *Landscape, Natural Beauty and the Arts*, ed. Salim Kemal and Ivan Gaskell. (Cambridge: Cambridge University Press, 1993), 228–43.

Aesthetics of Environment. (Philadelphia: Temple University Press, 1992).

Berlin, Isaiah. *The Roots of Romanticism*. (London: Chatto and Windus, 1999).

Bevis, Richard W. *The Road to Egdon Heath: The Aesthetics of the Great in Nature*. (Quebec: McGill-Queen's Press, 1999).

Bhagavad-Gita, trans. Barbara Stoler-Miller. (New York: Columbia University Press, 1987).

The Bible, Authorized King James Version with Apocrypha, ed. Robert Carroll and Stephen Prickett. (Oxford: Oxford University Press, 1997).

The Bible, New International Version. (London: Hodder and Stoughton, 2008).

Blair, Hugh. *Lectures on Rhetoric and Belles Lettres*, ed. Harold F. Harding, 2 vols. (Carbondale: Southern Illinois University Press, 1965).

Blake, William. "There Is No Natural Religion." In *Blake's Poetry and Designs*, ed. Mary Lynn Johnson and John E. Grant. (New York: W. W. Norton, 1979).

Blanc, Charles. *Grammaire des arts du dessin*. (Paris: Veuve Jules Renouard, 1867).

Bloch, Ruth H. *Visionary Republic: Millennial Themes in American Thought, 1756–1800*. (Cambridge: Cambridge University Press, 1985).

Blunt, Anthony. *Philibert Delorme*. (London: A. Zwemmer, 1958).

Boileau Despréaux, Nicolas. "Épitres." In *Oeuvres complètes* (Paris: Firmin Didot Frères, 1837; Elibron Classics Replica, 2007), 219–40.

L'art poétique. In *Oeuvres complètes* (Paris: Firmin Didot Frères, 1837; Elibron Classics Replica, 2007), 241–52.

Traité du sublime ou du merveilleux dans le discours. In *Oeuvres complètes* (Paris: Firmin Didot Frères, 1837; Elibron Classics Replica, 2007), 316–48.

Bonth, R. J. G. de. *De Aristarch van 't Y: De "grammatica" uit Balthazar Huydecopers Proeve van Taal- en Dichtkunde (1730)*. (Maastricht: Shaker, 1998).

Borgerhoff, E. B. O. *The Freedom of French Classicism*. (Princeton, NJ: Princeton University Press, 1950).

Borghini, Raffaello. *Il riposo*, trans. Lloyd H. Ellis, Jr. (Toronto: University of Toronto Press, 2008).

Bork, G. J. van, and P. J. Verkruijsse, eds. *De Nederlandse en Vlaamse auteurs van middeleeuwen tot heden*. (Weesp: De Haan, 1985).

Borsi, Stefano. *Giuliano da Sangallo: i disegni di architettura e dell'antico*. (Rome: Officina, 1985).

Boullée, Étienne-Louis. *Architecture: Essai sur l'art*, ed. Jean-Marie Pérouse de Montclos. (Paris: Hermann, 1968).

Brady, Emily. *Aesthetics of the Natural Environment*. (Edinburgh: Edinburgh University Press, 2003).

"Reassessing Aesthetic Appreciation of Nature in the Kantian Sublime." *Journal of Aesthetic Education* 46, 1 (2012), 91–109.

Brandt, Reinhard. "The Guiding Idea of Kant's Anthropology and the Vocation of the Human Being." In *Essays on Kant's Anthropology*, ed. Brian Jacobs and Patrick Kain. (Cambridge: Cambridge University Press, 2003), 85–104.

Bremond, Henri. *Histoire littéraire du sentiment religieux*. (Paris: Bloud et Gay, 1926), vol. 3.

Brody, Jules. *Boileau and Longinus*. (Geneva: Droz, 1958).

Brown, Chandos Michael. *Benjamin Silliman: A Life in the Young Republic*. (Princeton, NJ: Princeton University Press, 1989).

"Mary Wollstonecraft, or, the Female Illuminati: The Campaign Against Women and the 'Modern Philosophy' in the Early Republic." *Journal of the Early Republic*, Special Issue on Gender in the Early Republic, 15, 3 (1995), 389–424.

"Scientific Inquiry: The British Colonies." In *Encyclopedia of the North American Colonies*, ed. Jacob Ernest Cooke. (New York: Scribner, 1993), 3:165–75.
Brownlee, Kevin. "Phaeton's Fall and Dante's Ascent." *Dante Studies* 102 (1984), 135–44.
Brückner, Martin. *The Geographical Revolution in Early America: Maps, Literacy, and National Identity*. (Chapel Hill: Published for the Omohndro Institute of Early American History and Culture, Williamsburg, VA, by the University of North Carolina Press, 2006).
Bryant, William Cullen. "The Prairies." In *Poems*, 5th ed. (New York, 1840).
Budd, Malcolm. *The Aesthetic Appreciation of Nature*. (Oxford: Oxford University Press, 2002).
Buddensieg, T. "Criticism and Praise of the Pantheon in the Middle Ages and the Renaissance." In *Classical Influences on European Culture, A.D. 500–1500*, ed. R. R. Bolgar. (Cambridge: Cambridge University Press, 1971), 259–67.
"Criticism of Ancient Architecture in the Sixteenth and Seventeenth Centuries." In *Classical Influences on European Culture, A.D. 1500–1700*, ed. R. R. Bolgar. (Cambridge: Cambridge University Press, 1976), 335–48.
Bullough, Edward. "Psychical Distance." *British Journal of Psychology* 5 (1912), 87–117.
Bultmann, Rudolf. *New Testament and Mythology and Other Basic Writings*, ed. and trans. Schubert M. Ogden. (Philadelphia: Fortress Press, 1984).
Bungay, Stephen. *Beauty and Truth: A Study of Hegel's Aesthetics*. (Oxford: Oxford University Press, 1987).
Burke, Edmund. *A Philosophical Enquiry into the Origin of Our Ideas of the Sublime and Beautiful*, ed. James T. Boulton. (London: Routledge and Kegan Paul, 1958 [1759, 1st ed. 1757]).
Burke, Peter. *The Fabrication of Louis XIV*. (New Haven, CT: Yale University Press, 1994).
Bury, Emmanuel. *Le classicisme*. (Paris: Nathan, 1993).
Byron, Lord, George Gordon. *Byron's Poetical Works*, ed. Frederick Page; rev. John Jump. (Oxford: Oxford University Press, 1970).
Caesar, Michael, ed. *Dante: The Critical Heritage: 1314–1870*. (London: Routledge, 1989).
Çakmak, Ahmet Ş., Rabun M. Taylor, and Eser Durukal, "The Structural Configuration of the First Dome of Justinian's Hagia Sophia (A.D. 537–558): An Investigation Based on Structural Analysis and Literary Analysis." *Soil Dynamics and Earthquake Engineering* 29 (2009), 693–8.
Carey, Daniel. *Locke, Shaftesbury, and Hutcheson: Contesting Diversity in the Enlightenment and Beyond*. (Cambridge: Cambridge University Press, 2006).
Carlson, Allen. *Aesthetics and the Environment*. (New York: Routledge, 2000).
"Environmental Aesthetics." *Stanford Encyclopedia of Philosophy* (2007). http://plato.stanford.edu/entries/enviromental-aesthetics (accessed June 30, 2010).
Cassius Dio Cocceianus. *The History of Dion Cassius. Abridg'd by Xiphilin. Containing the Most Remarkable Passages under the Roman Emperors, from the Time of Pompey the Great, to the Reign of Alexander Severus*, trans. Francis Manning, 2 vols. (London: A. and J. Churchill, 1704).
Catalogue of Books, Sold by Noel and Hazard, at Their Book and Stationary Store, Next Door to the Merchants Coffee-House, Where the Public May Be Furnished with All Sorts of Books and Paper. [New York, 1772].
Catalogue of Books, to Be Sold, by Public Auction, at the City Vendue-Store, in Front-Street. [Philadelphia, 1769].
Cave, Terence. "Mimesis of Reading in the Renaissance." In *Mimesis: From Mirror to Method*, ed. John D. Lyons. (Aurora, CO: Davies Group, 2004).
Champlin, Edward. *Nero*. (Cambridge, MA: Harvard University Press, 2003).
Chantal, Jeanne de. *Oeuvres*. (Paris: Plon, 1875).
Chaplin, Joyce. *Subject Matter: Technology, the Body, and Science on the Anglo-American Frontier, 1500–1676*. (Cambridge, MA: Harvard University Press, 2001).
Chave, Anna C. *Mark Rothko: Subjects in Abstraction*. (New Haven, CT: Yale University Press, 1989).
Clark, A. F. B. *Boileau and the French Classical Critics in England*. (New York: Russell & Russell, 1965).
Clements, Robert J. "Marguerite de Navarre and Dante." *Italica* 18, 2 (1941), 37–50.
Clewis, Robert R. "A Case for Kantian Artistic Sublimity: A Response to Abaci." *Journal of Aesthetics and Art Criticism* 68, 2 (2010), 167–70.

The Kantian Sublime and the Revelation of Freedom. (Cambridge: Cambridge University Press, 2009).
Cohen, I. Bernard. *Science and the Founding Fathers: Science in the Political Thought of Thomas Jefferson, Benjamin Franklin, John Adams, and James Madison.* (New York: W. W. Norton, 1995).
Cohn, Jan, and Thomas H. Miles. "The Sublime: In Alchemy, Aesthetics and Psychoanalysis." *Modern Philology* 74, 3 (1977), 289–304.
Cole, Michael W. *Cellini and the Principles of Sculpture.* (Cambridge: Cambridge University Press, 2002).
Cole, Thomas. "Essay on American Scenery." *American Magazine*, New Series, Vol. I, January 1836. (Boston and New York, 1836).
Coleridge, Samuel Taylor. *On the Sublime*, ed. David Vallins. (Houndsmill, Hampshire: Palgrave Macmillan, 2003).
Collingwood, R. G. *The Principles of Art.* (Oxford: Oxford University Press, 1938).
Conihout, Isabelle de, and Patrick Michel, eds. *Mazarin, les lettres et les arts.* (Paris: Monelle Hayot, 2006).
Connor, Carolyn L. "The Epigram in the Church of Hagios Polyeuktos in Constantinople and Its Byzantine Response." *Byzantion* 69 (1999), 479–527.
Cooper, Anthony Ashley, third Earl of Shaftesbury. *Characteristicks of Men, Manners, Opinions, Times*, 3 vols. (Indianapolis, IN: Liberty Fund, 2001 [1711]).
Cooper, David E. *The Measure of Things: Humanism, Humility and Mystery.* (Oxford: Clarendon Press, 2002).
Cooper, James Fenimor. *The Prairie: A Tale*, ed. James P. Elliott. (Albany: State University of New York Press, 1985).
Cordellier, D., et al. *Primatice: Maître de Fontainebleau*, ed. D. Cordellier. Exhibition catalog, Paris: Musée du Louvre, September 22, 2004–January 3, 2005. (Paris: Réunion des Musées Nationaux, 2004).
Cosgrove, Denis. *Social Formation and Symbolic Landscape.* (London: Croom Helm, 1984).
Costelloe, Timothy M. *The British Aesthetic Tradition: From Shaftesbury to Wittgenstein.* (Cambridge: Cambridge University Press, forthcoming).
Croce, Benedetto. *The Aesthetic as the Science of Expression and of the Linguistic in General*, trans. Colin Lyas. (Cambridge: Cambridge University Press, 1992).
Crockett, Clayton. *A Theology of the Sublime.* (New York: Routledge, 2001).
Cronk, Nicholas. *The Classical Sublime: French Neoclassicism and the Language of Literature.* (Charlottesville, VA: Rockwood, 2002).
Cronon, William. "The Trouble with Wilderness; or, Getting Back to the Wrong Kind of Nature." In *Uncommon Ground: Rethinking the Human Place in Nature*, ed. William Cronon. (New York: W. W. Norton, 1996), 69–90.
Crotch, William. *Substance of Several Courses of Lectures on Music.* (London: Longman, Rees, Orme, Brown, and Green, 1831); reprint, ed. Bernarr Rainbow. (Clarabricken: Boethius Press, 1986).
Crowther, Paul. *The Kantian Sublime: From Morality to Art.* (Oxford: Clarendon Press, 1989).
d'Alembert, Jean le Rond. "Discours préliminaire." In *Encyclopédie, ou dictionnaire raisonné des sciences, des arts et des métiers*, ed. Denis Diderot and Jean le Rond d'Alembert. (Paris: Briasson, David, Le Breton, Durand, 1751), I:i–xlv.
Dante Alighieri. *The Divine Comedy. I. Inferno*, trans. John D. Sinclair. (New York: Oxford University Press, 1961).
The Divine Comedy, trans. Allen Mandelbaum. (New York: Everyman's Library / Alfred A. Knopf, 1995).
The Divine Comedy. Volume 1. Inferno, ed. and trans. Robert M. Durling; intro. and notes by Ronald L. Martinez and Robert M. Durling. (New York: Oxford University Press, 1996).
Danto, Arthur C. *After the End of Art: Contemporary Art and the Pale of History.* (Princeton, NJ: Princeton University Press, 1997).
"The End of Art." In *The Philosophical Disenfranchisement of Art.* (New York: Columbia University Press, 1986).
Davies, Brian. *The Thought of Thomas Aquinas.* (Oxford: Clarendon Press, 1993).
de Bolla, Peter. *The Discourse of the Sublime: Readings in History, Aesthetics, and the Subject.* (Oxford: Blackwell, 1989).

The Education of the Eye: Painting, Landscape, and Architecture in Eighteenth Century Britain. (Stanford, CA: Stanford University Press, 2003).

Delehanty, Anne T. "From Judgment to Sentiment: Changing Theories of the Sublime, 1674–1710." *Modern Language Quarterly* 66 (2005), 151–72.

Deleuze, Gilles. *Cinéma 1: L'Image-mouvement.* (Paris: Éditions de Minuit, 1983); *Cinema 1: The Movement-Image,* trans. Hugh Tomlinson and Barbara Habberjam. (Minneapolis: University of Minnesota Press, 1986).

Coldness and Cruelty. (New York: Zone, 1991).

Différence et Répétition. (Paris: Presses Universitaires de France, 1968); *Difference and Repetition,* trans. Paul Patton. (New York: Columbia University Press, 1994).

Francis Bacon: Logique de la sensation, 2 vols. (Paris: Éditions de la Différence, 1981); *Francis Bacon: The Logic of Sensation,* trans. Daniel W. Smith. (Minneapolis: University of Minnesota Press, 2003).

La Philosophie critique de Kant. (Paris: Presses Universitaires de France, 1963); *Kant's Critical Philosophy,* trans. Hugh Tomlinson and Barbara Habberjam. (London: Athlone Press, 1984).

"L'Idée de genèse dans l'esthétique de Kant." *Revue d'esthétique* XVI, 2 (1963), 113–36; "The Idea of Genesis in Kant's Esthetics," trans. Michael Taormina. In *Desert Islands and Other Texts,* ed. David Lapoujade. (New York: Semiotext(e), 2002), 56–71.

Seminar on Immanuel Kant, 3/28/1978, trans. Melissa McMahon. http://www.webdeleuze.com/php/texte.php?cle=68&groupe=Kant&langue=2 (accessed June 18, 2011).

Deleuze, Gilles, and Félix Guattari. *Mille Plateaux.* (Paris: Éditions de Minuit, 1980); *A Thousand Plateaus,* trans. Brian Massumi. (Minneapolis: University of Minnesota Press, 1987).

Deliyannis, Deborah Mauskopf. *Ravenna in Late Antiquity.* (Cambridge: Cambridge University Press, 2010).

Delorme, Philibert. *Le premier Tome de l'architecture.* (Paris: Federic Morel, 1567).

de Man, Paul. "Hegel on the Sublime." In *Aesthetic Ideology,* ed. Andrzej Warminski. (Minneapolis: University of Minnesota Press, 1996), 105–118.

"Phenomenality and Materiality in Kant." In *Aesthetic Ideology,* ed. Andrzej Warminski. (Minneapolis: University of Minnesota Press, 1996), 70–90.

Dennis, John. *Remarks of a Book Entitled, Prince Arthur* (1696). In *The Sublime: A Reader in Eighteenth-Century Aesthetic Theory,* ed. Andrew Ashfield and Peter de Bolla. (Cambridge: Cambridge University Press, 1996), 30–1.

Derrida, Jacques. *La Vérité en peinture.* (Paris: Flammarion, 1978); *The Truth in Painting,* trans. Geoffrey Bennington and Ian McLeod. (Chicago: University of Chicago Press, 1987).

Descartes, René. "Les passions de l'âme." In *Oeuvres,* ed. André Bridoux. (Paris: Gallimard, La Pléiade, 1953), 695–802.

"Description de la belle maison d'Anet, veu le mardy seconde feste de la Pentecoste 29 mai 1640." Bibliothèque Nationale de France. Manuscripts, Fonds Dupuy 550, fols. 198–202.

Desmond, William. *Art and the Absolute: A Study of Hegel's Aesthetics.* (Albany: State University of New York Press, 1986).

des Places, Édouard. *Numénius: Fragments,* Greek and French. (Paris: Les Belles Lettres, 1973).

de Tocqueville, Alexis. *Democracy in America,* trans. Henry Reeve. (New York, 1838).

Doueihi, Milad. "The Politics of Simplicity." *Modern Language Notes,* 107 (1992), 639–58.

Dunlop, Anne. "'El Vostro Poeta': The First Florentine Printing of Dante's *Commedia.*" *RACAR* 20, 1–2 (1993), 29–42.

Dwight, Timothy. *The Duty of Americans: At the Present Crisis, Illustrated in a Discourse, Preached on the Fourth of July, 1798.* (New Haven, CT, 1798).

Edwards, James. *The Plain Sense of Things.* (University Park: Pennsylvania State University Press, 1997).

Edwards, Jonathan. *A Treatise Concerning Religious Affections,* ed. John E. Smith. In *The Works of Jonathan Edwards,* 26 vols. (New Haven, CT: Yale University Press, 1959 [1746]), vol. 2.

Eisentein, Elizabeth L. *The Printing Revolution in Early Modern Europe.* (Cambridge: Cambridge University Press, 1983).

Eliot, George. *Felix Holt, the Radical,* ed. Fred C. Thomson. (Oxford: Oxford University Press, 1980).

Elkins, James. "Against the Sublime." In *Beyond the Finite: The Sublime in Art and Science*, ed. Roald Hoffman and Iain Boyd White. (Oxford: Oxford University Press, 2011).
Elledge, Scott, and Donald Schier, eds. *The Continental Model: Selected French Critical Essays of the Seventeenth Century, in English Translation*. (Ithaca, NY: Cornell University Press, 1970).
Emerson, Ralph W. "Over-Soul." In *Essays: First Series*. (Boston: James Munroe, 1850 [1841]).
Entrikin, Nicholas. "Afterword: The Unhandselled Globe." In *High Places: Geographies of Mountains, Ice and Science*, ed. Denis Cosgrove and Veronica Della Dora. (London: I.B. Tauris, 2009), 216–25.
Etlin, Richard A. "Aesthetics and the Spatial Sense of Self." *Journal of Aesthetics and Art Criticism*, 56, 1 (1998), 1–19.
  "Death in the Enchanted Palace: Philibert Delorme's Château d'Anet," archived webcast lecture, Bernard and Anne Spitzer School of Architecture, City College of New York, March 17, 2011. http://www.totalwebcasting.com/view/?id=ccnyssa.
  Modernism in Italian Architecture, 1890–1940. (Cambridge, MA: MIT Press, 1991).
  "The Pantheon in the Modern Era." In *The Pantheon*, ed. Todd Marder and Mark Wilson Jones. (Cambridge: Cambridge University Press, 2013).
  "The Parthenon in the Modern Era." In *The Parthenon: From Antiquity to the Present*, ed. Jenifer Neils. (Cambridge: Cambridge University Press, 2005), 362–95.
  "St. Peter's in the Modern Era: The Paradoxical Colossus." In *St. Peter's in the Vatican*, ed. William Tronzo. (Cambridge: Cambridge University Press, 2005), 270–304.
  Symbolic Space: French Enlightenment Architecture and Its Legacy. (Chicago: University of Chicago Press, 1994).
Fallacara, Giuseppe. "Philibert Delorme e l'*invenzione*." In Philibert Delorme, *Nouvelles inventions pour bien bastir et à petits fraiz*, ed. and trans. Maria Rita Campa. (Bari: Poliba, 2009), 129–45.
Feith, Rhijnvis. *Het Ideaal in de kunst*, ed. P. J. Buijnsters, 2nd rev. ed. (Den Haag: Martinus Nijhoff, 1979).
Ferguson, Frances. *Solitude and the Sublime: Romanticism and the Aesthetics of Individuation*. (New York: Routledge, 1992).
Force, Pierre. *Le problème herméneutique chez Pascal*. (Paris: Librairie Philosophique J. Vrin, 1989).
Forster, Kurt W., and Richard J. Tuttle. "The Palazzo del Te." *Journal of the Society of Architectural Historians* 30, 4 (1971), 267–93.
Franklin, Wayne. *James Fenimore Cooper: The Early Years*. (New Haven, CT: Yale University Press, 2007).
Freeman, Barbara Claire. *The Feminine Sublime: Gender and Excess in Women's Fiction*. (Berkeley: University of California Press, 1995).
Friederich, Werner P. *Dante's Fame Abroad, 1350–1850*. (Rome: Edizioni di Storia e Letteratura, 1950).
Fumaroli, Marc. "Crépuscule de l'enthousiasme." In *Héros et orateurs: rhétorique et dramaturgie cornéliennes*. (Geneva: Droz, 1990), 349–77.
  L'age de l'éloquence. (Geneva: Droz, 1980).
  "L'inspiration du poète de Poussin et l'allégorie du Parnasse." *Revue du Louvre et des Musées de France* 3 (1989), 194.
  "Rhétorique d'école et rhétorique adulte." *Revue d'histoire littéraire de la France* 86, 1 (1986), 33–51.
Gadamer, Hans-Georg. *Truth and Method*, trans. Joel Weinsheimer and Donald G. Marshall, 2nd ed. (London: Continuum, 2004).
Gallet, Michel. "L'Orme, Philibert de." *Praeger Encyclopedia of Art* (New York: Praeger, 1971), vol. 3.
Gallucci, Margaret A. *Benvenuto Cellini: Sexuality, Masculinity, and Artistic Identity in Renaissance Italy*. (New York: Palgrave Macmillan, 2003).
Geel, Jacob. *Gesprek op den Drachenfels: Een dialoog uit 1835 over de literatuur in de negentiende eeuw*, ed. J. C. Brandt Corstius. (Amsterdam: Atheneum-Polak & Van Gennep, 1968).
  Onderzoek en Phantasie. (Leiden: Van der Hoek, 1838).
Gerard, Alexander. *An Essay on Taste*. (London, 1759).
  An Essay on Taste, 3rd ed. (Edinburgh, 1780 [1759]); reprint, ed. Walter J. Hipple, Jr. (Gainesville, FL: Scholars' Facsimiles and Reprints, 1963).
Gethmann-Seifert, Annemarie. *Einführung in Hegels Ästhetik*. (Munich: Wilhelm Fink Verlag, 2005).
Gilby, Emma. *Sublime Worlds: Early Modern French Literature*. (Oxford: Legenda, 2006).

Gilby, Emma, ed. *Pseudo-Longin, "De la sublimité du discours."* (Chambéry: L'Act Mem, 2007).
Glare, P. G. W., ed. *Oxford Latin Dictionary*. (Oxford: Oxford University Press, 1983).
Godlovitch, Stan. "Icebreakers: Environmentalism and Natural Aesthetics." *Journal of Applied Philosophy* 11, 1 (1994), 15–30.
The Gospel of Thomas: The Hidden Sayings of Jesus, trans. and ed. Marvin Meyer. (San Francisco: Harper, 1992).
Gosse, E. *Gray*. (London: Macmillan, 1902 [1882]).
Goyet, Francis, ed. *Longin, Traité du sublime, trad. par Nicolas Boileau (1674)*. (Paris: LGF, Le Livre de Poche, 1995).
Grimm, C. L. W. *Clavis Novi Testamenti*. (Leipzig: Libraria Arnoldiana, 1879).
Guyer, Paul. "Eighteenth Century German Aesthetics." *Stanford Encyclopedia of Philosophy* (2007). http://plato.stanford.edu/entries/aesthetics-18th-german (accessed July 3, 2010).
  "The Harmony of the Faculties Revisited." In *Values of Beauty: Historical Essays in Aesthetics*. (Cambridge: Cambridge University Press, 2005), 77–109.
  Kant and the Experience of Freedom: Essays on Aesthetics and Morality. (Cambridge: Cambridge University Press, 1996).
  "The Origins of Modern Aesthetics: 1711–35." In *The Blackwell Guide to Aesthetics*, ed. Peter Kivy. (Oxford: Blackwell, 2004), 15–44.
  "Symbols of Freedom in Kant's Aesthetics." In *Values of Beauty: Historical Essays in Aesthetics* (Cambridge: Cambridge University Press, 2005), 222–41.
Hache, Sophie. *La langue du ciel: Le sublime en France au XVIIe siècle*, ed. Philippe Sellier. (Paris: Champion, 2000).
Haidu, P. "The Dialectics of Unspeakability." In *Probing the Limits of Representation*, ed. Saul Friedlander. (Cambridge, MA: Harvard University Press, 1992).
Hailwood, Simon. "The Value of Nature's Otherness." *Environmental Values* 9 (2000), 353–72.
[Hall, John]. *Peri Hupsous, or Dionysius Longinus of the Height of Eloquence Rendred out of the Originall by J[ohn] H[all]. Esq.* (London, 1652).
Halliwell, Stephen. *The Aesthetics of Mimesis: Ancient Texts and Modern Problems*. (Princeton, NJ: Princeton University Press, 2002).
Halttunen, Karen. *Confidence Men and Painted Women: A Study of Middle-Class Culture in America, 1830–1870*. (New Haven, CT: Yale University Press, 1982).
Hamilton, William. *Works of Sir William Hamilton*, 7 vols. (London, 1859).
Hammermeister, Kai. *The German Aesthetic Tradition*. (Cambridge: Cambridge University Press, 2002).
Hardy, Thomas. "The Return of the Native." *Belgravia Magazine* 34 (January 1878), 257–508.
Hart, Henry. "Robert Lowell and the Religious Sublime." *New England Review* 14, 1 (1991), 27–47.
Hartman, Geoffrey. *Wordsworth's Poetry 1787–1814*. (New Haven, CT: Yale University Press, 1964).
Heath, Malcolm. *Ancient Philosophical Poetics*. (Cambridge: Cambridge University Press, 2012).
  "Caecilius, Longinus and Photius." *Greek, Roman and Byzantine Studies* 39 (1998), 271–92.
  "Longinus *On Sublimity*." *Proceedings of the Cambridge Philological Society* 45 (1999), 43–74.
  "Longinus *On Sublimity* 35.1." *Classical Quarterly* 50 (2000), 320–3.
  Menander: A Rhetor in Context. (Oxford: Oxford University Press, 2004).
  "Platonists and the Teaching of Rhetoric in Late Antiquity." In *Late Antique Epistemology: Other Ways to Truth*, ed. Panayiota Vassilopoulou and Stephen R. L. Clark. (London: Palgrave Macmillan, 2009), 143–59.
Hegel, G. W. F. *Aesthetics: Lectures on Fine Art*, trans. T. M. Knox, 2 vols. (Oxford: Clarendon Press, 1975).
  Elements of the Philosophy of Right, trans. H. B. Nisbet; ed. Allen W. Wood. (Cambridge: Cambridge University Press, 1991 [1821]).
Heller, Agnes. *Renaissance Man*. (Boston: Routledge & Kegan Paul, 1984).
Hepburn, Ronald W. "The Concept of the Sublime: Has It Any Relevance for Philosophy Today?" *Dialectics and Humanism* 15 (1988), 137–55.
"Contemporary Aesthetics and the Neglect of Natural Beauty." In *Wonder and Other Essays: Eight Studies in Aesthetics and Neighbouring Fields*. (Edinburgh: Edinburgh University Press, 1984), 9–35.

"Landscape and Metaphysical Imagination." *Environmental Values* 5 (1996), 191–204.
"Mystery in an Aesthetic Context." Manuscript read to the Philosophy Department Research Seminar, University of Durham, 2003.
"Nature Humanised: Nature Respected." *Environmental Values* 7 (1998), 267–79.
The Reach of the Aesthetic. (Aldershot: Ashgate, 2001).
"Trivial and Serious in Aesthetic Appreciation of Nature." In *Landscape, Natural Beauty and the Arts*, ed. Salim Kemal and Ivan Gaskell. (Cambridge: Cambridge University Press, 1993), 65–80.
Herbert, Sir Thomas. *Some Yeares Travels into Divers Parts of Asia and Afrique, Describing Especially the Two Famous Empires the Persian and Great Mogull Weaved with the History of These Later Time, &c.*, 2nd ed. (London, 1638 [1634]).
Hertz, Neil. "The Notion of Blockage in the Literature of the Sublime." In *The End of the Line: Essays on Psychoanalysis and the Sublime*. (New York: Columbia University Press, 1985), 40–60.
Hetland, Lisa M. "Dating the Pantheon." *Journal of Roman Archaeology* 20 (2007), 95–112.
Hinds, Stephen. "Landscape with Figures: Aesthetics of Place in the *Metamorphoses* and Its Tradition." In *The Cambridge Companion to Ovid*, ed. Philip Hardie. (Cambridge: Cambridge University Press, 2002), 122–49.
Hipple, Walter J., Jr. *The Beautiful, the Sublime, and the Picturesque in Eighteenth-Century British Aesthetic Theory*. (Carbondale: Southern Illinois University Press, 1957).
Hitt, Christopher. "Toward an Ecological Sublime." *New Literary History* 30, 3 (1999), 603–23.
Hodder, Alan D. *Thoreau's Ecstatic Witness*. (New Haven, CT: Yale University Press, 2001).
Hoffmann, E. T. A. "Beethoven's Instrumental Music." In *Source Readings in Music History*, ed. William Oliver Strunk and Leo Treitler; trans. William Oliver Strunk, 2nd ed. (New York: W. W. Norton, 1998), 1193–8.
Hoffmann, Volker. "Donec Totum Impleat Orbem: Symbolisme impérial au temps de Henri II." *Bulletin de la Société de l'Histoire de l'art français*, année 1978 (1980), 29–42.
"Philibert Delorme und das Schloss Anet." *Architectura* 2 (1973), 131–52.
Hogarth, William. *The Analysis of Beauty*, ed. Ronald Paulson. (New Haven, CT: Yale University Press, 1997 [1753]).
Holbrook, Richard Thayer. *Portraits of Dante from Giotto to Raffael: A Critical Study, with a Concise Iconography*. (London: Philip Lee Warner, 1911).
Home, Henry, Lord Kames. *Elements of Criticism*, ed. Peter Jones, 2 vols. (Indianapolis, IN: Liberty Fund, 2005 [1785, 1st ed. 1762]).
"Our Attachment to Objects of Distress." In *Essays on the Principles of Morality and Natural Religion*, ed. Mary Catherine Moran. (Indianapolis, IN: Liberty Fund, 2005 [1779, 1st ed. 1758]).
Homer. *The Iliad*, trans. A. T. Murray, Loeb Classical Library, 2 vols. (London: William Heinemann; New York: G. P. Putnam's Sons, 1928).
The Odyssey, trans. A. T. Murray; rev. George E. Dimock. Loeb Classical Library. 2 vols. (Cambridge, MA: Harvard University Press, 1995).
Hooker, Edward Niles, ed. *The Critical Work of John Dennis*, 2 vols. (Baltimore: Johns Hopkins Press, 1939).
[Hopkins, Samuel]. *The Life and Character of the Late Reverend, Learned, and Pious Mr. Jonathan Edwards, President of the College of New-Jersey Together with Extracts from His Private Writings & Diary and Also Seventeen Select Sermons on Various Important Subjects*. (Northampton, MA, 1804).
Hopkins, Samuel. *A Treatise on the Millennium. Showing from Scripture Prophecy, That It Is Yet to Come; When It Will Come; in What It Will Consist; and the Events which Are First to Take Place, Introductory to It. By Samuel Hopkins, D.D. Pastor of the First Congregational Church in Newport, Rhode Island. [Two Lines from Psalms]*. (Boston, 1793).
Howe, Sarah. "General and Invariable Ideas of Nature: Joshua Reynolds and His Critical Descendants." *English* 54 (2005), 1–13.
Hugo, Victor. *Notre-Dame de Paris 1482*. (Paris: Garnier Frères, 1961 [1832]).
Hume, David. *An Inquiry Concerning the Principles of Morals*, ed. Tom Beauchamp. (Oxford: Oxford University Press, 1998).
"Of Tragedy." In *Essays: Moral, Political, and Literary*, ed. Eugene F. Miller. (Indianapolis, IN: Liberty Fund, 1987), 216–25.

Hutcheson, Francis. *An Inquiry into the Original of Our Ideas of Beauty and Virtue in Two Treatises*, 2nd ed. (Indianapolis, IN: Liberty Fund, 2004 [1726]).

Huydecoper, Balthazar. *Arsazes, of 't edelmoedig verraad*, 3rd ed. (Amsterdam: Izaak Duim, 1743).

Proeve van taal- en dichtkunde, in vrijmoedige aanmerkingen op Vondels vertaalde Herscheppingen van Ovidius, ed. Frans van Lelyveld and Nicolaas Hinlópen, 2nd ed. (Leiden: A. en J. Honkoop, 1782–1794).

Huyler, Jerome. *Locke in America: The Moral Philosophy of the Founding Era*. (Lawrence: University Press of Kansas, 1995).

[Ingersoll, Charles Jared]. *Inchiquin, the Jesuit's Letters, During a Late Residence in the United States of America ... Containing a Favourable View of the Manners, Literature, and State of Society, of the United States, and a Refutation of Many of the Aspersions Cast upon This Country by Former Residents and Tourists*. (New York, 1810).

Innes, D. C. "Longinus and Caecilius: Models of the Sublime." *Mnemosyne* 55 (2002), 259–84.

"Longinus: Structure and Unity." In *Greek Literary Theory after Aristotle: A Collection of Papers in Honour of D.M. Schenkeveld*, ed. J. G. J. Abbenes, S. R. Slings, and I. Sluiter. (Amsterdam: VU University Press, 1995), 111–24.

Jacks, Philip. *The Antiquarian and the Myth of Antiquity: The Origins of Rome in Renaissance Thought*. (Cambridge: Cambridge University Press, 1993).

James, William. *The Varieties of Religious Experience*. (New York: Touchstone, 1997 [1902]).

Jameson, Fredric. *The Political Unconscious: Narrative as a Socially Symbolic Act*. (Ithaca, NY: Cornell University Press, 1981).

Postmodernism, or the Cultural Logic of Late Capitalism. (Durham, NC: Duke University Press, 1991).

Janaway, Christopher. *Beyond Selflessness: Reading Nietzsche's Genealogy*. (Oxford: Oxford University Press, 2007).

Jeanneret, Michel. *Le défi des signes*. (Orléans: Paradigme, 1994).

Jefferson, Thomas. *Notes on the State of Virginia*, ed. William D. Peden. (New York: W. W. Norton, 1972).

Johnson, Mark Joseph. *The Roman Imperial Mausoleum in Late Antiquity*. (Cambridge: Cambridge University Press, 2009).

Johnson, Samuel. *A Dictionary of the English Language; in Which the Words Are Deduced from Their Originals and Illustrated in Their Different Significations by Examples from the Best Writers. To Which Are Prefixed, a History of the Language, and an English Grammar. By Samuel Johnson, A. M. In Two Volumes* (London, 1755).

Preface to Shakespeare, 1756. In *The Yale Edition of the Works of Samuel Johnson*, 18 vols. (New Haven, CT: Yale University Press, 1958–2004), vol. 8, *Johnson on Shakespeare*, ed. Arthur Sherbo (1968).

The Yale Edition of the Works of Samuel Johnson, 18 vols. (New Haven, CT: Yale University Press, 1958–2004), vol. 2, *The Idler and The Adventurer*, ed. W. J. Bate, John M. Bullitt, and L. F. Powell (1963).

Johnson, S. F. "Hardy and Burke's 'Sublime.'" In *Style in Prose Fiction: English Institute Essays*, ed. Harold C. Martin. (New York: Columbia University Press, 1958), 55–86.

Jones, Mark Wilson. *Principles of Roman Architecture*. (New Haven, CT: Yale University Press, 2000).

Joost-Gaugier, Christiane L. *Measuring Heaven: Pythagoras and His Influence on Thought and Art in Antiquity and the Middle Ages*. (Ithaca, NY: Cornell University Press, 2006).

Jusselin, Maurice. *Gabriel Syméon à Anet au temps de Diane de Poitiers*. (Chartres: Lainé and Tantet, 1935).

Kain, Philip J. *Schiller, Hegel, and Marx: State, Society, and the Aesthetic Ideal of Ancient Greece*. (Quebec: McGill-Queen's Press, 1982).

Kalbfleisch, K., ed. *Porphyry: Ad Gaurum*, Greek. In K. Kalbfleisch, "Die neuplatonische, fälschlich dem Galen zugeschriebene Schrift πρὸς Γαῦρον περὶ τοῦ πῶς ἐμψυχοῦται τὰ ἔμβρυα." *Abhandlungen der Preussischen Akadamie der Wissenschaft, philosophisch-historische Klasse* (1895), 33–62.

Kalff, G. *Geschiedenis der Nederlandsche letterkunde*, 7 vols. (Groningen: J. B. Wolters, 1906–1912).

Kammen, Michael. *A Machine that Would Go of Itself: The Constitution in American Culture*, 2nd ed. (New York: St. Martin's Press, 2006).

Kant, Immanuel. *Anthropology from a Pragmatic Point of View*, trans. Mary J. Gregor. (Den Haag: M. Nijhoff, 1974).

Anthropology, History, and Education, trans. and ed. Robert B. Louden and Günter Zöller. (Cambridge: Cambridge University Press, 2007).
Critique of Judgment, trans. Werner S. Pluhar. (Indianapolis, IN: Hackett, 1987).
Critique of Pure Reason, trans. Paul Guyer and Allen W. Wood. (Cambridge: Cambridge University Press, 1999).
Critique of the Power of Judgment, ed. Paul Guyer; trans. Paul Guyer and Eric Matthews. (Cambridge: Cambridge University Press, 2000).
Kant's gesammelte Schriften, Königlichen Preussischen (later Deutschen) Akademie der Wissenschaften, 29 vols. (Berlin: Reimer [later de Gruyter], 1900–).
Notes and Fragments, ed. Paul Guyer; trans. Curtis Bowman, Paul Guyer, and Frederick Rauscher. (Cambridge: Cambridge University Press, 2005).
Observations on the Feeling of the Beautiful and Sublime, trans. John T. Goldthwait, 2nd ed. (Berkeley: University of California Press, 2003 [1960]).
Observations on the Feeling of the Beautiful and Sublime and Other Writings, ed. and trans. Patrick Frierson and Paul Guyer. (Cambridge: Cambridge University Press, 2011).
Practical Philosophy, trans. and ed. Mary J. Gregor. (Cambridge: Cambridge University Press, 1996).
Religion within the Boundaries of Mere Reason. In *Immanuel Kant, Religion and Rational Theology*, trans. and ed. Allen E. Wood and George Di Giovanni. (Cambridge: Cambridge University Press, 1996).
Kearney, Richard. "Evil, Monstrosity, and the Sublime." *Revista Portuguesa de Filosofia* 57, 3 (July–September 2001), 485–502.
Keats, John. *Letters of John Keats*, ed. Robert Gittings. (Oxford: Oxford University Press, 1970).
Keller, Luzius. *Piranèse et les romantiques français: le mythe des escaliers en spirale*. (Paris: José Corti, 1966).
Kemble, Frances Ann. *Records of a Girlhood*, 2nd ed. (New York, 1879).
Kerslake, Lawrence. *Essays on the Sublime: Analyses of French Writings on the Sublime from Boileau to La Harpe*. (Berne: Peter Lang, 2000).
Kinker, Johannes. "Iets over het romantische: Eene voorlezing." *De recensent, ook der recensenten* 2 (1836), 329–50.
Kirwan, James. *Sublimity: The Non-Rational and the Irrational in the History of Aesthetics*. (New York: Routledge, 2005).
Kivy, Peter. *Antithetical Arts: On the Ancient Quarrel between Literature and Music*. (Oxford: Clarendon Press, 2009).
Philosophies of Arts: An Essay on Difference. (Cambridge: Cambridge University Press, 1997).
The Seventh Sense: Francis Hutcheson and Eighteenth-Century British Aesthetics, 2nd ed. (Cambridge: Cambridge University Press, 2003 [1976]).
Kivy, Peter, ed. *Thomas Reid's Lectures on the Fine Arts*, transcribed from the original manuscript with an introduction and notes. (Den Haag: Martinus Nijhoff, 1973).
Kleiner, John. *Mismapping the Underworld: Daring and Error in Dante's "Comedy."* (Stanford, CA: Stanford University Press, 1994).
Kneller, Jane. "Beauty, Autonomy, and Respect for Nature." In *Kant's Aesthetics*, ed. Herman Parret. (Berlin: Walter de Gruyter, 1998), 403–14.
Kollewijn, R. A. "Een taaldespoot uit de pruiketijd." *Taal en Letteren*, 16 (1906), 1–29.
Kostof, Spiro. *A History of Architecture: Settings and Rituals*. (Oxford: Oxford University Press, 1985).
The Orthodox Baptistery of Ravenna. (New Haven, CT: Yale University Press, 1965).
Kristeva, Julia. *Pouvoirs de l'horreur*. (Paris: Éditions du Seuil, 1980); *Powers of Horror: An Essay on Abjection*, trans. Leon S. Roudiez. (New York: Columbia University Press, 1982 [1980]).
Labacco, Antonio. *Libro d'Antonio Labacco appartenente a l'architettura*. (Rome: Casa Nostra, 1559).
Lap-chuen, Tsang. *The Sublime: Groundwork towards a Theory*. (Rochester, NY: University of Rochester, 1998).
Lawrence, D. H. *The Rainbow*. (Harmondsworth: Penguin, 1976).
Le Brun, Charles. "Sur l'expression des passions (7 avril et 5 mai 1668)." In *Les conférences de l'Académie royale de peinture et de sculpture*, ed. Alain Mérot. (Paris: ENSB, 1996), 145–62.
Lecoq, Anne-Marie, ed. *La Querelle des Anciens et des Modernes, XVIIe–XVIIIe siècles*. Prefaced by Marc Fumaroli, "Les abeilles et les araignées." (Paris: Gallimard, 2001).

Lee, Renssalaer W. *Ut Pictura Poesis*. (New York: W. W. Norton, 1967).
Lehmann, Karl. "The Dome of Heaven." *Art Bulletin* 27, 1 (1945), 1–27.
[Le Marquant]. *Description du Château d'Anet*. (Paris: G. Desprez, 1789).
Leroy, Julien-David. *Histoire de la disposition et des formes différentes que les Chrétiens ont données à leurs temples, depuis le règne de Constantin le Grand, jusqu'à nous*. (Paris: Desaint and Saillant, 1764).
Levine, Edward M. "Abstract Expressionism: The Mystical Experience." *Art Journal* 31, 1 (1971), 22–5.
Lichtenstein, Jacqueline, ed. *La peinture*. (Paris: Larousse, 1995).
Liddell, H. G., and R. Scott, eds. *Greek-English Lexicon, New Edition*, rev. Henry Stuart Jones. (Oxford: Oxford University Press, 1995).
Litman, Théodore A. *Le sublime en France (1660–1714)*. (Paris: Nizet, 1971).
Liu, Alan. "Wordsworth: The History in 'Imagination.'" *ELH* 51, 3 (1984), 505–48.
Locke, John. *An Essay Concerning Human Understanding*, ed. Peter H. Nidditch. (Oxford: Oxford University Press, 1975 [1689]).
Lockridge, Laurence. *The Ethics of Romanticism*. (Cambridge: Cambridge University Press, 1989).
Loerke, William. "A Rereading of the Interior Elevation of Hadrian's Rotunda." *Journal of the Society of Architectural Historians* 49, 1 (1990), 22–43.
Logan, John. "Longinus and the Sublime." In *The Cambridge History of Renaissance Criticism*, ed. Glyn P. Norton. (Cambridge: Cambridge University Press, 1999), 3:529–39.
Longinus. *An Essay on the Sublime: Translated from the Greek of Dionysius Longinus Cassius the Rhetorician. Compared with the French of Sieur Despréaux Boileau*, trans. anonymous. (Oxford, 1698).
  "Longinus" On the Sublime, ed., with an introduction by Donald A. Russell. (Oxford: Clarendon Press, 1964).
  On Great Writing (On the Sublime), trans. G. M. A. Grube. (New York: Bobbs-Merrill, 1957).
  "On the Sublime." In *Aristotle/Horace/Longinus, Classical Literary Criticism*, trans. T. S. Dorsch. (London: Penguin, 1965).
  On the Sublime, trans. W. Rhys Roberts. (Cambridge: Cambridge University Press, 1899).
  On the Sublime, trans. W. H. Fyfe; rev. Donald Russell. In *Aristotle: Poetics. Longinus: On the Sublime. Demetrius: On Style*, ed. Stephen Halliwell, Donald A. Russell, and Doreen C. Innes. Loeb Classical Library. (Cambridge, MA: Harvard University Press, 1995).
Longinus, Dionysius. *On the Sublime*, trans. William Smith. (London: J. Watts, 1739).
  On the Sublime, trans. William Smith, 2nd rev. ed. (London: B. Dod, 1743).
Low, David M. *Gibbon's Journal to January 28th, 1763*. (London: Chatto & Windus, 1929).
Lyotard, Jean-François. "The Communication of Sublime Feeling." In *Lyotard Reader and Guide*, ed. Keith Crome and James Williams. (Edinburgh: Edinburgh University Press, 2006).
  "Complexity and the Sublime," trans. Geoffrey Bennington. In *Postmodernism*, ed. Lisa Appignanesi. (London: Institute of Contemporary Arts, 1986), 10–12.
  Discours, figure. (Paris: Klincksieck, 1971); *Discourse, Figure*, trans. Antony Hudeck and Mary Lydon. (Minneapolis: University of Minnesota Press, 2011).
  Leçons sur l'analytique du sublime. (Paris: Galilée, 1991).
  Le Différend. (Paris: Éditions de Minuit, 1983); *The Differend*, trans. Georges Van Den Abbeele. (Minneapolis: University of Minnesota Press, 1988).
  Lessons on the Analytic of the Sublime, trans. Elizabeth Rottenberg. (Stanford, CA: Stanford University Press, 1994).
  "Le Sublime et l'Avant-garde." In *L'Inhumain: Causeries sur le temps*. (Paris: Galilée, 1988), 101–18.
  "Presenting the Unpresentable: The Sublime." *Artforum* 20, 8 (1982), 64–9.
  "Réponse à la question: qu'est-ce que le postmoderne?" *Critique* 419 (1982), 357–76; "Answering the Question: What Is Postmodernism?" trans. Régis Durand. In *The Postmodern Condition*, trans. Geoffrey Bennington and Brian Massumi. (Minneapolis: University of Minnesota Press, 1984), 71–82.
  "The Sublime and the Avant-Garde." In *The Lyotard Reader*, ed. Andrew Benjamin. (Oxford: Blackwell, 1989).
  "The Sublime and the Avant-Garde." In *The Inhuman: Reflections on Time*, trans. Geoffrey Bennington and Rachel Bowlby. (Cambridge: Polity Press, 1991), 89–107.

MacDonald, William L. *The Pantheon: Design, Meaning, and Progeny*. (Cambridge, MA: Harvard University Press, 1976).
Madelein, Christophe. "Juigchen in den adel der menschlijke natuur: Het verhevene in de Nederlanden (1770–1830)." PhD dissertation, Vakgroep Nederlandse literatuur, University of Ghent, 2008.
"Kant in de fout? Het verhevene in de Nederlanden." *De Achttiende Eeuw* 39, 1 (2007), 77–93.
Madelein, Christophe, and Jürgen Pieters, eds. *Bilderdijk, Kinker & Van Hemert: Als van hooger bestemming en aart*. (Groningen: Historische Uitgeverij, 2008).
Makkreel, Rudolf. *Imagination and Understanding in Kant*. (Chicago: Chicago University Press, 1994).
Mallgrave, Harry Francis, and Eleftherios Ikonomou, eds. and trans., *Empathy, Form, and Space: Problems in German Aesthetics, 1873–1893*. (Santa Monica, CA: The Getty Center for the History of Art and the Humanities, 1994).
Mango, Cyril. *The Art of the Byzantine Empire 312–1453: Sources and Documents*. (Englewood Cliffs, NJ: Prentice-Hall, 1972).
Marder, Tod. "Bernini and Alexander VII: Criticism and Praise of the Pantheon in the Seventeenth Century." *Art Bulletin* 71, 4 (1989), 628–45.
Marin, Louis. "Le sublime dans les années 1670: Un je ne sais quoi?" *Papers on French Seventeenth Century Literature: Biblio 17*, 25 (1986), 185–201.
Politiques de la représentation, ed. Alain Cantillon. (Paris: Kime, 2005).
Sublime Poussin, ed. Alain Badiou and Barbara Cassin. (Paris: Seuil, 1995).
Martin, Éva Madeleine. *Esthétiques de Port-Royal*. (Paris: Nolin, 2012).
Matelli, E. "Struttura e stile del περὶ ὕψους." *Aevum* 61 (1987), 137–247.
Mather, Cotton. *The Christian Philosopher*, ed. Winton L. Solberg. (Urbana-Champaign: University of Illinois Press, 1994 [1721]).
Mather, Increase. *A Discourse Concerning the Uncertainty of the Times of Men and the Necessity of Being Prepared for Sudden Changes and Death. Delivered in a Sermon Preached at Cambridge in New England. Decemb. 6. 1696. On Occasion of the Sudden Death of Two Scholars Belonging to Harvard Colledge*. (Boston, 1697).
Mayernik, David. "The Winds in the Corners: Giulio Romano, the Elements, and the Palazzo Te's *Fall of the Giants*." In *Aeolian Winds and the Spirit in Renaissance Architecture: Academia Eolia Revisited*, ed. Barbara Kenda. (New York: Routledge, 2006), 125–49.
McCoy, Drew. *The Elusive Republic: Political Economy in Jeffersonian America*. (Chapel Hill: Published for the Institute of Early American History and Culture, Williamsburg, VA, by the University of North Carolina Press, 1980).
McKinsey, Elizabeth R. *Niagara Falls: Icon of the American Sublime*. (Cambridge: Cambridge University Press, 1985).
Mellor, Anne K. *Romanticism and Gender*. (New York: Routledge, 1993).
Melville, Herman. *Moby Dick; or the Whale*. (Berkley: University of California Press, 1979).
Merritt, Melissa McBay. Review of Robert Clewis, *The Kantian Sublime and the Revelation of Freedom*. *British Journal for the History of Philosophy* 18, 3 (2010), 529–32.
Middleton, Robin D. "The Abbé de Cordemoy and the Graeco-Gothic Ideal: A Prelude to Romantic Classicism." *Journal of the Warburg and Courtauld Institutes* 25, 3–4 (1962), 278–320, and 26, 1–2 (1963), 90–123.
Miller, Angela. *The Empire of the Eye: Landscape Representation and American Cultural Politics, 1825–1875*. (Ithaca, NY: Cornell University Press, 1993).
"The Soil of an Unknown America: New World Lost Empires and the Debate over Cultural Origins." *American Art* 8, 3–4 (1994), 8–27.
"Thomas Cole and Jacksonian America: *The Course of Empire* as Political Allegory." *Prospects* 14 (1990), 65–92.
Miller, William F. *Signs of the Times, or the Sure Word of Prophecy: A Dissertation on the Prophecies of the Sixth and Seventh Vials, and on the Subsequent Great Day of Battle, Immediately Preceding the Millennium*. (Hartford, CT, 1803).
Milton, John. *Paradise Lost*, ed. David Hawkes. (New York: Barnes and Noble Classics, 2004).
Paradise Lost. Authoritative Text. Sources and Backgrounds. Criticism, ed. Gordon Teskey. (New York: W. W. Norton, 2005).

Minkowski, Eugène. *Vers une Cosmologie: fragments philosophiques*, 2nd rev. ed. (Paris: Aubier-Montaigne, 1936).
Mishra, Vijay. *The Gothic Sublime*. (Albany: State University of New York Press, 1994).
Modiano, Raimonda. "The Kantian Seduction: Wordsworth on the Sublime." In *Deutsche Romantik and English Romanticism*, ed. Theodore G. Gish and Sandra G. Frieden. (Munich: Fink, 1984), 17–26.
Monk, Samuel Holt. *The Sublime: A Study of Critical Theories in XVIII-Century England*. (Ann Arbor: University of Michigan Press, 1935).
Montaigne, Michel de. *Les essais*, ed. Pierre Villey, 3 vols. (Paris: Quadrige/Presses Universitaires de France).
Moore, Leslie. *Beautiful Sublime: The Making of Paradise Lost, 1701–1734*. (Stanford, CA: Stanford University Press, 1990).
Morello, Giovanni. "Sandro Botticelli's *Chart of Hell*." In *Sandro Botticelli: The Drawings for Dante's "Divine Comedy,"* ed. Hein-Th. Schulze Altcappenberg. (London: Royal Academy of Arts, 2000), 318–25.
Morris, David B. *The Religious Sublime: Christian Poetry and Critical Tradition in Eighteenth-Century England*. (Lexington: University Press of Kentucky, 1972).
Mothersill, Mary. *Beauty Restored*. (Oxford: Oxford University Press, 1986).
Motherwell, Robert. *The Collected Writings of Robert Motherwell*, ed. Stephanie Terenzio. (Oxford: Oxford University Press, 1992).
Muszynska-Wallace, E. Soteris. "The Sources of *The Prairie*." *American Literature* 21, 2 (1949), 191–200.
Nancy, Jean-Luc. "L'Offrande sublime." In *Du sublime*, ed. Jean-François Courtine et al. (Paris: Belin, 1988), 37–75.
  "The Sublime Offering." In *Of the Sublime: Presence in Question*, ed. Jean-François Courtine et al.; trans. Jeffrey S. Librett. (Albany: State University of New York Press, 1993 [1988]), 25–54.
Nehamas, Alexander. *Nietzsche: Life as Literature*. (Cambridge, MA: Harvard University Press, 1985).
Newman, Barnett. "The Sublime Is Now." In *Art in Theory, 1900–2000: An Anthology of Changing Ideas*, ed. Charles Harrison and Paul Wood, 2nd ed. (Malden, MA: Wiley-Blackwell, 2003), 580–2.
Newman, John Henry. *An Essay in Aid of a Grammar of Assent*, 9th ed. (London: Longmans and Green, 1903 [1870]).
Nicolson, Marjorie Hope. *Mountain Gloom and Mountain Glory: The Development of the Aesthetics of the Infinite*. (Seattle: University of Washington Press, 1997 [1959]).
Nicot, Jean. *Thresor de la Langue Françoyse, tant Ancienne que Moderne*. (Paris: David Douceur, 1606). Transcribed and digitalized without pagination at http://artfl-project.uchicago.edu/content/dictinonnaries-dautrefois.
Nietzsche, Friedrich. *The Birth of Tragedy and Other Writings*, ed. Raymond Geuss and Ronald Speirs; trans. Ronald Speirs. (Cambridge: Cambridge University Press, 1999).
  The Genealogy of Morals, ed. Keith Ansell-Pearson; trans. Carol Diethe. (Cambridge: Cambridge University Press, 2007).
  "Schopenhauer as Educator." In *Untimely Meditations*, trans. R. J. Hollingdale. (Cambridge: Cambridge University Press, 1983), 125–94.
Nikšić, Goran. "The Restoration of Diocletian's Palace – Mausoleum, Temple, and Porta Aurea (with the Analysis of the Original Architectural Design)." In *Diokletian und die Tetrarchie: Aspekte einer Zeitenwende*, ed. Alexander Demandt et al. (Berlin: Walter de Gruyter, 2004), 163–71.
Nobel, Louis Legrand. *The Life and Works of Thomas Cole, N.A.*, 3rd ed. (New York, 1856).
Norton, Charles Eliot, ed. *Correspondence of Thomas Carlyle and R. W. Emerson 1834–1872*, 2 vols. (Boston, 1884).
Omont, Henri. *Anciens Inventaires et catalogues de la Bibliothèque nationale*, 4 vols. (Paris: E. Leroux, 1908–1921).
O'Neill, Onora. "Kant on Duties Regarding Nonrational Nature." *Proceedings of the Aristotelian Society: Supplementary Volume* 72, 1 (2003), 211–28.
Onians, John. *Bearers of Meaning: The Classical Orders in Antiquity, the Middle Ages, and the Renaissance*. (Cambridge: Cambridge University Press, 1988).

Otto, Rudolf. *Das Heilige; über das Irrationale in der Idee des Göttlichen und sein Verhältnis zum Rationalen*. (Munich: Beck, 1963 [1917]).
   The Idea of the Holy, trans. John W. Harvey. (Oxford: Oxford University Press, 1923).
   The Idea of the Holy, trans. John W. Harvey, 2nd ed. (Oxford: Oxford University Press, 1950 [1923]).
Ovid. *The Metamorphoses of Ovid*, trans. Allen Mandelbaum. (New York: Harvest/Harcourt, 1993).
Paré, Ambroise. *Oeuvres*. (Paris: Gabriel Buon, 1575).
Parker, Deborah. *Commentary and Ideology: Dante in the Renaissance*. (Durham, NC: Duke University Press, 1993).
Parrish, Susan Scott. *American Curiosity: Cultures of Natural History in the Colonial British Atlantic World*. (Chapel Hill: Published for the Omohundro Institute of Early American History and Culture, Williamsburg, VA, by the University of North Carolina Press, 2006).
Parry, Elwood C., II. "Acts of God, Acts of Man: Geological Ideas and the Imaginary Landscapes of Thomas Cole." In *Two Hundred Years of Geology in America: Proceedings of the New Hampshire Conference on the History of Geology*, ed. Cecil J. Schneer. (Hanover, NH: University Press of New England, 1979).
   Nature and Culture: American Landscape Painting 1825–1875, 3rd ed. (Oxford: Oxford University Press, 2007).
Pascal, Blaise. *Pensées*. In *Oeuvres complètes*, ed. Louis Lafuma (Paris: Seuil, Intégrale, 1963 [1654]), 493–649.
   "Sur la conversion du pécheur." In *Oeuvres complètes*, ed. Louis Lafuma. (Paris: Seuil, Intégrale, 1963 [1654]), 290–1.
Patillon, Michel, and Luc Brisson. *Longin. Fragments. Art Rhétorique. Rufus. Art Rhétorique*. (Paris: Les Belles Lettres, 2001).
Patton, Paul. "Introduction." In *Deleuze: A Critical Reader*, ed. Paul Patton. (Malden, MA: Blackwell, 1996), 1–17.
Paulson, Ronald. *Representations of Revolution (1789–1820)*. (New Haven, CT: Yale University Press, 1983).
Pérouse de Montclos, Jean-Marie. *Philibert De l'Orme: Architecte du roi (1514–1570)*. (Paris: Mengès, 2000).
Pillow, Kirk. *Sublime Understanding: Aesthetic Reflection in Kant and Hegel*. (Cambridge, MA: MIT Press, 2000).
Pincus, Debra. "The Humanist and the Poet: Bernardo Bembo's Portrait of Dante." In *Patronage and Italian Renaissance Sculpture*, ed. Kathleen Wren Christian and David J. Drogin. (Farnham: Ashgate, 2010), 61–94.
Plato. *Early Socratic Dialogues*, ed. Trevor J. Saunders. (London: Penguin, 1987).
Pluche, Noël-Antoine. "From *The Spectacle of Nature* (1746)." In *Music and Culture in Eighteenth-Century Europe: A Source Book*, ed. Enrico Fubini; trans. Wolfgang Freis et al. (Chicago: University of Chicago Press, 1994), 79–83.
Poetzsch, Markus. *"Visionary Dreariness": Readings in Romanticism's Quotidian Sublime*. (New York: Routledge, 2006).
Pope, Alexander. *The Twickenham Edition of the Poems of Alexander Pope*, 6 vols. (London: Methuen, 1961), vol. 1, *Pastoral Poetry and An Essay on Criticism*, ed. E. Audra and Aubrey Williams.
Porter, James I. "Is Art Modern? Kristeller's 'Modern System of the Arts' Reconsidered." *British Journal of Aesthetics* 49, 1 (2009), 1–24.
   "Reply to Shiner." *British Journal of Aesthetics* 49, 2 (2009), 171–8.
Potkay, Adam. *The Fate of Eloquence in the Age of Hume*. (Ithaca, NY: Cornell University Press, 1994).
   "Romantic Transformations of the King James Bible: Wordsworth, Shelley, Blake." In *The King James Bible after Four Hundred Years: Literary, Linguistic, and Cultural Influences*, ed. Hannibal Hamlin and Norman W. Jones. (Cambridge: Cambridge University Press, 2011), 219–32.
   The Story of Joy from the Bible to Late Romanticism. (Cambridge: Cambridge University Press, 2007).
   "Theorizing Civic Eloquence in the Early Republic: The Road from David Hume to John Quincy Adams." *Early American Literature* 34, 2 (1999), 147–70.
Poulet, Georges. *Les Métamorphoses du cercle*. (Paris: Plon, 1961).
Poussin, Nicolas. *Lettres et propos sur l'art*, ed. Anthony Blunt. (Paris: Hermann, 1964).

Pownell, Thomas. *The Speech of Th-m-s P-wn-ll, Esq; Late G-v-rn-r of This Province, in the H – se of C-m – ns, in Favor of America*. (Boston, 1769).
Prager, Brad. *Aesthetic Vision and German Romanticism: Writing Images*. (Rochester, NY: Camden House, 2007).
Priestley, Joseph. *A Course of Lectures on Oratory and Criticism*, ed. Vincent M. Bevilacqua and Richard Murphy. (Carbondale: Southern Illinois University Press, 1965 [1777]).
Price, Uvedale. *Essays on the Picturesque, as Compared with the Sublime and the Beautiful, and on the Use of Studying Pictures, for the Purpose of Improving Real Landscape*. (London: J. Robson, 1796).
Prückner, Helmut, and Sebastian Storz. "Beobachtungen im Oktogon der Domus Aurea." *Mitteilungen des Deutschen Archaeologischen Instituts, Roemische* 81 (1974), 323–39.
[Pulteney, J.]. *A Treatise of the Loftiness or Elegance of Speech. Written Originally in Greek by Longinus; and Now Translated out of the French by Mr. J. P[ulteney]*. (London, 1680).
Quint, David. "Fear of Falling: Icarus, Phaethon, and Lucretius in *Paradise Lost*." *Renaissance Quarterly* 57, 3 (2004), 847–81.
Rabuse, Georg. *Der kosmische Aufbau der Jenseitsreiche Dantes*. (Graz and Cologne: Böhlau, 1958).
Radcliffe, Ann. *A Sicilian Romance*. (London: Hookham and Carpenter, 1792).
Rancière, Jacques. *Le Destin des images*. (Paris: La Fabrique, 2003); *The Future of the Image*, trans. Gregory Elliott. (New York: Verso, 2007).
Reath, Andrews. "Kant's Theory of Moral Sensibility." *Kant Studien* 80 (1989), 284–302.
Reeder, John. "The Relation of the Moral and the Numinous in Otto's Notion of the Holy." In *Religion and Morality*, ed. G. Outka and J. Reeder. (Garden City, NY: Doubleday, 1973), 255–92.
Reid, Thomas. *Essays on the Intellectual Powers of Man*. (University Park, PA: Pennsylvania State University Press, 2002 [1785]).
Reynolds, Joshua. *Discourses on Art*, ed. Robert W. Wark. (San Marino, CA: The Huntington Library, 1959; reprint, New Haven, CT: Yale University Press, 1997 [1975]).
Richardson, Lawrence, Jr. *A New Topographical Dictionary of Ancient Rome*. (Baltimore: Johns Hopkins University Press, 1992).
Richelet, César-Pierre. *Dictionnaire françois*. (Geneva: Jean Herman Widerhold, 1680).
Ricks, Christopher B. *Milton's Grand Style*. (Oxford: Clarendon Press, 1978 [1963]).
Rigolot, François. *Louise Labé Lyonnaise, ou La Renaissance au féminin*. (Paris: Champion, 1997).
Ripa, Cesare. *Iconologia*, ed. Edward A. Maser. (New York: Dover, 1971).
Rizzardi, Clementina. "I mosaici parietali di Ravenna da Galla Placidia a Giustiniano," in *Venezia e Bisanzio. Aspetti della cultura artistica bizantina da Ravenna a Venezia (V–XIV secolo)*, ed. Clementina Rizzardi (Venice: Istituto veneto di scienze, lettere ed arti, 2005).
Rosenberg, A. *Longinus in England bis zur Ende des 18: Jahrhunderts*. (Berlin: Meyer und Müller, 1917).
Rosenblum, Robert. "The Abstract Sublime." *Art News* (1961), 38–41 and 56–67.
   Modern Painting and the Northern Romantic Tradition: Friedrich to Rothko. (New York: Harper & Row, 1975).
Rosiek, Jan. *Maintaining the Sublime: Heidegger and Adorno*. (Bern: Peter Lang, 2000).
Rossi, Paolo. *The Dark Abyss of Time: The History of the Earth and the History of Nations from Hooke to Vico*, trans. Lydia G. Cochrane. (Chicago: Chicago University Press, 1984).
Rousseau, Jean-Jacques. *Œuvres complètes*, 5 vols. (Paris: Gallimard/Bibliothèque de la Pléiade, 1959).
Roussel, Pierre Désiré. *Histoire et description du Château d'Anet*. (Paris: D. Jouaust, 1875).
Rowland, Ingrid D. *The Culture of the High Renaissance: Ancients and Moderns in Sixteenth-Century Rome*. (Cambridge: Cambridge University Press, 1998).
Rudwick, Martin. *Bursting the Limits of Time: The Reconstruction of Geohistory in the Age of Revolution*. (Chicago: Chicago University Press, 2005).
Ruskin, John. *Modern Painters*, vol. I. In *The Complete Works of John Ruskin (Library Edition)*, ed. E. T. Cook and Alexander Wedderburn, 39 vols. (London: George Allen, 1903–1912), vol. 3.
Russell, Donald A. "Longinus Revisited." *Mnemosyne* 34 (1981), 72–86.
Russell, Donald A., ed. *Quintilian: The Orator's Education*, Latin text with English translation. (Cambridge, MA: Harvard University Press, 2001).

Russell, Donald A., and M. Winterbottom, eds. *Ancient Literary Criticism*. (Oxford: Clarendon Press, 1972).
  Classical Literary Criticism. (Oxford: Oxford University Press, 1989).
Ryan, Vanessa L. "The Physiological Sublime: Burke's Critique of Reason." *Journal of the History of Ideas* 62, 2 (2001), 265–79.
Saint Augustine. *The City of God*, trans. Gerald G. Walsh et al., abridged ed. (New York: Image Books/Doubleday, 1958).
Saint Girons, Baldine. "Avant-propos." In Edmund Burke, *Recherche philosophique sur l'origine de nos idées du sublime et du beau,* trans. Baldine Saint Girons. (Paris: Vrin, 1990),
  Fiat lux: Une philosophie du sublime. (Paris: Quai Voltaire, 1993).
  "Sublime." In *Vocabulaire européen des philosophies,* ed. Barbara Cassin. (Paris: Dictionnaires le Robert, Seuil, 2003).
Saito, Yuriko. "The Aesthetics of Unscenic Nature." *Journal of Aesthetics and Art Criticism* 56, 2 (1998), 101–11.
  "Appreciating Nature on Its Own Terms." *Environmental Ethics* 20 (1998), 135–49.
Sandler, Irving. *Mark Rothko: Paintings, 1948–69.* (New York: Pace Gallery, 1983).
Schelling, Friedrich Wilhelm Joseph. *The Philosophy of Art*, trans. and ed. Douglas W. Stott. (Minneapolis: University of Minnesota Press, 1989).
  System of Transcendental Idealism, trans. Peter L. Heath. (Charlottesville: University of Virginia Press, 1978).
Schiller, Friedrich von. *Essays*, ed. Walter Hinderer and Daniel O. Dahlstrom. (New York: Continuum, 1993).
  "On the Sublime." In *Naïve and Sentimental Poetry and On the Sublime: Two Essays*, trans. Julius A. Elias. (New York: Frederick Ungar, 1966), 193–212.
Schlegel, August Wilhelm. *Kritische Schriften und Briefe*. (Stuttgart: Kohlhammer, 1963), vol. 2, *Die Kunstlehre*.
Schleiermacher, Friedrich. *On Religion: Speeches to Its Cultured Despisers*, ed. and trans. R. Crouter. (Cambridge: Cambridge University Press, 1988 [1799]).
  On the Christian Faith, ed. and trans. H. R. Mackintosh and J. S. Stewart. (London: T & T Clark, 1999 [1821–1822]).
Scholar, Richard. *The Je-Ne-Sais-Quoi in Early Modern Europe*. (Oxford: Oxford University Press, 2005).
Schopenhauer, Arthur. *The World as Will and Representation*, trans. E. F. J. Payne, 2 vols. (Indian Springs, CO: Falcon's Wing Press, 1958).
Segal, C. P. "ὕψος and the Problem of Cultural Decline in the *De sublimitate*." *Harvard Studies in Classical Philology* 64 (1959), 121–46.
Segala, Elisabetta, and Ida Sciortino. *Domus Aurea*, trans. Colin Swift. (Milan: Electa/Soprintendenza Archaeologica di Roma, 1999).
Seznec, Jean. *The Survival of the Pagan Gods*, trans. Barbara F. Sessions. (Princeton, NJ: Princeton University Press, 1972 [1953]).
Shaw, Philip. *The Sublime*. (New York: Routledge, 2006).
Shearman, John K. G. *Funzione e illusione: Raffaello, Pontormo, Correggio*, ed. Alessandro Nova. (Milan: Il Saggiatore, 1983).
  Only Connect: Art and Spectator in the Italian Renaissance. (Princeton, NJ: Princeton University Press, 1992).
Shelley, Percy Bysshe. *Shelley's Poetry and Prose*, ed. Donald H. Reiman and Neil Fraistat, 2nd ed. (New York: Norton, 2002).
Shiner, Larry. "Continuity and Discontinuity in the Concept of Art." *British Journal of Aesthetics* 49, 2 (2009), 159–78.
  The Invention of Art: A Cultural History. (Chicago: University of Chicago Press, 2001).
Shusterman, Richard. *Body Consciousness: A Philosophy of Mindfulness and Somaesthetics.* (Cambridge: Cambridge University Press, 2008).
  "Somaesthetics and Burke's Sublime." *British Journal of Aesthetics* 45, 4 (2005), 323–41.
Signorini, Rodolfo. *Il Palazzo del Te e la Camera di Psiche: Miti e altre fantasie e storie antiche nella villa di Federico II Gonzaga ideata da Giulio Romano a Mantova*. (Mantua: Sometti, 2001).

Silk, M. S., and J. P. Stern. *Nietzsche on Tragedy*. (Cambridge: Cambridge University Press, 1981).
Simeoni, Gabriello. *Épitomé de l'origine et succession de la Duché de Ferrare, composé en langue Toscane par le seigneur Gabriel Symeon et traduict en François par luy mesme. Avec certaines Epistres à divers personnages, et aucuns Epigrammes sur la proprieté de la Lune par les douze signes du Ciel. Pour madame la Duchesse de Valentinois*. (Paris: Gilles Corrozet, 1553).
  Les illustres Observations antiques du seigneur Gabriel Symeon florentin en son dernier voyage d'Italie l'an 1557. (Lyon: Jan de Tournes, 1558).
Simpson, David. "Commentary: Updating the Sublime." *Studies in Romanticism* 26, 2 (1987), 245–58.
Simson, Otto von. *The Gothic Cathedral: Origins of Gothic Architecture and the Medieval Concept of Order*, 2nd rev. ed. (New York: Harper & Row/The Bollingen Library, 1962).
Sircello, Guy. "How Is a Theory of the Sublime Possible?" *Journal of Aesthetics and Art Criticism* 51, 4 (1993), 541–50.
Skinner, Quentin. *Reason and Rhetoric in the Philosophy of Hobbes*. (Cambridge: Cambridge University Press, 1996).
Smith, Andrew, ed. *Porphyrii philosophi fragmenta*, Greek. (Stuttgart: B.G. Teubner, 1993).
Smith, Daniel W. "Deleuze's Theory of Sensation: Overcoming the Kantian Duality." In *Deleuze: A Critical Reader*, ed. Paul Patton. (Malden, MA: Blackwell, 1996), 29–56.
Smith, E. Baldwin. *Architectural Symbolism of Imperial Rome and the Middle Ages*. (Princeton, NJ: Princeton University Press, 1956).
  The Dome: A Study in the History of Ideas. (Princeton, NJ: Princeton University Press, 1971 [1950]).
Smith, Nigel. *Is Milton Better than Shakespeare?* (Cambridge, MA: Harvard University Press, 2008).
Smith, Samuel Stanhope. *An Essay on the Causes of the Variety of Complexion and Figure in the Human Species*, 2nd ed. (New Brunswick, NJ, 1810).
Soper, Kate. "Looking at Landscape." *Capitalism, Nature, Socialism* 12, 2 (2001), 132–8.
Squier, E[phraim] G[eorge], and E[dwin] H[amilton] Davis. *Ancient Monuments of the Mississippi Valley*. (New York: Bartlett & Welford; Cincinnati: J. A. & U. P. James, 1848).
Stewart, Dugald. *Philosophical Essays*. In *Collected Works*, ed. William Hamilton, 11 vols. (Edinburgh: Thomas Constable, 1855).
Stinger, Charles L. *The Renaissance in Rome*. (Bloomington: Indiana University Press, 1985).
Stolnitz, Jerome. "On the Origins of 'Aesthetic Disinterestedness.'" *Journal of Aesthetics and Art Criticism* 20, 2 (1961), 131–44.
  "On the Significance of Lord Shaftesbury in Modern Aesthetic Theory." *Philosophical Quarterly* 11, 43 (1961), 97–113.
Stookey, Laurence Hull. "The Gothic Cathedral as the Heavenly Jerusalem: Liturgical and Theological Sources." *Gesta* 8, 1 (1969), 35–41.
Stott, Annette. *Holland Mania: The Unknown Dutch Period in American Art and Culture*. (Woodstock, NY: Overlook Press, 1998).
Suetonius. *Lives of the Caesars*. In *Suetonius*, trans. J. C. Rolfe, 2 vols. (Cambridge, MA: Harvard University Press; London: William Heinemann, 1979).
Sulzer, Johann Georg. "Art, Beaux-arts." In *Supplément à l'Encyclopédie*, ed. Jean-Baptiste Robinet. (Amsterdam: Marc-Michel Rey, 1776), 1:587–96.
  General Theory of the Fine Arts. In *Aesthetics and the Art of Musical Composition in the German Enlightenment: Selected Writings of Johann Georg Sulzer and Heinrich Christoph Koch*, ed. and trans. Nancy Kovaleff Baker and Thomas Christensen. (Cambridge: Cambridge University Press, 1995).
Tarrant, Harold. *Proclus: Commentary on Plato's Timaeus*. (Cambridge: Cambridge University Press, 2007), vol. 1.
Taylor, Rabun M. "A Literary and Structural Analysis of the First Dome on Justinian's Hagia Sophia." *Journal of the Society of Architectural Historians* 55, 1 (1996), 66–78.
Thayer, J. H. *A Greek-English Lexicon of the New Testament*. (New York: American Book, 1889).
Thoreau, Henry David. "Ktaadn." In *The Maine Woods*, ed. Joseph J. Moldenhauer. (Princeton, NJ: Princeton University Press, 1972).
Tower, Troy, and Jane Tylus, eds. *Gaspara Stampa: The Complete Poems*. (Chicago: University of Chicago Press, 2010).

Trapp, Michael. *Maximus of Tyre: The Philosophical Orations*. (Oxford: Oxford University Press, 1996).
Trapp, Michael, ed. *Maximus Tyrius: Dissertationes*. (Stuttgart: B.G. Teubner, 1994).
Tylus, Jane. "Gaspara Stampa and the Rediscovery of the Sublime in Early Modern Europe." Paper delivered to the Department of French and Italian, Princeton University, November 11, 2010.
Unglaub, Jonathan. *Poussin and the Poetics of Painting*. (Cambridge: Cambridge University Press, 2006).
Van Schepen, Randall K. "From the Form of Spirit to the Spirit of Form." In *Re-Enchantment*, ed. James Elkins and David Morgan. (New York: Routledge, 2008), 47–68.
Vasari, Giorgio. *Lives of the Painters, Sculptors and Architects*, trans. Gaston du C. de Vere, 2 vols. (New York: Alfred A. Knopf, 1996 [1912]).
Vickers, Brian. "Rhetoric and Poetics." In *The Cambridge History of Renaissance Philosophy*, ed. Charles B. Schmitt and Quentin Skinner. (Cambridge: Cambridge University Press, 1988), 715–45.
Viller, M., F. Cavallera, and J. de Guibert, eds. *Dictionnaire de spiritualité ascétique et mystique*, 17 vols. (Paris: Bauchesne, 1981).
Wagner, Richard. *Beethoven*, trans. Albert R. Parsons. (Indianapolis, IN: Benham Brothers, 1873).
Wallace, William E. *Michelangelo: The Artist, the Man, and His Times*. (Cambridge: Cambridge University Press, 2010).
Wallach, Alan. "Thomas Cole: Landscape and the Course of American Empire." In *Thomas Cole: Landscape into History*, ed. William H. Truettner and Alan Wallach. (New Haven, CT: Yale University Press, 1994), 23–111.
Walsh, G. B. "Sublime Method: Longinus on Language and Imitation." *Classical Antiquity* 7 (1988), 252–69.
Ward-Perkins, J. B. *Roman Imperial Architecture*. (Harmondsworth: Penguin, 1981).
Wardropper, Ian. "Le mécénat des Guise. Art, religion et politique au milieu du XVIe siècle." *Revue de l'art* 94 (1991), 27–44.
Weinberg, Bernard. "Translations and Commentaries of Longinus, *On the Sublime*, to 1600: A Bibliography." *Modern Philology* 57, 3 (1950), 145–51.
  "Une traduction française du 'Sublime' de Longin vers 1645." *Modern Philology* 59, 3 (1962), 159–201.
Weiskel, Thomas. *The Romantic Sublime: Studies in the Structure and Psychology of Transcendence*. (Baltimore: Johns Hopkins University Press, 1976).
[West, Stephen, D. D.], ed. *Sketches of the Life of the Late Rev. Samuel Hopkins, D. D., Pastor of the First Congregational Church in Newport Written by Himself, Interspersed with Marginal Notes Extracted from His Private Diary to which Is Added, a Dialogue, by the Same Hand, on the Nature and Extent of the Christian Submission Also, a Serious Address to Professing Christians, Closed by Dr. Hart's Sermon at His Funeral with an Introduction to the Whole by the Editor*. (Hartford, CT, 1805).
Whichcote, Benjamin. *Select Sermons*, with a preface by Anthony Ashley Cooper, third Earl of Shaftesbury. (London, 1698).
White, Stephen K. *Edmund Burke: Modernity, Politics, and Aesthetics*. (Newbury Park, CA: Sage, 1994).
Wilton, Andrew. *Turner and the Sublime*. (London: British Museum, 1980).
Winckelmann, Johann Joachim. *Reflections on the Painting and Sculpture of the Greeks* (1755), trans. Henry Fuseli. (London: A. Millar, 1765); reprinted in Johann Joachim Winckelmann. *Essays on the Philosophy and History of Art*, ed. Curtis Bowman, 3 vols. (Bristol: Thoemmes Press, 2001), vol. 1.
Wood, Allen W. "Self-Love, Self-Benevolence, and Self-Conceit." In *Kant, Aristotle, and the Stoics*, ed. Stephen Engstrom and Jennifer Whiting. (Cambridge: Cambridge University Press, 1996), 141–61.
Wood, Neal. "The Aesthetic Dimension of Burke's Political Thought." *Journal of British Studies* 4, 1 (1964), 41–64.
Wood, Theodore E. B. *The Word "Sublime" and Its Context, 1650–1760*. (Den Haag: Mouton, 1972).
Wordsworth, William. *The Excursion*, ed. Sally Bushell et al. (Ithaca, NY: Cornell University Press, 2007).
  A Guide through the District of the Lakes in the North of England, with a Description of the Scenery, &c. for the Use of Tourists and Residents, 5th ed., with Considerable Additions (Kendal and London, 1835). In *The Prose Works of William Wordsworth*, ed. W. J. B. Owen and Jane Worthington Smyser. (Oxford: Clarendon Press, 1974), vol. 3.

Lyrical Ballads 1798 and 1800, ed. Michael Gamer and Dahlia Porter. (Peterborough, ON: Broadview, 2008).
The Prelude: 1799, 1805, 1850, ed. Jonathan Wordsworth, M. H. Abrams, and Stephen Gill. (New York: W. W. Norton, 1979).
Wright, Wilmer Cave, ed. *Philostratus and Eunapius: Lives of the Sophists*. (Cambridge, MA: Harvard University Press, 1921), vol. 1.
Yeager, Patricia. "Toward a Female Sublime." In *Gender and Theory: Dialogues on Feminist Criticism*, ed. Linda Kauffman. (Oxford: Blackwell, 1989), 190–212.
Yerbury, J. C. "The 'Sons of Freedom' Doukhobors and the Canadian State." *Canadian Ethnic Studies* 16, 2 (1984), 47–70.
Yogananda, Paramhansa. *Autobiography of a Yogi*. (Los Angeles: Self-Realization Fellowship Press, 1946).
Zammito, John. *The Genesis of Kant's Critique of Judgment*. (Chicago: University of Chicago Press, 1992).
Zelle, Carsten. *Angenehmes Grauen*. (Hamburg: Meiner, 1987).
  Die doppelte Aesthetik der Moderne: Revisionen des Schönen von Boileau bis Nietzsche. (Stuttgart: J. B. Metzler, 1995).
Zerilli, Linda M. G. *Signifying Women: Culture and Chaos in Rousseau, Burke, and Mill*. (Ithaca, NY: Cornell University Press, 1994).
Zimmer, Robert. *Edmund Burke: Zur Einführung*. (Hamburg: Junius Verlag, 1995).
Zuckert, Rachel. "Awe or Envy: Herder Contra Kant on the Sublime." *Journal of Aesthetics and Art Criticism* 61, 3 (2003), 217–232.

Index

Note: f = figure

abjection. *See under* sublime
Abraham, William, 199
Accoliti, Pietro, 83
Ackerman, James S., 262
Addis, William, 251
Addison, Joseph. *See also* sublime
　cited by Samuel Johnson, 6
　and the fine arts, 223
　and history of aesthetics, 2, 184
　as imagination theorist, 57–9
　and Longinian tradition, 7, 58, 223–4
　on primary and secondary pleasures, 58
　on sight and seeing, 35, 58
admiration, 88–90. *See also* Kant, Immanuel
aesthetic
　eliminativism, 175, 176
　Greek origin of term, 2, 234
　intuition, 107
aesthetics, discipline of
　Dutch, 9, 135–6, 146
　environmental, 171, 182
　origins of, 2
Akenside, Mark, 212–13
Alamanni, Luigi, 266
alchemy. *See sublimatio*
Aldovrandi, Giovan Francesco, 266
Alexander, Samuel, 110
Alexander the Great, 18, 91
Algarotti, Francesco, 270
Alison, Archibald. *See also* associationism
　and Burke, 66
　on emotion, 67
　on simple and complex emotions, 66n12
　on sublime and beautiful, 66, 66n13
　on terror, 66
　on trains of ideas, 66, 75
ambition, as passion, 30–1
amplification. *See under* sublime

Amyot, Jacques, 81
Apollonian and Dionysian art.
　See under Nietzsche, Friedrich
Aquinas, Thomas, 30, 185
architectural sublime. *See also* Boullée, Étienne-Louis; Burke, Edmund; Kant, Immanuel; Longinus; *On the Sublime*
　and artificial infinite, 233–5, 270
　and Basilica of Maxentius, 251
　of Boullée, 235–7
　in Byzantine period, 247–54
　and Cathedral of Parma, 254
　and Château d'Anet (of Philibert Delorme), 254, 258–63, 259f, 260f, 267–8, 269, 272
　and Château de Fontainebleau, 264
　and Church of the Holy Apostles (Constantine's), 253–4
　and Domus Augustana (of Domitian), 243, 258
　Einfühlung and *Körpergefühl* in, 234–5, 241, 243, 267
　and Golden House of Nero, 239–43, 242f, 244, 245–6, 254, 257, 258, 260, 261n108, 271–2
　and Hagia Sophia, 251–4, 252f
　and Hall of Giants. *See* Palazzo del Te
　and influence of Dante Alighieri at Château d'Anet, 264–7, 278–9
　and literature, 237–8, 239–41, 270–2
　and Mausoleum of Diocletian, 247
　and Mausoleum of Galla Placida, 251
　and Mausoleum of Theodoric, 250f, 250–1, 253
　and Orthodox Baptistery, Ravenna, 248, 249f, 250, 251
　and Palazzo del Te (of Giulio Romano), 254–8, 255f, 256f, 263, 268
　and Pantheon, 243–7, 244f, 249, 250, 251, 254, 257, 271
　Renaissance, 254–69
　Roman, 239–47, 251

architecture, styles of, 247. *See also* architectural sublime
Aristotle, 18, 89. *See also* tragedy
Arnauld, Agnès, 100
art. *See* fine arts
Ashton, Dore, 228–9
associationism. *See also* Alison, Archibald; Gerard, Alexander; imagination; Kames, Lord; Stewart, Dugald; sublime
  art and sublimity in, 69, 76
  and Burke, 66–7, 73
  elevation, magnitude, and pride in, 64–5, 66, 67, 70, 71, 73
  and family-resemblance concept of sublime, 72–4
  and Hume, 68nn17–18, 72n27
  and internal sense, 67
  and Longinian tradition, 66, 70, 70n21, 73
  paradigm of sublime objects in, 64, 70, 75
  pleasure and sublime in, 67–9
  sublime in, 66–7, 69–72, 74–6
Audran, Jean, *Ravissement*, 96f
Augustine of Hippo, 85, 93
Avison, Charles, 227

Bach, J. S., 220
Bacon, Francis, 124, 148, 149, 151. *See also* Deleuze, Gilles
Baillie, John, 184, 232
Ball, Larry, 243
Balzac, Guez de, 4, 79, 80, 82, 89, 93–4
Bartram, William, 152–3, 157
Bat, Dr. Obed, 165, 166
Batteux, Charles, 219, 222, 228. *See also* fine arts
Baugin, Lubin, 86, 98
  Le dessert aux gaufrettes (*Sill Life with Wafers*), 88f
Baumgarten, Alexander Gottlieb, 2, 103–4
Beattie, James, 178, 221
beauty. *See also* Burke, Edmund; sublime
  compared to the sublime, 64, 108, 109–10, 114, 115, 171, 182, 225
  criticisms of concept of, 74–5
  and morality in Kant, 46
  of nature and art in Reynolds, 61
  paradigm of in Burke, 33
  and proportion in Burke, 31–2
  qualities of in Burke, 35
  as rational contemplation in Shaftesbury, 52
  Reid on use of term, 54
  and relation to sublime in Burke, 26, 33–4
  as social passion in Burke, 29–30
  and society in Burke, 29
  three orders of in Shaftesbury, 52–3
  and ugliness in Burke, 32
Beck, G., *Great Falls of the Potomac*, 156f
Béguin, Sylvie, 259
Bembo, Pietro, 266
Berlin, Isaiah, 181
Bhagavad-Gita, 184, 185
Bilderdijk, Willem, 136, 141, 142
Blair, Hugh, 209
Blake, William, 204, 205–6, 207, 211
Blanc, Charles, 230
Bodin, Jean, 83
Boileau Despréaux, Nicolas, 92, 101, 138, 139, 204. *See also* hupsos/hupsous; *Traité du sublime ou du merveilleux dans le discours*
  and history of "sublime," 4–5, 77
  influences on, 79
  and Racine, 82
Borghini, Raffaello, 80, 83
Bosanquet, Bernard, 117
Botticelli, 265
Bouhours, Dominique, 77
Boullée, Étienne-Louis, 254, 263, 273. *See also* architectural sublime
  and Cenotaph to Sir Isaac Newton, 230, 231f, 233, 236, 247, 272
  and Metropolitan Church, 235f, 235–6, 273
Boulton, James T., criticism of Burke, 26
Brownlee, Kevin, 268
Brunelleschi, Filippo, 265, 266
Bryant, William Cullen, 163, 166
Buijnsters, P. J., 140–1
Bullough, Edward, 53
Bultmann, Rudolf, 197
Burke, Edmund. *See also Philosophical Enquiry into the Sublime and Beautiful, A*
  on architecture, 224–5
  break with Longinian tradition, 26
  "double aesthetics" of (Carsten Zelle), 26, 27
  and fine arts, 224–5, 227–8
  general influence of, 148–9, 172
  Newtonian methodology of, 25
  relation between aesthetic and political ideas of, 2n1
  sensualist aesthetics of, 24, 25
  on the standard of taste, 25
Byron, Lord, 204, 207, 212

Caecilius. *See under On the Sublime*
Caesar, Michael, 266
Carlyle, Thomas, 152–3
Castiglione, Baldassare, 80
categorical imperative. *See under* Kant, Immanuel

Index

Cave, Terence, 85
Céline, Louis-Ferdinand, and Kristeva, 129
Cellini, Benvenuto, 266
Champlin, Edward, 239, 240
Chaucer, Geoffrey, 5
Church, Frederick Edwin, *The Natural Bridge, Virginia*, 155f
Cicero, Marcus Tullius, 12
Clement VII, Pope, 268
Clewis, Robert, 179
Cole, Thomas, 157–8, 160–1, 164, 167
  Course of Empire: Desolation, The, 168f
  Course of Empire: Destruction, The, 167f
  View of the Mountain Pass Called the Notch of the White Mountains, 162f
  View of the Round-Top in the Catskill Mountains, 161f
Coleridge, Samuel Taylor, 204, 205, 207
Collingwood, R. G., 110
Cooper, Anthony Ashley. *See* Shaftesbury, third Earl of
Cooper, James Fenimore, 163–6, 167. *See also* prairies, the American
Corneille, Pierre, 79, 89, 94
Correggio, 254, 255
Cranach, Lucas, the Elder, 189
  The Crucifixion with the Converted Centurion, 190f
critical philosophy. *See under* Kant, Immanuel
Critique of Practical Reason (Immanuel Kant), 46, 207, 231n6. *See also* Kant, Immanuel
Critique of Pure Reason (Immanuel Kant), 41, 120, 124. *See also* Kant, Immanuel
Critique of the Power of Judgment (Immanuel Kant). *See also* Kant, Immanuel; sublime
  and Dutch intellectual tradition, 136, 145
  "enthusiasm" in, 46
  "idea of reason" in, 38, 39
  moral source of sublime in, 38
  and music, 220
  sublime and architecture in, 230
  sublime in nature in, 39–40
  treatment of colors in, 63
Croce, Benedetto, 110, 117
Cronon, William, 178
Crotch, William, 227
Cuyp, Aelbert, 135

da Falgano, Niccolò, 4
D'Alembert, Jean le Rond, 220, 221
Dante Alighieri. *See under* architectural sublime
Darwin, Charles, 158
da Vinci, Leonardo, 80
de Beauvais, Vincent, 264
de Bérulle, Pierre, 95
de Buffon, Comte, 15
de Castrobello, Stephanus, 6n27
de' Cavalieri, Tommaso, 268
de Champaigne, Philippe, 96, 98, 101
  Portrait de mère Agnès Arnauld et de soeur Catherine de Sainte-Suzanne (*Portrait of Mother Agnès Arnauld and Sister Catherine de Sainte-Suzanne*), 100f
  Saint Augustine, 99f
de Kooning, Willem, 222
de La Tour, Georges, 86
  La Madeleine à la veilleuse (*The Magdalene with the Nightlight*), 87f
Deleuze, Gilles, 118, 123–7. *See also* postmodernism
  on Bacon, 124–6
  and Kant, 123, 124
  and Lyotard compared, 126–7
  and primacy of sensation, 123
  on rhythm and catastrophe, 124, 125–6
Deliyannis, Deborah Mauskopf, 248–9
Delorme, Philibert. *See under* architectural sublime
de' Medici, Cardinal Ippolito, 268
de' Medici, Lorenzo, 265
de Muret, Marc-Antoine, 78, 79
de Navarre, Marguerite, 87, 266
Dennis, John, 7, 51, 57, 177
de Petra, Gabriel, 4, 79, 82, 83, 84
de Poitiers, Diane, Duchess of Valentinois, 254, 261–4. *See also* Henri II, Duke of Mantua
de Sacy, Lemaistre, 85, 99
de Sales, François, 85, 99
de Sangallo, Giuliano, 266
Descartes, René, 89, 95
Desmarets, Jean de Saint-Sorlin, 94
d'Étaples, Jacques Lefèvre, 85
de Tocqueville, Alexis, 161
Dictionnaire étymologique de la langue latine, histoire des mots (A. Ernout and A. Meillet), 3, 4
di Michelino, Domenico, 265
Dionysius of Halicarnassus, 15
Doukhobor sect. *See* Freedomites
Doueihi, Milad, 80
Dudith, Andreas, 79
Dürer, Albrecht, 31
Dutch Golden Age, 138, 145
duty, Kantian, 45, 46
Dwight, Timothy, President of Yale, 158–9

Edwards, James, 197
Edwards, Jonathan, 147, 148, 153, 166, 192n20
Eichler, Gottfried, the Younger, 91, 93
Einfühlung. See under architectural sublime

Eliot, George, 204
Eliot, T. S., 270
Elkins, James, 1n1, 197, 201
Emerson, Ralph Waldo, 152, 158, 194
emotion. *See under* sublime
Entrikin, Nick, 174, 180
Essay on Criticism, An (Alexander Pope), 6, 6n27
Euripides, 237, 242
evil, 198–9

feeling. *See under* Kant, Immanuel; *under* sublime
Feith, Rhijnvis, 136, 140–2, 146
Ferrier, Susan, 211
fine arts, 69, 116, 171, 173. *See also* architectural sublime; Burke, Edmund; Kristeva, Julia; Lyotard, Jean-François; sublime
    Batteux on, 219–21
    Enlightenment definitions of, 218–21
    in the nineteenth century, 107–8, 121–2, 225–8
    style and content of, 221–5
    sublime and, 37, 65, 121–2, 129, 141–2, 218, 219
Force, Pierre, 87
Forster, Kurt, 257, 258
François I, King, 266
Freedomites, 195–6
French Academy of Painting and Sculpture, 83
Friedrich, Caspar David, 226
Fumaroli, Marc, 78

Gallet, Michel, 263
Gallucci, Margaret, 266
Gainsborough, Thomas, 59
Gassendi, Pierre, 81
Geel, Jacob, 136, 142–5, 146
geology, 156. *See also* natural history; nature
    and nationalism, 157–61
    and Neptunism, 150–1
    and religion, 152–3, 158–9, 162–3
    and volcanism, 150–1
Genesis. *See* Holy Bible
genius, 113
Gerard, Alexander. *See also* associationism
    and criticism of Longinus, 70n21
    on emotion, 67
    on imaginative identification, 68
    influence on Kant of, 103
    on nature, 178–9
    on sublime, 70–1
    on terror, 66, 73
Gibbon, Edward, 15
Gilby, Emma, 82
Godlovitch, Stan, 181
Goethe, Johann Wolfgang von, 226
Golden House (Domus Aurea). *See under* architectural sublime

Gorham, Dr. John, 150, 157
Gospels. *See* Holy Bible
Gray, Thomas, 188
Greek New Testament. *See* Holy Bible

Hache, Sophie, 80
Hadrian, 261
Hardouin-Mansart, Jules, 236–7
Hardy, Thomas, 225
Heath, Malcolm, 208
Heidegger, Martin, 122
Hegel, G. W. F., 102, 109–12
    on beauty and sublimity, 109–10
    on "death of art," 110
    Elements of the Philosophy of Right, 1, 7
    on forms of art, 111–12
    Phenomenology of Spirit, 53
Henri II, Duke of Mantua, 254, 258, 261, 262, 264, 267
Hepburn, Ronald, 175–6, 180–1
Herder, Johann Gottfried, and Kant compared, 175n12
Hesiod, 242, 258, 267, 271. *See also* architectural sublime
Heywood, Major Duncan, 166
Hoffman, E. T. A., 227–8
Hogarth, William, 35, 60
Holland Society of Fine Arts and Sciences, 143
Holy Bible, 16, 94, 189, 195–6, 199, 206, 216–17, 251
Home, Henry. *See* Kames, Lord
Homer, 17, 18, 19, 238, 241, 253, 265, 271
Horace, 80
Hudson, J., 6
Huet, Pierre Daniel, 77
Hume, David, 25, 27. *See also* associationism; tragedy
humīlis. *See under sublīmis*
humility. *See under* nature; *under sublīmis*
hupsos/hupsous (ὕψος/ὕψους). *See also* sublime
    Longinus's conception of, 12
    and *magnificence*, 90
    meanings and renditions of, 2, 4, 78
    and *merveilleux*, 94
Hutcheson, Francis, 2, 24, 31, 51, 55, 67
Hutton, James, 150
Huydecoper, Balthazar, 136, 137–40

imagination. *See also* Burke, Edmund; Kant, Immanuel; Wordsworth, William
    and associationism, 65, 69, 75
    in Lyotard, 120, 121
    "metaphysical" of Hepburn, 175, 176–7
Ingersoll, Charles Jared, 159
internal sense. *See under* associationism; *under* Reid, Thomas; *under* sublime

James, William, 192
Jameson, Frederic, 118, 119, 210
  contrasted with Deleuze, Lyotard, and Kristeva, 129–30
  as critic of postmodernism, 129–30
  and Kant, 130
Jeanneret, Michel, 87
Jefferson, Thomas, 160, 161, 163
  and Declaration of Independence, 154
  on the falls at Harpers Ferry, 154–7
  Notes on the State of Virginia, 154
Jodelle, Étienne, 78
John of the Cross, Saint, 99
Johnson, Samuel, 6, 60, 270
Joost-Gaugier, Christiane, 245
jouissance. *See under* sublime
Julius II, Pope, 266
Justinian, 252

Kames, Lord. *See also* associationism
  and Longinian tradition, 7, 209
  on sources of pleasure, 67
  on sublimity and grandeur, 65n6, 70n24
  on sublime feeling, 72–3n30
  on terror, 66
Kant, Immanuel, 102, 171, 172. *See also* moral feeling, in Kant; sublime
  on admiration and respect, 47–8
  and Akenside compared, 213
  and British Romantics, 172, 181, 205, 209, 215
  and categorical imperative, 42
  critical philosophy of, 37, 41, 46, 107, 124, 207, 231n6
  and disinterestedness, 53
  and Dutch aesthetic tradition, 135–6, 141, 143, 144
  on Dutch taste, 135, 145
  and duty, 45, 46
  early and mature theories of sublime in compared, 48–9
  feeling in, 176–7, 231
  and fine arts, 224–5
  on freedom, 38n7, 41, 42
  on free play of the faculties, 105
  and German Idealist tradition, 102
  and Herder compared, 175n12
  on human beings as rational animals, 38, 42–3
  and imagination, 38, 39, 102, 104, 176–7
  on judgment, 48, 105, 179
  and Kristeva compared, 128
  and the Longinian tradition, 7
  and the monstrous (*das Ungeheure*), 199
  and the moral law, 42, 43, 45, 47
  and postmodern sublime, 118–19, 120–1, 123–4, 127–8, 130
  on practical (and theoretical) reason, 43, 102, 103
  religion and sublime in, 184, 186–8
  and Schelling contrasted, 108
  and Schopenhauer contrasted, 112–13
  on sensible and supersensible, 39, 40, 41–2
  on sublime in nature, 38, 38nn7–8, 174–5, 176–7, 179
  on theoretical and practical knowledge, 41
Keats, John, 208, 209
Keller, Luzius, 267
Kemble, Fanny, 159
King James Bible. *See* Holy Bible
Kinker, Johannes, 136, 141, 142
Kivy, Peter, 220
Kleiner, John, 265
Körpergefühl. *See under* architectural sublime
Kostof, Spiro, 253
Kristeva, Julia, 118, 119, 127–9, 199. *See also* Kant, Immanuel; postmodernism; sublime
  and Lacan, 127, 128
  and Céline, 129
  compared with Deleuze and Lyotard, 128, 129
  on fine art, 129
  and Plato, 127

Labacco, Antonio, 261
Labé, Louise, 79
Lacan, Jacques, and Kristeva, 127, 128
Landino, Cristoforo, 265, 266
landscapes. *See* nature
Langbaine, Gerard, 5
Lawrence, D. H., 204
Le Brun, Charles, 89, 91, 92, 94, 95–6, 98
  Entrée d'Alexandre dans Babylone (*Entrance of Alexander into Babylon*), 95f
  La Franche-Comté conquise pour la seconde fois (*The Second Conquest of the Franche-Comté*), 92f
  Surprise et admiration (*Admiration and Astonishment*), 90f
Leclerc, George-Louis, 154
Le Fèvre, Tanneguy, 4, 79, 84
Leiden University, 137, 143
Le Nain, Louis, *Famille de paysans dans un intérieur* (*Peasant Family in an Interior*), 86f
Lewis and Clark expedition, 164–5
  A Map of Lewis and Clark's Track, 165f
Lippi, Filippino, 265
Locke, John, 51, 55, 147–8
Loerke, William, 243–5
Logan, John, 79

Longinus. *See also On the Sublime*
  as author of *On the Sublime*, 3
  and Poussin, 86
  reception and influence of, 78–9, 80, 83, 204, 208, 211
  and sublime in architecture, 230, 232–3
Longinus, Cassius, 11, 15
Louis XIV, 82, 83
Low Countries, 135–6. *See also On the Sublime*
Lucretius, 272
Luke, Gospel of. *See* Holy Bible
Lyell, Charles, 158
Lynagh, Sarah-Jane, 199
  Mute, 200f
Lyotard, Jean-François, 117, 118, 119–23, 131.
  See also Deleuze, Gilles; sublime
  on avant-garde art, 121–2
  and history of "sublime," 77, 88, 173
  and *le differend*, 121
  and sublime in nature, 180

MacDonald, William, 246
Macrobius, Ambrosius Theodorius, 262, 267
Madelein, Christophe, 135, 136
Malevich, Kasimir, 217
Manetti, Antonio, 265, 266
Mantegna, 262
Manutius, Paulus, 4, 16
Mark, Gospel of. *See* Holy Bible
Martin, Éva Madeleine, 4, 269
Mather, Cotton, 151, 152
Mather, Increase, 152
Matthew, Gospel of. *See* Holy Bible
Maximus of Tyre, 13
Mayernik, David, 257
Mazarin, Cardinal Jules, 82, 83, 91, 96
Mellor, Anne, 211
Melville, Herman, 167
Mersenne, Marin, 85
Michelangelo, 262, 266, 268
Middleton, Captain Duncan Uncas, 165
Miller, William F., 158
Milton, John, 216. See also *Philosophical Enquiry into the Sublime and Beautiful, A*
  Paradise Lost, 58, 151, 186–7, 223, 270–2
  reference to Longinus in, 5
Minkowski, Eugène, 232–3
Monk, Samuel, 58, 66n14, 74
Montaigne, Michel de, 78, 80, 88, 89, 98
moral feeling, in Kant
  and *Critique of the Power of Judgment*, 40
  and humiliation, 44–5
  and the moral law, 43, 45
  and self-love, 44
  and the sublime, 46–7
  and sublime in nature, 40, 43
moral law. *See under* Kant, Immanuel
Morris, David, 192–3
Mothersill, Mary, 171
Motherwell, Robert, 217, 221, 222, 228.
  See also On the Sublime
Mound Builders. *See under* prairies, the American
music. *See* fine arts

Nancy, Jean-Luc, 118n2, 228
Natalis, Michel, 95
  Le ravissement de saint Paul (*The Ecstasy of Saint Paul*), 97
Natty's grave. *See Prairie, The*
natural history, 150–1, 152–7. *See also* geology; Protestantism, in North America
nature. *See also* geology; Lyotard, Jean-François; natural history; *On the Sublime*; sublime
  aesthetic appreciation of, 175–6, 206
  and American sublime, 147, 155–6
  and fine art, 69, 224–5
  and humility, 176–7, 179, 180
  and sublime in Shaftesbury, 53
  and sublimity in Kant, 37, 48
  and taste in landscape, 173–4
  and technology, 174
Nero, 239, 240, 243. *See also* architectural sublime
new historicism in literary studies, 209–10.
  See also Jameson, Frederic
Newman, Barnett, 173, 180, 228
Newman, John Henry, 191
Newton, Sir Isaac, 24, 148. *See also* Boullée, Étienne-Louis
Nicot, Jean, 95
Nietzsche, Friedrich, 102, 109, 114–17
  on Apollonian and Dionysian art, 115, 116–17
  on music and dance, 116
  and Schopenhauer, 115, 117
Numenius, 16

Observations on the Feeling of the Beautiful and Sublime, 37, 48, 135, 136, 231n6.
  See also Kant, Immanuel
Onians, John, 251
On the Sublime (*Peri hupsous*).
  See also Longinus; sublime
  Aeschylus in, 257–8
  Ajax in, 18, 19, 214
  amplification in, 17, 18, 19
  and architectural sublime, 230, 232, 237–8
  Caecilius on Plato in, 13, 22
  Cicero and Demosthenes compared in, 19

and concept of sublime, 3–4, 14
Demosthenes in, 19, 23
emotion in, 17
ethics and politics of sublime in, 20–2, 210–11
Euripides in, 20, 237–8
French translation history of, 4–5, 79–80, 83–4, 88
Genesis in, 209
greatness of nature in, 17–18, 20
greatness of thought in, 17
Homer in, 17, 79, 232, 237
Hyperides in, 23
images of the divine in, 18, 188
imagination in, 19, 20
imitation in, 18
and influence in Low Countries, 137, 138, 139
and influence in North America, 148n4
Lysias compared to Plato in, 16, 22, 23
Moses in, 79
Motherwell on, 221
natural talent and genius in, 22
nature and art in, 20, 22–3
publication history of, 78
as response to Caecilius, 13, 16, 17
and rhetorical style, 5, 14, 15, 25, 221–2
and Romantic sublime, 204, 208–9
Sappho in, 79, 82, 208
selection and combination in, 17
transmission and attribution of, 15–16, 172, 204n2
Otto, Rudolf, 184, 198, 232
Ovid, 240–1, 242, 258, 267–8, 270.
  See also architectural sublime
Owensen, Sydney, 211

Paganus, Petrus, 4, 82
pain. *See under* pleasure
painting. *See* fine arts
Pannini, Giovanni Paolo, 247
Pantheon, the. *See under* architectural sublime
Paradise Lost. See under Milton, John
Paré, Ambroise, 80
Pascal, Blaise, 85–6, 87–8, 100, 185
Paul, first epistle to the Corinthians. *See* Holy Bible
Pearce, Zachary, 6
Peri hupsous (Longinus). *See On the Sublime*
Philosophical Enquiry into the Sublime and Beautiful, A (Edmund Burke).
  See also architecture, styles of; beauty; Burke, Edmund; sublime
  as aesthetics of an "event," 36
  artificial infinite in, 233
  beautiful and sublime connected in, 26

criticism of utility and perfection in, 32
and eighteenth-century aesthetic tradition, 24, 25, 29, 32, 58, 184, 221
and history of "sublime," 7
and influence on Kant's *Critique of the Power of Judgment*, 37–8, 103, 172
love in, 30–1
Milton in, 224, 270
opposition of beautiful and sublime in, 26
pain and pleasure in, 27, 66
religion and sublime in, 184, 186–8
role of imagination in, 27
self-preservation in, 28
terror in, 25, 27, 28
Photius, 15
Picasso, Pablo, 222
Pincus, Debra, 265
Pinelli, Niccolo, 82
Plato, 19, 89, 113
  Symposium, 50
  Timaeus, 11, 12, 15, 20, 127
Platonism, 79
  of Reynolds, 60–1
  of Schopenhauer, 112–14
  of Shaftesbury, 50–1
pleasure (and pain), 67. *See also* associationism; *Philosophical Enquiry into the Sublime and Beautiful, A*; sublime
  in Addison, 59
  in Hume, 27
  in Kant, 37, 39, 44, 105
  in Lyotard, 120
  Plotinus, 50
  and sublime, 64
Plutarch, 221
Poerson, Charles, *Louis XIV en Jupiter, vainqueur de la Fronde* (*Louis XIV as Jupiter, Conquerer of the Frond*), 91f
Pope, Alexander. *See under An Essay on Criticism*
Porphyry, 11, 15
Port-Royal, 81, 82, 96, 98, 100
Portus, Franciscus, 4
postmodernism. *See also* sublime
  and Kant, 118–19, 121, 123
  sublime as crisis in, 118–19
Poussin, Nicolas, 79, 80, 85, 86, 95–6
  L'hiver, or *Le deluge* (*Winter*, or *The Flood*), 81f
  L'inspiration du poète (*Inspiration of the Poet*), 98f
Prairie, The (James Fenimore Cooper), 163, 164, 166, 167–70. *See also* Cooper, James Fenimore

prairies, the American, 163–7. *See also* natural history; nature
  and Mound Builders, 163, 166, 168
Priestly, Joseph, 205, 214
primary and secondary qualities, 55, 65. *See also* Reid, Thomas
Primaticcio, Francesco, 259, 264, 268, 269
privation, 198–9
Proclus, 11
Procopius, 252, 253, 254
Protestantism, in North America, 148, 151–2, 157–8
Proust, Marcel, 122
Pulteney, J., 5
Puritanism. *See* Protestantism, in North America

Quint, David, 242, 261

Rabelais, François, 87
Rabuse, Georg, 267
Racine, Jean, 82
Radcliffe, Ann, 150, 191–2, 211
Raphael, 116
Rapin, René, 77
Reid, Thomas. *See also* sublime
  and critique of aesthetic tradition, 54
  on excellence, 57
  as internal sense theorist, 50, 54–7
  and Longinian tradition, 7
  perception contrasted with judgment in, 55
  on primary and secondary qualities, 55
  on taste as intellectual power, 55
religion. *See also* geology; Kant, Immanuel; Protestantism, in North America; sublime
  and British Romantics, 207
  and conversional spiritualistic sublime, 194
  and conversional theistic sublime, 184, 188–91
  and corroborative spiritualistic sublime, 194–5
  and corroborative theistic sublime, 191–3
  and demythologistic sublime, 184, 196–8
  and grace, 189–90
  and nontheistic sublime, 184, 198–9
  and spiritualistic sublime, 184, 193
  and transformative spiritualistic sublime, 195–6
  and transformative theistic sublime, 192–3
respect. *See under* Kant, Immanuel
Reynolds, Sir Joshua, 222. *See also* beauty; Platonism; sublime
  and eighteenth-century aesthetics, 60
  and the "grand style," 60, 62–3
  on history of art, 62–3
  as imagination theorist, 59–63
  and Kant compared, 63

Mrs. Siddons as the Tragic Muse, 62
  and Royal Academy of Arts, 59
Richelet, Pierre, 81, 82
Rigolot, François, 79
Ripa, Césare, 90
Rizzardi, Clementina, 249–50
Robortello, Francesco, 4, 78, 79
Rolfe, J. C., 239
Romano, Giulio. *See under* architectural sublime
"romantic," meaning of, 143
Romanticism, 144, 172–3, 175, 181, 221. *See also On the Sublime*; sublime; Wordsworth, William
Ronsard, Pierre, 78
Rosenblum, Robert, 217
Rothko, Mark, 217, 218, 221, 228
Rousseau, Jean-Jacques, 234
Royal Society of London for the Improvement of Natural Knowledge, 148
Ruskin, John, 226–7

Sappho, 12, 17, 79, 209. *See also On the Sublime*
Sarpi, Paolo, 83
Scaliger, Joseph, 78, 83
Schelling, Wilhelm Joseph, 102, 107–9
Schiller, Friedrich von, 102, 105–7, 141, 144, 208, 226
Schlegel, August Wilhelm, 26
Schmarsow, August, 234–5, 243
Scholar, Richard, 78
Schopenhauer, Arthur, 102, 112–14, 115, 117. *See also* Nietzsche, Friedrich
Schouwburgh Theater, Amsterdam, 137, 138
Schröder, J. F. L., 136
Shaftesbury, third Earl of. *See also* Platonism; sublime
  and Cambridge Platonists, 51
  concept of disinterestedness in, 53–4
  and history of aesthetics, 2, 51
  and Longinian tradition, 7, 51–2
  on rules of art, 62–3
Shearman, John, 254
Shelley, Percy Bysshe, 207, 209, 214
Shusterman, Richard, 233, 263
Sidney, Philip, 138
Silentiarius, Paulus, 252–3
Silliman, Benjamin, 150, 152, 153, 157
Simeoni, Gabriello, 260
Simpson, David, 210
Smith, Daniel, 123, 126
Smith, E. Baldwin, 258
Smith, Samuel Stanhope, 147
Smith, William, 6, 232, 237, 242
Smithson, John, 168
Smithsonian, 168

Spencer, Herbert, 5
Squier, E. G., and E. H. Davis, 168–70
  Ancient Monuments of the Mississippi Valley, 169f
Sterne, Laurence, 145
Stewart, Dugald. *See also* associationism; sublime
  beauty compared to sublime in, 72n28
  criticism of Burke, 66
  distinction between imagination and association in, 69n19
  on elevation, 66
  and family-resemblance concept of sublime, 72–4
  on terror, 66
  on transference, 72–4, 75
Stoddard, Solomon, 153
sublimatio, 3, 80, 81
sublime, the (sublimity). *See also* architectural sublime; beauty; fine arts; Kant, Immanuel; religion; *sublīmis*
  as abjection, 127–8, 129, 199
  Addison's conception of, 58–9, 184
  as admiration and respect, 47–8, 66
  American, 148, 157, 159
  and amplification (spatial sublime), 233–5, 241, 264–9
  as associative category, 69
  and astonishment in Burke, 28, 29
  as astonishment or amazement in Addison, 59
  attractive aspect of in Kant, 40, 44
  and British Romanticism, 172, 181
  "camp" or "hysterical," 130
  and capitalism, 129–30
  of Cicero, 19
  contemporary meanings of, 184
  as delight in Burke, 29
  and dimension in Burke, 217–18
  egotistical, 208
  and enthusiasm in Kant, 46
  environmental, 171
  as epiphany, 185, 186, 201, 236
  ethics of in Longinus, 20–2
  etymology of term, 3
  examples of, 65, 70
  as family-resemblance concept, 65, 72–4
  and fear, 40
  figurative, 71, 72–5
  first American, 161–7
  five sources of in Longinus, 17–19
  German term for (*das Erhabene*), 42, 185
  and "great" or "grand," 52, 56, 58, 60, 146
  Greek, of Byron, 212–15
  history of as philosophical concept, 3–7
  ideological American, 148–56
  and internal sense in Shaftesbury, 50–4
  and irrationalism in Burke, 29
  as *jouissance*, 127, 128, 129
  Kantian, 103–5, 108, 109, 184–6, 221
  Latin origin of term, 2–3
  as literary style in Shaftesbury, 51
  "logical," in Kant, 46
  Longinus's conception of, 12–14, 16–19
  mathematical and dynamical, in Kant, 39–40, 104–5, 106, 172, 208, 215, 227–8
  modes of in Kant, 47f
  moral, in British Romantics, 205, 206–7, 212–16
  and moral feeling in Kant, 46, 177–8
  and moral vocation in Kant, 42–3
  in music, 220, 227–8
  and mystery, 180, 181, 200–1
  nationalist, 157–61
  and nature, 69, 106, 113–14, 147–57, 171, 179
  nonrational, 115, 117
  and painting, 225–6
  and permanent revolution, 123
  political use of term, 90–4
  positive and negative in Weiskel, 208
  postmodern, 64, 77, 118n2, 119
  prehistory of in early modern France, 78–84
  as presentation of the unpresentable (negative presentation), 120–1
  "problem" of, 65
  quasi- or mini- in Dutch aesthetics, 146
  Reid's conception of, 56–7
  and religion, 184, 185–6, 199–200, 201–2
  Reynold's conception of, 60
  rhetorical, 223
  Romantic, 203–5
  Sapphic, 209
  as secondary quality, 65
  as second-order pleasure in Alison, 66
  self- and human-regarding, 177
  stages of, 184–5, 186–7, 199
  as state of mind (vibration) in Kant, 37, 38, 43
  "subtler," in Dutch aesthetics, 136
  "Theoclean," in Shaftesbury, 53–4
  and transcendence, 203–4
  as transformative experience, 201
  Wordsworth's conception of, 63
sublīmis. *See also* sublime
  and aesthetic experience, 78
  and astronomy, 81
  and *humīlis*, 78, 81, 101
  meanings of, 2–3, 4, 93–4
  and *miraculum*, 99
  and natural science, 80–1

sublimité. See also Balzac, Guez de; sublime
  in early modern codex, 82–4
  as interdisciplinary semantic field, 80–2
  meaning of, 78, 79, 82, 90
Suetonius, 239
Sulzer, J. G., 220, 234

Tacitus, 210
Taemssoon, Cornelis, 138–9
Tasso, Torquato, 78, 80
Taylor, Rabun, 253
Teresa of Avila, 99
Theodoric, King. *See under* architectural sublime
Thirty Years' War, 83, 92
Thomas, Gospel of. *See* Holy Bible
Thoreau, Henry David, 159–60, 194
Tollens, Hendrik, 146
tragedy, 64, 64n1, 106, 108–9
  Aristotle on, 64n1
  Hume on, 64n1, 220
  paradox of, 64
Traité du sublime ou du merveilleux dans le discours, 94. *See also* Boileau Despréaux, Nicolas
  influence of, 4
  meaning of *hupsos* in, 78, 90–101
  as translation of Longinus, 83–5
Turner, J. M. W., 217, 226
Tuttle, Richard, 257, 258

Utrecht University, 137

van den Vondel, Joost, 138
van Goyen, Jan, 145
van Hemert, P., 136
van Lennep, D. J., 142
van Mander, Karel, 138
van Rijn, Rembrandt, 145
Van Schepen, Randall, 197–8
van Swinderen, T., 136
Vasari, Giorgio, 255, 265
Vickers, Brian, 80
Vignola, Jacomo, 83
Virgil, 241–2, 251. *See also* architectural sublime

Wachsmuth, Jeremias, *Magnificentia*, 93f
Wagner, Richard, 228
Wallace, William, 268
Walpole, Horace, 188
Walpole, Robert, 210–11
Ward-Perkins, J. B., 244
Weinberg, Bernard, 82, 83, 84
Weiskel, Thomas, 197, 207–9. *See also* sublime
Werner, Abraham Gottlob, 150
Whichcote, Benjamin, 51
Williams, Helen Maria, 211
William the Silent, 137
Wordsworth, William, 172, 208. *See also* sublime
  Guide through the District of the Lakes, A, 63
  and imagination, 203
  "Lines Composed a Few Miles above Tintern Abbey," 63, 206, 215
  Michael: A Pastoral Poem, 205
  moral sublime in, 206, 215–16
  Prelude, The, 153, 173, 178, 203, 206, 215
  "Sublime and the Beautiful, The," 215

Xenophon, 12

Yogananda, Paramhansa, 194–5

Zenobia of Palmyra, 15